Your Reading

Committee on the Junior High and Middle School Booklist

Jane Christensen, Chair; Associate Executive Director, National Council of Teachers of English

Ronald A. Finelli, Everitt Junior High School, Wheat Ridge, Colorado

Peggy A. Flood, Northglenn Junior High School, Boulder, Colorado (formerly)

Beverly Haley, Fort Morgan High School, Fort Morgan, Colorado (formerly)

James Hobbs, Smiley Junior High School, Denver, Colorado

John F. Specht, Cole Junior High School, Denver, Colorado

Imogene Springer, Office of Curriculum Development, Denver Public Schools

Melva J. Yeaman, Everitt Junior High School, Wheat Ridge, Colorado

Robert Squires, *ex officio*

Paul O'Dea, NCTE Staff Liaison

Your Reading

A Booklist for Junior High and Middle School Students

New Edition

Jane Christensen, Chair,
and the Committee on the Junior High
and Middle School Booklist
of the National Council of Teachers of English

71663

National Council of Teachers of English
1111 Kenyon Road, Urbana, Illinois 61801

Library of Congress Cataloging in Publication Data
Main entry under title:

Your reading, a booklist for junior high and middle
    school students.

    Continues: Your reading : a booklist for junior high
students. c1975.
    Includes index.
    Summary: An annotated listing of over 3000 fiction and
non-fiction books recommended for junior high and middle
school students.
    1. Children's literature—Bibliography. 2. Bibliog-
raphy—Best books—Children's literature. 3. School
libraries—Book lists. [1. Bibliography—Best books]
I. Christensen, Jane, 1934–   . II. National Council
of Teachers of English. Committee on the Junior High
and Middle School Booklist. III. Your reading : a
booklist for junior high students.
Z1037.Y68   1983 [PN1009.A1]   011'.62   83-17426
ISBN 0-8141-5938-9

Contents

Acknowledgments

A booklist committee is made up of unbelievable people—unbelievable for endurance, dedication, and unpaid professional service. Only the committee to direct the decade-long writing project for the *Encyclopedia Britannica* might excel in perseverance—but they were paid.

All the volunteer booklist committee members for this edition of *Your Reading* touched student lives in some way every day: Ronald A. Finelli, Peggy A. Flood, Beverly Haley, James Hobbs, John F. Specht, Imogene Springer, Melva J. Yeaman.

All these seven people have a passion for reading, but unlike most readers, they disciplined themselves to read adolescent books for review—to write for younger readers. I'm still impressed with their discipline, care, and cooperation.

These professionals carried untold numbers of books to their homes for midnight reading or to the classrooms for student reading. Many of the 3,100 annotations were written by students, and some of the adult annotations were even edited by students for more appeal at the student level. Reading and writing stretched over five years and included appropriate level books published from 1975 to the present—books submitted by publishers for consideration. To these publishers, our sincere appreciation for generously supplying all copies of books reviewed.

Also, thank you to all the students who joined our forces to make this book possible. We needed your personal touch and tone, but mostly your love of reading.

Commendation should also be given to NCTE Editorial Staff, especially editors Jane Curran and Alexander Doty for their time, good cheer, and obvious talent. Lois Haig, Director of Editorial and Production Services, and Paul O'Dea, Director of Publications, kept their guiding eyes on the project and showed great patience as they made important suggestions.

A special note of gratitude goes to Elizabeth Carroll, who served as secretary for the project and who displayed a wide range of skills and care as "keeper of the books." She gave home space to mountains of books—hundreds at a time—and took great pride in the project and in the distinct book aroma that permeated the rooms. Often it was her sanguine nature that kept us positive. She reminded us that some day this book would indeed be published.

vii

When the time was extended for the book reading and writing of annotations, other individuals gave helpful assistance: Carolyn McMahon, Patricia Motherway, Elizabeth Siebel, and Rona Smith.

As editor, I had the unique experience during my term of moving from the field of teaching to NCTE headquarters to serve as Associate Executive Director. Rarely do booklist chairs serve half a term with one view and the other half term with another. What I gained was a deep appreciation for all the substantial help given to me at NCTE after my move, when I was not able to devote as much time to the project, and I also feel gratitude for the committee readers who, in my absence, continued their disciplined reading and writing, beyond their appointed terms. I wonder if all editors feel this superfluous.

Jane Christensen
Committee Chair

Introduction to the Student

"I read because I can't help it."

When a large group of students was asked to tell why they read, this was the only response that would not fit into a computer category. It's probably the most important reason for reading, even though all the other reasons are more conventional. No matter what other reason we give for our reading, those of us who love reading "just can't seem to help it." Something pulls us toward it, even with the strong competition of busy lives. Pleasure, escape, assignment, curiosity—all bring us to the open page and to a private world of the author and us.

Since a private world exists between author and reader, you should choose your own books as you choose your friends. However, the world is set up in such a way, especially in school, that you can't always choose all those books. But this book is a boost in that direction—choosing. You may have certain familiar subjects that *always* interest you; then again you may wish to find out about new but intriguing subjects; or you may begin reading the same book as someone special in your life simply because that person is reading it.

Let's begin with your favorite author or title. Check the Author Index or Title Index in the back of the book before you start flipping pages. These "yellow pages" of the book have been designed to save you time. If your favorite book has not been included, don't be dismayed. We were limited by space, publication date (since 1975), and publishers who were willing to submit titles. Also, we worked to include books of appropriate age level and tried to choose those with some measure of literary merit.

Next check the Table of Contents, mainly to find out the main subject or theme groupings of the books. For example, if you are wild about horses, check under *Animals* for inclusion of books about horses. If you can't resist a good mystery book, check the *Mysteries* section. Sometimes we found a book that crossed over several categories and could be included under several different subjects. We had to choose the one category most appropriate for each book, so we suggest that you read through book descriptions in several related categories. For example, see *Fantasy and Folklore, Science Fiction and the Future,* and *The Supernatural* for books with imaginary elements.

You will also notice that the standard classification of Fiction and Nonfiction has been duly observed. *Humor and Satire, Poetry, Plays, Short Story Collections*, and *Information Please* are also included.

There is a separate entry for each book. First comes the author's name, with the last name listed first. Then in boldface or dark type is the title of the book. Following that are the publisher of the book, the year of publication, and the number of pages. The summary or "annotation" consists of a few lines about what's in the book. Each annotation is designed to give you an overview of the book, the general plot or outline, and other extra information such as photos or charts. You'll notice that the reviews do not give away the ending of the story; that's for you to discover. If the book is easy or difficult to read, that has been noted. If the book contains mature subject matter or language, that caution is also included. And when known, book awards are listed at the end of the annotation.

You may just skim a book such as this, not paying attention to any categories until you come across an annotation that sounds exciting, interesting, or weird. It captures your interest in some way. Copy down the information and check your school library. If the book is not there, don't stop searching. Check the local community library. If the book isn't there, begin pleading with the librarian to locate the book for you. Librarians love persistent readers.

You might not think the Directory of Publishers in the back "yellow pages" of the book is very important to your concerns. Wrong. If you have enjoyed a particular book, sit down and write to the author. Be bold. Write your letter to the author in care of the publisher at the address listed. Many publishers and authors consider such a letter an honor, and many authors respond personally. Be sure to include your return address.

We address you as reader in this foreword and wish you hours of pleasure in reading and stretching your imagination. Many important memories will be tied to books.

Whether it's the world of nature, technology, or people—it's your world, reshaped through your eyes. Keep books close—neatly on your bookshelf, scattered over your bed, stacked on the floor. Many readers become writers, and we challenge you to repay the world with a book of your own. We'll be ready to review it for this booklist. Meanwhile, keep reading—because you can't help it.

The Editors

Your Reading

Adventure

Adkins, Jan. **Moving On: Stories of Four Travelers.** Charles Scribner's Sons, 1978. 95 pp.

In each of these stories, the characters love outdoor sports, and they fish, ski, backpack, or bicycle. The stories are all very simple and do not have plots. They tell about how people move around the country and learn about themselves and life in general from their sports and from their observations of nature.

Aiken, Joan. **Arabel and Mortimer.** Illus. Quentin Blake. Doubleday & Co., 1981. 143 pp.

Mortimer is one unusual raven. He loves to answer the phone, croaking out the one human word he knows: "nevermore." He hates to fly, except in emergencies. Unfortunately, when Mortimer is around, there are plenty of emergencies! But Arabel adores him, in spite of all the trouble he causes, and together they share adventure after adventure. Easy reading.

Aiken, Joan. **Go Saddle the Sea.** Doubleday & Co., 1977. 311 pp.

Felix Brooke is an orphan who runs away from his grandfather's house in Spain to find his father's family in England. On his way, though, he is accused of murder and thrown in jail. After he is released, Felix finds himself involved in a series of adventures and dangers that includes being captured by a band of gypsies.

Ames, Mildred. **Is There Life on a Plastic Planet?** E. P. Dutton, 1975. 134 pp.

Hollis doesn't like her fat body, her nagging mother, or even her name. School seems horrible, too, until the day Hollis meets a young woman who runs an experimental doll shop. Hollis asks for a life-size doll that looks like her. She decides to send the doll to school while she escapes to play. But how long will the doll fool everyone?

3

Anderson, Margaret J. **Light in the Mountain.** Alfred A. Knopf, 1982.
177 pp.

Eight-year-old Rana is chosen to be sacrificed to the god inside a
mountain. When the sun sets, she will be thrown into a volcano.
But Matakana has a plan to become his tribe's chief. And to do so,
he will need to save Rana and use her father's influence to convince
the tribe to leave the island for a new home in the distant Land of
the Long White Cloud. Rana begins to feel Matakana's plans are
more selfish and destructive to her people than anyone believes. But
how can she tell them about this threat?

Annixter, Jane, and Paul Annixter. **The Last Monster.** Harcourt Brace
Jovanovich, 1980. 84 pp.

Ron, a teenage boy, still remembers how he failed to help his father
many years ago when he was being mauled by a grizzly bear. Ron
swore to revenge himself and kill the grizzly, but he didn't know
how much that encounter would change him, and his life, forever.

Ashley, Bernard. **Break in the Sun.** Illus. Charles Keeping. S. G. Phillips,
1980. 185 pp.

Patsy Bleigh is unhappy living with her stepfather, so she sneaks on
board a ship belonging to a theatrical group. A search begins for
Patsy, who's having a great time on the ship—she even gets a small
part in a play. Will her stepfather and friends be able to convince
Patsy to return home?

Ashley, Bernard. **A Kind of Wild Justice.** Illus. Charles Keeping. S. G.
Phillips, 1978. 182 pp.

Young Ronnie is left alone when his father is caught driving a
getaway car in a robbery and his mother leaves home. Now the
same gang that forced his father to be a criminal is threatening him
and his best friend. Ronnie must figure out a way to escape these
dangerous criminals.

Avi. **The History of Helpless Harry.** Illus. Paul O. Zelinsky. Pantheon
Books, 1980. 179 pp.

Horatio Stockton Edgeworth, who prefers to be called Harry, wears
an innocent look that makes others think he is helpless. So when
his parents plan a trip, they decide to leave him at home in the care
of the minister's ward, Miss Annie Trowbridge, a person Harry
detests. A mystery soon develops around Miss Annie that triggers a
series of hilarious and suspenseful adventures in the England of the
mid-1800s.

Avi. **A Place Called Ugly.** Pantheon Books, 1981. 141 pp.

Everyone thinks the Coughlin's rented vacation cottage on Green-low's Island is an eyesore. They are glad it's going to be torn down. They are even more glad that a resort hotel will be built in its place, because this hotel will be the only hope for anyone on the island to make some money. But to Owen Coughlin, the cottage is the only place he can call home after a lifetime of constant moves and changes. When his family get on the ferry on their way to another home, Owen hides. He is determined to stay alone in the cottage and do anything to preserve it. But what can a fourteen-year-old do?

Bachman, Richard. **The Long Walk.** Signet Books, 1979. 245 pp.

The Long Walk is a walking contest across America where one hundred teenage boys race against each other. The winner gets everything—prizes, money, honor. But the losers must all die. Mature language and situations.

Baker, Charlotte. **Cockleburr Quarters.** Illus. Robert Owens. Camelot Books, 1973. 175 pp.

A young black boy, Dolph, and his friends find a litter of puppies under the Cockleburr Street Kingdom of Heaven Church. The preacher, Brother Biggers, wants the puppies moved out. He promises Dolph and the boys a dime for every puppy they can get out. But Dolph overhears Brother Biggers talking to his wife and learns they are going to leave the puppies to die at the dump. Dolph decides to save the puppies at all cost. Easy reading. (Book World Children's Spring Book Festival Award)

Bawden, Nina. **Rebel on a Rock.** J. B. Lippincott Co., 1978. 158 pp.

The kingdom of Ithaca has just come under the rule of a cruel dictator, and Jo's family becomes involved in a plot to seize the throne from the wicked ruler. Jo begins to suspect that her step-father is a spy. When government soldiers attack, Jo and her family must act quickly to save themselves.

Belden, Wilanne Schneider. **Mind-Call.** Argo Books, 1981. 246 pp.

Tallie has just slept through the greatest earthquake the continent has ever experienced. But when she awakes, she knows what she must do—her dreams have told her. With Pandora, a cat, Tallie sets out in her sailboat *Pride* and finds her way to the place her dreams have told her she must camp. But first she has to rescue a baby and make a dangerous trip to a house built high into a cliff. Once she gets to the house, Tallie is joined by other children who have been brought together by mysterious mental forces. Here they soon realize their survival instincts will be tested. But can they all face the challenge?

Beresford, Elisabeth. **The Treasure Hunters.** Elsevier/Nelson Books, 1980. 96 pp.

Cuddy used to tell stories about hidden treasures to visitors from London to make the small English seaside village he lived in seem more exciting. But now Cuddy begins to believe his stories are true. So he and some friends form the Lost Treasure Company, pool their money, and buy a metal detector. Can the group really find treasures of silver and gold? The members of the Treasure Company soon discover that the word "treasure" means different things to different people.

Bermant, Chaim. **Belshazzar: A Cat's Story for Humans.** Illus. Meg Rutherford. Bard Books, 1979. 64 pp.

Belshazzar, a cat supposedly descended from Egyptian royalty, tells his life story for mere humans, whom he thinks of as his servants. The world looks very different through Belshazzar's eyes, as he describes his activities and his owners-servants.

Bethancourt, T. Ernesto. **The Dog Days of Arthur Cane.** Holiday House, 1976. 160 pp.

Arthur Cane had everything: a beautiful home, a wealthy family, a comfortable life, and a long tail. One day Arthur awakes to find he has been mysteriously transformed from a purebred to a mongrel dog. He is now chased by dogcatchers and teased by strangers. Arthur runs to Greenwich Village and becomes a Seeing Eye dog for a street musician. But he is soon separated from his new friend, captured, and condemned to death in the dog pound gas chamber.

Bodelson, Anders (translator Joan Tate). **Operation Cobra.** Elsevier/ Nelson Books, 1979. 121 pp.

Life in Denmark becomes stranger and stranger for friends Dan, Arim, and Fredrik as they begin to notice taxis that look like sports cars and Englishmen driving Danish furniture vans. Little do they realize they are becoming trapped in Operation Cobra—a plan to assassinate an American statesman.

Brand, Max. **Dan Barry's Daughter.** Warner Books, 1976. 254 pp.

Harry Gloster is accused of murdering his two mining camp partners. He knows that he can't prove his innocence, so he decides to hide in Mexico. On his way, he meets Joan Daniels and falls in love with her. Now he must decide whether love is worth the risk of hanging.

Brand, Max. **The Long Chance.** Warner Books, 1981. 254 pp.

Sam Cross, at age twenty-one, is a famous gunfighter in the Old West. One day he realizes he's no better than a murderer, so he decides to give up gunfighting and start a new life. But what will he do when people call him a coward?

Brand, Max. **Mistral.** Warner Books, 1980. 224 pp.

Mistral was a proud and wild stallion, but Blister was determined to tame him. Time after time Mistral threw the cowboy off, one time almost killing him. Now Blister's friends are afraid that his promise to break the horse's spirit may cost the cowboy his life.

Brand, Max. **Storm on the Range.** Warner Books, 1980. 221 pp.

Visconti, the hated moneylender, is accidentally killed at Tom Fernald's isolated mountain cabin. Tom steals the dead man's hidden treasure and uses it to gamble himself into a fortune. He soon makes himself the most feared gunfighter in the area. Falling in love with Julie, however, begins to make Tom doubt the value of his life.

Brand, Max. **The White Wolf.** Warner Books, 1980. 204 pp.

All the pups born to the dog of a trapper are killed by the Black Wolf—except one. This small dog finds his way into a pack of wolves where he is raised to become their leader. His wolflike quickness and doglike agility are dramatically tested when he battles the Black Wolf. But his instincts confuse him, and he must choose between being a friend to humans or their fiercest enemy.

Branscum, Robbie. **To the Tune of a Hickory Stick.** Doubleday & Co., 1978. 119 pp.

When their mother is no longer able to support them, Nell and Peckerwood are sent to their uncle's cabin in the woods. But they soon find life unbearable as Uncle Jock makes them work like slaves. One night he savagely beats Peckerwood, so Nell flees to an abandoned schoolhouse with her sick brother. Will the pair be able to take care of themselves—and keep their hideout a secret?

Brown, Irene Bennett. **Skitterbrain.** Thomas Nelson, 1978. 112 pp.

Larnie, a young pioneer girl, is in charge of getting milk for her baby brother from Bessie, the family cow. One day Larnie accidentally lets the cow wander off. To save her brother's life and restore her own confidence, Larnie must search for Bessie across the vast Kansas prairie.

Bulgakov, Mikhail (translator Michael Glenny). **A Country Doctor's Notebook.** Bantam Books, 1975. 177 pp.

There is much sickness and suffering in the remote Russian area when the young doctor arrives. And he is nervous and unsure of himself. The people there have more confidence in him than he does. But the disease and pain will not wait, so the doctor finds he has to perform things like amputations and births quickly and under rough conditions.

Butterworth, Ben, and Bill Stockdale. **Danger in the Mountains.** Illus. Maureen Gray and Gordon Gray. Methuen, 1977. 64 pp.

British spy Jim Hunter's life is filled with close escapes from death. On his latest mission to stop a forgery plot, Jim, his dog, Radar, and another agent are trapped in an avalanche in the Canadian Rockies. Can they all escape nature's deep freeze in time to save the British Empire from economic disaster?

Butterworth, Ben, and Bill Stockdale. **The Desert Chase.** Illus. Maureen Gray and Gordon Gray. Methuen, 1976. 64 pp.

Jim Hunter, British agent, searches for the kidnapped son of a wealthy Arab sheik in the deserts of the Middle East. But before he can find the boy, Jim and his dog, Radar, are ambushed and taken to a lonely stockade. Escape seems almost impossible as the sand around the stockade is filled with powerful explosive mines.

Butterworth, Ben, and Bill Stockdale. **The Diamond Smugglers.** Illus. Maureen Gray and Gordon Gray. Methuen, 1977. 64 pp.

A British spy is killed before he can pass on vital information about diamond smuggling to fellow agent Jim Hunter. Left to solve the mystery alone, Jim travels to the Monaco Grand Prix. Soon, he begins to suspect a famous racer is an important part of the notorious gem-smuggling scheme.

Butterworth, Ben, and Bill Stockdale. **The Island of Helos.** Illus. Maureen Gray and Gordon Gray. Methuen, 1976. 64 pp.

Two agents have already been killed and one has disappeared when Jim Hunter is assigned to a case of international espionage. With the help of two female agents Jim uncovers a ring of criminals on the Greek island of Helos. Jim and his partners must now find the link between these criminals and the murdered agents—before they themselves are discovered and killed.

Butterworth, Ben, and Bill Stockdale. **Jim and the Dolphin.** Illus. Maureen Gray and Gordon Gray. Methuen, 1975. 30 pp.

In this adventure, British secret agent Jim Hunter works with a trained dolphin in an effort to stop enemy agents from stealing the secret plans for the building of a new midget submarine.

Butterworth, Ben, and Bill Stockdale. **Jim and the Sun Goddess.** Illus. Maureen Gray and Gordon Gray. Methuen, 1975. 30 pp.

Who would be foolhardy enough to attempt to recover some valuable microfilm hidden at the temple of the sun goddess in an extinct volcano? British agent Jim Hunter and his dog, Radar, try to do just this while enemy agents threaten them every step of the way.

Butterworth, Ben, and Bill Stockdale. **Jim in Training.** Illus. Maureen Gray and Gordon Gray. Methuen, 1975. 64 pp.

To qualify for a promotion, British agent Jim Hunter goes to a special training camp. But things begin to go terrifyingly wrong—he almost drowns, he crashes while using a jet pack, he sees his instructor shot by a poison dart, and he almost detonates a bomb. Hunter begins to suspect another British agent is behind the "accidents."

Butterworth, Ben, and Bill Stockdale. **The Missing Aircraft.** Illus. Maureen Gray and Gordon Gray. Methuen, 1975. 64 pp.

British agent Jim Hunter is sent to a South American country to find his commander's missing friend, Harry Hammond. Once there Jim meets a CIA agent who is also looking for Harry because the country's gold, an airplane, and Hammond all disappeared at the same time. Jim finds it hard to believe, but could his chief's friend be a crook?

Butterworth, Ben, and Bill Stockdale. **Prisoner of Pedro Cay.** Illus. Maureen Gray and Gordon Gray. Methuen, 1978. 64 pp.

Rubber dummies, hang gliding, and a trained dog named Radar are all part of British spy Jim Hunter's latest mission—to locate a missing painter and some forged works of art. But how long can he fool a group of vicious enemy agents before they discover he is a threat to them?

Butterworth, Ben, and Bill Stockdale. **The Shipwreckers.** Illus. Maureen Gray and Gordon Gray. Methuen, 1976. 80 pp.

Three ships carrying gold and diamonds have mysteriously sunk off the coast of Cornwall, England. British spy Jim Hunter must use all his diving skills and a series of special underwater weapons to expose and defeat a gang of modern shipwreckers.

Butterworth, Ben, and Bill Stockdale. **The Sniper at Zimba.** Illus. Maureen Gray and Gordon Gray. Methuen, 1978. 64 pp.

A gang of assassins wants to kill President Komo, leader of an African country. Agent Jim Hunter is sent to stop the gang from carrying out the murderous plot. If he fails, President Komo's people will be robbed of all their valuable iron and gold deposits by some big European companies.

Butterworth, Ben, and Bill Stockdale. **The Temple of Mantos.** Illus. Maureen Gray and Gordon Gray. Methuen, 1976. 80 pp.

What secrets are held within an ancient golden temple in Brazil? Agent Jim Hunter tries to find out, but before he can reach the temple, he must battle dangerous Indians, flesh-eating piranha fish, and poisonous snakes.

Byars, Betsy. **Trouble River.** Illus. Rocco Negri. Camelot Books, 1975. 158 pp.

A wild band of Indian savages forces twelve-year-old Dewey and his grandmother to flee for their lives. The pair begin a long and dangerous journey down Trouble River on Dewey's homemade raft. Grandmother and grandson survive the perils of wolf attacks and rushing rapids but soon discover that more dangerous encounters lie ahead of them.

Byars, Betsy C. **Rama the Gypsy Cat.** Illus. Peggy Bacon. Camelot Books, 1976. 109 pp.

Rama is a cat who seems to have nine lives. His travels lead him to several masters, but he always moves on to look for adventure. Using his wits and skill, Rama survives fights with tough wharf cats, flooded rivers, and near starvation.

Cameron, Ian. **The White Ship.** Avon Books, 1977. 207 pp.

Susan Kent tells zoology teacher Dave Seymour a strange tale all about golden seals on a desolate island near Antarctica. Then, weird things happen to Susan. She experiences a type of transformation in which someone seems to possess her body, speaking a strange language and calling for help. Feeling this transformation has something to do with the mysterious island of seals, Susan and Dave travel there as members of the British Antarctic survey team.

Campbell, Archie. **Diamonds in the Dirt.** Illus. John Lytle. Fearon-Pitman Publishers, 1977. 44 pp.

A new motocross track is plagued with a series of accidents. But why? The members of the club are determined to find out and keep their track open and safe no matter what the cost. This is only one in a series of ten easy-to-read adventure books that includes *The Money Game, Flight to Fear, The Time Trap, The Candy Man,* and *Dream of the Dead.*

Campbell, Hope. **A Peak beneath the Moon.** Four Winds Press, 1979. 133 pp.

Maggie Sanderson loves to fantasize in and around a marvelous old stone tower on the vacant lot next door. When she discovers it will be torn down, Maggie works hard to save the tower. Maggie's detective work about the tower leads her to uncover the strange story of Miguel Sanchez Oliver St. James, the man who had begun building the tower years ago and then disappeared, leaving the structure unfinished.

Carter, Lin. **The Nemesis of Evil.** Popular Library, 1978. 219 pp.

The Omega men are a highly specialized crime-fighting force that crosses swords with all the fiendish supercriminals of the world. Led by Prince Zarkon, the Omega crew will meet their toughest challenge when they battle a monstrous creature who calls himself Lucifer. This criminal and his satanic slaves are using their knowledge of the black arts to gain power and threaten humankind.

Carter, Lin. **The Volcano Ogre.** Popular Library, 1976. 224 pp.

Prince Zarkon comes from the future to fight evil with his superior knowledge and training. His men are all handpicked for their special talents. The Prince and his force have been called to the tiny island of Rangatoa to get rid of the terrifying fire devil, a lava-dripping creature who lives in the island's volcano.

Cervantes Saavedra, Miguel de (translator J. M. Cohen; abridged by Olive Jones). **The Adventures of Don Quixote.** Illus. George Him. Methuen, 1980. 207 pp.

Don Quixote is a popular figure who has turned up throughout Spanish literature in plays, musicals, and comedies. He is a Spanish gentleman who has a horse called Rocinante and a squire called Sancho Panza. They wander through the country imagining themselves on special missions of rescue. Along the way Quixote tilts at windmills, thinking they are giants. This is a shortened version of the long novel written in 1604.

Chester, Deborah. **The Sign of the Owl.** Four Winds Press, 1981. 219 pp.

Fifteen-year-old Wint, son of the Duke of Gaumont, discovers his uncle and cousin are plotting to take his father's title and lands.

Wint warns his father, but it is too late. One night his uncle, his cousin, and a band of traitors kill the duke. Wint is determined to regain control of what is now rightfully his. But first he must find the sacred sword.

Clark, Ann Nolan. **Year Walk.** Viking Press, 1975. 197 pp.

Sixteen-year-old Kepa is excited to leave his Basque village and help Tio Maro herd sheep across the wilds of Idaho. When Tio becomes ill, Kepa is forced to herd sheep alone over 400 miles. Kepa must depend on his own courage and survival instincts to complete this dangerous but necessary job.

Cleaver, Vera, and Bill Cleaver. **Trial Valley.** J. B. Lippincott Co., 1977. 158 pp.

When their father dies, the three Luther children are left alone in their wilderness home in the Great Smokey Mountains. Determined to survive, they learn the value of hard work and courage. Then a small child is abandoned near their home, and the three Luthers must decide if they can care for the child by themselves.

Cohen, Peter Zachary. **Deadly Game at Stony Creek.** Illus. Michael J. Deas. Dial Press, 1978. 107 pp.

Cliff's parents are away when a pack of wild dogs begins to roam the countryside near Cliff's home. But Cliff does more than sit and watch from the ranch window—he goes after them. Before long, Cliff realizes he is no match for the wild, crazed beasts, but by that time he has gone too far into the dense forest that surrounds the ranch.

Conn, Martha Orr. **Crazy to Fly.** Illus. Richard Cuffari. Atheneum Publishers, 1978. 179 pp.

When young Tommy Davison first sees an airplane, he is living on a farm with his parents. It is just after World War I, a period when flying circuses and barnstorming are popular. Tommy, fascinated with planes, wants to learn all about them, but his father is opposed. So Tommy runs away from home to join a group of flyers led by Mrs. Kelly. Tommy works on engines and performs as a stunt man while learning that exhibition flying is a more serious, and dangerous, profession than he had thought.

Corcoran, Barbara. **Cabin in the Sky.** Atheneum Publishers, 1977. 197 pp.

In a small town in Maine, Tom Fortier dreams about becoming a great stage director. With high hopes, he journeys to the heart of theater activity—New York City. But instead of a warm reception, he is ignored and made fun of. Slowly, Tom begins to realize he must continue to have faith in his abilities and fight for recognition if he is to succeed at all.

Corlett, William. **The Dark Side of the Moon.** Bradbury Press, 1976. 159 pp.

David Mason is kidnapped from Ruggles Military Academy for no apparent reason. No ransom is demanded in the notes sent back— only messages that the world is a mess. At the same time Major Wayne Andrews is on his way to Mars. How these two events begin to relate to each other forms the strange story of this adventure novel.

Cormier, Robert. **After the First Death.** Pantheon Books, 1979. 233 pp.

A school bus of preschool children, four terrorists, the military, a general and his son, and a top-secret organization known as Inner Delta are all involved in this story of international intrigue. The book asks readers to decide how far they feel it is right to go in fighting for a cause. Mature situations.

Cowen, Eve. **Jungle Jenny.** Illus. Mary Burkhardt. Fearon-Pitman Publishers, 1979. 57 pp.

Jenny agrees to marry Cliff and live with him as a pioneer in the Brazilian jungle. But soon after her arrival she is shocked by stories of an uprising and by Cliff's apparent abandonment of her. How will Jenny survive in the jungle? Can she trust anybody? Easy reading.

Credle, Ellis. **Big Doin's on Razorback Ridge.** Illus. by author. Thomas Nelson, 1978. 125 pp.

The president is coming to Razorback Ridge to give a speech to open a new dam that will bring electricity to the mountain people. But many people, like cousins Nancy and Jodey, don't want their old way of life to change. Nancy and Jodey want to show the president some traditional mountain dances at the celebration for him, so their Uncle Badger, the witchman, decides to help the pair. Easy reading.

Crompton, Anne Eliot. **The Rain-Cloud Pony.** Illus. Paul Frame. Holiday House, 1977. 127 pp.

Pat Dunfield dreams about riding horses. Then she meets Angel, a beautiful, sophisticated girl who owns a horse. The girls decide to switch roles so Pat can be with the horse and Angel can spend time with her boyfriend. But their perfect scheme backfires.

Crume, Vic, and Arthur R. Dubs. **Wilderness Family, Part 2.** Scholastic Book Services, 1979. 122 pp.

To the Robinson family, a log cabin, mountain air, and summer warmth is a dream come true after living in smoggy California. But the arrival of winter ushers in new challenges and hardships. Soon the Robinsons are plagued by hungry bears, giant avalanches, and fierce wolves. Their only hope is that spring will come soon, but meanwhile they must survive.

Cummings, Betty Sue. **Now, Ameriky.** Atheneum Publishers, 1980. 175 pp.

It is the 1840s—the time of the terrible potato famine in Ireland. Brigid N. Clery realizes she must leave for America and, once there, must raise enough money to send for her family. The dream of America quickly turns into a nightmare as Brigid must spend the long voyage in a crowded and dirty ship. Worse yet, she has paid for food but is getting none. Now she has the choice of being a prostitute for the crew and being fed, or starving. Luckily, two fellow passengers decide to help Brigid during the voyage. But there are more hardships awaiting her in the poor Irish settlement she is forced to live in once she lands in "Ameriky."

Cunningham, Julia. **Dear Rat.** Illus. Walter Lorraine. Camelot Books, 1977. 126 pp.

Andrew the rat may look tough, but he has a tender heart. Coming to France from Humpton, Wyoming, Andrew wants nothing but peace and quiet. Instead, he's soon involved in a plot to steal the Chartres Cathedral jewels and dispose of them at the royal court. Soon Andrew is running from murderous mobsters through the sewers of Paris. Easy reading.

Curry, Jane Louise. **The Wolves of Aam.** Argo Books. 1981. 192 pp.

With his lucky "dreamstone" gone, Runner was in great danger from the "Dread Ones"—great wolves who walked the land—and from evil Lord Naghar. Now Runner must find the stone before Lord Naghar's men do. To help in his quest are Fith and Cat, two huge Ice Folk, and the magical wolves of Aam. Even with these friends, however, Runner realizes that death could be waiting for him at any moment during his trip through Iceland to find the mystic stone.

Dahlin, Doris (translator Joan Tate). **The Sit-In Game.** Avon Books, 1977. 124 pp.

Seventeen Swedish students decide to let everyone know how frustrated they are with their school system by staging a sit-in demonstration. By the end of the book we learn how all seventeen students feel about the demonstration, as well as how the sit-in started, how it developed, and how it ended.

Dank, Milton. **Game's End.** J. B. Lippincott Co., 1979. 158 pp.

Half French, half American, Charles Marceau is now a British spy working behind German lines to support the upcoming Allied invasion of Normandy. Charles and his friends usually fight against the Germans, but they also must battle traitors within their own organization. Through their acts of sabotage and espionage, Charles and his fellow agents hope to help speed the end of World War II.

Dank, Milton. **Red Flight Two.** Delacorte Press, 1981. 185 pp.

This novel traces the story of Edward Burton who, at only eighteen, has earned medals in World War I and won victories. But he has also suffered a breakdown because of a friend's death. Now a flight instructor in England, he finds himself forced to return to France where he has to cope with the pressure of readying undertrained men for war. His battle with his conscience in choosing men to send out on dangerous missions, and his responsibilities in leading his old squadron, make life difficult for Edward.

Davies, Andrew. **Conrad's War.** Crown Publishers, 1980. 120 pp.

Conrad has an unusual hobby—war. His parents don't think much of it, and when he decides to build a tank, they refuse to help him. So he builds it himself out of bicycle wheels, wood, and cardboard. He has a great time driving the tank; it gives him a sense of real power and makes him feel as if he is in World War II. But when Conrad suddenly becomes the enemy, his own private war becomes very scary indeed. (Horn Book Award for Fiction)

Davis, Paxton. **Ned.** Illus. Harold Little. Atheneum Publishers, 1978. 140 pp.

Even when Ned (later known as Lawrence of Arabia) was a small child in England, he showed signs of being a strong leader. Now a soldier in World War I, Ned is given the important job of advising British troops in Arabia. Suddenly, he runs away from this high position and leads the Arabs in a bloody revolt against the Turks. When Britain becomes the enemy of Arabia, Ned must choose between his homeland and the country for which he has been fighting.

Davis, Robert P. **Control Tower.** G. P. Putnam's Sons, 1980. 322 pp.

A fierce storm over Miami leads a Concorde airliner into a collision course with a private plane. One veteran air controller slowly realizes he may not be able to handle the pressure that this dangerous situation is creating for him. Will he snap under it? Or can he and the other men in the airport control tower prevent the two planes from crashing?

Defoe, Daniel. **Robinson Crusoe.** Watermill Press, 1980. 448 pp.

Robinson Crusoe, shipwrecked on an island, must survive and fight against boredom and loneliness. He finds most of his time taken up with finding food, avoiding cannibals, and teaching English and civilized manners to Friday, a native slave he saves from death. Originally published in 1719.

Degens, T. **The Game on Thatcher Island.** Viking Press, 1977. 148 pp.

Harry didn't want to play the mysterious game on Thatcher Island. But the other kids forced him, and now, with the sea between himself and safety, he must face a horror worse than he had ever dreamed. Harry is trapped in a huge game of death, where friends turn on each other with fury in their eyes and weapons in their hands.

Dickinson, Peter. **Annerton Pit.** Atlantic Monthly Press, 1977. 175 pp.

Jake Bertold is worried when the weekly postcards stop coming from his ghost-hunting grandfather. Jake is blind, and his "sixth sense" tells him his grandfather is in trouble. But exactly what kind of trouble? To find out, Jake and his brother Martin set out on a new motorcycle to trace their grandfather's route and finally locate him in northern England. Their problems are far from over, however, because Grampa is being held prisoner by a group of dangerous revolutionaries. How can two boys overcome these armed men?

Dickinson, Peter. **The Seventh Raven.** Unicorn Books, 1981. 192 pp.

Doll Jacobs, a hundred other children, her own mother, and a few parents from their London neighborhood are taken hostage at a church opera rehearsal. For the first time in her life, Doll tastes fear. Then the revolutionaries begin a terrible game. The morality of art and politics is put on mock trial, and Doll and her mother are forced to judge their own values. Doll realizes that the gun at her head is held by a woman from a different sort of world—a world that Doll must try to understand.

Dickinson, Peter. **Tulku.** Unicorn Books, 1979. 286 pp.

In China, a boy whose father's mission is destroyed decides to travel with Mrs. Jones, an eccentric, gun-toting plant collector. Together they enter a great gold-domed monastery where an old lama holds them as prisoners. Will the supernatural powers in the area help them escape—or will they help the lama?

Dixon, Paige. **Pimm's Cup for Everybody.** Atheneum Publishers, 1976. 142 pp.

Derek Fillmore, high school basketball star, learns life is more than running up and down a court when he meets old Mr. Pimm, a former bartender. An Englishman, Mr. Pimm is on vacation in America. His trip is being paid for by the company that is advertising "Mr. Pimm's Rum," and it soon becomes clear to Derek and Mr. Pimm that greed is what made the company send the old man to America. Derek and Mr. Pimm become close traveling companions, venturing into the wilderness to escape the falsities of big business.

Dixon, Paige. **The Search for Charlie.** Atheneum Publishers, 1976. 90 pp.

When her younger brother Charlie is reported kidnapped, Jane decides to take matters into her own hands. With the help of an Indian friend named Vic, Jane desperately searches the mountains of Montana for her brother. She becomes even more determined when the police officers involved in the search turn out to be lazy and uncaring. Then, after three exhausting days, Jane meets the true test of her courage and of her love for her brother.

Dixon, Paige. **Skipper.** Atheneum Publishers, 1980. 110 pp.

Skipper's brother is dead, so he decides to move on and find a life of his own. First, Skipper goes to North Carolina to find the father he has never seen. To his surprise, Skipper discovers his family is a wealthy, landowning dynasty ruled by his half brother, Gerald. Adjusting to so many relatives, and to Gerald's view of the world, becomes almost more than Skipper feels he can cope with.

Dixon, Paige. **Walk My Way.** Atheneum Publishers, 1980. 139 pp.

Kitty Le Blanc was fourteen, nearly six feet tall, broad shouldered— and afraid. She did not ever feel sure of herself and did not know how to handle her widowed father, who often beat her. One night, one of her father's friends tries to kiss her. Panic-stricken, Kitty pushes him backward and watches in horror as he hits his head on a radiator. Certain he is dead, Kitty rushes off into the woods to hide. Her goal is her Aunt Lee's house, fifty miles away. But before she reaches her Aunt Lee's, Kitty will have adventures that teach her about other people and herself.

Domke, Todd. **Grounded.** Alfred A. Knopf, 1982. 186 pp.

Anyone can build a glider. But can anyone fly it? And what about getting the money to build one in the first place? Parker and Zeke dream up a scheme to produce a play to earn that money for a glider, but they end up making the front page of every newspaper, and getting some television coverage. When they become involved with some very famous people, including the president, they realize their project has gotten out of their control. The results of the project contain both suspense and laughter.

Dunne, Mary Collins. **Hoby and Stub.** Atheneum Publishers, 1981. 156 pp.

Hoby is a thirteen-year-old boy whose mother and father are both dead. Until a foster home is found for Hoby, he has to stay with his mother's boyfriend, Virgil, who is a violent man. When Virgil brings a dog home, Hoby falls in love with him and names him Stub for "stubborn." Soon Hoby decides to run away with Stub, and go to his one relative, who lives a long way from Texas. He finds life on the road harder than he expects, but he also experiences some kindness along the way.

East, Ben, as told to (editors Jerolyn Nentland and Howard Schroeder). **Danger in the Air.** Illus. Jack Dahl. Crestwood House, 1979.

In the isolated islands of the Florida Keys, Les Tassell is possessed by the uncomfortable and frightening feeling that danger waits for him on the water. But Les tries to shake off his fears as he prepares for another day of deep-sea fishing and diving. Will he survive the next twenty-four hours? Are his instincts to be trusted? This is one in a series of eight adventure stories that includes: *Frozen Terror, Trapped in Devil's Hole, Grizzly, Found Alive,* and *Four Days Lost.*

Edwards, G. B. **The Book of Ebenezer Le Page.** Avon Books, 1982. 400 pp.

Crusty, funny, contrary old Ebenezer Le Page remembers his long and interesting life in this novel. Ebenezer's life is tied to the sea around the Channel Islands. Through stories of his loves, feuds, sorrows, friendships, and family ties, Ebenezer gives readers a clear feeling for what life is like on those isolated islands between England and France.

Eisenberg, Lisa. **Falling Star.** Fearon-Pitman Publishers, 1980. 57 pp.

When Laura Brewster's favorite actor appears to have been murdered, she takes it upon herself to investigate the case. His car has crashed, but no body has been found. Is the actor's manager responsible for tampering with the car's brakes—or is the actor's wife to blame?

Eisenberg, Lisa. **Fast-Food King.** Fearon-Pitman Publishers, 1980. 58 pp.

Laura Brewster travels to Sydney, Australia, to investigate the disappearance of a famous secret sauce recipe. It seems that Reginald Bumpo, the inventor of the sauce, has been murdered just before unveiling the new Bumpo Burger. Little does Laura suspect that her search for the murderer (and the secret sauce) will lead her to an encounter with a shark and a fall from a building.

Eisenberg, Lisa. **Golden Idol.** Fearon-Pitman Publishers, 1980. 59 pp.

Laura Brewster, an international insurance agent, is off to Hong Kong to recover a golden idol stolen from a client. An American taxi driver, a private investigator, and an Oriental sea goddess all become involved with Laura in the search for the priceless statue.

Eisenberg, Lisa. **Killer Music.** Fearon-Pitman Publishers, 1980. 60 pp.

Insurance investigator Laura Brewster flies to London to help rock star Roddy Moon discover who is stealing his music—and holding it for ransom. Before he can discover the criminals, however, Roddy is killed. Laura's life is now in danger as she decides to uncover the killer's identity.

Eisenberg, Lisa. **Tiger Rose.** Fearon-Pitman Publishers, 1980. 59 pp.

In Mexico, Laura Brewster takes the place of a dead horse-trainer in an attempt to discover who is killing racehorses insured by her company. After a close escape from death caused by a spooked horse, Laura becomes suspicious about the news that champion racer Tiger Rose is dead. Could fellow racehorse Big Bay be a fraud?

Elwood, Ann, and John Raht. **Walking Out.** Tempo Books, 1979. 169 pp.

Sixteen-year-old Lisa parachutes into the dense forest when the small airplane she is in has engine trouble. Alone in the Alaskan wilderness, she must use her common sense and her few possessions to survive. For days she wanders in search of help; then she encounters something that turns the lonely wilderness into a nightmare.

Eyerly, Jeannette. **The Leonardo Touch.** J. B. Lippincott Co., 1976. 156 pp.

When Elizabeth's artist father is injured, the trip to England that she has dreamed of seems ruined. But her father urges Elizabeth to go on alone and choose a painting to add to their collection. But when she follows his instructions, Elizabeth discovers a hidden secret and finds herself in grave danger.

Eyerly, Jeannette. **See Dave Run.** J. B. Lippincott Co., 1978. 126 pp.

Fifteen-year-old Dave Hendry runs away from his strict stepfather and alcoholic mother in search of his real father. He travels across America, working on farms and at restaurants. Then a criminal look-alike escapes from prison, and the police arrest Dave instead. Behind bars he makes a dramatic decision when he realizes that he will be sent back to his unhappy family.

Farley, Walter. **The Black Stallion.** Random House, 1982. 187 pp.

In a small Arabian port on the Red Sea, young Alec Ramsay first sees his black stallion—a horse destined to play an important part in his life. The pair develop an understanding between them after surviving a shipwreck and life alone on a deserted island. Their final adventure is a famous horserace in America—and it threatens to separate them forever. Originally published in 1941.

Forman, James D. **Call Back Yesterday.** Charles Scribner's Sons, 1981. 163 pp.

Cindy Cooper is the sole survivor of the violent and bloody take-over of an American embassy in Saudi Arabia. Her family and friends all appear to be dead. Now government officials want to force her to relive the terror by remembering the events. If she does not, a major world conflict could occur. So Cindy painfully pieces her story together from that carefree moment she left her boarding school in Switzerland on Christmas Day, 1988.

Fox, Michael. **Whitepaws: A Coyote-Dog.** Illus. Stephen Gammell. Coward, McCann & Geoghegan, 1979. 73 pp.

Whitepaws is a "coydog," a cross between a coyote and a dog. Some young children decide to take Whitepaws out of the country to live with them in the city. But Whitepaws still has many wild, natural instincts, and the children must decide if they should keep Whitepaws chained up or take her back to the country. Easy reading.

French, Michael. **Pursuit.** Delacorte Press, 1982. 181 pp.

After Gordy's brother Martin plunges to his death off the steep Sierra rockface, Roger claims the fall was an accident. But Gordy knows that Roger had cut Martin's safety rope. Gordy must get to town and notify the sheriff, and he sets off alone. But Roger, a star athlete with a brilliant college future, pursues him. With his superior wilderness skills, Roger has dozens of ways of stopping Gordy. Gordy has only one advantage: his fierce determination to outwit and outlast his pursuer.

Garfield, Leon. **The Confidence Man.** Viking Press, 1979. 279 pp.

Young Hans Ruppert, the village loafer, is haunted by secret visions of great wealth. When Captain von Stumpfel, a mysterious soldier dressed in black with a skull on his cap, offers to lead a group of persecuted Germans to Virginia, Hans feels that his dreams could easily come true. When the group reaches London, von Stumpfel abandons them. Hans will not give up his dream, however, and he becomes leader of the group. But can Hans get the group from England to America?

Gathorne-Hardy, Jonathan. **The Airship "Ladyship" Adventure.** Illus. Glo Coalson. J. B. Lippincott Co., 1977. 218 pp.

Jane Charrington's father has invented the world's first nuclear-powered airship. When the ship accidentally launches, with Jane and her housekeeper aboard, Jane begins a series of adventures that includes a narrow escape from an avalanche and encounters with the "Tiger Man" and the savage Mub. Easy reading.

George, Jean. **My Side of the Mountain.** Illus. by author. E. P. Dutton, 1975. 166 pp.

No one takes the childish threats of young Sam Gribley seriously until he actually does run away. Sam is determined to take care of himself without any store-bought food or clothing. A large hollowed-out hemlock tree becomes his home, and small game and roots make up his meals. But the newspapers soon betray his hiding place, and Sam must take steps to fight for his new secluded home.

George, Jean Craighead. **River Rats, Inc.** E. P. Dutton, 1979. 136 pp.

Joe Zero and Crowbar smell "something fishy" when their uncle asks them to take a dangerous raft trip to dispose of the ashes of

Roland Streeter, as requested in his will. The boys soon realize that a federal agent and the "Lizard Boy" are following them—a discovery that signals the beginning of a period of terror and intrigue.

Goudge, Elizabeth. **Linnets and Valerians.** Avon Books, 1978. 280 pp.

Four children run away from their grandmother's house and are taken in by a lost uncle living in the strange town of High Barton. Someone has cast a sinister spell on the people there. The children are in danger of being overcome by the dark magic, unless they can learn to reverse its powers.

Green, Phyllis. **The Empty Seat.** Elsevier/Nelson Books, 1980. 128 pp.

Young Michael is excited about staying with his grandparents in Ocean City for the summer. But when his grandmother, Tweety-Bird, becomes ill, Michael decides to team up with Donald and his English girlfriend to rescue Donald's sister from a religious cult.

Greene, Constance C. **Dotty's Suitcase.** Viking Press, 1980. 147 pp.

The suitcase filled with money and lying beside the road is like a dream come true to Dotty and Jud, who have often wished to go on a long vacation. Without telling their parents, the two youngsters set out right away, hitching a ride with a stranger. But their hopes of vacation fun are ruined when a car accident, a fierce blizzard, and other mishaps cross their path.

Griese, Arnold A. **The Wind Is Not a River.** Illus. Glo Coalson. Thomas Y. Crowell Co., 1978. 108 pp.

What will happen to Sasan and her brother Sidak? They had always lived a very peaceful life in their village on the island of Attu, off the Alaskan coast, but now World War II has begun. Japanese soldiers have taken over their tiny village, and everyone has been captured but Sasan and Sidak. Will the children be able to survive on their own? Easy reading.

Griffiths, Helen. **Dancing Horses.** Holiday House, 1981. 152 pp.

Francisco Javier is a child wandering alone in post-Civil War Spain after running away from an orphanage. When he finds a job taking care of an old mare, he also finds an opportunity to give freely of his affection—to Gavilan, the golden colt of the mare. But this colt is wild and hates people. Francisco's dream of riding Gavilan as part of a mounted bullfight begins a series of adventures.

Griffiths, Helen. **Just a Dog.** Illus. Victor Ambrus. Holiday House, 1975. 160 pp.

To most people, Shadow was just another unwanted stray dog. After a group of boys attempts to kill her and a woman tries to bind her with a chain, Shadow decides to lead the life of a vagabond. But in the course of her travels she mets a human vagabond who may change her sad and lonely life.

Halacy, D. S., Jr. **The Sky Trap.** Thomas Nelson, 1975. 124 pp.

Teenager Grant Stone's troubles begin when he lands his home-built glider in an abandoned airfield in Arizona. Here Grant runs into a gang of drug smugglers who blackmail him into helping them bring drugs into the United States from Mexico.

Hall, Lynn. **Ride a Wild Dream.** Camelot Books, 1978. 160 pp.

The moment Jon first sets eyes on Sun God at the auction, he knows that it is the horse he's always dreamed of. But after several months of joyous rides, Jon begins to realize that there is something terribly wrong with his dream horse, something that endangers Jon's own life. As a result, a desperate struggle develops between Jon's love for Sun God and his own conscience.

Hallman, Ruth. **Rescue Chopper.** Laurel-Leaf Library, 1981. 94 pp.

Danger—Commander Scott Keane and his Coast Guard crew face it every day aboard their rescue helicopter. They are the men called upon to save victims of floods, boating accidents, and other disasters. Sometimes they have problems working together in these situations, but the chopper team always puts safety first.

Hallstead, William F. **Conqueror of the Clouds.** Elsevier/Nelson Books, 1980. 185 pp.

In 1912 young Ben Horner is working in his uncle's blacksmith shop, but his heart is in the air with the spectacular barnstorming stunt pilots. So Ben runs away from home to join barnstormers Murf and Fos, learns to fly, and tests his courage in daring aerial acrobatics, including the perilous "Dive of Death."

Hallstead, William F. **The Man Downstairs.** Elsevier/Nelson Books, 1979. 158 pp.

After Don Ellison, a city employee, ignores a request for a political contribution, he and his new wife are threatened. Don is torn between speaking out against the political party's corruption and keeping quiet in order to further his career. His decision to go against the party throws him into a new series of dangers.

Hancock, Niel. **Dragon Winter.** Popular Library, 1978. 351 pp.

Because they face a fierce winter, the worried animals in one forest persuade Bramble Otter to visit Old Bark, the wise and revered silver bear, to find out what they can do to protect themselves. But the Forest Council representatives are attacked by killer wolves and barely escape being trapped in a forest fire. Their most dangerous encounter, however, is with Olwin, who wants to become True King. The mysterious Blackpaw soon joins the group and helps devise a plan to outwit Olwin and find Old Bark.

Hardy, Thomas. **Our Exploits at West Poley.** Illus. John Lawrence. Oxford University Press, 1978. 79 pp.

While exploring a cave, cousins Lenny and Steve find a mysterious underground stream. Their discovery provides them with some amusement as they attempt to change its course. What they don't realize is that their playful efforts threaten the lives of the local villagers and may cause irreversible damage to the area.

Hartley, Norman. **Quicksilver.** Avon Books, 1980. 237 pp.

Weary of his life as a terrorist-for-hire, Major Peter Dallman retires to a Zen monastery. But when his best friend's daughter, Silver, places herself in a dangerous situation, Peter agrees to become her bodyguard. Soon both Peter and Silver are involved in a battle against a vast computer empire and the evil mastermind who controls it. Mature language and situations.

Haugaard, Erik Christian. **Leif the Unlucky.** Houghton Mifflin Co., 1982. 206 pp.

Young Leif Magnusson finds himself in a life-and-death struggle in fifteenth-century Greenland. Life in the Norwegian colony there has been getting worse and worse. The elders dream of the past and wait for supply ships that never come. So Leif and a group of colonists decide to do something to save themselves and Greenland. But they first have to overcome the ambituous Egil Sigurdson, who wants to restore the worship of ancient gods and make himself master of all Greenland.

Hayes, Richard. **The Secret Army.** Viking Press, 1977. 212 pp.

The Nosotros, a secret terrorist organization, is kidnapping the teachers at Lindown Primary School for ransom money. Three students, John, Brian, and Juniper, do their best to find the teachers, but they have to deal with helicopters, tranquilizer darts, and the gigantic underground Nosotros headquarters. Can a small band of teachers and students foil the mad plot of the Nosotros to take over the world?

Henderson, Lois T. **Touch of the Golden Scepter.** Chariot Books, 1981. 144 pp.

It is 485 B.C., and young Hadassah is an orphan who can depend only on her wits and her Uncle Mordecai. One day her beauty attracts the attention of some officers of King Ahasuerus, and Hadassah is taken away to court. Hadassah—now called Esther—is finally told the reason behind her treatment: she is to compete to be the next queen of Persia.

Hinton, Nigel. **Collision Course.** Thomas Nelson, 1976. 159 pp.

Fifteen-year-old Ray steals a motorcycle and accidentally kills an old woman. Now Ray is afraid of losing his friends and disgracing his father, so he begins to cover up his crime. Finally Ray's conscience begins to bother him, threatening the elaborate web of lies he has created.

Hinton, S. E. **Rumble Fish.** Delacorte Press, 1979. 122 pp.

Motorcycles, gangs, and gang fights are not unusual in Rusty James's town. Together with his brother, the rough and respected "Motorcycle Boy," Rusty fights and scrambles his way through high school. Close scrapes with death and the law are part of his life as a "rumble fish," but underneath the toughness Rusty has deep feelings and hurts.

Hodge, Jane Aiken. **Last Act.** Coward, McCann & Geoghegan, 1979. 251 pp.

Tragedy seems to follow tragedy for Anne. First her young husband is killed in a car accident and she is left penniless. Now the doctors tell her that she has only a few months to live. So Anne accepts an offer to sing in a new opera as a way of forgetting her pain. But she soon finds herself involved in international intrigue—someone is determined that the opera will not be performed.

Hostetler, Marian. **Fear in Algeria.** Illus. James Converse. Herald Press, 1979. 126 pp.

Fourteen-year-old Zina from South Bend, Indiana, is excited by the chance to visit her birthplace in Algeria during spring vacation. However, one problem after another happens after she arrives. No matter where Zina goes, she has the feeling she is being followed. Is the mysterious man in blue really spying on her?

Hostetler, Marian. **Journey to Jerusalem.** Illus. Allan Eitzen. Herald Press, 1978. 126 pp.

Mim's world changes dramatically when her mother accepts a job that throws the two of them into the middle of the Jewish-Arab conflict. Plunged into a life-and-death struggle, the curious twelve-year-old learns there are two sides to every issue.

Household, Geoffrey. **Escape into Daylight.** Atlantic Monthly Press, 1976. 139 pp.

One minute Mike is watching a familiar-looking man writing graffiti on a wall, and the next he is being drugged and pushed into a van. Mike has unwittingly seen the father of a kidnap victim trying to make contact with her captors. Now he, too, is kidnapped and being held with the girl, Carrie, in the underground chambers of a ruined church. He and Carrie plot their escape, but they soon find freedom is worse than being captive—they are being hunted like animals in unfamiliar country.

Houston, James. **Frozen Fire: A Tale of Courage.** Illus. by author. McElderry Books, 1978. 149 pp.

Matthew Morgan's father, a geologist searching for rare minerals, is lost in the Canadian Arctic when his helicopter is forced down by a blizzard. Matthew and his Eskimo friend, Kayak, set off in a snowmobile on a perilous search for Mr. Morgan. Struggling against fierce wind storms, starvation, wild animals, and wild men, the two fight desperately for life—theirs and that of Matthew's father.

Houston, James. **River Runners: A Tale of Hardship and Bravery.** Illus. by author. McElderry Books, 1979. 142 pp.

This is a fictionalized account of Andrew Stewart, a fifteen-year-old apprentice at a fur-trading post on the Hudson Strait. An Indian boy called Pashak joins Andrew, and they set off to start a fur outpost on distant Ghost Lake. But bitter life and death experiences happen to them during the brutal winter that arrives that year.

Houston, James. **Spirit Wrestler.** Avon Books, 1981. 277 pp.

One night a body is carried into a camp in the frozen north of the Canadian territories. It is Shoona, the feared and respected shaman—a man with magic powers. But the spirit still lives on in Shoona, and though dead, he tells his story. It is a tale of tattooed giants, sorcery, sacred relics, and angry sea goddesses.

Houston, Robert. **Cholo.** Avon Books, 1981. 175 pp.

He was once the poorest of the poor, an Indian, a "cholo" who lived in the slums of Lima, Peru. But there may be a way out for him. The Chinaman controls every black market in the country. All this powerful man's crimes are written in a book. Now the cholo has the secret records, and with them the Chinaman's money. He is now the richest man in Peru. But he is also the most wanted. Mature language and situations.

Hubert, Cam. **Dreamspeaker.** Avon Books, 1980. 85 pp.

Peter has been committed to an institution for delinquent boys. Something haunts him—some unnamed evil. In a desperate attempt to escape, he runs deep into the forests of British Columbia. There he is adopted by an old Indian, the Dreamspeaker, and his mute companion, He Who Would Sing. Through their strange teachings, Peter learns the power of the Indian spirit—and the courage to face his own terror. (Gibson Literary Award)

Hunter, Kristin. **Lou in the Limelight.** Charles Scribner's Sons, 1981. 296 pp.

Singer-composer Lou and her three friends leave home to make their marks in the world of popular music. Their first record album gets them jobs in New York clubs and then an opening at a Las Vegas casino, where they proceed to fall into most of the traps that await inexperienced performers. They even become involved with criminal underworld figures. Their rescuer turns out to be a surprise to everyone.

Hyde, Dayton O. **Strange Companion.** Scholastic Book Services, 1975. 234 pp.

David's mean stepfather has threatened him once too often, so David decides to run away from home. He hides in the cargo hold of a small plane. But when the plane crashes in the icy wilderness, the boy finds himself in a desperate struggle to stay alive. Who will survive—the runaway, the injured pilot, or their strange companion? (Dutton Animal Book Award)

Jablonski, David, editor. **Behold the Mighty Dinosaur.** Elsevier/Nelson Books, 1981. 256 pp.

What happens when people of the present and the future travel back to prehistoric times and meet dinosaurs? This collection of stories suggests a number of exciting ideas—for example, the use of mental telepathy by people of the future in dealing with the huge and ferocious creatures of the Stone Age.

Johnson, Annabel, and Edgar Johnson. **Finders, Keepers.** Four Winds
Press, 1981. 117 pp.

Thirteen-year-old Burr McKenna gets suspended and sent home
from school one May afternoon. Meanwhile a radio newscaster begs
some man to stop circling a nuclear power plant just outside Denver.
At the same time, Burr's rebellious older sister, Alex, gathers some
food and other essentials into a knapsack and decides to run away.
Then it happens. The man carries out his threat to crash into the
plant's containment building. Mass hysteria follows as a deadly
cloud of radiation moves over the city. Burr and Alex leave for the
mountains on foot, but Burr breaks his leg on the way. How will
the pair be able to survive the nuclear disaster now?

Jones, Diana Wynne. **The Spellcoats.** Argo Books, 1979. 250 pp.

Tanaqui has spent nearly all her young life uncertain of the future.
Her country is at war with the savage Heathens, and her father and
oldest brother have left to fight them. Only Tanaqui's brother
returns, but by that time the townspeople have become suspicious
of her family. At about the same time, a great flood drives Tanaqui
and her brothers and sisters away from the village. During their
journey on the Great River, Tanaqui meets her dead mother, the
king of the Heathens, and the evil Kankredin, who threatens
everyone. Tanaqui soon realizes that she is the only one who can
defeat the fearful Kankredin.

Jones, Thomas Firth. **Rebel Gold.** Westminster Press, 1975. 158 pp.

Ike Cooper is recovering from an illness in Mexico City when he
meets Terry and the Gorillas, a tough motorcycle gang. Ike discovers
that Terry's big plan is to steal the gold left in a poor Mexican
village by a band of Confederates at the end of the Civil War. Ike
decides he must stop the Gorillas and warn the villagers, although
he is outnumbered six to one.

Joslin, Sesyle. **The Gentle Savages.** McElderry Books, 1979. 176 pp.

Twelve-year-old Dorcas and thirteen-year-old Peter would rather
run off together than be separated. So when the ship they and their
parents are traveling on docks at a North African port, the pair
escape. The newspapers call it an "elopement," but it seems less
romantic than dangerous to Dorcas and Peter at first. While their
parents search frantically for them, the two learn to fend for themselves and deal with problems never encountered at home.

Judd, Denis. **The Adventures of Long John Silver.** Avon Books, 1979. 208 pp.

How did Long John Silver get mixed up with a band of pirates in the first place? How did these pirates gain their fabulous treasure? Why did they need to bury their treasure on Captain Kidd's island? The answers to these and other questions (left unanswered in *Treasure Island*) are in this adventure novel.

Karr, Lee. **The House-Sitter.** Avon Books, 1980. 221 pp.

Lori Martin had come to Denver to spend her summer quietly housesitting for a vacationing couple, but suddenly she found herself impersonating another woman as part of an international political plot. If she doesn't go through with the masquerade, Lori is told she may never see her boyfriend—a POW in Cambodia—alive again.

Kästner, Erich (translator James Kirkup). **The Little Man.** Camelot Books, 1980. 184 pp.

When two-inch-tall Maxie Pichelsteiner's thumb-sized parents are swept off the Eiffel Tower, he is put in the custody of circus magician Hokus von Pokus. Soon Maxie becomes an apprentice to Hokus, and the two practice picking the pockets of innocent members of the circus audience. Their fun is suddenly interrupted when a group of criminals decides to kidnap Maxie.

King, Clive. **Me and My Million.** Thomas Y. Crowell Co., 1976. 180 pp.

Young Ringo's criminal abilities are so masterful that he manages to steal a painting worth one million pounds from a London art museum. Then things go wrong. He gets on the wrong bus, goes to the wrong town, is surrounded by a wild gang, is chased by the police, and has to hide on a shabby boat. But against these incredible odds, and with the help of a counterfeit painting, Ringo manages to escape . . . or does he?

Kipling, Rudyard. **Captains Courageous.** Watermill Press, 1981. 196 pp.

Harvey Cheyne, a spoiled teenager, is swept overboard while traveling on an ocean liner. He is saved by a passing fishing boat but must work for his keep. Angry and resentful, Harvey is forced to work as a member of a team. But what can the snobbish young man learn from the crew of a fishing boat? Originally published in 1897.

Kipling, Rudyard. **The Jungle Book.** Watermill Press, 1980. 222 pp.

Mowgli wandered deep into the jungle as a baby and was found and raised by a family of wolves. Through several interlocking stories, this book describes the many adventures Mowgli has with tigers, seals, elephants, and other jungle animals as he tries to become accepted as part of their world. Originally published in 1894.

Kipling, Rudyard. **Kim.** Watermill Press, 1981. 396 pp.

Kimball O'Hara, or Kim, is the orphan son of an Irish soldier. Kim is now living as a beggar in India with some Hindus who have taken him in. Then he is found by a member of his father's regiment and is sent away to be educated. Because of his firsthand knowledge of India and the ways of the Indians, Kim is drawn into the British Secret Service. He now must use his keen powers of observation as an agent for England. Originally published in 1901.

Kjelgaard, Jim. **Boomerang Hunter.** Illus. W. T. Mars. Camelot Books, 1978. 171 pp.

Balulu is an Australian aborigine boy whose tribe is having trouble finding food during a drought. When Balulu will not let his pet dingo-dog be eaten, he is forced to leave the tribe and find food on his own. Armed with only a couple of boomerangs and two spears, Balulu begins a series of adventures where he meets wild beasts and enemy tribesmen.

Kornfeld, Anita Clay. **In a Bluebird's Eye.** Holt, Rinehart & Winston, 1975. 260 pp.

Honor Whitfield, a spunky young prankster, lives in a small town during the Great Depression. When her black friend Lola, on parole from jail, decides to escape, Honor agrees to help. Planning a night flight for Lola through the backwoods is only part of Honor's adventures, though. She also hides her father from the law and spies on the town flirt. But not all of Honor's playful jokes have happy endings, and soon the young girl finds herself in grave danger.

Kotzwinkle, William. **The Leopard's Tooth.** Illus. Joe Servello. Camelot Books, 1978. 95 pp.

The moment he sets his foot on the African soil, Charles Pickett senses danger. Years ago, the witch doctor of a primitive tribe cursed his father and warned him not to return. Now, a peculiar skull on a cave floor triggers a series of weird events. When Charles finally learns the secret of the leopard's tooth, he knows that it is up to him to break the witch doctor's spell and save his father's life.

Krasilovsky, Phyllis. **The First Tulips in Holland.** Illus. S. D. Schindler. Doubleday & Co., 1982. 32 pp.

Did you know that the first tulip bulbs were brought to Holland from Persia in the sixteenth century? Well, that's how this novel explains the arrival of the Dutch national flower. Colorful illustrations and easy-to-read text fully explain the story of these famous blooms.

Kraske, Robert. **The Sea Robbers.** Harcourt Brace Jovanovich, 1977. 147 pp.

Hugh and his older brother are kidnapped and taken aboard a pirate vessel captained by the crooked Chief Hood. Hood forces the two captives to take part in recovering a treasure he has hidden from the crew, so Hugh must travel to a secluded cave on Skull Island. Then the crew discovers the plan, and the young boy tumbles into dangerous, hair-raising adventures with the pirates.

Leeson, Robert. **Silver's Revenge.** William Collins Publishers, 1978. 196 pp.

Remember *Treasure Island* and Captain Long John Silver? This book continues the story of Treasure Island. The main character here is young Tom Carter, a runaway apprentice who is befriended by Dr. Livesey. When Tom overhears talk of buried silver and a hidden map, the adventures begin. Now fifteen years after its first voyage to Treasure Island, the *Hispaniola* sails again, and it proves just as dangerous to be aboard the ship now as then.

Levin, Betty. **The Beast on the Brink.** Illus. Marian Parry. Camelot Books, 1980. 158 pp.

When Lena invents an endangered animal for a school report, she never dreams that the creature actually exists. Neither does she suspect that this animal, called a thylacine, will lead her into a strange adventure at the zoo. With the help of two platypuses, a tautara, and a loris, Lena sets out to rescue the beast.

Levin, Betty. **Landfall.** McElderry Books, 1979. 198 pp.

Liddy, an American, visits her pen pal on an island off the Scottish coast. Here she becomes involved in a chain of events concerning seals. She also finds a modern crime that is linked with an ancient myth. One day, while watching the seals frolic in the water, Liddy is suddenly faced with the sight of a stranger named Bres. And this is only one of the mysterious events that begin to happen on this Scottish island.

Lingard, Joan. **The File on Fräulein Berg.** Elsevier/Nelson Books, 1980. 153 pp.

In 1944, Kate, Sally, and Harriet, Irish schoolgirls, decide to follow their new substitute teacher, Fräulein Berg. They pursue her out of the city, destroy her new romance, and cause her to give up a treasured gift because they think she is a German spy. But the truth about the mysterious Fräulein Berg astounds even them!

Lingard, Joan. **Snake among the Sunflowers.** Thomas Nelson, 1977. 142 pp.

Each summer the Grant children—Claudine, Sophie and Paul—and their parents leave Scotland to spend time in the south of France. This summer, Claudine decides to get down to the bottom of the mystery of a strange house called "Les Tournesols," or "The Sunflowers." As the Grant children set about to solve the mystery, they are surprised to learn that their Aunt Nicole and their grandparents play an important part in the puzzle.

London, Jack. **The Call of the Wild.** Watermill Press, 1980. 137 pp.

Buck, a large friendly dog, is stolen from his home in California and is sold to an abusive master. Buck makes an excellent sled dog in Alaska, but he suffers frequent maltreatment. A kind man saves him from near death, and Buck must now choose between his loyalty to this new master and a strange desire to run free with the wild wolves. Originally published in 1903.

London, Jack. **White Fang.** Watermill Press, 1980. 311 pp.

White Fang, half dog, half wolf, is sold to Beauty Smith, who tortures the dog to increase his ferocity and his value as a fighter. After several successful fights, White Fang meets his match and is badly injured. Weedon Scott sees the pathetic dog and buys him from Smith. Scott and White Fang begin a strong friendship in which each trusts and protects the other. Originally published in 1905.

Love, Sandra. **Dive for the Sun.** Houghton Mifflin Co., 1982. 209 pp.

For years Kris Ramsey's father and his crew of divers have searched for the wreckage of the *Concepción*, queen of all the lost Spanish treasure ships. But they have no luck. Sometimes it seems to Kris that his father is sacrificing all their lives to this quest. Then comes a terrible night when lives are indeed lost, and Kris rebels. But though he stubbornly turns his back on the diving operation, his mysterious encounters with the boy Apu-Raoul end up drawing him even closer to the treasure ship.

Ludlum, Robert. **The Bourne Identity.** Richard Marek Publishers, 1980. 523 pp.

A man rescued from the ocean, more dead than alive, awakens with no memory of who or what he is. It seems that others know him and fear him, however—they fear him enough to try to kill him. In his attempts to discover his identity, this man finds that he must risk his life and the lives of others. But the more he learns, the more horrified he becomes. Could he really be a paid assassin, responsible for a number of deaths?

Lyle, Katie Letcher. **The Golden Shores of Heaven.** J. B. Lippincott Co., 1976. 189 pp.

Eighteen-year-old singer Mary Curlew's one goal is to make it to Nashville and the Grand Ole Opry. But she realizes she has to do it on her own, and the beginning of her career may be the coffeehouse advertising for a folksinger. This job does start Mary on a singing career, one filled with satisfaction and disappointment.

MacLeod, Charlotte. **We Dare Not Go A-Hunting.** Atheneum Publishers, 1981. 188 pp.

Last summer, Annette Sotherby, the daughter of one of the wealthy summer people of Netaquid Island, was kidnapped. The native islanders, who depended on the summer people, spent days looking for the girl. Yet once she was returned, the summer people ignored the islanders. This summer, Molly Bassett is hired to care for four-year-old Sammy Truell, the son of other summer people. As the summer goes on, Molly discovers the truth about the earlier kidnapping and becomes involved in an even more disastrous kidnapping. Molly decides she must solve the new crime to help the islanders regain the favor of the summer people.

Mannix, Daniel P. **The Wolves of Paris.** Illus. Janny Wurts. Avon Books, 1979. 235 pp.

During the winter of 1439 the city of Paris is attacked by a wild pack of wolves led by a legendary man-eater—the dog-wolf Courtaud. Driven by starvation, Courtaud and his mate Silver lead the pack into the city to challenge the most powerful human hunter, Bosselier. Traps are set, but who will be the hunter and who the hunted?

Marks, J. M. **Border Kidnap.** Thomas Nelson, 1977. 187 pp.

Jason's trip to Thailand becomes a test of survival when he and three other people are captured first by Burmese rebels and then by guerilla fighters. Tension mounts even more when Jason and his friends try to escape with heroin worth a million dollars.

Marks, J. M. **Hijacked!** Thomas Nelson, 1979. 167 pp.

Jason, a potential Olympic swimmer, is caught up in international intrigue when the airplane he is on is hijacked by Japanese terrorists. After the terrorists force the plane to land on a deserted beach in Thailand, Jason escapes, but he is pursued by one of the hijackers.

Martin, Les. **Raiders of the Lost Ark: The Storybook Based on the Movie.** Random House, 1981. 58 pp.

Indiana "Indy" Jones must prevent the Nazis from locating a sacred Hebrew relic that has supernatural powers. Indy's adventures take him all over the world as he gets into—and out of—one dangerous situation after another. Many color photographs from the movie accompany the text. Based on the screenplay by George Lucas and Philip Kaufman.

Masterman-Smith, Virginia. **The Great Egyptian Heist.** Four Winds Press, 1982. 180 pp.

Angel's father is an archeologist, and when the Egyptian coffin arrives for him, so does adventure for Angel and Billy Beak, her next-door neighbor. Angel and Billy find a false bottom in the coffin and, under that, a compartment full of diamonds. The rest of the story takes Angel and Billy through events that are surprising, suspenseful, and even humorous.

Mazer, Norma Fox, and Harry Mazer. **The Solid Gold Kid.** Delacorte Press, 1979. 219 pp.

Derek Chapman, the son of a millionaire, is kidnapped with five other classmates. They are gagged, bound, and locked in an old cabin in the woods. Suddenly the teenagers become possessed with the need to escape, even though they have no food or water. An isolated boat house, an old fire tower, and a loaded pistol are all part of the boys' terrifying adventure with two mad killers.

McCarthy, Gary. **The Legend of the Lone Ranger.** Ballantine Books, 1981. 188 pp.

This is the story of the legendary masked Western hero, his faithful Indian friend Tonto, and a magnificent stallion named Silver. Whenever someone needs help, wherever there is lawlessness, the Lone Ranger seems to be there. This book is based on the recent film.

McInerney, Judith Whitelock. **Judge Benjamin: Superdog.** Illus. Leslie Morrill. Holiday House, 1982. 142 pp.

Judge Benjamin, a St. Bernard, tells this humorous story from his point of view. It seems that Judge Benjamin ends up rescuing his family from one tricky situation after another. The only trouble is that his family, the O'Rileys, don't have a day go by without some kind of disaster.

Mewshaw, Michael. **Land without Shadow.** Avon Books, 1981. 254 pp.

The members of a movie company find themselves faced with trouble and danger when war breaks out in the North African country they are filming in. Jack Cordell, actress Helen Soray, and director Tucker Garland must now choose sides in a political battle that threatens to destroy their personal relationships. Mature situations.

Miles, Betty. **Maudie and Me and the Dirty Book.** Alfred A. Knopf, 1980. 160 pp.

For her school project, Kate Harris innocently reads to first graders from a picture book about a mother dog giving birth. The incident starts a controversy in the community about what is called "the dirty book." Everyone seems to take sides as the demands for censorship increase. The incident produces both humorous and tense situations for Kate and the entire town.

Miller, Frances A. **The Truth Trap.** Unicorn Books, 1980. 248 pp.

When Matt's parents are killed in a car accident, all of his neighbors agree that his deaf sister, Katie, should be put in a special school. Fearing separation, the brother and sister run away to California, where Matt is forced to look for a job. Then Matt is hurled into a nightmare when he is blamed for a murder. His courage crumbles, and his honesty is put to the test.

Millstead, Thomas. **Cave of the Moving Shadows.** Dial Press, 1979. 213 pp.

Kimba is a teenaged Cro-Magnon caveman who becomes the apprentice of Ultrec the Sorcerer, the leader of magic dances and secret ceremonies. When his foster father is wounded, Kimba sets out on an impossible mission to save his life: he must bring back a tusk of the great hairy beast, the Mastodon. Kimba ventures into the

Forbidden Mountains, befriends a wild dog, and walks straight into the hands of the wicked Neanderthal men.

Milton, Hilary. **Blind Flight.** Vagabond Books, 1980. 154 pp.

Debbie is in a state of shock. She is 3,000 feet above sea level in a small plane. The pilot is unconscious and the windshield is broken. To survive, Debbie must try to land the plane herself. But she has never flown alone—and she is blind.

Moeri, Louise. **A Horse for X.Y.Z.** Illus. Gail Owens. Scholastic Book Services, 1977. 120 pp.

Solveig Nilsson was glad to leave Camp Ahwanee. All she heard for weeks was that she was too young, too small, or too inexperienced to do anything. If she was sorry to leave anything behind, it was the horse Snake Dancer. If only she could have ridden it once. Then, without thinking, Solveig slips off the bus taking her back to school, and she returns to ride Snake Dancer before anyone can notice she is gone. But her ride will take Solveig into danger and terror as she becomes lost in the woods—and becomes the target of a mysterious man with a gun.

Molarsky, Osmond. **The Peasant and the Fly.** Illus. Katherine Coville. Harcourt Brace Jovanovich, 1980. 36 pp.

When Czar Dimitri the Foolish of Russia is bothered by a fly, he orders the fly to be arrested and executed. But the fly eludes all his pursuers, until the peasant Pirigov comes to the Czar's rescue. This is an easy-to-read fable with colorful illustrations.

Montgomery, R. A. **House of Danger.** Illus. Ralph Reese. Bantam Books, 1982. 115 pp.

You are a detective and psychic investigator. One day you receive an urgent phone call, which you quickly trace to a big, strange-looking house. The front door is opened by a mysterious woman who vanishes before your eyes! You soon discover that each room in the house contains a deadly surprise. Can you think fast enough to survive? What happens in this story depends on the choices *you* make! (From the Choose Your Own Adventure series)

Morey, Walt. **The Lemon Meringue Dog.** E. P. Dutton, 1980. 165 pp.

Coast Guardsman Chris George and his German shepherd, Mike, fail in their first attempt at a drug-bust operation because Mike devours a lemon meringue pie and misses the drugs. Then two men try to kill Mike. The action becomes more exciting as Chris tries to save Mike without becoming involved in a drug smuggling operation.

Morey, Walt. **Run Far, Run Fast.** Camelot Books, 1979. 174 pp.

Sixteen-year-old Nick Lyons hops on a freight train to avoid being placed in a home when he is orphaned. He meets Idaho Jamieson, a professional "knight-of-the-road," who helps educate Nick on their way to California. Then Nick meets a troubled logging family in the Pacific Northwest and becomes torn between offering help or running away again.

Morey, Walt. **Sandy and the Rock Star.** E. P. Dutton, 1979. 171 pp.

Paul Winters, the popular lead singer of a local rock band, runs away from home to escape his parent's restrictions. Paul dives into a motorboat to dodge the police but finds himself being taken to an island by Mr. McKinzie, a rich big-game hunter who brings wild game to his home for sport. On the island, Paul breaks free and meets a tame mountain lion. When Mr. McKinzie decides to go after them, the boy and the cougar must race against time in a deadly hunt.

Morgan, Alison. **At Willie Tucker's Place.** Illus. Trevor Stubley. Thomas Nelson, 1975. 95 pp.

Dan and his friend Willie have one goal in life: to one day become army colonels. At first, they are content with playing "war" in their backyards, but then they decide to sneak onto the nearby army base. There Dan and Willie are faced with the important mission of saving the life of a soldier.

Mukerji, Dhan Gopal. **Gay-Neck: The Story of a Pigeon.** Illus. Boris Artzybasheff. E. P. Dutton, 1968. 191 pp.

In the isolated land near the Himalayas, young Gay-Neck is trained to be a carrier pigeon by the hunter Ghond. First he must prove himself worthy of being selected for dangerous World War I missions by battling fierce hawks and rescuing close friends. After this, Gay-Neck becomes a key part of the military, bearing important messages to the battle line. (Newbery Award)

Munch, Theodore W., and Robert D. Winthrop. **Thunder on Forbidden Mountain.** Westminster Press, 1976. 155 pp.

Darby Driscoll isn't very impressed with his cousin Kevin's life in Arizona. Kevin and his Apache friend Ramona think Darby is a snob. They plot to teach him a lesson by taking him up to the Superstition Mountains and scaring him with stories of unsolved murders and Indian spirits who protect the mountains. But their plan backfires when they all get trapped in the mountains without food or water.

Munves, James. **The Treasure of Diogenes Sampuez.** Four Winds Press, 1979. 186 pp.

Young Diogenes's happy and carefree life suddenly changes when his father dies of a heart attack and his uncle comes to take care of the family and the farm. Diogenes is angry that his mother is made to do all the work while his uncle claims the property for himself. But the bitterest hurt comes when his uncle announces he is planning to sell The Frog, Diogenes's beloved horse. The young boy quickly puts together a plan to slip away one night with his horse, his best friend, Pedro, and his little sister, Consuelo. Their travels across the rugged Columbian mountains are a very dangerous but fascinating experience for the courageous trio.

Murphy, Shirley Rousseau. **The Wolf Bell.** Argo Books, 1979. 182 pp.

Ram, a boy living in the dark mountains of the planet Ere, is trained to use his magical powers to control wolves. He also uses these powers to fight the evil of the Seer of Pelli, who seeks to control the world. An evil city filled with hidden gold, a magical Wolf Bell, and a charmed runestone all become part of Ram's mission on this extraordinary planet.

Noyes, Beppie. **Mosby, the Kennedy Center Cat.** Illus. by author. Acropolis Books, 1978. 127 pp.

Mosby is a stray cat who lives in the Kennedy Center in Washington, D.C. Mosby begins to cause trouble by howling during concerts and by eating the shrimp and caviar prepared for special guests. But catching Mosby is a problem—for no human knows the hiding places around the Kennedy Center as well as Mosby does.

Nye, Peter. **The Storm.** Franklin Watts, 1982. 92 pp.

When the marina is set on fire, all the evidence points to Mike. He decides to run away and becomes a stowaway on his friend's boat. A terrible storm erupts just as Mike discovers that his friend is a drug dealer. This series of events forces him to think about human nature, friendship, and responsibility. Easy reading.

Oleksy, Walter. **The Pirates of Deadman's Cay.** Hiway Books, 1982. 112 pp.

Randy Kiley and his father set out on the *Esmeralda* for the outer islands of the Bahamas. Their object is sunken treasure. But on the way they discover the *Martha Anne,* the Norland family, and some modern-day pirates. When these pirates take over both ships, Randy manages to escape. But will he be able single-handedly to rescue his father and the Norlands, especially their daughter Kathy, with whom he has fallen in love?

Packard, Edward. **Underground Kingdom.** Illus. Anthony Kramer. Bantam Books, 1983. 108 pp.

You are exploring the underground kingdom and you decide to climb the Shining Mountains there. But should you try Weightless Peak or the Hills of Diamonds? This is just one of the crucial choices you get to make as you read this book. And your choices will determine the course of the story—and the chances of your survival in a land filled with Kota beasts and barbarian tribes. (From the Choose Your Own Adventure series)

Paterson, Katherine. **The Master Puppeteer.** Illus. Haru Wells. Thomas Y. Crowell Co., 1975. 179 pp.

When famine sweeps the Japanese countryside, Jiro parts with his hungry, dying family and joins a puppet theater. Though peasant uprisings and a mysterious Robin Hood hero threaten the young boy's life, he works hard to please the master puppeteer. But his new career brings him in close touch with danger, death, and evildoers.

Paterson, Katherine. **Of Nightingales That Weep.** Illus. Haru Wells. Camelot Books, 1980. 170 pp.

Takiko, a samurai's daughter, is young, gifted, and beautiful. When her family is killed by the plague, the heartbroken girl becomes a musician to the Princess Aai. There she meets and falls in love with Hideo, a soldier in the enemy army. Soon Takiko finds herself in the hands of the enemy, and she must fight for freedom, love, and pride alone.

Paulsen, Gary. **The Foxman.** Thomas Nelson, 1977. 125 pp.

A seventeen-year-old boy who is living with his uncle on a farm in northern Minnesota likes to hunt deer and fox. Adventure and intrigue suddenly break the monotony of his hard life when the boy and his companion chase a prized fox too far north. Lost, the boys meet a strange old man—the Foxman—who offers hospitality and then friendship. Eventually the boys and the Foxman learn to depend upon each other to survive.

Paulsen, Gary. **Tiltawhirl John.** Thomas Nelson, 1977. 127 pp.

A young boy decides to run away from his farm home and explore the world on his own. He begins his adventure by hitching a ride and finding a job chopping sugar beets. He soon leaves this tedious job and is quickly introduced to the world of carnival people, whose creed is "Us against Them." He meets Tiltawhirl John and finds excitement, but the razzle-dazzle of the carnival hides violence and danger.

Peck, Robert Newton. **Kirk's Law.** Doubleday & Co., 1981. 204 pp.

If life looked grim to Collin Pepper before, it is much worse now. He has been dismissed from his prep school, and he now finds life totally boring. So his father arranges for him to spend time with Wishbone Kirk, who lives with few modern conveniences up in the Green Mountains. Collin soon discovers he must learn to survive by developing skills such as hunting, shooting, and chopping firewood. He must also learn to love and respect other people to get along in the world.

Peck, Robert Newton. **Wild Cat.** Illus. Hal Frenk. Camelot Books, 1977. 64 pp.

A new calico kitten is born to a stray cat. What does life have in store for it? First, the love of its mother. But then a series of dangers: an angry dog, a fierce rat, and other unknown perils. Can the kitten survive these dangers while also searching for food to stay alive?

Petersen, P. J. **Nobody Else Can Walk It for You.** Delacorte Press, 1982. 215 pp.

At first the three motorcyclists seem friendly. But soon their taunts terrorize eight teenage girls. What starts out as a challenging wilderness backpacking trip turns into a frightening experience. Can eighteeen-year-old Laura and her young friends outwit the bikers?

Peterson, Bernard. **The Peripheral Spy.** Coward, McCann & Geoghegan, 1980. 209 pp.

Harry Stockdale didn't even know he was in the spy business until the day he found himself in London with two unfriendly men holding a gun on him. But Harry had been tricked—he was only a messenger who took unknown information from France to England. Now, Harry must find out who his real enemy is.

Peyton, K. M. **Prove Yourself a Hero.** William Collins Publishers, 1978. 182 pp.

What sixteen-year-old thinks of being kidnapped? Not Jonathan Meredith. Coming home from a guitar lesson, Jonathan is taken captive in a plumber's van and is held three days for ransom. He is freed, but his adventures continue when he recognizes the voice of one of his captors. Jonathan has more than just the ransom money to think about—he has something to prove to himself.

Pfeffer, Susan Beth. **A Matter of Principle.** Delacorte Press, 1982. 181 pp.

A group of high school students feel that they have been deprived of their constitutional rights. They publish an underground newspaper and, as a result, get suspended from school. This makes them feel they must fight even harder for their rights. Through their protests, the students learn many things about courage and honor.

Phipson, Joan. **The Cats.** McElderry Books, 1977. 169 pp.

Kidnapped! Jim and Willy realize now they should not have told everyone their parents won a lottery prize. But they did, and now they face danger and hardship at the hands of their abductors. The kidnappers plan to hide the boys in a deserted old farm until the ransom is paid. But things begin to go wrong—floods, windstorms, and a pack of wild cats threaten the boys and their jailers.

Phipson, Joan. **When the City Stopped.** McElderry Books, 1978. 181 pp.

Nick and his sister, Binkie, find themselves trapped in a city paralyzed by strikes and labor disputes. Their mother fails to return from work one evening, and the food and money supply dwindles. In an effort to save themselves, they are forced to face the cruel city with their maid and her crippled husband.

Picard, Barbara Leonie, retold by. **The Odyssey of Homer.** Illus. Joan Kiddell-Monroe. Oxford University Press, 1979. 272 pp.

Homer, the blind poet of Greece, wrote his great tale of Odysseus (or Ulysses, in Latin mythology) in the form of a long poem. In this book the author retells the myth in a manner more easily understood today. Odysseus, the King of Ithaca, is victorious in his bloody war with Troy. But it takes him ten years to return home. During these ten years he and his men have adventures with such legendary creatures and characters as Calypso, the Cyclops, Circe, and King Nestor.

Pohlmann, Lillian. **The Unsuitable Behavior of America Martin.** Westminster Press, 1976. 155 pp.

America Martin is a young girl of the 1870s who is being raised by an aunt and uncle to become a proper Southern belle. "Mer" wants adventure, though. Her affection is captured by Ned Massie of Nevada City, and she follows him west. But once there, Mer can find no trace of Ned. Will she be able to endure the long, hard winter and support herself in the Wild West?

Pollock, Bruce. **It's Only Rock and Roll.** Houghton Mifflin Co., 1980. 232 pp.

Eugene Maybloom is the local music hero of Elvira, New York. This story centers on Eugene's exciting experiences in the world of entertainment. It is a life filled with nervousness, exhaustion, and frustration for Eugene, but there is also fame and fortune to make things worthwhile.

Putnam, Alice. **Spy Doll.** Elsevier/Nelson Books, 1979. 128 pp.

A brave Baltimore women and her daughter, Belle, undertake the task of smuggling desperately needed quinine and morphine to the Southern troops by hiding the medicine inside Belle's china doll. They must make their way through enemy Yankee patrols and many other dangers before they can accomplish their mission of mercy.

Rabe, Berniece. **Naomi.** Thomas Nelson, 1975. 192 pp.

Young Naomi is living on a small farm in Missouri during the Great Depression. She tries hard to please her parents and to get along with her sister, Grace. However, nothing ever seems to work out well for her and she is pleasing no one, not even herself. Then the town's fortune teller predicts Naomi will die before her fourteenth birthday. As this birthday draws closer, she becomes more terror-stricken and wonders just what is going to happen to her.

Reader, Dennis J. **Coming Back Alive.** Random House, 1981. 233 pp.

When Bridget and her friend Dylan feel their lives are falling apart—hers because of her parents' death, his because of his parents' divorce—they decide to get away from it all, from all the people who might try to hurt them. They go high up in the mountains of northern California to live off the land as the Indians did. But living off the land—and avoiding other people—turns out to be much harder than they thought. Eventually, they realize they must make some decision about the future.

Reeves, Bruce. **Street Smarts.** Beaufort Books, 1981. 222 pp.

Twelve-year-old T. C. feels she is different from her school friends because she has grown up in a commune. She resents the lack of privacy and the total sharing this life-style represents. When she meets eight-year-old Caper, an abused neighborhood boy, they decide to run away to San Francisco. Are they prepared for the dangers and temptations of their new way of life?

Rice, Earl, Jr. **The Animals.** Illus. Jim Sanford. Fearon-Pitman Publishers, 1979. 58 pp.

During World War II, Captain Clay Denison's bomber is shot down over France, and he is captured by the Germans. Through a French resistance group whose members use animal names to protect their identities, Clay learns that the Germans are planning a raid to kill the British Prime Minister, Winston Churchill. It now becomes a suspenseful race against time as Clay and the Animals attempt to warn the British government. Easy reading.

Rivers-Coffey, Rachel. **A Horse like Mr. Ragman.** Charles Scribner's Sons, 1977. 150 pp.

Twelve-year-old Elizabeth always wanted a thoroughbred jumping horse, but instead she gets a shaggy pinto named Mr. Ragman. In spite of her shame over Mr. Ragman, she learns that he is a natural performer, and she begins to win ribbons in horse exhibitions. She competes with some of the best riders around, and then she receives an offer to buy Mr. Ragman. She now has to decide if she wants to sell Mr. Ragman and buy her dream thoroughbred.

Roach, Marilynne K. **Presto; or, The Adventures of a Turnspit Dog.** Illus. by author. Houghton Mifflin Co., 1979. 146 pp.

From behind cage bars in a dark inn, life is grim for Presto, a small dog that knows nothing but hard work. Then a traveling puppeteer brings new excitement to Presto's life with tales of laughter, children, and adventure. Immediately, Presto begins to plan his escape.

Robinson, Joan G. **The Dark House of the Sea Witch.** Coward, McCann & Geoghegan, 1979. 128 pp.

Meg and Maxie are left in the care of the housemaid, Hannah, for two days. But Hannah abandons them at the beach, and the two girls are left to wander alone. There they meet Mrs. Jarvis, who everyone thinks is a witch. Meg and Maxie soon realize that they have no choice but to spend the night in her dark, mysterious house.

Rossman, Parker. **Pirate Slave.** Thomas Nelson, 1977. 148 pp.

Sandy, a young cabin boy on an American ship, is the lone survivor when a gang of pirates raids the vessel. Scared and sick, he is taken aboard a ship filled with pirates who hope to sell him for a high price because of his blond hair. But in the meantime, Sandy will be responsible for tending the filthy, unorganized ship—and its blood-thirsty crew.

Roth, Arthur. **Two for Survival.** Charles Scribner's Sons, 1976. 126 pp.

Four high school seniors are flying home after a weekend in Maine when a hijacker threatens the pilot, and the plane crashes in a mountain woods. Six passengers survive, including the four teen-agers. John and Mark, the least injured, find an isolated mountain cabin for the others to remain in while they hike out for help. Through wilderness and storms, the two teenage boys must depend on each other in their attempt to bring help to the remaining passengers.

Rounds, Glen. **Whitey and the Colt-Killer.** Illus. by author. Camelot Books, 1982. 90 pp.

Can Whitey and his cousin Josie catch the wolf before it kills their pinto colt? There's a two-hundred-dollar ransom on the wolf, but so far nobody's been able to catch it—not even the wolf trappers. Whitey and Josie, though, are determined to save their colt. Easy reading.

Rounds, Glen. **Whitey's First Roundup.** Illus. by author. Camelot Books, 1982. 94 pp.

As the youngest and least experienced cowhand, Whitey is always stuck with the most boring jobs—like helping the cook or chopping wood. He dreams of roping cattle and riding on the range. Now, finally, Whitey will get a chance to prove himself. The other cow-hands have decided to let him come along on a real roundup. Whitey is nervous, but determined to show the others just what he can do. Easy reading.

Rubinstein, Robert E. **When Sirens Scream.** Dodd, Mead & Co., 1981. 206 pp.

Ned Turner's town didn't have much to keep it alive until the nuclear plant came, bringing with it money and jobs. But it also brought the sirens and the fear of what would happen if a nuclear accident took place. When such an accident does occur, the townspeople react strangely because it is hard to be afraid of something that cannot be seen.

Rubinstein, Robert E. **Who Wants to be a Hero!** Dodd, Mead & Co., 1979. 158 pp.

When Jason saves the school janitor from Jimmy Cardon's tough gang, he becomes a hero. He also becomes the prime target of Jimmy's gang. His books are ripped to pieces, he receives threatening phone calls, and his family is tormented. Jason begins to wonder if he should continue to uphold justice or fight to protect his life.

Salkey, Andrew. **Hurricane.** Oxford University Press, 1979. 88 pp.

In Jamaica, Joe and Mary wonder if the radio weather forecast warning of heavy showers could be the first sign of a hurricane. They feel both curious and afraid—wanting and not wanting the storm. Then the hurricane hits, and a few hours become an eternity of nightmares for the family.

Schellie, Don. **Kidnapping Mr. Tubbs.** Vagabond Books, 1978. 197 pp.

How did he get into this mess? Sixteen-year-old A. J. Zander suddenly finds himself driving along an Arizona highway in an old VW with a strange girl, a smelly saddle, a fat basset hound, and a 100-year-old ex-cowboy he and the girl, Eloise, have just kidnapped. Why had he listened to Eloise? What could she possibly have in mind for them and the old cowboy?

Schellie, Don. **Maybe Next Summer.** Four Winds Press, 1980. 244 pp.

Seventeen-year-old Matt Althaus has his heart set on becoming an investigative reporter, so he is delighted to be spending the summer in Crandall, Arizona, working for his father's best friend, Mitch Garrity, the editor and general manager of the *Chronicle*. He is encouraged by Shannon, Garrity's young daughter, to push forward with his investigation of illegal aliens. As Matt digs deeper into the story, he discovers that someone in the newspaper office is involved in smuggling the illegal aliens into Arizona.

Smith, Dodie. **The Hundred and One Dalmatians.** Avon Books, 1979. 199 pp.

All over the country, dalmatian puppies are being dognapped by Cruella de Vil, a wicked woman who wants to use them for fur coats. Among the stolen ones are the fifteen little puppies of Pongo and Missis. Pongo courageously begins a desperate search, calling all the dogs of London to his aid, running through the countryside, and going without food. When he finally reaches Cruella's hideout, he finds not only his puppies, but eighty-four others. Now, in the middle of a blizzard, Pongo must escape with all ninety-nine puppies. Originally published in 1956.

Smith, Pauline C. **Brush Fire!** Westminster Press, 1979. 96 pp.

Johnny is about to drop out of high school and run away from his aunt's home when he is offered the job of taking care of the house and animals of Mr. Miller, his shop teacher. This is the first time anyone has trusted Johnny to be responsible for something important. In the days that follow, Johnny must protect the house from brush fires and motorcycle gangs.

Southall, Ivan. **The Golden Goose.** Greenwillow Books, 1981. 180 pp.

Everyone believes thirteen-year-old Custard can sense where gold is, so he is kidnapped by Preacher Tom's sons. Preacher Tom rescues Custard from his sons, but the idea of easy riches makes the preacher decide to use the boy to prospect for gold. The disappearance of Preacher Tom and Custard—the "Golden Goose"—starts rumors that set off both a search for the boy and a wild gold rush in Custard's area of Australia. Sequel to *King of the Sticks*.

Sparks, Ted. **Hot Lead and Cold Feet.** Scholastic Book Services, 1978. 118 pp.

Jasper has a huge fortune and wants to leave it to the son who can win a series of racing contests. Problems begin right away because neither son, Wild Billy, the local tough guy, nor Brother Eli, the tenderfoot man of the Bible, has any idea that he has a twin brother. Based on the Walt Disney movie. Easy reading.

Spier, Peter. **Rain.** Illus. by author. Doubleday & Co., 1982. 32 pp.

This wordless picture book tells the story of two children as they go out and play on a rainy day. All the common experiences of playing in the rain are displayed in this colorful book.

Stahl, Ben. **Blackbeard's Ghost.** Illus. by author. Scholastic Book Services, 1976. 174 pp.

J. D. decides to try out a magic spell one day. But who could he conjure up? He decides on Blackbeard, the greatest pirate who ever sailed the seas. So J. D. chants the secret words, and the pirate's ghost really does appear. Now there is only one problem—Blackbeard has decided to take over the town where J. D. lives!

Steele, Mary Q. **Journey Outside.** Puffin Books, 1979. 127 pp.

Dilar's grandfather claims that they are following the underground river in search of the "Better Place." The Raft People have never seen the outside world, but Dilar finds a way out. He meets people he never imagined existed and experiences many strange and beautiful adventures. But he must find a way back to his people so they too can share this "Better Place."

Steig, William. **Abel's Island.** Farrar, Straus & Giroux, 1980. 117 pp.

Abel is a happy mouse who lives in a comfortable home and has an easy life. One stormy day, however, flood waters carry him off, away from his wife, Amanda, and dump him onto an island. Forced to spend weeks and months here, Abel loses his soft ways and begins to toughen up as he faces basic survival every day. Even better, Abel finds he has talents that he never imagined he had.

Stevenson, Anne. **Mask of Treason.** G. P. Putnam's Sons, 1979. 262 pp.

Fiona Grant leaves London for a Scottish holiday at her parents' home, little dreaming that her life will soon become quite different. Accidentally, Fiona becomes involved in a deadly game of international intrigue. Soon she and her parents are accused of being foreign spies. She is plunged into a world of agents, counterspies, and romance.

Stevenson, Robert Louis. **Kidnapped.** Watermill Press, 1980. 317 pp.

Seventeen-year-old David Balfour is tricked out of his rightful inheritance by his wealthy uncle. He finds himself kidnapped and aboard a ship filled with cutthroat seamen. He must endure a frightening voyage before he is forced to survive alone on a deserted island. David is now determined to do something about his uncle's evil actions against him. Originally published in 1886.

Stevenson, Robert Louis. **Treasure Island.** Illus. N. C. Wyeth. Charles Scribner's Sons, 1981. 273 pp.

This story involves Jim Hawkins and his friends. They begin their ocean adventure with the treasure map of Billy Bones, a sea pirate who dies in Jim's boarding house. The map leads the boys through many dangerous situations and tense encounters with all kinds of people. Long John Silver, the notorious pirate, becomes the major obstacle between the boys and the treasure. Originally published in 1883.

Stewart, A. C. **Ossian House.** S. G. Phillips, 1976. 179 pp.

When the grandfather of eleven-year-old John Murray dies, he leaves John his estate in Scotland. John is thrilled to own the mansion, where he is to spend eight weeks of every summer. After convincing his mother that it will be safe, John begins a two-month adventure—alone in the heart of Scotland.

Stohlman, Richard. **An Overflowing Rain.** Avon Books, 1979. 266 pp.

Colonel Katzhak of the NKVD uncovers a secret Soviet plot to launch a surprise attack on Israel. Katzhak, however, has a dream vision in which he sees the Soviet forces suffer massive defeat because of weather and the hand of God. But the colonel still feels some action needs to be taken to stop the attack.

Story, Bettie Wilson. **The Other Side of the Tell.** Illus. Seymour Fleishman. David C. Cook Publishing Co., 1977. 150 pp.

Jeff and his family are spending the summer in Israel taking part in an archaeological excavation at the Tel Gezer, an ancient city dating back to Biblical times. Jeff is fascinated with the mysteries which could be solved about ancient peoples through bits of pottery and utensils. However, young Jeff is soon confronted with a present-day mystery—who is the young Arab, Kermin, who guards the opening to the dangerous cave?

Story, Bettie Wilson. **River of Fire.** Chariot Books, 1979. 217 pp.

When Malinda Sharp's mother dies of yellow fever, her father decides it will be best for Malinda to live with her Aunt Eliza in Mobile, Alabama. During the second night of her journey the riverboat explodes and Malinda escapes. She awakens to find that she is in a secluded grove of trees suffering from "the fever" and being tended by Jasmine, a slave girl. Malinda develops a friendship with Jasmine and knows that if the slave girl is caught, she will suffer a beating or even death. Can Malinda abandon Jasmine when the chance for rescue comes?

Sutcliff, Rosemary. **Blood Feud.** E. P. Dutton, 1977. 147 pp.

Young Jestyn is taken into slavery by the Danes who invade the English coast in the tenth century. Jestyn fights for his new master, Thormond; he not only wins freedom but also becomes involved in a blood feud when two brothers murder Thormond's father. The feud takes the characters through Russia to Constantinople (now the city of Istanbul, Turkey), where Jestyn must choose between two opposing sets of values.

Sutcliff, Rosemary. **Frontier Wolf.** E. P. Dutton, 1981. 196 pp.

The Germanic barbarians have attacked, the Roman commanding officers have been killed, and suddenly Alexios is left in command. In a panic, he makes a decision that he will regret for years to come: to abandon the fort he is defending. After a nightmarish enemy interrogation, he is sent to the Empire's frontier in Ireland.

Alexios struggles to gain the confidence of his men, a group of amateur soldiers called the Frontier Wolves. Then the nomadic tribes of the area rise in revolt, and Alexios must once again make the agonizing decision to abandon the fort—but this time there are surprising results.

Sutcliff, Rosemary. **The Light beyond the Forest: The Quest for the Holy Grail.** Illus. Shirley Felts. E. P. Dutton, 1980. 144 pp.

Galahad has pulled the sword from the stone and, in doing so, has earned the right to search for the Holy Grail—Christ's cup from the Last Supper. So this "perfect knight" sets out with the blessings of King Arthur on the dangerous and exciting search for the holy treasure.

Taber, Anthony. **Cats' Eyes.** Thomas Congdon Books, 1980. 78 pp.

Did you ever wonder what the world looks like to a cat? Imagine viewing everything from ten inches off the floor. This story explains how one particular striped feline named Tiger sees his world. Illustrations help the text create a total sense of a cat's view of things.

Taylor, Robert Lewis. **The Travels of Jaimie McPheeters.** Ace Books, 1981. 544 pp.

Follow young Jaimie McPheeters and his family on an astounding trip across nineteenth-century America. The McPheeters ride riverboats, forge streams in covered wagons, and deal with pioneers, Indians, shady characters, and downright villains as they seek their fortunes in the goldfields of California. (Pulitzer Prize)

Taylor, Theodore. **The Odyssey of Ben O'Neal.** Illus. Richard Cuffari. Camelot Books, 1979. 208 pp.

When thirteen-year-old Ben O'Neal's mother dies in 1899, Ben decides to sign on as a sailor and search for his older brother, Reuben. But problems begin to mount for Ben: a young girl called Teetoncey and a dog called Boo follow him when he boards a sailing vessel that has been described as a "hellship." Ben feels responsible for the girl, but she keeps getting in the way of his adventures. (Third volume in the Cape Hatteras trilogy)

Taylor, Theodore. **Teetoncey.** Illus. Richard Cuffari. Camelot Books, 1975. 153 pp.

A raging storm brings more than driftwood to the shores of young Ben O'Neal's island home. It brings Teetoncey, a scared, ragged girl who the doctors say is a deaf mute. Ben and his widowed mother care for the girl in their home, and Ben is sure that he does not just imagine the light in her eyes. To protect Teetoncey from life in an institution, Ben searches for the secret of her background—and also finds out some secrets about his own father's death. (First volume in the Cape Hatteras trilogy)

Taylor, Theodore. **Teetoncey and Ben O'Neal.** Illus. Richard Cuffari. Camelot Books, 1976. 185 pp.

Teetoncey is the sole survivor of a shipwreck. She tells a secret to young Ben O'Neal that sets in motion a series of exciting and tragic events whose effects are felt long past that memorable winter of 1899. (Second volume in the Cape Hatteras trilogy)

Thayer, James Stewart. **The Stettin Secret.** G. P. Putnam's Sons, 1979. 321 pp.

Andrew Jay has been sent to Stettin, Poland, to blow up the *Graf Zeppelin* before the Soviets can add it to their list of World War II prizes. Besides opposition from both the Soviet Union and Poland, Andrew must fight against the plots of others interested in the aircraft carrier for their own selfish purposes. Andrew begins to feel he is on an impossible mission.

Thiam, Djibi (translator Mercer Cook). **My Sister, the Panther.** Dodd, Mead & Co., 1980. 203 pp.

In Guinea, Africa, Mina and her four-year-old son wait in their hut for the return home of her husband, Bamou. How would she tell Bamou of the mysterious and frightening death of his faithful dog, Couti? It was incredible even to think that Couti had been killed by the revered panther, the symbol of the tribe's unity with nature. When he hears the story, Bamou sets out traveling from hamlet to hamlet to follow the retreating panther's trail. But he soon wonders if the panther is not actually trailing him.

Thiele, Colin. **The Fire in the Stone.** Puffin Books, 1981. 228 pp.

It is a rough and lawless part of Australia, and Ernie cannot count on his alcoholic father for anything. The boy has to take care of himself or starve. He digs up a collection of precious opals from the rocky fields around him to sell. But when the opals are stolen, Ernie is forced to face the dangerous countryside in a search for the thief. His dreams of wealth soon turn into a series of nightmares.

Trivers, James. **Hamburger Heaven.** Avon Books, 1980. 125 pp.

With such boring duties and such low pay, Kenny wonders why he stays at his summer job at Benny's Burger Restaurant. Then he gets the idea he can pick up extra money by cheating at the cash register and stealing some of the extra income made during the Benny Festival. But can such a crooked scheme succeed?

Twain, Mark. **The Adventures of Huckleberry Finn.** Signet Books, 1959. 288 pp.

In the early nineteenth century, a young boy, Huckleberry Finn, is on the run. His father is a brutal alcoholic who kidnapped Huck to blackmail Huck's guardian. On the Mississippi River, Huck joins a runaway slave, Jim. Together they travel down the river on a raft. Along the way Huck must make many important decisions about his own feelings and those of society. Huck and Jim's adventures include witnessing robberies, murders, and feuds. Originally published in 1884.

Twain, Mark. **The Prince and the Pauper.** Signet Books, 1964. 223 pp.

Tom Canty and Edward Tudor have little in common. Tom is a child from the London slums, and Edward is heir to the throne. Tom has had nothing. Edward has had everything. But the one thing they do have in common is that they look exactly alike. By a strange accident the two boys exchange places, the prince roaming the London streets and the waif living in a palace. The adventures that follow for each boy reveal the courage, cleverness, and maturity of both. Originally published in 1882.

Verne, Jules. **Around the World in 80 Days.** Watermill Press, 1981. 272 pp.

Phineas Fogg and his French valet, Passepartout, undertake a hasty trip around the world as a result of a $40,000 bet made at Fogg's London men's club. Via boat, railroad, and sled, the two adventurers overcome obstacle after obstacle in an attempt to complete their journey within eighty days. In 1872, this task is assumed impossible; nevertheless, Fogg believes he will win the wager. Originally published in 1873.

Verne, Jules (adapter Andrea M. Clare). **20,000 Leagues under the Sea.** Illus. David Grove. Fearon-Pitman Publishers, 1973. 92 pp.

For over twelve weeks the ship *Abraham Lincoln* sails around the Pacific in search of the large sea monster that plagues sailors in the

Pacific and Atlantic oceans. Professor Aronnax and his good friend, Conseil, have been summoned by Commander Farragut to pursue this enormous whalelike creature and make the seas safe again. Little do they know that the "monster" is a submarine, the *Nautilus,* commanded by the eccentric Captain Nemo, who will show these men a part of the sea they have never explored before. Originally published in 1870. Easy reading.

Way, Peter. **Icarus.** Avon Books, 1981.

Project Icarus is a top-secret plan to build the world's first nuclear reactor to extract the sun's energy from seawater. But scientist Michael French's work on the project is being sabotaged. Are the Russians behind the destructive plot? Or could it be one of Michael's fellow workers? Michael does not know who to trust any more. And now he finds out someone wants him dead.

Weinberg, Larry, adapter. **Dragonslayer: The Storybook Based on the Movie.** Random House, 1981. 60 pp.

When a dragon begins killing all the young girls in a kingdom, the villagers come to the last of the great magicians for help. Aided by the wizard, a young man and a young woman disguised as a man eventually do battle with the dragon and her terrifying brood of children. Based on the Walt Disney film. Easy reading.

Westheimer, David. **Von Ryan's Return.** Coward, McCann & Geoghegan, 1980. 271 pp.

During World War II American Colonel "Von" Ryan escapes from the Germans in a hijacked prison train. Now Von Ryan must get even with the man who betrayed him—a dangerous imposter who is somewhere in Italy spying on the Allies. But Von Ryan is compelled to make the treacherous trip into enemy territory to find this man before he has a chance to betray anyone else.

White, Robb. **The Long Way Down.** Doubleday & Co., 1977. 185 pp.

A life of glamor and adventure in the circus is a wish that many girls share, but for Tina it is more than a dream. Tina runs away to the traveling circus in search of the famous trapeze artist Danny York. At first, Danny is reluctant to take in an apprentice, but he changes his mind when he sees how determined Tina is. But for Tina, this chance of a lifetime is marred by the hardships of circus life. The young girl struggles with love and tears as she strives for fame and success.

Wilder, Laura Ingalls. **Little House on the Prairie.** Illus. Garth Williams. Scholastic Book Services, 1963. 335 pp.

This is the story of young Laura Ingalls and her family as they travel by covered wagon to a new home on the prairie. Crossing a dangerous river, they lose their dog, and at night they are surrounded by wolves. And this is just the beginning of their adventures and hardships. The book contains illustrations of important moments in their journey. It was also the basis for the television series. Originally published in 1935. Easy reading.

Wilson, Ron. **Lost in the Shenandoahs.** Chariot Books, 1981. 118 pp.

Fourteen-year-old Ken Brindle and a group of boys find themselves trapped in a winter storm during a backpacking trip. They all are determined to get out of the icy wilderness alive. But things begin to go wrong for the boys, and Ken starts to suspect Chip Dreiser of foul play.

Winters, Jon. **The Drakov Memoranda.** Avon Books, 1979. 252 pp.

Anton Drakov slyly involves several people in a plot for Soviet control of a key Western area. Neville Conyers of British Intelligence and Comrade Novetsky, a retired Soviet military hero, combine forces, but they are unwittingly fulfilling Drakov's plans. Mature language.

Wuorio, Eva-Lis. **Detour to Danger.** Delacorte Press, 1981. 186 pp.

Sixteen-year-old Nando takes a small detour on his way to Spain to check on his Aunt Jane's house in Andalusia. It doesn't take long for Nando to discover that a group of neo-Nazis have taken over the villa next door. International terrorism threatens Nando when he and an old friend learn that the group is planning a violent demonstration and has hired an assassin. The boys decide it is up to them to stop the destructive plans.

Wyss, Johann. **The Swiss Family Robinson.** Watermill Press, 1980. 422 pp.

A terrible storm at sea leaves the Robinson family shipwrecked and stranded on an unknown deserted island. Rescuing a few important items from the sinking ship, the family begins to carve out a life for themselves on what is now their private island. They must rely on their own ingenuity and the resources of the island in order to survive. Originally published in 1814.

Family Situations

Aaron, Chester. **Catch Calico!** E. P. Dutton, 1979. 148 pp.

Louis's life changes when his grandfather becomes ill and his cat, Calico, dies. Louis is fourteen years old and must grow up in a hurry. But without the companionship of his grandfather and Calico, it seems life will be empty.

Aaron, Chester. **Spill.** McElderry Books, 1977. 214 pp.

The Taylor family lives on a California ranch near the ocean. Young Judy Taylor puts her energy into caring for sick farm animals, but her brother Jeff escapes his problems by hanging out with the wild Mother Earth gang. When two oil tankers collide near the coast, the entire family rushes to save the endangered birds and animals there. As Judy and Jeff rub shoulders with death, fear and danger erase their differences and bind them together.

Adler, C. S. **In Our House Scott Is My Brother.** Macmillan Publishing Co., 1980. 139 pp.

At first Jodi thinks it might be fun to have a stepmother and stepbrother. She has been pretty lonely since her own mother died three years ago. Before long, however, Jodi can't decide whether to be mad at them for messing up her life or sorry for them because they have big problems. Her dad wants so desperately for all of them to get along—but is this possible?

Adler, C. S. **Shelter on Blue Barns Road.** Signet Vista Books, 1982. 150 pp.

When Betsy's father loses his teaching job in New York City, the whole family falls apart. A move to the country seems only to complicate matters and make everyone more miserable. Then Betsy discovers an animal shelter near her home and begins a crusade to save a supposedly vicious Doberman pinscher called Zoro.

Ames, Mildred. **The Dancing Madness.** Delacorte Press, 1980. 134 pp.

Pressured by the loss of her job and her mother's desire that she become a star, Mary's sister teams up with an ex-vaudeville trouper for a dance marathon at Gaiety Beach. Winning the thousand-dollar prize may be the only way the Reillys can end the life of poverty brought on by the Great Depression. Mary watches her sister endure a grueling test of strength for her family. But when the dancing stops, both Mary and her sister must come to terms with life in their own ways.

Amoss, Berthe. **Secret Lives.** Atlantic Monthly Press, 1979. 180 pp.

If her upbringing were left up to Aunt Eveline, Addie would grow old on prunes and castor oil, rehearsing her catechism. She would never know the truth behind the legends that surround her mother, Pasie, who died when Addie was five. Everyone says that Pasie was perfect. But who was Pasie, really? Addie begins a search that is both funny and moving—a search that exposes truths which in time free Addie to come into her own.

Anderson, Margaret J. **The Journey of the Shadow Bairns.** Alfred A. Knopf, 1980. 177 pp.

Will Elspeth and her little brother Robbie be able to make it from Scotland to Canada all by themselves? When their parents die and they learn they are to be put in an orphanage, Elspeth decides they should try to fulfill their father's dream of going to Canada to start a new life. The trip is difficult, but the worst part comes afterwards when Elspeth becomes sick and loses little Robbie. Will she ever find him again? Easy reading.

Anderson, Mary. **The Rise and Fall of a Teen-Age Wacko.** Atheneum Publishers, 1981. 169 pp.

Laura loved the fancy stores in New York City like Bloomingdale's. They were the center of her world, with their great clothes, chic customers, and fantastic sales. So Laura is less than thrilled when she is forced to rough it in the mountains with her family. They may get excited by all the scenery and with hiking and swimming, but Laura is bored. When the chance comes for a part-time job back in New York, Laura begs her parents to let her take it. Little does she realize her trip to New York will throw her into the world of movies—and Woody Allen movies at that!

Anderson, Mary. **You Can't Get There from Here.** Atheneum Publishers, 1982. 194 pp.

Reggie always wanted to be an actress, so after high school she enters Adam Bentley's Acting School and begins to have a new feeling about herself and her craft. Taking the role of Vicki in a new play is not only hard work, but it begins to confuse her emotions about her family and the other people at school. But her teacher, Adam, and her brother, Jamie, help her realize the boundaries between her life and her art.

Andrew, Prudence. **Close within My Own Circle.** Elsevier/Nelson Books, 1978. 160 pp.

All of the Talbot family's hopes and pride are centered in their oldest son, Daniel. He's the one with all the brains, it seems. Then one day Daniel refuses to go to school any more. He becomes involved with an older woman and mysteriously builds a raft in his father's shed. Because all their dreams appear to vanish as Daniel loses touch, the family disintegrates.

Angell, Judie. **Dear Lola, or How to Build Your Own Family.** Laurel-Leaf Library, 1982. 176 pp.

When ten-year-old Annie, her twin brothers, and four other kids run away from St. Theresa's Orphanage, they decide to stick together and form a family. Led by eighteen-year-old Lola, the group find a house in the small town of Sweet River and make it their home. But their neighbors begin to notice there are no adults in the family. Soon the kids are hatching crazy plots to keep the snoopy neighbors and the authorities from looking too closely into their family situation.

Angell, Judie. **What's Best for You.** Bradbury Press, 1981. 187 pp.

Lee's parents have split up. Her brother and sister are going to live with their mother, but Lee is going to stay with her father for the summer. That's where she wants to be. Her father understands her and doesn't criticize. But when a boy enters Lee's life and her father starts dating again, will things ever be the same for them?

Arthur, Ruth M. **An Old Magic.** Illus. Margery Gill. Atheneum Publishers, 1977. 175 pp.

Hannah, a young woman of the nineteenth century, is fascinated by the stories, songs, and customs of the gypsies that visit her home in Wales. When her son, Davey, marries a gypsy woman, her family is tied with them forever. But gypsy blood begins to act like a curse on the family, and the mysterious magic that Hannah once loved rapidly becomes a dangerous threat.

Avi. **Sometimes I Think I Hear My Name.** Pantheon Books, 1982. 144 pp.

Conrad begins to feel his parents are ignoring him. First he is sent to live with his aunt and uncle in St. Louis. Then he hears his mother has agreed to send him to London to spend spring vacation with his cousins. But Conrad has been looking forward to spending the time with her. Something is wrong. Conrad decides to go to New York City on his own to find his mother and uncover the mystery. Now he is a stranger in a strange city. Perhaps Nancy, a girl he meets along the way, can help him. But she seems a bit odd.

Babbitt, Natalie. **Herbert Rowbarge.** Farrar, Straus & Giroux, 1981. 216 pp.

Herbert Rowbarge has an identical twin he never finds out about. All he knows is that his twin daughters make him jealous and that mirrors make him feel funny. Is he going mad? But even with all these psychological confusions, Herbert has been able to realize his childhood dream—to create a giant amusement park. His personal life is less than amusing, though, as those people closest to him often find it difficult to communicate with him.

Bates, Betty. **Bugs in Your Ears.** Holiday House, 1977. 128 pp.

When her mother marries Dominic, problems begin for Carrie. She doesn't want a new father and a new family. Her stepfather's children won't listen to her, and no one is sympathetic with the anxiety she is going through in adjusting to being an adopted child.

Bates, Betty. **It Must've Been the Fish Sticks.** Holiday House, 1982. 136 pp.

Brian's world is shaken when he finds out that his natural mother is still alive. Angry and confused, he can hardly face his adoptive parents, and he insists on meeting his real mother. He then has another problem: the conflicting loyalties he feels toward the woman who gave him birth and the stepmother who raised him as her own son.

Bates, Betty. **My Mom, the Money Nut.** Holiday House, 1979. 158 pp.

When Fritzi Zimmer moves into a rich neighborhood with her mother and father, she is self-conscious about being poor and overweight. Fritzi longs to talk things over with her mother, but she is always tired from her job and wants to be left alone. Fritzi's new friend Hope gets her to join a few music groups at the junior high, and soon Fritzi finds in the vocal director, Mrs. Torcom, a friend and a confidant.

Bates, Betty. **The Ups and Downs of Jorie Jenkins.** Holiday House, 1978. 126 pp.

Jorie Jenkins's father, a doctor, seems athletic and tireless to her. But one evening, Dr. Jenkins has a heart attack and collapses. Jorie feels frightened, angry, and alone. Her older sister is busy with her own life and problems, and their mother spends all her time at the hospital. Even her father begins to act differently toward her. Then one night Jorie is alone with him when he goes through a crisis—and that changes everything for them both.

Bess, Clayton. **Story for a Black Night.** Parnassus Press, 1982. 84 pp.

One evening an African father decides to tell his children about an exciting event in his childhood. It was another night when a knock came at his family's door—a knock that was to change their lives. A baby with smallpox has been abandoned at their house. What to do? The decisions that follow bring both pain and joy to the family and the village around them.

Blos, Joan W. **A Gathering of Days: A New England Girl's Journal, 1830–32.** Charles Scribner's Sons, 1979. 145 pp.

Thirteen-year-old Catherine Hall keeps a journal of her last year on a small New Hampshire farm where she keeps house for her widowed father. The journal shows the kindness, the determination, and the strength of the people around her. It also reveals Catherine's growth and maturation as she learns to cope with increased responsibilities. (Newbery Award)

Blume, Judy. **Superfudge.** E. P. Dutton, 1980. 166 pp.

Kindergarten-aged Fudge drives his eleven-year-old brother crazy and makes his mother hysterical when a new baby sister joins the family. Jealous of the new arrival, Fudge plots to get rid of the infant. When hiding her in the closet fails, he tries selling her for a quarter. But that plan also has an unsuccessful—but unusual—ending. When the family takes a trip to the country, it seems to Fudge a wonderful opportunity to make more mischief.

Bograd, Larry. **The Kolokol Papers.** Farrar, Straus & Giroux, 1981. 168 pp.

In the middle of the night, men take Lev's father away in a big black car. Because his parents have openly opposed the Soviet government, his father is arrested and sentenced to a long prison term. Lev decides to write the story of his family's life in Moscow. Will he be able to sneak it out of the Soviet Union for publication in the West?

Bond, Nancy. **The Best of Enemies.** Atheneum Publishers, 1978. 248 pp.

When Charlotte Paige's family make summer plans that don't include her, she decides to get involved with the town's Patriot's Day celebration. In the course of planning activities, Charlotte becomes mixed up with some of the town's oddest citizens. But her experiences help Charlotte become more independent and self-sufficient.

Bond, Nancy. **Country of Broken Stone.** McElderry Books, 1981. 271 pp.

Fourteen-year-old Pennie and her family move to Wintergap, an old country house in England. The house is bleak and unwelcoming. And Pennie has her own problems adjusting to her new life. Besides this she discovers some unpleasantness about the history of the area through Randall, the brother of a local farmer. A fire tests Pennie's feelings for her family and for Randall.

Brancato, Robin F. **Blinded by the Light.** Alfred A. Knopf, 1978. 215 pp.

Gail Brower infiltrates the religious cult called "Light of the World" in a desperate search for her brother Jim, who cut all ties with his past life when he pledged himself to the cult. Half fearing facing her brainwashed brother, and half fearing for her own safety, Gail tries to unravel tangled clues while keeping her identity a secret. Mature situations.

Brancato, Robin F. **Sweet Bells Jangled Out of Tune.** Alfred A. Knopf, 1982. 200 pp.

Why should her mother forbid fifteen-year-old Ellen Dohrman from seeing her own grandmother? Well, this grandmother, Eva, has become a "bag lady," an eccentric old woman whom people laugh at and feel sorry for. Ellen has not seen Eva in years, and she wants to have a reunion. But can Ellen handle all the family trouble that follows? (ALA Best Book for Young Adults)

Branscum, Robbie. **Toby Alone.** Avon Books, 1980. 94 pp.

When her grandmother dies, Toby finds herself all alone. Now she must decide how she is to live on her own. Will Toby ever be able to find someone who is as friendly and supportive as her grandmother? Easy reading.

Brenner, Barbara. **A Year in the Life of Rosie Bernard.** Camelot Books, 1975. 179 pp.

Ten-year-old Rosie Bernard's father is an actor who must travel from city to city during the depression in the 1930s. When her mother dies, Rosie goes to live in Brooklyn with her grandparents, uncles, aunts, and cousins. Rosie feels very out of place, and when her father brings back a new wife the stubborn young girl decides to run away from home.

Bridgers, Sue Ellen. **All Together Now.** Alfred A. Knopf, 1979. 238 pp.

Twelve-year-old Casey Flanagan comes to spend the summer in the small Southern town where her grandparents live. She meets Dwayne Pickens, a thirty-three-year-old man whose mind has never grown beyond that of a boy of twelve. When Dwayne's vulnerability leads to disaster, Casey, her family, and the community pull together in an unselfish act to save him.

Buchan, Stuart. **A Space of His Own.** Charles Scribner's Sons, 1979. 197 pp.

Do you know anyone who has served time at a state correctional farm? Starting life over at eighteen is difficult! Michael is determined to stay out of trouble but finds that crime is not so easily left behind. Will he be able to find a space of his own and win the struggle to become his own person?

Buchan, Stuart. **When We Lived with Pete.** Charles Scribner's Sons, 1978. 147 pp.

Tommy's mother wants to be an actress but has trouble getting even modeling jobs. Alone much of the time, Tommy decides to explore an abandoned mansion, where he makes friends with a runaway and an Indian recluse. But even with his new friends, Tommy longs for how things used to be when they lived with Pete—and so he does something about it.

Bunting, Eve. **Blackbird Singing.** Illus. Stephen Gammell. Macmillan Publishing Co., 1980. 92 pp.

Do you know how it feels to be caught in the middle of a fight between your mom and dad? This argument begins over what to do with the thousands of blackbirds that are roosting in the farmyard trees. Young Marcus doesn't know whose side he is on. But he does know that his stuttering, which had disappeared, has started again. Can Marcus adapt?

Burch, Robert. **Ida Early Comes over the Mountain.** Camelot Books, 1982. 145 pp.

For the four Sutton kids, life in the Blue Ridge Mountains of Georgia is rough. Their mother is dead, and their father is always at work. But when unpredictable Ida Early is hired as housekeeper, life becomes a lot more exciting. Ida brings laughter back into the Sutton house, and the kids love the tall tales she tells. But their friendship is put to the test when they discover there is more to Ida Early than just her funny ways. (ALA Notable Book; Junior Literary Guild Selection)

Butler, Beverly. **My Sister's Keeper.** Dodd, Mead & Co., 1980. 219 pp.

When Mary goes to Wisconsin in 1871 to visit her sister, little does she expect that this trip will be filled with romance and adventure. The two sisters never got along very well, and now that Mary is befriended by her sister's husband, things are becoming worse. However, all of these emotional problems are pushed into the background for a while when a raging forest fire threatens the survival of the entire community.

Butterworth, W. E. **Leroy and the Old Man.** Four Winds Press, 1980. 154 pp.

After witnessing a ruthless robbery in a Chicago housing project, Leroy is sent to live with his grandfather in rural Mississippi to escape possible harm from the criminals. There he must learn to love the old man, who seems stupid and dull to Leroy. But their experiences together on the river reveal surprising secrets, and Leroy is faced with a challenge that tests his true feelings toward his grandfather.

Butterworth, W. E. **A Member of the Family.** Four Winds Press, 1982. 172 pp.

Mrs. Lockwood wants to fill the gap in fourteen-year-old Tom's life when his older brother goes off to college, so she buys him a seven-inch ball of fluff that's destined to become a one-hundred-twenty-five-pound Old English sheepdog. As a puppy, Precious eagerly assumes the role of protector, but it isn't long before he looks as if he might bite—and badly. Tom tries to hide the truth, but it finally becomes clear to everyone that Precious is a sick animal, a victim of inbreeding. The Lockwoods know what they must do, but none can bear to do it. Then Precious threatens Dr. Lockwood's life, and Tom must find the courage to act.

Byars, Betsy. **The Animal, the Vegetable, and John D. Jones.** Illus. Ruth Sanderson. Delacorte Press, 1982. 150 pp.

Clara and Deanie are happy and excited about spending summer vacation with their father. But when they discover that Dad is bringing his woman friend and her son along, they decide this may be two weeks in the wrong place with the wrong people. It takes a terrible mistake to change their opinion.

Byars, Betsy. **The Night Swimmers.** Illus. Troy Howell. Delacorte Press, 1980. 131 pp.

Retta, Johnny, and Roy live with their father, a country-western singer. Since he works nights and sleeps most of the day, it is up to Retta to help raise her brothers. The three have the most fun when they can sneak into a private swimming pool down the street at night. But the children are soon forced to realize that nighttime swims will have to give way to more serious matters if they want to help each other grow up. Easy reading.

Byrd, Elizabeth. **It Had to Be You.** Viking Press, 1982. 159 pp.

Kitty's biggest frustration was Johnny. Did he even notice her? This story takes place in New York during the depression of 1931. A weekend at West Point, an interesting school assignment, and her sister's wedding all keep Kitty from getting too discouraged over the bad times and Johnny's lack of attention.

Calvert, Patricia. **The Money Creek Mare.** Charles Scribner's Sons, 1981. 135 pp.

It's tough to be mature. Ella Rae Carmody knows because she is stuck running the family diner and taking care of her younger brothers and sisters while her mother is in Hollywood and her father is looking for a fast horse. When her father finds a crippled red mare, they plan to breed her with Dark Victory, a stallion at nearby Fairfield Farms. Ella Rae takes a job as housemaid at Fairfield and hopes for the chance to breed the horses and to work for a new home. But everything does not go smoothly for Ella Rae. Will she have to go back to being the family drudge?

Cameron, Eleanor. **To the Green Mountains.** E. P. Dutton, 1975. 180 pp.

In her family's drab hotel in Ohio, Kath Rule dreams about returning to her grandmother's house in the Green Mountains. Kath's desire increases when her best friend, Tissie, changes so much that Kath becomes frightened of her. A tragedy that occurs after her mother leaves her father may help Kath return to her grandmother and the Green Mountains sooner than she expected, however.

Carris, Joan Davenport. **The Revolt of 10-X.** Harcourt Brace Jovanovich, 1980. 128 pp.

"HALLELUJAH! GIVE ME A JOB," typed out the computer on its screen. Young Taylor punched in "LIFE HAS BOMBED." No sooner does she put in the last word, however, than all the electrical circuits in the house go out. So Taylor next types "100%" as a compliment to the computer, and all the electrical equipment comes on again. Taylor realizes that with the computer she can now control all the electricity in the house. But how will she use this power? And does she even want to keep the computer now that her father is dead?

Cate, Dick. **A Nice Day Out?** Illus. Trevor Stubley. Elsevier/Nelson Books, 1979. 94 pp.

Who would have thought that a baby's losing her pacifier would begin a series of disasters for Billy and his family? But this is just what happens, as Billy almost drowns while swimming to a raft, and Grandma disappears mysteriously during a picnic at the beach.

Cavanna, Betty. **The Surfer and the City Girl.** Westminster Press, 1981. 95 pp.

Anne is not quite prepared for what she encounters in Florida. Living with her grandmother seems safe enough. She even meets a great surfer named Swifty, who is friendly and fun to be with. But then Anne realizes her grandmother is an alcoholic. What can Anne do to help?

Cazzola, Gus. **To Touch the Deer.** Westminster Press, 1981. 127 pp.

Robert is having a hard time getting along with his new stepfather. When the family members are in a car accident and Robert thinks his mother is dead, he runs away. He just can't face living with his stepfather. Alone in the Pine Barrens of New Jersey, Robert learns how to survive in the wilderness and makes a difficult decision about his life.

Chaikin, Miriam. **I Should Worry, I Should Care.** Illus. Richard Egielski. Yearling Books, 1979. 103 pp.

No one even asked Molly if she wanted to move. Mama and Papa just announced one day that the family was moving. Molly is worried about going to a new school. Will she make friends or will she be miserable? What will it really be like to live in a new neighborhood? Easy reading.

Chetin, Helen. **How Far Is Berkeley?** Harcourt Brace Jovanovich, 1977. 122 pp.

Twelve-year-old Michael and her single mother undergo many changes when they move to the free-thinking community of Berkeley, California. Mike explores the colorful neighborhood with her new friend David, who is handicapped. Mike soon has to deal with her confused feelings when she realizes her mother is developing a serious relationship with a man. But the young girl's sense of humor and common sense help her cope with her new life.

Clarke, Joan. **Early Rising.** J. B. Lippincott Co., 1976. 249 pp.

The harder Erica tries to be good, the more she gets into trouble. But she likes to play tricks on her two older sisters, her brother, and her friends. And when she and her sisters play outdoors, it's Erica who comes in all muddy. Erica has what seems a natural rebelliousness that doesn't fit into society's ideas of what girls are supposed to act like in the 1880s. At times, Erica feels lonely for the dead mother she has never seen, especially since her father, who has married a second time, is usually too tired to spend time with her. But Erica follows her conscience throughout her childhood years, and at seventeen, she is determined to make a career of her own away from the family.

Cleary, Beverly. **Ramona the Brave.** Illus. Alan Tiegreen. Scholastic Book Services, 1975. 124 pp.

Meet Ramona the Brave. Ramona is only a first grader, but she has just told all the sixth-grade boys that they are bad for calling her sister "Jesus-Beezus." Her sister is embarrassed, and her mother is laughing. What can Ramona do now but get into more trouble?

Cleaver, Vera, and Bill Cleaver. **Dust of the Earth.** J. B. Lippincott Co., 1975. 159 pp.

Fern and her family move to a farm in South Dakota, near some property left to them by her grandfather. But as soon as they arrive, the family must deal with stress and pressure when they decide to sell the land. Then Fern faces the challenge of a lifetime when she discovers the danger that surrounds them.

Cleaver, Vera, and Bill Cleaver. **Queen of Hearts.** J. B. Lippincott Co., 1978. 158 pp.

Twelve-year-old Wilma Lincoln finds herself being a companion to her grandmother for the summer. Wilma feels no love for the grumpy seventy-nine-year-old, yet when Wilma tries to get a replacement her grandmother objects. Eventually, Wilma learns the hard way about love, life, and giving through her grandmother.

Clewes, Dorothy. **Missing from Home.** Harcourt Brace Jovanovich, 1978. 150 pp.

Carrie and Maxwell Grant are young English children living in France. To keep their parents from getting a divorce, the children plan a wild kidnapping scheme. But their plan backfires with terrifying results.

Colman, Hila. **Sometimes I Don't Love My Mother.** Scholastic Book Services, 1977. 184 pp.

The happy life of seventeen-year-old Dallas Davis is suddenly turned upside down when her father dies of a heart attack. As an only child, she tries very hard to comfort her mother, but Dallas soon finds that her mother is becoming much too dependent upon her. The young girl feels trapped and realizes that her love for her mother is turning into anger. With the help of her friends, Dallas is able to find a life for herself and to convince her mother that she can make it on her own too.

Colman, Hila. **Tell Me No Lies.** Crown Publishers, 1978. 74 pp.

Angela has never known her father; her mother told her they had been divorced when Angela was just a baby and that her father now lives in Saudi Arabia. When Angela's mother remarries, her new husband wants to adopt Angela. It is then that she learns the truth—that her mother was not married when Angela was born. Angry and resentful, Angela goes looking for her real father, and she ends up finding herself. Easy reading.

Colman, Hila. **What's the Matter with the Dobsons?** Crown Publishers, 1980. 113 pp.

The Dobsons appear to be the ideal American family, but they are really very troubled. Thirteen-year-old Amanda thinks her father picks on her and favors her young sister, Lisa. And Lisa thinks her mother and Amanda deliberately ignore her. Mr. and Mrs. Dobson's arguments become so serious that they decide to separate. After the family gets back together, Amanda and Lisa are forced to accept the fact that some things can't be changed.

Corcoran, Barbara. **The Faraway Island.** Atheneum Publishers, 1977. 158 pp.

Fourteen-year-old Lynn bursts into tears when her father announces that the family will be going to Brussels, Belgium. She is too shy to go to a strange country, and besides, she can't speak the language. Lynn is so upset that her mother and father agree to let her stay with her grandmother on Nantucket Island. It has been two years since Lynn has seen her grandmother, and Lynn finds her to be confused, forgetful, and much older than she remembered. Lynn's problems begin when she becomes so wrapped up in looking after her grandmother that she "forgets" to enroll in school.

Corcoran, Barbara. **Hey, That's My Soul You're Stomping On.** Atheneum Publishers, 1978. 122 pp.

When Rachel's parents send her off to spend a few weeks with her grandparents in California, she knows it's because they are quarreling again. Since her grandparents live in a resort for retired people, Rachel misses being with other young people. Then she meets cool and assured Ariadne and Ariadne's brother, Alan. Gradually, Rachel discovers that her problems are nothing compared to Ariadne's.

Corcoran, Barbara. **Make No Sound.** Atheneum Publishers, 1977. 148 pp.

Melody, her mother, and two half brothers have just moved again, this time from California to Hawaii. Melody's family quarrel all the time, and she doesn't like her older brother's wild new friends. Melody's only consolation is the late-night talk show with Kahuna, who tells of gods, goddesses, and magic. Frightening events begin to happen when Melody is threatened by a bully after school one day.

Cormier, Robert. **I Am the Cheese.** Pantheon Books, 1977. 233 pp.

What would you do if you suddenly found out that you were someone else? Young Adam Farmer goes on a journey to find his father and his past. Adam's quest becomes filled with mystery and tragedy as the young boy faces family secrets connected with the evils of organized crime and government intelligence.

Cornish, Sam. **Grandmother's Pictures.** Illus. Jeanne Johns. Camelot Books, 1978.

This book presents a poetic collection of stories from the past. A young black boy recaptures his family's history by viewing the many pictures in his grandmother's old photo album.

Crompton, Anne Eliot. **Queen of Swords.** Methuen, 1980. 139 pp.

Abandoned by her husband, teenage Susan lives alone with her one-year-old son, Jason. Life is difficult, and Susan's only comfort lies in her artwork. Her dreams seem to come true when she wins a scholarship to South Beach Design, one of the leading commercial art schools in the country. But when she calls home to share the good news, she finds her family shattered by separation. Susan struggles to help her parents and to find a sense of inner confidence.

Danziger, Paula. **Can You Sue Your Parents for Malpractice?** Delacorte Press, 1979. 152 pp.

Lauren had been looking forward to ninth grade, but so far everything seems to be going wrong. Her mother and father quarrel, her older sister moves out, and her boyfriend leaves her for a cheerleader. When Lauren meets Zack Davies, her friends laugh at her new love because he is a year younger. Then Lauren's new class, "Law for Children and Young People," begins to give her new courage and determination, and soon she is out to change the world.

Danziger, Paula. **The Divorce Express.** Delacorte Press, 1982. 148 pp.

Fourteen-year-old Phoebe spends weekdays with her father in Woodstock, New York, and commutes on the bus called the Divorce Express for weekends with her mother in New York City. It seems that joint custody means more problems for her than for either parent. She's got to deal with all the crises in their lives, and it's hard to become a part of things in Woodstock when she's not around on the weekends. Her life improves when she becomes friends with Rosie, an offbeat Divorce Express regular, and when Dave, her secret crush, asks her for a date. But just when everything seems to be going well, her mother announces that she's planning to marry a man Phoebe can't stand.

Danziger, Paula. **The Pistachio Prescription.** Delacorte Press, 1979. 154 pp.

Cassandra Stephens feels out of place at home and at school. Things take a turn for the better when she runs for ninth-grade class president and meets good-looking Bernie. But her happiness at home vanishes when her parents consider divorce. As Cassie struggles with adult decisions, she learns about life's hardships.

Dawson, Cleo. **She Came to the Valley: A Novel of the Lower Rio Grande Valley, Mission, Texas.** Ballantine Books, 1978. 405 pp.

Willy Westall finds life in the territory of Texas in the early 1900s terribly hard. The Mexican revolutionary Pancho Villa is threatening war, and her husband becomes crippled in an accident. Now Willy must find a way to support her husband and two daughters.

de Messieres, Nicole. **Reina the Galgo.** Elsevier/Nelson Books, 1981. 211 pp.

When Colette and her family brought home their sickly little puppy, they never imagined she would live up to her name—Reina, Spanish for "queen." But even though her high-spirited nature occasionally got her into trouble, Reina did seem to be all that her name promised—beautiful, free, and strong. And she was a true friend to Colette, a source of comfort in all the bad times—until that one tragic event that only Manuel, Colette's childhood friend from Peru, could help her get over.

Donahue, Marilyn Cram. **The Crooked Gate.** David C. Cook Publishing Co., 1979. 208 pp.

For Cass, a summer with Aunt Mathilda means being stuck with two pesky brothers and a strange aunt in a weird house that looks like a three-layer chocolate cake. But as the summer passes, Cass is plunged into mystery and romance as she discovers the secret of the third floor of the house and meets Hal, a deaf boy with whom she must learn to communicate.

Douglass, Barbara. **Sizzle Wheels.** Illus. James McLaughlin. Westminster Press, 1981. 173 pp.

Tori and the Sizzle Wheels skating group just have to win first prize at the big parade. Tori knows her father would be proud of her then. And that is what she wants more than anything else. But things don't go smoothly. Tori collides with old Mr. Cooper on the sidewalk, and his 375 ladybugs get loose. Now his prize roses are sure to be eaten without the ladybugs there to feast on the aphids. So Tori must help Mr. Cooper in his garden. How will she ever have the time to practice with the Sizzle Wheels?

Dunlop, Eileen. **The House on Mayferry Street.** Illus. Phillida Gili. Holt, Rinehart & Winston, 1976. 204 pp.

At age nine, Colin Ramsay enters what looks like the worst period of his life. His father dies of a heart attack one day at work, and soon after that his thirteen-year-old sister Marion is hit by traffic and becomes an invalid. Now, three years later, sister and brother live with their mother in a run-down house on Mayferry Street in Edinburgh, Scotland. Their sadness and loneliness fade when a ghost appears—a ghost that holds the keys to hidden secrets of the past, and the key to their future happiness. (Honor Book, Committee for the International Reading Association's Annual Children's Book Award)

Elfman, Blossom. **Butterfly Girl.** Houghton Mifflin Co., 1980. 146 pp.

A sixteen-year-old girl becomes pregnant and runs away to a poverty-stricken area where she finds comfort from other troubled girls. Through these girls' help and advice, her talks with religious groups, and the experience of giving birth to a child, the girl matures. Then she decides to return home to her family, not knowing if she faces acceptance or rejection.

Elliot, Bruce. **Village.** Avon Books, 1982. 584 pp.

In the nineteenth century, Tom Endicott decides to move to New York's Greenwich Village in order to raise his family in an exciting and liberating place. Throughout the next 130 years, the Endicott family remain closely linked with the Village. They help build the subway system, produce works of art, and struggle through the Great Depression, changing and growing with the Village. Mature language and situations.

Ellis, Joyce K. **The Big Split.** Thomas Nelson, 1979. 168 pp.

Rod's life seems to be falling apart. He can't get his mind on school or football, and he nearly ruins his chance to play on the high school team. When his mother leaves, the only comfort he finds is his aunt Mattie and his sister Jodi. But Rod feels he needs outside help, so he becomes a Christian and decides to change his life with the support of his family and his religious faith.

Ellis, Mel. **An Eagle to the Wind.** Holt, Rinehart & Winston, 1978. 141 pp.

Dyland Pinchot lives a lonely life—not just because he and his parents live in a backwoods cabin in Michigan during the late 1800s, where neighbors are few and far between. What makes life really lonely for Dyland is that he and his father are so different. Gifford Pinchot is a rough, practical lumberman, while his son loves intellectual tasks, likes protecting nature, and has fun growing the family's food. One day while returning from an errand to the city for his father, Dyland makes a trip that threatens him with danger, but that also leads him into manhood.

Etchison, Birdie L. **Me and Greenley.** Illus. James Converse. Herald Press, 1981. 124 pp.

Robin wonders what she has done to deserve her life. Her mother has debilitating multiple sclerosis, her sister is a troublemaker, and her grandmother wants to put her mother into a nursing home. Now her best friend, Greenley Hinson, is leaving. In her confusion, Robin turns to God. She comes to find that God does answer prayers in unexpected ways.

Ewing, Kathryn. **Things Won't Be the Same.** Scholastic Book Services, 1980. 92 pp.

A new house, a new school, and a new father! Things sure have been different ever since Marcy's mother got married again. Marcy feels left out, especially when her stepfather's daughter comes to visit and is treated like a special guest. Marcy begins to think more and more about living with her father and his new wife in California. So she writes him a letter. Then Marcy changes her mind. What will her mother say when she finds out about the letter? Easy reading.

Farley, Carol. **Twilight Waves.** Atheneum Publishers, 1981. 131 pp.

Browning Wilds never knew his father, who supposedly drowned when a freighter sank in Lake Michigan. Browning's grandmother says his father was no good because he ran off and left Browning's mother. But Browning wants to discover the truth about his father himself, so he goes to Lake Michigan. Will he be able to find his father? Or is he dead?

Feagles, Anita MacRae. **Sophia Scarlotti and CeeCee.** Atheneum Publishers, 1979. 164 pp.

For her family, vacation is a time of relaxation, but for CeeCee, it is just the beginning of her troubles. First, her boyfriend dumps her for a snobbish rival. When her grandfather dies, her family is split apart. Worst of all, she keeps having nightmares that trouble even her waking hours. Then an unexpected call seems to end all her unhappiness.

Feagles, Anita MacRae. **The Year the Dreams Came Back.** Atheneum Pubishers, 1978. 146 pp.

A year after her mother committed suicide, Nell is still depressed and feels herself growing away from her family. When her father falls in love and plans to remarry, Nell feels unable to accept the situation.

Nell, her father, and her stepmother-to-be must all work hard at understanding each other's feelings.

Fitzhugh, Louise. **Sport.** Delacorte Press, 1979. 218 pp.

Eleven-year-old Sport lives happily with his absent-minded father— until his wealthy grandfather dies and leaves him twenty million dollars. The trouble comes when his cruel mother schemes to get some of the fortune. Soon Sport finds himself kidnapped and alone in a locked hotel room. His chance of escape is slim until Sport puts a daring plan in action.

Fleming, Susan. **Countdown at 37 Pinecrest Drive.** Illus. Beth Krush and Joe Krush. Westminster Press, 1982. 128 pp.

Joel has wild daydreams: of being a NASA astronaut, of making contact with Pluto, of being awarded the Congressional Medal of Honor. And it all began when he got his own gas mask, which Joel thought looked futuristic and astronautic. But when Joel, his brother Terry, and his sister Olivia stumble onto clues relating to a series of robberies, it seems there will be more real-life adventure than Joel can handle.

Fleming, Susan. **The Pig at 37 Pinecrest Drive.** Illus. Beth Krush and Joe Krush. Westminster Press, 1981. 127 pp.

Terry Blodgett wants to be noticed, to be somebody. If only he could be captain of the baseball team. Then one day something comes into his life that gets him noticed. It is a small pink and white pig named Cadillac. Suddenly Terry is somebody in town, but somebody everyone laughs at. If someone calls him "piggy" once more he will leave town, Terry decides. Even the baseball coach is laughing. Then Cadillac turns detective and amazes everyone—especially Terry.

Forbes, Tom H. **Quincy's Harvest.** J. B. Lippincott Co., 1976. 143 pp.

Quincy's life as a sharecropper's son had never been easy, but this year his friendship with Stump, an old black man, has helped. When hard rains wash away his family's crops, Quincy knows he must help by doing the one thing he hates—killing animals for their meat and fur. But Stump again gives Quincy comfort and guidance to survive this new ordeal.

Fox, Paula. **The Stone-Faced Boy.** Illus. Donald A. Mackay. Bradbury Press, 1975. 106 pp.

Gus is trapped behind a face that never smiles or frowns, and he is also trapped in the middle of a family of five children. Then Serena asks him to find her dog, who is lost in the woods and possibly even caught in a fox trap. Even more unusual is the arrival of Gus's strange Great-Aunt Harriet that same night. She takes over Gus's room and is able to read his thoughts. What can all this mean?

Gauch, Patricia Lee. **Kate Alone.** G. P. Putnam's Sons, 1980. 107 pp.

Unlike most teenage girls, Kate Arthur has few friends and spends most of her time with her dog, Duffy. When Duffy returns from obedience school, however, Kate begins to realize that something terrible has happened to him; Duffy is no longer the loveable friend he used to be. Now afraid of Duffy, Kate searches for an explanation for her pet's strange behavior.

Gerson, Corinne. **How I Put My Mother through College.** Atheneum Publishers, 1981. 136 pp.

What do you do when your newly divorced mother decides to become a college freshman? If you are thirteen-year-old Jessica, you listen to her worries about papers, advise her about courses, make suggestions about dating, and even give her permission to stay out late. But Jessica does not know how long she can stand this role reversal, especially when she discovers she has nobody to tell her own troubles to.

Gerson, Corinne. **Son for a Day.** Illus. Velma Ilsley. Atheneum Publishers, 1982. 140 pp.

With his mother living on the West Coast and his aunt working nights and weekends, Danny is left pretty much on his own. So he thinks up a very unusual hobby. He adopts lots of families by getting to know divorced fathers and their sons when they visit the Bronx Zoo. It was a good idea—but even the best of schemes sometimes goes wrong. Easy reading.

Gerson, Corinne. **Tread Softly.** Dial Press, 1979. 133 pp.

Kitten Tate is an orphan who has romantic ideas about families. Though she lives a comfortable life with her grandparents, she spends most of her spare time inventing an imaginary family. This fantasy endangers her real relationships when Kitten lies about her family to get a job.

Gessner, Lynne. **Danny.** Illus. Donald Schlegel. Harvey House, Publishers, 1979. 216 pp.

Sixteen-year-old Danny Heber and his fifteen-year-old sister, Claudia, must grow up rapidly as they travel with their family to Oregon in a wagon train. On the Oregon Trail, Danny learns that his father has become a Mormon and has taken a second wife. Danny and his mother are so angry that they decide to leave the father in Salt Lake City and go to Oregon without him.

Giff, Patricia Reilly. **The Gift of the Pirate Queen.** Illus. Jenny Rutherford. Delacorte Press, 1982. 164 pp.

Ever since her mother died, Grace O'Malley has been doing fine caring for her father and her younger sister, Amy. But now cousin Fiona is coming all the way from Ireland and threatening to upset her ways; Amy has diabetes and isn't following her doctor's orders; and Grace breaks her teacher's prize Christmas bell and is too afraid to confess. Then, through Fiona's great gift of storytelling, Grace is whirled back to a time when a brave and bold pirate queen named Grace O'Malley ruled the seas. "You're like the other Grace O'Malley," Fiona tells her. But Grace wonders if she really has the courage of the Pirate Queen.

Girion, Barbara. **Like Everybody Else.** Charles Scribner's Sons, 1980. 169 pp.

What's it like to be a seventh grader with an unusual mother? Ask Samantha Gold. Everything is fine until her mother decides to write an adult novel. Soon her mother is having magazine interviews and going on publicity tours. But her novel is about a subject Samantha wishes her mother had not written about—marital infidelity. Soon Samantha is caught up with this unwanted publicity, starting junior high school, and planning her bas mitzvah. Can she handle it all?

Girion, Barbara. **Misty and Me.** Charles Scribner's Sons, 1979. 139 pp.

Kim's parents have come close to promising her a dog, but now that her mother has taken a full-time job, it's clear that getting a puppy is out of the question. Then Kim gets a bright idea: she thinks of a way that she can keep her parents happy *and* have her very own puppy. The plan works well until something completely unexpected happens—long before Kim is ready for it.

Glaser, Dianne. **Summer Secrets.** Holiday House, 1977. 126 pp.

Fourteen-year-old Worthy Meadows is spending a whole summer with her great aunt in Tulip, Alabama. Worthy plans to make two dreams come true during these summer months: to have a beautiful horse of her own and to find out about the places and the people that her dead mother knew when she was young. When handsome sixteen-year-old Iago Poke offers to help her with her new horse, Rascal, Worthy is warned that Iago is not someone to be friends with. For Worthy, a summer filled with mysteries, surprises, pain, and joy has just begun.

Goins, Ellen H. **Big Diamond's Boy.** Thomas Nelson, 1977. 160 pp.

Cotton has never gone to school. Instead, he leads an exciting life with his father—battling rattlesnakes, dealing bootleg whiskey, and playing poker with gamblers. The trouble begins when his grandmother steps in and demands that he have an education. Suddenly, Cotton finds himself faced with the most important decision of his life.

Gottschalk, Elin Toona. **In Search of Coffee Mountains.** Thomas Nelson, 1977. 203 pp.

Katrin begins to wonder if she and her grandmother will ever find a permanent home. It is shortly after World War II, and all Lotukata (Katrin's pet name) knows is the lonely and difficult life in refugee camps. Her father has gone in search of a better life in Brazil. Her mother is in England, waiting for word from him. So Lotukata must also wait, hoping for the day when she will be reunited with her parents in a land of gold and coffee across the sea.

Grant, Cynthia D. **Big Time.** Atheneum Publishers, 1982. 158 pp.

Missy, a Hollywood star? Dory's father and mother are sure her little sister can be more famous than Shirley Temple and Judy Garland. And Missy herself says she is ready to be in the movies. But there is not much chance of meeting a Hollywood agent in Deadwood, Oklahoma. Then one day a stranger comes to town and promises to introduce Missy to the right people in Hollywood. So Dory, her boyfriend, her mother, and Missy go west with Robert, the talent scout. But soon Dory begins to suspect Robert is not what he says he is.

Grant, Cynthia D. **Joshua Fortune.** Atheneum Publishers, 1980. 152 pp.

What can you do when your parents are hippies? Joshua Fortune lived in a world of protest marches, no rules, and kids with strange names like Peace, Love, and Civil Disobedience. Even his sister was named Sarah Sunshine. Josh's father has dreams of seeing the world, so one day he gets up and leaves—just like that. Left alone, Josh's mother becomes involved with a man called Harley. The next thing Josh knows, he is living in Santa Rosa, California. If anything, the kids there are crazier than those he left behind in San Francisco, but in a different way.

Grant, Cynthia D. **Summer Home.** Atheneum Publishers, 1981. 150 pp.

Vacations are supposed to be free of conflict, but tensions are about all Max finds in his three weeks at Summer Home. He fights with his "Dracula-like" sister, is disappointed in his reading, is afraid of water, and encounters many other problems. But through these episodes, many of them humorous, Max learns to understand other people, and himself.

Green, Phyllis. **Grandmother Orphan.** Thomas Nelson, 1977. 76 pp.

When eleven-year-old Christy is suspended from school and arrested for shoplifting, her parents decide to take drastic actions. The best punishment, they decide, is for her to spend a week with Grandmother Matthews, a tough-talking and grouchy old woman. For Christy, it seems anything is better than having to live with her grandmother. But she changes her mind when Grandmother Matthews does some wild and crazy things. Christy decides she might be able to learn a thing or two from her grandmother after all.

Greene, Constance C. **Getting Nowhere.** Viking Press, 1977. 121 pp.

Ever since his father's remarraige a year ago, fourteen-year-old Mark Johnson's hatred has grown into a rage. As an outlet for his anger, one night Mark takes his younger brother's fencing foil and scratches the new silver car his father bought his stepmother for their first anniversary. But that's only the beginning. The chain of events that follows leads Mark and his entire family to the brink of tragedy.

Greenwald, Sheila. **It All Began with *Jane Eyre*.** Laurel-Leaf Library, 1981. 123 pp.

Franny Dillman loves to read books, and when her mother gives her some modern problem novels about teens, Franny decides to keep a journal. Since her own life seems dull, she borrows incidents from the problem novels and writes these in her journal. But her imagination soon gets her in trouble, and she begins to lose control of her fantasy life.

Griffiths, Helen. **Grip: A Dog Story.** Illus. Douglas Hall. Holiday House, 1978. 129 pp.

Eleven-year-old Dudley Kershaw's world is filled with champion fighting dogs and a strict father who doesn't believe in obeying the law or sending Dudley to school. A loner, the young boy finds it very hard to talk to people, so he reacts to difficult situations with his fists. Dudley's world begins to change when he is given a puppy called Grip to train. But the boy is soon faced with a tense situation when Grip refuses to fight and his father commands him to destroy the dog.

Griffiths, Helen. **Running Wild.** Illus. Victor Ambrus. Holiday House, 1977. 192 pp.

Pablo lives with his grandparents on their small farm in the Spanish mountains while his parents work in a factory in the city. Although he loves his grandparents, he is lonely until his grandfather gives him a dog of his own. After his grandfather destroys the dog's first litter of puppies, Pablo helps her hide her second litter in the forest. But the hidden puppies grow to be wild, vicious dogs, teaching Pablo a painful lesson about nature.

Groch, Judith. **Play the Bach, Dear!** Doubleday & Co., 1978. 191 pp.

Musically untalented, Hilary enlists her little brother's aid in reciting the words to a magic spell that she believes will make her play the piano better. With the December recital fast approaching, Hilary becomes more and more desperate. Then her magic spell takes an unexpected turn—something that amazes everyone.

Guest, Judith. **Ordinary People.** Viking Press, 1976. 263 pp.

Conrad Jarrett has just returned from six months in a mental institution after attempting suicide. Instead of a warm welcome at home, he receives nervous comments from his mother and silence from his father. And always, the memory of his dead brother bothers everyone. With the help of a psychologist, Conrad struggles to build his own confidence and to understand the tense situation at home.

Guy, Rosa. **Mirror of Her Own.** Delacorte Press, 1981. 183 pp.

This is the first summer that seventeen-year-old Mary Abbot can enter into the social whirl of the upper class, which includes parties, yachts, and drugs. She meets an African prince, and in the dizzy high of new ways, she feels her shyness fall away. But her relationship with her older sister—the beautiful, ambitious Roxanne—is painful. How can Mary even hope to be like her? Finally, Mary's attraction to Roxanne's wealthy boyfriend makes her realize that she must go after what she wants, no matter what the cost.

Hall, Lynn. **Danza!** Charles Scribner's Sons, 1981. 185 pp.

It took a trip from Puerto Rico to the United States for Paulo to discover his deep love for horses. But this bond was almost a family trait. Paulo's grandfather was a great horse rider and horse breeder. Now, on his grandfather's ranch, Paulo discovers Danza, a Paso Fino stallion. The boy decides to devote all his time and energy to caring for it. However, Paulo quickly discovers love may not be enough when Danza becomes seriously ill.

Hamilton, Dorothy. **Amanda Fair.** Herald Press, 1981. 115 pp.

Amanda's family has been split apart by her parents' divorce. Now Amanda feels she and her sister might be losing touch with each other. Connie seems to be acting more secretive and mysterious every day. Then Amanda discovers the awful truth—Connie is involved in a shoplifting gang. Amanda wonders what she can do to help her sister. Should she tell the rest of the family?

Hamilton, Dorothy. **Cricket.** Illus. Paul Van Demark. Herald Press, 1975. 113 pp.

Dale's greatest desire is to have a pony. As long as his family lives in a town, his wish has to remain just a dream. But then he and his family move to a farm. Now, if he can only convince his mother he will not be hurt, he can have his dream pony. Easy reading.

Hamilton, Dorothy. **Eric's Discovery.** Illus. Betty Wind. Herald Press, 1979. 111 pp.

Eric Markely is burdened with guilt after he sees Ron Cranor's gang destroy the church windows. Afraid to confide in his family or friends, Eric keeps the information secret. But as vandalism sweeps the town, he must battle with his conscience to keep quiet. Then Eric makes a decision that endangers his life.

Hamilton, Dorothy. **Gina In-Between.** Illus. James Converse. Herald Press, 1982. 122 pp.

Gina's father was killed in a car accident, and now Gina's mother is dating Alan. Gina's brother hates Alan and gets angry every time his mother mentions Alan's name. Sometimes Gina feels sorry for her mother, but sometimes she agrees with her brother. Who is right? And how will Gina's family ever be happy again? Easy reading.

Hamilton, Dorothy. **Ken's Hideout.** Illus. James Converse. Herald Press, 1979. 84 pp.

Twelve-year-old Ken and his mother have survived together ever since his father died four years ago. His mother's boyfriend, Bert, is eager for marriage, but he seems to dislike Ken. Confused and hurt, Ken runs away. With the help of a friend named Mr. Trent, Ken tries to organize his life again.

Hamilton, Dorothy. **Mari's Mountain.** Illus. Esther Rose Graber. Herald Press, 1978. 130 pp.

Mari, a high school student, leaves home to escape the anger of her alcoholic father. She rapidly learns the many problems involved in finding a job and a place to live. Mari meets many interesting people during her adventures, including her cousin Patty. Together the girls help each other face the pressures in their lives.

Hamilton, Dorothy. **Neva's Patchwork Pillow.** Illus. Esther Rose Graber. Herald Press, 1975. 111 pp.

Neva Vance moves north to the big city to live with Miss Mary, but she soon misses her family back in the Appalachian Mountains. Neva decides to stay, however, because she has a chance for a better life with Miss Mary. The patchwork pillow Neva's mother made for her helps comfort her while it gives her an idea that brings Christmas happiness to her family.

Hamilton, Dorothy. **Rosalie at Eleven.** Illus. Unada. Herald Press, 1980. 110 pp.

It is Fair Week, but Marie Marker plans a number of alternate activities for her family so they can save money. Her husband and children are not certain they like the idea. A strain grows between Marie and her husband over this issue. For young Rosalie, the tension in her house soon becomes worse than the thought of missing merry-go-round rides and seeing horse races.

Hamilton, Dorothy. **Straight Mark.** Illus. Paul Van Demark. Herald Press, 1976. 126 pp.

Mark Owens is a good student and an equally good basketball player at his junior high. But he becomes confused when he discovers that one of the high school basketball players is a drug dealer. Should he tell someone? How many others are involved? Mark tries to come to a decision about his knowledge of the drug problem. But can he do it without making his life more difficult at school and at home?

Hamilton, Dorothy. **Winter Girl.** Illus. Allan Eitzen. Herald Press, 1976. 119 pp.

Dalice is startled when she realizes that her younger sister, Anita, is intensely jealous of her. Now Dalice understands why Anita has broken away from her friends and become a loner. Dalice is confused and hurt, but she begins to take steps to draw her younger sister out of her shell of envy.

Hayes, Sheila. **The Carousel Horse.** Thomas Nelson, 1978. 127 pp.

Fran is ready for a relaxing vacation. But she isn't ready for the announcement that her family will be separated for the summer. Her father has taken a job with a Long Island yacht club, and her mother has agreed to work as a cook for the Fairfields, a wealthy family in Merriweather. Fran is to stay with her mother, which means that she will be under the same roof with Andrea Fairchild, the "town snot." However, as the summer wears on, Fran gets to know Andrea and to understand that things are not always what they seem.

Heck, Bessie Holland. **Golden Arrow.** Illus. Charles Robinson. Charles Scribner's Sons, 1981. 136 pp.

For thirteen-year-old Randy Colson, life means riding motorcycles. His father tries to discourage Randy's desire to become a professional racer, but he cannot seem to reach his son. What does reach Randy is Golden Arrow, a beautiful palomino colt born on his grandfather's farm. Now all Randy can think of is turning the farm into a horse ranch.

Hill, Margaret. **Turn the Page, Wendy.** Abingdon Press, 1981. 176 pp.

Wendy survived a childhood of abandonment, neglect, and terrible poverty only to spend her adolescence moving from one institution to another. Then she is given a second chance at Virginia Hall—a chance at a good foster home and a future. Will she give it all up—risk everything—to try to find the mother she has never known?

Hinton, S. E. **Tex.** Delacorte Press, 1979. 194 pp.

Tex and his brother, Mace, are forced to take care of themselves since their father is a cowboy on the rodeo circuit and is rarely home. Tex, a fifteen-year-old, is in love with his horse, Negrito, and his friend's blue-eyed sister, Jamie. Things begin to get tough for the brothers when their father stops sending them money.

Hodges, Hollis. **Why Would I Lie?** Avon Books, 1980. 220 pp.

Cletus Hayworth, a carefree bachelor, an unconventional social worker, and a master liar, suddenly becomes the adopted father of a six-year-old boy. As he begins to care more and more for the boy, Cletus becomes obsessed with finding the boy's missing mother. Originally published as *The Fabricator.*

Hogarth, Grace. **A Sister for Helen.** Illus. Pat Marriott. André Deutsch, 1976. 139 pp.

Helen, a twelve-year-old girl living in the early 1900s, is overjoyed when the new housekeeper brings her daughter Katie along to live with them. Now Helen has a playmate with whom to spend the lonely hours of the day. Helen becomes strangely afraid of Katie's mother, but she keeps quiet about her fears. She finally tries to calm her doubts by finding out more about the woman. The search leads her to an unexpected tragedy.

Holland, Isabelle. **Dinah and the Green Fat Kingdom.** J. B. Lippincott Co., 1978. 189 pp.

Life is hard when you are a "fatty" in a family of thin people. In fact, the only good things are eating and knowing that in the Green Fat Kingdom you are not fat enough to be Fat Princess. At least this is how it is for Dinah, whose life is made even worse by her mother's insistence that she go on a diet and give up all sweets. Having Francis, her fat puppy, helps, but even he will be taken away if she is caught eating candy or ice cream.

Holland, Isabelle. **Hitchhike.** J. B. Lippincott Co., 1977. 156 pp.

Pud, a sixteen-year-old girl, feels let down by her father because he backs out of a promise to take her backpacking. She is so hurt that she decides to get revenge by hitchhiking home from school since "that always drives parents wild." Pud is sure it will be safe enough if she avoids the "creeps" and takes rides only from people who look trustworthy. Unfortunately, it is difficult to tell whom to trust, and Pud's journey home takes longer than she planned.

Holland, Isabelle. **Of Love and Death and Other Journeys.** J. B. Lippincott Co., 1975. 159 pp.

Young Meg Grant is happy and carefree as she moves about Europe with her unpredictable mother and loving stepfather. Life is always exciting and sometimes even crazy. However, the summer of her fifteenth year brings some important changes for Meg. Most important, her real father, whom she has never met, comes to visit her in Italy. But his visit becomes a bad omen as Meg begins to find her days filled with sorrow and grief.

Hostetler, Marian. **African Adventure.** Illus. Esther Rose Graber. Herald Press, 1976. 124 pp.

Instead of just talking about the world's food shortage, Denise's father decides to do something about it. He is a professor of agriculture at a church college in Illinois. His mission begins when he decides to take his family to the African nation of Chad to serve as an agricultural advisor. Unusual adventures begin when the family arrives in their new home.

Howard, Jean G. **Half a Cage.** Illus. by author. Tidal Press, 1978. 319 pp.

Have you ever wondered what it would be like to have a monkey for a pet? When Ann Carpenter and her family take in a spider monkey named Diana, their lives are turned upside down. Diana is charming and fun, but also a lot of trouble. After a while Ann is faced with a difficult decision. Should she give Diana up?

Hunt, Irene. **William.** Charles Scribner's Sons, 1977. 188 pp.

William is only eight when his mother dies, leaving him with his thirteen-year-old sister, Amy, and a younger, blind sister, Carla. Soon a new friend, who is only sixteen and the mother of a baby girl, becomes part of the family. Now this newly assembled family must face many hardships that test the strength of their love for each other.

Irwin, Hadley. **Bring to a Boil and Separate.** McElderry Books, 1981. 123 pp.

Katie Warner is thirteen, but already her life seems to be falling apart. Her parents have decided to get a divorce. And when Katie tries to talk to her brother Dinty about it, he refuses. With her close friend Marti gone, Katie tries to fill her days with tennis and horseback riding. Then Marti comes back, and with her come both more trouble and a chance for Katie to solve her problems.

Johnson, Maud. **Sixteen Can Be Sweet.** Scholastic Book Services, 1978. 158 pp.

Jenny's sixteenth birthday is spent in the waiting room of a hospital. Her father has been seriously injured in a car accident, and the doctor says he must be in a quiet place for many months to recuperate. So Jenny's summer will be spent on a lonely North Carolina beach. How will she fill the hours? Keith Ericson, a handsome, gentle seventeen-year-old, seems to be the answer.

Johnston, Norma. **If You Love Me, Let Me Go.** Atheneum Publishers, 1979. 162 pp.

Sixteen-year-old Allison greets the autumn with joy and disbelief. She seems to have become a new person over the summer—the person she has always wanted to be, confident and likeable. Yet the brightness fades as the new school year grows older. Her grandmother's health grows ever worse, bringing both embarrassment and sorrow to the family. Her relationship with her best friend, Lisa, becomes strained as Lisa's family breaks apart. Then her father's business begins to fail, while her brother's unhappiness at school creates other complications. As many of her old dreams and plans die, Allison tries to understand what is happening to her and to grow stronger as a result.

Johnston, Norma. **The Sanctuary Tree.** Atheneum Publishers, 1977. 219 pp.

Fish Sterling is independent, active in church, and very good at helping other people with their problems. Then Fish begins to have some problems of her own: her boyfriend moves away, her father enters the hospital, her dream of acting in the school play is shattered, and her aunt does her best to find fault in everything the girl does. Only her love of writing helps Fish to endure the troubles, until Christmas brings a series of happy surprises.

Johnston, Norma. **A Striving after Wind.** Atheneum Publishers, 1976. 250 pp.

The Vandevers are a famous, talented Southern family. They, like everyone else in 1861, are caught up in the Civil War. Bridget, the sixteen-year-old daughter, tries to make sense of her life while all around her the war destroys so many things and people she holds dear. Only the strange solitary man she names Mr. Odysseus can really help Bridget understand what is happening around her and to her. Mature situations.

Johnston, Norma. **The Swallow's Song.** Atheneum Publishers, 1979. 192 pp.

In the summer of 1920, Alison Standish takes a trip to New Jersey, where her grandmother lives. Alison is amazed at the ease of life in the "rich city" and becomes ashamed of her humble country family back home. But the city can harbor danger and evil, she later learns, as her love and pride get her involved with criminals.

Jones, Hettie. **I Hate to Talk about Your Mother.** Delacorte Press, 1980. 248 pp.

Alicia is reluctant to go on a vacation to the ocean with her swinging, drinking mother. But her trip is soon filled with excitement as a handsome lifeguard saves her from being trapped in a lighthouse, and she becomes involved with the problems of an emotionally disturbed girl. Then Alicia meets her biggest challenge: resolving the bitterness in her relationship with her mother.

Kelly, Rosalie. **Addie's Year.** Beaufort Books, 1981. 155 pp.

Eleven-year-old Addie's family may not be rich, but they have lots of fun together. It is during the 1920s, and this summer promises to be filled with picnics, boat rides, and adventures for Addie. Her special friend is Ruth, a rich girl whose parents lavish all kinds of treats on her. Over this particular summer, Addie and Ruth will learn even more interesting secrets about each other and also will discover that friendships can be hard work.

Kibbe, Pat. **The Hocus-Pocus Dilemma.** Illus. Dan Jones. Alfred A. Knopf, 1979. 125 pp.

When B.J. Pinkerton is convinced she has ESP, she decides to go into the fortune-telling business. She starts reading books that promise to help develop her "natural talent" and she even buys a crystal ball. B.J. tries to use her powers to help her family, but somehow something always goes wrong. Easy reading.

Kingman, Lee. **The Refiner's Fire.** Houghton Mifflin Co., 1981. 218 pp.

Since Sara's mother died, she has lived with her grandmother while her father traveled and studied ceramics. But then Gran gets sick, and Sara is going to live with her father again—and with several new people too, for her father now lives in an artists' cooperative in a big old barn in New Hampshire. Getting to know these artists is quite a task for Sara, but in the process she comes to know herself better too.

Klass, Sheila Solomon. **To See My Mother Dance.** Charles Scribner's Sons, 1981. 154 pp.

Thirteen-year-old Jessica Van Norden longs for the mother who abandoned her as a baby. And she prefers the fantasy of her missing mother to the reality of her stepmother. Jessica is sure her real mother is now a successful dancer. She finds some comfort in her best friend, Brookie, who lost her father the same way Jessica lost her mother. But this is never enough for Jessica. How far can she allow her fantasies to take her, though, before there are problems?

Klein, Norma. **Breaking Up.** Pantheon Books, 1980. 207 pp.

She has always tried to please everyone. Maybe that's why fifteen-year-old Alison finds making changes hard, for changes mean learning all over again what other people expect of her. Now Alison and her older brother, Martin, are leaving the home in New York they share with their mother and her friend Peggy to spend the summer in California with their father and stepmother. Once there, Alison falls in love with her best friend's brother, but keeps her love a secret. Then she learns that her mother and Peggy are more than just friends. Finally Alison becomes the center of a fight between her parents over who is to keep her.

Konigsburg, E. L. **Journey to an 800 Number.** Atheneum Publishers, 1982. 138 pp.

Maximillian Stubbs is used to first-class treatment. So he is not very happy when his mother sends him to stay with his father while she goes off on a honeymoon trip with her second husband. Max's father is a camel keeper, and Max does not really like Ahmed the camel. But during the month Max stays with his father, the camel's jobs at state fairs, dude ranches, and night clubs bring Max into contact with strange and bizarre people. Max begins to think that maybe being first class does not always mean having money.

Lee, Joanna. **I Want to Keep My Baby!** Signet Books, 1977. 166 pp.

Sue Ann Cunningham is fifteen years old—old enough to have a baby. But is she old enough to be a mother? Find out how one teenage mother copes with her parents, social workers, school, boyfriends, and a job in order to keep the baby she loves more than anything else. Mature situations.

Lehmann, Linda. **Better Than a Princess.** Thomas Nelson, 1978. 95 pp.

Tilli has a hard life with Mother Baelk: she does the hardest chores and is not allowed to go to school. Tilli is sure her real mother is a royal princess and will send for her soon. Then one day the letter comes—Tilli is going from Germany to America to be with her mother. Her journey by riverboat, steamship, and finally railroad is a series of surprises all the way. And the surprises continue for the young girl when she is reunited with her mother.

Lehmann, Linda. **Tilli's New World.** Elsevier/Nelson Books, 1981. 154 pp.

Tilli is so excited she could cry. At last, after months of travel, she is going to be reunited with her family in America. Together again, Tilli's family must share hard work and sacrifices to keep their Missouri farm going. Tilli's dream is to go to school, but the nearest school is miles away. Besides, she is needed on the farm. Even though she does not speak English, Tilli is determined to find some way to fulfill her dream.

LeRoy, Gen. **Cold Feet.** Laurel-Leaf Library, 1981. 187 pp.

Geneva Michellini really wanted that job in the penny arcade. But they wanted to hire a boy. So with her hair slicked down with olive oil and a set of new clothes, Geneva becomes Johnny Bertolli and is soon working at the arcade. It all seems like a great joke at first. But Geneva-Johnny quickly becomes entangled in misadventures with gamblers and gangsters. On top of all this, her double life is beginning to change her relationship with her family.

Levine, Betty K. **The Great Burgerland Disaster.** Atheneum Publishers, 1981. 104 pp.

Fifteen-year-old Mike Whitland is a great cook. He has even started his own catering service. But when the Raleigh Grand Prix ten-speed bike he uses to make deliveries is stolen, Mike is reduced to working at Burgerland. Mike tries to interest Mr. Metro, Burgerland's manager, in adding some unusual dishes to Burgerland's menu. Mr. Metro is not thrilled with the idea, but after tasting Mike's cooking, he decides to give it a try. The new menu items work so well that the fast-food service begins to get rave reviews from local restaurant critics. For Mike, however, all this attention and success only seem to create problems between himself and his parents.

Lifton, Betty Jean. **I'm Still Me.** Alfred A. Knopf, 1981. 243 pp.

Lori Elkins knows she is adopted, but it isn't until she does an American history assignment to trace her family roots that she decides to find her biological parents. She begins the search but does not tell her adopted parents. Her other friends—Maggie, Bottomless Pit, and Chris—quietly aid her in the search. Lori wonders what she will eventually find out about her first parents, little realizing that everything she is doing is developing her character and telling her more about who she really is.

Lingard, Joan. **Odd Girl Out.** Elsevier/Nelson Books, 1979. 187 pp.

Tall, red-haired Ellie is upset when her mother decides to remarry. She finds comfort talking with a seventy-year-old friend and musician, but she remains stubbornly opposed to the marriage. The situation worsens when Ellie keeps mentioning her long-dead father. Then her mother tells Ellie a shocking secret about her father-to-be that completely changes her attitude.

Lingard, Joan. **A Proper Place.** Thomas Nelson, 1975. 159 pp.

Kevin and Sadie McCoy flee war-torn Belfast, Ireland, for the slums of Liverpool, England. They have escaped the bombs of Ireland but not the many problems of coping with life and keeping their marriage together. They have an infant son to care for, and Kevin's job as a laborer does not bring in enough money. Sadie's mother and Kevin's brother arrive and make matters worse by their interference. Finally, Kevin and Sadie decide that they must find "a proper place" for themselves, so they move to a farm in Cheshire. There they hope that with spunk and courage they can build the peaceful life they have been searching for.

Lingard, Joan. **The Resettling.** Thomas Nelson, 1975. 166 pp.

When their old apartment building in Glasgow, Scotland, is scheduled to be torn down, sixteen-year-old Maggie McKinley decides to convince her father to open his own plumbing business so the family could rent a shop and an apartment together. After she finally convinces him, however, Maggie must back her talk with action and help her father get the business going. But how long can the young girl work at the store, help in the family, keep up with her schoolwork, and carry on a relationship with a boy in another city?

Lorimer, L. T. **Secrets.** Holt, Rinehart & Winston, 1981. 192 pp.

Maggie's father is a popular, respected minister. But one day Maggie catches him lying about an evening visit to a parishioner, and doubts about her father begin. After her father rescues her from an evening with a drunken date, Maggie wonders how he can lie about it so easily to her mother. And why does he insist that a troubled young woman become the new adviser to the Youth Group instead of the members' choice? When Maggie guesses her father's secret, she realizes that he has another side to his personality and learns that the truth, no matter how terrible, can be a relief. Mature situations.

Lowry, Lois. **Anastasia Again!** Yearling Books, 1982. 145 pp.

Anastasia already has said good-bye too many times—when her grandmother died and again when her goldfish was flushed down the toilet. But when she has to say good-bye to the house she has lived in since she was born, that is the hardest good-bye of all. Is it possible that her move to the suburbs will have more to offer than Anastasia expects? (ALA Notable Book)

Lowry, Lois. **Autumn Street.** Houghton Mifflin Co., 1980. 175 pp.

With her father off at war, Elizabeth is forced to move with her mother and older sister into her grandmother's big, gloomy house. The only times Elizabeth looks forward to are the times she and Charles, the grandson of the family cook, go adventuring together.

Tragedy awaits the pair one winter day, however, when Elizabeth decides to try out her new sled.

Ludman, Barbara. **The Strays.** Thomas Nelson, 1976. 149 pp.

The small town of Monroe isn't friendly to strangers. So when the Shanks family move in, it isn't surprising that the only family around to welcome them is the Allens, who seem to have time and love for everyone and everything. The Allens soon find that they are drawn into the personal problems of the Shanks family. In fact, they are faced with some tough decisions when Billy Shanks breaks the law. However, with understanding and caring, the Allens help the Shanks to find a place in the community.

Lyle, Katie Letcher. **Dark But Full of Diamonds.** Bantam Books, 1983. 174 pp.

Scott and his doctor father just seemed to settle down into separate lives since Scott's mother died—every day growing further and further apart. The situation worsens when Scott's swimming teacher from a few years back is hired as a high school teacher at his school. Scott has strong feelings for Hilah Brown, but so does his dad. Can Scott accept her as a stepmother? Mature language and situations.

Majerus, Janet. **Grandpa and Frank.** J. B. Lippincott Co., 1976. 192 pp.

Sarah fears that her uncle Frank, who runs the family farm, wants to gain complete control and ownership of the farm by proving that Grandpa is senile. Sarah and her friend Joey decide to carry out a daring last-ditch plan to save Grandpa from life in a nursing home. The three set out in the old truck for Chicago, where they hope to find a doctor to prove that Grandpa is sane. Not knowing how to drive, Joey zooms into a hilarious adventure. And soon, what started out to be an easy, quick escape turns into disaster.

Major, Kevin. **Hold Fast.** Delacorte Press, 1978. 168 pp.

When a drunk driver kills Michael's parents in an auto accident, Michael's rage and grief are uncontrollable. Just fourteen years old, he knows his relatives won't let him and his seven-year-old brother, Brent, stay alone in the house. The adults decide that Brent is to stay with Grandfather and Aunt Flo, and that Michael must go to St. Albert to live with an aunt and uncle. Michael misses his home in the country in Newfoundland, filled with memories of hunting and fishing with his father and grandfather, but for two months he tries hard to adjust to life in St. Albert. One day Michael gets in trouble and decides to leave. His cousin Curtis goes too—and the pair set out to try to survive on their own. Mature language.

Marangell, Virginia J. **Gianna Mia.** Dodd, Mead & Co., 1979. 224 pp.

Thirteen-year-old Gianna Mia lives in an Italian community in New Haven, Connecticut, in 1937. She leads a sheltered, secure life there, but things change when her favorite brother dies, and she must learn to live in a home filled with bitterness. Even worse, she must watch as her father suffers from grief and guilt over the marriage of her sister. Gianna Mia is left alone much of the time now, and she must use her own wit and courage to determine whether she will build a successful life for herself or leave it in shambles.

Martini, Teri. **All Because of Jill.** Westminster Press, 1976. 155 pp.

The Wainwright family revolves around the beautiful eldest child, Jill. Mrs. Wainwright has taken a job to help put Jill through college and Mr. Wainwright works extra hours at his store for his daughter. Beth and Jeff are left to take charge of the house and meals—and are also left alone much of the time. Beth feels plain and unpopular beside Jill. But Beth's best friend, Andrea, gives her a new haircut, shows her how to be less awkward with boys, and encourages her to develop her own special talents. When Carl, the new boy in school, asks Beth for her first date, Beth feels flattered. But Carl is a "foreigner" and some of the kids call him a Nazi. Can these two outsiders stick together against the pressures they face?

Mays, Lucinda. **The Candle and the Mirror.** Atheneum Publishers, 1982. 182 pp.

How could Anne Simmons ever live up to her mother's example? In 1895 women were supposed to stay home, keep house, and take care of children. But Emily Simmons traveled and lectured to other women about finding their own identities and using their intelligence. Her husband did not like it, but Emily continued. After his death, Emily takes on the job of organizing labor unions for miners who are underpaid and overworked. Anne joins her mother in this work. But she also tries to get out from under her mother's shadow and make her own special contribution to the cause.

Mays, Lucinda. **The Other Shore.** Atheneum Publishers, 1979. 223 pp.

Gabriella wonders how long she can lead a double life. She is taking an active part in regular American high school life. But she is also part of a tradition-bound society at home in the Little Italy section of New York City. It is 1911, and most of the Italian girls Gabriella knows do not go to high school. And hardly any of them have a secret American boyfriend, as she does. Her father sympathizes with Gabriella's plans for a full education. But her mother and most of her other relatives feel Gabriella should be married or working. Is there any way for Gabriella to balance her two worlds and make everybody happy?

Mazer, Harry. **The Island Keeper.** Delacorte Press, 1981. 165 pp.

Cleo Murphy, fat, rich, and miserable, is alone in the world. Her mother and sister are dead. In despair, she secretly runs away to a desolate island her father owns in Canada. She wants some time alone there to rest and to think about her scrambled life.

Mazer, Norma Fox. **Taking Terri Mueller.** Flare Books, 1981. 189 pp.

Why are Terri and her adored father always on the move? What are they running from? Why won't Terri's father ever tell her about her dead mother? Is it possible that Terri's mother didn't die after all? As thirteen-year-old Terri Mueller struggles to answer these questions, she finds herself torn between the two people who love her the most.

McCord, Jean. **Turkeylegs Thompson.** Atheneum Publishers, 1979. 242 pp.

No boy could fight Turkeylegs and win. Is she made so angry by the kids at school? Or is it because her father has left the family and her mother has to go to work, and now she must take care of her younger brother and sister? But this is only the beginning of her desperation—the months of fighting that school year are nothing compared to the wretchedness of the summer that follows.

McGraw, Eloise Jarvis. **A Really Weird Summer.** Illus. Allen Davis. McElderry Books, 1977. 216 pp.

After his parents' divorce, twelve-year-old Nils Anderson is sent to stay with some strange relatives. Shut away in an old inn with these relatives, Nils finds it pleasant to escape and explore the secret rooms in the inn and to enjoy the company of the person who lives in these rooms. But is Alan real? Is he a ghost? Or could he be a relative from another time?

McHargue, Georgess. **Stoneflight.** Illus. Arvis Stewart. Camelot Books, 1976. 223 pp.

When Jamie's parents begin to fight, her summer becomes terrible. Then she meets and awakens a stone griffin, an animal that is part eagle and part lion. Her life becomes enchanted and exciting with her griffin and the other sculptured creatures in New York, until she is forced to make an important decision about her living stone menagerie. Mature language.

McKay, Robert. **Bordy.** Thomas Nelson, 1977. 141 pp.

Just out of high school, Bordy Masterson searches for answers to confusing questions about life. First he seeks a job in an employment center and finds himself in a speedboat heading straight toward work on a freighter. Later he is asked to play psychologist to his mixed-up younger sister. Bordy gets tangled up with the law when he rebels against his parents and joins his sister in using drugs.

Mearian, Judy Frank. **Someone Slightly Different.** Dial Press, 1980. 197 pp.

Marty cannot bear the taunting of the other kids at school. Can she help it that her father walked out, her mother works, and she is left with all the housework? Then her grandmother comes to the rescue. Not only does she do the chores for Marty, but she reveals a brighter side of life to the girl. Then Marty must use all that she has learned from her grandmother when she has to cope with the death of a loved one.

Mearian, Judy Frank. **Two Ways about It.** Dial Press, 1979. 166 pp.

Annie Reynolds, an only child, is enjoying a happy and carefree year. The only real problem she faces is her two-week summer visit with her bossy and difficult cousin, Lou. However, life suddenly changes for Annie when she learns that her mother has cancer. Strangely, it is Lou who is the most help to her during this difficult time. Both girls learn a great deal about each other, the importance of families, and their own inner strengths.

Mendonca, Susan. **Tough Choices.** Dial Press, 1980. 136 pp.

Crystal's self-confidence is crushed when her parents get divorced and her mother begins drifting across the state to live with boyfriend after boyfriend. The court decides to put Crystal in her father's home, but things aren't much better. Here, though, Crystal finds a new friend, and together they decide to run away and try to leave their troubles behind forever.

Meyer, Carolyn. **C. C. Poindexter.** McElderry Books, 1979. 208 pp.

C. C. (Cynthia Charlotte) Poindexter is fifteen years old, six feet one inch tall, and still growing. Her parents are divorced; her best friend, Laura, is completely wrapped up in labeling relationships; her Aunt Charlotte is a militant feminist; and her little sister, Allison, is a brat. With all this in her life, will things ever run smoothly for C. C.?

Meyer, Carolyn. **Eskimos: Growing Up in a Changing Culture.** McElderry Books, 1977. 215 pp.

Life in a typical Eskimo village is sometimes a blending, but mostly a conflict, of the old and the new. The problems of drinking, boredom, and trying to accept the white culture are mixed with the pleasures of storytelling, hunting, fishing, and the closeness of the family in this tale of the struggles and joys of native Alaskans.

Miklowitz, Gloria D. **Did You Hear What Happened to Andrea?** Delacorte Press, 1979. 168 pp.

On a ride back from the beach, fifteen-year-old Andrea is attacked and raped by a stranger. She finds her troubles have just begun as she realizes she must deal not only with her own emotional problems but also with tension with her parents, who appear to be drawing away from her. Without their support and understanding, Andrea wonders how she will ever be able to rebuild her life.

Miles, Betty. **Just the Beginning.** Camelot Books, 1978. 143 pp.

Everything seems to be going wrong so far in eighth grade for Cathy Myers. She gets suspended from school for breaking a minor rule and is always being compared to her "perfect" sister, who is the yearbook editor and class valedictorian. Worst of all, she faces the humiliation of her mother becoming a cleaning lady. Everyone else in town *has* a cleaning lady. Cathy begins to wonder what she can do to begin feeling better about herself.

Milton, Hilary. **The Gitaway Box.** Chariot Books, 1980. 231 pp.

Jock has always been "Paw-Paw" to his grandson Chris, but he is forced to become more than just a loving grandfather when the young boy's parents are killed in an automobile accident. The two now face extremely difficult times. They have very little money, and the social worker wants to place the young boy in a foster home. However, the pair are determined that their courage and devotion, as well as the "gitaway box" and their willingness to take a chance, will help them to remain together and to preserve their dignity.

Moore, Emily. **Something to Count On.** Unicorn Books, 1980. 103 pp.

Lorraine has a hard time fitting in at school. She finds schoolwork and IQ tests boring, and she is always getting into fights. The only bright spot in her day is her favorite teacher, whom she has nick-named "Wolfman." Lorraine's real problem is the fact that her father, who has moved away from home, is always promising to come to see them but never does. She feels guilty and thinks the reason he doesn't come home is because she and her younger brother, Jason, are not good enough. One day Lorraine and Jason come up with a plan to find out if their father really loves them. But the answers they discover surprise and shock them.

Morey, Walt. **The Year of the Black Pony.** E. P. Dutton, 1976. 152 pp.

When his father dies in the early 1900s, Christopher must devote all his time to chores around the ranch. He becomes disappointed when he realizes he can no longer ride up to Christmas Ridge to see his dream horse, a black stallion named Lucifer. But when his mother arranges to marry a nearby rancher to gain additional help for her ranch, Christopher's dream comes true. However, the great stallion becomes like a curse on the new family, and the young boy learns to use tragedy to dissolve bitterness.

Morgan, Alison. **All Kinds of Prickles.** Elsevier/Nelson Books, 1980. 175 pp.

Paul is a young orphan who comes to live with his aunt Jean Dawkes and her family. Unfortunately, Paul's pet goat, Davy, has a hard time being accepted by the family. Paul's uncle quickly becomes very angry at Davy's pranks, and it looks as if Paul may soon have to part with his beloved pet.

Morgenroth, Barbara. **Ride a Proud Horse.** Atheneum Publishers, 1978. 177 pp.

Horses are a way of life for Corey Mathis. She has no big dreams of being rich or famous from riding them—all she wants is to be with them, to care for them, and to develop her own abilities in training them. But ever since her mother was killed by a horse years ago, Corey and her father have moved from place to place, barely making a living. When her father ruins a job opportunity at Windaway Stable, Corey decides it's time to break from him and to make a life of her own.

Mueller, Amelia. **Sissy Kid Brother.** Illus. Paul Van Demark. Herald Press, 1975. 234 pp.

Ken, almost fourteen, feels his family won't give him the chance to accept responsibilities. But when he spends the summer with his older brothers cutting wheat from Oklahoma to North Dakota, he finds plenty of responsibilities and gains some maturity in dealing with them.

Myers, Walter Dean. **It Ain't All for Nothin'.** Viking Press, 1978. 217 pp.

Twelve-year-old Tippy lives with his Grandma Carrie in Harlem, where his life is happy, secure, and protected from much of the violence and crime in the neighborhood. However, all of this is suddenly changed when Grandma Carrie becomes ill and is placed in a nursing home, and he is sent to live with his father, a man he barely knows. Here Tippy is introduced to the world of drugs, theft, and violence. Now Tippy must learn the hard way to stick up for his own values and beliefs. Mature language and situations.

Myers, Walter Dean. **Won't Know Till I Get There.** Viking Press, 1982. 176 pp.

What do fourteen-year-old kids and a group of senior citizens have in common? This is what Steve and his gang find out when they are sentenced to help at a retirement home after he is caught writing graffiti on a subway car. His involvement with the senior citizens helps Steve understand himself better and his new foster brother, Earl.

Naylor, Phyllis Reynolds. **Faces in the Water.** Atheneum Publishers, 1981. 167 pp.

Dan Roberts watches helplessly as his father grows weaker and weaker in a hospital with what may be the start of Huntington's disease—a hereditary illness. A worried Dan is sent to Pennsylvania to spend the summer with his grandmother. When he gets there, however, a strange apparition haunts Dan and his grandmother. She is sure it is someone out of her past, but Dan is not as certain. Could this ghostly face and the mysterious, yet somehow familiar, people Dan keeps meeting be trying to warn him about his future?

Naylor, Phyllis Reynolds. **Shadows on the Wall.** Atheneum Publishers, 1980. 165 pp.

Dan Roberts is very confused. Why have his parents decided to take him out of school in the middle of the year for a visit to England? Who are the people his mother is always visiting? Why do his parents begin to seem afraid from time to time? And why does he have a strange feeling of horror when he gets near the ruins of an ancient Roman city? Dan decides to look for answers to these questions and confront his fears. But he soon realizes he risks stirring up problems in his search for knowledge.

Naylor, Phyllis Reynolds. **Walking through the Dark.** Atheneum Publishers, 1976. 211 pp.

Ruth Wheeler's family is a normal, happy family and luckier than many because they are buying their own house even though it is the depression and times are hard. Then Mr. Wheeler loses the job he's held for nineteen years and can find only occasional work. Life for the Wheelers quickly goes from bad to worse. Ruth's big ambition is to become a teacher, but now she despairs of getting the money for that. A chance encounter with her English teacher, though, may provide Ruth with the opportunity to make her dreams of teaching become a reality.

Neigoff, Mike. **It Will Never Be the Same Again.** Illus. Gwen Brodkin. Holt, Rinehart & Winston, 1979. 191 pp.

For Sid Kaplan, life is not easy. Ever since his father was fired, everything has gone wrong. The ski trip he hoped for is now too expensive, and his father is getting crabbier by the day. Then Sid's new job as a film developer leads to some happy surprises and unexpected discoveries.

Nelson, Carol. **Dear Angie, Your Family's Getting a Divorce.** Chariot Books, 1980. 119 pp.

Angie doesn't fit in with some of the sophisticated girls at school. But that doesn't really depress her. What is really bothering her is that her mother and father are constantly fighting and yelling at each other. Young Angie begins to fear that she will soon have to face the possibility that her parents might be planning a divorce.

Neufeld, John. **Freddy's Book.** Camelot Books, 1975. 132 pp.

Freddy isn't stupid, but he certainly feels stupid when a certain word that he doesn't understand keeps leaping out at him. He sees it on fences, sidewalks, and bathroom walls. So Freddy begins to ask all kinds of people, whenever the opportunity seems right, if they know what the word means. He talks to his best friend, his mother, his father, the librarian. He even looks it up in the dictionary. No one seems comfortable about giving him a clear definition. But this makes Freddy even more determined to solve the dilemma.

Neufeld, John. **Sunday Father.** Signet Books, 1977. 159 pp.

Will Tessa's mother and father get back together someday? This is Tessa's dream until her dad tells her that he is marrying someone else. She is angry and hurt until she learns what love and growing up are all about.

Neville, Emily Cheney. **Garden of Broken Glass.** Delacorte Press, 1975. 215 pp.

Brian Moody is a junior high student who looks forward to going to school because only there does he feel safe, even though he's one of the few white kids in his grade. Brian dreads his home life, especially facing an alcoholic mother every day. Besides, his older sister bosses him, and his younger brother is the spoiled pet of the family. Then a black family befriends Brian and helps show him that he is a valuable person. Brian soon learns how to feel alive and decides to help rebuild his own family.

Newton, Suzanne. **M. V. Sexton Speaking.** Viking Press, 1981. 196 pp.

She would not have believed it a year ago, but a summer job at a bakery is changing Martha Venable Sexton's life. An orphan, M. V. has been lonely and confused for most of her life. She does not know if she wants to "blend in" with everyone else or remain independent. And M. V. certainly does not know how to communicate with the great-aunt and great-uncle she lives with. But this bakery job is giving M. V. a sense of worth, and she is meeting all sorts of interesting people there besides.

O'Dell, Scott. **The Spanish Smile.** Houghton Mifflin Co., 1982. 182 pp.

Lucinda's life on Isla del Oro, an island off the coast of California, has always been like that of a princess. Her father, Don Enrique, surrounds her with luxuries, but he shelters her too. Newspapers, radios, televisions, and books never reach the island. Don Enrique makes sure that his daughter knows nothing of the "barbarians" on the mainland. So it is not until the young archaeologist Christopher Dawson arrives on the island that Lucinda begins to question her world. Slowly, horrifyingly, the truth about Isla del Oro and its master begins to emerge.

Oldham, Mary. **The White Pony.** Hastings House Publishers, 1981. 119 pp.

Barbara's dreams of riding her way to fame seem almost in reach when she moves next door to a riding school. From the start, there is a special warmth between her and Bianca, the gentle, blind pony. Barbara imagines herself, thin and glamorous, taking fences and hurdles with ease on Bianca. But Barbara isn't thin and glamorous. Her parents bribe and nag her to diet, until she doesn't even know if she wants to lose weight for her own reasons or theirs. Before anything else, Barbara wants to make her own choices—and she'll decide when and how.

Osborne, Mary Pope. **Run, Run, as Fast as You Can.** Dial Press, 1982. 149 pp.

When her family move to Holden Beach, Hallie sees this as her chance to get in with the popular crowd—the girls with boyfriends and good figures. She is eleven now—too old to play with dolls and her little brother, Mickey. But when tragedy strikes her family, she does some fast growing up and comes to see the popular girls for what they really are. Easy reading.

Parker, Richard. **He Is Your Brother.** Thomas Nelson, 1976. 98 pp.

Orry is an autistic child—he is withdrawn and pays little attention to his family or to what is happening around him. Then one day Orry becomes interested in his brother Mike's hobby of trains and railroad equipment. Orry wants to learn about trains too, and he and Mike start becoming close. As the two visit dump sites and explore dangerous, unused tunnels, they share adventure, excitement, and respect.

Parker, Richard. **The Runaway.** Thomas Nelson, 1977. 125 pp.

Fourteen-year-old Hugo is tired of his parents' quarreling and feels partly to blame for the rocky marriage. Hugo decides to bring his parents together by running away and pretending he has been kidnapped. He thinks that his parents will be so concerned for his safety that they will stop fighting. But Hugo's pretended danger becomes real, and the only person who can help is his new friend, Caroline.

Pascal, Francine. **The Hand-Me-Down Kid.** Yearling Books, 1982. 172 pp.

It is not easy for eleven-year-old Ari Jacobs to be the youngest in her family. All she gets are her sister Elizabeth's used things: clothes, beds, bicycles. One day Rhona, the school bully, talks Ari into borrowing her sister's new ten-speed bike for a race. When the bike is stolen, Ari begins to lie to her family while she frantically searches for the bike herself. But can she find it without being forced to admit her part in its disappearance?

Paterson, Katherine. **The Great Gilly Hopkins.** Thomas Y. Crowell Co., 1978. 148 pp.

Gilly Hopkins is a child who has had little discipline. After six foster homes, she is sent to the dusty, broken-down house of Mrs. Trotter. During her stay, Gilly struggles with prejudices toward a blind, black neighbor and Mrs. Trotter's withdrawn son. Finally Gilly can stand it no longer and runs away to find her mother. (National Book Award and Newbery Honor Book)

Paterson, Katherine. **Jacob Have I Loved.** Flare Books, 1980. 175 pp.

Louise is a twin and feels much like the biblical character Esau because her sister Caroline is like a Jacob who is favored and loved by everyone. Louise finds conflicts of all kinds where her sister is concerned. Caroline seems to rob her of any pleasure from school, friends, her mother, and even her name. The family lives on a remote island in Chesapeake Bay in the early 1940s, so Louise decides to become a waterman like her father and hopes the life-style will help her become her own person. (American Book Award and Newbery Award)

Peck, Richard. **Don't Look and It Won't Hurt.** Avon Books, 1979. 158 pp.

Nothing about Carol's life is right. Her family lives on the wrong side of the tracks, her wardrobe is even older than last year's styles, her older sister is in Chicago at a home for unwed mothers, and her mother works as a hostess at an all-night truck stop. She is hardly a member of the "in" crowd. But she does have some things going for her: her brains, her first boyfriend, and the independence of going to Chicago from Claypitts to see for herself how her older sister is getting along.

Peck, Richard. **Father Figure.** Signet Books, 1979. 182 pp.

Dad had been erased from the family for Jim and Byron Atwater. They were very young when he left, and they have not seen or heard from him since. But when their mother dies, the boys' grandmother insists they visit their father in Florida. Byron likes the idea, but Jim is jealous and angry. He is the only father his little brother needs. Once in Florida, both boys find their feelings about their father are more confused than they thought.

Peyton, K. M. **Marion's Angels.** Illus. Robert Micklewright. Oxford University Press, 1979. 152 pp.

The people in the village think of Marion as mentally unstable, like her dead mother. The lonely girl's favorite companions are the beautiful carved angels on the ceiling of the crumbling medieval church near her father's cottage. When a handsome young pianist enters the church to give a concert to help pay for rebuilding the church, Marion's life suddenly becomes exciting. It all seems to come about because Marion has prayed so long and so hard. But it seems that Marion's angels have added trouble to her blessings.

Platt, Kin. **Chloris and the Freaks.** Bradbury Press, 1975. 217 pp.

Chloris Carpenter consults her horoscope every morning for advice. Her mother is having trouble with her second marriage, and her weird older sister claims that their dead father talks to her. Divorce and madness seem to be in the air, but Chloris doesn't give up trying to keep control of her life, or helping those around her.

Platt, Kin. **Chloris and the Weirdos.** Bradbury Press, 1978. 231 pp.

Chloris Carpenter, at thirteen, is in love with Harold (The Hawk) Osborne, champion skateboarder. Chloris's older sister, Jenny, is so depressing that she drives everyone crazy, and Chloris's mother is working on her third marriage. Their lives become even more hectic when Jenny disappears one weekend with Wayne Gavin, a notorious "pizza freak."

Rabe, Berniece. **The Girl Who Had No Name.** E. P. Dutton, 1977. 149 pp.

When Girlie is cast out of her home by her angry father, she seeks refuge in the homes of her many older sisters. She learns the pain of poverty in one house, the deception of beauty in another, and a deep family secret in the last. Girlie deals with confusion and hurt as she seeks peace in the lonely outside world.

Rabe, Berniece. **The Orphans.** E. P. Dutton, 1978. 184 pp.

Little Adam and Eva Braggs, two orphan twins, seem to attract bad luck. After their parents' deaths, they are shipped from home to home and cause mischief wherever they go. A seventy-five-year-old grandmother, a scraggly hound pup, and lots of close calls with the law are all part of their crazy adventures.

Radley, Gail. **The World Turned Inside Out.** Crown Publishers, 1982. 116 pp.

The Chase family just seemed to fall apart after the suicide of Tyler Chase. Now fifteen-year-old Jeremy loses a sister when she angrily decides to leave home. Isolated and frustrated, Jeremy takes a job at a hot-dog stand on the boardwalk. Soon he finds himself feeling more at ease, especially after becoming friends with Gina. However, when a job offer comes from Seaside Mental Hospital, Jeremy is once again plunged into confusion and doubt. Seaside is the place where his brother Tyler was a patient. Jeremy wonders if working at Seaside will help him understand his brother's death, or will it make Tyler's suicide even harder to accept?

Reiff, Tana. **So Long, Snowman.** Fearon-Pitman Publishers, 1979. 59 pp.

Billy's life is tough in the slums. He is kicked out of school, caught stealing, and sent to a boys' training school. When he gets out, in spite of his promise to do better, he gets hooked on drugs. Now, however, he has a wife and a son, and as an eighteen-year-old adult, he faces prison. Other titles in the Lifeline series are *The Family from Vietnam, A Time to Choose, Mollie's Year, Juan and Lucy, A Place for Everyone,* and *The Shoplifting Game.* Easy reading.

Richard, Adrienne. **Into the Road.** Atlantic Monthly Press, 1976. 206 pp.

Nat is about to graduate from high school when his older brother, Cy, comes home. Four years ago, Cy left home, leaving his aunt and uncle sorry and angry. Now Cy is back, and he wants Nat to leave home and go with him, touring on motorcycles. Nat is uncertain of what he should do. Can he betray the aunt and uncle who have raised him to go with his brother and meet the adventures of the open road?

Richards, Judith. **Summer Lightning.** Avon Books, 1979. 264 pp.

In the 1940s, Gerald Calder is concerned about his job as the New Deal director of a farm workers' camp. Mickey Calder, who is expecting her second child, is concerned about the kind of life this child will have to face. However, Terry, their young son, is busy with all kinds of adventures in the Everglades. He is not concerned about school or the world, but about friendship, beauty in nature, and learning survival skills from McCree, who lives outside the law.

Rinaldi, Ann. **Promises Are for Keeping.** Walker & Co., 1982. 187 pp.

Nicole has many difficult experiences that teach her about responsibility. She struggles between doing what is expected of her and her desire for independence. She loves her two older brothers, but lately Nicole always seems to be in trouble. Once she even steals birth control pills for a friend. In the midst of prank phone calls and drug problems with other friends, Nicole must discover who she really is.

Roberts, Thom. **Summerdog.** Camelot Books, 1978. 128 pp.

City dwellers Becky Norman and her family have the whole summer ahead to live in the country. First they must battle to keep the raccoons out of the garbage. Then one morning Becky's brother, Adam, finds that a long-haired, muddy dog is caught in one of their raccoon traps. They name him Hobo and learn to love him, but what will happen when summer is over and they must return to the city? Based on the screenplay.

Roberts, Willo Davis. **Don't Hurt Laurie!** Illus. Ruth Sanderson. Atheneum Publishers, 1977. 166 pp.

No one knows that Laurie is abused by her mother. Her stepfather is often gone, and her family moves often—too often for her to make lasting friendships. Then Laurie meets George, an ailing boy who becomes her secret companion and best friend. Together they share their dreams and discuss them with their pet dog, which is kept hidden from everyone. Then the situation with her mother worsens, and Laurie must choose between leaving her best friend or living a tortured life at home.

Robinson, Barbara. **The Best Christmas Pageant Ever.** Illus. Judith Gwyn Brown. Avon Books, 1979. 80 pp.

The Herdmans, six skinny, stringy-haired kids who live over a garage at the bottom of Sproul Street, are the terrors of Woodrow Wilson School. They smoke cigars, cuss, hit little kids, and have even set fire to Fred Shoemaker's old broken-down tool house. Their outrageous behavior and dirty tricks are known all over town, so it comes as a shock when Imogene Herdman volunteers all her brothers and sisters for the church's Christmas pageant. But it is an even greater shock when Mrs. Armstrong and the Ladies' Aid Bazaar agree to give them parts. Rehearsals and the actual performance are wild and hilarious, as the Herdmans seem to have a different idea about the Christmas story than everyone else.

Rockwood, Joyce. **Enoch's Place.** Holt, Rinehart & Winston, 1980. 205 pp.

Fifteen-year-old Enoch Callahan lives in a rural area of North Carolina. His parents were hippies in the 1960s and now live a very different life from most people. For one thing, their house has no electricity or other modern conveniences. Enoch begins to feel the need to explore the world, so he decides to go off to the city to live with his uncle's family.

Rodowsky, Colby. **The Gathering Room.** Farrar, Straus & Giroux, 1981. 186 pp.

Talk about unusual work! Mudge's parents are the caretakers at a cemetery. What is even more curious are Mudge's playmates. He skips stones with Little Dorro, who was killed by a milk wagon; he listens to the recitations of the Butterfly Lady; and he runs messages for two veterans of the War of 1812. But then something happens that changes Mudge's life forever. Easy reading.

Rushforth, Peter. **Kindergarten.** Bard Books, 1981. 190 pp.

In a peaceful English village, three children and their grandmother try to celebrate an old-fashioned Christmas. But the television and newspapers keep reminding them of all the violence loose in the world—violence that killed the children's mother. Disturbed by this memory, the grandmother decides to tell the children about her terrifying life as a Jew in World War II Germany.

Salassi, Otto R. **On the Ropes.** Bantam Books, 1982. 241 pp.

Squint and Julie's dad ran off six years ago, their mom has just died, and they can't pay the mortgage on the farm. They set out to find their father and discover that he's a changed man. Claudius Gains is a pool shark, con artist, wrestling manager, and about a hundred other things. When he returns to the farm with a caravan of performers and Seymour, the tea-drinking bear, Squint and Julie's lives are changed forever. But can their father's quick talking save the farm?

Sallis, Susan. **A Time for Everything.** Harper & Row Publishers, 1979. 218 pp.

At first World War II didn't seem to touch young Lily Freeman and her family as they went about the usual routine in Gloucester, England. However, times soon change, and the war comes to the Freemans when Lily's aunt and retarded cousin, Phillipa, come to live with them to escape the bombings in London. Then Lily's father enlists in the army, and the family is asked to care for an eight-year-old evacuee, Mavis. Now Lily has to work hard caring for Phillipa, teaching English to Mavis, and trying to get a scholarship so that she can continue school. But from her work Lily learns about responsibility and sacrifice.

Samuels, Gertrude, **Adam's Daughter.** Thomas Y. Crowell Co., 1977. 209 pp.

After seven years in prison, Robyn's father is released. But his carefree life does not return to him easily. It becomes a hard task for Robyn to help her father learn about life again. Added to this, she has to face rejection from her mother, who feels a bitter hatred against everyone. Then Robyn must make a painful decision when her father turns his back on the law forever.

Sargent, Sarah. **Secret Lies.** Crown Publishers, 1981. 118 pp.

When Elvira's mother elopes, leaving Elvira all alone, the school social worker sends her off to stay with her aunt in Virginia. But Elvira is lonely there, and she turns to her daydreams for comfort. She fantasizes about the father she has never known; she imagines him to be distinguished, loving, and rich—all the things her mother is not. But a chance meeting with her father's sister shatters Elvira's dreams and forces her to realize that she must give up her fantasies in order to get the love and acceptance she has always wanted.

Schiffman, Ruth. **Turning the Corner.** Dial Press, 1981. 170 pp.

It is 1935—the depth of the Great Depression. Rebecca Levin is a graduating senior with hopes for a life beyond the one she has in Forgetown, Pennsylvania. But there is no money for college, and no promise of an immediate out-of-town job. Just when Rebecca begins to despair, though, she finds her family and friends there to encourage her to pursue her dreams.

Seavy, Susan. **The Liberation of Samantha Carson.** Thomas Nelson, 1978. 151 pp.

When Samantha Carson's first husband dies, she meets Will Monahan, a shiftless fortune hunter. Samantha is treated badly by Will, which might be expected. What is unexpected, however, is that Samantha becomes a strong feminist because of her experiences.

Sebestyen, Ouida. **IOU's.** Atlantic Monthly Press, 1982. 188 pp.

Stowe Garrett is determined to repay his mother for taking care of him alone during the past thirteen years and for trying to make life fun. So when his dying grandfather asks him to come, but doesn't ask for his mother, Stowe and his friend Brownie try to resolve the family problem. Then Stowe discovers that at his grandfather's house he will meet his father. (ALA Best Book of the Year)

Shaw, Richard. **Hard Way Home.** Thomas Nelson, 1977. 127 pp.

Gary is tired of his parents constantly bothering him, especially his father. As if his dad's rules and constant sarcasm weren't bad enough, his father has cut the cord to his stereo. So Gary runs away from home. Once on his own, however, he finds that everyone has rules, some even worse than his father's. Even the commune he joins has rules, and the members are all kids his age! They expect him to get up for dawn meetings and to hand over his entire paycheck. Gary just can't live that way, but to his dismay everyone kicks him out before he has a chance to leave first. He begins to think maybe he is doing something wrong.

Shaw, Richard. **Shape Up, Burke.** Thomas Nelson, 1976. 142 pp.

Pat and his father, a former policeman, don't agree on many things, so Pat is sent to a military school to "shape up." The first step in the process is a survival camp in Vermont where Pat thinks the training is too tough even for marines. In this funny story about the generation gap, Pat Burke does change, but not before he and his father learn something about themselves and each other.

Shreve, Susan. **The Masquerade.** Laurel-Leaf Library, 1981. 192 pp.

Disaster and tragedy strike the Walker family when father Edward is arrested for embezzlement. Everything has to be auctioned to repay the millions of dollars owed to clients of Walker & Lutrec. Then, before the trial begins, Mrs. Walker's mind snaps, and she is found one night wandering the streets in her high school formal. The four Walker children decide to put up a united front against the outside world. But each must struggle alone with their confused feelings about their father.

Shura, Mary Francis. **The Season of Silence.** Illus. Ruth Sanderson. Atheneum Publishers, 1976. 123 pp.

Susie Spinner was sick for a long time. When she gets better she is startled to learn how many things have changed in her life. There is now a strange tension between her parents and her sister Carrie, and Carrie's boyfriend doesn't come around any more. In addition, Susie's best friend Lindy ignores her to spend time with a boy who has always been a bully. By the time Susie meets Derek, a very strange and troubled boy, she has done a lot of growing up. Easy reading.

Shyer, Marlene Fanta. **My Brother, the Thief.** Charles Scribner's Sons, 1980. 138 pp.

Twelve-year-old Carolyn Desmond knows that her brother, Richard, is a thief. She watches painfully as Richard gets himself deeper and deeper into trouble. Finally, some valuable items are missing from the house next door, and Carolyn herself must answer a police officer's questions. Will she lie for her brother?

Simons, Wendy. **Harper's Mother.** Prentice-Hall, 1980. 220 pp.

Harper O'Leary has never really known a secure life with her mother. Harper's mother goes from one boyfriend to the next, and from one town to another before Harper can get used to anyone or anything. She loves her mother, but sometimes Harper wishes the two of them would settle down somewhere, alone and together. Mature language and situations.

Smith, Alison. **Help! There's a Cat Washing in Here!** Illus. Amy Rowen.
E. P. Dutton, 1981. 152 pp.

Young Henry has his hands full when he is put in charge of caring
for his younger brother and sister for two weeks. First, little Annie
announces that she needs an important school costume the next
day, and it is up to Henry to sew it. Then Henry tries cooking
dinner for the first time, and disaster follows. But the real challenge
comes when Annie runs away from home, and the household is
turned upside down.

Smith, Alison. **Reserved for Mark Anthony Crowder.** E. P. Dutton, 1978.
123 pp.

Mark Anthony's dream is to have a place of his own. But after his
plans for a treehouse mansion fall through, there seems to be no
hope. If only he could escape the snickers of the kids at school and
the disappointment on his father's face. Could he help it if he was
born tall, skinny, and anything but athletic? Then, when Mark is
put in charge of the family vegetable garden, things take a turn for
the better.

Smith, Doris Buchanan. **Last Was Lloyd.** Yearling Books, 1982. 124 pp.

Lloyd is always the last one chosen at recess baseball games because
the kids all think he is too fat and unable to run fast. But Lloyd can
always turn to his mother for comfort. He and his mother say they
only need each other for company. Then Lloyd's classmates discover
he is really a great ballplayer. Now Lloyd has the chance to fit in
with the other kids—but what will his mother say about his new
popularity?

Smith, Doris Buchanan. **Moonshadow of Cherry Mountain.** Four Winds
Press, 1982. 154 pp.

For as long as Moonshadow can remember, the mountain has been
hers. She was just a puppy when the Rileys brought her home, and
there had been nothing on Cherry Mountain then. Now the Rileys
have adopted a girl who is allergic to dogs, and Moonshadow is
banished from the house. Then people start to arrive on the
mountain, altering the land and building houses. Moonshadow's
territory dwindles, and she is forbidden to chase the dogs or tree the
cats. Greg knows that Moonshadow would never hurt another
animal, but Mr. Riley reluctantly agrees that if a cat is killed,
Moonshadow will meet the same fate.

Snyder, Anne. **First Step.** Holt, Rinehart & Winston, 1975. 128 pp.

For Cindy the first and hardest step is to recognize her mother for what she is—an alcoholic. She soon finds that other kids in school share her problem. Then she begins to attend meetings of Alateen. Through this group's help, Cindy is able to start to live with her mother and her mother's problem.

Snyder, Carol. **The Great Condominium Rebellion.** Illus. Anthony Kramer. Delacorte Press, 1981. 149 pp.

The Lemon Cove condominium in Florida sounds great to thirteen-year-old Stacy and twelve-year-old Marc. It has a pool, a recreation room, and plenty of yard. But once they go there to visit their grandparents, they realize they are being treated more like criminals than guests. Lemon Cove has hundreds of rules that keep Stacy and Marc from doing anything fun. The pair, along with their new friends Lisa and Paul, decide they have to fight for their rights, even if it throws the whole condominium development into an uproar.

Spencer, Zane, and Jay Leech. **Cry of the Wolf.** Westminster Press, 1977. 144 pp.

Young Jim Tyler is driving one night when he loses control of the truck and his father is killed. The accident leaves Jim in a wheelchair, feeling guilty, and with no will to get better. He doesn't even snap out of it when his mother is threatened with the loss of their farm. Can Jim ever overcome his depression and rebuild his life?

St. George, Judith. **The Girl with Spunk.** Illus. Charles Robinson. Scholastic Book Services, 1975. 182 pp.

Why is Mrs. Brown kicking her out? Fourteen-year-old Josie Dexter is angry and afraid. She really hasn't done anything wrong and wants to keep working as Mrs. Brown's hired girl. Now she will be forced to go back to her cruel stepfather—and back to working in a dark, airless knitting mill. Josie would do anything to escape this fate.

Stanley, Carol. **Take Care of My Girl.** Scholastic Book Services, 1978. 234 pp.

Sixteen-year-old Kate wonders why she isn't popular, but she has resigned herself to be content with her life as it is. Then she learns her father's job will force her to spend her junior year living in another town with her aunt, uncle, and cousin Julie. What happens to Kate is gradual, but it makes things startlingly different from her former life.

Stewart, John Craig. **The Last to Know.** Tempo Books, 1981. 185 pp.

Bruce is excited about going to Mobile, Alabama, for a number of reasons. He will have a chance to work on his uncle's fishing boat and to meet his only living relatives. But once Bruce arrives, he finds his Uncle Walton is hard to get to know. His cousin, Louise, however, is friendly and pretty. Between them, they make Bruce's seventeenth summer a memorable experience in growing up.

Stren, Patti. **There's a Rainbow in My Closet.** Harper & Row Publishers, 1979. 136 pp.

Emma's mother is off to Europe as the public relations manager for a ballet company, so Emma is stuck with a grandmother she doesn't even know. However, after the sulking and tantrums are over, Emma finds out that her grandmother is a very special person. She understands Emma's purple paintings, plays games with Emma, takes her fishing, and teaches her how to paint stars. One day she even makes a rainbow for Emma as a magical surprise. But most of all, her grandmother makes Emma feel good about herself as she teaches her that it's all right to be different.

Sullivan, Mary W. **The VW Connection.** Elsevier/Nelson Books, 1981. 84 pp.

When Gordon's family moves from Sacramento to a twenty-acre farm, his brother Joe threatens to leave and return to his girlfriend. In an attempt to keep the family together, Gordon meets a challenge from Joe—a challenge that demands strength, wit, and luck. Gordon begins to comb the community for a pretty girl with a Volkswagen, and his funny adventures have only begun.

Thrasher, Crystal. **Between Dark and Daylight.** McElderry Books, 1979. 251 pp.

Twelve-year-old Seely's father wanted to move the family out of the dark hills of southern Indiana. The depression was almost over, and he had a job in another part of the state. But before they travel very far, the family truck breaks down. Seely and her family are forced to seek shelter in an empty house in the woods—and there they settle. But Seely does not mind because she soon meets friendly Johnny Meaders and his family. Everything is fine, except for the threats the Fender twins keep making against Johnny and his family. Soon everyone's nerves are on edge as they wait for violence from the twins.

Tolan, Stephanie S. **Grandpa and Me.** Charles Scribner's Sons, 1978. 120 pp.

Kerry's grandfather had always been a part of her life and that of the family. But now Kerry and her brother, Matt, have other interests and other friends. Grandpa begins doing crazy things like wearing his pants wrong side out and jumping in the pool with all his clothes on. Should Grandpa be put in a nursing home? Or can he really decide what should happen to him?

Tolan, Stephanie S. **The Liberation of Tansy Warner.** Charles Scribner's Sons, 1980. 137 pp.

Tansy is so excited when she wins the part of Anne Frank in the school play that she rushes home to tell her mother. But when she arrives, all Tansy finds is a note on the kitchen table. Her mother has decided to leave to find out who she is and what her value to the world is—and she will not be coming back. Tansy is desperate. Since she cannot really talk to her father, Tansy turns to her friend Vickie for advice. Vickie urges her to look for her mother. But where to begin?

Tolan, Stephanie S. **No Safe Harbors.** Charles Scribner's Sons, 1981. 184 pp.

At sixteen, Amanda Sterling is the daughter of the mayor of an Ohio city and lives in a safe world. That world is shattered, however, when her father is accused of taking a bribe. Amanda can't believe her father is wrong, and her friend Joe Schmidt, the son of the other accused man, can't believe his father is guilty either. Both Amanda and Joe must learn to look beneath the surface and to accept human nature and human weaknesses.

Towne, Mary. **First Serve.** Illus. Ruth Sanderson. Atheneum Publishers, 1976. 214 pp.

As long as she can remember, Dulcie has been surrounded by talk about her sister—what a good tennis player she is, how much potential she has, how many trophies she's won. Though proud of her sister's accomplishments, Dulcie has never really thought about tennis seriously; for her, it is just a relaxing pastime. Then the former tennis pro, Mrs. Trask, comes to watch her sister play. But instead, Mrs. Trask decides to coach Dulcie. Suddenly, Dulcie sees tennis as a career and a commitment—but what about her sister?

Voigt, Cynthia. **Homecoming.** Atheneum Publishers, 1982. 312 pp.

Four children are left by their mother in a parked car at a shopping center. Thirteen-year-old Dicey, the oldest, is afraid to go to the police for fear they will separate her from her siblings. So with less than ten dollars, the children begin their long walk to Connecticut, a trip that will take many days. They hope to reach Great-Aunt Cilla, whose address they find on a crumpled piece of paper in the car. But they discover they must make a second journey before they have a true homecoming.

Walker, Diana. **The Hundred Thousand Dollar Farm**. Abelard-Schuman Books, 1977. 182 pp.

The McKinnon girls find more than the mushrooms they set out to pick in the back pasture of a farm on Prince Edward Island. They find Australian Charlie Hancock, sick and nearly dead. When nursed back to health, Charlie becomes a lifelong friend, aiding the McKinnons in their search for money, happiness, and a new life in the city.

Walker, Diana. **Mother Wants a Horse**. Abelard-Schuman Books, 1978. 186 pp.

Failing her English class triggers many other problems for Joanna. Instead of riding horses at Holmwood Farms every Saturday, she will have to be tutored by old Mrs. Williams. In a fit of anger, Joanna gallops off into the country on a prize horse—an action she will regret for many months to come.

Wallace-Brodeur, Ruth. **The Kenton Year**. McElderry Books, 1980. 93 pp.

Mandy McPherson is only nine when her father is killed in an accident. Too shocked to fully accept this, Mandy becomes confused. To help both of them face a new life, Mandy's mother decides to rent a house in Kenton, Vermont, where she had been happy as a child. It is here that Mandy and her mother must learn to rebuild their lives. Mandy is helped in this by Carrie, a girl her own age, and Shanden, the strange village recluse.

Wallin, Luke. **The Redneck Poacher's Son**. Bradbury Press, 1981. 245 pp.

Jesse Watersmith used to love his life with his father and his brothers in the swamps of Alabama. But now something is disturbing him. He has grown to hate Paw, for Jesse suspects that Paw killed his mother years ago. So Jesse plans to revenge his mother's death. He gets a pistol and waits for Paw to come home along the trail one day. Mature situations.

Wartski, Maureen Crane. **My Brother Is Special.** Signet Books, 1981. 138 pp.

Everyone always asks Noni what's wrong with her brother. Kip is retarded, but Noni sees him as a special person. When her parents seem to lose the spirit to push Kip on, Noni decides to help her brother make it to the Special Olympics. She is determined Kip will become a winner at something, even if it means creating problems for herself with family and friends.

Weiman, Eiveen. **It Takes Brains.** Atheneum Publishers, 1982. 261 pp.

Barbara Brainard's nickname was Brains, but she rarely lived up to it. She was always in trouble, seldom got good grades, and had no friends. So when her parents announce they are moving to Ohio, she is glad to go; she thinks things might be better there. But things are the same—until the day she punches Herbie in the stomach and is sent to a new class where she finally fits in.

Weiman, Eiveen. **Which Way Courage.** Atheneum Publishers, 1981. 132 pp.

Courage Kunstler is an Amish girl who increasingly questions the Amish way of life, especially those rules about no further schooling past eighth grade and no medical attention for her handicapped brother. She eventually leaves the Pennsylvania farm for the city to find some answers for herself.

Wells, Rosemary. **None of the Above.** Avon Books, 1975. 172 pp.

Seventeen-year-old Marcia Mills doesn't fit in with her father's new wife and family, especially Chrissy. Chrissy is the original "all American girl," while Marcia is overweight and mousy. So Marcia's first strategy is withdrawal—she stays in her room, reads, and eats. Then she tries other tactics; she begins making good grades and finding her own friends. But, strangely enough, the fear of success becomes as great as the fear of failure. By the time it's graduation night, Marcia has limited her alternatives for the future to two—but both are undesirable and even terrifying. Mature situations.

Westall, Robert. **The Scarecrows.** Greenwillow Books, 1981. 185 pp.

Those scarecrows in his stepfather's turnip field become more than just odd sights to thirteen-year-old Simon Wood. They are symbols of his anger and jealousy—anger at his mother for having married again, and jealousy toward his stepfather for taking his mother's love away from him. What is worse, however, is that all Simon's held-in emotions seem to have strange effects on him. Does he really see the three scarecrows in the field becoming people?

Wideman, John Edgar. **Damballah.** Bard Books, 1981. 205 pp.

This is a connected series of stories tracing the 100-year history of a black American family. In the 1860s, Sybela and Charlie arrive in Pittsburgh with two children. Twenty-five years later, there are eighteen more. These children, and their children, include John French, a gambler; Gert Hollinger, who has her children out of wedlock; and Lizabeth French, who begins life in an alley snowdrift. Mature language and situations.

Wideman, John Edgar. **Hiding Place.** Bard Books, 1981. 158 pp.

Mother Bess is a crazy and mean old woman who lives in a shack. But she is the only person Tommy can turn to when he is suspected of murder and attempted robbery. Mother Bess is hiding too—but from herself. She has secrets that Tommy only slowly begins to discover. Just maybe, Tommy and Bess will be able to help each other. Mature language and situations.

Wiggin, Kate Douglas. **Rebecca of Sunnybrook Farm.** Watermill Press, 1981. 303 pp.

Rebecca Rowena Randall is not an ordinary eleven-year-old girl. Her delightful, sunny disposition has a positive effect on everyone in Riverboro. She has been sent to live with her two strict unmarried aunts and to receive a good eduation there. Unfortunately, Aunt Miranda Sawyer doesn't seem to appreciate Rebecca's captivating personality, or even to want her around the house. Can Rebecca's sunny, positive attitude overcome the gloomy atmosphere of her aunt's home? Originally published in 1902.

Winthrop, Elizabeth. **Knock, Knock, Who's There?** Holiday House, 1978. 192 pp.

For two years, Sam and Michael watched their father die. Now they wonder how can they go on without him. Then their mother begins having days of strange moods, foul language, and little accidents. What is wrong with her? Kathleen knows, and finally she tells the boys. At first they avoid the problem. But eventually the boys find the courage to confront their mother with the truth.

Woiwode, Larry. **Beyond the Bedroom Wall.** Bard Books, 1979. 610 pp.

This is the story of four generations of the Neumiller family from North Dakota. Martin Neumiller is seen through the eyes of his father and grandfather, and then, in turn, Martin examines the personalities of his own children as they grow up. Despite the changes in the family, the deaths and tragedies, the births and celebrations, the family's basic respect for the land does not change. The Neumillers seem to inherit a common bond from one generation to the next, and that bond is in the land itself. Mature situations.

Wolkoff, Judie. **Where the Elf King Sings.** Bradbury Press, 1980. 178 pp.

When Marcie's father, a Vietnam veteran, can't escape the nightmares of war, he loses his job and turns to drinking. Marcie watches sadly as her beautiful mother works as a waitress at a dirty cafe to support the family, and as her alcoholic father decides to leave the house. She finds comfort in the company of eccentric Mrs. King, but she still struggles with her family situation. Then letters from her father bring unexpected hope.

Wood, Phyllis Anderson. **Get a Little Lost, Tia.** Westminster Press, 1978. 172 pp.

When Jason gets a note during English class to telephone his sister's school, he heaves a big sigh. What now? At thirteen, Tia is one long series of aggravations. But Jason is responsible for her since their father's death and their mother's taking a full-time job. He almost wishes Tia would just get lost—at least long enough to give him a break. This time, though, fate holds a new twist for both Jason and Tia. Celia, the lovely dark-haired student office clerk who delivers the message about Tia, comes up with some answers that transform Tia. Then on a Sunday outing with Celia's family, Tia does get lost, and there is a frantic search for her.

Wood, Phyllis Anderson. **Win Me and You Lose.** Westminster Press, 1977. 137 pp.

Seventeen-year-old Matt's parents were divorced and had a bitter custody battle for the teen. Matt is now living with his father, a move that means the two have to adjust to setting up a new apartment and getting to know each other. Soon Matt meets Rebecca Javez, who also lives in the apartment complex. The two find that they have many interests in common and that they enjoy each other's company. But their good times are soon clouded by fear, for Rebecca is sure that someone is following her. Then a stranger in an Acme Plumbing Company suit appears, and fear becomes terror—first for Rebecca, and then for Matt.

Yep, Laurence. **Sea Glass.** Harper & Row Publishers, 1979. 213 pp.

Young Craig Chin is torn between keeping his Chinese culture and learning to speak the language better, and trying to fit in with his American neighbors and classmates. The kids think of him as a little fat foreigner, and the older Chinese think of him as American. He feels that he doesn't belong any place. He also has a hard time living up to the expectations of his father, who made the all-city varsity team in his high school days and who expects his son to be a champion, too. Finally, it is Craig's Uncle Quail who introduces him to the joys of collecting seashells and who, during their afternoons at the seashore, helps Craig to see himself as a real person.

Friendship

Adler, C. S. **Footsteps on the Stairs.** Delacorte Press, 1982. 151 pp.

Dodie thinks that the creaky old house by the marsh is a weird place to spend the summer. She's also not too keen on the reason for being there—so she can get to know her new stepsister, Anne, and stepbrother, Chip. When Anne says she hears footsteps on the stairs, Dodie wonders if it's just Anne's way of paying her back for the "ghostly" trick she played on them when they first arrived. But soon Dodie hears the footsteps too, and the two girls work together to find out more about the ghosts of two long-dead sisters.

Alexander, Anne. **Connie.** Illus. Gail Owens. Atheneum Publishers, 1976. 179 pp.

Connie's life is turned upside-down when her father's job forces the family to move. Worse still, ninety-year-old Aunt Berta moves in, and Connie has to share a room with the cranky old lady. Connie also has problems adjusting to her new school, until handsome Joel starts to work in Aunt Berta's garden and strange things start to happen.

Anderson, Mary. **. . . Forever, Ahbra.** Atheneum Publishers, 1981. 200 pp.

Sixteen-year-old Larry Rostovich is assigned to see the King Tut treasures and write a paper about them with Ahbra, an Egyptian student at the High School of Music and Art. But Ahbra seems frightened by the treasures. Larry also notices that she dresses like "the ghost of Cleopatra" and has sudden attacks of unconsciousness at school. What is wrong with her? Is she on drugs? Or is she under the spell of some strange power? Larry decides to solve the mysteries surrounding Ahbra, but in doing so he begins to question his own life and his values.

Angell, Judie. **In Summertime It's Tuffy.** Bradbury Press, 1977. 230 pp.

For ten months of the year, eleven-year-old Elizabeth is "Betsy"; but for the two months she spends at summer camp, she is just plain "Tuffy." This summer she needs to be tougher than ever since the head camp counselor, who likes to be called "Uncle" Otto, is just about the most unfair adult she has ever met. He never listens to any side but his own, and he even fires Sheila, their bunk counselor. The girls of bunk ten, with Tuffy as their leader, decide to try a little magic against Uncle Otto with the help of a voodoo doll. The results could be coincidence, but who wants to take that chance?

Angell, Judie. **Ronnie and Rosey.** Bradbury Press, 1977. 283 pp.

Eighth-grader Ronnie Rachman is entering a new school, and she feels very alone until she literally runs into Robert Rose. Soon another new friend, Evelyn, invites Ronnie to a party where she meets Robert again. They later go out on dates—until tragedy strikes on Halloween night. Ronnie's mother becomes hard to live with and refuses to let Ronnie see Robert. The two teenagers do what they can to keep their friendship alive.

Angell, Judie. **Tina Gogo.** Bradbury Press, 1978. 196 pp.

Sarajane is spending a peaceful, relaxing summer at Lake Meridian, working in her parents' restaurant. She meets Tina Gogo, and the two rapidly become good friends. Sarajane, the first real friend Tina has ever had, begins to unravel the mystery of the young girl's strange behavior. Tina has been living in foster homes ever since she was six years old, but her mother recently reappeared to ask Tina to come back to New York to live with her. This invitation poses problems for Tina. However, as she goes through the agony of deciding to accept or reject her mother's invitation, Tina finds that she has a true friend in Sarajane.

Angell, Judie. **A Word from Our Sponsor; or, My Friend Alfred.** Laurel-Leaf Library, 1981. 123 pp.

Twelve-year-old science mastermind Alfred Caro has made a shocking discovery. The ceramic mug his little brother is using is covered with a glaze containing dangerous levels of lead. What makes matters even worse is that Alfred's father worked on the campaign to sell these mugs. But Alfred still decides to organize some of his friends into a consumer protection group. Now Alfred wants to get the group on national television.

Asher, Sandy. **Just like Jenny.** Delacorte Press, 1982. 148 pp.

Ever since their first ballet class together seven years ago, Stephie and Jenny have been best friends and have shared the same dream—

to be real dancers. This fall, their teacher says, is the crucial time when "the gutsy few" will break through into the world of professional dance. But lately Stephie can't seem to stop making mistakes. And when Stephie and Jenny go to audition for the prestigious Workshop, Jenny is thrilled, but Stephie loses her nerve. Suddenly it seems that Jenny will cross over easily into the world of "the gutsy few," and that Stephie will be left behind.

Ashley, Bernard. **All My Men.** S. G. Phillips, 1978. 159 pp.

Paul and his parents move from London to a small country town with high hopes of making friends and establishing a successful family business. Paul's hopes are shattered, though, when he is forced to earn his right to be included in the "in" group at school. Even to be on the school soccer team, there is a high price to pay. Soon Paul finds himself trapped in a pattern of corruption, and he surprises himself by turning against his parents.

Bawden, Nina. **The Peppermint Pig.** J. B. Lippincott Co., 1975. 189 pp.

Polly and Theo miss their father terribly when he moves from England to America. Then they save the life of a small pig and find comfort in this new friend. Polly spends many afternoons feeding and cuddling the animal, and Theo often shares his troubles with the pig. But the brother and sister learn that something terrible is going to happen to their dear animal friend, something they cannot prevent.

Bawden, Nina. **The Robbers.** Laurel-Leaf Library, 1981. 170 pp.

When Phillip has to leave his grandmother and the castle they have always lived in, he feels angry and cheated. The boy thinks that just because his father has remarried doesn't mean he has the right to ruin Phillip's safe and happy life. Life in the city frightens Phillip, but he does become good friends with Darcy, a poor boy. But Phillip isn't really aware of Darcy's poverty until Darcy gets himself and Phillip into trouble by stealing. Phillip is more scared than he ever dreamed possible. The incident puts his loyalty to Darcy, and his own courage, to the test.

Beckman, Delores. **My Own Private Sky.** E. P. Dutton, 1980. 154 pp.

Could a middle-aged, muscular woman draped in jewelry actually be Arthur's summer babysitter? Arthur is disappointed with his mother's choice until his days begin to fill with exciting stories of the Old West and funny episodes with a know-it-all girl. But a terrible accident throws Arthur's happy life into turmoil.

Bethancourt, T. Ernesto. **New York City Too Far from Tampa Blues.**
Holiday House, 1975. 190 pp.

Tom, a Spanish-American boy, has just moved to New York City
from Tampa, Florida, and is unprepared for life in the big city.
During his first month in the neighborhood, he is involved in a
street gang fight, is expelled from school, and finds himself without
many close friends. The only good thing about all of his difficulties
is that he finds his father really believes in him and will support him
when he gets in trouble. When Tom meets Aurelio, a feisty young
Italian boy who make his spending money by shining shoes, it is
instant friendship. Tom learns that Aurelio's first love is music and
that he has two guitars, a Fender bass, a full set of drums, and a big
amp. The boys soon give up the shoe-shining business and decide to
try the world of rock music.

Blume, Judy. **Starring Sally J. Freedman as Herself.** Bradbury Press,
1977. 298 pp.

Sally Freedman moves with her family to Florida for the winter.
There she learns some strange facts about the ferocious man-o'-war
fish and about tiny creatures that lay eggs in people's hair. She also
meets Peter Hornstein, the cutest boy in the class, and snobby
Harriet Goodman, who is out to get Peter. Before winter is over,
Sally makes some decisions with bittersweet results.

Bond, Ann Sharpless. **Saturdays in the City.** Illus. Leonard Shortall.
Houghton Mifflin Co., 1979. 147 pp.

Best friends Adam Tyler and Noah Carter constantly find themselves in the middle of some wild adventure. They experience everything from a visit to an interesting museum to an appearance on a
television talk show. Somehow, the pair of nine-year-olds manage
to have wild fun without causing too many serious problems.

Bosse, Malcolm J. **The 79 Squares.** Thomas Y. Crowell Co., 1979.
185 pp.

Everyone is suspicious when Eric, on probation for vandalism,
starts spending time with an ex-convict. Eric likes talking with the
old man, but something strange that he cannot describe sometimes
freezes his courage when he's with the man. His fears surface when
he is ordered to divide a garden into seventy-nine equal squares—
for a reason Eric does not dare to guess.

Bridgers, Sue Ellen. **Home before Dark.** Alfred A. Knopf, 1976. 176 pp.

Stella Willis loves her sharecropper's cabin even if it is old. She's spent most of her life traveling in an old station wagon, so she now enjoys being in one place. But Stella soon learns that although she has self-confidence, she is not really ready to handle such situations as a first love, a tragic death, and a friendship. She discovers there is more to life than just finding one place to live.

Brooks, Jerome. **The Testing of Charlie Hammelman.** E. P. Dutton, 1977. 129 pp.

Charlie has problems: the best teacher in the world (and his friend) has just died; he can't talk to his parents; he is ashamed of his fat, unathletic body; he can't swim, and just this year his school makes being able to swim a graduation requirement. All this makes Charlie wonder if he might go mad. At least he has Hicks, who may be a jock but who is an understanding friend. Then Shirl comes along, and he, Charlie Hammelman, finds he has a steady girlfriend who likes him just for being himself.

Butterworth, W. E. **Flunking Out.** Four Winds Press, 1981. 216 pp.

Charley Taylor has always been a whiz at school, so in his first year at the U of Franklin, all he does is drink cocktails, go out with girls, and hang out. But for his friend Eddy, school has always been impossible. Eddy studies hard to please his father, but it's no use. As soon as he learns something, he forgets it. Both boys are getting uncomfortably close to flunking out. But that isn't their only problem. When Eddy falls in love with Charley's girlfriend, a great friendship is threatened.

Butterworth, W. E. **Under the Influence.** Four Winds Press, 1979. 247 pp.

Keith Stevens, a student at Stockton High, has a severe drinking problem. Allan Corelli befriends Keith but finds himself constantly pulling his drunken friend out of fights. Allan is perplexed about his new friend's need to drink. The problem worsens until it seems inevitable that it will result in disaster for Keith.

Byars, Betsy. **After the Goat Man.** Illus. Ronald Himler. Camelot Books, 1975. 126 pp.

Harold Coleman, feeling fat and unhappy, thinks that no one else has problems quite like he does. Even his good friend Ada doesn't really understand him. Then Figgy, a new boy in the neighborhood, enters their Monopoly game and everything changes. The three youngsters face the world together as they search for Figgy's desperate, eccentric grandfather—the Goat Man.

Campbell, Barbara. **A Girl Called Bob and a Horse Called Yoki.** Dial Press, 1982. 167 pp.

Yoki is the horse that pulls the milk wagon, and Bob is the girl who befriends the horse. All her life nothing has been simple for Bob— from the day of her baptism to her attempt to save Yoki from the glue factory. She does things that seem wrong to others, but that are really right. She has trouble explaining all this to her father, however.

Cebulash, Mel. **The Spring Street Boys Settle a Score.** Illus. Robert Sabin. Scholastic Book Services, 1981. 90 pp.

If the smallest kid in your neighborhood group was threatened by older teenagers, what would you do about it? That is what the Spring Street Boys have to decide. A car accident, a championship basketball game, and a lack of information all complicate matters.

Cebulash, Mel. **The Spring Street Boys Team Up.** Illus. Robert Sabin. Scholastic Book Services, 1981. 90 pp.

When the tough North Bergen Lions call Tony and his friends chicken and challenge them to a football game, the Spring Street Boys accept. But the Lions have everything Tony and his friends don't have: uniforms, helmets, a good football field, and a big team. How can the Spring Street Boys get ready for the big game in just two weeks? Easy reading.

Chaikin, Miriam. **Finders Weepers.** Illus. Richard Egielski. Yearling Books, 1982. 120 pp.

Molly can't believe her luck when she finds a small gold ring on the school playground. Certain that there is no way to locate its owner, she happily slips it on her finger. Then Molly learns that the ring belongs to a girl in her class! She knows she should return the ring—but how can she when it is stuck on her finger?

Cheatham, K. Follis. **Bring Home the Ghost.** Harcourt Brace Jovanovich, 1980. 288 pp.

Tolin and Jason grew up together on an Alabama plantation. Now they decide to share the excitement and danger of life on the Western frontier of the 1830s. But there is one big problem that complicates their lives wherever they go—Tolin is white and Jason black. They must overcome physical obstacles and the emotional barriers of prejudice as they fight for a new life in a new land.

Cleary, Beverly. **Ribsy.** Illus. Louis Darling. Yearling Books, 1982. 192 pp.

Ribsy, Henry Huggins's lovable dog, is lost. Henry's father offers to buy the boy another dog, but Henry would rather have no pet if he can't find Ribsy. Meanwhile, Ribsy is struggling to come home, but he becomes caught up in misadventures along the way. Someone even attempts to give him a violet-scented bubble bath!

Clifford, Mary Louise. **Salah of Sierra Leone.** Illus. Eliza Moon. Thomas Y. Crowell Co., 1975. 184 pp.

Luke and Salah are best friends who go to the same school in the African wilderness of Sierra Leone and share a love for soccer. Things change when Salah is accused of sending his father to prison and Luke feels responsible for the death of a child. Soon these problems become a barrier in their friendship, but instead of tearing the walls down, Luke and Salah build them higher.

Cohen, Barbara. **Fat Jack.** Atheneum Publishers, 1980. 182 pp.

Judy Goldstein has been hurt too many times by false friends, so she decides to keep to herself. Jack Muldoon is an overweight senior transfer student in Judy's high school whom everyone likes to pick on. They are two loners who desperately need a real friend. Then one day, Mr. Sharf, the school librarian, is chosen to direct a play. He chooses Shakespeare's *Henry IV, Part One* and decides to cast Judy and Jack. The whole school predicts disaster, but Judy and Jack work hard to make the play a success and even become close friends in the process.

Corcoran, Barbara. **"Me and You and a Dog Named Blue."** Atheneum Publishers, 1979. 179 pp.

Maggie Clarke is relieved when CoCo, an eccentric old woman, saves her from being put behind bars. But what she doesn't count on is having the woman watch over her all the time like a hawk. CoCo even comes to Maggie's baseball practices. To escape this watchful woman, Maggie plans to run away to Chicago, where the women's pro baseball team practices. But the scheme turns out to be more interesting than Maggie ever dreamed.

Crane, William B. **Oom-Pah.** Atheneum Publishers, 1981. 196 pp.

Why had this tuba player moved from Texas to her high school? Darleen was perfectly happy as the only tuba player in her high school marching band. Then Fred arrived. He is always late for rehearsals, he asks silly questions, and he gets Darleen into trouble all the time. The worst experience is the halftime show during a big game. Fred is late and has to run across the field with his tuba. And he tries to get dressed in his uniform on the way! Darleen quickly realizes her life, and the school band, will never be the same.

Crawford, Charles P. **Letter Perfect.** E. P. Dutton, 1977. 167 pp.

Chad Winston and his friends, B. J. and Toad, are bored with school, so they think up practical jokes and pranks. As they become more and more involved with these antics, they decide to try a real crime, a perfect crime. But the boys nearly destroy the life of their victim when they carry out their plan.

Cross, Gillian. **The Iron Way.** Oxford University Press, 1979. 131 pp.

When Conor O'Flynn came looking for respectable lodgings, Kate Penfold was upset at the idea of a railway laborer in her house. But that all changes when busybody Mrs. Neville, the rector's wife, starts telling Kate and her brother Jem what to do about O'Flynn. Then something terrible happens in the English village. The villagers threaten to blow up the Crayston Railway Tunnel, but if that happens the laborers promise to attack the village. Kate wonders if Conor O'Flynn can reason with the villagers.

Cunningham, Julia. **Come to the Edge.** Camelot Books, 1978. 79 pp.

Fourteen-year-old Gravel runs away from the foster farm when he discovers that his father doesn't want him and that his best friend is gone. Gravel soon discovers three people who need him, but he can't decide whether to stay or keep on running.

Cunningham, Julia. **Flight of the Sparrow.** Pantheon Books, 1980. 130 pp.

Little Cigarette owed a lot to Mago. He took her from the orphanage, gave her a home, and even gave her her name. But most of all, he gave her love and the courage to survive. Will this be enough for Little Cigarette when she finds herself alone once more?

Cunningham, Julia. **The Silent Voice.** Unicorn Books, 1981. 145 pp.

An orphan and a mute, fourteen-year-old Auguste wandered around Paris more dead than alive. Then Astair, a street singer, rescues Auguste and decides to get him a position in the house of M. Bernard, a famous mime and teacher. Madame Louva, M. Bernard's housekeeper, keeps watch over Auguste as he learns to be a mime.

Everyone is happy with the new arrangements, until a jealous student of M. Bernard's decides to destroy his teacher and Auguste.

Cuyler, Margery. **The Trouble with Soap.** Unicorn Books, 1982. 104 pp.

Sometimes Laurie thinks her friend Soap has too much imagination. She is always thinking up crazy stunts that get them both into trouble. After one particular prank gets Laurie and Soap suspended from school, the girls are sent to a fancy private school. Laurie quickly makes new friends, but Soap decides she hates everyone. Now Laurie has to make a painful choice between Soap and her new friends.

Delton, Jina. **Two Blocks Down.** Signet Vista Books, 1982. 124 pp.

Sixteen-year-old Star is popular with a college crowd, so what does she need with high school dances, dating, or friends her own age? But before she knows it, Star allows herself to be drawn into the world of teenage schoolmates Justina, Leslie, and Roddy. Now she wonders how long she can keep her two groups of friends from meeting each other.

Dengler, Marianna. **Catch the Passing Breeze.** Illus. Marlies Najaka. Holt, Rinehart & Winston, 1977. 127 pp.

Vicki lives with her mother in a small, shabby apartment near the ocean in California. She is in love with the sea and the idea of sailing across its waves, but her disapproving mother and her poverty prevent her from fulfilling her dream—until she meets Bob Schaffer, a kindly sailing instructor. After seeing Vicki's excitement over sailing, Bob promises to give her his old, broken-down sailboat if she will restore it. Along with Tak, a Japanese schoolmate, Vicki sets out to make her dreams of sailing the sea a reality.

Dexter, Pat Egan. **Arrow in the Wind.** Thomas Nelson, 1978. 160 pp.

Sixth-grader Ben Arrow discovers that his parents are going to get a divorce. At first he can't believe it, but his father moves out and Ben must help make money to keep the rest of his family together. Ben takes on a paper route but must deal with the local bully, Joe Tepper. Ben tries to be friends with Joe. However, this friendship may lead Ben into trouble at home, at school, and with the law.

Dodson, Susan. **Have You Seen This Girl?** Four Winds Press, 1982. 182 pp.

Tom was on a search for the girl of his dreams. He thought it might be Kathy, who had problems at home. Then Kathy runs away from Michigan to New York. Tom is determined to find her, so he stays with his Aunt Maggie in the city. But his dreams of running away with Kathy seem to remain just dreams. Tom quickly discovers all the traps there are in New York for homeless runaways. And in the process of looking for Kathy, he finds some answers about life for himself, even if they aren't the answers to his dreams. Mature situations.

Donahue, Marilyn Cram. **To Catch a Golden Ring.** Chariot Books, 1980. 223 pp.

They lived in a slum called Bundy Street. Now Angie and Con feel a need to get away from the rundown buildings, the glaring neon signs, and the oddball people who roam the street. Con decides to escape through a college scholarship, and he urges Angie to join him. But the pair's plan of escape turns from dreams to nightmares when Con tries to find another way to get them out of Bundy Street.

Draper, Cena C. **The Worst Hound Around.** Westminster Press, 1979. 115 pp.

Jorie's favorite friend is his dog, Blue Hound. Blue Hound's only problem is that he won't hunt coons. Instead, he chases cats and climbs ladders. Jorie finds it hard to take the taunts of his classmates about Blue Hound. Then his three girl cousins arrive for a visit. Together, they attempt to turn the "good-for-nothing" dog into a true hunter.

Elfman, Blossom. **The Return of the Whistler.** Houghton Mifflin Co., 1981. 163 pp.

Arnie Schlatter and Francesca de la Paula, both outsiders in the adult world, help each other to find a place in life. Disappointed with their parents, Arnie and Francie aid each other through the shame and guilt they feel.

Ellis, Ella Thorp. **Sleepwalker's Moon.** Atheneum Publishers, 1980. 234 pp.

In 1942, Anna's father decides to join the army, so Anna must stay with the Raymonds, a family she has always dearly loved. After all, she has spent summers with them before, and she always wanted to be a Raymond. Yet under the image of the perfect family, Anna finds tensions and problems she hadn't seen before. Will she be able to deal with these "new" Raymonds?

Etchison, Birdie L. **Strawberry Mountain.** Illus. James Converse. Herald Press, 1982. 131 pp.

Twelve-year-old Ben is a foster child sent to live with a farm family. Ben hates farmwork—he would rather draw in his sketchbook. But Ben's biggest problem is Quint, a tough, older foster kid. Quint laughs at Ben's treasured sketches and accuses Ben of killing his pet squirrel. Ben is angry and frustrated. What can he do? Find out how a haunted house and a mysterious old man help Ben to practice his Christian beliefs.

Farrar, Susan Clement. **Samantha on Stage.** Illus. Ruth Sanderson. Dial Press, 1979. 164 pp.

Samantha takes a blow to her pride when Russian-born Lizinka, an experienced dancer, joins her ballet class. Samantha, feeling the pangs of envy, establishes a strong friendship with the Russian girl. But difficulties arise when the two girls compete for the leading role in the Christmas ballet, and their friendship is put to the test when a tragedy occurs the night before the performance.

First, Julia. **Flat on My Face.** Camelot Books, 1975. 95 pp.

Eleven-year-old Laura Loring is a great baseball player, but she wants to be popular like the other girls in her sixth-grade class. Then she meets Georgie, a cerebral palsy victim who is confined to a wheelchair, and she discovers a new approach to happiness and popularity.

Fox, Paula. **A Place Apart.** Signet Books, 1982. 151 pp.

Thirteen-year-old Victoria Finch has just experienced two traumatic events—the death of her father and the move with her mother from a beautiful old house to a dumpy home in a small town. Then she meets Hugh Todd, who is like nobody she has ever known. But why do none of the other kids like him? For the moment, though, Victoria is very happy with her new friend. The arrival of a new boy, Tom, quickly changes everything, however.

Galbraith, Kathryn Osebold. **Come Spring.** McElderry Books, 1980. 198 pp.

Reenie's family moves all the time. But maybe this move will be different. Reenie dreams the family will stay in one place, and that she will be able to find new friends and a dog of her own. But it takes more than wishing to make dreams come true, so Reenie works to make her life the way she would like it.

Gauch, Patricia Lee. **Fridays.** G. P. Putnam's Sons, 1979. 160 pp.

Corey belongs to "The Eight," a secret club of teenage girls. Every Friday night until the spring dance they have agreed to have a party. The late-night excursions are fun at first, then things begin to get out of hand. But like the others, Corey doesn't dare to disobey such a solemn pact—not even when something strange and frightening threatens their lives.

Gilbert, Harriett. **Running Away.** Harper & Row Publishers, 1979. 266 pp.

At her English school, sixteen-year-old Jane feels scared and lonely. Around her, the world seems to be crumbling. Her mother is in a hospital far away; her best friend, Audrey, is burdened with family problems, and distance has sprung up between the girls. Then Jane is involved in a car accident, and she struggles to piece her life together.

Gilbert, Nan. **The Strange New World across the Street.** Camelot Books, 1979. 167 pp.

Eleven-year-old Robbie has been living with his grandparents in Iowa. Then his father wins custody of Robbie, and the boy has to move into a strange environment with a man he barely knows. He makes friends with Janet Kernan and her family, and through Janet's friendship and help, Robbie gains new confidence and decides to get to know his father.

Goldreich, Gloria. **Lori.** Holt, Rinehart & Winston, 1979. 181 pp.

When sixteen-year-old Lori Mandell is suspended from school for smoking pot, her grandfather arranges for Lori to leave New York and spend a year and a half in Israel. Lori, preferring to stay with her friends, goes reluctantly. But once in Israel she meets Rina, a girl her own age, and Rina's family. Lori learns that life in Israel can be difficult when she becomes very close to a young Arab girl and a young Israeli soldier.

Graeber, Charlotte Towner. **Grey Cloud.** Illus. Lloyd Bloom. Four Winds Press, 1979. 124 pp.

Grey Cloud is a racing pigeon who belongs to Orville Breen—the boy all the kids say is crazy. But Tom likes Orville's quiet ways, and he begins working with him to train other pigeons for a big race. The special friendship between Orville and Tom is threatened when Tom can't resist taking a dare.

Green, Phyllis. **Wild Violets.** Thomas Nelson, 1977. 104 pp.

Ruthie Hickory, a poor girl who feels she has and is nothing in life, adores Cornelia Lee, the richest and most popular girl in fourth grade. But events like illness and the coming of World War II create changes in her life that Ruthie never dreamed possible. Easy reading.

Greenberg, Jan. **The Iceberg and Its Shadow.** Laurel-Leaf Library, 1982. 123 pp.

Anabeth and Rachel are best friends until glamorous Mindy, the new girl in the class, splits them apart. When Mindy turns the class against Rachel, Anabeth feels helpless against her meanness. And when Anabeth herself becomes Mindy's next victim, she realizes how powerless she has become. Anabeth knows she must fight back. But how?

Greene, Bette. **Get On out of Here, Philip Hall.** Dial Press, 1981. 150 pp.

Beth Lambert is expecting to win the Abner Jerome Brady Leadership Award given out each year by her church. Who deserves it more than she does? She is the number one student in her class, the president of the Pretty Pennies Club, and an all-around celebrity in Pocahontas, Arkansas—she's even been in the newspaper. But the winner is Philip Hall—Beth's sometime crush and frequent enemy. What will Beth do now?

Greene, Constance C. **Double-Dare O'Toole.** Viking Press, 1981. 158 pp.

If anybody double-dares Fex O'Toole, he has to act—even if it means trouble. One time he even put a picture of a pig on the principal's desk. Many people try to help Fex break his need to pull pranks and take dares, but nothing seems to work. Fex's brother is too busy thinking about sex to notice Fex's problems. Fex is confused by all his brother's talk about French kissing and making out. But he soon gets a chance to learn what it all means when the lights go out at a party, and someone whispers in his ear "I double-dare you."

Greene, Constance C. **Your Old Pal, Al.** Viking Press, 1979. 149 pp.

Al is always waiting for a letter. First she hopes her father will write, then she hopes to hear from a boy she met at her father's wedding to his new wife. Al becomes jealous when her best friend invites Polly to stay with her while Polly's parents are in Africa.

Greenwald, Sheila. **Blissful Joy and the SATs: A Multiple-Choice Romance.** Atlantic Monthly Press, 1982. 143 pp.

Bliss Bowman wants to attend Vassar College, but her 450 score on the SATs is too low. She wonders if there is any way to conquer the SATs. Suddenly hilarious complications begin to muddle her life, including being befriended by a persistent stray dog. But Bliss eventually learns by these experiences that there may be more to life than her definition of "success."

Grohskopf, Bernice. **Children in the Wind.** Atheneum Publishers, 1977. 190 pp.

Lenore is fascinated and intrigued by Chris Rivers, the new girl in school. When she finally gets to know the mysterious Chris, however, Lenore finds she is able to work out her own problems more easily. But friendship and human relationships are not without failure and pain, as Lenore discovers.

Hall, Lynn. **Flowers of Anger.** Avon Books, 1978. 112 pp.

Carey and Ann's common interest in horses makes them the best of friends. But the night before an important show, tragedy strikes Ann's horse. Suddenly what was once a beautiful friendship changes into blind hatred and revenge. Soon there is a slow, horrible change in Ann, a change that Carey cannot prevent.

Hall, Lynn. **The Horse Trader.** Charles Scribner's Sons, 1981. 121 pp.

Karen has a special friendship with Harley Williams, a horse trainer, just as her mother once had. He promised her a mare of her own when she was fifteen, and now she has Lady Bay. But there is a secret about the horse that Harley sold her. There is also another secret between Karen and Harley—she has a crush on him. What will happen when all this hidden information is revealed?

Hall, Lynn. **New Day for Dragon.** Illus. Joseph Cellini. Camelot Books, 1976. 122 pp.

Dragon, a fifteen-year-old horse, is befriended by fourteen-year-old Lyle Hunter. The boy is unaware of Dragon's history in Mexico or of the animal's terrible experiences with humans. Lyle hopes that his understanding can help this unbroken horse become a champion.

Hall, Lynn. **Stray.** Illus. Joseph Cellini. Camelot Books, 1975. 93 pp.

Lonely Rhody feels unloved by her parents and shunned by her friends. Then she finds Royal, a stray dog that becomes her pet and only friend. But even Royal fails to return her love; instead, he attempts to escape and run free. Rhody tries desperately to find an answer to Royal's behavior, but this search brings the dog close to death.

Hall, Lynn. **Troublemaker.** Illus. Joseph Cellini. Camelot Books, 1976. 94 pp.

Willis, a troubled, motherless boy, finds his only friend in a dog he steals from the pound. But when Willis's stealing and fighting get him tangled up with the law, the friendship is endangered. The boy is sent to a special training school and is not allowed to see his dog. Then in desperation Willis plans a daring escape.

Hallman, Ruth. **Tough Is Not Enough.** Hiway Books, 1981. 110 pp.

Kurt was streetwise and tough—he could handle anything. Hadn't he been taking care of himself and his little brother, Timmy, ever since their parents left? So when Kurt is sent on a camping trip with other boys from the home he and Timmy live in, he runs away, figuring that he can make it on his own. But when he has to seek the help of a mountain girl named Laura Mae in order to survive, Kurt learns that tough is not always enough.

Hamilton, Dorothy. **Bittersweet Days.** Illus. Esther Rose Graber. Herald Press, 1978. 123 pp.

When Kathy decides she wants out of the "in group" at school, she learns it's not that simple. The loneliness, the cutting remarks, and the empty hours all hurt. With help, she begins long days of building a new way of life suited to her own style.

Hamilton, Dorothy. **The Castle.** Illus. Esther Rose Graber. Herald Press, 1975. 111 pp.

Carol Retherford envies Veronica Kingsbury for her wealth until she learns some of the disadvantages of being rich. As Carol begins to know Veronica and understand life in the Castle, she draws the entire Kingsbury family closer to their neighbors. Easy reading.

Hamilton, Dorothy. **Rosalie.** Illus. Unada. Herald Press, 1977. 120 pp.

Rosalie is growing up on a farm near Muncie, Indiana, just after World War I. The car, the "horseless carriage," has just been introduced; all telephones are on party lines so some neighbors listen to each other's conversations; and Victrolas play marvelous records. Although sensitive and shy, thirteen-year-old Rosalie finds she does have the courage to stand up for what she believes in and will not let others try to make her feel bad. Doris, the school gossip, learns of Rosalie's determination to stand by her friends and by Virginia, a new student at school, and soon Doris learns what it is to have a true friend.

Hamilton, Dorothy. **Scamp and the Blizzard Boys.** Illus. James Converse. Herald Press, 1980. 78 pp.

A wild snowmobile ride through a blizzard brings Craig and his dog Scamp to Doug's house. Craig, Doug, Doug's mother, and even Scamp soon realize they will have to work closely together to survive the storm. Meanwhile, the entire community is working to fight against this natural disaster. But Doug and Craig begin to wonder how long it will take for the townspeople to realize they are trapped and to dig them out. Easy reading.

Hayes, Sheila. **Me and My Mona Lisa Smile.** Elsevier/Nelson Books, 1981. 116 pp.

Sixteen-year-old Rowena Smith changes overnight when the new English teacher invites her to a poetry reading. This once shy girl turns into an outgoing grownup. Rowena's values change too; she forms new attitudes toward boys, herself, and even her best friend. But after a few months of her so-called loose new life, Rowena learns how important friends can be.

Heide, Florence Parry. **Time's Up!** Illus. Marylin Hafner. Holiday House, 1982. 119 pp.

Noah is new in the neighborhood and doesn't have any friends. His mother is busy studying and usually can't be bothered with his problems. So Noah does work for his father to fill the time. But what Noah hates the worst about all the jobs his father gives him is that his father expects him to do the jobs in a certain way—his father's way. However, Noah discovers that sometimes doing something wrong turns out to be the right thing after all when he meets a clever girl named Bib and an unusual housepainter named Bruce Dooster.

Heide, Florence Parry. **When the Sad One Comes to Stay.** J. B. Lippincott Co., 1975. 74 pp.

Sara, a fatherless young girl, moves into a high-class neighborhood. Though her mother urges her to be popular, Sara doesn't make any friends. Then she meets Maisie, an old woman with love to give and stories to tell. But even this special friend can't seem to soothe her hurt, until Sara makes a painful decision.

Hinton, S. E. **The Outsiders.** Laurel-Leaf Library, 1982. 156 pp.

Johnny's father is a drunk, and his mother is a selfish slob. Two-Bit's mother works as a barmaid to support him and his kid sister. Dally turns into a hoodlum because he'll die if he doesn't. Darry is getting old before his time trying to raise a family and work two jobs. But the Socs have so much spare time and money that they jump other kids for kicks and have beer blasts and river-bottom parties because they don't know what else to do. To Ponyboy, it just doesn't seem right. What will he do to change things? Originally published in 1967. Mature situations.

Hodges, Margaret. **The High Riders.** Charles Scribner's Sons, 1980. 172 pp.

Larry Dunlap is excited to be chosen as a junior oarsman on his school team to compete in Henley, England. He's good at math, he has a passport, and he has the money. But his late arrival forces him to live alone, away from the team, in ancient Horse Shoe Inn, where he is the only guest. There he meets older people who change his prejudices about adults, and he comes to enjoy their love of horses. But Larry also discovers some of their ghosts at the Inn.

Holland, Isabelle. **Alan and the Animal Kingdom.** J. B. Lippincott Co., 1977. 190 pp.

Alan McAndrews walks into the hospital and finds that his aunt, his only guardian, is dead. Afraid of being sent to a strange home away from his collection of pets, he decides to tell no one of the death. All is well until a crisis threatens Alan's peaceful family of animals. Then Alan's cash supply dwindles, and some school authorities become suspicious.

Hopkins, Lee Bennett. **Wonder Wheels.** Alfred A. Knopf, 1979. 163 pp.

Mick's world is roller skating, and he lives only for the thrill of skating. That is, until he meets Kitty Rhoades. It isn't until he has known her for a while that he finds out much about Kitty's life, and then Kitty shares all her problems—except one. When this problem is revealed right before the big skating competition, Mick is left alone to work out his life.

Howe, Fanny. **The Blue Hills.** Flare Books, 1981. 127 pp.

Casey wakes up one morning to find her Aunt Bonnie gone. While her aunt's boyfriend says she left for a vacation, Casey is sure he is lying. With the help of an old friend, Willie, Casey decides to search the Blue Hills for her aunt. In the process, the two teenagers learn more about themselves and their feelings for each other than they expected. Mature situation.

Howe, Fanny. **Yeah, But.** Flare Books, 1982. 125 pp.

When Casey and her Aunt Bonnie move to the rich part of town, Casey's boyfriend, Willie, doesn't like it. He says Casey is acting differently. Then Casey meets Treat, a real preppy, and Casey and Willie grow further apart. But when a freak accident kills a local bum, Casey sees Treat for what he is—and appreciates Willie for what he is. But what does Willie think of her?

Irwin, Hadley. **The Lilith Summer.** Feminist Press, 1979. 109 pp.

For Ellen, staying with a seventy-seven-year-old woman all summer was a terrible job, but it paid fifteen dollars a week and meant the ten-speed bicycle in the department store window would be hers. So Ellen takes the job and counts the days until her job will be over, but Lilith, the old woman, can be interesting at times. She certainly doesn't always act like all the other old people Ellen knows—she has lots of ideas, and she really listens to what Ellen has to say.

Irwin, Hadley. **Moon and Me.** McElderry Books, 1982. 150 pp.

Fourteen-year-old E. J. was ready for love and friendship to sweep her up this summer. But what chance does she have stuck out in the country with her grandparents? Then Moon comes along. He seems smart and interesting enough, but he is only twelve. Rick Adams seems a much more likely candidate for romance to E. J. It is Moon, however, who talks E. J. into a hundred-mile horseback endurance ride. He even plans and manages her training. E. J. soon begins to think she has been wrong about Moon's possibilities.

Johnston, Norma. **The Crucible Year.** Atheneum Publishers, 1979. 166 pp.

When Elizabeth returns from vacation in 1963, she realizes how much values and ways of thinking are changing. In her new high school, she deals with problems in her friendships and discovers the difficulty of getting along with her parents. Then Elizabeth must make some important decisions when she comes into contact with drugs, homosexuality, and violence. Mature situations.

Johnston, Norma. **A Mustard Seed of Magic.** Atheneum Publishers, 1978. 184 pp.

Fifteen-year-old Tish has the gift of writing. She loves to spin stories and descriptions from her heart to her pen and then onto paper. But her English teacher, Mrs. Owens, keeps demanding writing assignments that are hard to fulfill—like writing structured, clear paragraphs. And that's not all that Tish struggles with. Problems at home and inner emotional battles bring much heartache. So Tish learns how to use her writing to help heal the wounds.

Johnston, Norma. **Myself and I**. Atheneum Publishers, 1981. 210 pp.

Saranne has always defended Paul Hodge when people criticized him for being "wild." She even made it possible for Paul to leave and start a new life. But what about her life? Saranne wonders why she cannot like Tim in the same way he likes her. And then Paul returns, and she understands why—she loves him. Because of this love, Saranne is drawn into Paul's often painful and troublesome search for his real father. Once again Saranne realizes she risks losing herself in her desire to help someone else. Can she afford to ignore her own needs again?

Johnston, Norma. **A Nice Girl like You**. Atheneum Publishers, 1981. 222 pp.

How had she ever become involved with Paul Hodge? Saranne Albright was shy, quiet, a good student, and the daughter of Bronwyn Sterling Albright, one of the leaders of the women's rights movement, while Paul Hodge was from a family no one liked. The family's only claim to fame was a movie-star daughter they had disowned. Besides, Paul always seems to be in trouble—even his parents do not appear to like him. But Saranne begins to feel sorry for Paul, so she decides to help him by suggesting he play Shylock in their high school's production of Shakespeare's *The Merchant of Venice*. This sign of concern, however, is only the start of trouble for Saranne.

Klevin, Jill Ross. **The Turtle Street Trading Co**. Illus. Linda Strauss Edwards. Delacorte Press, 1982. 138 pp.

The kids who live on Turtle Street—Morgan, P. J. (for Priscilla Jane), Mikey, and Fergy—need money to do fun things like going to Disneyland. But how can they get money when they're too young to have jobs? That's when the idea of the Turtle Street Trading Company is born—a business run by kids for kids. The Turtles soon learn that there's more to running a business than they had thought, but pretty soon they are written up in the paper, filmed for the evening news, and hailed as teenage tycoons. Everything's perfect until Fergy's family problems threaten to break up the group, and the Turtles must find a way to live up to their motto, "Turtles together forever!"

Klevin, Jill Ross. **Turtles Together Forever!** Illus. Linda Strauss Edwards. Delacorte Press, 1982. 156 pp.

Fergy, the treasurer of the Turtle Street Trading Company, a business run by kids for kids, has to move to San Francisco, so the other Turtles decide it's the perfect opportunity to open a branch office. But Fergy's not so sure. He knows it will be hard to start a new business in a strange town. Sure enough, life in San Francisco keeps him hopping and he puts off starting the business, even though he knows the other Turtles will be up soon to check on his progress. Then one day he and his new friend, Joey Tew, stumble on a method for making the best ice cream ever, which just might turn out to be the solution to Fergy's problem!

Knowles, John. **Peace Breaks Out.** Bantam Books, 1982. 178 pp.

All the time that Pete is in the Army during World War II, he looks forward to returning to his teaching job at the Devon School for boys. Who could predict that his contacts with the students Nick, Tug, Cotty, and the bright but troublesome Wexford would come to such a shocking climax?

Kullman, Harry. **The Battle Horse.** Bradbury Press, 1981. 183 pp.

In Stockholm, Sweden, in the 1930s, a neighborhood takes on a make-believe game of knights and horses in a jousting battle. The knights are the wealthy children, and the horses are played by poor public school kids. Roland is fascinated with it all—and even more fascinated when a certain Black Knight appears. But just as fascinating is Kossan, the girl who carries the Black Knight's conqueror. (Newbery Award)

Lampman, Evelyn Sibley. **Three Knocks on the Wall.** McElderry Books, 1980. 182 pp.

During the early days of World War I, Marty Hitchinson lives in a small town in Oregon where not much happens. However, an adventure begins on a day when she hears three knocks from behind the ten-foot-high outdoor wall. Her neighbor, Mrs. Hutchinson, is supposed to be crazy. What can she be up to now? Marty soon learns the reason for the knocking, and how it relates to her neighbor, but she can't find a way to help until a major flu epidemic throws everyone's life into chaos.

L'Engle, Madeleine. **A Ring of Endless Light.** Laurel-Leaf Library, 1980. 332 pp.

During a summer on beautiful Seven Bay Island, a young girl faces many problems. A friend of hers has just died, and now her grandfather is dying of cancer. To add to her complications, she finds herself the center of attention for three very different boys. (Newbery Honor Book)

Levitin, Sonia. **The Year of Sweet Senior Insanity.** Atheneum Publishers, 1982. 192 pp.

Leni wonders how she will ever make it through her senior year in high school and keep from going crazy. Just that past summer she and her two friends Angie and Rhonda had planned to save their money for an end-of-school trip to Hawaii. But now that she is in the middle of the madness of senior year, the trip to Hawaii seems a million years away to Leni. There are so many things to consider first: the senior prom, recognition day, and her relationship with Blair Justin, a college student. Some days Leni wonders why she was so eager for her senior year to arrive.

Levoy, Myron. **A Shadow like a Leopard.** Signet Vista Books, 1982. 138 pp.

Fourteen-year-old Ramon Santiago lives alone in a roach-infested slum, and the only way he can stay alive is to join a gang and be as macho as his switchblade can make him. Seventy-six-year-old Arnold Glasser used to be a well-known artist, but now he is flat broke, confined to a wheelchair, and bitter towards the whole human race. They meet when Ramon breaks into Glasser's apartment. Arnold and Ramon, an old man who is tired of life and a young man who hasn't had much chance to really live—can they teach each other what living is all about? Mature language. (ALA Best Book for Young Adults)

Lipp, Frederick J. **Some Lose Their Way.** McElderry Books, 1981. 118 pp.

They have been enemies for a long time. Could Vanessa and David now try to be friends? They were both outsiders who hid from the world. And they had something else in common—a love for nature. Slowly over one memorable summer, David and Vanessa learn to like and respect each other. They even work together on an environmental study of bird life in an area called the Bottoms. David and Vanessa suddenly do not want the summer to end. But it does, and with a near tragedy for them both.

Luger, Harriett. **The Elephant Tree.** Laurel-Leaf Library, 1982. 94 pp.

Dave and Louis are from rival gangs and hate each other. They constantly fight in school and on the streets—that is, until the day they are forced to go on a supervised camping trip. If they cause trouble here, they will go to juvenile court. So the boys keep their cool by staying away from each other. Then Dave and Louis get lost in the desert. Without food, water, or proper clothing, they are forced to struggle together to stay alive.

Malmgren, Ulf (translator Joan Tate). **When the Leaves Begin to Fall.** Harper & Row Publishers, 1978. 118 pp.

When Joel and Lena, two shy twelve-year-olds, become friends, they agree that their secret friendship will last until "the leaves begin to fall." This somehow makes their friendship more special and almost perfect, but it is also bittersweet, for the two know just when it will end.

Mark, Jan. **Thunder and Lightnings.** Illus. Jim Russell. Thomas Y. Crowell Co., 1976. 181 pp.

When Andrew and his family move from London to Norfolk, England, they have to get used to the constant sonic booms of passing aircraft from a nearby military base. Even Andrew's new friend, Victor, has his own model air force on display in his room. Although Victor is considered a slow learner, he knows more mechanical details about airplanes than most adults. As the friendship between the two boys grows, Andrew begins to take on Victor's concern over the phasing out of one of his favorite airplanes, the *Lightning.*

Mayerson, Evelyn Wilde. **Coydog.** Charles Scribner's Sons, 1981. 152 pp.

Kiko Adonia, the twelve-year-old son of a Greek immigrant, is a sensitive, artistic boy. He is lonely until he discovers Coydog hiding in an alley near his home. Coydog is the only survivor of a litter of pups born to a German shepherd and a coyote. But what will happen when people find out the real heritage of Coydog? In the face of this problem, Kiko finds a new talent, and a new friend, to help him and Coydog.

Mazer, Norma Fox. **Mrs. Fish, Ape, and Me, the Dump Queen.** E. P. Dutton, 1980. 138 pp.

After her feelings are deeply wounded by schoolmates, Joyce's father forbids her to trust another human being with her feelings again. Joyce obeys, until she meets Mrs. Fish, the school custodian.

She finds a reliable friend in the silly, lively woman. Then her father discovers the friendship, and a terrible accident forces Joyce to make a painful decision about her new friend.

McHargue, Georgess. **The Horseman's Word.** Delacorte Press, 1981. 259 pp.

A summer of horses and Scotland—the invitation to manage her sick uncle's pony-trekking business is too good for champion rider Leigh Powers to pass up. Then Leigh overhears plans for the secret ceremony of the Horseman's Word, an ancient charm that is supposed to give people uncanny power over horses. Leigh decides to learn more about it by having her friend, handsome Rob Tinto, sneak her in. But her plan backfires, with potentially grave consequences for Rob. Leigh knows she must use all her ingenuity and courage to repair the damage she's done.

McKillip, Patricia A. **The Night Gift.** Illus. Kathy McKillip. Atheneum Publishers, 1976. 156 pp.

Barbara's brother, Joe, tried to take his life because "It's so ugly." Now that he is to leave the hospital, his sister and her two friends try to make his room beautiful for his return. For each of the girls, the room begins to take on a different, special meaning. Their work on the room really solves no one's problems, but it gives all of them a gift of knowledge and love.

Meredith, Don. **Morning Line.** Avon Books, 1980. 206 pp.

Fern comes to the sleepy little desert town to forget herself and her past. Ritchie comes to the same town to bet on the horses, while Angel comes to rely on Ritchie and his gambling knowledge. All are losers, or they wouldn't have ended up here. But this trio's finding each other does not make things much better. Instead, all are driven to a near disaster when both men discover they love Fern. Mature situations.

Miles, Betty. **Looking On.** Camelot Books, 1979. 187 pp.

Rosalie is a fourteen-year-old girl who takes a negative view of herself—she is tall and overweight and her life seems boring. But then something happens. A young married couple move into a trailer behind Rosalie's home. The Judsons appear to be the perfect couple, and Rosalie dreams of becoming their friend. Rosalie soon loses interest in her own friends and school, but she also discovers that the Judsons have problems just like other people.

Miles, Betty. **The Real Me.** Camelot Books, 1975. 122 pp.

Barbara Fisher's first day at Jefferson Middle School triggers a series of battles for her. First she has to sign up for "slimnastics" when she wanted to take tennis. Only boys can take tennis. Then the *Plainview Journal* refuses to give her a job delivering newspapers in her neighborhood, even though she's been substituting for her brother Richard while he tries out for the basketball team. Her customers sign a petition on her behalf, but the editor doesn't relent. So Barbara decides to change things. What happens brings some interesting pains and surprises for Barbara—and also some fame!

Miles, Betty. **The Trouble with Thirteen.** Alfred A. Knopf, 1979. 108 pp.

Annie and Rachel want everything to stay just the way it is: to be best friends, have silly adventures, and stay twelve forever. Then things start changing around them that they can't stop. Their other friends begin to act older and different, Annie's dog dies, and Rachel's parents get a divorce. And the grown-up world that they are unwilling to enter starts to threaten their special friendship.

Miller, Ruth White. **The City Rose: Dee Bristol.** Avon Books, 1978. 128 pp.

Eleven-year-old Dee Bristol loses her home and family in a devastating fire and is sent to live with her aunt and uncle in the South. She has a hard time adjusting to her uncle's coldness, but she soon makes a friend named Wendy. They spend time in the lonely woods that hide a menacing secret that will determine Wendy's future.

Mills, Claudia. **At the Back of the Woods.** Four Winds Press, 1982. 86 pp.

Clarisse would give anything to be as brave and honest as Emily, the new girl. Emily can climb high trees quickly, swing on branches gracefully, leap down great distances, confront the town "witch," and talk openly about things like mental illness. Then something happens to Emily. For the first time, Clarisse sees that Emily is afraid. Easy reading.

Milton, Hilary. **The Brats and Mr. Jack.** Beaufort Books, 1980. 220 pp.

A twelve-year-old boy and his thirteen-year-old sister run away from the orphanage and meet a strange old man. Together the three share many adventures as they take up residence in a boarded-up mansion.

Moore, Ruth Nulton. **Tomás and the Talking Birds.** Illus. Esther Rose Graber. Herald Press, 1979. 115 pp.

The move from Puerto Rico to Pennsylvania is a hard one for Tomás and his mother. Tomás feels sad and friendless until he visits Sam's pet shop. He decides to teach a miserable Mexican parrot to talk. This task helps Tomás to learn English and to make new friends. Easy reading.

Morey, Walt. **Gentle Ben.** Illus. John Schoenherr. Camelot Books, 1976. 191 pp.

Mark is only thirteen when he befriends a brown bear cub that he names Ben. The special love between these two convinces Mark's father that Ben is a safe pet. Some of the people in their small Alaskan town disagree, however, and Mark faces several challenges in order to save his lovable friend. (ALA Notable Book; Sequoyah Children's Book Award; Dutton Junior Animal Book Award)

Murphy, Barbara Beasley, and Judie Wolkoff. **Ace Hits the Big Time.** Delacorte Press, 1981. 181 pp.

"They're going to kill you." These were the words his sister Nora yelled at Horace as he left for his first day at Kennedy High School. "They" were the Purple Falcons, a tough gang who beat up anyone they think looks funny. And today, Horace looks funny with a large sty in his eye. But Horace decides to face the Falcons. His tangles with them, and with a beautiful girl at school, begin a series of hilarious and crazy adventures for Horace.

Newton, Suzanne. **Reubella and the Old Focus Home.** Westminster Press, 1978. 197 pp.

Reubella is a young girl who wants to run away from home. Then she meets three wacky elderly women and begins to see her life in a different way. Her conversations and adventures with these women are strange and funny.

Ney, John. **Ox under Pressure.** J. B. Lippincott Co., 1976. 253 pp.

When Ox meets nervous, witty Arabella on his vacation in New York, he doesn't realize the fun that is in store for him—or the danger that awaits him. When the two friends are caught trespassing, the legal authorities investigate closely. That's when they discover Arabella's fantasy word—a cruel, elaborate world of make-believe where she rules as queen. Now they are threatening to put her in a mental institution, so Ox fights to prove Arabella's sanity.

Nostlinger, Christine (translator Anthea Bell). **Luke and Angela.** Harcourt Brace Jovanovich, 1980. 144 pp.

When Luke returns to Austria from a summer in England, he's not the person Angela has known for years. He turns up at school wearing the wildest clothing combinations imaginable, and he makes loud, outrageous statements. This new behavior turns him into the class hero. For Angela, though, Luke's return is painful because he's now ignoring her deliberately, and he's fallen in love with an older girl. Confused, angry, and lonely, Angela doesn't know what she might do.

O'Connor, Jane. **Yours Till Niagara Falls, Abby.** Illus. Margot Apple. Hastings House Publishers, 1979. 128 pp.

Abby Kimmel is spending eight weeks at Camp Pinecrest without her best friend, Merle. The first few weeks are anything but fun for this first-time camper. First of all, she is extremely annoyed at the pranks her roommates play on her. Then she is unable to pass her swimming test; she gets a major case of poison ivy; and she is bored with the food, games, and most of the girls. Add to all this the three straight days of rain. But life changes with the arrival of Roberta, her missing roommate. The girls become instant friends, and Roberta, a seasoned camper, teaches Abby all about life at Pinecrest.

Oppenheimer, Joan. **Working on It.** Harcourt Brace Jovanovich, 1980. 136 pp.

Tracy Ayres hates being fifteen. Not only does she have weird hair and no figure, but she is suffering from a terminal case of shyness. Her handsome, jock brother doesn't make it any easier for his klutzy kid sister. Even her parents are winners—popular, talented, and good-looking. Then Tracy and her one true friend decide to sign up for the drama class to help improve their self-confidence. How could Tracy know that her teacher, Miss Lindsay, would play such an important role in her own personal growth?

Orgel, Doris. **Next-Door Neighbors.** Illus. Dale Payson. Harper & Row Publishers, 1979. 160 pp.

Patricia is a loner, but not because she wants to be. More than anything she wants a friend who will like her for what she is and who will help her overlook the nicknames, like "Fatsy Patsy," that the boys call her. Patricia is lucky, and her wish comes true. Dorothy moves in next door, and right away life begins to change. With her new friend's help, she gets even with Bill and Charlie for their name-calling and ends up being their friend too. Originally published as *Next-Door to Xanadu.*

Parker, Richard. **Quarter Boy.** Thomas Nelson, 1976. 92 pp.

Charlie has held eight different jobs since he left school five weeks ago. His newest job allows him to use his artistic talent by painting the Indian figure on the clock mechanism atop the town hall. His efforts to paint the Indian and be friendly with a very shy girl lead to conflicts and confusion, but also to a new outlook on life.

Paterson, Katherine. **Bridge to Terabithia.** Illus. Donna Diamond. Thomas Y. Crowell Co., 1977. 128 pp.

Jess Aarons feels lonely and discouraged until Leslie moves nearby, for with Leslie comes Terabithia, a magical land where they reign as king and queen. Together they battle imaginary enemies and talk about real ones. Jess's confidence grows, and his friendship with Leslie strengthens. Then the real test of Jess's courage comes when he must face the reality of death. (Newbery Award)

Patterson, Gardner. **Docker.** McElderry Books, 1980. 145 pp.

Docker (whose real name is Jonathan Bradley Coe III) sometimes wonders why his family ever moved from St. Louis to Connecticut. The kids at his junior high school are crazy. But they soon bring out a practical-joker streak in Docker. After a while, there is nothing Docker will not do to get a laugh. Once he hires the town eccentric to pretend to be a famous scientist and address the school at at assembly. Another time, Docker falls through the ceiling of a friend's house while trying to scare someone. But Docker finds that jokes can often lead to trouble when he is first chased by burglars and later talked into a boxing match.

Paulsen, Gary. **The Night the White Deer Died.** Thomas Nelson, 1978. 96 pp.

Janet and her mother are nearly the only non-Native Americans in the small mountain town of Tres Pinos, New Mexico. Her mother is a sculptor, and Janet is a loner with few close friends. But Janet is happy enough with life except for a recurring dream she has about an Indian brave whose just-released arrow is speeding toward a deer at the edge of a pool. Janet is finally able to figure out some meaning to her strange dream when, by chance, she befriends Peter Honcho, an old Indian who is just out of jail and who is an alcoholic. What follows is an unlikely story of friendship and of a kind of love that is filled with understanding.

Paulsen, Gary. **Winterkill.** Thomas Nelson, 1976. 142 pp.

The unlikely friendship between an abused teenager and a tough and bitter cop develops into a story of mystery and suspense. Duda, the tough cop, has no use for the sassy kid, but when his harsh foster father nearly beats the boy to death, it is Duda who comes to the rescue. The uneasy relationship between the two builds throughout the novel to a surprising and tragic climax.

Peck, Richard. **Representing Super Doll.** Laurel-Leaf Library, 1982. 126 pp.

Whenever people turn to stare at and admire teenage beauty Darlene Hoffmeister, she always seems to take it in stride. But when she is chosen to be Teen Super Doll and is whisked off to New York City with her friend Verna, a startling change takes place. Can Darlene's appearance make up for what she lacks? Should Verna cover up for her friend when the going gets rough? Not many girls can live a dream. If Darlene and Verna dare to, will their lives ever be the same?

Peck, Richard. **Secrets of the Shopping Mall.** Delacorte Press, 1979. 185 pp.

Barnie and Theresa are unlikely friends who face trouble with a gang of kids at school. The King Kobra gang is after them, and the two eighth-graders run for their lives. They decide to hide out in a large department store at a shopping center. Everything appears cozy and safe until Barnie and Theresa find out that they are not alone in the night.

Peck, Robert Newton. **Mr. Little.** Illus. Ben Stahl. Doubleday & Co., 1979. 87 pp.

At first, Stan and Finley feel there isn't much to look forward to at school. But then they find out they are to be in Miss Kellogg's class, and she is the prettiest teacher in the school. When the first day finds a Mr. Little in front of the class instead, Stan and Finley decide to play their worst tricks on him. What the boys don't figure on, though, is Mr. Little being so incredible. In fact, he is the exact opposite of his name.

Peck, Robert Newton. **Trig Sees Red.** Illus. Pamela Johnson. Yearling Books, 1982. 59 pp.

Will Trig stand by and let her friend Pop the Cop be replaced by a new traffic light? Not on your life! Watch out as Trig's plan to get Pop his job back goes off with a bang. Easy reading.

Petersen, P. J. **Would You Settle for Improbable?** Delacorte Press, 1981. 185 pp.

For Michael Parker and his friends, their last year at Marshall Martin Junior High turns out to be much different than they could have imagined. For starters they have a student teacher whose enthusiasm for learning excites them. Then this teacher's moonlighting job at Juvenile Hall gets them involved with Arnold, a juvenile offender released to attend their school. It is going to be rough, but Ms. Karnisian asks them to try to be his friends.

Pfeffer, Susan Beth. **Kid Power.** Illus. Leigh Grant. Scholastic Book Services, 1977. 121 pp.

Janie believes she has found her true calling when she organizes a group of her friends into a work force called Kid Power. With the motto "No job too big or small," these kids go out and do all sorts of work for less than the minimum wage. But soon the success of Kid Power threatens to wreck Janie's social life—especially her relationship with her best friend Lisa. Easy reading.

Pfeffer, Susan Beth. **Starting with Melodie.** Four Winds Press, 1982. 122 pp.

Fifteen-year-old Elaine Zuckerman would give anything to have a name and a glamorous life-style like her best friend, Melodie St. Clare Ashford, whose parents are celebrities. Elaine thinks her own parents are dull, so she spends most of her time at Melodie's mansion. But when she meets Steve, her life suddenly doesn't seem so ordinary. But now Melodie has a big problem—her parents are getting a divorce and fighting over custody. Elaine can't desert Melodie just when she really needs a friend. But how can she pass up her first chance at excitement and romance?

Phillips, Kathleen C. **Katie McCrary and the Wiggins Crusade.** Elsevier/ Nelson Books, 1980. 188 pp.

Katie McCrary wonders if she will ever do anything right. She uses the wrong door at school, she votes to read the wrong book, and worst of all, she chooses being nice to the Wigginses as her personal crusade as a member of the Crusaders' Club. Sure, some of the Wigginses are mean and selfish, but Katie has discovered there are nice members of the family. Jeff is quiet and kind, Marva Mae is direct and honest, and Pansy-Lily-and-Rose is shy and sweet. And then there is Oscar, who likes everything about Katie. When Oscar is jailed, Katie is pressured to give up her crusade. But she sticks by Oscar, and finds herself with the whole town against her.

Phipson, Joan. **Fly Free.** McElderry Books, 1979. 134 pp.

They have the chance to go on an exciting school trip to a remote island, but Wilfred and Johnny just do not have the money. So the two boys team up to trap animals like rabbits and foxes to sell. Wilfred, shy and fearful, is reluctant at first, but Johnny convinces him of how easy it is. Then Johnny gets involved with poachers who want to trap rare birds to sell illegally. One day Johnny gets caught in one of these bird traps, and it is up to Wilfred to save his friend without calling the authorities.

Phipson, Joan. **A Tide Flowing.** McElderry Books, 1981. 156 pp.

Mark's life has not been a happy one. His mother has died and his father has gone to another part of Australia to start a new life without his son. Left with his grandparents, Mark is close to despair. His grandparents are kind and loving, but they cannot quite understand the torment Mark feels because of his mother's death and his father's rejection of him. Then Mark gets to know Connie, a quadriplegic who slowly teaches him that the human spirit can survive and grow strong even under the roughest conditions.

Porter, Sheena. **Nordy Bank.** Illus. Annette Macarthur-Onslow. Oxford University Press, 1979. 122 pp.

Bron, a shy fifteen-year-old English girl, is like a magnet to dogs. So why does she fear the wolflike Alsatian? Surprisingly, she fights not only to save the Alsatian but to keep him—even risking a separation from her family.

Rees, David. **Risks.** Thomas Nelson, 1977. 92 pp.

When Derek Lockwood's older brother calls from London to ask Derek and his friend Ian to spend the weekend with him, they jump at the chance. The two boys set out hitchhiking to London, but what happens along the way will have a terrible effect upon the rest of Derek's life.

Robinson, Margaret A. **Arrivals and Departures.** Charles Scribner's Sons, 1981. 169 pp.

Sophie teaches high school in Philadelphia and has enjoyed a short love affair with Tim. Now she must readjust her life. And she has some wonderful friends to help her: Marie, Lois, Joe Dodge, and even Dog, the mutt she adopts. But Sophie feels that people come into and leave other people's lives too fast. Life begins to seem like a train station with constant arrivals and departures. Can she ever do anything about this, Sophie wonders?

Robinson, Nancy K. **Wendy and the Bullies.** Illus. Ingrid Fetz. Hastings House Publishers, 1980. 128 pp.

Who likes bullies? Wendy Kent has a classification system that helps her deal with bullies. But then her best friend Karen gets sick, and Wendy is left to handle Stanley Kane, a "class A" bully. Just when she thinks all is lost, Wendy discovers a most surprising and unexpected thing about bullies and about herself.

Rockwell, Thomas. **The Thief.** Illus. Gail Rockwell. Delacorte Press, 1977. 81 pp.

Tim fears his two older brothers. They taunt him, tease him, and torture him behind his parents' backs. At least Dwayne, his only friend, understands. Dwayne builds his confidence and makes him able to endure the ridiculing. But Tim knows that something is wrong when Dwayne vandalizes an old man's shack and then begins to steal things from Tim's own pockets. With growing regret, he realizes that his best friend is a thief.

Roe, Kathy Gibson. **Goodbye, Secret Place.** Houghton Mifflin Co., 1982. 164 pp.

When Robin and Whitney started seventh grade, they made a pact to be friends forever. But Whitney can't believe that pretty and popular Robin would really want to be her friend. This friendship is very important to Whitney, but will she destroy it with her jealousy?

Ross, Marianne. **Good-bye, Atlantis.** Elsevier/Nelson Books, 1980. 172 pp.

Ann thinks that her senior year will be the same as any other year, but Jonathan Williamson changes her mind. This all-around athlete and straight A student draws up the mysterious Atlantis Charter. The truths of this secret document affect Ann deeply and inspire her, but Jonathan turns to cheating and teasing. Then Ann is the object of a terrible tragedy, and the two friends must struggle with the strength of their friendship and the powers of the Atlantis Charter.

Roth, David. **The Hermit of Fog Hollow Station.** Beaufort Books, 1980. 96 pp.

Twelve-year-old Alex moves with his family from Boston to the country. To get over his loneliness, Alex goes fishing with some boys. But trouble comes when they run into the dreaded Old Man Turner, who supposedly eats young boys alive. How Alex and the old man become friends is a surprising story about the needs and feelings of friends.

Sachar, Louis. **Johnny's in the Basement.** Flare Books, 1981. 126 pp.

Johnny has a great life—a great bike, a great best friend, and the World's Greatest Bottle Cap Collection. Not bad for a ten-year-old kid. But when he turns eleven, his parents decide he must grow up. That means washing the dishes, taking out the garbage, and—worst of all—dancing lessons! Things look pretty bad to Johnny until he meets Valerie, who hates dancing school as much as he does. Suddenly, growing up isn't so awful after all.

Sachs, Marilyn. **Bus Ride.** Illus. Amy Rowen. Skinny Books, 1980. 107 pp.

The usual bus ride to and from school is the usual bore for Judy until she meets Ernie at the bus stop one morning. Judy, who considers herself just average, is flattered by Ernie's attention. However, she is soon hurt when it seems that all Ernie is interested in is getting to know her friend Karen, one of the most popular girls in school. As the bus rides continue, however, Judy and Ernie become friends and are able to prove to themselves that neither of them is a loser.

Sachs, Marilyn. **Class Pictures.** E. P. Dutton, 1980. 138 pp.

Pat and Lolly met in kindergarten; Pat bit Lolly on the cheek and that was the start of a beautiful friendship. Every year, from kindergarten through high school, the two share each other's problems and triumphs. And as their friendship matures, so do they.

Sachs, Marilyn. **A Secret Friend.** Doubleday & Co., 1978. 111 pp.

Jessica and her best friend, Wendy, exchange lockets and invent crazy adventures. Then Wendy turns on Jessica and becomes friends with Barbara. Life is miserable for Jessica until she starts to receive mysterious notes from an unknown friend. Strange things begin to happen to Wendy and Barbara, and the web of friendships begins to get tangled.

Sachs, Marilyn. **A Summer's Lease.** E. P. Dutton, 1979. 143 pp.

Gloria decides to use genius, not popularity, to get some attention at school. She plans to prove her genius by becoming the editor of the school's literary magazine. But when the magazine's advisor tells her she will be sharing that editorship with Jerry Lieberman, Gloria is furious. To top it all off, the advisor, Mrs. Horne, asks both Jerry and Gloria to work for her at her summer home during the vacation months. While Gloria is dying to get away from home, she doesn't want to share Mrs. Horne, or the editorship, with Jerry!

Schellie, Don. **Shadow and the Gunner.** Four Winds Press, 1982. 136 pp.

The best person in the world, thinks eleven-year-old Bobby, is his friend Gunner. Gunner is seven years older than Bobby, but he always has time for the kid he calls Shadow. But when Gunner comes home from World War II on furlough and falls in love with Bobby's snotty sister Shirley, Bobby is lonely and hurt. Will Gunner help him deal with the sorrow of losing someone?

Schwartz, Lynne Sharon. **Balancing Acts.** Harper & Row, Publishers, 1981. 216 pp.

Alison Markman, age thirteen, and Max Friend, a seventy-six-year-old retired circus performer, make a strange pair. Alison makes Max her hero when he comes to give tumbling lessons at her school. Their friendship sets off many amusing incidents that involve other people, and it also provides Alison with some important lessons in dealing with adolescence.

Scott, Jane. **Cross Fox.** McElderry Books, 1980. 130 pp.

Jamie feels strange and lonely in the new countryside home his parents have moved into. Then he begins to explore the woods around his house and catches sight of a cross fox—a rare fox with a dark line down its back and across its shoulders. Soon Jamie is spending each day tracing the fox's movements. By doing this, Jamie begins to feel closer to the mysterious animal. One day Jamie and his friend Ellie hear that the neighborhood is out to hunt the cross fox because he has been raiding henhouses. The boy knows he must do something to stop the killing—no matter what horrible consequences result.

Shura, Mary Francis. **Chester.** Illus. Susan Swan. Dodd, Mead & Co., 1980. 92 pp.

Chester moves into the old Owens house in the Fillmore School District on Saturday. That same day he meets Amy, Zack, George, James, and Edie—members of the very special Fillmore Gang. But Chester soon finds out that he has some unique qualities too. First of all, he has forty-three freckles, and Jamie has only two. He also proves himself in a foot race and amazes everyone in the Great Goat Chase. In fact, in just seven days Chester proves himself to be just as special as any member of the gang.

Shura, Mary Francis. **My Friend Natalie.** Scholastic Book Services, 1979. 154 pp.

When her "best friend," Natalie, moves away, Jane seems to lose everything that's important to her. First her special dog, Stilts, disappears. Then she notices that her other friend, Margaret, is spending more and more time away from her. Doesn't she have any friends left? When a letter from Natalie finally arrives in the mail, Jane begins to learn what it means to make and be a friend. Originally published as *The Barkley Street Six-Pack.*

Singer, Marilyn. **No Applause, Please.** E. P. Dutton, 1977. 122 pp.

Ruthie doesn't fit in with the usual high school crowd. She likes to write poetry and to listen to Tchaikovsky rather than spend all her time talking about clothes, boys, or television. Her friend Laurie is the only one who understands and appreciates her interests. They form a singing act and manage to win second place in a high school talent show. This win convinces Laurie's mother that her talented daughter can be sucessful in show business. Soon Laurie launches a career on her own as a singer at the Capri Club. But the splitting up of the singing act tests the girls' friendship and Ruthie's ability to keep her sense of humor.

Slote, Alfred. **Tony and Me.** Camelot Books, 1976. 156 pp.

Bill's best friend in the strange new town is his teammate Tony. Everyone admires the way Tony can hit, pitch, and run—especially Bill. Then Bill discovers something terrible about his new friend: Tony steals things . . . all the time. And before Bill can think twice, Tony's shoplifting habits begin to be a part of his life.

Smith, Doris Buchanan. **Dreams and Drummers.** Thomas Y. Crowell Co., 1978. 180 pp.

As first-chair drummer, Stephanie has the advantage of hearing lots of gossip from the band kids and is able to tell her best friends revealing secrets about their boyfriends. Then Stephanie has love problems of her own when the cute trumpet player begins slipping her love notes. But her troubles are just beginning: her runaway brother causes family quarrels, and her best friend tries to break the chain of restrictions set upon her. Stephanie escapes to her private island, where strife is banished and peace reigns.

Smith, Doris Buchanan. **Salted Lemons.** Four Winds Press, 1980. 233 pp.

In a hot August during World War II, ten-year-old Darby Bannister and her parents complete their move from Washington, D.C., to

Atlanta. What promises to be excitement and adventure in a new city turns into boredom and loneliness when Darby finds out how difficult it is to make friends in Atlanta. She is considered a Yankee, and the Southerners want nothing to do with such "foreigners." The young outcast soon finds out, however, that there are others who are also not accepted in Atlanta. Mr. Kaigler, a German, and Yoko, a Japanese, are also rejected. Darby is faced with the problem of surviving and making and keeping friends in a community that seems to reflect the problems of World War II.

Snyder, Anne, and Louis Pelletier. **Counter Play.** Signet Books, 1981. 166 pp.

Brad Stevens is a star football player on a winning team—a nice guy who plans on going to West Point. His best friend, Alex, has told Brad that he is gay. Now Brad must decide if he can remain friends with Alex. People in the community and friends at school find out about Alex and try to pressure Brad from even talking to Alex. What should Brad do? Mature language and situations.

Snyder, Anne, and Louis Pelletier. **Two Point Zero.** Signet Vista Books, 1982. 154 pp.

Kate Fleming desperately needs money to stay in college, so she agrees to write class papers for the football team's star kicker. But Kate's problems are only beginning. She becomes involved with Doug Hollis, who is writing an article exposing the kind of cheating Kate has become involved with. If the story is published, it would mean the end of the football star's career—and of Kate's hope to go to law school.

Sorensen, Virginia. **Friends of the Road.** McElderry Books, 1978. 180 pp.

Cathy moves all around the world. Most people would think Cathy's way of life exciting, yet Cathy longs to stay in one place for a while. When Cathy's father is sent to Morocco, Cathy begs to take along her dog, Foxy. Soon after the move, though, Foxy is killed in the streets, and depression seems to fill Cathy's life. Then she meets another diplomat's daughter, Pippa, and Cathy makes an immediate friend. A pet lamb, Boots, replaces Foxy, and Cathy now feels she can begin to absorb the wonders of this new culture. But one day danger threatens Cathy's and Pippa's lives.

Spence, Eleanor. **A Candle for Saint Antony.** Oxford University Press, 1977. 140 pp.

When Justin, a fifteen-year-old Australian, and Rudi, an Austrian-born Catholic, meet for the first time, the sparks fly. Later, however, religious differences are resolved, and the two build a strong friendship—one that lasts through many hours of preparation for a trip to Germany. But when the two chums arrive at Rudi's birthplace, Rudi tells Justin some unusual and disturbing secrets that threaten to cut the strong bond between them.

Stein, R. Conrad. **Me and Dirty Arnie.** Harcourt Brace Jovanovich, 1982. 144 pp.

When eleven-year-old Dan moves to Chicago with his family, he feels he needs to meet someone who knows the city. Enter Dirty Arnie, who knows all the special tricks of getting along in the city, even though they often lead him to trouble. But when he and Dan begin to dig for dinosaur bones, the results are surprising.

Strasser, Todd. **Rock 'n' Roll Nights.** Delacorte Press, 1982. 217 pp.

Will Gary's band ever get their big break? Gary knows it's not easy to make it to the top of the music business, but he has so many headaches: his keyboard player has endless tantrums; their manager is the drummer's flaky, ex-hippie mother; and the only girl Gary's attracted to is their bass player Susan, who also happens to be his cousin. But despite these obstacles, Gary knows that their big break could come any day now. Mature language and situations. (ALA Best Book of the Year)

Taylor, Theodore. **The Trouble with Tuck.** Doubleday & Co., 1981. 110 pp.

When Helen's young Labrador retriever, Friar Tuck, begins to go blind, the young girl thinks of ways to help him. She is worried that the dog will be put to sleep. She doesn't want Tuck chained up, but she is afraid he will get hit by a car if he runs loose. In a moment of desperation, Helen thinks about getting Tuck a guide dog, the kind that aid blind people. But can one dog get used to leading another? Easy reading.

Tchudi, Stephen. **The Burg-O-Rama Man.** Laurel-Leaf Library, 1983. 183 pp.

Five Crawford High students may soon become commercial stars. Burg-O-Rama, a new fast-food chain, wants a group of typical American teenagers to promote their restaurants on television. But who will be chosen? Karen Wexler, the school paper editor, begins to notice that the competition is causing jealousies to develop and friendships to split. She begins to wonder if the Burg-O-Rama search will do Crawford High more harm than good.

Terris, Susan. **Stage Brat.** Four Winds Press, 1980. 179 pp.

For young Linnet Purcell, life is real only when she is on stage. Offstage she is always imagining and acting. It is only at the Dell'Arte Repertory Theatre that she feels she can really belong. Linnet gets along with the young kids in the company by always playing the comedian. They love her antics, but the adults think she is suffering from a case of "terminal cuteness." When she is given the lead role in *Peter Pan* she comes into direct conflict with leading lady Hilda Cane, who is jealous because she didn't get the star role.

Terris, Susan. **Tucker and the Horse Thief.** Four Winds Press, 1979. 188 pp.

It is the time of the Old West, and Tucker Delaney is a girl who disguises herself as a boy. She soon meets a young Jewish boy, Solomon Weil, who believes that Tucker really is a boy. Together they form a plan to escape from Tucker's crazy father.

Thrasher, Crystal. **Julie's Summer.** McElderry Books, 1981. 263 pp.

Near the end of the Great Depression, Julie's parents must move out of Indiana, but she is to remain behind to finish her last year of high school so she can become a teacher. Julie stays with her best friend, whose mother runs a dress shop. It isn't easy for Julie to adjust to the strict rules in the house, but she has Floyd Perry as a good friend. Then Chance Cooper appears in town. Julie likes them both, so why should she choose? Then she finds out how vicious gossip can become when rumors are spread about her, Floyd, and Chance.

Voigt, Cynthia. **Tell Me If the Lovers Are Losers.** Atheneum Publishers, 1982. 241 pp.

What will Ann find at Stanford College for Women? Until she goes there she has everything so under control, but she is totally unprepared for her roommates: the brash and vulgar Niki and Hildy, the serene farm girl from North Dakota. The three girls clash instantly, but eventually they find common ground on the volleyball court, where they manage to work out their differences. There they discover a friendship that gives them strength to fall back on when tragedy strikes. (ALA Best Book of the Year)

Walker, Mary Alexander. **Maggot.** Atheneum Publishers, 1980. 142 pp.

Three young people in San Francisco in the 1970s find their lives deeply affected by each other. Maggot cares only for dancing,

Elephant only for her sister, and Josh for something he can't quite define. Each one of them has periods of crises, and each learns to count on one another for help.

Webster, Jean. **Daddy-Long-Legs.** Bantam Books, 1982. 151 pp.

After living in the ward of an orphanage for eighteen years with twenty roommates, Jerusha is delighted to have a room of her own. In a collection of letters written to the man who pays her way through college, Jerusha tells of the friendships she makes, the books she reads, and the other exciting things that happen to her— which include falling in love for the first time.

Willard, Nancy. **The Marzipan Moon.** Illus. Marcia Sewall. Harcourt Brace Jovanovich, 1981. 48 pp.

Is this a big joke? Or is it a dream? For the second day in a row the priest finds a marzipan moon treat on his kitchen table. He wished for it on his birthday, but all he received from his friends were mufflers and an old crock. That was it! The crock must be magic. Maybe it can grant more wishes. Easy reading.

Williams, Barbara. **Where Are You, Angela von Hauptmann, Now That I Need You?** Holt, Rinehart & Winston, 1979. 192 pp.

For Woody Jones, canceling Field Day is bad enough, but to have a dance for seventh-grade graduation is even worse, especially when his partner is Angela von Hauptmann, the know-it-all, trouble-maker, and newcomer to the school. But Angela turns out to be a wonder—she makes Miss Sutherland change her mind about Field Day, makes Madeline Fisher change her mind about baths, makes Ben Brady change his mind about getting involved in sports, and makes Woody Jones himself change his mind about everything, including dances and Angela von Hauptmann. But it is also 1939, when everyone is afraid of Germans and possible Nazi spies. A girl as different as Angela with a name like von Hauptmann is bound to come under suspicion. And she does—by Woody's father.

Williams, Ursula Moray. **No Ponies for Miss Pobjoy.** Thomas Nelson, 1975. 159 pp.

Frances and Megan return for the new school year at Canterdown Girls' School in England to find that the new headmistress, Miss Pobjoy, plans to change the institution from a riding school to a school centered on studies. But the girls will have no part of the plan. They love Canterdown just the way it is—rundown, unorganized, and allowing a life filled with ponies and riding. So Frances and Megan set about to organize protests and other activities to outsmart the new headmistress. The girls are assisted in their plotting by Hilary, a new student who has an imaginary pony, and Bella, the school donkey. The hilarious events that follow bring surprises for everyone at Canterdown.

Wilson, Gina. **Cora Ravenwing.** McElderry Books, 1980. 161 pp.

Prejudice often twists people's minds. Becky Stokes finds this out when she makes friends with Cora Ravenwing, a strange, motherless girl whose father is a gravedigger. Becky likes her and spends time with her, until she begins to pay attention to the local gossip about Cora. Should she really believe it? Becky soon finds her secret alliance with Cora threatens to bring a disaster to both their lives.

Winthrop, Elizabeth. **Marathon Miranda.** Holiday House, 1979. 155 pp.

Everything is going wrong for Miranda: she suffers from asthma, her best friend deserts her, and her favorite older person disappoints her. Things begin to brighten up when she makes friends with Phoebe, an enthusiastic jogger. As Miranda joins Phoebe in her workouts, a close relationship develops. With Phoebe's encouragement, Miranda becomes a stronger runner, and both girls decide to enter a marathon race. Easy reading.

Wood, James Playsted. **Chase Scene.** Elsevier/Nelson Books, 1979. 170 pp.

Hugh and Tap wake in the blackness of night to see a man huddled over the glow of their campfire. The man soon forces them into Hugh's rebuilt Model T. Abner Nye, as the boys learn, has just escaped from the nearby asylum for the criminally insane—he's a convicted murderer! The adventure begins when Abner convinces the boys of his innocence, and they help him elude the police. During the trio's escape, Hugh gets mugged in Central Park and Tap disguises himself as a girl so he can go out for supplies. Soon, the newspapers, radio, and television are filled with wild stories about them.

Wood, Phyllis Anderson. **A Five-Color Buick and a Blue-Eyed Cat.** Westminster Press, 1977. 125 pp.

Fred, a teenager, meets Randy while looking for a summer job. Both boys apply for a job transporting pets for a pet shop. They need a good car to impress the boss, but all they have is a fourteen-year-old, five-color Buick. Mr. Palmer likes the car and hires the boys, and now Fred can earn money for himself and to help pay for car insurance. During the summer Fred and Randy learn how to handle all sorts of pets, including an obscene parrot and neurotic cat.

York, Carol Beach. **The Look-Alike Girl.** Beaufort Books, 1980. 125 pp.

Fifteen-year-old Charlene does not want to spend the summer babysitting her eight-year-old cousin, Gracie. When Charlene and her friend discover that Gracie resembles old Mrs. Mayfield's long-dead daughter, they try to encourage a friendship so Mrs. Mayfield will give her wealth to Gracie. The relationship that results is a touching and maturing experience for all the girls.

York, Carol Beach. **Stray Dog.** Beaufort Books, 1981. 96 pp.

What is Frankie to do? The Doberman followed him home from school, but his mother said no animals in the house. So Frankie keeps the dog in the barn all winter, and his brother and sister and his friend Velma help him take care of it. The children learn a lot from caring for Dog, and when they find out she will have puppies they are delighted. But after Dog's puppies are born, the children have to learn a harder lesson than they had bargained for. Easy reading.

Dating and Love

Angell, Judie. **Secret Selves.** Bradbury Press, 1979. 177 pp.

Julie is surprised at herself when she suddenly starts noticing how cute Rusty Parmette is. She's surprised because Rusty Parmette is the most chauvinistic, snobbish boy in the whole school. Julie sees another side of Rusty's personality, though, when she disguises her voice on the phone and holds a long conversation with him. These phone calls become more and more frequent, until the two build a close relationship. But off the phone it is a different story, and Julie and Rusty struggle to fit their secret conversations into their everyday life.

Austen, Jane. **Pride and Prejudice.** Signet Books, 1980. 332 pp.

In eighteenth-century England, two opinionated young people clash romantically. Elizabeth Bennet is both fascinated and annoyed by the arrogant Mr. Darcy. The courtship of the two—one too snobbish, the other too quick to judge on first impressions—makes for an enjoyable story of courtship patterns of the past. Originally published in 1813.

Baldwin, James. **If Beale Street Could Talk.** Signet Books, 1975. 242 pp.

Tish is nineteen and pregnant. Fonny is twenty-two and in jail for a crime he did not commit. Both are afraid and in love. Once they get together, they find they must stand up against daily threats and dangers in the world around them. Luckily, they have their families and each other to turn to when life becomes too tough. Mature language and situations.

Ball, John. **Miss One Thousand Spring Blossoms.** Avon Books, 1980. 272 pp.

Dick Seaton visits Japan on assignment for his American engineering company. There Dick, who has always been extremely shy with women, is introduced to the most attractive geisha, Miss One Thousand Spring Blossoms. They soon become very close friends, and even begin to fall in love. Now Dick must cope with the language barrier on both a business and personal level, but he's learning much about his host country's customs. Dick's growing respect and love for Japan lead him to find a real home for himself at last.

Borisoff, Norman. **Bewitched and Bewildered: A Spooky Love Story.** Illus. Harold Roth. Laurel-Leaf Library, 1982. 107 pp.

Nicole is more beautiful and interesting than anyone Michael has ever met. So when Nicole announces that she is going on a vacation for three weeks, Michael begs her to stay. Nicole promises that they will still see each other—even while she's away. Michael is haunted by her words, especially when they turn out to be true. Is Michael just bewildered—or has he been bewitched?

Bowen, Elizabeth. **To the North.** Avon Books, 1979. 260 pp.

London in the early twentieth century is the setting for this story of a young widow, Cecilia Summers, and her sister-in-law, Emmeline Summers, who live together in a secure and peaceful pattern. However, when they both meet a young lawyer, Mark Linkwater, their lives are thrown into emotional confusion. The relationship of the two women, and their own sense of independence in the world, are seriously affected by the new roles they must assume because of Mark. Originally published in 1932.

Brontë, Charlotte. **Jane Eyre.** Signet Books, 1960. 460 pp.

Orphaned at birth, Jane Eyre's first ten years of life are spent in the cruel and harsh care of an aunt. She is later sent to Lowood School, a charitable institution for girls. Here she learns to become a governess. Her employment by Mr. Rochester is the beginning of a strange love affair that is threatened by some evil secret hidden away in a little room in the attic of the Rochester house. Originally published in 1847.

Brontë, Emily. **Wuthering Heights.** Signet Books, 1959. 320 pp.

This is a violently romantic love story set in the English countryside in the nineteenth century. A poor young man, Heathcliff, falls madly in love with rich Catherine Earnshaw, the daughter of his benefactor. But their love only brings confusion and misery to themselves and those around them. When Catherine decides to marry neighbor Edgar Linton, Heathcliff vows eternal revenge. Originally published in 1847.

Bunn, Scott. **Just Hold On.** Delacorte Press, 1982, 151 pp.

All through high school, Charlotte Maag and Stephen Herndon have been outsiders, wounded and cut off from life at school by family troubles. But during their senior year they discover in each other new possibilities for comfort, understanding, and affection. Now, as a couple, they are suddenly welcomed into the school's inner circle, which includes handsome Rolf and his girl friend, Helen. But there are moments when Charlotte seems withdrawn from reality, moments when Stephen feels his hold on her is slipping. At times, too, Stephen senses an undercurrent to Rolf's friendship that threatens to pull him away from Charlotte. How many forms can love take—and how will he ever know which one fits him best? Mature situations.

Byrd, Elizabeth. **I'll Get By.** Viking Press, 1981. 196 pp.

Fifteen-year-old Julie Willis is "denied absolutely nothing but sex and clichés." Even so, Julie must try to reconcile her practical mother with her dashing but often absent father. When she falls in love with a college student, the poised, aspiring actress must defy both a mother and an aunt who find him "unsuitable." But nothing can erase her thoughts of handsome Rick. The glamour and glitter of the Prohibition era—just before the stock market crash—pervade this riches-to-rags story.

Cavanna, Betty. **Catchpenny Street.** Westminster Press, 1975. 223 pp.

Ellen isn't ready to decide on a husband yet—what she really wants is a career in nursing. But in the midst of World War I, the society in Camden, New Jersey, looks at nurses as just above the servant class. Ellen, not wanting to disappoint those who have sacrificed so much for her, gives up the idea of nursing instruction. She makes herself believe that waiting for marriage to Gordon is the right choice. Then Tony, a fun-loving, premed student, moves into the neighborhood, and Ellen's indecision starts all over again.

Chang, Diana. **The Gift of Love.** Ballantine Books, 1978. 185 pp.

Beth Atherton, daughter of a fabulously wealthy man, can have anything she wants—except her onetime love, Rudi Miller. He is a poor immigrant who would rather die than be without Beth. How will they ever be able to share their love with class differences forcing them apart? Based on a teleplay by Caryl Ledner.

Christman, Elizabeth. **Flesh and Spirit.** Avon Books, 1980. 176 pp.

Bridgit becomes a nun because she sees no better way to be of service to other people. This remains true until she meets Larry and his two little girls, all of whom so desperately need someone to take care of them. When Larry asks her to marry him, she is shaken. Can she break her vows? Could being a wife and mother really be what God wants her to do?

Claypool, Jane. **Jasmine Finds Love.** Westminster Press, 1982. 112 pp.

Jasmine Chan works at her father's store in Honolulu, Hawaii. Life is pleasant, but a little dull until Sammy Santiago enters her life. Soon the two become close friends as they surf, go to the zoo, and eat at fancy restaurants. But their growing love is threatened by Tom, who also likes Jasmine. The tension between the two rivals threatens to explode as the summer progresses. And Jasmine feels helpless to prevent the violence.

Claypool, Jane. **A Love for Violet.** Westminster Press, 1982. 96 pp.

Violet felt like an outsider at her school, especially when she was around Sylvia and the other girls on the basketball team. They all had pretty clothes, got good grades, and were popular. Then Tony Dawson, one the the best-looking boys around, began to notice her. Violet could hardly believe it. She thought he was Sylvia's boyfriend. What will the other girls do now that Violet seems to be taking away some of their popularity?

Conford, Ellen. **Dear Lovey Hart, I Am Desperate.** Vagabond Books, 1975. 153 pp.

Carrie is having a great time writing a column of advice to the lovelorn for her school paper. An added benefit is that she gets to be around Chip, the paper's handsome editor. But when the letters to "Lovey Hart" become more serious, Carrie does not know what to do. People are taking her advice, and trouble is usually the result. What is worse, though, is that Chip seems to be interested in Carrie's best friend Claudia. Now Carrie feels she needs some advice!

Drake, Elizabeth. **The Last Score.** Four Winds Press, 1981. 183 pp.

Tasha's father is a professional burglar, and Tasha herself can cop a mean score. Tasha has to lie to everyone about her parents and herself—except to Toby Morrison, who likes Tasha a lot. But

Toby's mother and stepfather torment him, and Tasha knows how close Toby is to running away. How can Tasha fall in love with him? But then again, how can she refuse? Mature situations.

Ellis, Carol. **Small Town Summer.** Tempo Books, 1982. 154 pp.

Maggie Papers thought she had never been as bored as she was this summer. Bailey was a dull town, and her boyfriend, Joey, was just average. Suddenly, Maggie meets an exciting new boy. There is even excitement all around her hometown as it begins to get busy carrying out a new urban renewal program. But Maggie soon begins to wonder if she can cope with all the changes in her life.

Eyerly, Jeannette. **He's My Baby, Now.** J. B. Lippincott Co., 1977. 156 pp.

Charles and Daisy, two high school lovers, find themselves in a heated debate about what to do with the baby that surprises them. Daisy wants to put the baby up for adoption, but Charles feels responsible. A wise social worker cannot smooth out the differences between them. Then, unknown to his family and friends, Charles begins a daring plan: he sets out to kidnap the baby from its hospital crib. Mature situations.

Fine, Anne. **The Summer-House Loon.** Thomas Y. Crowell Co., 1978. 127 pp.

Ione does some matchmaking over the summer with the help of her father, a blind history professor. Carolyn Hope, her father's secretary, and brilliant, unemployed Ned Hump are in love, but they have one serious problem keeping them apart: Ned refuses to get a job. Ione tricks and prods the young man into making a decision, then Ned surprises everyone when he brings home an unusual gift.

Fitzgerald, Nancy. **Mayfair.** Popular Library, 1978. 319 pp.

For Sibilla and her younger sister, the London Season is their chance to find suitable husbands, but that will take some work, as all the young women of London society are their competition. Sibilla faces even greater odds because she is determined not to make the same mistakes in choosing a husband as did her four older sisters. She wants to be happy, and to her that means more than wealth and social standing; it also means having a husband who will accept her as an equal with an intellect of her own. But Sibilla is living in the late 1800s, so finding this perfect husband is going to be a difficult task.

Foley, June. **It's No Crush, I'm in Love!** Delacorte Press, 1982. 215 pp.

Annie Cassidy must find some way to make her ninth-grade English teacher love her the same way she loves him. But it takes hard work to make a fantasy come true, so Annie gets some advice from her friend Susanna, who has much more experience with men. Their outrageous schemes are often humorous, especially one in which Annie tries to fit her teacher into her life by playing the role of her favorite heroine from *Pride and Prejudice,* Elizabeth Bennet.

Gerber, Merrill Joan. **Please Don't Kiss Me Now.** Dial Press, 1981. 218 pp.

Leslie can't figure out how her life can be so wrong: her mother and father are divorced; her mother has several new boyfriends; her father is newly married; and a favorite teacher proves unreliable. Leslie's best friend and her new boyfriend only seem to add to her confusion. Then a great tragedy helps Leslie realize some important truths about life.

Greene, Bette. **Summer of My German Soldier.** Dial Press, 1978. 230 pp.

Patty Bergen is a Jewish girl growing up in a small Arkansas town during World War II. She has been taught to hate the German POWs at a nearby internment camp. Then she meets a young Nazi soldier who changes all her resentment into admiration. When Anton escapes from prison, Patty hides him in a secret room and tends to his wounds. Then her German-hating father suspects mischief, and Patty's love for the soldier is put to the test.

Grossman, Mort. **The Summer Ends Too Soon.** Westminster Press, 1975. 159 pp.

Despite her father's protests, Diane Elizabeth takes a job as a camp counselor for the summer. Diane is assigned to assist the drama coach, Marc Gordon. She finds herself immediately attracted to him, and Marc falls in love with her. There is one potential problem—Diane is the only Protestant among the Jewish counseling and administrative staff. For the moment, Diane and Marc are involved with their work and fun, and the difference seems small. But when camp is over and Marc and Diane return to the outside world, will their feelings for one another survive?

Guest, Elissa Haden. **The Handsome Man.** Laurel-Leaf Library, 1981. 176 pp.

Who is that good-looking man? Alexandra Barnes wants to know because she thinks she is falling in love with this stranger. So Alex and her friend Angela begin to keep a record of all his moves. Soon Alex's crush becomes an obsession, and she fantasizes going out on dates with the mysterious stranger. Angela, her family, her other activities—all these begin to fade away as Alex pursues her dream man. But how can she get him to notice her?

Hall, Lynn. **Gently Touch the Milkweed.** Avon Books, 1977. 126 pp.

As more families settle in Willard's Ford, it becomes a prospering boom town. Janet, a large and awkward girl, begins to wonder if she will ever find the right man and raise her own family. She becomes friendly with the Makinichs, and it is Mr. Makinich who awakens Janet to her inner beauty and sensitivity. But then rumors start flying about a new gold discovery in nearby Kansas, and it appears that Janet must part with her new friend.

Hall, Lynn. **The Shy Ones.** Illus. Greta Elgaard. Camelot Books, 1977. 188 pp.

Robin knows that being shy is being miserable. But she doesn't know what to do or how to change either her personality or her plain looks. Then Robin saves a dog that is even more shy than she is. No one claims the dog, so Robin takes it home and names it Kate. She also gets a part-time summer job with the veterinarian who healed Kate. These two events begin to change Robin's life. Through Kate, Robin's first romance begins—and so do a number of other new and exciting things.

Hamilton, Gail. **Love Comes to Eunice K. O'Herlihy.** Atheneum Publishers, 1977. 131 pp.

The Hawaiian family that arrive at the airport have no place to stay in the Montana town, so Eunice's father brings them home. Eunice records this in her diary, just as she records every important thing that happens. But soon her diary becomes more than just a record of events. It becomes a record of her feelings, because the Hawaiian boy is beginning to attract her attention.

Hannay, Allen. **Love and Other Natural Disasters.** Atlantic Monthly Press, 1982. 241 pp.

Bubber Drumm, a nineteen-year-old in the town of Merry, Texas, is casual and good-natured about life, but he has a restless curiosity. In just one day he wrestles a tiger, has twenty-three stitches put in his leg, and thinks he has fallen in love with the divorced mother of a girl he dates. Because of this last situation, Shirley, his girlfriend, plots a wonderful revenge. Mature situations.

Hart, Bruce, and Carole Hart. **Sooner or Later.** Avon Books, 1978. 125 pp.

Thirteen-year-old Jessie is ready for romance. She wants love to be real when it does come to her, but patience is not one of Jessie's virtues. When she first sees seventeen-year-old Michael and his band entertaining at a shopping mall, Jessie is afraid he'll think she's too young. She tells him she is sixteen and asks him to give her guitar lessons. Is she also asking for trouble? She is uncertain whether she can handle Michael, her feelings about him, and the lie she's told him about her age.

Hinton, Nigel. **Getting Free.** Thomas Nelson, 1978. 189 pp.

Two English teenagers, Jo and Pete, run away to escape pressure from their families. They travel by night across Europe, fleeing their parents' search. Then Jo discovers she is pregnant, and Pete must battle a deathly blizzard as he tries to save their child.

Holmes, Marjorie. **Follow Your Dreams.** Laurel-Leaf Library, 1982. 221 pp.

Tracey has always wanted to work for a veterinarian. Now she has the chance for a summer job at a local animal hospital. Tracey soon finds herself interested in Whit, the medical assistant at the hospital. When he shows no signs of interest, though, Tracey decides to force him to notice her. Then Diane shows up and threatens her romantic plans.

Holmes, Marjorie. **Saturday Night.** Laurel-Leaf Library, 1982. 221 pp.

Can Danny Keller, the most popular boy in town, really be interested in her? Carly's friends warn her Danny is unpredictable, but she is too much in love to notice. Going out with him is a dream come true for Carly. It is only little by little that she begins to think her friends might be right about her new boyfriend.

Holmes, Marjorie. **Senior Trip.** Laurel-Leaf Library, 1982. 237 pp.

Being senior class president is not easy. Day-to-day problems are bad enough, but Fran finds that organizing and raising the money for a class trip to Washington, D.C., is taking up all her time and energy. But everything seems worth the trouble when the class arrives in the nation's capital. Fran's trip becomes even more memorable when she meets Vance Crandall. Can she really be in love? But what about Nick, her hometown boyfriend?

Holmes, Marjorie. **Sunday Morning.** Laurel-Leaf Library, 1982. 192 pp.

After a stormy romance with Danny Keller, Carly Williams finds it hard to recover. Going out with Chuck Richards has helped, for Carly finds him kind and considerate. Then Danny returns to town after a time in the army. Carly soon discovers her old feelings for Danny have not completely died away. What is she supposed to do now? Originally published as *Love Is a Hopscotch Thing.*

Klevin, Jill Ross. **The Summer of the Sky-Blue Bikini.** Scholastic Book Services, 1978. 136 pp.

Fifteen-year-old Abby isn't exactly looking forward to spending her summer on Castle Island with her lawyer mother and her pesky younger sister, Mel. However, the prospects of a boring summer vacation quickly change when she meets Guy. He is not only handsome but also intelligent and understanding. Abby finds herself in love for the first time. The only problem is that Abby's new friends on the island don't approve of Guy due to gossip about his family. Because of her relationship with Guy, Abby learns that she can stand up for what she believes in.

Koehn, Ilse. **Tilla.** Greenwillow Books, 1981. 240 pp.

World War II is coming to an end in Germany. In Dresden, fifteen-year-old Tilla is returning home after a thirty-mile bicycle ride into the countryside for potatoes. To her horror, she finds the buildings on her street are now just a pile of rubble. Her mother and brother are dead. Now Tilla and her friend Rolf must establish a life for themselves in what is left of their country.

Kropp, Paul. **Wilted.** Coward, McCann & Geoghegan, 1980. 111 pp.

Anyone who must wear glasses already has a ruined life. Or at least that's what it seems like to fourteen-year-old Danny. In fact, nothing seems to be going right for him. Then Danny meets Samantha, the girl of his dreams. But how can he get her attention? There are incredible odds facing Danny—such as competing against the class jock—but he finally gets his big chance to get to know his dream girl.

Lee, Mildred. **The People Therein.** Signet Vista Books, 1982. 230 pp.

At eighteen, Lanthy Farr has long resigned herself to the fact that no one in the Great Smoky Mountains wants a lame girl for a wife. Then Drew Thorndike, the tall handsome stranger from Boston, shows up in Dewfall Gap, looking for a place to stay. Theirs is a magical romance. The two give no thought to the future—a future in which both have to pay a terrible price for their few brief moments of love.

Linden, Catherine. **Close Associates.** Avon Books, 1980. 208 pp.

Bright, ambitious, beautiful, and sensible Elena Perry receives a promotion in her real estate office. She takes it because it's a challenge, and Elena loves challenges. The assignment takes her out of the city and to a charming New England village. Elena soon learns, though, that the outward simplicity and loveliness of the place and its people are dangerously deceptive. A powerful little group will stop at nothing to keep their town the way it is. Their energies at the moment are directed against housing contractor Luke Maxwell, with whom Elena must work. Mature situations.

Lingard, Joan. **No Place for Love.** Scholastic Book Services, 1973. 189 pp.

Kevin and Sally are in love. That is not a problem for most people, but Kevin is Catholic and Sally is Protestant, and they both live in Belfast, Northern Ireland. The only sensible thing for them to do is to get married and move to London. Once in London, however, they begin to wonder if their love can survive in such a strange, impersonal, even hostile city. They begin to think that moving home, with all its religious strife, might be better after all. Originally published as *Into Exile.*

Lingard, Joan. **The Pilgrimage.** Thomas Nelson, 1976. 158 pp.

Two young lovers, Maggie and James, take a trip to Scotland in hopes of learning about their ancestors. But as they discover the secrets of the past, they discover some frightening things about their own relationship. Instead of bringing them closer, their research seems to be feeding hidden grudges in each of them. Then this journey into the past brings them an adventure that carries them to a world much wilder than any they had ever dreamed of.

Lingard, Joan. **The Reunion.** Thomas Nelson, 1978. 158 pp.

After saving her money and flying from Scotland to visit Phil, her Canadian boyfriend, Maggie is brokenhearted to learn that he has another lover. Maggie refuses the job that awaits her and runs to the city, searching for comfort. And just as she is beginning to recover from her hurt, Phil shows up.

Mazer, Norma Fox. **Up in Seth's Room.** Delacorte Press, 1979. 199 pp.

From the very first moment that Finn saw Seth, she knew she loved him. Seth was handsome, smart, and daring; why, he was the one that set up all the secret night meetings so her parents wouldn't be suspicious. And now that he's rented a room, their meetings will be cozy and comfortable. But Seth has some new ideas about their relationship, and Finn isn't sure she is ready for the grown-up things he wants to do. Mature situations.

Monjo, F. N. **The Porcelain Pagoda.** Illus. Richard Egielski. Viking Press, 1976. 243 pp.

Kitty, a sixteen-year-old girl in the early nineteenth century, is incurably romantic. Her desire for adventure is satisfied when her father takes his entire family on a voyage from New York to China in hopes of making his fortune in the trading of silk and spices. Kitty meets a dashing opium smuggler on the high seas, and she must make a decision that will drastically change her life.

Mulford, Philippa Greene. **If It's Not Funny, Why Am I Laughing?** Delacorte Press, 1982. 166 pp.

For Mimi Canfield, adjusting to her mother's Hollywood career and her father's remarriage is easier than adjusting to the sexual pressures at high school. The tension is maddening. Her best friend won't stop talking about her love life, and handsome Lars keeps pushing Mimi for a "relationship." Yet it seems that just about everything, including sex, makes Mimi laugh. She starts giggling at all the wrong moments. "What's so funny?" Mimi keeps asking herself. "And why don't I want to get involved with Lars?"

Murphy, James F., Jr. **The Mill.** Avon Books, 1981. 312 pp.

With only hunger and poverty facing her in Ireland, Mary Roark decides to try her luck in America. But the young nation is filled with immigrants like Mary, and she must work as a cheap laborer in a textile mill. Mary's beauty soon catches the attention of a rich and powerful man who decides to help her. Little does Mary realize that her childhood love, Brendan McMahon, has come to America to find her. Mature situations.

Ogilvie, Elisabeth. **A Steady Kind of Love.** Scholastic Book Services, 1959. 187 pp.

Ellen looks forward to a summer at home before beginning the adventure and challenge of art school in Boston. But the events of the summer and her changing relationship with Joey bring confusion and indecision. Should she risk change, or is her island where she truly belongs? There are no "right" answers. Originally published as *How Wide the Heart*.

Oppenheimer, Joan. **The Voices of Julie.** Wildfire Books, 1979. 156 pp.

Julie wonders why Tony feels he can boss her around. She has a great life except for this—parties, few chores, and an easygoing aunt to live with. If only Tony would leave her alone, Julie thinks. But her opinion of him begins to change one horrible night when she becomes lost in a fog.

Pascal, Francine. **My First Love and Other Disasters.** Laurel-Leaf Library, 1981. 173 pp.

Victoria is fifteen and in love with a boy who doesn't even know she exists. She takes a summer job as a mother's helper on Fire Island just to be near him. She has to spend her days doing endless household chores, but it's all worth it because Jim begins to notice her and even to like her. But is this really what Victoria wants? Mature situation.

Peck, Richard. **Close Enough to Touch.** Delacorte Press, 1981. 133 pp.

After Matt Moran loses Dory, his first and only love, he finds it impossible to hang around with her rich friends any longer. He's trapped in his pain over Dory, and it almost seems as though he doesn't want to get out. That is, until he meets Margaret Chasen. She refuses to indulge his self-pity, but she provides a chance for Matt to take some new views on life.

Pilcher, Rosamunde. **The Carousel.** St. Martin's Press, 1982. 184 pp.

Prue Shackleton is intelligent, artistic, and independent—and thoroughly bored with her dreary job in London. But her vacation at her Aunt Phoebe's cottage in Cornwall is destined to change her life. First she meets Charlotte Collis, a timid but most unusual child. Then she meets the handsome, unpredictable artist Daniel, a man unlike any she has known in stuffy London society. But it is in energetic, creative Aunt Phoebe, whose heart is big enough to hold them all, that the three come together—almost before they are ready.

Posner, Grace. **In My Sister's Eyes.** Beaufort Books, 1980. 144 pp.

Billy's senior year of high school is turning out to be pretty good. He's on the tennis team, playing much better than the year before, and Chrissie, the school's prettiest cheerleader, is interested in him! But life is not all rosy; both Billy and Chrissie have serious problems they must face on their own.

Rees, Barbara. **Harriet Dark: Branwell Brontë's Lost Novel.** Warner Books, 1980. 223 pp.

In this story, based on a novel supposedly written by the brother of the Brontë sisters but never found among his papers, five-year-old Harriet Dark is brought to Thirleby Hall in the 1820s by its owner, Mr. Ogilvy. She is put to work as a kitchen servant, but she discovers the life of the lords and ladies and decides she wants that for herself in spite of advice to stay in her own place. Years later, as a twenty-two-year-old woman, Harriet must decide between her selfish plans and the love of a young man.

Robins, Denise. **The Long Shadow.** Avon Books, 1979. 191 pp.

Candida's love for a young American singer, Vincent Rhiner, blinds her to the wishes of her mother and the warnings of her friends. A terrible secret from the past may ruin Candida's life if she doesn't discover it in time.

Robins, Denise. **The Seagull's Cry.** Avon Books, 1979. 191 pp.

The Seagull's Cry is a small hotel in a village in Cornwall, England. Because the hotel used to be the property of a well-liked family in that village, the local people are not very friendly toward the hotel's new owner, Martin Wyde. Only young Tansy Trehearn is willing to go to work for Martin as his business secretary. Despite several rumors that hint at a scandal in Martin's past, Tansy tries to remain loyal. When the gossip concerns Tansy's own sister, however, the relationship between Tansy and Martin becomes very strained. Finally, a ferocious storm causes everyone to come to important decisions.

Snyder, Zilpha Keatley. **A Fabulous Creature.** Atheneum Publishers, 1981. 240 pp.

James Archer Fielding is sixteen when he decides to try to become a ladies' man over the summer. But he runs into a snag: his parents insist he go with them to the Sierras. James is sure the wilderness is the last place he wants to be. Once there, however, he quickly discovers a number of interesting diversions, including an awesome buck and two very different, but very interesting, girls. One of the girls, Diane, is a hunter, and Jim soon becomes worried that the buck will become her next target.

Springstubb, Tricia. **Give and Take.** Laurel-Leaf Library, 1982. 253 pp.

Polly and Naomi have been best friends for seven years, ever since fourth grade. Shy, sensitive Naomi knows she can always count on popular Polly for sound advice, particularly when it comes to boys. But when Naomi uses Polly's words of wisdom on her new boyfriend, Danny, she quickly regrets it. And as Polly becomes more and more involved with Crow, a boy who doesn't quite fit in with her popular friends, she realizes that her relationship with him is jeopardizing her place in the crowd. New loves, old friends—does growing up mean choosing between them?

Taylor, Sydney. **Ella of All of a Kind Family.** Illus. Gail Owens. E. P. Dutton, 1978. 133 pp.

Eighteen-year-old Ella, the oldest of six children, wants privacy, especially now that Jules is back from World War I. Ella also wants the glamour of a singing career since being discovered by a famous talent scout. Now she must decide between marrying Jules or the excitement of being a professional singer.

Vaughter, Carolyn. **West Wind Wild.** Avon Books, 1981. 409 pp.

She grew up on the Oklahoma prairie, as young and strong as the frontier she lived on. Her father, a preacher, nicknamed her Miss Rowdy. She was the love of his life, and the Indians were his bitterest foe. Then Miss Rowdy falls deeply in love with a full-blooded Indian, and her peaceful family life is shattered. Miss Rowdy is as headstrong as her father. Their feud stuns all Oklahoma. Mature situations.

Vogelman, Joyce. **Getting It Right.** Avon Books, 1981. 204 pp.

Julie was lonely and felt like an outsider teaching high school out in farming country. Then, by accident, she meets Tony Harrison. He is not much interested in books and cultural things, but he is considerate and kind. He is also in love with Julie. But Julie begins to wonder if Tony's love is enough for her to build a life upon. If only Tony will wait for her while she goes after her own ambitions and dreams.

Walsh, Jill Paton. **Fireweed.** Avon Books, 1972. 141 pp.

Bill and Julie survive the terrible London blitz of World War II and find friendship and love in the chaos of the war. Their strength together helps them get through the destruction, but they realize they will bear some psychological scars long after the battles are over.

Wood, Phyllis Anderson. **I Think This Is Where We Came In.** Westminster Press, 1977. 155 pp.

Three young friends set out for a vacation in the Sierra wilderness. But things are bound to change when Maggie, Paul's sister, becomes Mike's girl. This is a story about how friendship turns to love, and how love can create joys and tensions between people.

Woodford, Peggy. **Please Don't Go.** Avon Books, 1975. 192 pp.

Mary is a fifteen-year-old English girl who spends a summer in France. She lives with a French family and spends most of her time with Mic, a French girl, and Joël, a sixteen-year-old boy. When Mary returns to England, she realizes how much she misses Joël and what he means to her. The two young people write letters during the year, and Mary returns to France the next summer. But Mary's summer of love seems to be heading for tragedy.

Yolen, Jane. **The Gift of Sarah Barker.** Viking Press, 1981. 155 pp.

Though set in a Shaker community in the mid-1800s, this love story of Sarah and Abel has elements that make it very much like those of young people in love today. But in New Vale, where Sarah and Abel live, they have the added problem that the sexes are separated and are not even permitted to speak to one another alone. Under these conditions Sarah and Abel wonder how they can continue their love for one another.

Zindel, Paul. **The Girl Who Wanted a Boy.** Bantam Books, 1982. 123 pp.

Sibella Cametta is an unusual fifteen-year-old. She loves electronic, automotive, and mechanical problems, and her dream is to own and operate a gas station when she graduates from high school. With all her brains, though, Sibella still has not come up with a plan to get a boy interested in her. So she decides to take drastic measures. Sibella spots her perfect boy in a newspaper picture. Now she is ready to use all her intelligence and energy to attract his attention. Mature situation.

Racial, Ethnic, or Religious Groups

Aleichem, Sholom (translator Tamara Kanana). **The Adventures of Menahem-Mendl.** Paragon Books, 1979. 222 pp.

In Czarist Russia, the letters Menahem-Mendl sends his loyal wife Sheineh-Sheindle help them share the new and bewildering experience of being separated. Always one to look on the bright side, Menahem-Mendl tells his wife of funny and frustrating experiences with a series of strange characters, like the author who cannot write.

Arrick, Fran. **Chernowitz!** Bradbury Press, 1981. 165 pp.

For two years all that Bobby Cherno hears from Emmett Sundback is vicious name calling whenever the two pass each other in Middleboro High. Soon Emmett convinces others to bother Bobby. He is able to take the harassment quietly until he finds even his best friends are calling him names. When Emmett's meanness hurts Bobby's parents, Bobby decides to teach Emmett a lesson. But the plan for revenge becomes more complicated than Bobby expects.

Asher, Sandy. **Daughters of the Law.** Beaufort Books, 1980. 157 pp.

Ruthie Morgenthau has a hard decision to make. Should she be bas mitzvah or not? Her Jewish heritage requires it, and her Aunt Sarah is in favor of the idea. But Ruthie's father, now dead, hated religion, and Ruthie doesn't want to be disloyal to him. Ruthie's mother is no help; she just sits and thinks about her tragic past. When the political situation in Ruthie's town becomes difficult, she realizes what she must do.

Asher, Sandy. **Summer Begins.** Elsevier/Nelson Books, 1980. 173 pp.

After much debate, Summer Smith finally decides what to write as her editorial assignment for her eighth-grade class newspaper. She writes about how non-Christians must feel to be acting and singing in the Christmas program every year at school. Surely, Summer thinks, this story can't be too controversial. But she is wrong—soon the entire school is arguing about her article. Summer's article makes headlines in the town paper, her English teacher resigns, and the principal becomes angry. With the help of two friends, Summer tries to straighten out the mess her article has caused.

Baer, Edith. **A Frost in the Night.** Pantheon Books, 1980. 208 pp.

If you are Jewish in the late 1930s and Hitler is rising to power, Germany is not a safe place to live. This story contrasts Eva's warm safe family life with the frightening and puzzling incidents that are occurring all around her. Although this is a fictional book, it is written by a woman who lost her entire family in the Holocaust; the events that she describes might really have happened.

Barrett, William. **The Lilies of the Field.** Illus. Bert Silverman. Popular Library, 1975. 127 pp.

Homer Smith, a young black man, is traveling around the Southwest in the early twentieth century, picking up odd jobs here and there to finance his "sightseeing tour." Little does he know when he hires himself out to a group of German nuns that his one day's work will turn out to be the major achievement of his life. Homer and the nuns are faced with almost impossible obstacles to overcome before their dream can be fulfilled.

Bosse, Malcolm J. **Ganesh.** Thomas Y. Crowell Co., 1981. 185 pp.

When his father dies, young Jeffrey Moore (called Ganesh) must leave India to live with his aunt. But Aunt Betty lives a world away in the American Midwest. His father never told him anything about America, so everything is new, exciting, and a bit disturbing for Ganesh. As he learns about American culture, he wants to make friends. But his schoolmates find his interests—Hinduism, yoga, and mantra—strange. Ganesh begins to wonder if he will ever be able to be really close to anyone his own age.

Brooks, Jerome. **Make Me a Hero.** E. P. Dutton, 1980. 152 pp.

In the 1940s, when Jake decides it's time to strike out on his own, he doesn't know which way to turn. Then he finds a job and meets Harry, a boy who is about to be officially recognized as "grown-up" at his bar mitzvah. As a result of meeting Harry, Jake does some serious thinking about religion, values, and manhood.

Brown, Irene Bennett. **Morning Glory Afternoon.** Atheneum Publishers, 1981. 219 pp.

Jessamyn Farmer tries to escape her past by becoming a telephone switchboard operator in Ardensville, Kansas, in 1924. But soon the peaceful town is disturbed by a series of incidents that reveal the strong prejudice of a certain group of people against anyone who is different. When some of Jessy's friends are persecuted, she decides to forget her personal sorrows and take a stand against the group of Ku Klux Klan members who have been the source of all the trouble.

Chamberlain, Barbara. **The Prisoners' Sword.** Illus. Arnie Kohn. David C. Cook Publishing Co., 1978. 117 pp.

Young Nathan, a Quaker growing up in seventeenth-century London, doesn't understand why he has to continue to dress in a plain gray suit, Quaker fashion. Such dress only makes him the passive target for jokes and abuses of those who don't believe in religious freedom. When he and his family are forced to flee the city to escape the Black Plague, they are captured and imprisoned by English soldiers for going against the King's church. In a filthy jail cell, Nathan begins to understand what his religious faith means.

Cheatham, K. Follis. **Life on a Cool Plastic Ice Floe.** Westminster Press, 1978. 180 pp.

Danny Raynor is an American Indian boy who has been in and out of detention centers. But he risks trouble once more to prevent a white family from adopting his sister.

Childress, Alice. **A Short Walk.** Bard Books, 1981. 333 pp.

America changed a lot between 1900 and 1950, and so does Cora James. She was born into the world of the deep South—a world where a black woman had to learn "her place." But when Cora moves north to Harlem and discovers Marcus Garvey and his ideas of African Nationalism, she learns to feel pride in being black. Mature language and situation.

Collier, James Lincoln, and Christopher Collier. **Jump Ship to Freedom.** Delacorte Press, 1981. 198 pp.

Jack Arabus, a slave during the mid-1700s, earns his family's freedom from their Connecticut master, Captain Ivers, by fighting in the Revolutionary War. But Jack drowns at sea, so the captain refuses to turn over the military notes that will free son Daniel and his mother. Daniel, age fourteen, makes a daring move to recover those notes. Instead he finds himself on board a ship bound for the West Indies, where he discovers he's to be sold.

Dodson, Owen. **Boy at the Window.** Popular Library, 1977. 174 pp.

Life has bitter lessons for a poor black boy growing up in Brooklyn in the 1920s. At nine, Coin Foreman is too young to have to cope with all the terrible things that happen to him: learning what the word "nigger" means, discovering that miracles happen only in the movies, watching his mother die, and finding and immediately losing a friend. Even Uncle Troy, who seems at first to want him, eventually abandons him.

Dodson, Owen. **Come Home Early, Child.** Popular Library, 1977. 221 pp.

When both Coin's mother and father die, it is up to his older sister, Agnes, to keep the family together. It is a job Agnes feels she can handle better if she joins forces with Miss Lucy, a family friend. To Coin, Miss Lucy is no friend, but a mean, spiteful woman whose every word and action bring him pain. When Agnes also dies, Coin finds that escape from Miss Lucy means running off to join the navy. There Coin begins to find himself and the peace he has been denied.

Dunnahoo, Terry. **This Is Espie Sanchez.** E. P. Dutton, 1976. 156 pp.

"Don't get involved" is advice Esperanza (Espie) Sanchez finds hard to follow. Espie now works for the police department that picked her up as a runaway a year ago. When beautiful Teresa Hernandes walks into the police department late one night, Espie feels sorry for her. Her work as an Explorer Scout leads her to discover the body of a dead boy as well as to become involved in a series of dangerous adventures revolving around Teresa.

Dunnahoo, Terry. **Who Cares about Espie Sanchez?** E. P. Dutton, 1975. 152 pp.

Espie Sanchez is fed up with her life. Thinking there is absolutely no one who cares a thing about her, she has spent the last few years running away from a bad home situation. Now Espie is faced with either going to a juvenile hall or moving in with Mrs. Garcia, who would be her guardian. Espie slowly learns that Mrs. Garcia cares about her and so does her roommate, Denise, who introduces her to the Law Enforcement Explorer Group. Espie's spirits and her outlook brighten even more when she meets handsome Carlos Medina, one of the young Explorers.

Dunnahoo, Terry. **Who Needs Espie Sanchez?** E. P. Dutton, 1977.
138 pp.

At home, Espie's parents have always warned her not to get
involved in the world. But Espie has always needed more than what
she has, so she runs away. She becomes a scout with the Los
Angeles Law Enforcement Explorer Group, and now she is involved
in the life of a young girl who has just had a tragic accident.
Desperately, Espie tries to rebuild the crushed hope of the young
woman, while she tries to find a meaningful life of her own.

Dyer, T. A. **The Whipman Is Watching.** Houghton Mifflin Co., 1979.
177 pp.

Thirteen-year-old Angie tries desperately to keep her family from
showing their Indian ways to the white world outside the reservation. At school, she is embarrassed by her troublemaker cousin,
Cultus. The final blow to Angie's pride comes when her stubborn,
traditional grandmother preaches Indian values to the school principal. Then Cultus is sent to a juvenile home, and Angie is forced to
deal with painful feelings about her family and her culture.

Evans, Mari. **JD.** Illus. Jerry Pinkney. Camelot Books, 1975. 61 pp.

Eight-year-old JD is black and lives in a housing project called
Meadow Hill. His day-to-day life is hard and cold as he has to
defend his little brother from bullies and worry about whether his
mother can pay the rent. But he has other problems: he tries hard to
figure out a way to pay his book rental fee at school, and he watches,
brokenhearted, as his neighborhood sports hero shoots heroin.

Fiedler, Jean. **The Year the World Was out of Step with Jancy Fried.**
Harcourt Brace Jovanovich, 1981. 156 pp.

Being Jewish was not really much of an issue in Jancy's life until
her twelfth birthday in 1936. Soon world events begin to touch
Jancy in disturbing ways, making her more aware of her religious
heritage. Her cousin in Austria writes of the troubles Jews are
already experiencing because of the Nazi party. Then one of Jancy's
friends decides Jancy needs a lecture on "being Jewish." Jancy
realizes it is time for her to discover her place in the world.

Gessner, Lynne. **Brother to the Navajo.** Elsevier/Nelson Books, 1979.
144 pp.

In 1909, young Paul Corbett, his widowed mother, his uncle, and
his retarded brother are stranded and face death in the Arizona
desert. Eventually, Paul's family comes to a trading post run by a

white man. They are afraid of the Indians, but the trader, Fletch, calms them down. Fletch explains the Navajos trade for goods and explains their bartering practices. Paul likes Fletch, and because of Fletch's explanations, he makes friends with some of the Navajo boys. But Paul's mother wants to leave Arizona, and Paul tries some tricks to get her to stay.

Gessner, Lynne. **To See a Witch.** Thomas Nelson, 1978. 144 pp.

Twelve-year-old Kopi loves the cliff dwellings of Big Tree Village because here he can hunt and have all kinds of fun. This peacefulness is disturbed one day when a witch predicts that only disaster awaits him. When he returns home, he finds that his mother has taken in a young girl abandoned by another Indian tribe. He becomes extremely jealous of his family's attention to the newcomer. Later, Kopi becomes angry when his cousin Chongova shoots his dog, claiming the dog is a witch. Most disturbing, however, is the fact he had not been accepted into the mysteries of the kiva, a special ceremonial place for men. A series of strange events helps Kopi lose some of his childishness and prove his manhood in spite of the witch's predictions.

Graham, Lorenz. **Return to South Town.** Thomas Y. Crowell Co., 1976. 245 pp.

David Williams and his family left South Town because of its fierce racial hatred. Now he is returning to the Virginia town as a doctor. They say things have changed in fifteen years, but have they? Will the town accept a black doctor? He will soon find out, for David is determined to make a success in the town that once scorned him.

Hale, Janet Campbell. **The Owl's Song.** Avon Books, 1976. 144 pp.

Fourteen-year-old Billy White Hawk feels trapped and alone in Benewah, an Idaho Indian reservation. His mother and his best friend are dead, and it seems only old people are left in Benewah. So Billy decides to begin a new life in California with his half-sister. Once there, he finds fulfillment in painting scenes of Indian land and culture. But every day Billy becomes more aware that the tensions and prejudices around him threaten to change his character for the worse.

Hamilton, Dorothy. **Linda's Rain Tree.** Illus. Ivan Moon. Herald Press, 1975. 118 pp.

Linda's friends suddenly want to do things that, at age eleven, Linda doesn't want to do. Why doesn't she fit in any more? Her family's love, her joy in people who have high standards, and her excitement for learning set Linda apart from most people her age. She is lonely much of the time, but she finds that seeing life in a different way has its own rewards for this black girl. Easy reading.

Hassler, Jon. **Jemmy.** McElderry Books, 1981. 175 pp.

At seventeen, Jemmy Stott seems destined for a life of poverty. Her father orders her to quit school and take care of him and the family because her Indian mother is dead. However, a chance friendship with the Chapmans leads to Jemmy's discovery of her real talent as an artist. This discovery gives her some hope for a future away from the family.

Henderson, Lois T. **The Blessing Deer.** Chariot Books, 1980. 207 pp.

Ellen is just beginning to cope with her mother's death. She is planning to take an exciting art class with Clarisse, her best friend. She is learning to cook and to take care of the house for her father. However, racial tensions erupt, and Clarisse, who is black, tells her that they can never be friends again. Ellen decides to escape the strife by spending some time with her aunt in Canada. Ellen doesn't find the quiet that she wants in Canada, but she does find the inner strength to deal with some of the harsh bigotry and hatred in the world.

Hentoff, Nat. **The Day They Came to Arrest the Book.** Delacorte Press, 1982. 169 pp.

Maybe Mark Twain was just showing life the way it was, but a group of students at George Mason High School insist that *Huckleberry Finn* is not fit to read. Demands lead to more demands, and townspeople begin to choose sides and take a stand on censorship within the schools. Before long, the conflict draws national attention. Will the school board find Mark Twain guilty of being a racist and sexist—a writer of an immoral book?

Herman, Charlotte. **What Happened to Heather Hopkowitz?** E. P. Dutton, 1981. 186 pp.

Heather is fourteen when her parents tell her they plan to take a Caribbean cruise. They decide Heather will stay with Orthodox Jewish friends, the Greenwalds. She hardly looks forward to a bleak month without her junk food. But suddenly food becomes less important when Heather meets Heshy Rabinowitz, a boy in her synagogue youth group. Heather soon realizes that her food habits are not the only changes taking place in her life.

Heyman, Anita. **Exit from Home.** Crown Publishers, 1977. 277 pp.

Samuel, a Jewish boy living in a small village in Russia at the turn of the century, is doing well in his religious studies. But he is becoming more and more discontented; he no longer wants to become a rabbi. He is more excited with the struggles taking place in Russian society, so he begins reading underground books and helps to defend his village against the attacks on the Jews. Eventually, he gives up his religious studies altogether to take part in the Revolution of 1905. When it fails, he risks everything for a chance at a better life.

Holman, Felice. **The Murderer.** Charles Scribner's Sons, 1978. 151 pp.

The children of Polish miners in Ashlymine, Pennsylvania, call Hershy a "murderer" because he's Jewish. They bully him, tease him, and beat him up. Confused and hurt, Hershy also listens to the daily news about the Great Depression, Roosevelt—and Hitler persecuting German Jews. If Jews are God's chosen people, it seems to Hershy God's forgotten them.

Hope, Christopher. **A Separate Development.** Charles Scribner's Sons, 1980. 199 pp.

Harry Moto, a black boy growing up in South Africa, has no ID card. Having no ID card means having no protection under the law. Thus, when Harry is caught with a rich, white girlfriend, he feels it is necessary to flee to avoid charges under the Immorality Act. Displaced and misclassified, he tries to disappear into the squalid life-style of the underprivileged. But Harry soon discovers that he isn't safe anywhere. And he learns even more about the system that controls his life when he is forced to write a "confession" in exchange for freedom. Mature situations.

Hunter, Kristin. **The Lakestown Rebellion.** Charles Scribner's Sons, 1978. 314 pp.

The small black community in Lakestown is threatened when plans are made to build a new highway right through town, destroying homes and businesses. The whites call this progress, but the blacks call it disaster and decide to sabotage the construction efforts. Abe, the black mayor, is willing to go along with the construction of the highway because he's been promised a better job. His wife, Bella, however, is a rebel who has some ideas of her own. So Bella, an off-beat professor, and an eccentric doctor conspire to keep the highway from being built. The rebellion is on, filled with hilarious events, tragedy, courage, and ingenuity.

Hunter, Kristin. **The Soul Brothers and Sister Lou.** Avon Books, 1975. 192 pp.

In the ghetto of a big city, Lou Hawkins lives in a small apartment with her big family. Life is discouraging until she finds a way to have fun. In the front room of her brother's print shop she forms a club with five other blacks. After much work and imagination, Lou and her friends form a successful singing group. But their adventures are not over, for the rough city life tests their courage more than once. (Lewis Carroll Shelf Award)

Karp, Naomie J. **The Turning Point.** Harcourt Brace Jovanovich, 1976. 154 pp.

Hannah Brand, age twelve, loves her life in the Bronx—she has a close family, close friends, and things to look forward to at school. So when her parents buy their dream house in the suburbs, Hannah is angry about leaving her familiar world. Hannah brightens when she first sees the new house, though, but before long her sharp tongue makes her enemies, not friends, with the neighborhood kids and with students and teachers at school. Hannah suddenly is an outsider. But it isn't just her sharp tongue that makes her an outcast—it's also the fact that she's Jewish and living in a Protestant community. When Hannah's best friend, Shirley, comes for a visit, though, she causes a real sensation in this smug neighborhood.

Kata, Elizabeth. **A Patch of Blue.** Popular Library, 1975. 142 pp.

Selina has been blind since that day long ago when she was hit in the face with the acid her mother threw at her father. In her world she can remember blue, red, and white—and black. Black is not pleasant for it is the color of her mother's heart and of her world. Then one day in the park she meets Gordon, who opens up her world, gives her hope, and offers her love. Gordon is black, but for the moment, Selina doesn't realize this.

Lee, Harper. **To Kill a Mockingbird.** Popular Library, 1977. 284 pp.

Atticus Finch, a lawyer in a small Southern town in about 1930, defends a black man wrongly accused of rape. The town reacts violently against this, putting Atticus and his two children, Scout and Jem, in danger. As seen through Scout's eyes, the story shows the bigotry present in the town and forces readers to evaluate their own attitudes toward justice and social change. (Pulitzer Prize)

Marger, Mary Ann. **Justice at Peachtree.** Elsevier/Nelson Books, 1980. 140 pp.

In 1950, Cary Bowen, a senior who is now working on the town newspaper, is becoming more aware of the racial prejudice in Peachtree, South Carolina. Cary soon becomes personally involved in the exciting movement to work out the racial problems in her Southern town.

Mathis, Sharon Bell. **Listen for the Fig Tree.** Avon Books, 1975. 143 pp.

Sixteen-year-old Marvina (Muffin), blind since she was a small child, struggles to help her alcoholic mother survive the death of her husband. When Muffin's father was shot in the streets of New York on Christmas Day a year ago, her mother turned to drinking and now refuses all sympathy and help. It is at Kwanza—a seven-day Afro-American celebration that begins on Christmas night—that Muffin decides to face the reality of her mother's condition and her own growing up.

Mills, Claudia. **Luisa's American Dream.** Four Winds Press, 1981. 155 pp.

Luisa Ruiz is secretly ashamed of her Cuban family; they're poor, noisy, and fat, and they speak English with an accent. When she meets and falls for a well-to-do white American boy, she's sure he wouldn't love her if he knew her background, so she lies about her family. Finally, she comes to realize that what she really wants has been right under her nose all the time.

Myers, Walter Dean. **Fast Sam, Cool Clyde, and Stuff.** Avon Books, 1978. 159 pp.

When "Stuff" Williams moves to the black and Puerto Rican neighborhood of Harlem's 116th Street, he learns that the street life is tough, but he makes friends with Fast Sam and Cool Clyde. The three join with some neighborhood girls to form a society called the 116th Street Good People. Together they try to help one another and people in need, including Carnation Charlie, a junkie.

Ofek, Uriel (translator Israel I. Taslitt). **Smoke over Golan.** Illus. Lloyd Bloom. Harper & Row, Publishers, 1979. 184 pp.

Eita Avivi learned that life in Israel is full of surprises. His mother arranged for a state teacher to come live at the farm and teach Eita in a toolshed converted into a classroom. Then one day a jeep comes to the farm, and a man in military uniform orders his father and the farmhand, Albert, to join their assigned army unit immediately. It is the beginning of the 1973 Yom Kippur War between Israel and Egypt and Syria. And Eita, his family, and his friends are soon faced with excitement and danger on their homes near the war front.

Powers, John R. **The Last Catholic in America: A Fictionalized Memoir.** Popular Library, 1976. 224 pp.

Eddie Ryan's experiences at St. Bastion's Grammar School during the 1950s are both funny and revealing. Eddie's Catholic school education shows him how his religion will affect his life forever. The nuns, the other students, the strict discipline, the classwork, and the religious lessons are all important parts of Eddie's school days.

Richter, Conrad. **A Country of Strangers.** Schocken Books, 1982. 169 pp.

In the late 1700s young Stone Girl was taken captive and adopted by Indians. She soon became accustomed to their way of life. However, when she is fifteen the Indians give up their captives, and Stone Girl returns to her white family, only to discover that they no longer have anything in common. This sends Stone Girl on a strange journey.

Rockwood, Joyce. **Long Man's Song.** Holt, Rinehart & Winston, 1975. 207 pp.

When Soaring Hawk, a pre-Columbian Cherokee Indian, diagnoses his sister's illness as caused by angry fish-spirits, he is confident of his future as a great medicine man. But the illness changes suddenly, and his sister is near death. Plagued by self-doubt, Soaring Hawk must enter into a desperate battle of mystical power with Scratcher, the evil rival of Soaring Hawk's powerful uncle.

Rockwood, Joyce. **To Spoil the Sun.** Holt, Rinehart & Winston, 1976. 180 pp.

A rattlesnake in a cornfield in the dead of winter? This is the first of four omens to cause Rain Dove, Mink, and the Cherokee people of the Seven Clans to fear for their lives. It is the sixteenth century and the Indians are being killed by an "invisible fire" they cannot understand. The fire turns out to be smallpox brought to America by European explorers. And it soon seems that the disease will destroy the Cherokee way of life forever.

Rose, Anne. **Refugee.** Dial Press, 1977. 118 pp.

What would it be like to adjust to America as a twelve-year-old Belgian Jewish girl who has been forced to leave home in the late 1930s because of Hitler's army? Elke has this adjustment problem and is also worried about those people still trapped in Europe. Can Elke ever get used to a strange new country and feel inner peace as long as people she cares about are still threatened by the Nazis? Mature situations.

Sebestyen, Ouida. **Words by Heart.** Atlantic Monthly Press, 1979. 162 pp.

It is 1910, and Lena and her family are the only black people in Bethel Springs, a small town in the Southwest. Lena soon learns she has a good mind, and she uses it to win a scripture-reciting contest. Lena's father dreams of a better future for the family in this town, but Lena learns she must struggle to make these dreams come true. Even with her cleverness and courage, Lena finds the path to advancement a rough one.

Smucker, Barbara Claassen. **Days of Terror.** Herald Press, 1979. 152 pp.

Otto Neufeld defies Mennonite beliefs when he decides to join the Russian army and fight against Germany. When he returns to his family after the end of World War I, new terrors begin. As the family members struggle against invading bandits, disease, and hunger, and as they suffer the loss of freedom to practice their own religious beliefs, they make the decision to begin a new life in Manitoba, Canada. That decision means leaving friends and relatives, leaving all that is familiar and loved, and facing unknown problems and dangers.

Steele, William O. **The Man with the Silver Eyes.** Harcourt Brace Jovanovich, 1976. 147 pp.

Talatu, a young Cherokee boy living on the American frontier of 1780, has grown up hating all whites. He feels they are all guilty of taking his people's land and driving them deep into the wilderness. When the boy's great-uncle tells him that he must live with a white man, Talatu is stunned because all he dreams of is the day when he can join other warriors in attacks on white settlers. It is only when trust develops between the two that Talatu begins to understand the meaning of friendship.

Stoddard, Sandol. **Five Who Found the Kingdom: New Testament Stories.** Illus. Robert Sabin. Doubleday & Co., 1981. 117 pp.

How might the children who knew Jesus during his lifetime view him? Meet Joshua, who welcomed Mary and Joseph to the stable, and Naomi, who was Jesus's childhood playmate. These fictional children and others tell stories of the Jesus they knew and how each of their lives was given new meaning through their contact with Christ.

Suhl, Yuri. **The Purim Goat.** Illus. Kaethe Zemach. Four Winds Press, 1980. 60 pp.

Ten-year-old Yossele is a poor Jewish girl living in a small European town. Her mother has a scheme to make money that involves buying a goat and selling the milk to a man for his ailing son. But Yossele discovers that this goat produces more than milk—it creates trouble. Now the goat seems destined for the butcher, unless Yossele can think of a way to save it. Easy reading.

Taylor, Mildred D. **Let the Circle Be Unbroken.** Dial Press, 1981. 394 pp.

It is 1935, and the close-knit Logan family find many problems to overcome: their friend T. J. is charged with murder, local sharecroppers are being cheated by landowners, and daughter Stacey begins to resent being kept at home. These and other trials will test the Logan children's lessons in pride and self-respect. Sequel to *Roll of Thunder, Hear My Cry.*

Taylor, Mildred D. **Roll of Thunder, Hear My Cry.** Dial Press, 1977. 276 pp.

It is the time of the Great Depression, but Cassie Logan's family is doing fairly well on their farm in Mississippi. They own their land, a fact which allows them to live with pride and independence—something that their sharecropper neighbors cannot do and that their white neighbors would like to see taken away. Cassie has grown up protected from trouble, but she has also grown up strong. This strength will be tested, however, when Cassie decides to face the outside world and demand her rights as a human being. (Newbery Award)

Taylor, Mildred D. **Song of the Trees.** Illus. Jerry Pinkney. Dial Press, 1975. 48 pp.

With her large black family suffering from the Great Depression and her father out searching for work, Cassie finds her greatest comfort in the company of the trees. Tall, friendly trees surround her house and seem to whisper among themselves and the wind. But Cassie's greatest joy is threatened when white loggers offer lots of money to cut down the timber.

Thayer, Marjorie, and Elizabeth Emanuel. **Climbing Sun: The Story of a Hopi Indian Boy.** Illus. Anne Siberell. Dodd, Mead & Co., 1980. 95 pp.

During the 1920s, eleven-year-old Hubert Honanie, whose Indian name is Climbing Sun, leaves his Hopi village to travel to the Sherman Indian Institute in California to continue his education and to learn to live like the white man. Hubert finds he must struggle with two life-styles and two cultures. This novel is based on a true story.

Trivilpiece, Laurel. **During Water Peaches.** J. B. Lippincott Co., 1979. 160 pp.

LaVerne Honeycutt, the daughter of "Okie" peach pickers in California, decides to pull herself up out of the troubles of her life. The brightest person in her class and a whiz at math, LaVerne hopes to win a scholarship to the state university. Meanwhile, she gets a government job in an office supervising Mexican migrant workers brought in to harvest the peach crops during World War II. LaVerne falls in love with a handsome Mexican student whose culture is vastly different from her own. She must now come to terms with herself and her heritage. Mature situations.

Turner, Ann. **A Hunter Comes Home.** Crown Publishers, 1980. 118 pp.

Jonas didn't really fit in at the big school for Indian and Eskimo children. After one very lonely year there, he was happy to return home to his tiny village in northern Alaska. There he tries to learn the old ways of hunting that his grandfather is so proud of. But it seems that the harder Jonas tries, the less he succeeds. Then something happens that forces Jonas to very quickly become the man his grandfather wanted him to be.

Uchida, Yoshiko. **A Jar of Dreams.** McElderry Books, 1981.

Rinko, an eleven-year-old Japanese girl, has a difficult time living in California during the Great Depression. Because she is Japanese, she often is made to feel different and is left out of games by her classmates. She and her family also experience prejudice of various kinds. Aunt Waka comes to visit and helps the family feel better about life by leading them to discover their dreams and their inner strengths. Rinko's dream is to go to college and become a teacher, so Aunt Waka encourages her to develop her own self-confidence and pride.

Van Der Veer, Judy. **Higher Than the Arrow.** Illus. F. Leslie Matthews. Camelot Books, 1975. 132 pp.

Francie is as proud of her Indian heritage as she is of her blossoming artistic talent. She dreams of keeping both of them alive by living always on the reservation in the shadow of the mountain called Higher Than the Arrow. It's here on the mountain that she becomes friends with a spindly young coyote and becomes inspired to make a statue of Saint Francis. Then terrible things happen that force Francie to grow up quickly before she can begin to make her dreams come true.

Veglahn, Nancy J. **Fellowship of the Seven Stars.** Abingdon Press, 1981. 175 pp.

Mazie Ffoulke, a preacher's daughter, is not someone you'd expect to get involved in a religious cult. But this group offers Mazie a sense of belonging she has never felt before, so she leaves home to become a Messenger and a member of the Fellowship. Mazie must endure discomfort, hard work, lack of sleep, and participation in phony fund-raising activities to experience the warmth of belonging and the joy of worshipping with her new friends. Gradually, though, her questioning mind begins to discover some disturbing secrets about the group. Now she wants to leave—but can she?

Walker, Mary Alexander. **To Catch a Zombi.** Atheneum Publishers, 1979. 193 pp.

How are Vance and his family ever going to have a better life when all their money goes to a witch doctor? But Vance's mother is sure the family needs to raise a zombi to protect their father, a runaway slave who escaped to the North in the mid-1800s. The money their father sent them was meant to pay for the trip north to join him. Now that it is gone on the zombi, however, Vance is sure he will never see his father again. But there are other problems close at hand. Vance's friend Shanta is pregnant, and he wants to buy her freedom. So Vance decides to go to New Orleans and seek his fortune.

Wartski, Maureen Crane. **A Long Way from Home.** Signet Vista Books, 1982. 135 pp.

Can a Vietnamese boy from a refugee camp be happy in America? Kien's brother and sister fit in well with their new family, but Kien finds nothing but trouble. He runs away to Travor, a town with many other Vietnamese, and gets caught in a battle between the local people and the new immigrants. A close brush with disaster makes Kien realize that to be free of his troubles, he must face up to them.

Young, Al. **Snakes.** Creative Arts Book Co., 1981. 149 pp.

When a young black man makes a record that is a modest success, he also sets his path for his future. But starting out so young in a successful career in music confuses this singer, leading him from a secure family life to a life on the road with his band. Problems with drugs and love follow, forcing the young man into a new maturity.

Young, Alida E. **Land of the Iron Dragon.** Doubleday & Co., 1978. 211 pp.

Lim Yan-sung is a fourteen-year-old immigrant from China who lives with his father in San Francisco's Chinatown in the mid-1800s. One night their store is burned and Lim Yan-sung's father is killed. The boy travels to Sacramento and joins a crew laying tracks for the "Iron Dragon," the nickname for the transcontinental railroad.

Sports

Cox, William R. **Home Court Is Where You Find It.** Dodd, Mead & Co., 1980. 207 pp.

Willy Crowell is a rich kid who has been bounced back and forth between his famous parents for most of his life. But Willy is a great basketball player, and at Harper School he begins to fit in. He even finds a girl he can talk to. Then, last year's stars on the basketball team begin to resent it when Willy seems to be taking away their glory on the court.

French, Michael. **The Throwing Season.** Delacorte Press, 1980. 216 pp.

Indian, who is half Cherokee, is a junior in high school in Arkansas. He knows how people were prejudiced against his father, but things seem to be going fairly well for Indian. He is a shot-put champion on the track team and is known as one of the best athletes in the state. Then two things happen to Indian: he meets Golly, a bragger who wants to take the shot-put title, and he is offered a bribe to throw the track meet. A local businessman threatens that if Indian doesn't accept the bribe he will get hurt.

Gault, William Campbell. **Super Bowl Bound.** Dodd, Mead & Co., 1980. 153 pp.

Tom Cavanaugh's career in football begins in California, where he is pushed into the game by his grandfather. However, by junior high, Tom is nicknamed "the judge" because he's always sitting on the bench. In high school, Tom is able to replace the quarterback and gains a close friend, Amos Hawkins, a wide receiver. He and Hawkins attend college together and bring fame to Weston College. When he and Amos finally join the Pumas, a professional team, their job is to lead their new team through the long season to finish at the Super Bowl. But it soon begins to look as if Tom will be sitting on the bench again.

Gault, William Campbell. **Thin Ice.** E. P. Dutton, 1978. 151 pp.

The Raiders, a new National Hockey League team, like their games filled with action. The relationship between two players with very different playing styles may provide the kind of exciting teamwork that will help the team win the championship.

Guy, David. **Football Dreams.** Signet Vista Books, 1982. 275 pp.

Dan can hardly wait to study football and girls! Who will win the championship game? Will Sara ever say yes to a date? How can he make his father proud of him, especially now that Dad is so ill? These are some of Dan's concerns during his high school years. Mature language and situation.

Henry, Marguerite. **One Man's Horse.** Illus. Wesley Dennis. Rand McNally & Co., 1977. 104 pp.

One horse began it all. He was Hambletonian, the great trotting horse of a Dutchman named Rysdyk. Hambletonian was trained to be a winner, and he was. After a glorious history as a racer, Hambletonian began to sire a long line of champion horses. This is a fictionalized story of a legendary horse's career and of his descendents' fame.

Kaplan, Janice. **First Ride.** Flare Books, 1982. 125 pp.

Rodeo comes naturally to fourteen-year-old Cadmy Stevens. But when her school rodeo team goes to the finals, Cadmy discovers that some boys can't stand to see a girl compete. Cadmy and her boyfriend, Michael, have a lot of learning to do—about bulls and about love—before Cadmy can become the person she knows she was born to be.

Knudson, R. R. **Fox Running.** Illus. Ilse Koehn. Avon Books, 1977. 125 pp.

Olympic champion runner Kathy "Sudden" Hart begins to lose her desire to compete. Then she meets Fox Running, a Mescalero Apache who is wild and talented and who has amazing endurance. The two girls begin working and running together, each finding in the other what she lacks in herself. Their story provides an inside view of the pain, hard work, and determination that go into making champion athletes.

Leitch, Patricia. **The Fields of Praise.** J. B. Lippincott Co., 1975. 191 pp.

Gillian, a twelve-year-old girl with a dream of winning the big horse race at Wembley, finds life hard in her new country neighborhood. Then Mr. Ramsey shows her Perdita, a prize race horse, and he begins preparing Gillian for her dream. A sudden death tests Gillian's courage, and she must now battle her way to Wembley.

Levy, Elizabeth. **The Tryouts.** Illus. Jacquie Hann. Four Winds Press, 1979. 102 pp.

Eighth-graders Matt, Diggy, Spider, and Ritchie are all looking forward to the basketball team tryouts until they hear that girls can be on the team. Not only will they be the laughing stock of the league, but some of the girls, especially tall Donna Findley, just might get one of their spots on the team.

Love, Sandra. **Melissa's Medley.** Harcourt Brace Jovanovich, 1978. 137 pp.

Melissa (Moe) Hayes loves to swim, and out of that love comes competitive swimming. Moe's coach thinks she has a chance for a berth in the Olympics. But such a goal means long hours of training and practice; it means taking criticisms from the coach and one's teammates; and it means learning to cope with the pressures of traveling and competing in meets. Moe wants to make it to the Olympics—but if she does win the berth, then she's got to convince her reluctant mother and stepfather that it's the right thing to do.

McCrackin, Mark. **A Winning Position.** Laurel-Leaf Library, 1982. 92 pp.

Alec wants to win his first car race—not just for himself, but for Sam, his coach and close friend. But the road to the big competition is filled with personal problems for Alec. His girlfriend Jenny tells him if he really cared for her he would give up racing. And his parents want him to start thinking about college. Then Sam gets injured in a racetrack brawl, and Alec's decision becomes even more difficult to make. Whom should he try to please?

McKay, Robert. **The Running Back.** Harcourt Brace Jovanovich, 1979. 146 pp.

When Jack Delaney finally leaves the Juvenile Delinquent Center to come to Hollbrook, his troubles are far from over. Losing the football game in the last few seconds for Hollbrook High School doesn't help him make friends quickly. As the season continues, though, Jack struggles for confidence, new friends, and a place back on the team.

Meltzoff, Nancy. **A Sense of Balance.** Westminster Press, 1978. 157 pp.

The only time eighth-grader Gail Penski feels truly comfortable is when she is dressed in a gym suit, going through her gymnastic routines. So she is thrilled when she wins the chance to go to Summer Gymnastics Camp where she will compete for a place on Coach Fritzler's championship team, a stepping-stone to the National Team, and then to the Olympic Team. Life at the summer camp runs smoothly until she meets a very special boy named J. J. She finds that she can't keep up with the rigorous gymnastics training and yet find time for dates with J. J. and picnics with her friends. Gail has to decide if she is really willing to sacrifice all her social life and friends in order to achieve her goal of the Olympics.

Morgenroth, Barbara. **Last Junior Year.** Atheneum Publishers, 1978. 180 pp.

Kim has a dream—a dream to ride so well she'll make the United States Equestrian Team. She's fighting heavy odds, though, to make her dream come true. Her father doesn't approve of her goal and doesn't have the money it takes to help Kim reach a goal like that. At seventeen, Kim is in her last year as a junior rider, so she needs a lucky break, and she needs it soon. Then Kim meets someone who changes her luck. Incredible things begin to happen, and Kim learns another dimension to riding as she begins to reorder her life.

Myers, Walter Dean. **Hoops.** Delacorte Press, 1981. 183 pp.

Lonnie Jackson, a teenage basketball player from Harlem, has a chance to play in a basketball tournament for players who did not play on high school teams. It is his big chance to be seen by college scouts. But Lonnie is an angry young man who seems to be his own worst enemy. Then he meets an ex-basketball player who lost his career because he was caught "shaving" points. The man doesn't want Lonnie to ruin his opportunities, but there are others who lure Lonnie into trouble. Mature language and situations.

Ogan, Margaret, and George Ogan. **Donavan's Dusters.** Westminster Press, 1975. 156 pp.

Carl Donavan, just out of the army, decides to work for his step-father at an auto repair shop. His career plans change, however, when he saves the life of motorcycle daredevil Easy Jackson. With

Easy's help, Carl moves from simple motocross races to World Cup competition. Then Carl wonders if giving up his girlfriend and flirting with death are worth the success.

Ogan, Margaret, and George Ogan. **Grand National Racer.** Hiway Books, 1977. 114 pp.

The thrills of stock car racing fill this story of a young man who is following in his father's footsteps as a racer. In his first season of racing, Shelby finds himself in the middle of a rivalry between his father and the father of the girl he loves. This more than competitive rivalry may spell death for one of them.

Ogan, Margaret, and George Ogan. **Green Thirteen.** Hiway Books, 1978. 126 pp.

Jim Justin is a guy who likes to race cars. During a certain race, his Triumph TR4 is hit from the rear and Jim goes off the track, breaks through a fence, and ends up in the hospital. In the bed next to him is Dennis Johnson, the driver who rammed Jim's car. Dennis and Jim are angry at first, but they become close friends when they are both asked to drive Firebirds in an All-Am series—races in which American sports cars are driven by professional race drivers. Both Dennis and Jim are new to the racing circuit, and they experience dangers and fears that leave both of them wondering about their futures as race car drivers. Easy reading.

Peyton, K. M. **The Team.** Illus. by author. Thomas Y. Crowell Co., 1975. 213 pp.

Ruth is determined to prove to her Pony Club coach that she is a good rider. Her big break comes when she spots a pony for sale. But this is not just an ordinary pony. It is Toadhill-Flax, a champion show pony. Ruth discovers that she is willing to do anything to get it.

Seed, David. **Stream Runner.** Four Winds Press, 1979. 185 pp.

Fourteen-year-old Leif Collins is an unusual boy who spends his time thinking about the present instead of the future. He refuses to wear a wristwatch because he believes watches make you concerned about what you should be doing twenty minutes from now instead of enjoying what you are doing now, this minute. So Leif enjoys a "now" that includes trout fishing, his favorite pastime, and also running, swimming, and playing practical jokes with his friends.

Slote, Alfred. **The Biggest Victory!** Camelot Books, 1977. 154 pp.

Randy knows that quitting the baseball team would break his father's heart, but he dreads the long practices and the mocking laughter of his teammates. His real dream is to become a skilled fisherman and to be able to drop a line in the Huron River whenever he wishes. Somehow, Randy must show his father that reeling in a prize fish is just as important as winning a baseball game.

Slote, Alfred. **Matt Gargan's Boy.** Camelot Books, 1977. 158 pp.

Danny Gargan is a boy with big dreams. As star pitcher for his hometown baseball team, he hopes to grow up to play in the major leagues like his father, a catcher for the Chicago White Sox. The other part of his dream is that one day his father will remarry his mother. Then the Warren family moves to town. Mr. Warren, a handsome widower, works where Danny's mother does. And young Susie Warren announces she's going to try out for the second base spot on Danny's team! Danny has to do some quick thinking and some fast growing up to cope with these twists in his life.

Slote, Alfred. **My Father, the Coach.** Camelot Books, 1977. 157 pp.

Young Ezel Corkins and his friends like sports. They get a chance to play Little League baseball when Ezel's father decides to become a coach. Ezel is worried, though, because his father doesn't know anything about coaching. His father seems only to want to get revenge by beating a team coached by his employer. But things begin to look better when Obey, Ezel's best friend, starts telling everyone what to do. But then the baseball season begins, and Ezel's father and Obey have a clash.

Vockings, John. **Goal.** Illus. Len Epstein. Harvey House, Publishers, 1979. 79 pp.

The excitement of soccer is the center of this story about two boys. Both Jimmy and Alan want to be captain of the school soccer team. But the one finally chosen quickly finds out that being the leader of a group of energetic boys can be a difficult job.

Wallace, Barbara Brooks. **Hawkins and the Soccer Solution.** Illus. Gloria Kamen. Abingdon Press, 1981. 126 pp.

Talk about a rotten soccer season. It hasn't even started, but all the plans and hopes of Harvey Small and his teammates are already wrecked. First of all, the team's sponsor went out of business, leaving them with no uniforms or equipment. Now the team loses its coach and faces being kicked out of the league. In desperation, the group turns to Hawkins, the town's most famous "gentleman's gentleman." So the team has a new coach and a new name—Doody's Doobies. But there is only one small problem—they still cannot play soccer very well.

Wells, Rosemary. **When No One Was Looking.** Dial Press, 1980. 218 pp.

Kathy Bardy was considered ordinary until she was twelve. Then she discovered her talent for tennis. Soon she is being coached and encouraged to enter every competition. Her parents push her career for the money, status, and reflected fame it will bring the family. So for Kathy, winning becomes an obsession. But it is an obsession that threatens to ruin her life.

Physical Handicaps

Blume, Judy. **Deenie.** Bradbury Press, 1979. 159 pp.

Pretty Deenie Fenner, almost thirteen, doesn't really want to be a model, but her mother is set on it. Deenie would rather be with friends Midge and Janet, or dating the captain of the football team, or listening to Buddy Brader play his drums. Then, suddenly, Deenie doesn't have to worry about anything—but a frightening adjustment to a body brace.

Brancato, Robin F. **Winning.** Alfred A. Knopf, 1977. 213 pp.

Gary Madden was a football player. Now he is alone and paralyzed, the unlucky victim of a simple tackle. How will he continue his life? His girlfriend promises to wait for him, but his other friends either try to avoid him or use humor to hide their feelings. Then Ann Treer, a young English teacher who has suffered a recent tragedy, begins to tutor Gary. Ann wants to help Gary to become more than just a survivor—she wants to help him become a true winner.

Brooks, Jerome. **The Big Dipper Marathon.** E. P. Dutton, 1979. 134 pp.

For Ace Zweig, riding the roller coaster is more than an excuse for thrills; it is a test of how to face life. For Ace is a victim of polio, and his crippled legs seem to curse his life. Now, as the giant silver tracks loom before him, Ace must muster all the courage he has to ride the Big Dipper. But he never suspects how dangerous the amusement park ride really is.

Callen, Larry. **Sorrow's Song.** Illus. Marvin Friedman. Atlantic Monthly Press, 1979. 150 pp.

Sorrow Nix, who is unable to speak, and her friend Pinch struggle to save a whooping crane from death. They nurse the crippled bird in a secluded pen near the riverbank until the town discovers the valuable creature. Sorrow must fight to overcome her handicap as she and Pinch protect the bird from a life of captivity.

Cook, Marjorie. **To Walk on Two Feet.** Westminster Press, 1978. 93 pp.

A freak car accident confines fifteen-year-old Carrie to a wheelchair and leaves her with a new dread of the world. One night, from her bedroom window, Carrie views a crime being committed. She places her life in danger by reporting the crime, but she feels she is doing something to make her life have meaning again.

Corcoran, Barbara. **Axe-Time, Sword-Time.** Atheneum Publishers, 1976. 203 pp.

Elinor Golden has a reading disability; simple sentences and words are a challenge to her. Relying on teachers, parents, and friends for encouragement, Elinor keeps struggling to overcome her handicap. Then, in the confusion of World War II, she finds a curious way to prove her worth.

Cowley, Joy. **The Silent One.** Illus. Hermann Greissle. Alfred A. Knopf, 1981. 136 pp.

Jonasi is a deaf-mute boy who lives in the South Pacific. He feels separated from his people because they think a demon plugged his ears and held his tongue so he couldn't hear or speak. They also feel Jonasi will only bring bad luck to any hunt the men go on. When he is paddling alone one day, Jonasi sees a white turtle. He knows the turtle will win him a special place with the men, but he also knows he can never kill so rare a creature. Even alive, however, the white turtle proves to be an answer to Jonasi's loneliness.

Dacquino, V. T. **Kiss the Candy Days Good-Bye.** Delacorte Press, 1982. 129 pp.

If Jimmy wants to be captain of the junior high wrestling team, he's got to put on a few pounds. But no matter how much he eats, he loses weight. And lately he's always irritable, dizzy, and hungry. Then one day he collapses and is rushed to the hospital, where he finds out that he has diabetes. Suddenly it seems that his whole life has changed. In the first days out of the hospital, Jimmy, his family, and his girl friend, Margaret, must begin to adjust to everything that's happened.

Evans, Jessica. **Blind Sunday.** Scholastic Book Services, 1978. 167 pp.

Fifteen-year-old Jeff is so shy that he decides to give up trying to meet girls or even talking with anyone as long as he lives. But suddenly Lee comes into his life. She is beautiful, intelligent, witty, and easy to talk with. She is also blind. Although Jeff enjoys being with Lee, he is faced with several problems. First of all, he wonders what his friends will think if he dates a blind girl. Then he wonders if he could ever really understand Lee's sightless world.

García, Ann O'Neal. **Spirit on the Wall.** Holiday House, 1982. 192 pp.

This is the story of three fiercely independent people of ancient times. Em is handicapped but becomes an artist in spite of it. Mat-Maw, her grandmother, is known as a rebellious troublemaker. Em's brother, who is a talented cave painter, joins the two women so hated by the others to set up a life-style of their own.

Gerson, Corinne. **Passing Through.** Dial Press, 1978. 193 pp.

Liz is looking forward to tutoring French until she learns that her pupil is a boy her own age with cerebral palsy. Secretly, she has always hated physical weaknesses like this. To her surprise, she finds herself liking Sam, then loving him. Now it is her parents' turn to be irritated. Somehow, Liz must find a way to show them the Sam underneath their ideas about him.

Girion, Barbara. **A Handful of Stars.** Charles Scribner's Sons, 1981. 179 pp.

Why her? Why did this have to happen to her? Julie has everything going for her. She loves high school and wouldn't change places with anyone in the world. Then suddenly she starts having epileptic seizures. How can she get through those days when she is sick or unhappy from the seizures, the medication, or the reactions of uninformed people? (ALA Best Book for Young Adults)

Hallman, Ruth. **Breakaway.** Westminster Press, 1981. 93 pp.

Kate realizes her boyfriend Rob's mother is trying to keep everyone away from her son after he becomes deaf. So Kate convinces Rob to break away from his mother and start a life of his own. But the only way the pair are able to do this is to run away to Georgia. Kate begins to wonder, though, if this new beginning will really help Rob overcome his handicap.

Hanlon, Emily. **The Swing.** Bradbury Press, 1979. 209 pp.

For Beth, the swing under the old oak has always been her refuge whenever the hearing world becomes too much for her deafness to bear. But this summer she has to share her refuge with Danny, who is escaping the stepfather he can't accept and the mother he can no longer understand. Neither wants to share the swing, nor the tragedy that is to befall them later, but together they learn to keep going past the lies, cruelty, and hurt brought about by others.

Hermes, Patricia. **What If They Knew?** Harcourt Brace Jovanovich, 1980. 121 pp.

Jeremy has a secret—she is an epileptic. During one summer while her parents are abroad, she lives with her grandparents in Brooklyn. Jeremy meets many new friends, including twins Mimi and Libby and tattletale Corrie. But Jeremy feels uneasy because she doesn't know how her friends will react if they find out that she has epilepsy.

Little, Jean. **Listen for the Singing.** E. P. Dutton, 1977. 215 pp.

The Nazis that are taking over Germany, her country across the seas, are not the major concern on Anna's mind. Public high school in Canada is beginning, and for Anna, who has spent all of her years at a school for the blind, the experience is traumatic. Anna is forced into many uncomfortable situations with her teachers and friends. Then the war in Europe directly affects her family when her brother is wounded in battle. It is now up to Anna to draw him out of his self-made shell.

Rosen, Lillian. **Just like Everybody Else.** Harcourt Brace Jovanovich, 1981. 155 pp.

Jenny was a normal fifteen-year-old girl until a school bus accident caused her to lose her hearing. Suddenly her life is a nightmare. She doesn't know how to cope with her new, soundless world, and she feels confused and very much alone. But when Joe Benton, who has never known what it is to hear, enters her life, Jenny finds the courage to go on.

Sallis, Susan. **Only Love.** Harper & Row, Publishers, 1982. 251 pp.

Fran spends her life in a wheelchair because she is paralyzed from the waist down. But she is determined to make every minute worthwhile. Everyone is amused by her pranks except Lucas, the victim of a motorcycle accident who refuses to leave his room. Can Fran convince Lucas to take an active part at Thornton Hall? (ALA Best Book for Young Adults)

Savitz, Harriet May. **On the Move.** Avon Books, 1979. 123 pp.

A beautiful young woman has decided it's easier to stay at home in her room than to reach out for independence. Her equally beautiful but physically active sister is determined to bring her out of that room of false protection. The sisters become involved with a winning basketball team, the Zippers, composed of young wheelchair athletes. Soon all of these people are fighting together against a society that wants to hide certain people away and protect them because they are "different"; because society does not understand them; and because society fears them.

Savitz, Harriet May. **Run, Don't Walk.** Signet Vista Books, 1980. 132 pp.

Samantha loved sports—running, swimming, hiking. She also enjoyed dancing. But that was before the diving accident that left her in a wheelchair. Now all Samantha wants to do is quietly blend into the crowd at Scot High. But Johnny Jay, the only other wheelchair student, will not let her withdraw. Then Samantha is kept from entering a marathon race, and she decides to join Johnny in his fight to make all the school facilities available to the handicapped.

Slepian, Jan. **Lester's Turn.** Macmillan Publishing Co., 1981. 139 pp.

It is not unusual to have a friend over for the weekend, but this visit is really a kidnapping attempt. It occurs because Lester, who has cerebral palsy, fears that his friend Alfie, who is mentally retarded, is wasting away in the hospital. However, the outcome is a disaster that causes Lester to examine his motives. Mature language and situations.

Story, Bettie Wilson. **Summer of Jubilee.** Illus. Arnie Kohn. David C. Cook Publishing Co., 1978. 132 pp.

After moving to a new community on the beaches of Alabama, Marte Drake must contend not only with an adjustment to new friends and customs (like the celebration of a group of sea creatures who mysteriously land on the beach), but also with her own frustrations about her artificial leg and its limitations. To complicate her life, Marte must accept into her family her difficult cousin Julia, who has suddenly been orphaned. Marte is surprised by the strength she finds inside herself. What is even more surprising is that she finds this new strength as she conquers the greatest fear in her life.

Wartski, Maureen Crane. **The Lake Is on Fire.** Westminster Press, 1981. 130 pp.

Ricky Talese, blinded in an auto crash, wishes he'd been killed along with three of the other passengers. But he survives, an angry and bitter version of his once energetic self. When friends invite Ricky to spend a weekend with them and their new dog at their White Mountain cabin, Ricky thinks it is a trick but decides to go. At one point, Ricky and the dog are left alone as an electrical storm gathers force. Suddenly Ricky realizes the pines behind the cabin are on fire, and then he senses the cabin itself is burning. How can a blind boy and a dog survive the raging flames?

Young, Helen. **What Difference Does It Make, Danny?** Illus. Quentin Blake. André Deutsch, 1980. 93 pp.

Danny Blane was a perfectly ordinary boy. He was good at sports and good at schoolwork. But he had epilepsy. This didn't bother Danny, but one teacher became frightened of it and banned Danny from most sports. Confused and hurt, Danny decides to become the worst kid in school as revenge.

Mental and Emotional Problems

Albert, Louise. **But I'm Ready to Go.** Bradbury Press, 1976. 230 pp.

School is tougher for Judy than for most students because a part of her brain doesn't work as it should. She finds it hard to work with numbers, and when things start going wrong, her hands shake. Judy has few friends. Even her own family doesn't seem to understand how she feels. Judy is pretty good with words, though, so like Anne Frank she creates a diary friend, Lisa, to whom she can pour out all her troubles and share her secret plan for becoming somebody. Her secret plan keeps her hopeful; now if only she can make her plan work, then no one will laugh at her again.

Ashley, Bernard. **Terry on the Fence.** Illus. Charles Keeping. S. G. Phillips, 1975. 196 pp.

After a family quarrel, life takes a turn for the worse for Terry, a good-natured eleven-year-old. He runs from his warm home into the pouring rain and seeks shelter in the park bandstand. But Terry isn't the only one hiding there. Rough boys from the bad part of town meet there to devise ways to dodge the law. Soon Terry becomes part of a criminal plan.

Belair, Richard L. **Double Take.** Laurel-Leaf Library, 1982. 191 pp.

Big and clumsy Beau always acted as the class clown. Then he learns about cameras and becomes a photographer's assistant. But when the photographer's studio is robbed, Beau is a prime suspect. Beau goes undercover to find the thief, and finds himself as well.

Bonham, Frank. **Gimme an _H_, Gimme an _E_, Gimme an _L_, Gimme a _P_.** Charles Scribner's Sons, 1980. 210 pp.

Dana Furlong is attracted to Katie Norman, a high school cheerleader. He finds her fun loving and delightful, but he soon finds she also her periods of chronic depression and suicidal tendencies. She looks to Dana for help, but sometimes he feels he can hardly handle his own problems, much less Katie's. Dana wonders if he can really help Katie, or if she will just bring trouble into his life.

Bridgers, Sue Ellen. **Notes for Another Life.** Alfred A. Knopf, 1981.
252 pp.

For Wren Jackson, the summer before her fourteenth birthday is
one she will never forget. It is the summer her father comes home
from a mental institution, only to slip off again into his own world.
It is the summer her mother decides she wants to get a divorce and
move to a different city by herself. It is the summer her tennis
champion brother breaks his arm, and Wren herself feels the first
stirrings of love. It is also the summer that their grandmother's
wisdom helps them to find the courage to begin their new lives.

Carlson, Dale. **Triple Boy.** Atheneum Publishers, 1977. 172 pp.

Upset by his brother's death and his parents' divorce, sixteen-year-
old Paul develops a split personality. When two other personalities
take over his body, Paul forgets what happens to him and does
things he cannot remember doing. At last Paul is given help, and he
begins the difficult process of dealing with the problem of having a
multiple personality.

Cheatham, K. Follis. **The Best Way Out.** Harcourt Brace Jovanovich,
1982. 192 pp.

Haywood Romby is only thirteen, but his life already seems messed
up. He is in the seventh grade for the second time, and he has even
been forced to go to a new school. Haywood turns to alcohol to
relieve the pain, and he soon feels he has ruined any chance he had
to succeed. Fortunately, people close to him have more faith in
Haywood than he has in himself.

Conford, Ellen. **To All My Fans, with Love, from Sylvie.** Little, Brown
& Co., 1982. 192 pp.

Sylvie is fifteen, pretty, and living in a foster home. Since she is
afraid of her foster father's advances, she runs away. She is aided by
Walter and Vic, but she soon discovers they have hidden motives
for helping her. Sylvie believes life is like her movie fan magazines,
so she isn't prepared for the hardships she encounters.

Culin, Charlotte. **Cages of Glass, Flowers of Time.** Bradbury Press, 1979.
316 pp.

The terms *child abuse* and *battered children* take on clear meaning
in this story of Claire Burden. Claire's father abandoned her, and
her mother often beats her when she is drunk. But Claire tries to protect
those who hurt her, even when they keep her from what she loves
best, drawing. The girl struggles to survive her harsh life with the
help of several caring friends.

Daly, Jay. **Walls.** Laurel-Leaf Library, 1981. 204 pp.

Life is both wonderful and terrible for Frankie O'Day. He is his high school's star basketball player, but at home he has to face an unemployed, alcoholic father. In order to cope with this situation, Frankie begins to write graffiti on walls under the name The Shadow. Then he meets Laurel Travers, and her love helps Frankie deal with his problems. But all his progress is threatened when Frankie's friends involve him in a stupid prank, and the police begin to misunderstand The Shadow's graffiti messages.

Davidson, Mary S. **A Superstar Called Sweetpea.** Viking Press, 1980. 134 pp.

Ever since she was little, Elizabeth has dreamed of singing and dancing in front of large audiences. So when a job at the local nightclub opens up, she can't resist—even if it means lying to her parents. But Elizabeth discovers that being a superstar isn't easy; soon she is being pulled emotionally in all directions. Now Elizabeth must choose between her present, ordinary life and her dream of fame.

Degens, T. **Friends.** Viking Press, 1981. 161 pp.

When hardships begin to accumulate, people must learn to become mentally and emotionally tough to survive. Nell Atwood, an eleven-year-old, must learn this lesson. Her life is filled with harmless mischief until more serious matters appear—things like the Vietnam War, her mother's walking out, and her father's retreat into alcohol. Nell must learn to stand alone, yet she first needs to accept help from the special people around her—like eighteen-year-old Gene. Mature language and situations.

Dengler, Marianna. **A Pebble in Newcomb's Pond.** Illus. Kathleen Garry-McCord. Holt, Rinehart & Winston, 1979. 160 pp.

Eighteen-year-old Mara knows something is wrong with her when a turtle beckons her to come to Newcomb's pond and shows her a pile of white pebbles with a hidden meaning. When Mara's friends and parents learn of her hallucination, they fear for her mental health. Mara is sent to a hospital for treatment of schizophrenia.

Dizenzo, Patricia. **Why Me? The Story of Jenny.** Avon Books, 1976. 142 pp.

Jenny accepts a ride home with a guy she knows—and she gets raped. She's scared to tell anyone but feels a desperate need for help. What if she's pregnant? How can she get the help she needs and still keep her secret? Slowly, the mental and physical anguish become too great, and Jenny makes attempts to reach out for help. Mature situation.

Dodson, Susan. **The Creep.** Four Winds Press, 1979. 218 pp.

Summer starts on a wrong note for fifteen-year-old Brina when she and Pete, who she hoped would become more than best friends, go their separate directions. Then she rescues Annie from a child molester's attack, and her summer suddenly becomes filled with danger, challenge, and many changes. Mature situations.

Dorman, N. B. **Laughter in the Background.** Elsevier/Nelson Books, 1980. 158 pp.

Marcie's one wish in life is that her mother stop drinking. Then there would be no more of her mother wobbling home on weekends, or running off to a local bar and coming home with strangers. When her mother decides to give up drinking, however, she becomes strict and bad-tempered. So Marcie decides to go to meetings for children with alcoholic parents. There Marcie learns more about how to communicate with her mother. Things begin to seem brighter for Marcie, but only for a while.

Garden, Nancy. **Annie on My Mind.** Farrar, Straus & Giroux, 1982. 234 pp.

What happens between Liza and Annie that makes it impossible for Liza to answer Annie's letters? Liza wants to face the situation—the frightening things, but the good things too. Even after the two girls finally accept their love for one another, they cannot be open about it. What if someone finds out? How will their relationship threaten and hurt other people? Mature situations. (ALA Best Book for Young Adults)

Garrigue, Sheila. **Between Friends.** Bradbury Press, 1978. 160 pp.

Making friends in a new town is hard enough, but when almost everyone your own age is away for the summer, it can seem impossible. This was what Jill was feeling when she met Dede, the only girl her age who lived nearby. But Dede was retarded. From her relationship with Dede, Jill found out what being friends really means.

Grace, Fran. **Branigan's Dog.** Bradbury Press, 1981. 188 pp.

How will Casey Branigan survive without his dog Denver—his beautiful and only friend? After his mother's remarriage, Casey withdraws into himself and his fantasy life as an Old West gunslinger and talks only through Denver. But his hobby of setting fires gets him into trouble, and he is sent to a youth home. There a psychologist finally helps Casey come out of his fantasies and face the world.

Hallman, Ruth. **I Gotta Be Free.** Hiway Books, 1977. 92 pp.

Jay's father always seems to criticize the boy, telling him he's not good enough to hold a job and keep his grades up at school, that he wastes money, and that he should go out for basketball. He also gives Jay many other orders Jay doesn't want to follow. So Jay walks out and hitches a ride with a fellow named Lee and his sister Linda. Then Jay realizes Lee is involved in something shady, and that he himself is being forced into the dealings. But just when Jay decides to leave Lee and Linda, he's arrested and thrown in jail.

Hanlon, Emily. **It's Too Late for Sorry.** Bradbury Press, 1978. 222 pp.

Fifteen-year-old Kenny wants to make the school football team and dreams of becoming a professional football player. But when he enters high school, he meets a few problems. A new family moves into his neighborhood with a retarded son named Harold. Kenny, a popular boy, is now kidded by his friends because he lives on the same block as a "retard." But Kenny likes Harold, and Kenny meets Rachel, who also gets to like Harold. The three friends soon provide a valuable lesson for the whole neighborhood.

Haugen, Tormod (translator Sheila La Farge). **The Night Birds.** Delacorte Press/Seymour Lawrence, 1982. 135 pp.

Jake was particularly terrified of what might "live" in his closet— that is why he turned the key in the lock and pulled it out as fast as he could. He was always scared, but even more so when his father was away from home. Now Jake's father is ill, and Jake can't depend on him for protection against the night birds with their black wings, screeching beaks, and eyes that glow in the darkness of the room. How can Jake make the night birds disappear? And were they even real?

Heide, Florence Parry. **Growing Anyway Up.** J. B. Lippincott Co., 1976. 128 pp.

Florence Stirkel is a young girl who is thought of as overly nervous. When she is in new situations, she performs little rituals to protect herself. Florence gradually begins a journey out of her shell with the help of an aunt who shows her the joys and excitement of facing the outside world.

Heide, Florence Parry. **Secret Dreamer, Secret Dreams.** J. B. Lippincott Co., 1978. 95 pp.

Caroline, age thirteen, cannot read or write. She says only a few words, even though she hears words in her mind. Caroline is a special student who goes to a special school because she is not considered "normal." She knows she angers her older sister, Amy. She knows her mother resents staying home to look after her. And she hears people talk about her as if she weren't there. Only her father seems to accept her as she is. Caroline searches for the key that will open communication with others. Then one day Caroline's family visits an aquarium. The eyes of a turtle there draw Caroline's eyes, and she sees a secret lying behind them that she feels will help her with her problems.

Hopper, Nancy J. **The Seven ½ Sins of Stacey Kendall.** E. P. Dutton, 1982. 106 pp.

What is beauty? Could it be like the gold in Jill's newly pierced ears? Stacey Kendall thinks so and spends hours reading *1,001 Ways to Be Beautiful* (under a book cover for *Life of the Seal*), and wondering about how she could improve her ordinary brown hair, brown eyes, and figure like an ironing board. When she goes into the ear-piercing business for herself, however, trouble begins. But in the end she does find out answers to questions about what true beauty is.

Hull, Eleanor. **Alice with Golden Hair.** Atheneum Publishers, 1981. 186 pp.

Alice is eighteen years old and is mentally retarded. When her mother became sick, Alice lived in institutions. Now she is trying to find a life of her own by taking a job in a nursing home. As she works here she encounters many problems, but she also finds friendship and a feeling of self-worth.

Hunt, Irene. **The Lottery Rose.** Charles Scribner's Sons, 1976. 185 pp.

At age seven, Georgie Burgess lives in a world filled with fear and loneliness. He is laughed at by the other children in school, and he is afraid to go home at night, for Georgie is a victim of child abuse. It is not until he is nearly killed by his mother's boyfriend that the neighbors and the legal authorities step in to save him. It may be possible to save Georgie's body, but what can be done to help him love and trust people once again? The rose bush he won in a grocery store lottery may hold the key, for at least Georgie loves the beauty of flowers.

Jacobs, Anita. **Where Has Deedie Wooster Been All These Years?** Delacorte Press, 1981. 230 pp.

Life at fourteen seems to thrust too many problems at Deedie Wooster. First, her older brother dies, making her an only child. At school she's a dawdler and an underachiever. At parties she gets stuck having to wear clothes her mother picks out, and she is usually trapped dancing with Joey Falcaro, who is a head shorter than she and who calls her "Piano Legs." The only solution, Deedie decides, is to write about her troubles—but then she finds that writing comes with its own peculiar set of problems.

Lee, Joanna, and T. S. Cook. **Mary Jane Harper Cried Last Night.** Signet Books, 1978. 152 pp.

Mary Jane is a little girl whose mother has been abandoned by her husband, and now her mother is having trouble taking care of her. When Mary Jane is brought into the emergency room after an accident, Dr. Angela Buccieri suspects child abuse, but this is hard to prove. Can anyone save Mary Jane from further abuse?

Levenkron, Steven. **The Best Little Girl in the World.** Warner Books, 1979. 253 pp.

Alexandra Dietrich, fifteen and the youngest of three children, has always been a model daughter. But during ballet lessons, another personality begins to develop and gain power over Alexandra. This new girl living inside her is "Kessa." Kessa shuns the idea of ugly little rolls and dimples of fat. Greasy, messy food disgusts Kessa. Her goddess is thinness, bone structure, and dance. Pounds begin melting away from Alexandra's already thin frame. At first Alexandra's parents are concerned and irritated, then angry and panic-stricken. As Kessa gains more and more power over Alexandra, the girl is forced toward death from starvation. It seems no one can stop that fatal journey, until Sandy comes along.

Levy, Elizabeth. **Come Out Smiling.** Delacorte Press, 1981. 186 pp.

Fourteen-year-old Jenny is eager to go to Camp Sacajawea. Peggy, her favorite counselor and her riding instructor, is there to meet her. Ann, Peggy's new assistant, also seems very nice. The days go by filled with sports, crafts, and fun. Then Jenny discovers Peggy and Ann have a closer relationship than she had thought. Shocked and upset, Jenny retreats into herself. She is even ready to give up her dreams of competing in the Midsummer Horse Show. Jenny wonders how she will ever be able to understand and trust Peggy again.

Luger, Harriett. **Lauren.** Laurel-Leaf Library, 1981. 176 pp.

Lauren is seventeen and pregnant. Her parents, her girlfriends, and even her boyfriend think she should have an abortion. Lauren does not really know what she wants. So in order to think things out for herself, Lauren leaves home. In going away to solve one problem, though, Lauren discovers others within herself. She is confused, lonely, and afraid being on her own. But she also realizes it is time for her to struggle with her emotions and make some choices about her life. Mature situations.

Mann, Peggy. **Twelve Is Too Old.** Doubleday & Co., 1980. 139 pp.

When Jody turns twelve, everything seems to go wrong. Her parents get divorced, and her older sister, Linda, starts smoking pot. Worst of all, Linda pressures Jody to smoke too. Confused and upset, Jody fights for what she thinks is right. But it takes more than good intentions to change things, and soon Jody is involved in a serious and terrifying accident.

Minahan, John. **Nunzio.** Ballantine Books, 1978. 195 pp.

Thirty-two-year-old Nunzio Sabatini suffered brain damage at birth. He now has a learning problem that he is struggling to overcome. Nunzio lives with his mother and works delivering groceries. He has a great desire to help other people, and that is why he wears a cape and calls himself Superman. A friendly priest listens to Nunzio's dreams, fears, and problems and helps Nunzio cope with the world.

Moeri, Louise. **The Girl Who Lived on the Ferris Wheel.** E. P. Dutton, 1979. 117 pp.

Til's parents are divorced. Til dreads the long weekdays with her mother, who demands perfection and a perfectly tidy house. She is so obsessed with neatness that Til lives in constant fear of her mother's anger and physical abuse. The only time Til can escape the burden of her mother's demands is on Saturdays, when she is with her father. The two of them have a ritual of events each Saturday. They laugh, talk, and always ride the ferris wheel to end the day. Til wants to tell her father of her fears about her mother but never finds the right moment. Then one day her mother chases after her with a newly sharpened knife, and Til runs in terror through the streets of the city trying to find her father.

Morgenroth, Barbara. **Demons at My Door.** Atheneum Publishers, 1980. 145 pp.

Aly is an overachiever who pushes herself, but she may soon reach a point where she can't push any further. Socially, Aly is a part of everything. She is brilliant, is enrolled in the independent studies program, and has no trouble reaching her goals. But somehow she can't seem to handle things as smoothly as before, and she thinks of the "demons" inside people that she once heard Indians talk of. Even her boyfriend Rick is getting on her nerves. What is happening to her?

Morgenroth, Barbara. **Will the Real Renie Lake Please Stand Up?** Atheneum Publishers, 1982. 164 pp.

After her parents divorce, Renie's mother decides to live in a poor section of town without her father's help. It seems Renie's new high school friends major in drugs, gangs, and trouble. Soon Renie is in a gang, though, and it is not long until she and her boyfriend are caught in a stolen car containing drugs. Saved from reform school by her father, Renie tries to get along with her new stepmother and stepsister, Gretchen. However, it soon becomes clear that Gretchen wants to get Renie out of the house.

Murphy, Barbara Beasley. **No Place to Run.** Bradbury Press, 1977. 176 pp.

Moving to New York City from Potsdam is a big change for Billy and his family, but Billy is determined to adjust. He has to become streetwise, so Milo "the Cougar" teaches him what he needs to know. Everything is going along well, until a certain night in the park when the boys play a prank on a tramp and he dies. Was it really their fault? Could he and Milo be responsible for the death of someone? Billy wonders how he can live with himself and with his family now.

Neufeld, John. **Lisa, Bright and Dark.** S. G. Phillips, 1976. 125 pp.

Sixteen-year-old Lisa Shilling is losing her mind, and her parents refuse to recognize that. Her friends don't understand it at first, because many days she is her usual bright self. But there are those other days when she is violent, deceitful, and confused. Mary Nell Fickett is the first of Lisa's friends to recognize the truth and to realize that Lisa's friends must help her. Lisa doesn't make that job easy, though, and the long time she spends in group therapy and with doctors is alternately filled with hope and despair for her, and for her concerned friends.

Oneal, Zibby. **The Language of Goldfish.** Viking Press, 1980. 192 pp.

Carrie Stokes loves being a child, especially playing with the goldfish in the backyard pond. She and her sister, Moira, have learned to communicate with the goldfish by scattering crumbs and whistling softly. Suddenly Carrie finds she slips into strange mental states where she sees colored rocks sliding, hears voices like glass, and feels the sensation of floating. But she can't remember what happens during these times, so she is sent to see a psychiatrist each day after school. Her talent in drawing seems the only hope Carrie has to pull herself out of her mental confusion.

Peck, Robert Newton. **Clunie.** Alfred A. Knopf, 1979. 124 pp.

Clunie Finn's world was as simple and happy as waking up to the scent of lilacs in spring. But then bullies began chasing her home more each day after school, and other kids tease her and shout at her. Clunie is mentally retarded. Braddy Macon hates what he sees happening to Clunie so much that he risks losing his own popularity, and his girlfriend, to protect Clunie from the cruelty and ignorance of others.

Pfeffer, Susan Beth. **About David.** Laurel-Leaf Library, 1982. 173 pp.

Lynn just will not believe it. Her friend and neighbor could not have murdered his parents and then committed suicide. Confused and scared, Lynn tries to piece together David's past life from entries in his secret journal. Yet even with this information, Lynn finds it hard to face the truth.

Pfeffer, Susan Beth. **Just between Us.** Illus. Lorna Tomei. Delacorte Press, 1980. 116 pp.

Like most other teenagers, Cass Miller has trouble keeping secrets— except that her problem is worse because she can't tell the difference between a real secret and imaginary ones. Then her mother, who is taking a course in behavioral psychology, decides to help. With the promise of a dollar a day if she can keep a secret, Cass tries her best to keep her mouth shut. But no one tells her that keeping information confidential can lead to difficulty, and Cass finds herself trapped between two friends.

Pfeffer, Susan Beth. **What Do You Do When Your Mouth Won't Open?**
Illus. Lorna Tomei. Yearling Books, 1982. 114 pp.

Reesa is excited when she learns her essay about America has been
chosen to represent her junior high in a nationwide contest. But her
excitement turns into panic when she realizes she will have to read
the essay in front of five hundred people. Reesa finally decides she
must overcome her fear. But how can she do it in just two weeks?

Platt, Kin. **The Ape inside Me.** J. B. Lippincott Co., 1979. 117 pp.

Eddie's temper is like an animal inside him—fierce and bitter, it
springs out without warning. Maybe that is why Eddie has named it
"Kong," after the angry ape. Eddie tries to control it, but without
success. Then he meets Debbie, a girl with a similar problem.
Together, they work to harness the savage beasts inside them.

Rhue, Morton. **The Wave.** Delacorte Press, 1981. 143 pp.

Mr. Ross, a young high school social studies teacher, sets out to
conduct a harmless experiment in group psychology. He establishes
an elitist group known as The Wave, but what he doesn't expect is
that The Wave will sweep the entire school and grow out of control.
Friendships are severed, and parents no longer recognize their
children after The Wave has touched them. This chilling experiment
shows how easily individuals can give up their freedom to a group
without even realizing it.

Savitz, Harriet May. **Wait until Tomorrow.** Signet Vista Books, 1981.
150 pp.

When Shawn Blake's mother dies, Shawn realizes the event means
more than the loss of someone he loves. He finds himself suddenly
cut off from everything and everyone he knows. His father, whom
he has not seen in years, now wants Shawn to come to Arizona to
live with him. His grandfather has troubles of his own. And Shawn's
girlfriend, Robin, seems to give all her time and energy to social
problems and crusades. Suicide begins to look like the only answer
to Shawn's problems.

Shreve, Susan. **Loveletters.** Alfred A. Knopf, 1978. 217 pp.

As children, Kate would dare most things, and Tommy would dare
anything at all. Only in their teens do the two friends split apart—
Tommy to some wild, dark place in his mind, and Kate to the
seeming security of a bittersweet love affair with a minister who is

young, and married. When Kate becomes pregnant, her parents send her to a home for unwed mothers that takes "girls of good breeding who have only done it once." Kate fights to keep her child. When she returns home, she is haunted by a fear of Tommy and his madness. When Tommy makes one last violent attempt to possess her, Kate discovers the strength of her own character. Mature situations.

Shyer, Marlene Fanta. **Welcome Home, Jellybean.** Charles Scribner's Sons, 1978. 152 pp.

At the age of thirteen, Gerri Oxley comes home to stay after having lived most of her life in institutions for the retarded. No one in the family realized how hard it would be for them to take care of her, especially not her twelve-year-old brother, Neil, who tells this story of frustration, pain, loyalty, and love.

Smith, Nancy Covert. **The Falling-Apart Winter.** Walker & Co., 1982. 128 pp.

Addam Hanley moves from a small Ohio town to Washington, D.C., and leaves his friends, his dog, and his confidence behind. To complicate matters, he feels he can't communicate with his father, and his mother begins to act strangely. Addam's winter brings depression and mental health problems that demand a solution.

Snyder, Anne. **Goodbye, Paper Doll.** Signet Books, 1980. 155 pp.

Seventeen, beautiful, and bright, Rosemary has everything—so why is she starving herself to death? This is a realistic story about a young girl who has anorexia nervosa and the attempt made to save her life. Mature reading.

Snyder, Anne. **My Name Is Davy: I'm an Alcoholic.** Signet Vista Books, 1978. 133 pp.

Davy Kimble took his first drink on New Year's Eve when he was home alone. It tasted harsh, but a few more drinks helped him forget about being lonely. Now, a year later, he drinks all the time and has to steal and lie to get enough liquor. Soon Davy and his new girlfriend, Maxi, discover they are drinking themselves into more mental and physical problems than they can handle alone.

Sorel, Julia. **Dawn: Portrait of a Teenage Runaway.** Ballantine Books, 1977. 122 pp.

Fifteen-year-old Dawn Wetherby wants what she cannot have: a loving mother who doesn't drink. So, for Dawn, running away seems to be the only answer to finding out who she is. But Hollywood is a cold, lonely place that makes Dawn desperate enough to sell herself for money. Mature situations.

Sullivan, Mary W. **What's This about Pete?** Thomas Nelson, 1976. 125 pp.

Fifteen-year-old Peter Hanson faces a problem. He likes to sew and help his mother in her bridal shop, but he also wants to please his father, who is a motorcycle lover. Peter is very frail and doesn't like sports. This makes him wonder if he is ever going to grow up to be a man like his father. Peter questions if he is really different from other boys. Could he be a homosexual?

Thomas, Joyce Carol. **Marked by Fire.** Flare Books, 1982. 172 pp.

Abyssinia, a black girl growing up in the South, is admired for her beautiful singing voice. Her father's disappearance, a destructive tornado, and the bitter sting of poverty cannot stop her from singing. But when she is raped, Abyssinia seems to lose her voice for good. Mature situations. (ALA Best Book of the Year)

Van Leeuwen, Jean. **Seems Like This Road Goes On Forever.** Dial Press, 1979. 214 pp.

Being a preacher's daughter doesn't prevent Mary Alice from shoplifting a beautiful sweater. No one would have known, if it hadn't been for the terrible car accident that happened when she sped away from the store. Now in traction at the hospital, Mary Alice struggles with her confused feelings and remains mute. Dr. Nyquist, a soft-spoken woman psychiatrist, leads Mary Alice back to the events of the past that forced her on her destructive journey.

Wagner, Robin S. **Sarah T.—Portrait of a Teen-Age Alcoholic.** Ballantine Books, 1978. 120 pp.

Not all alcoholics are adults drinking cheap wine from paper sacks. Not all alcoholics are businesspeople who start relieving pressure with several martinis at lunch and dinner. A half million of America's alcoholics are underage juveniles. Sarah T. is one of these kids who has become almost totally dependent on liquor. Her story is one of desperate need for alcohol and her fight to control her addiction. With the support of a few friends, Sarah T. eventually takes the first hard step toward sobriety.

Death and Dying

Arrick, Fran. **Tunnel Vision.** Bradbury Press, 1980. 167 pp.

Tragedy strikes when fifteen-year-old Anthony Hamil, a near genius, commits suicide. He leaves no note, no explanation. Anthony's parents and friends search for answers to his death as they deal with feelings of guilt and bewilderment.

Blume, Judy. **Tiger Eyes.** Bradbury Press, 1981. 206 pp.

Davey's father is killed during a robbery of his grocery store in Atlantic City. To help the family recover from the tragedy, Davey, her mother, and her younger brother, Jason, visit her father's sister in Los Alamos, New Mexico. Will Davey be able to work through her pain and confusion and return to everyday life?

Brenner, Barbara. **A Killing Season.** Four Winds Press, 1981. 182 pp.

How can people live with bears without killing them and without letting the bears take over? That is a question Allie Turner faces when her brother kills her favorite bear. A biologist tries to explain some facts about bears to Allie. But the bear had been a way for Allie to forget her scarred hand, and its death has added to her pain as she remembers other deaths—those of her parents. Now she must find a new way to make her life worthwhile. Allie hopes developing an interest in photography will be the answer.

Brown, Harry. **The Gathering.** Ballantine Books, 1978. 250 pp.

Long ago, they were a happy family. Adam and Kate Thornton lived in a comfortable house with their two sons and two daughters. But too many times Adam was tough and unbending. Finally, all six family members went their separate ways, each harboring a private bitterness, hardness, and hatred—all, that is, except Kate. When Kate learns that Adam is dying of an inoperable brain tumor, she calls the family together without giving the reason. The clan gathers, and the magic of Christmas and the reunion works a miracle. Based on the screenplay by James Poe. Mature reading.

Cameron, Eleanor. **Beyond Silence.** E. P. Dutton, 1980. 197 pp.

Fifteen-year-old Andrew has nightmares about his dead brother, Hoagy. No matter how hard he tries, Andy cannot stop thinking about Hoagy. To help him forget, Andy's father takes the boy to the family castle in Scotland. But the past seems to be all around this place where his father spent his childhood days. Andy soon realizes, however, that the past he is encountering is not his own, but that of one of his ancestors.

Clifford, Eth. **The Killer Swan.** Houghton Mifflin Co., 1980. 114 pp.

It has been a tough year for fourteen-year-old Lex Mebbin. The suicide of his father and moving from the city are too much for him to handle. But he has no idea yet of the great impact on his life that will be caused by the swans who settle on the lake near his house.

Cormier, Robert. **Now and at the Hour.** Avon Books, 1980. 140 pp.

Alph LeBlanc, the father of five children, has been working in a factory for forty-six years. He discovers that he is very ill and will soon die. Now Alph and his family must struggle against pain and the fear of dying.

Dixon, Paige. **A Time to Love, a Time to Mourn.** Vagabond Books, 1975. 284 pp.

Jordan Phillips had a wonderful life. He was talented, had a great relationship with his family, and was in love with Susan. Then one day he finds he has the same disease that killed baseball star Lou Gehrig. Jordan first feels anger, horror, and fear. But he quickly decides to fight his depression and despair so that he can make his last days his best days.

Freeman, Gail. **Out from Under.** Bradbury Press, 1982. 166 pp.

Emily is still mourning the death of her father until she meets Tank—a forty-year-old ex-hippie school bus driver and a weaving teacher, whom she gets a crush on. But then Tank meets Emily's mother, and the two of them become friends, making Emily feel left out. A boy named Ernie helps Emily get over Tank and learn a few things about herself besides.

Girion, Barbara. **A Tangle of Roots.** Charles Scribner's Sons, 1979. 154 pp.

The principal of Millburn High School tells Beth Frankle that her mother is dead, and suddenly sixteen-year-old Beth finds her life

totally changed. Her father's loneliness, her grandmother's atten-
tions, and her boyfriend's annoyance when she spends less time with
him and more with her family—all add to the pain, which at first
seems so great that she can't stand it. Angry, grieving, and lonely,
Beth must deal with her loss and somehow find the strength to
rebuild her life. (American Jewish Committee's *Present Tense* award
for juvenile fiction; ALA Best Book for Young Adults)

Hermes, Patricia. **Nobody's Fault.** Harcourt Brace Jovanivich, 1981.
107 pp.

Guilt. This is all Emily can feel after her brother's death in an
accident. She knows she did not actually cause the accident, but she
had wanted to get back at Monse for teasing and pestering her. All
she had planned to do, though, was put a dead snake in his bed.
Now Emily feels she cannot face her family or herself because she
had once wished ill for Monse.

Kidd, Ronald. **That's What Friends Are For.** Elsevier/Nelson Books,
1978. 127 pp.

Gary meets Scott in science class on the first day of school. Scott is
big and burly and looks like a bully. However, Gary soon finds out
that Scott hates violence, and that he loves playing chess, listening
to music by Doc Watson, Pete Seeger, and the Dillards, and
watching people. Gary and Scott become best friends and share
many things, including the honor of participating in a special
summer science program. But then Scott becomes ill, and Gary
learns that the illness is terminal. Facing the death of a good friend
tears Gary apart. He spends as much time as possible with Scott,
but he also tries to be alone with himself to try to understand what
is happening.

Korschunow, Irina (translator Eva L. Mayer). **Who Killed Christopher?**
William Collins Publishers, 1980. 125 pp.

Martin is shocked when Christopher dies. He, like everyone else,
wonders if it happened by accident or if the death was a suicide.
Christopher seemed confident and happy, but perhaps he hid loneliness and depression beneath the smiles. Upset yet curious, Martin
tries to piece together the truth.

Mann, Peggy. **There Are Two Kinds of Terrible.** Camelot Books, 1979.
132 pp.

Just as summer vacation begins, Robbie falls off his bike and
breaks his arm. Then he discovers something more terrible than not

being able to swim and play baseball. He learns that his mother has cancer. Robbie is very close to his mother, but he hardly knows his father. Through the illness and death of his mother, however, Robbie and his father come to understand their relationship.

Oneal, Zibby. **A Formal Feeling.** Viking Press, 1982. 162 pp.

Is it ever easy to accept a stepmother? Sixteen-year-old Anne, home from boarding school for the holidays, has difficulty accepting her new stepmother because the house holds so many memories of her dead mother. Can she find her solution in such activities as cross-country running and ice skating? (ALA Best Book for Young Adults)

Orgel, Doris. **The Mulberry Music.** Illus. Dale Payson. Harper & Row, Publishers, 1979. 130 pp.

Libby's Grandmother Liza calls her Liboosh, and Libby loves it. In fact she loves everything about her free-spirited grandmother who takes her swimming at dawn, plays mulberry music on the piano, and even wears a mulberry sweat suit when she jogs. However, one morning Grandmother calls to say she can't take Libby swimming. At first Libby is hurt, thinking that her grandmother is deserting her. But when she finds out her grandmother is seriously ill and is to be admitted to the hospital, Libby is frantic. She finds out that she is too young to be admitted to her grandmother's hospital room, so Libby decides to plot and plan to get into the hospital. Her plan is successful, but she finds that she is not ready to face the awful truth she learns once inside.

Rinaldi, Ann. **Term Paper.** Walker & Co., 1980. 202 pp.

Nicki thinks she is responsible for the heart attack that caused her father's death. Her feelings of guilt continue to grow until she can't handle them. Then her brother, who is also her English teacher, assigns her a term paper on the topic of death in their family. Will doing the paper help Nicki adjust to the loss of her father—or lead to even greater emotional stress? Mature language.

Schell, Jessie. **Sudina.** Avon books, 1977. 208 pp.

Sudina feels safe in her room and never wants to leave it. She doesn't want anyone breaking into the mental walls that enclose her, either. Sudina's mother died—abandoned her, in Sudina's mind. Her professor father is kind and loving, but he is busy with his own life. Worst of all, the grandmother she adores leaves her too. Sudina is certain that if she allows herself to care, to love, there will be more abandonment, more pain, more loneliness. But Dr. Bridges barges into Sudina's room at the sanitarium and makes her angry and afraid—he forces her into the real world. Mature reading.

Schotter, Roni. **A Matter of Time.** Tempo Books, 1981. 126 pp.

Sixteen-year-old Lisl Gilbert's life is less than perfect. But when she learns that her mother is dying of cancer, she feels as though she's living in a bad dream. Lisl painfully comes to understand and appreciate her mother, her family, her friends, and, most of all, herself.

Sedgewick, Rae. **The White Frame House.** Delacorte Press, 1980. 137 pp.

Eight-year-old B. J. Aiken is determined to fly. So her best friend, Press, and her grandfather, Paps, help her in a hilarious adventure. Then the death of a loved one brings her down to earth, and her dreams take a dive. B. J. begins to search deep inside herself for answers to her painful questions. Easy reading.

Strasser, Todd. **Friends till the End.** Delacorte Press. 1981. 199 pp.

David Gilbert has a full life with soccer, a girlfriend, and his studies. He has little or no time for Howie Jamison, a newcomer, until Howie is hospitalized with leukemia. Through David's visits to Howie, he learns another side of life, a more serious side. When David gives up a soccer scholarship to study premed in college, no one seems to understand. Even Howie's parents don't want the boys' friendship to upset the important treatment coming up for Howie.

Wallace-Brodeur, Ruth. **One April Vacation.** McElderry Books, 1981. 80 pp.

That school know-it-all Harlan Atwater said you would die in a week if you lost a nose hair. It is too silly to be true. But what if it is true, Kate wonders. She had pulled out a nose hair but does not feel any different. Just to make sure, though, Kate decides that if it is her last week on earth, it will be a good one. So Kate sets out to do whatever she feels like doing, whenever she feels like it. It turns out to be an exciting, crazy week for Kate—and one full of surprises.

Whelan, Gloria. **A Time to Keep Silent.** G. P. Putnam's Sons, 1979. 127 pp.

When thirteen-year-old Clair Lothrop's mother dies, she stops talking. In an effort to help Clair and himself, her minister father moves to the back country of northern Michigan. Clair meets a girl her own age, Dorrie, who has an alcoholic father. Clair soon becomes involved in the lives of others, and this helps her solve her own problems.

Wyatt, Molly. **Kim's Winter.** Signet Vista Books, 1982. 155 pp.

Can Kim adjust to life in a small town when she's used to the glamour and excitement of traveling all over the world? This is what she must do when she goes to live with her grandmother after her parents are killed in a plane crash. But Gram helps Kim realize that she won't be truly happy until she learns to put her memories behind her and live for the present. Mature situation.

York, Carol Beach. **Remember Me When I Am Dead.** Elsevier/Nelson Books, 1980. 94 pp.

Sara and Jenny's mother was killed in a railway accident in Switzerland almost a year ago. The girls are now finding that their lives are changing quickly. Their father remarried just a month ago, and their new stepmother is trying hard to become a part of the family and get everything ready for the Christmas holidays. However, neither of the young girls is in a holiday mood. Strange things keep happening to remind them of their mother. One day, for example, the girls glimpse, from a distance, the figure of their mother's long-vanished friend. Another time, they find a scrap of mistletoe where Mother always placed mistletoe, and they also discover a Christmas package with a label "From Momma." Now the girls must go through a painful growing-up experience before they are able to cut the ties of the past and look forward to the future.

Mysteries

Allan, Mabel Esther. **The Horns of Danger.** Dodd, Mead & Co., 1981. 190 pp.

When eighteen-year-old Marissa gets a phone call from her orphaned friend, Sabrina, her hot, boring summer turns into a dangerous, mysterious adventure. Sabinra is afraid because "the horns are out in the wood." Marissa doesn't believe in ghosts, until she herself sees the horns in the wood. Are the horns of Deer Darkling ghostly beings, or is there a practical explanation of why these symbols of an ancient fertility dance appear in the wood, when they are supposed to be locked up in the church?

Anderson, Mary. **Step on a Crack.** Atheneum Publishers, 1978. 179 pp.

Young Sarah Carpenter dreads going to sleep because of nightmares in which she becomes insane and kills her mother. Frightened and confused, she asks her friend Josie to help find the meaning of her dreams. Together, the two girls use hypnotism to delve into Sarah's past, and there they find some terrifying facts about her childhood.

Arden, William. **Alfred Hitchcock and the Three Investigators in The Mystery of the Deadly Double.** Random House, 1981. 140 pp.

Jupiter Jones is one of the Three Investigators—a group of young boys who solve crimes. But in this mystery, Jupiter is kidnapped because he looks like the son of an African prime minister. So now the leader of the Three Investigators is helpless and must rely on his friends to save him. Easy reading.

Arden, William. **Alfred Hitchcock and the Three Investigators in The Secret of the Shark Reef.** Random House, 1979. 181 pp.

Three young boys uncover a deadly mystery hidden since World War II in an area filled with sharks. Danger and death now threaten the boys—and all they wanted to do was help an environmentalist fight against the drilling for offshore oil wells. Easy reading.

Asimov, Isaac. **The Key Word and Other Mysteries.** Illus. Rod Burke. Camelot Books, 1979. 54 pp.

Young Larry's detective skills baffle even the police, as he solves mystery after mystery in New York's active crime scene. Larry finds the criminal hidden in a crossword puzzle, explains why a rare coin is found in a Santa Claus collection bucket, and prevents a bombing of the United Nations. Each case leads Larry into thrilling adventure—and grave danger.

Babbitt, Natalie. **Goody Hall.** Illus. by author. Camelot Books, 1976. 176 pp.

Hercules Feltwright, who could never quite get his lines straight when he was a traveling actor, decides to be a tutor at the Goody mansion. His young student, Willet, persuades him to become involved in a search for the answer to his father's myserious death. This search takes both tutor and student through an adventure with gypsies, hidden jewels, and a dark-cloaked stranger.

Baker, Will. **Chip.** Harcourt Brace Jovanovich, 1979. 206 pp.

Chip, a young cowboy, drifts into a small Idaho town and makes friends with Mutt, a boy working in a gas station. Although Chip is a friendly fellow with a variety of skills, his background seems a little suspicious. When a murder is committed in the town, Chip is arrested. Mutt and a young friend set out to find the real murderer and to prove Chip is innocent. Their detective work leads them to the town's banker, and the two devise a plan to trap the guilty party.

Barth, Richard. **A Ragged Plot.** Avon Books, 1982. 175 pp.

Gary-haired Margaret Binton is an amateur detective. During one hot summer in New York, she is gardening with friends and discovers hidden diamonds and a buried corpse! What, Margaret wonders, can be the story behind the jewels and body?

Bennett, Jay. **The Birthday Murderer.** Delacorte Press, 1977. 150 pp.

As his seventeenth birthday nears, Shan Rouke begins to hate and fear his mother's boyfriend, Paul. Perhaps it has something to do with the death of Paul's seventeen-year-old son long ago. Shan's fears are confirmed when he receives mysterious threatening notes. But one thing stands in the way of accusing Paul: the notes are written in Shan's own handwriting.

Bennett, Jay. **The Pigeon.** Methuen, 1980. 147 pp.

When seventeen-year-old Brian Crowley gets a pleading phone call from his girlfriend, Donna, he never expects to find her dead in her apartment. When the police suspect that he is the killer, Brian flees to the home of an understanding teacher. There he launches a desperate search to find Donna's murderer, a search that leads Brian closer to his own death.

Bennett, Jay. **Say Hello to the Hit Man.** Delacorte Press, 1978. 133 pp.

Fred's life seems ordinary enough; he is a student at New York University, spends time with his girlfriend, and dreams of being a schoolteacher. But things take a drastic turn when he starts to receive life-threatening phone calls and notes from a madman killer. Fred is watched all the time by the unseen criminal. And soon it is not only Fred who is in danger. His girlfriend, his father, and an uncle are also threatened. Fred looks desperately for a way to escape the madman.

Bethancourt, T. Ernesto. **Doris Fein: Deadly Aphrodite.** Holiday House, 1982. 151 pp.

Aphrodite's is the most exclusive health spa in the world, and wealthy Doris Fein goes there to lose some excess pounds. While there, she encounters celebrities and sudden death. Doris feels she must both solve the murder mystery in this place of health and beauty, and expose the dangers of becoming hooked on weight loss and health fads. But she finds she can't do this without the help of Bruno and a message from someone beyond the grave.

Bethancourt, T. Ernesto. **Dr. Doom: Superstar.** Holiday House, 1978. 160 pp.

Larry Small, music critic and editor of the high school newspaper, gets his big chance. All he has to do is get an exclusive interview with superstar Dr. Doom when he reviews the rock concert for the paper. If he gets the interview, his chances for getting on the staff of *Rolling Stone* magazine will be very good. But murder interrupts Larry's plan. Now Larry risks his life to uncover the mysterious plot behind the killing. He also discovers the corruption that lies beneath the neon lights of the rock scene.

Bolton, Carole. **Little Girl Lost.** Elsevier/Nelson Books, 1980. 176 pp.

Nineteen-year-old Elizabeth Hobart's sister Carrie mysteriously disappeared twenty years ago. Now her mother wants Elizabeth to help find her lost sister. Elizabeth's attempts lead her into strange situations and romance.

Bonham, Frank. **Devilhorn.** E. P. Dutton, 1978. 153 pp.

There is nothing sixteen-year-old Tom likes to do better than graze his small herd of goats on the grassy hillside. When his angry father threatens to kill them, Tom runs away. Hoping to live a peaceful life with his animal friends, he rents some mountain land. Then Tom discovers that a fierce creature roams free in the area, and that a drunken man seeks his blood.

Branscum, Robbie. **Toby, Granny and George.** Illus. Glen Rounds. Avon Books, 1977. 109 pp.

Toby doesn't believe that Preacher Davis has killed Minnie Lou Jackson. Granny, Toby's guardian, doesn't think so either, and both distrust mean Deacon Treat. But then Deacon Treat is shot and killed, and Toby, with her dog George, makes some startling discoveries—in the deep woods they find a freshly dug grave.

Bromley, Dudley. **Bad Moon.** Fearon-Pitman Publishers, 1979. 56 pp.

Karl Baumer finds himself involved in the murder of a famous magician. Because of this, he meets a mysterious man called No-Name and is lured to the House of Tricks. Through the use of a "haunted television" Karl must solve the murder mystery or risk losing his life. Easy reading.

Butler, Gwendoline. **The Red Staircase.** Coward, McCann & Geoghegan, 1979. 431 pp.

Young Russian girls of nobility were never allowed to go anywhere without a proper companion. English governess Rose Gowrie had sailed to St. Petersburg to act as companion to the young daughter of the Countess Dolly Denisov. Little did Rose realize she would live with her young charge, Ariadne, in an enormous house centered around a red staircase that wound up and up in three curving flights to a mysterious oak door.

Calter, Paul. **Magic Squares.** Thomas Nelson, 1977. 143 pp.

Matrix Inverse, a Computer-Assisted Detective (CAD), fights with a mad scientist who plans to destroy all computers and throw the world into chaos. But Mat must work through a series of mathematical and computer problems before he can solve the mystery. Readers are invited to work out with Mat many vital clues involving figures and logic.

Cameron, Eleanor. **The Court of the Stone Children.** E. P. Dutton, 1973. 191 pp.

Nina has recently moved from Nevada to an apartment in San Francisco, and she is lonely in the large city. Her desire to be a museum curator takes her to a large French museum. She finds that the stone children in the courtyard come to life for her, and there she meets Dominique, a ghost who cannot find peace until she solves the mystery of an old murder. Nina soon finds herself slipping into the seventeenth century, where a lost diary helps her discover secrets of the past. (National Book Award)

Campbell, Jeffrey. **The Homing.** G. P. Putnam's Sons, 1980. 275 pp.

George Kenner can't believe his daughter would turn against her beliefs and goals to become the docile little homemaker that he now sees before him. Something is wrong, and he is determined to find out what. But George is experiencing problems of his own. He has strange dreams, precognitions, and headaches. He doesn't even believe in ESP, but how else can he predict conversations and events? Yes, something is wrong. He is going to find out what, and then he'll get himself and his daughter out of that weird town.

Carey, M. V. **Alfred Hitchcock and the Three Investigators in The Mystery of Death Trap Mine.** Random House, 1980. 145 pp.

Why does a millionaire suddenly insist on buying a worthless old silver mine? And why does he get an attack dog to guard the entrance? The Three Investigators decide that the only way to find out is to sneak into the mine themselves. But once inside, the trio fall into a maze of dreadful secrets. Easy reading.

Carey, M. V. **The Three Investigators in The Mystery of the Blazing Cliffs.** Random House, 1981. 180 pp.

Can a flying saucer really be invading Rancho Valverde? Ranch owner Charles Barron seems to think so, and he sends out a posse of armed men to meet the invaders. Three young boys have some doubts about this alien activity, however, so they set out to investigate the mystery. The boys quickly discover that UFOs are only part of their troubles. Easy reading.

Chance, Stephen. **The Stone of Offering: A Septimus Mystery.** Thomas Nelson, 1977. 191 pp.

Septimus is challenged with a weird mystery in the thick woods of the Welsh mountains. Someone in the little valley is using an old black-magic formula to prevent a dam from being built. A white bird, a silver fish, and a black lamb have been sacrificed as part of the formula to call forth the power of the old gods to protect the valley. The next victim that the magic demands is a child. Septimus must race against time to find the killer.

Christie, Agatha. **Death in the Air.** Popular Library, 1975. 189 pp.

When Hercule Poirot boards the flight from the Riviera to London, he was hoping for a pleasant, uneventful journey. His hopes are dashed when an inflight murder is committed and none of the passengers, including Hercule, can prove their innocence. The other suspects are a strange mixture of beautiful people and suspicious characters. Can you unravel the clues to the guilty party before Poirot does? Originally published in 1935.

Claire, Keith. **The Otherwise Girl.** Holt, Rinehart & Winston, 1976. 147 pp.

Matt takes the midnight London coach to the small village of Elverley. While he looks for his friend, he becomes fascinated, almost hypnotized, by a huge bonfire flaming up in the night sky with masked dancers moving around it. He is suddenly startled when a beautiful young girl addresses him by name. The young girl, Chloe, continues to mystify Matt throughout his stay in Elverley. But Chloe has an eerie past that Matt finds hard to believe.

Clark, Margaret Goff. **Who Stole Kathy Young?** Dodd, Mead & Co., 1980. 191 pp.

When Meg sees the brown van pull over beside her deaf friend Kathy, she thinks it is only two tourists asking for directions. But her quiet musing shifts to alarm when she sees Kathy being shoved inside. Meg begins a desperate search, a search with many dead ends and false clues. And around every corner, there is danger.

Collins, Wilkie (abridged and adapted by Carli Laklan). **The Moonstone.** Illus. Meredith Brooks. Fearon-Pitman Publishers, 1967. 92 pp.

How could Rachel have known that the lovely diamond she fell heir to was the much sought after "Moonstone" from the Moon God statue of India? Why hadn't she noticed the mysterious men with turbans following her? But Betteredge, the houseman, is very much aware of these strangers and of the real story behind the Moonstone's curse. But can he do anything to prevent this curse from harming Rachel? Originally published in 1868.

Corcoran, Barbara. **The Person in the Potting Shed.** Atheneum Publishers, 1980. 121 pp.

When their father was killed in an accident during a trip to England, Dorothy and Franklin did not expect it would take their mother a year to come home. Now here she is, and with a stepfather for them. There is another surprise in store for Dorothy and Franklin—a move to Belle Reve, a spooky Southern plantation. Much to their horror, the children discover a murder on the plantation. But they decide to risk their lives to track down the killer.

Curry, Jane Louise. **The Birdstones.** McElderry Books, 1977. 204 pp.

When Mike Pucci finds the birdstone in the rubble of ancient ruins on Apple Island, he never dreams of its evil powers. The birdstone seems innocent enough—a bird chiseled out of stone—but it is so realistic that it looks as if it might fly away. Its magic suddenly turns a girlish prank into a nightmare as it haunts Apple Island with a mystery from the past.

Curry, Jane Louise. **Ghost Lane.** McElderry Books, 1979. 158 pp.

Richard Morgan is spending his summer in the charming English village of Gosford. However, the dull routine of Richard's summer quickly changes when he learns about a series of mysterious burglaries at Goslings, an ancient manor house rumored to be haunted. With the help of the owner of the house and some new friends, Richard decides to track down the burglars. During their search, the trio sight a ghostly figure on the manor terrace, discover a secret passageway, and come upon an old warehouse filled with broken furniture. Their adventure almost ends in tragedy when Nolly, a strange little boy who cannot talk, disappears. However, Richard shows courage and good detective work in his efforts to find Nolly and to unravel the strange and mysterious happenings at the old manor house.

DeAndrea, William L. **The Hog Murders.** Avon Books, 1979. 205 pp.

A mass murderer is terrorizing the citizens of Sparta, New York. There is no pattern nor reason, making the crimes even more horrible. All would have seemed like accidents, except for one small detail that reveals they were really murders. The police are baffled, so an expert is called in to assist a special team trying to stop this maniac.

de Toledano, Ralph. **Devil Take Him.** G. P. Putnam's Sons, 1979. 283 pp.

Paul Castelar, aristrocrat and famous author, is constantly drawn to the bizarre. But even with all of his experience with weird events, one night he sees something at his window that brings about a fatal heart attack. Peter Minot is given the task of honoring the dead writer, but he discovers unexpected sides to his idol's personality. Peter pieces together a picture of Castelar so shocking that he doesn't dare reveal it. It is knowledge that even places Peter's own soul in danger.

DeWeese, Gene. **Major Corby and the Unidentified Flapping Object.** Doubleday & Co., 1979. 109 pp.

Young Russ Nelson is out to visit a cousin in the country when he stumbles on what appears to be a UFO. Russ wants to tell other people what he has seen, but he is afraid no one will believe him. Soon Major Corby, a spy, becomes part of the UFO mystery. Then Russ and a girlfriend, Cindy, capture a huge bat that eventually helps Russ to solve the mystery of Major Corby and the UFO. Easy reading.

Dickens, Charles (concluded by Leon Garfield). **The Mystery of Edwin Drood.** Illus. Antony Maitland. Pantheon Books, 1980. 327 pp.

Charles Dickens's uncompleted novel, *The Mystery of Edwin Drood,* is concluded here to reveal who really killed Edwin Drood. Was it his opium-addict uncle? Or the brooding Neville Landless? But whoever the murderer is, the added nineteen chapters bring Dickens's last work to a thrilling climax.

Dicks, Terrance. **The Baker Street Irregulars in The Case of the Cinema Swindle.** Elsevier/Nelson Books, 1981. 119 pp.

Four English sleuths try to unravel the mystery of a suspicious fire at a movie theater. One clue after another leads the gang to several possibilities. They bait the trap and wait for the criminal to step forward. But not one of them realizes the grave danger they are in.

Dicks, Terrance. **The Baker Street Irregulars in The Case of the Crooked Kids.** Elsevier/Nelson Books, 1980. 125 pp.

The Baker Street Irregulars are a group of young English sleuths who like to solve mysteries. When a series of robberies occurs, Dan Robinson and his gang have some ideas about the criminals are.

They think a group of teenagers is responsible, but the police think otherwise. Using Sherlock Holmes's detective methods, the Baker Street Irregulars swing into action to prove their theory.

Dicks, Terrance. **The Baker Street Irregulars in The Case of the Ghost Grabbers.** Elsevier/Nelson Books, 1981. 120 pp.

A ghost haunting the house of an English squire? This is a case for the Baker Street Irregulars, a group of teenage detectives who risk their lives to solve mysteries. They piece together clues in an attempt to track down the cause of strange—and terrible—happenings in the old house. Even when one sleuth's life is threatened, these four brave teenagers continue to search for an answer.

Dicks, Terrance. **The Baker Street Irregulars in The Case of the Missing Masterpiece.** Elsevier/Nelson Books, 1979. 141 pp.

A stolen piece of artwork and a dare from a classmate bring adventure for Dan and his three friends. In trying to solve the crime, the group finds that adults aren't always helpful, and that even the police seem to need guidance. Each teenager involved in the case has some very narrow escapes before the thieves are brought to justice and the painting returned to its rightful owner.

Dixon, Franklin W. **Mystery of the Samurai Sword.** Illus. Leslie Morrill. Wanderer Books, 1979. 179 pp.

When Mr. Satoya, a wealthy Japanese businessman, arrives in America, it is the job of Frank and Joe Hardy to protect him. When Mr. Satoya disappears without a trace, it is up to the Hardy boys to solve the mystery. A stolen samurai sword, undercover criminals, and a motorcycle gang are all part of their adventure.

Dixon, Franklin W. **Night of the Werewolf.** Illus. Leslie Morrill. Wanderer Books, 1979. 181 pp.

John Tabor begins to act suspiciously when werewolves begin to terrorize a small town, so the Hardy boys step in to solve the mystery. In daylight and darkness they search to find the source of the trouble in an attempt to prove John's innocence. Then an ancient silver tomahawk and a sinister business deal lead Frank, Joe, and friend Chet Morton into the heart of danger.

Doyle, Sir Arthur Conan. **The Hound of the Baskervilles.** Watermill Press, 1980. 231 pp.

The Bakerville family is being haunted by a huge, ferocious dog. Terrified, they ask Sherlock Holmes and Dr. Watson for help. Is the hound a supernatural creature fulfilling an ancient family curse? Is it a part of an evil plot to conceal a mysterious secret? Holmes and Watson must use all their wits to solve this baffling case. Originally published in 1902.

du Maurier, Daphne. **Rebecca.** Avon Books, 1971. 380 pp.

This mystery-romance reveals the story of the second Mrs. deWinter, a quiet and plain young woman who is completely enchanted by her handsome, mature, wealthy husband and his lavish estate. But her marriage immediately becomes mixed with surprises, shocks, fears— and the oppressive memory of Rebecca, the first Mrs. deWinter. At every turn in the house, in every corner of the grounds, in the whispers and looks of servants and friends, the beautiful and evil Rebecca mocks the new Mrs. deWinter, traps her, and threatens to take away any happiness she hopes to gain in her marriage. Originally published in 1938. Mature situations.

Duncan, Lois. **Daughters of Eve.** Little, Brown & Co., 1979. 239 pp.

Ten girls and a teacher, Irene Stark, become involved in a story of innocence turning evil. The school year begins for these girls in an elite group that gets together for fun and to decide ways to be of service to the school and the community. Each girl belongs to the club for different reasons, but gradually they all come under the influence of the twisted personality of their faculty sponsor, Irene Stark. As individuals change, the group changes. Violence and destruction become a way of life for them now, and each girl must suffer some painful consequence.

Duncan, Lois. **Killing Mr. Griffin.** Little, Brown & Co., 1978. 243 pp.

He gives the lowest grades. He demands the most work. He refuses to turn his classroom into a place where students have fun. Are these grounds for murder? Maybe not, but two teenage students decide to punish their English teacher, Mr. Griffin, by frightening him. But the boys' plans don't have exactly the results they expected. (ALA Best Book for Young Adults)

Duncan, Lois. **They Never Came Home.** Avon Books, 1980. 189 pp.

Dan Cotwell and Larry Drayfus, two high school friends out for a camping adventure, never return home. Even after an extensive search, no trace of them can be found. But Larry's sister Joan begins to suspect the truth as she pieces together bits of information: a missing two thousand dollars, a drug-smuggling ring, and Dan's unexpected appearance in California. Something strange happened to Dan and Larry on the camping trip, and Joan is determined to find out exactly what it is.

Eagar, Frances. **Time Tangle.** Thomas Nelson, 1976. 126 pp.

Life at a convent school in England begins to get interesting when Beth meets Adam, a boy who seems to be out-of-date about everything. Then she begins to develop a theory: Adam could be a remnant of the sixteenth century . . . a ghost caught in a time tangle. A strange silver cross leads Beth into peril as she attempts to help Adam return to his own century.

Ecke, Wolfgang (translators Stella Humphries and Vernon Humphries). **The Stolen Paintings.** Illus. Rolf Rettich. Prentice-Hall, 1981. 140 pp.

Here are seventeen mysteries that the reader is asked to solve. These short mystery stories have a wide range of difficulty in their solutions. All contain numerous clues, and the explanations and solutions are given at the back of the book. Included are "The Case of the Stolen Paintings," "The Smugglers," "A Ransom Demand," and "The House of the Ninety-Nine Ghosts."

Elmblad, Mary. **Outrageous Fortune.** Avon Books, 1981. 176 pp.

One morning, American Jane Berquist discovers a body on the English moors. The police think she is responsible for the murder, while the real killer sets a trap for Jane. Fellow American Bill Clay and Inspector Mackenzie offer Jane their help, but she does not know if she can trust them. Even more terrifying, however, is the prospect of facing the killer alone.

Elmore, Patricia. **Susannah and the Blue House Mystery.** Illus. John C. Wallner. E. P. Dutton, 1980. 164 pp.

Susannah and Lucy's newly formed detective agency seems to have no purpose since there are no cases to solve. But that changes when a kindly old man disappears. The only place to look for clues is his blue house, among the antique collection. In their search, the girls find puzzles and leads, and they discover they are in competition with someone else who wants to know all the secrets as well.

Evarts, Hal G. **Jay-Jay and the Peking Monster.** Charles Scribner's Sons, 1978. 185 pp.

When teenagers Jay-Jay and Carla discover the lost bones of the prehistoric Peking Man, they become involved with hoodlums, marines, real estate agents, and two Chinese governments. At first,

Jay-Jay tries to hide the bones on his Southern California farm, but his Aunt Hattie's experiments with electricity and fertilizer create some weird and frightening problems.

Evarts, Hal G. **The Purple Eagle Mystery.** Charles Scribner's Sons, 1976. 218 pp.

The most important project for Bix Ballard right now is to raise enough money to save his uncle's antique shop. Bix first goes to Reno, where he hopes to borrow the money from his mother, a nightclub entertainer. When that visit ends unsuccessfully, he does some research on the Flying Eagle, a rare decorated bottle that would be worth a good deal of money on the antique market. His search for the Flying Eagle leads to mystery, intrigue, and danger.

Farley, Carol. **Ms. Isabelle Cornell, Herself.** Atheneum Publishers, 1980. 145 pp.

Ibby Cornell is unhappy because she must move to Korea. She finds the crowding and noise worse than she imagined once she arrives. Add to this the fact that she does not care for her new stepfather, and you have one miserable girl. But she meets Mary Beth Pike and develops a friendship with Rick and Raymond. These new companions lead her to a class where they learn to speak and write Korean. Then a baffling mystery comes into their lives, and Ibby takes a part in solving it.

Fleischman, Sid. **Humbug Mountain.** Illus. Eric von Schmidt. Atlantic Monthly Press, 1978. 149 pp.

Young Wiley and his family are leaving Mulesburg forever to seek a new life in Sunrise, where Grandfather lives and where Wiley's father will start a newspaper. After a strange trip down the Missouri River on the Prairie Buzzard with Captain Cully, the family finally reaches Sunrise, at the base of Humbug Mountain. When the family arrives, Grandfather is missing, but they do run into Shagnasty and Fool Killer, well-known villains of the West, and Wiley's young sister discovers a petrified man. Immediately, the family searches for Grandfather and tries to capture some outlaws.

Franzén, Nils-Olof (translator Evelyn Ramsden). **Agaton Sax and the Diamond Thieves.** Illus. Quentin Blake. André Deutsch, 1980. 110 pp.

On a fine Saturday in June, Agaton Sax, the editor-in-chief of the Swedish newspaper *Bykoping Post,* sits happily at his desk and lights his pipe. But the message on one telegram catches his eye—

the police are looking for two thieves who both have long noses. This news starts Agaton on an attempt to solve another crime that has Scotland Yard baffled. Agaton's Aunt Mary worries that he'll irritate the police by working on his own solution. Before the end of the case, though, Agaton is in for a number of surprises from the police.

Freeman, Barbara C. **A Pocket of Silence.** Illus. by author. E. P. Dutton, 1978. 171 pp.

Caroline dreams that she must return to her home in Mariston on her sixteenth birthday because of something to do with a cottage and children who are lost. So she returns to Mariston and buys a book that discusses the history of the town. In it Caroline reads the story of the young girl in her dreams who seemed to call her back to Mariston. Now Caroline realizes there is a mystery connecting her life with the life of a young girl who lived in the eighteenth century. Caroline is determined to find out who or what is behind her dreams.

Gallico, Paul. **The House That Wouldn't Go Away.** Delacorte Press, 1979. 234 pp.

After Miranda has a bizarre vision of a Victorian house, she can think of nothing else. Then she finds some old blueprints that date back to 1873 and realizes that the house in her vision once stood on the very ground that her apartment now occupies. In the old papers she also discovers some odd coincidences about the location of the old house's rooms and those of the new apartments. Then another vision complicates the mystery.

Garfield, Leon. **Footsteps.** Delacorte Press, 1980. 196 pp.

When his father dies, twelve-year-old William is left with a mystery on his hands. A gold watch, an unsolved murder, and a shady business deal lead him to the dark alleys of London. There William confides in the street people. Some of them are honest friends, but some will do anything to keep him from uncovering their secrets.

George, Jean Craighead. **Hook a Fish, Catch a Mountain.** E. P. Dutton, 1975. 129 pp.

No one knows why the giant cutthroats are disappearing from the waters of the Snake River. Skinner Shafter and her cousin Al pursue the mystery while on an ecological campout, and they soon realize that something terrible is driving all the creatures of the river into a crazed fear. Alone against the powers of nature, the two friends set out to save the wildlife of Snake River.

Giff, Patricia Reilly. **Have You Seen Hyacinth Macaw?** Illus. Anthony Kramer. Yearling Books, 1982. 135 pp.

With a memo book full of strange notes, junior detective Abby Jones and her pal Potsie piece together confusing clues. They soon discover there is more than one mystery they must solve as they look for Hyacinth Macaw. Sneaking into empty apartments and slithering around subway trains are only some of the crazy things these two sleuths must do to solve their case.

Gosling, Paul. **The Zero Trap.** Coward, McCann & Geoghegan, 1980. 286 pp.

On a plane heading for Oslo, Norway, nine passengers are captured by the crew and taken to a mountain cabin in Finland. As they are held hostage, a brutal murder turns tension into chaos, and the remaining eight live in fear of the mysterious criminal in their midst. Then they become desperate as fire and cold weather drive the group from the safe cabin into the wilderness, where rescue by Laplanders seems to be their only hope.

Goudge, Elizabeth. **The Little White Horse.** Avon Books, 1978. 219 pp.

Beautiful young Maria Merryweathers is bothered by all kinds of mysterious and strange people. First there is her crotchety, bitter uncle who hates all women. Then there is a familiar looking young boy who appears at the castle every night. Finally, there are the Black Men, a band of outlaws who are terrorizing the countryside. Young Maria sets out to unravel the mysteries behind these people and unlock their secrets.

Green, Thomas J. **The Flowered Box.** Beaufort Books, 1980. 187 pp.

A tramp is found murdered by what appears to have been a severe electrical shock. When the police come up with nothing suspicious about the death, the man's sister insists her brother was not a tramp and hires two private detectives to find the killer. They have only one clue—an empty box covered with painted flowers.

Guy, Rosa. **The Disappearance.** Delacorte Press, 1979. 246 pp.

When a Harlem court finds young Imamu innocent of murder charges, a kindly social worker takes him into her own family. Then her seven-year-old daughter disappears, and Imamu is accused of having something to do with her disappearance. Desperately, the boy tries to prove his innocence as a terrible truth about the missing girl is revealed.

Hall, Marjory. **Mystery at October House.** Westminster Press, 1977. 163 pp.

In nineteenth-century Georgia, a group of visitors come to October House. But few of the guests are as handsome and mysterious as Darien Richards or have his keen interest in the nearby old Indian mounds. But the guests ask too many questions. One night there are unexpected sounds and a shot in the dark.

Hallman, Ruth. **Gimme Something, Mister!** Hiway Books, 1978. 103 pp.

Jackie wants to be in the Mardi Gras parade like everyone else, but Aunt Voletta forbids it. She feels there is too much danger in the middle of a sea of dancing masked people. You never know what lurks behind a disguise. But Jackie talks the maid Bertha into helping her. Scarcely does Jackie reach the edge of the crowd when a masked man dressed in black and with snake skins wrapped round him looks threateningly at her. Voodoo, a visit to the grave-yard, a hair-raising chase, a young portrait artist, a couple of determined thieves, and a threat to her own life all await Jackie during Mardi Gras.

Haynes, Betsy. **The Ghost of the Gravestone Hearth.** Thomas Nelson, 1977. 128 pp.

Charlie Porter is stuck with his mother and younger sister in an old beach house for the summer. However, Charlie's life is soon filled with strange and mysterious events. First, defective wiring causes a fire in his bedroom. As the firemen are tearing down one of the walls to put out the fire, they discover an old hearth that years earlier was plastered over. Later, Charlie makes a discovery on his own. This fireplace is the home of the ghost of Able Blackman, a sailor who died in 1712. Able has been waiting in the hearth to find a friend who will help him search for a lost pirate treasure. Charlie's summer is now anything but boring as he sets out to help Able find the missing gold.

Hildick, E. W. **The Top-Flight, Fully-Automated Junior High School Girl Detective.** Illus. Iris Schweitzer. Doubleday & Co., 1977. 195 pp.

Alison McNair, future detective, has been hoping for a case like this. Emmeline's father misplaced his credit card, and now money is being taken from his account. When Alison first investigates, no one has seen a strange character picking up the card. But she is determined to solve the crime. But when her clues begin to accumulate, they don't make much sense.

Hiller, Doris. **Little Big Top.** Illus. Dugald Stermer. Fearon-Pitman Publishers, 1979. 59 pp.

Pancho Cardoza is a young man who decides to use his strength in a job at the circus. As he helps set up the tents, works at concession stands, and trains on the trapeze, Pancho begins to sense he has enemies. When he is charged with stealing from the other circus people, Pancho must decide whether he should stay and remain a suspect until he can catch the real thief, or whether he should quit the circus. Easy reading.

Hoppe, Joanne. **The Lesson Is Murder.** Harcourt Brace Jovanovich, 1977. 149 pp.

Why are the members of Mr. Sanders' handpicked high school humanities class being murdered one by one? Can clues taken from reading studied in the class reveal the killer? Muffy Montgomery begins to suspect and fear she will be the next victim. When Muffy's parents go away for the weekend, the killer seizes the opportunity to strike. Things don't work out quite according to the murderer's plan, though, and Muffy must experience one terrifying event after another until the identity of the guilty person can be revealed through a clever plan.

Hostetler, Marian. **Secret in the City.** Illus. James Converse. Herald Press, 1980. 106 pp.

Jo Clifford is excited about the idea of her family leaving their small-town home and spending a year in the big city doing volunteer work for the church. Through her new friend Van, Jo quickly learns what it is like to be poor in the city. But while she is learning about life, Jo also stumbles upon some mysteries. Is the treasure of the 10th Street Gang still somewhere in the old Arnold House she is helping her dad repair? And who is that dangerous-looking person Jo sees every time she looks out the window?

Jeffries, Roderic. **Against Time!** Harper Trophy Books, 1979. 151 pp.

Peter Dunn wins a special tennis match, but he never makes it home for lunch. Two members of the Charles Meppam gang kidnap Peter just as he is leaving the match. He soon learns that the price of his ransom is his detective father's promise not to testify at the trial of Charles Meppam, a criminal apprehended by the detective. Peter knows these gang members mean what they say, so he watches his actions very carefully. However, when he has the chance to speak with his father by phone during the ransom negotiations, he manages to slip in a secret message. The message begins a tense search for Peter before time runs out on the ransom threat.

Kay, Mara. **A House Full of Echoes.** Crown Publishers, 1981. 168 pp.

Why is the ballroom at Astrovo all lit up when the rest of the house is dark? Whose footsteps are heard in the hall? Mademoiselle has explanations for everything, but Marguerite doesn't believe her. When Marguerite learns of Astrovo's tragic past, she begins to suspect the truth—a truth that may destroy two of her classmates.

Keene, Carolyn. **The Triple Hoax.** Illus. Ruth Sanderson. Wanderer Books, 1979. 184 pp.

Three baffling mysteries send Nancy Drew and her friends Bess and George to New York, Los Angeles, and even Mexico. First, two men are cheated out of three thousand dollars with the promise of a world tour. Then, a valuable vial filled with poison is stolen. And to complicate matters, a young girl is kidnapped. Quick thinking and intuition help put Nancy on the trail of a band of tricky magicians, hurling her into excitement.

Keller, Beverly. **The Sea Watch.** Four Winds Press, 1981. 134 pp.

Fortney has been given the opportunity of a lifetime: the chance to be untroubled by his pollen and dust allergies as he sails to France with his Aunt Elena. But the trip is not as peaceful and relaxing as Fortney had imagined it would be. There's a mystery on board, and Fortney's allergies help him sniff out the solution.

Kelley, Leo P. **Night of Fire and Blood.** Fearon-Pitman Publishers, 1979. 59 pp.

Marilyn doesn't know who is trying to hurt her, but somebody certainly is. She wants to trust her husband, so she decides the source of her problems is an ex-boyfriend. Then everything seems to become suddenly clear when she reads *The Book of the Dead.*

Kenny, Kathryn. **The Mystery at Mead's Mountain.** Golden Press, 1978. 210 pp.

When Trixie Belden and the Bob-Whites accept the job of investigating the business possibilities of developing a mountain area as a natural recreation resort, it sounds like a paid vacation. But an angry and elusive ghost, missing valuables, counterfeit money, an avalanche, and a kidnapping combine for an exciting mystery.

Kenny, Kathryn. **The Mystery of the Castaway Children.** Golden Press, 1978. 213 pp.

On a hot August night, the Beldens find an abandoned baby in their dog's house. Trixie Belden and the Bob-White gang team up with police Sergeant Molinson to try to solve the mysterious runaway-kidnapping case of the baby and his older brother.

Kenny, Kathryn. **The Mystery of the Midnight Marauder.** Golden Press, 1980. 211 pp.

Trixie Belden has a way of becoming involved in mysteries. This time she must trap the mysterious criminal who vandalizes buildings and leaves behind messages in spray paint. Things get worse when her brother Mart becomes the chief suspect, and it is up to Trixie and her friends to catch the real culprit and prove Mart's innocence.

Konigsburg, E. L. **Father's Arcane Daughter.** Atheneum Publishers, 1978. 118 pp.

Winston Carmichael and his handicapped sister are children of a millionaire father. One day Winston discovers an old secret: seventeen years before, during his father's first marriage, a daughter named Caroline was kidnapped and has never been found. When a strange young woman shows up at the Carmichael house claiming to be that daughter, Winston decides to learn the true identity of the stranger.

Kyle, Duncan. **White Out!** Avon Books, 1977. 224 pp.

On the freezing Arctic plains sits Camp Hundred, an experimental survival base for three hundred scientists. They keep alive by advanced technology and a complex computer system. Then something mysterious begins to happen to the system—something evil, deadly, and uncontrollable. When Harry Bowes is sent to investigate, he never suspects the grave danger his life is in.

L'Engle, Madeleine. **Dragon in the Waters.** Laurel-Leaf Library, 1982. 330 pp.

This ocean voyage produces a stolen portrait, a murder of a cousin, danger, and newfound friends. Thirteen-year-old Simon Renier knows only that he and his cousin are on their way to Venezuela to return a family heirloom, a portrait of freedom fighter Simón Bolívar, to its rightful place. But then the shipboard adventure begins, and everyone on the ship becomes a suspect.

Leonard, Constance. **The Marina Mystery.** Dodd, Mead & Co., 1981. 159 pp.

Tracy James loves boats and Pete, who looks on her as a pesky kid. So when she arrives at the marina where Pete works, she is not exactly welcome. Tracy's suspicions about a certain yacht seem to cause Pete nothing but trouble. But the discovery of a body under the pier changes Pete's mind. Maybe he should have listened to Tracy after all.

Levitin, Sonia. **The Mark of Conte.** Illus. Bill Negron. Atheneum Publishers, 1978. 226 pp.

Computers are wonderful machines until you try to correct one of their errors. A computer at Conte Mark's school is convinced that he is really two students—Mark Conte and Conte Mark. Conte decides to use this computer error to help him finish four years of high school in two years. He enlists several odd characters with special skills to help with his devilish plan. Eccentric teachers and counselors add ridiculous twists to Conte's masterplan.

Lilius, Irmelin Sandman (translator Marianne Helweg). **Gold Crown Lane.** Illus. Ionicus. Merloyd Lawrence Books, 1980. 101 pp.

In the Finnish village of Tulavall in the late nineteenth century, there is mystery and intrigue. A customs official has died under strange circumstances, and the suspect has disappeared. Now the Halter family becomes involved in tense events as it is linked to the son of the suspected murderer. Crooked politics and smuggling also enter the picture to make life even more hectic for the Halters.

Malone, Ruth. **Mystery of the Golden Ram.** Westminster Press, 1976. 128 pp.

Three young people become involved in mystery. When a priceless art treasure is stolen, these amateur detectives decide to investigate. Their search takes them to a strange hiding place—and danger. Easy reading.

Marston, Elsa. **The Cliffs of Cairo.** Beaufort Books, 1981. 124 pp.

Tabby is the only one of her family interested in exploring Cairo's culture. She loves to wander around the ancient parts of the city and learn about Egyptian history this way. But during one of these strolls, Tabby buys an old relic. Little does she realize this purchase will plunge her into mystery, intrigue, and danger. There are men now following Tabby who will stop at nothing to get back what she has just bought.

Martin, Albert. **Secret Spy.** Fearon-Pitman Publishers, 1979. 56 pp.

Jeff Avery is returning from a visit to Kenya. As he goes through the customs inspection before entering the United States, a foreign spy secretly switches tape recorders with Jeff, and Jeff leaves the airport with very important secret information. He soon finds that someone is trying to kill him to get the tapes.

Masterman-Smith, Virginia. **The Treasure Trap.** Illus. Roseanne Litzinger. Four Winds Press, 1979. 200 pp.

When Angel moves into the haunted mansion nearby, Billy doesn't waste any time telling her about the sinister murder that happened there eight years ago. Unafraid, Angel invites Billy to be her partner, and together they piece together the real story of the murder. Secret knowledge of certain townspeople, a hidden tunnel, and a curious treasure map lead the two sleuths to a big surprise.

McDaniel, Suellen R. **Serpent Treasure.** John F. Blair, Publisher, 1978. 129 pp.

A fascinating legend of Aztec civilization and golden treasure draw sixteen-year-old Chris and his father to a rocky Texas canyon where danger and excitement await them. As they come closer to finding the hidden riches, their lives are threatened. Everywhere they turn, Chris and his father find evidence of criminal work and sabotage. And then they realize just how important locating the treasure really is.

Mcdonald, Gregory. **Who Took Toby Rinaldi?** G. P. Putnam's Sons, 1980. 264 pp.

The son of a United Nations ambassador mysteriously disappears on a flight from New York to San Francisco. He has been kidnapped to prevent his father from aiding the passage of a United Nations resolution important to continued peace in the Middle East. The ambassador's young American wife, Christina, decides to undertake the search for her son herself. But the boy has been hidden among the exhibits of an amusement park, making it impossible to tell exactly what is false and what is real.

McHargue, Georgess. **The Talking Table Mystery.** Illus. Emanuel Schongut. Yearling Books, 1982. 140 pp.

Why is Aunt Dove's old table making such weird noises? Annie and How just wanted to help clean out the basement and maybe find a stand for How's guinea pig cage. Instead, they are faced with a moaning desk and some strange diaries written by Annie's great-grandfather. Now someone is writing Annie and How threatening letters demanding the diaries.

McHargue, Georgess. **The Turquoise Toad Mystery.** Delacorte Press, 1982. 137 pp.

Little does Ben know what he will find when he sets out to look for Indian artifacts in the Arizona desert. Strange tire tracks, CB messages, and deadly scorpions are all part of the puzzle. This is not the usual way to spend a Christmas vacation!

Moore, Ruth Nulton. **The Ghost Bird Mystery.** Illus. Ivan Moon. Herald Press, 1977. 143 pp.

The Yoder family moves from Indiana to the Blue Mountains of Pennsylvania where Mr. Yoder, an ornithologist, wants to establish a refuge for migrating hawks. Soon young Mark and Katie find their life on Hawk Ridge filled with beauty and mystery when the neighbors tell them their house is haunted. Then Mark and Katie glimpse a figure moving through the dark pines and hear the shrill whistle of someone calling a falcon. Finally they see the famous "ghost bird" that supposedly has returned to haunt the murderer of his master. Mark and Katie attempt to solve the mysteries with the help of their new friends, Myrna and Andy.

Moore, Ruth Nulton. **Mystery at Indian Rocks.** Herald Press, 1981. 183 pp.

"Back Mountain Girl"— that is what everyone calls Betty Jo. They only think of her as the daughter of a good-for-nothing without a job. Betty Jo hopes her summer job as a tour guide at Pioneer Village will change people's minds about her. Then a series of robberies occurs, and Betty Jo's father is accused. So Betty Jo and her friend Hal Turner decide to find the real thief. It is a search that takes them to a haunted rock-shelter and an encounter with an Indian spirit.

Moore, Ruth Nulton. **Mystery of the Lost Treasure.** Illus. James L. Converse. Herald Press, 1978. 177 pp.

The Howard twins are not especially looking forward to spending part of their summer vacation with their great-aunt Melinda on her Pocono Mountain farm in Pennsylvania. However, their visit turns exciting when Joey and Jan discover an old family diary telling of a hidden treasure buried somewhere on the farm. In their search for the gold, the pair find a secret room in the attic, explore a mysterious tunnel between the house and the barn, and visit a deserted island where they encounter a strange young boy.

Myers, Walter Dean. **Mojo and the Russians.** Viking Press, 1977. 151 pp.

While racing a friend on a bicycle, Dean crashes into an old voodoo woman named Drusilla. The shaken and angry witch threatens to put a mojo (a magic spell) on the boy. With the help of friends, Dean eavesdrops to discover Drusilla's plans, then races against time to expose what seems to be a Russian spy ring and to save himself from the wicked Mojo Lady.

Namioka, Lensey. **Valley of the Broken Cherry Trees.** Delacorte Press, 1980. 218 pp.

Zenta, an unemployed samurai, and his traveling companion Matsuzo stop at the inn of an old friend. The Japanese valley in which the sixteenth-century inn lies is known for its beautiful cherry trees, but someone is breaking the branches off the finest ones. When Zenta and Matsuzo begin to investigate, the clues lead them into the hands of powerful people. Soon they are in grave danger, and the two wanderers are forced to make a decision that will determine the fate of the entire valley.

Newman, Robert. **Night Spell.** Illus. Peter Burchard. Atheneum Publishers, 1977. 189 pp.

Tad, a recently orphaned boy, is not happy when he learns that he must live with a long-lost relative, Mr. Gorham. But inside Mr. Gorham's large and lonely house, a mystery surrounding a lost painting provides much excitement. Tad's strange dreams seem to predict the future, and they help him unravel this mystery. Then, on the verge of discovery, a hurricane strikes and Tad is swept away into more adventure.

Newton, Suzanne. **What Are You up to, William Thomas?** Westminster Press, 1977. 191 pp.

In 1923, fifteen-year-old William Thomas is busy keeping up with his schoolwork and working in his aunt's bookstore. But one afternoon he arrives for work and finds a "closed" sign on the bookstore door. He learns that Aunt Jessica is bankrupt and that Dr. Benson, one of the town's influential citizens, has angrily accused her of forcing his wife into giving money to the library. Then Dr. Benson dies mysteriously. William decides to turn detective and to unravel the mysteries.

Nixon, Joan Lowery. **Casey and the Great Idea.** Illus. Amy Rowen. E. P.
Dutton, 1980. 136 pp.

Twelve-year-old Casey fights for women's rights with what she
thinks are great ideas, but these ideas keep backfiring. For example,
when she tries to help her old friend regain a job, it leads to
threatening phone calls and an unexpected mystery.

Nixon, Joan Lowery. **The Kidnapping of Christina Lattimore.** Harcourt
Brace Jovanovich, 1979. 179 pp.

Christina Lattimore is kidnapped! The police rescue her, but the
kidnappers claim that Christina masterminded the plot to get
money from her wealthy grandmother. Christina attempts to prove
her innocence to her disbelieving family and friends. Her investigation brings Christina some frightening moments, clues about her
captors, and new insights into her values.

Nixon, Joan Lowery. **The Séance.** Harcourt Brace Jovanovich, 1980.
142 pp.

When seventeen-year-old Sara Martin disappears from a séance,
Lauren thinks she has run away—until Sara's body is discovered.
When another girl is killed, Lauren fears that she will be next. Is
there anyone she can trust?

Nixon, Joan Lowery. **The Specter.** Delacorte Press, 1982. 184 pp.

While she's in the hospital, Dina, a seventeen-year-old orphan with
Hodgkin's disease, takes an interest in nine-year-old Julie, who is
recovering from the car accident that killed her parents. In return,
Julie clings to Dina, telling her that a man named Sikes caused the
accident and that he's planning to kill Julie, too. When Dina moves
to a foster home, she arranges to take Julie with her, but the little
girl's attachment to her only grows more desperate. Why is Julie so
angry about the time Dina spends with her new friend, Dave? Who
is Sikes, and why can't Julie stop talking about him? Dina slowly
begins to realize that in befriending Julie, she may have made herself the target of a dangerous killer.

Norman, Elizabeth. **Castle Cloud.** Avon Books, 1977. 598 pp.

Vivian invites Mary to visit the castle, but when Mary arrives, Lord
and Lady Clareham and their son, Edmond, tell her Vivian is in
London. The family seems eager to be rid of the unexpected guest.
When Mary discovers possible lies in their stories, however, she

knows she must stay to find Vivian and learn the truth about Clareham Castle. Mature language and situations.

O'Donnell, Lillian. **Falling Star.** G. P. Putnam's Sons, 1979. 252 pp.

Mici Anhalt is thirty-three and dedicated to her job with the New York State Crime Victims Compensation Board. It is in this job of providing aid to crime victims that she first meets Julia Schuyler, an out-of-work actress now living in a run-down building and frequently a victim of muggers. Mici learns that between drunken periods Julia is writing a book about the scandalous life of her father, the late John Malcolm Schuyler, a famous actor in his time. However, this writing project is suddenly ended when Julia is found murdered in her apartment. Mici immediately puts all her detective skills to work to find out who killed Julia and why.

Orgel, Doris. **A Certain Magic.** Dial Press, 1976. 176 pp.

Jenny is feeding the cat in Aunt Trudl's apartment when she accidentally stumbles upon the copybook her aunt was given as a little girl. The copybook reveals Trudl's mysterious past to Jenny. Soon Jenny is reliving the childhood problems and fears of Trudl as a young German Jew and discovering a mystery involving an old emerald and her aunt.

Paulsen, Gary. **The Spitball Gang.** Elsevier/Nelson Books, 1980. 125 pp.

Greg and Stu are first-rate police detectives in Denver who earned the respect of their superior officers because they usually solve their cases quickly and efficiently. However, even these two are baffled by the newest case to cross their desk—a bank robbery by a gang of ten-year-olds. Operating with no clues but with plenty of luck, Greg and Stu are finally able to learn the identity of the gang members, as well as discover the bizarre way the gang was formed and manipulated through mind control.

Peck, Richard. **Through a Brief Darkness.** Laurel-Leaf Library, 1982. 141 pp.

Karen is sixteen, but she still can't forget those hateful words scrawled on the washroom mirror in sixth grade: "Karen's old man is a CROOK." After being shuffled from one boarding school to another, she is suddenly whisked away from New York City to live in England with relatives she's never met. She tries desperately to get some explanation from her father, but her efforts are in vain. When communication from home stops completely, her life becomes a nightmare. Can she bear to discover the truth?

Peyton, K. M. **A Midsummer Night's Death.** William Collins Publishers, 1979. 138 pp.

The suicide of Robinson, the most hated teacher at Meddington School, stuns everyone. But most of all, it bothers the students in the sixth form. On the afternoon of the teacher's death, that class had sent him screaming from the room. One member of the class, Jonathan Meredith, hated the English instructor as much as anyone else, but he has reason to doubt the death is a suicide. As he puts the clues together, Jonathan fears that Charles Hugo—the man he admires more than anyone in the world—may have murdered Robinson. Before many days have passed, Jonathan has reason to fear for his own life too.

Phipson, Joan. **Fly into Danger.** McElderry Books, 1978. 152 pp.

Thirteen-year-old Margaret, on a flight from Sydney to London, has bird smuggling on her mind. Just the day before, she discovered poachers near her home in the Australian countryside. When she reported the incident to the park ranger, she learned that smuggling brilliantly feathered wild parrots into other countries is extremely profitable. As Margaret settles down for her long flight, she becomes aware that the older couple sitting near her are acting very strangely. Their coats and hand luggage seem suspiciously bulky. Could they be smugglers?

Quentin, Patrick. **Puzzle for Players.** Avon Books, 1979. 238 pp.

Peter Duluth was planning a comeback on Broadway as a producer/ director of a promising new play. Success seemed close at hand, for Peter had a great cast and brilliant script. But he didn't count on having to cope with a ghost named Lillian haunting his theater.

Rabe, Berniece. **Who's Afraid?** Illus. Maribeth Olson. Skinny Books, 1980. 87 pp.

Sixteen-year-old Billie Jo is travelling by bus from her home in Arkansas to Illinois for a visit with her sister Mary Glen. But the long trip is made considerably more interesting when a handsome young man takes the seat next to Billie Jo's on the bus. She discovers that his name is Dart and that the two have many interests in common. Billie Jo enjoys the conversation and is surprised, but delighted, when Dart gives her a heavy metal box.

However, she soon finds that the mystery gift is changing her life. She begins to see strange shadows outside her window and realizes that someone is trying to steal the metal box. Anxious and confused, Billie Jo wonders how Dart is mixed up in the strange events.

Raskin, Ellen. **The Tattooed Potato and Other Clues.** E. P. Dutton, 1975. 170 pp.

When seventeen-year-old Dickory Dock is hired by the well-known artist Garson, he never suspects the adventures that await him. A deaf-mute giant and an obese apartment landlord are the suspects that lead him to a huge scandal. Then a hairdresser steals thousands of dollars from customers who wake up bald the next day. These mysteries, and more, are part of Dickory's new and exciting life as an artist's apprentice.

Raskin, Ellen. **The Westing Game.** E. P. Dutton, 1978. 185 pp.

When wealthy Samuel Westing is discovered dead, his heirs find themselves entangled in the "Westing Game," a dangerous fight for their share of the family fortune. In this game, designed to reveal Mr. Westing's murderer, the heirs are split into pairs and each pair reads the will. Ten thousand dollars and a set of clues are then given to each pair, and the search begins. The game turns out to be a little more dangerous than anyone dreams, however.

Read, Mary Lyle. **The Ghost of Emma Louise.** Illus. Ingrid Koepcke. Abingdon Press, 1980. 128 pp.

Emma Louise Jones is a nine-year-old girl who doesn't believe in ghosts. Then she meets her great-great-grandmother's ghost, who tells the young girl about their family history and how the family inheritance has fallen into evil hands. Emma Louise and a friend try to solve the crime and save the family fortune. Easy reading.

Rosenbloom, Joseph. **Maximilian, You're the Greatest.** Elsevier/Nelson Books, 1980. 142 pp.

Here are the sixteen most thrilling cases of young detective Maximilian Augustus Adams. The mysteries Maximilian is called upon to solve involve stamps, comets, tunnels, ballerina statues, Antarctic explorers, peanut bags, vanishing creams, and little green men. Match wits with Maximilian, and see if you can discover the answers before he can. Each story saves the solution for a separate section at the end of the book.

Sadler, Catherine Edwards, editor and adapter. **Sir Arthur Conan Doyle's The Adventures of Sherlock Holmes: Book One.** Illus. Andrew Glass. Camelot Books, 1981. 143 pp.

These are adaptations of famous Sherlock Holmes detective stories written in the late 1800s and early 1900s. Included are the stories "A Study in Scarlet," "The Red-Headed League," and "The Man with the Twisted Lips." In "A Study in Scarlet" Sherlock Holmes and his future assistant, Dr. Watson, meet for the first time.

Sadler, Catherine Edwards, editor and adapter. **Sir Arthur Conan Doyle's The Adventures of Sherlock Holmes: Book Two.** Illus. Andrew Glass. Camelot Books, 1981. 157 pp.

Three Sherlock Holmes mystery stories adapted for younger readers fill this volume. In "The Sign of the Four," Sherlock Holmes must solve a murder mystery. "The Adventure of the Blue Carbuncle" finds Holmes and Dr. Watson looking for a stolen diamond. Perhaps one of Holmes's most interesting cases is revealed in "The Adventure of the Speckled Band."

Sadler, Catherine Edwards, editor and adapter. **Sir Arthur Conan Doyle's The Adventures of Sherlock Holmes: Book Three.** Illus. Andrew Glass. Camelot Books, 1981. 109 pp.

Here are four of the mystery stories that made super sleuth Sherlock Holmes famous in the late 1800s. In "The Adventure of the Engineer's Thumb," Holmes and his assistant, Dr. Watson, investigate a mansion that houses deadly criminals. A priceless crown of jewels is stolen in "The Adventure of the Beryl Coronet," while an expensive and famous racehorse disappears in "The Adventure of Silver Blaze." The genius of the great detective is finally challenged in "The Adventure of the Musgrave Ritual."

Sadler, Catherine Edwards, editor and adapter. **Sir Arthur Conan Doyle's The Adventures of Sherlock Holmes: Book Four.** Illus. Andrew Glass. Camelot Books, 1981. 110 pp.

Sherlock Holmes and Dr. Watson use all their powers of detection to solve four tricky cases. In one story, Holmes and Dr. Watson must unravel a case of murder and blackmail. In another case, you get to meet Sherlock Holmes's older brother, Mycroft Holmes. The titles of the four cases reveal their subjects: "The Adventure of the Reigate Puzzle," "The Adventure of the Crooked Man," "The Adventure of the Greek Interpreter," and "The Adventure of the Naval Treaty."

Shea, George. **I Died Here.** Fearon-Pitman Publishers, 1979. 60 pp.

Larry Arkos has been having bad dreams. Every night he dreams that strangers chase him through a cemetery near a town called Drokola. But Drokola is in Greece, and Larry lives in the United States. The dreams are so strong and seem so real that Larry goes to Drokola. There he learns about another life he lived and about a time when he was murdered there. Easy reading.

Shearer, John. **Billy Jo Jive and the Walkie-Talkie Caper.** Illus. Ted Shearer. Yearling Books, 1982. 47 pp.

Steam Boat Louis is in real trouble. The Bugaloo Smackers paid him ten dollars to build a secret communications system for their club, but someone has stolen the walkie-talkies. There is only one thing to do now—call Billy Jo Jive and Susie Sunset to track down the thieves. Easy reading.

Shreve, Susan. **The Nightmares of Geranium Street.** Avon Books, 1979. 125 pp.

Twelve-year-old Elizabeth DuBois, the leader of the Nightmares, tries to uncover some of the secrets surrounding the mysterious woman, Tess Janario, who lives across the street. When Amanda visits her Aunt Tess, the Nightmares take her into the gang in order to find out more about the girl's aunt. Mature language.

Smaridge, Norah. **The Mystery at Greystone Hall.** Illus. Robert Hand-ville. Dodd, Mead & Co., 1979. 169 pp.

An eccentric old woman, a disappearing painting, and an old mansion add excitement to Robin's vacation in London. But Robin must risk her life to solve the mystery at Greystone Hall. Item after item seems to vanish from the old house, and even the police are baffled by the mystery. Then Robin and her friends discover some strange clues and set out to capture the criminal.

St. John, Wylly Folk. **The Mystery Book Mystery.** Viking Press, 1976. 209 pp.

A strange mystery develops at a conference of mystery-book writers. Soon after seventeen-year-old Libby Clark arrives at the conference, hoping to learn how to write detective stories, the star speaker is found dead. Add to the murder an assortment of rather strange personalities connected in some way with the victim, and it's easy to see why Libby wonders if she can make this mystery story about a real murder sound like fiction for her conference novel. Just when she thinks she has an idea that will work, another victim appears!

St. John, Wylly Folk. **The Mystery of the Other Girl.** Illus. Frank Aloise. Camelot Books, 1978. 159 pp.

After Stevie, short for Stephanie, receives a strange phone call from someone named Morna Ross, she and her brother try to solve the mystery of Morna's identity in spite of the dangers they encounter. Who is Morna Ross, and why did she get in touch with Stevie?

St. John, Wylly Folk. **The Secret of the Seven Crows.** Illus. Judith Gwyn Brown. Camelot Books, 1976. 188 pp.

Gale Franklin has a mystery to solve. And someone, some mysterious man, is trying to keep her from solving it. Gale has seven clues and a strange riddle to help her. A wedding, silver, gold, and an old secret are all part of Gale's unusual quest along the Mississippi shoreline.

St. John, Wylly Folk. **The Secrets of Hidden Creek.** Illus. Paul Galdone. Camelot Books, 1976. 160 pp.

Becky, Jenny, and Chuck are spending the summer in the Blue Ridge Mountains when they stumble upon a mystery. Together they search Winwood, the haunted estate of a dead Civil War colonel, for a lost treasure. A secret tunnel, an old diary, and an unsolved murder lead the three sleuths to Hidden Creek, where more mystery awaits them.

Tomlinson, Gerald. **On a Field of Black.** Nellen Publishing Co., 1980. 224 pp.

A local mine owner with no known enemies is murdered in a small Pennsylvania coal mining town. The Molly Maguires, a secret society of coal miners, are somehow involved as they terrorize the area with threats and random killings. The mine owner's beautiful widow hires Seth Warriner, a detective with unusual methods of investigation, to find her husband's murderer. As the investigation proceeds, corruption almost shields the real murderer.

Townsend, John Rowe. **The Visitors.** J. B. Lippincott Co., 1977. 221 pp.

John Dunham, a high school student in Cambridge, England, has a strange encounter with a group of foreigners. He initially thinks these people are tourists, but there is something different about them that he can't identify. Then, after he asks if he can help them, a dizzy spell comes over him. When he awakes, the strangers are standing over him, staring. John will soon discover that these tourists are from the future, and this knowledge will have a major effect on his life.

Walden, Amelia. **Escape on Skis.** Westminster Press, 1975. 173 pp.

While training for the Olympics, ski champion Kim Merrill is panic-stricken by the disappearance of her boyfriend, Clint. Carefully she collects clue after clue in an effort to locate him. Then she meets Tom Patterson, who puts her onto Clint's trail. But Kim never suspects that she is falling into the same deadly trap that lured her boyfriend.

Waldron, Ann. **The Blueberry Collection.** E. P. Dutton, 1981. 121 pp.

When Bessie moves from Texas to New Jersey, she never expects the adventures in store for her. But when she meets a strange woman who lives in an octagon-shaped house, Bessie senses a mystery. Then, the town seems to turn on her when she learns about an illegal underground gambling ring involving millions of dollars. Against her father's advice, Bessie sets out to find the criminals running the ring.

Waldron, Ann. **The French Detection.** E. P. Dutton, 1979. 129 pp.

Bessie Hightower is a strong-willed, thirteen-year-old Texan who is finally spending the summer in France, just as she has always wanted to do. Her classroom French is seeing her through most situations well enough, and she is enjoying life in the charming boarding house in the village of Argenon. However, the pace of her life quickens when she learns that someone is trying to evict the hosts of the boarding house. Added to this is her discovery of some statues in an antique shop that she knows have been stolen from a nearby castle. So Bessie assumes the role of detective.

Walsh, Jill Paton. **Unleaving.** Avon Books, 1977. 140 pp.

Madge, an Oxford University student, is spending the summer in the house she just inherited from her grandmother. Not only does this old house have a perfect view of the English shoreline, but it holds beautiful memories for Madge of happy summers spent here with her loving grandmother and family. The summer brightens even more when her brother Paul joins her for a few weeks and when she meets handsome young Patrick Fielding. Then comes the day at the shore when Patrick's younger sister, Molly, falls from a cliff. Or was she pushed? Madge's summer turns into nightmare and tragedy as she tries to decide what happened to Molly.

Warfel, Diantha. **The Violin Case Case.** E. P. Dutton, 1978. 151 pp.

Bax is only twelve, but he's on his way to becoming a fine musician—and an amateur detective! It seems odd to Bax when his aunt stops in at their mobile home on her way to San Francisco and asks to borrow Bax's violin. She promises him the use of her fancy German one so he can try out for the summer symphony. But Bax suspects why his aunt has made this bargain: she must think the violin will be safer with him. Soon it becomes obvious that someone wants the violin and its lovely case very much, because strange things begin to happen. Bax sets out to expose the would-be thief but ends up getting into some dangerous and embarrassing situations.

Wheeler, W. H. **Counterfeit!** Fearon-Pitman Publishers, 1979. 60 pp.

In this mystery, three agents from the international police force called Interpol must find out who is making fake money. They must solve this mystery quickly before all German, French, and American money becomes worthless. The agents' search for the counterfeiters takes them on an elaborate chase with a ship called the *Carib Queen*. Easy reading.

White, Wallace. **One Dark Night.** Photographs by Bill Aron. Triumph Books, 1981. 90 pp.

Greg is sent to spend the summer with his uncle after his father catches him using drugs. He has always admired Uncle Roy, who is a sheriff in a small town. But now his uncle seems mean, and it is rumored that he tried to kill a man. Can Greg stop a sheriff from breaking the law?

Whitney, Phyllis A. **Domino.** Doubleday & Co., 1979. 351 pp.

Laurie Morgan has been troubled for years with spells that are triggered by bits of her past, a past she has blocked out of her memory. Then one lovely summer day, a telegram arrives from her grandmother, asking her to return to Domino, the Colorado mining town that holds the key to her forgotten past. Laurie is afraid to go, afraid to remember, yet she is also afraid not to. Besides, her grandmother has asked for her help. Laurie returns to her past, to a Colorado where nothing is the same except the terror that certain noises, lights, or objects awaken in her memory.

Whitney, Phyllis A. **Secret of Haunted Mesa.** Westminster Press, 1975. 144 pp.

From the moment Jenny and her family arrive in New Mexico from Long Island for her father's lectures on ecology, a string of strange events begins. Objects disappear from various places—carved figures, a kachina doll, a drum from a museum. But there is always a crudely carved snake left in the missing object's place. Soon, a strange figure begins to appear and disappear on the peak of a nearby mesa, while the Indian Charlie Curtis always seems to be lurking around and then running away to hide. Jenny wants to know what is behind all this mystery.

Whitney, Phyllis A. **Secret of the Stone Face.** Westminster Press, 1977. 143 pp.

Jo couldn't stand the thought of her mother marrying another man so soon after the death of her father. So meeting Liza seemed like a miracle; not only did Liza understand, but she also was trying to stop her own mother's remarriage. But Liza only seemed to get Jo into more and more trouble and to increase her confusion. Meeting Erik didn't help either. She liked Erik, but he liked Scott, her prospective stepfather. Only the appearance of what looked like an unlawful scheme involving Scott gave Jo hope.

Windsor, Patricia. **Killing Time.** Harper & Row, Publishers, 1980. 188 pp.

Life in New York City is dangerous; life in a small country town is safer. Sam probably would agree with these statements, but New York has been his home for sixteen years. When he and his father move to Galeville, he finds the town very boring. Then mysterious things begin to happen. Can he and his girlfriend Tookey figure out what evils lurk here? Mature language and situations.

Wosmek, Frances. **Mystery of the Eagle's Claw.** Westminster Press, 1979. 129 pp.

When Quail's adoptive parents both die, she is sent to live with her father's aunt in the mountains of New England. Aunt Louise is very old, and her memory fails her from time to time, even to the point of forgetting who Quail is and why she is there. Quail discovers that some people are taking advantage of her aunt's problem and are using it to try to take her inn away from her. If they are successful, Quail will then really be alone. Somehow she must stop them.

Wosmek, Frances. **Never Mind Murder.** Westminster Press, 1977. 140 pp.

Sandy Douglas and her mother rent an old Victorian house in a small Massachusetts coastal town and are haunted by the ghost of a young artist who was murdered there. But why wasn't anyone interested in solving this two-year-old murder except Sandy?

Yep, Laurence. **The Mark Twain Murders.** Four Winds Press, 1982.
152 pp.

Famous author Mark Twain once spent two years as a reporter
when he was a young man. This book imagines Mark Twain during
those days in the 1860s as he is befriended by a fifteen-year-old
boy, the Duke of Baywater. Both of them investigate the murder
of the Duke's stepfather and find themselves in a Confederate plot
that involves stolen coins and disappearing corpses. But is this
mystery a real one or another hoax by Mark?

York, Carol Beach. **The Witch Lady Mystery.** Thomas Nelson, 1976.
86 pp.

Oliver has known for a long time about Mrs. Prichard, the old
witch lady who lives alone in a spooky old house with a black cat
and boarded-up rooms. He and his friends are certain that there is
something sinister connected with the old woman and her house. So
Oliver isn't too happy when he learns that Mrs. Prichard has made
the highest bid at the school auction for his services to rake her
leaves. Oliver waits until the last possible moment to keep his part
of the bargain, but he finally finds the courage to go up to the old
house and rake the leaves. Oliver is not ready for the frightening
experiences that follow, however, nor for the secret that he learns
about the strange woman.

Historical Novels

Allan, Mabel Esther. **A Lovely Tomorrow.** Dodd, Mead & Co., 1979. 190 pp.

Frue and her family ignored the war, staying on in London. In spite of nightly bombings, they were untouched except for food rationing, until New Year's Eve, 1945. Then, a final rocket attack killed both her parents, sending Frue to stay with her Great-Aunt Mildred, away from London and the acting school she so dearly loved. How could life so suddenly be so completely different? Would her dreams of being an actress ever be anything more than dreams?

Avi. **Encounter at Easton.** Pantheon Books, 1980. 138 pp.

The testimony provided at a Pennsylvania courthouse in 1768 becomes the painful story of young Elizabeth Mawes and Robert Linnly, runaway indentured servants. What had begun as a journey for jobs, security, and freedom becomes a nightmare. Elizabeth falls seriously ill, and the pair are forced to rely upon the mysterious Mad Moll. Then an offer of work to Robert delivers him into enemy hands. A chain of unlucky events follows that involves the characters with death and destruction. Sequel to *Night Journeys.*

Avi. **Night Journeys.** Scholastic Book Services, 1979. 139 pp.

In 1767, Peter York is orphaned at twelve when his parents die from a fever. His Pennsylvania Quaker community holds a meeting to decide what to do with this poor young man who has only the family mare, Jumper, to his name. They turn him over to the pious and strict Mr. Everett Shinn. Young Peter soon forgets his own problems, though, when two escaped bondsmen are seen in the area. Whoever turns them in can claim a reward of twelve pounds! Mr. Shinn allows Peter to go along on the hunt, but Peter cannot know in advance the dangers and decisions he will face on this quest.

Brady, Esther Wood. **Toliver's Secret.** Illus. Richard Cuffari. Camelot Books, 1979. 166 pp.

Ten-year-old Ellen Toliver is a young girl living with her mother and grandfather during the Revolutionary War. The British army controls New York, and Ellen's grandfather must deliver an important message to General Washington. It is decided that Ellen will take the message to New Jersey. Her hair is cut, and she dresses as a boy. Now Ellen must set out on a very perilous journey of espionage.

Branson, Karen. **The Potato Eaters.** Illus. Jane Sterrett. G. P. Putnam's Sons, 1979. 160 pp.

Maureen O'Connor is a young girl living with her family in County Cork, Ireland. It is 1846, and many people are starving because of a potato famine. Maureen learns that her family may leave for England or even go to America. This young girl loves the Irish land, but she knows she must face adult responsibilities and help provide food and shelter for her family.

Branson, Karen. **Streets of Gold.** G. P. Putnam's Sons, 1981. 176 pp.

Fourteen-year-old Maureen O'Connor left Ireland because of the potato famine of the 1840s. The ocean trip to New York is stormy and unpleasant. Next she and her family are upset over the difficulties they have finding a place to live and getting jobs. Besides, Maureen is lonely and homesick. Is America really the land of freedom and opportunity she had looked forward to finding?

Burton, Hester. **Kate Ryder.** Illus. Victor G. Ambrus. Thomas Y. Crowell Co., 1975. 177 pp.

In 1646, the English Civil War means tears and hardships to fifteen-year-old Kate Ryder. Her father has been fighting for the Parliament for so long that he is just a distant memory, and her older brother has joined the Royalist troops. When her favorite brother leaves to become a sailor, Kate is left alone with her bitter mother. Then the young girl is sent on a mission to Colchester and finds herself trapped in a besieged city with little food and water.

Calvert, Patricia. **The Snowbird.** Charles Scribner's Sons, 1980. 146 pp.

When her parents die in a suspicious fire, Willie Bannerman and her little brother, TJ, find themselves on a train bound for the Dakota Territory in the 1880s. The loss of her parents has left Willie with "lots of parts and pieces . . . but no whole." But through her bond with the mysterious horse called the Snowbird and her uncle's spirited Irish wife, Belle, Willie begins to put her life back together again. Certainly she cannot be hurt again. Or can she?

Carr, Philippa. **The Song of the Siren.** G. P. Putnam's Sons, 1979. 336 pp.

Carlotta lives in an exciting time in England, a time when men are scheming to return the exiled King James to the throne that Queen Anne holds. Carlotta finds life particularly exciting because she is beautiful, sought after by handsome men, and pampered. When she is abducted to France by the adventurous Jacobite leader, Hessenfield, she discovers that beauty can also be deadly and bring much pain. Demaris, the half sister she has always pitied for being plain, has been the victim of her cruelty in the past. But now Carlotta must turn to Demaris for help.

Chamberlain, Barbara. **Ride the West Wind.** David C. Cook Publishing Co., 1979. 182 pp.

Thirteen-year-old Nathan Cowell, his family, and other Quaker families are leaving their English prison and King George in search of freedom in America. In this story, based on the actual crossing of the Quaker ship *The Welcome,* the voyage seems doomed to disaster because of the terrifying appearance of the unknown Halley's comet in the sky. The prejudice of the crew and an outbreak of smallpox add to their troubles. The faith of Nathan and the other Quakers is truly put to test on this voyage.

Chester, Deborah. **A Love So Wild.** Coward, McCann & Geoghegan, 1980. 270 pp.

In early nineteenth-century England, Mary Clampton is rescued from the filth and rats of Newgate Prison only to face a new horror—becoming a thief in order to prevent being returned to jail. Her rescuer has no regard for her as a person, only a need for the criminal talents he assumes she possesses. But Mary has been wrongfully accused. Can she do the things he asks? Can she risk becoming a traitor to her country to avoid that awful prison? Falling in love with Lord Menton, the man for whom she is to steal, is complicating matters. What is she to do? Can she possibly escape?

Chukovsky, Kornei (translator Beatrice Stillman). **The Silver Crest: My Russian Boyhood.** Holt, Rinehart & Winston, 1976. 182 pp.

The school says they expelled the boy because he was restless and unruly and was therefore a bad influence on his classmates. The truth is that he was dismissed because his mother was not of a desirable class. She takes in laundry to feed and educate her two children. People on the street ridicule him and call him names as he goes about the town looking for odd jobs. This is all a very unlikely beginning for a person who grows up to become one of Russia's most beloved and respected storytellers. This is a fictionalized account of Chukovsky's life.

Clark, Margaret Goff. **Freedom Crossing.** Scholastic Book Services, 1980. 164 pp.

Laura and Bert Eastman risk their lives to smuggle the runaway slave boy Martin across the Canadian border. Find out how the two work together to outwit snooping neighbors, hound dogs, and ruthless slave catchers in this book based on actual facts about the Underground Railway.

Collins, Meghan. **Maiden Crown.** Houghton Mifflin Co., 1979. 229 pp.

Sixteen-year-old Sophie leaves her native Russia with great expectations, for she is to marry King Valdemar of Denmark. She throws herself into her new life with great joy, forgetting that the marriage is only a political arrangement. Soon she is threatened by clever enemies who act like friends. But Sophie is spirited, however, and turns her energies to battle against the court intrigue of twelfth-century Denmark.

Crane, Stephen. **The Red Badge of Courage.** Watermill Press, 1981. 192 pp.

Henry Fleming, a youthful private in the U.S. Army, is unsure of himself and his comrades as he prepares to battle Confederate soldiers during the Civil War. He thinks of soldiers at one moment as heroes, but at other times he sees them as cowards. His own insecurity and cowardice cause him to desert during a bloody battle, forcing him to consider his own worth as a soldier and a human being. Originally published in 1895.

Crompton, Anne Eliot. **A Woman's Place.** Illus. Ted Lewin. Atlantic Monthly Press, 1978. 233 pp.

The house no longer stands in the lovely wooded area in Massachusetts, but the lilacs still bloom by the rocks that were used as the original doorsteps. It's a strange house with a fascinating history. The five stories in the book trace the lives of five young women who have lived in the house during the past two hundred and fifty years. The first story begins in 1700 when Mary Stone helps her family survive a long winter storm. The following stories concern her descendants at times of great crisis in their lives. In 1950, the last Stone descendant sells the house to a young couple with children. But this young woman decides the only solution to her crisis is to destroy the old house and, she thinks, all its memories.

Cummings, Betty Sue. **Hew against the Grain.** Atheneum Publishers, 1978. 174 pp.

When the Civil War finally breaks out, Mattilda is only twelve. She watches as her family members divide their loyalties and as her brothers and her loved ones are killed. But by sheer will power, she keeps from giving up hope. Then, just as the war ends, she too must face a problem that threatens to break her spirit.

Dank, Milton. **The Dangerous Game.** J. B. Lippincott Co., 1977. 157 pp.

Charles is a teenager living in Paris at the time of the Nazi invasion. He joins an underground movement to resist German rule. This group sends him on dangerous missions across the country, delivering coded messages and smuggling goods. Then Charles walks into the hands of the enemy, an enemy that will torture him to get the truth.

Dank, Milton. **Khaki Wings.** Delacorte Press, 1980. 180 pp.

The year is 1914, and Great Britain has just declared war on Germany. Edward Burton is too young to enlist in the military, but he manages to get into the Royal Flying Corps and is assigned as a mechanic and observer in France. What begins as adventure and excitement for the young observer, however, soon turns into horror as the skies blaze with dogfights. Edward is finally able to prove himself courageous, but he pays a great price.

Darke, Marjorie. **A Question of Courage.** Thomas Y. Crowell Co., 1975. 208 pp.

In 1912, a female English dressmaker does not get paid much. To escape the drudgery, Emily Palmer goes for a spin on her new bicycle one evening and rides straight into a women's rights meeting. Fascinated and inspired, Emily begins a new career, one that brings her excitement and danger. Now she battles the law for her rights with all her energy and devotion.

Davis, Paxton. **Three Days.** Illus. Richard Rosenblum. Atheneum Publishers, 1980. 103 pp.

In this novel, the reader sees the Battle of Gettysburg through the eyes of Robert E. Lee. The story follows the general from the time he enters Pennsylvania to the disastrous conclusion of the Civil War for the Confederate troops. Mixed with Lee's account of these events is the story of one anonymous Confederate soldier fighting the war.

Degens, T. **The Visit.** Viking Press, 1982. 150 pp.

It was reading the diary that made everything different. Before that, Kate had been very fond of her Aunt Sylvia, but learning about her aunt's past as a Hitler Youth during World War II changed Kate's opinion. Sylvia's long-dead sister was never mentioned by the family. What was Aunt Sylvia's connection with her sister's death? The diary holds the answers.

Dickens, Charles. **A Tale of Two Cities.** Signet Books, 1980. 379 pp.

The French Revolution was a time of terror, fear, and also great patriotism. This is a story of people caught up in this conflict. Everyone, from the noble, aristocratic Sydney Carton to the blood-thirsty and harsh Madame De Farge, works in their own way to pull their country through this period of crisis. Originally published in 1859.

Donaldson, Margaret. **Journey into War.** Illus. Joanna Stubbs. André Deutsch, 1980. 152 pp.

During the German occupation of France around 1940, Janey becomes an undercover agent to help her people to become free again. Pursued by the enemy, she smuggles children to safety, rescues prisoners, and learns sabotage. Then she is captured and put in prison. But Janey's adventures have really only begun.

Donaldson, Margaret. **The Moon's on Fire.** Illus. Joanna Stubbs. André Deutsch, 1980. 138 pp.

The year is 1940, and there are three children in London who recently escaped from occupied France: Janey, an English girl, and the Polish twins, Tadek and Stefek, who are her friends. They have been left in the care of Janey's aunt and uncle. The uncle says the war is ruining his business, and the children angrily assume that if he doesn't hate Hitler he must be a spy. Tadek and Stefek decide to tail him, hoping to get evidence of his treachery, but their efforts fail badly and they are forced to run away. When the bombing begins, the boys are wandering the streets, and Janey is isolated from them, with increasing troubles of her own.

Ellison, Lucile Watkins. **Butter on Both Sides.** Illus. Judith Gwyn Brown. Charles Scribner's Sons, 1979. 150 pp.

Lucy is one of six kids in a close-knit farm family in Alabama in the early 1900s. Along with the hard work and the worry when Daddy is ill, there are good times too. The exciting overnight trip on a steamer up the Tombigbee River and the celebration of the Fourth-of-July-Christmas when the family is reunited are particularly special. Easy reading.

Fast, Howard. **The Magic Door.** Illus. Bonnie B. Mettler. Camelot Books, 1980. 80 pp.

No one but Tony knows about the secret door in his tenement backyard that leads him to Manhattan Island as it was hundreds of years ago. When he tries to tell his parents and teachers of his adventures with the Indians and Dutch settlers, they don't believe him. To prove his fantasy land is real, Tony sets out on a daring mission through the magic door. Originally published under the title *Tony and the Wonderful Door.*

Fenton, Edward. **The Refugee Summer.** Delacorte Press, 1982. 261 pp.

It is the summer of 1922 in a sleepy little town in Greece, and Nikolas and his American friends are bored, so they form a secret society. They call themselves the Pallikars and vow to do secret good and to wage war against suffering, injustice, and certain grownups. It is all a game to them until the Turks burn the city of Smyrna and send thousands of refugees fleeing all over Greece. Then the Pallikars' adventures really begin.

Fife, Dale. **North of Danger.** Illus. Haakon Sœther. Unicorn Books, 1978. 72 pp.

Twelve-year-old Arne trembles when he sees the Nazis surround his small Norwegian town, and he feels the danger in the air. Fearing that his father may return from his glacier studies in the far north and be captured by the Germans, he takes the matter into his own hands. Alone and pursued by the enemy soldiers, Arne sets out on a two-hundred-mile journey on skis over the frozen arctic to save his father.

Finlayson, Ann. **The Silver Bullet.** Thomas Nelson, 1978. 223 pp.

In the summer of 1777, Sergeant John Luckless volunteers to carry a secret message from General Burgoyne on Lake Champlain to

General Howe in New York City. To do so, the English soldier must travel undetected through the rebel American lines. But everything that can go wrong does go wrong: he sprains his knee; his mission is discovered and news of it spreads all over Albany; and he falls into the hands of ruthless American soldiers. This adventure tale, which has some basis in fact, is filled with the spies, Tories, and Indian raids that were part of the American Revolution.

Fisher, Leonard Everett. **A Russian Farewell.** Illus. by author. Four Winds Press, 1980. 133 pp.

This is the story of one family's suffering and courage. In the early years of the twentieth century, Benjamin Shapiro, his wife, and his family of eleven children must leave the Russian Ukraine and escape to America. Since they are Jews, they have been persecuted for years and are harrassed by peasants wherever they go. America seems their only hope for religious freedom.

Garrigue, Sheila. **All the Children Were Sent Away.** Scholastic Book Services, 1976. 171 pp.

Every night enemy planes roar overhead, bombing the cities and towns. It is 1940 and the war is coming closer and closer to England, so all the children must be sent away. Sara is being sent to live with her uncle in Canada. Stern Lady Drume will watch over her on the long sea voyage. But Lady Drume is a tyrant and a snob. She won't let Sara make friends or do anything! So Sara declares a war of her own—against the horrible Lady Drume.

Gedge, Pauline. **Child of the Morning.** Popular Library, 1978. 512 pp.

Hatshepsut was female and therefore not in line to rule as pharaoh of Egypt. But her father, Thothmes, saw in her a stronger and wiser ruler than in his son. So she did become pharaoh in spite of tradition and in spite of opposition, but it was a difficult reign, demanding Hatshepsut constantly look out for those who wanted a male pharaoh. Hatshepsut succeeds peacefully for a time because she surrounded herself with men who loved and worshipped her as a god, as a ruler, and as a woman. This is a fictionalized account of Egypt's only female pharaoh.

Glaser, Dianne. **The Diary of Trilby Frost.** Holiday House, 1976. 189 pp.

Living in a country home in Tennessee at the turn of the century, thirteen-year-old Trilby Frost has many things to write about. Every night she records in her diary the funny, touching, and frightening moments of her day. Then, when some of those people closest to her die, Trilby's diary becomes her most comforting friend.

Groseclose, Elgin. **The Kiowa.** David C. Cook Publishing Co., 1978. 187 pp.

Sanjak is the strong, handsome leader of the Kiowa Indians. I-leeta is a beautiful, young Mexican woman who has been kidnapped from her village. When these two meet, they are immediately caught up in a cultural conflict that only adds to their problems dealing with white traders, soldiers, and buffalo hunters who are trying to force the Indians off their land in the mid-1800s.

Harder, Janet D. **Letters from Carrie.** Illus. Bonney C. Schermerhorn. North Country Books, 1980. 137 pp.

Do you like to get letters? Theo does. Especially those that come all the way to New England from his spirited cousin Carrie in upstate New York in the early 1850s. Carrie always has some kind of adventure to report—like the time she took up with the gypsies or when her father helped the runaway slaves escape to Canada. How Theo must wish he could visit Carrie in person!

Haugaard, Erik Christian. **Catch Me, Catch Nobody!** Houghton Mifflin Co., 1980. 209 pp.

In 1937, Erik Hansen, a slightly snobbish Dane, goes on a school trip to Germany with his German class. On the ferry, a strange man in a gray coat slips Erik a small package and instructs him to deliver it to a certain inn. Then the secret contents of the package are revealed, and Erik gets involved with the anti-Nazi underground. Soon he must try to escape the pursuit of German government police and return to Denmark.

Hawthorne, Nathaniel. *The Scarlet Letter* **and** *The House of the Seven Gables: A Romance.* Signet Books, 1981. 277 pp.

In *The Scarlet Letter,* a man and woman living in colonial America fall in love, but they do not marry. When a child is born to Hester, she is forced to wear the red "A" that brands her as evil and an outcast in the Puritan town. The father of her child conceals his identity from the townsfolk. *The House of the Seven Gables* is concerned with a house cursed by a man who was hanged for witchcraft. Both novels were originally published in the 1850s. Mature reading.

Hegarty, Walter. **An Age for Fortunes.** Coward, McCann & Geoghegan, 1979. 395 pp.

In spite of the famine and rebellion in Ireland in the mid-1800s, a fortune can be made if one is smart and willing to take chances.

Shane O'Malley, an Irish peasant, and Jamie Campsie, an Irish lord, are two such fortune seekers. They are friends and business partners in spite of their different backgrounds and social standings. But they are also rivals for the love of the same woman.

Jennings, Gary. **The Terrible Teague Bunch.** Avon Books, 1982. 224 pp.

What happens when a group of good guys in the Old West decide to become bad guys? When times get hard, four men agree that robbing a train is the easiest answer to their money troubles. But their plans quickly become more and more confused—and hilarious—when a herd of sick cattle, a stubborn woman, and a young girl become involved in the daring plot.

Jones, Douglas C. **A Creek Called Wounded Knee.** Warner Books, 1979. 287 pp.

Here is a fictionalized account of the Battle of Wounded Knee, a battle that started with an accidental shot and resulted in the deaths of many Sioux Indians and U.S. soldiers. This story presents a picture of the starving Sioux suffering a loss of dignity by being forced to live on reservations and learn the white man's ways. But their religion eventually gives them hope, and they see a chance to regain their lands. This frightens the whites, who overreact and set off the tragic conflicts that followed.

Keith, Harold. **The Obstinate Land.** Thomas Y. Crowell Co., 1977. 214 pp.

Fourteen-year-old Fritz Romberg and his family leave a German settlement in Texas to take part in the Oklahoma land rush of the late 1800s. But when they come to claim their land, they find that someone has cheated and already claimed the land. The Rombergs take a poor section of land instead and must face such hardships as drought, storms, and the anger of cattle ranchers. One day Mr. Romberg is caught in a blizzard and freezes to death. Now Fritz must assume his father's position as head of the family and learn how to get along with the ranchers while keeping the family's land productive.

King, Clive. **Ninny's Boat.** Macmillan, 1980. 243 pp.

Ninny is a young slave to the Angles, a people of Germanic origin. Ninny goes with them on their flight to Britain in the fifth century. There he witnesses the final battle and death of King Arthur. But this is not the last of his adventures!

La Croix, Mary. **The Remnant.** Avon Books, 1981. 529 pp.

In this fictional account, three women reveal their special views of Jeshua (Jesus). Judith, whose father believes she must be educated even though she is female, becomes teacher to Jeshua, one of the greatest of teachers. Ruth, as Jeshua's younger sister, experiences the love of a brother who would change the world by spreading the idea of a new kind of love for others. And Sara, an innkeeper's daughter, witnesses Jeshua's birth, watches as he grows into the man who performs miracles, and stays near him at his crucifixion.

Lampman, Evelyn Sibley. **Bargain Bride.** McElderry Books, 1979. 180 pp.

Ginny was only ten years old when her cousins married her off to man nearly forty, but he agreed not to come for her until she is fifteen. Such marriages were not uncommon in the mid-1800s since married settlers could claim twice as much land as bachelors. But Ginny's husband died of a stroke their first night as husband and wife. Now, at fifteen, Ginny is a very rich widow with many suitors—all of whom appear to be after her money.

Leekley, John. **The Blue and the Gray.** Dell, 1982. 303 pp.

The Geysers and the Hales: one set of cousins sweated its living from the soil, the other from a small-town newspaper. The Geysers and the Hales were a family bonded by blood, faith, and love— until the Civil War splits the states into North and South and they have to face each other from opposite sides of the Mason-Dixon line. Does love no longer have any meaning?

Levitin, Sonia. **The No-Return Trail.** Harcourt Brace Jovanovich, 1978. 154 pp.

In this fictionalized account of the famous Bidwell-Bartleson Expedition of 1841, seventeen-year-old Nancy Kelsey, her husband, Ben, and their infant daughter Ann join the members of an expedition from Missouri to California to find a better life. Nancy loves the wide open spaces, but as the journey progresses, she begins to experience periods of weariness and doubt. Before the journey ends, however, she finds that she can face her life as a stronger, more determined, and more understanding person.

Mace, Elisabeth. **Brother Enemy.** Beaufort Books, 1979. 175 pp.

Will Andreas ever get back to Germany? That's what he wants, more than anything. He doesn't really understand why he's in England; his mother sent him there at the start of World War II to be with his father. She said that since Andreas was part Jewish, he would be safer in England. But as Andreas gets shuffled from one foster family to another, he doesn't feel that he belongs anywhere, and he longs for his old home in Germany.

Marcuse, Katherine. **The Devil's Workshop.** Illus. Paul Zepelinsky. Abingdon Press, 1979. 157 pp.

This is the story of what it might have been like to have been apprenticed to Johann Gutenberg in the mid-1400s as he worked to perfect his printing press and print the first Bible. Gutenberg's dream was to make books cheaply enough so that everyone, not just the rich, could afford them. Many things stood in his way, not the least of which were too little money and neighbors who feared his work as the work of the devil.

Mazer, Harry. **The Last Mission.** Delacorte Press, 1979. 182 pp.

During World War II, fifteen-year-old Jack Raab runs away from home and joins the U.S. Air Force. Jack is Jewish and dreams of saving the world from Hitler. But Jack's romantic view of the war is soon shattered when his buddies are killed and he is taken as prisoner of war. Jack begins to consider war wasteful and sense-lessly destructive. Mature language.

Moeri, Louise. **Save Queen of Sheba.** E. P. Dutton, 1981. 116 pp.

Twelve-year-old King David thinks he is the only one alive after the Sioux Indian raid on the wagon train. But then he finds his six-year-old sister, Queen of Sheba, under a feather bed where someone must have hidden her. And he hopes that Ma and Pa are still alive, too—somewhere ahead on the Oregon Trail. He has to find them, and he has to save his frail little sister by somehow getting her through the nearly impossible journey that lies ahead.

Moore, Barbara. **The Fever Called Living.** Doubleday & Co., 1976. 350 pp.

In the mid-1800s, Edgar Allan Poe wrote some of the most famous horror stories the world has known. But he was hated and mis-understood both by his family and by literary critics in America. So he set out to fight their dislike by writing stories and poems that would attract their attention and praise. It worked for a while. Then everything began to go wrong, and Poe risked losing his wife, his fame, and his life. Poe's life is retold in this fictional account.

Moore, Ruth Nulton. **Peace Treaty.** Illus. Marvin Espe. Herald Press, 1977. 153 pp.

Young Peter Andreas is captured by the Indians during the French and Indian War. Even though Peter's friends and family have been killed, he is given the responsibility of accepting or rejecting the peace plans offered to the Indians by the leader of the Moravians, a religious group who believe in peace and brotherhood. Easy reading.

Moore, Ruth Nulton. **Wilderness Journey.** Illus. Allan Eitzen. Herald Press, 1979. 182 pp.

James and John Graham and their parents leave Ireland in 1799 to start a new life in America, free from the political and religious wars in Ireland. But the boys' father dies during the hazardous sea voyage, and when they arrive in Pennsylvania, the boys are put to work for a cruel man. Their mother has gone farther west to find a homestead, so they finally decide to run away and search for her. A friendly religious circuit rider helps the boys on their adventures.

O'Dell, Scott. **The Captive.** Houghton Mifflin Co., 1979. 211 pp.

The *Santa Margarita,* a cargo ship of the 1500s, was not outfitted with bunks or hammocks—all available space was used for its cargo. But the ship still had a large crew of dangerous men. Young Julián Escobar, a Jesuit seminarian sailing for the first time, is put in charge of the drinking-water rations. It soon becomes clear to Julián that the crew is out to exploit and enslave the Mayan people of Mexico. Can he stand by silently while an entire civilization faces possible extinction?

O'Dell, Scott. **The Feathered Serpent.** Houghton Mifflin Co., 1981. 211 pp.

The Mayans believe Julián Escobar, a young man from Spain, is one of their gods. Taking advantage of this, Julián tries to change some of their inhumane customs while he deals with an old enemy who has become lord of a rival city. Finally, the battles between the explorer Cortés and the emperor Montezuma overwhelm Julián as he tries to survive in the magnificent but terrifying 1500s.

O'Dell, Scott. **Sarah Bishop.** Vagabond Books, 1980. 230 pp.

It is the time of the American Revolution, and Sarah Bishop has good reason to be afraid. Her father has been tarred and feathered.

Her brother has been captured by the enemy and has starved to death on a prison ship. So Sarah decides to flee from the British and to travel into the wilderness. Now with only a musket for protection, Sarah must defend herself against wild animals, hostile townspeople, and enemy soldiers.

Orgel, Doris. **The Devil in Vienna.** Dial Press, 1978. 246 pp.

Inge and Lieselotte vow they will always be best friends. But the time is 1938, and the place is Vienna, Austria, and the thirteen-year-old girls are suddenly torn apart by the coming of World War II. Lieselotte's family moves away and she becomes a member of Hitler's Youth Camp. Inge, in grave danger because she is Jewish, remains behind. Their letters are intercepted, and the girls' persistent attempts to keep in touch endanger themselves and their families. Now Inge's family begins to make escape plans, but their chances look slim. This is a true story of friendship in the face of danger and death.

Prokop, Phyllis S. **The Sword and the Sundial.** Chariot Books, 1981. 141 pp.

With enemy armies rushing to destroy his home in Jerusalem, it seems strange that young Hezekiah finds himself most afraid of his father, King Ahaz. The king has decided to make a special human sacrifice to the pagan gods to protect Jerusalem. But Hezekiah wonders who the victim will be. His baby brother? Himself? He also wonders if his own God will be able to help him now.

Rayner, Claire. **Charing Cross.** G. P. Putnam's Sons, 1979. 306 pp.

When Sophie Lackland receives a large inheritance, she finds herself able to pursue her dream of becoming a surgeon. But this is no easy goal for a woman in nineteenth-century England. Her career is further complicated by her love for two men, an exciting actor and an understanding old friend.

Rees, David. **The Exeter Blitz.** Elsevier/Nelson Books, 1978. 128 pp.

Fourteen-year-old Colin Lockwood lives in England during the time of German bombings in World War II. Since his father is a church official at Exeter Cathedral, Colin often climbs to the highest part of the building. One day the Nazis attack when he is up there, but Colin survives. Now he is faced with the difficult and dangerous task of saving his captured family from the Germans.

Rydberg, Lou, and Ernie Rydberg. **The Shadow Army.** Thomas Nelson, 1976. 160 pp.

Thirteen-year-old Demetrios Makakis awakes one morning in 1941 to find German troops invading his home island of Crete. Demetrios, his young brother, and his mother decide to flee to the safety of the mountains. But his mother is captured, and Demetrios joins the "Shadow Army," a group of underground fighters who battle the Germans.

Schlee, Ann. **Ask Me No Questions.** Holt, Rinehart & Winston, 1976. 228 pp.

It's 1848, and Laura is staying with her aunt in the country to escape the cholera epidemic in London, where her parents live. But she finds her aunt's house strange. Why is her aunt so cruel to her? Who are the children who steal the pig's food from her uncle's barn? What is going on in the house next door? The answers to these questions turn out to be more horrible than anything Laura could have imagined.

Skurzynski, Gloria. **What Happened in Hamelin.** Four Winds Press, 1979. 173 pp.

History tells of a stranger who appears in a small German town and offers to get rid of the rats, but instead he takes the children with him. This is a story about what could have happened. Geist, a young orphan and baker's assistant, becomes friends with the mysterious stranger and watches as he charms the town with his silver flute. Then Geist realizes with horror the Pied Piper's terrible plan and faces his own guilt when the piper uses him to carry it out.

Slaughter, Frank G. **The Passionate Rebel.** Doubleday & Co., 1979. 445 pp.

When the Civil War breaks out in the United States, Countess Moritza LeClerc is returning from France. Her husband recently died, so she is coming home to help the South. Moritza becomes a war correspondent, but later she becomes involved with spy work for the Confederate Secret Service.

Smucker, Barbara. **Runaway to Freedom: A Story of the Underground Railway.** Illus. Charles Lilly. Harper Trophy Books, 1979. 154 pp.

Life on master Hensen's plantation isn't easy for twelve-year-old Julilly, but at least she has her Mammy Sally to love and protect her. Then the day comes when mother and daughter are cruelly separated and sold to separate masters. Julilly finds herself on a plantation where she must pick cotton from morning to night and where slaves are whipped. The only person who can help her is Liza, a young slave who talks about escape to Canada. With the help of Lester, a fellow slave who plots the escape, and of Quaker friends and the Underground Railway, the girls are off on an exciting, but extremely dangerous, adventure. Their own ingenuity, courage, and determination help to see them through their journey to Canada.

Stiles, Martha Bennett. **The Star in the Forest: A Mystery of the Dark Ages.** Four Winds Press, 1979. 206 pp.

In the year 583, Valrada is ordered by her father, wealthy Lord Eurik of Poijou, to marry her cousin Rikimer. Yet Valrada loves Alarik, a poor man who is away on a long journey. She also believes that Rikimer is responsible for the death of her only brother, Berto, heir to her father's estate. Somehow Valrada must work out a solution to her plight without going against society's strict rules for women.

Suhl, Yuri. **On the Other Side of the Gate.** Avon Books, 1976. 126 pp.

Lena and her husband are determined to keep their spirits strong, even though the Nazis have invaded Poland in 1939 and are herding them and other Jews into a ghetto. Then Lena becomes pregnant, a dangerous situation, for if the Nazis find out, they will destroy the child. With all the courage she can summon, Lena decides to have the baby anyway. And now she and her husband must smuggle the child under the noses of the cruel soldiers to a new life outside the ghetto.

Sutcliff, Rosemary. **The Lantern Bearers.** Oxford University Press, 1979. 248 pp.

In early England the Roman legions once patrolled the land to keep it from enemy hands. Young Aquila is a warrior in this Roman outpost who lives there with his family. But when the Roman soldiers plan to return home, Aquila decides to stay in Britain and defend the land with other Britons. Mature reading.

Sutcliff, Rosemary. **Song for a Dark Queen.** Thomas Y. Crowell Co., 1979. 181 pp.

In 62 A.D., Queen Boadicea, who has been trained from infancy to lead men in battle, has inherited her royal father's sword. She is now leading British tribes in a courageous attempt to stop the Roman conquest. In this battle, the legendary Dark Queen is fighting not only against the Romans, but also to seek private vengeance and defend an ancient tribal culture.

Sutcliff, Rosemary. **Sun Horse, Moon Horse.** Illus. Shirley Felts. E. P. Dutton, 1978. 112 pp.

As a child in pre-Roman England, Lubrin, the chieftain's son, tries to capture the beautiful movement of galloping horses in his drawings. Years later, with only a small group of people remaining in his tribe, Lubrin tries to gain their freedom with his magnificent art.

Taylor, Robert Lewis. **Niagara.** G. P. Putnam's Sons, 1980. 500 pp.

In the early twentieth century, reporter William Morrison goes to Niagara Falls to write about the area and its wealthy vacationers. Through this job, he learns a great deal about the people and even becomes a part of their lives. Interesting facts, along with the beautiful but deadly spell of the falls, begin to surround William as he discovers life and develops a new sense of maturity.

Treece, Henry. **Man with a Sword.** Oxford University Press, 1979. 182 pp.

Hereward, an eleventh-century professional fighter and champion of the Empress of Germany, meets King Harold of Norway and shares adventures with him in Scandinavia, Russia, and Byzantium. Then, while stranded in England, Hereward becomes an enemy of William the Conqueror and uses all his skills to avoid execution at this ruler's hands.

Turner, Ann. **The Way Home.** Crown Publishers, 1982. 116 pp.

Her harelip made her feared, hated, and mocked. But young Anne was really just an average girl who wanted to be liked and accepted. Then a mysterious disease swept the land—the plague—and somehow Anne was blamed for it. The death of the local baron finally forces Anne to flee into the great marsh. Anne must now survive by trapping her own food and gathering herbs. It will be months before she can safely return home. But can Anne hold out that long alone?

Vernon, Louise A. **A Heart Strangely Warmed.** Illus. Allan Eitzen. Herald Press, 1975. 125 pp.

It is the mid-1700s, and young Robert Upton is peddling his father's wares on the streets of London. It is a world where traders smuggle goods into the country to avoid paying taxes and where men pick up children in the streets and force them to work long days in the mills. One day Robert meets David, a young smuggler who wants to buy some pots and pans from him so that his group can disturb the meeting of the Methodists. This religious sect is led by John Wesley, whose preachings are against the laws of England. In the days that follow, Robert meets Wesley and he eventually finds himself moved by Wesley's ideas to change his life.

Vernon, Louise A. **The Man Who Laid the Egg.** Illus. Allan Eitzen. Herald Press, 1977. 118 pp.

During the 1500s, a young Swiss orphan, Gerhard, runs away from his thieving uncles and goes to live where he can study with Erasmus, a religious leader. But Gerhard cannot understand if Erasmus is a Catholic or a Lutheran. Through his experiences, however, Gerhard learns many things about religion and life.

Von Canon, Claudia. **The Moonclock.** Houghton Mifflin Co., 1979. 159 pp.

The Turks have invaded Austria, and Barbara Cammerloherin is sent to Innsbruck by her husband. How long will they be separated? Will the Turks finally succeed in winning the entire country? Barbara writes her friend Thresl for comfort and advice. The two women and their husbands have always written letters to each other. Through these letters the four people reveal the exciting private and political events in central Europe during the seventeenth century.

Waldo, Anna Lee. **Sacajawea.** Avon Books, 1980. 1,342 pp.

Grass Child, daughter of Chief No Retreat, asks questions and wants to say and do things forbidden to Indian girls. Safe in the circle of her people, she looks forward to womanhood. But then the Hidatsas raid the Shoshoni tribe, and Grass Child is among the prisoners. The life of the young Indian princess is transformed into a life of slavery. Here she gains her new name, Sacajawea. And it is Sacajawea, the Bird Woman, whose sharp curiosity and knowledge lead to her selection as a guide and interpreter on the Lewis and Clark expedition to the Pacific Ocean in the early 1800s. Mature reading and situations.

Welch, Ronald. **Knight Crusader.** Oxford University Press, 1979. 246 pp.

Philip is seventeen and an inexperienced knight when he goes to battle against the Saracen leader, Saladin, in the twelfth century.

Although Philip fights well, he is captured. But Philip survives captivity to join King Richard in the Third Crusade. Finally he is able to return to England to claim his family estate.

Wheatcroft, Anita. **The Promise to Joel.** Illus. Robert H. Cassell. Abingdon Press, 1980. 80 pp.

A young boy, Joel, encounters Jesus Christ and decides to follow Jesus around for a time. As he travels with him, Joel is able to witness firsthand the experiences of this great religious leader.

Wisler, G. Clifton. **Winter of the Wolf.** Elsevier/Nelson Books, 1981. 124 pp.

The winter of 1864 brought more to T. J., the fourteen-year-old protector of his family, than the fear of Comanches raiding unprotected settlements. A huge wolf, which bullets can't seem to kill, is marauding, and people say the wolf is not a living creature but a legendary one. High adventure begins as T. J. and his Comanche friend set out to kill the mysterious monster.

Zei, Alki (translator Edward Fenton). **The Sound of the Dragon's Feet.** E. P. Dutton, 1979. 113 pp.

Sasha is a young girl living in Russia at the turn of the last century. All around her is hunger, poverty, and despair. Even her best friend Yulga is too sick to walk. But Sasha's tutor whispers of a revolution to end all the pain and suffering. Suddenly Sasha's eyes are opened to the world around her, and she begins to reevaluate what she believes in.

Science Fiction and the Future

Ames, Mildred. **Anna to the Infinite Power.** Charles Scribner's Sons, 1981. 200 pp.

Twelve-year-old Anna is almost a human computer. She can play music mechanically and click off numerical figures rapidly. However, she is a strangely cold person, even for the 1990 society in which she lives. When Anna finds she is an experiment in genetic engineering, she becomes emotionally shaken. Scientists are playing God, she thinks, and Anna decides to get others to help defend human values.

Beatty, Jerome, Jr. **Maria Looney and the Cosmic Circus.** Camelot Books, 1978. 160 pp.

Maria Looney and the Moonsters find themselves in grave danger when Bill Bailey's circus comes to the moon. Maria learns of an evil plan to steal the Moonsters' secret L-bomb, so she begins a search for the criminals. But can she crack a secret code in time to save the planet from destruction? Easy reading.

Beatty, Jerome, Jr. **Maria Looney and the Remarkable Robot.** Illus. Gahan Wilson. Camelot Books, 1979. 144 pp.

Young moon-dweller Maria Looney is sent to summer camp in the wilderness and soon becomes lost on Angel Island. There she meets Captain Smith, a shipwrecked astronaut who has a robot named Tommy Tonn. Smith uses Maria to teach Tommy Tonn to speak. But when Maria learns she is to be held on the island, she and Tommy Tonn escape. The robot learns to do Maria's homework and the family housework until it is robotnapped by Robinson K. Russo. Maria decides she must rescue Tommy Tonn—and the hunt is on. Easy reading.

Beatty, Jerome, Jr. **Maria Looney on the Red Planet.** Illus. Gahan Wilson. Camelot Books, 1977. 160 pp.

Maria Looney, a young girl, lives on the moon. As a class assignment she decides to do a report on Pocksum, which is our planet

Mars. But Maria can't find any information on Pocksum, so she goes to her brother, Space Commander Matthew Looney. He tells her about an old man called Digger who has been to Pocksum. Digger tells Maria about the people on Mars, the Wild Rubians. Maria has to see them for herself, though, so she takes off to visit the "Red Planet." Easy reading.

Bethancourt, T. Ernesto. **Instruments of Darkness.** Holiday House, 1979. 158 pp.

Someone is trying to rule the earth by controlling the minds of young people from all over the world. Millions call him a messiah. But to those few who have known his evil touch, he has another name: Devil. As he conducts a 3,000-mile "holy" walk from California to New York, his ranks continue to swell. Who is going to stop him? The only hope rests with a sixteen-year-old youth with powers far beyond the ordinary.

Bethancourt, T. Ernesto. **The Mortal Instruments.** Bantam Books, 1979. 145 pp.

Once Eddie was just an ordinary teenager from Spanish Harlem. Then he recovers from a coma with baffling powers over objects, people, and events. From inside a giant computer, the new EDUARDO controls nuclear warheads that could split the earth. What follows is a nightmare of supernatural terror.

Bishop, Michael. **Transfigurations.** Berkley Publishing Corp., 1979. 362 pp.

Egan Chaney, an anthropologist, has disappeared while studying the Asadi, the native race of the colonized planet BoskVeld. Now his daughter comes to the planet to discover the truth about her father's disappearance. She finds ancient Asadi rituals, and fearsome, mysterious rain forests, before learning the horrible fate of her father.

Bond, Nancy. **The Voyage Begun.** Argo Books, 1981. 319 pp.

There is an energy crisis on Earth in the not-so-distant future. There have also been disastrous shifts in climate that seem to be caused by pollution like toxic waste, oil spills, and radiation leaks. Sixteen-year-old Paul begins to do some exploring on his own in an area around Cape Cod. He comes upon some abandoned summer colonies and quickly becomes involved with a group of oddball local people and a gang of destructive looters called the Salvages.

Bonham, Frank. **The Forever Formula.** E. P. Dutton, 1979. 181 pp.

Evan Clark is frozen alive by a twentieth-century cryogenics expert and wakes up in the year 2164. The world is overpopulated and overaged, yet the people of this society wish to live forever. Hoping to find the secret, they extract the formula from Evan's brain and immediately begin working on the substance. Then a rebellion against overpopulation involves Evan in a savage war in this strange world of the future.

Bonham, Frank. **The Missing Persons League.** E. P. Dutton, 1976. 157 pp.

Brian lives in the California of the year 2400, a California in which cities are numbered, food is rationed, and laws are enforced by computer. Then Brian's family disappears, and he begins to hunt for them. On this search he discovers a secret plot concerning the incredible trick that the world government is playing on the people. Somehow Brian must rescue his family and warn the people of Earth.

Bova, Ben. **City of Darkness.** Charles Scribner's Sons, 1976. 150 pp.

Ron Morgan, excited and frightened by what his future holds, boards the plastic shell of a train for a weekend fling in the city. Once there, he meets a girl, is beaten and robbed, is prevented from leaving, and is forced to join a gang. By winter's end, Ron knows that slavery comes in many forms. Mature situations.

Bradley, Marion Zimmer, and Paul Edwin Zimmer. **The Survivors.** DAW Books, 1979. 238 pp.

Dane, Rianna, and Aratak are the only ones who managed to survive the terrible hunt of the Red Moon. But will they be able to discover the mystery of the Closed World? Their luck so far has made them over-confident, and the Closed World with its dread ghosts of white dragons may prove to be too dangerous for even these three heroes.

Bunting, Eve. **The Cloverdale Switch.** J. B. Lippincott Co., 1979. 119 pp.

John is walking in the woods outside of Cloverdale when the world seems to change—everything begins to pale. Confused, John searches for Cindy, and when he finds her, she seems to be in a trance. The world returns to normal, but Cindy appears frightened and very secretive about a black box she has in her purse. John is curious about the box. But does he dare take a look inside?

Burnham, Jeremy, and Trevor Ray. **Children of the Stones.** Charles Scribner's Sons, 1979. 200 pp.

Adam Brake, an astrophysicist, settles with his son Matthew in an ancient English village to study prehistoric stones supposedly set up in 3000 B.C. A visit to an antique shop and the purchase of a picture of a man and a boy are the beginning of an unsettling surprise as father and son find themselves caught in a time trap.

Carlile, Clancy. **Spore 7.** Avon Books, 1980. 280 pp.

The changing of ordinary people into mutants, creatures whose skin secretes slime and who become angry and hostile, reaches epidemic proportions and threatens to engulf the world. But the origin of the disease remains a mystery. Events build to a climax as the People's Republic of China resorts to nuclear weapons in an attempt to end the epidemic, and the United States prepares to follow this example. Mature situations and mature reading.

Carter, Bruce. **Buzzbugs.** Camelot Books, 1979. 133 pp.

In Millbeck, a small village in northwestern England, Lucy and John like to study insects outdoors. Instead of an innocent summer of bugwatching, however, Lucy and John are thrust into a bizarre search for the answer to the Buzzbugs, giant blood-draining creatures. As the animals in the area—and then the humans—become the prey of these monsters, Lucy's father and a team of entomologists try to resolve the mystery of these creatures' origin.

Cherryh, C. J. **The Pride of Chanur.** DAW Books, 1982. 224 pp.

No one at Meetpoint Station has ever seen a creature like the Outsider. It has no hide and is blunt-toothed and blunt-fingered. Actually, Tully, the Outsider, is a human—the only survivor of his space exploration group. Now his is the prisoner of a group of violent kifs. Tully's only escape seems to be aboard the hani ship, *The Pride of Chanur.* But his presence among the hani soon becomes a threat to them and to the peace of the entire universe.

Christopher, John. **Empty World.** E. P. Dutton, 1978. 134 pp.

Neil Miller, a teenager in London during the twenty-first century, finds himelf one of ten survivors of a plague that has swept the world. Strangely, having most of London to himself is not enjoyable for Neil. The other nine survivors are filled with greed and desire to rule the entire city alone. Suddenly, in this empty world Neil is caught up in a vicious battle for survival.

Christopher, John. **The Fireball.** E. P. Dutton, 1981. 148 pp.

The British woods seem quiet and refreshing to the two cousins, Brad and Simon. Then, from nowhere, a dazzling ball of electricity engulfs them and alters time, transporting the boys back hundreds of years to when the country was under Roman rule. Tomb robbers, slave owners, and horseback battles are all part of their adventures in the Britain of long ago.

Clarke, Arthur C. **2001: A Space Odyssey.** Signet Books, 1980. 221 pp.

Discovery, a space craft of the twenty-first century traveling at 100,000 miles per hour, is destined for a planet on the farthest edge of our solar system. Hal, a chatty computer, guides two astronauts through the vastness of space. But computers are not perfect. What will happen when this computer has a nervous breakdown? Based on the screenplay of 1968 by Stanley Kubrick and Arthur C. Clarke.

Compton, D. G. **Windows.** Berkley Publishing Corp., 1979. 255 pp.

Rod is the ultimate reporter and now, thanks to the wonders of microsurgery, he is the man with the "TV" eyes. Unfortunately, these mechanical eyes allow him to see into people's souls, and the horrors that he sees change his life forever.

Corbett, Scott. **The Deadly Hoax.** Unicorn Books, 1981. 86 pp.

Morgan and Sid, two young men born in a future time, stare at the message flashing across the screen during the blackout on Earth. It brings warning of alien invaders, the Nimbus, who intend to take over Earth with powerful weapons to prevent a nuclear war. Slowly, the two friends realize that humanity is in danger of being converted into the same humorless, unisex society to which the Nimbus belong. In a brave plan, they decide to use the aliens' own technology to defeat their plot.

Daley, Brian. **Han Solo and the Lost Legacy: From the Adventures of Luke Skywalker.** Del Rey Books, 1980. 186 pp.

Han Solo and his Wookiee partner Chewbacca are honest space smugglers until the pleadings of an old spacebum and a small misunderstanding set them on a dangerous quest for legendary treasure. The deadliest gunner in the galaxy, assassins, and an army of killer robots are just a few of the people and things they meet along the way.

Daley, Brian. **Han Solo at Stars' End: From the Adventures of Luke Skywalker.** Del Rey Books, 1981. 183 pp.

Han Solo and his Wookiee friend Chewbacca have to get their ship repaired if they want to keep on freewheeling around the galaxy. But only Jessa knows how to make the necessary repairs, and her price is high. She tells Han and Chewbacca that they must pick up some undercover agents on the Planet Orron III and then find her missing father. Will Han and Chewbacca be able to complete this dangerous mission, or will they meet disaster at the mysterious Stars' End?

Daley, Brian. **Han Solo's Revenge: From the Adventures of Luke Skywalker.** Del Rey Books, 1979. 198 pp.

Here is another adventure for *Star Wars* fans. This time spaceman Han Solo and his huge Wookiee copilot, Chewbacca, use their ship, the *Millennium Falcon,* for smuggling. There are friendly androids, warring space clans, and even a mysterious woman who may or may not be trustworthy.

Dicks, Terrance. **Doctor Who and the Genesis of the Daleks.** Pinnacle Books, 1979. 144 pp.

Doctor Who is a mysterious and zany 750-year-old Time Lord who hurtles through space in a stolen time machine. But, since there's a problem with the steering, he never lands exactly when or where he plans to. This inexactness, his desire to bring law and order to the galaxies, and his insatiable curiosity constantly lead him to weird and often wild circumstances. Now Doctor Who is given a chance to eliminate his most deadly enemy, the Daleks. Based on the popular BBC television series.

Donaldson, Stephen R. **Lord Foul's Bane: The Chronicle of Thomas Covenant the Unbeliever.** Del Rey Books, 1979. 480 pp.

Thomas Covenant finds himself thrust into a strange alternate world after being struck by a speeding police car. The people of this magical land revere Thomas as the reincarnation of their greatest hero. He is equipped with the mystic power of White Gold, which is supposed to protect the ruler of the Land from the ancient evil of Lord Foul. Thomas travels through the Land, learning its lore, meeting strange creatures, and eluding death using the magic he now possesses. This is the first volume in the first series of three chronicles of Thomas Covenant.

Eldridge, Roger. **The Shadow of the Gloom-World.** E. P. Dutton, 1977. 191 pp.

Fernfeather is clearly different from the other cave dwellers. It is he alone who challenges the Mystery, the great force of life; he alone who believes that there is a land beyond the glow-rocks and lichen of the caverns. But when he questions the authorities, he is sent to the caverns of the Gloom-World for punishment. But all is not lost, for there he finds a companion who shares the same beliefs, and together they enter into a new world.

Engdahl, Sylvia Louise. **The Doors of the Universe.** Argo Books, 1981. 262 pp.

Noren's people had been driven from their home planet by a nova. Now they are trapped on a planet that has little metal ore and whose soil and water are poisonous. People who drink untreated water or eat food grown in untreated soil begin to suffer from strange genetic changes. Noren's genius sees that there is only one way to save his people—genetic engineering. But he is the only one ready to experiment. How can Noren convince everyone that without genetic engineering there will be no chance for survival on the planet?

Fisk, Nicholas. **A Rag, a Bone, and a Hank of Hair.** Crown Publishers, 1982. 123 pp.

This story of the future concerns Brin, a young person who has an exceptionally high IQ. Because of this, he is chosen to monitor the Reborns, people who are produced chemically due to the drastic drop in Earth's birthrate. Brin's reaction to the Reborns, and to the way they behave, makes him face some basic questions about people's desire for free choice.

Foster, Alan Dean. **Splinter of the Mind's Eye.** Del Rey Books, 1978. 199 pp.

Luke Skywalker and Princess Leia of *Star Wars* continue their battle against the Empire. Stranded on a jungle planet and chased by Imperial Storm Troopers, the pair race to claim the Kaiburr crystal, a mysterious gem that has powers over the Force. Accompanied by their two faithful droids, Luke and Princess Leia again must confront the dark lord, Darth Vader. But can they escape his evil a second time?

Gee, Maurice. **Under the Mountain.** Oxford University Press, 1979. 155 pp.

Twins Rachel and Theo begin a quiet holiday with their aunt and uncle in New Zealand, but they soon find they have a strange link to the past. A Mr. Jones appears, and they remember him as the person who saved them from death when they were little children. Now Mr. Jones calls upon the children to help him fight against forces that are trying to overtake the world.

Harrison, Harry. **Bill, the Galactic Hero.** Avon Books, 1979. 185 pp.

In a future era, Bill's ambition is to be a Technical Fertilizer Operator on a farm. One day, though, Bill is recruited into the military, where he is taught to dig latrines and to hate the dreaded Chingers. Bill's story is one of combat misadventure as he follows his fearless leader, Petty Officer Deathwish Drang, into battle.

Harrison, Harry. **The Men from P.I.G. and R.O.B.O.T.** Atheneum Publishers, 1979. 141 pp.

A commanding officer addresses the graduates about to enter The Patrol, trying to convince them to sign up for the Special Assignments section. As background, the officer informs the graduates about P.I.G., the Porcine Interstellar Guard. He tells the story of Bron and his pigs who went to fight ghosts on the planet Frowbri. After this, he repeats the tale of Henry Venn, his robots, and the problems on the planet Slagter. What are the recent graduates to make of these stories?

Hill, Douglas. **Day of the Starwind.** Argo Books, 1981. 124 pp.

Space warrior Keill Randor and his alien companion Glr set out for the uninhabited planet of Rilyn to investigate some strange activities begun by the evil Warlord and his agents, the Deathwing. Once there, Keill and Glr encounter weird and deadly forms of life— and the golden figure of Altern, the leader of the Deathwing. Keill quickly realizes that he not only must battle the Deathwing band, but must survive the destructive Starwind that regularly blows across the planet.

Hill, Douglas. **Deathwing over Veynaa.** Argo Books, 1981. 125 pp.

Keill Randor saw his planet Moros destroyed by the evil genius Quern. Now he must outwit Quern and deactivate his secret weapon, or the planet Veynaa will be destroyed as Moros was. But first Keill must battle an out-of-control robot, destroy five enemy ships, and have a combat to the death with a Warlord's servant. Even if he survives all this, there is still a second Deathwing agent on Veynaa waiting for Keill. And Keill knows nothing about him.

Hoover, H. M. **Another Heaven, Another Earth.** Viking Press, 1981. 173 pp.

Gareth is the only one in her family left on Xilan, the planet that her ancestors colonized hundreds of years ago to escape the over-crowded Earth. When their machines failed, the people of Xilan had to relearn the ancient skills of farming, carpentry, and folk medicine. An exploratory party from Earth discovers these people, and Gareth and her people are forced to choose between two worlds—a simple but doomed life on Xilan or a new world of leisure and dazzling technology that includes boredom and lack of self-expression.

Hoover, H. M. **The Delikon.** Viking Press, 1977. 148 pp.

The Earth on which Aron lives has no freedom. Instead, the world is ruled by the Delikon, a powerful, evil group of space creatures. Aron is safe if he stays within the boundaries laid out by the Ruling House. But he and his family accidentally cross the boundary, and their lives are now in danger. And at the same time, a revolt is brewing. So Aron tries desperately to escape all the trouble.

Hoover, H. M. **The Lost Star.** Viking Press, 1979. 150 pp.

Lian Webster is a young astrophysicist who is bored with her life until she becomes involved in an archaeological excavation on Balthor, a Class Five planet. There she meets the lumpies, gray smiling creatures who hide a secret behind their expressionless eyes. Lian stumbles across their secret by accident and then must make a difficult decision. How much about the lumpies will she reveal to the rest of the world?

Hoover, H. M. **The Rains of Eridan.** Viking Press, 1977. 183 pp.

On a strangely beautiful planet in the year 2763, a small group of scientists explore a cave where they discover huge caterpillarlike creatures that appear to be dead. When the rains of Eridan arrive and flood the land for weeks, the enormous creatures come to life, beginning a period of confusion and horror.

Hoover, H. M. **Return to Earth: A Novel of the Future.** Viking Press, 1980. 172 pp.

Galen Innes, Governor-General of the colony of Marsat, seeks rest and a likely successor to his post, so he returns to Earth. What he finds, though, is that Samara, the young daughter of the director of one of the corporations ruling Earth, needs his advice and help. But Samara's plea for aid involves them in political intrigue due to a religious cult threatening the well-being of the Earth's populace.

Hoskins, Robert. **Jack-in-the-Box Planet.** Westminster Press, 1978. 155 pp.

Willie lives in a future world that has been at war. He has survived, and now he lives in a sealed house where he is served by robots. It seems like an easy life, but Willie discovers that he is actually in a dangerous situation. Easy reading.

Hughes, Monica. **Beyond the Dark River.** Atheneum Publishers, 1981. 152 pp.

A nuclear war has stripped Canada of all technology. In this barren land, Indian girl Daughter-of-She-Who-Came meets a white boy, Benjamin Gross. The Indian girl has healed many of the Old Ones who come to her crippled and maimed from the destroyed city nearby. But Benjamin is an Old One who is not ill. He has come from a Hutterite community to ask the Indian girl to help find a cure for the children of his village, who are sick with a mysterious ailment.

Hughes, Monica. **Crisis on Conshelf Ten.** Atheneum Publishers, 1977. 114 pp.

Kepler Masterman, son of the Moon Governor, travels to Earth with his father on a special mission. But while the guest of his aunt, uncle, and cousin in a peaceful undersea colony, Kepler stumbles into a revolutionary plot and nearly loses his life—more than once.

Hughes, Monica. **The Keeper of the Isis Light.** Argo Books, 1981. 136 pp.

Olwen Pendennis has lived on the planet Isis all her life. When her parents die, she takes over their job as Keeper of the Isis Light—a lighthouse in space built to guide ships with settlers from Earth. While she waits for these people, Olwen has only Guardian, a robot, to talk to. One day Olwen is surprised when Guardian brings her a new dress and tells her to prepare for some settlers. Olwen wonders if she will be able to communicate with these strange people. But then she falls in love with one of them and begins to think her life was much easier when she had only a robot to communicate with.

Hughes, Zach. **Thunderworld.** Signet Books, 1982. 151 pp.

When the crew of the spaceship first sight the new planet, they dub it "Worthless." But the people of Earth have to find a new home, and time is running out. So Don and Zees land on the alien planet to study it. Suddenly, there is a planetwide convulsion that kills many of the primitive life forms, and the two crew members are left stranded. They would never have guessed that the next meal they ate would change the future of a planet.

Hulke, Malcolm. **Doctor Who and the Dinosaur Invasion.** Pinnacle Books, 1979. 138 pp.

Doctor Who is a Time Lord who travels about in a Time Machine. He and his journalist companion, Sarah Jane Smith, arrive back in present-day London only to find that dinosaurs have taken over the city. Doctor Who must work quickly to discover who is behind this plot to return the world to the past by destroying all traces of the present, and all hope for the future.

Johnson, Annabel, and Edgar Johnson. **An Alien Music.** Four Winds Press, 1982. 184 pp.

A buildup of carbon dioxide in the atmosphere makes it so hot on Earth that people begin to die. Fifteen-year-old Jesse knows that unless she can get aboard the NASA Sky-Lab that is going to colonize another planet, she will die too. Jesse's plan succeeds, but discipline aboard the ship is strict, and the feisty young girl seems to get punished for everything she does. Eventually, quarrels among the crew members turn into fights—and finally into a mutiny. Then the Sky-Lab crashes into a piece of floating space debris and loses all power. They are doomed to drift in space forever unless someone on board can work a miracle.

Jones, Diana Wynne. **The Homeward Bounders.** Greenwillow Books, 1981. 224 pp.

Twelve-year-old Jamie is catapulted through space and time in a series of unexpected adventures. It happens when he becomes part of a game played by a powerful group he calls THEM. At first he is too shocked to make much sense of what is happening. But eventually he works out an unusual solution.

Jones, McClure. **Cast Down the Stars.** Holt, Rinehart & Winston, 1978. 186 pp.

Glory is a young girl and the Second Starcaster of Solstice Tower. She soon learns that the use of science must be mixed with feelings, especially when she becomes involved in a war with nomadic barbarian tribes.

Karl, Jean E. **But We Are Not of Earth.** E. P. Dutton, 1981. 170 pp.

Two boys and two girls live with their instructor at a school complex on an artificial planet. When the students show a remarkable ability to maneuver mind-controlled ships, they are sent on an exploratory mission with their teacher. But good turns to evil, and the four friends fight for their lives on a remote planet in space.

Kelley, Leo P. **Backward in Time.** Fearon-Pitman Publishers, 1979. 57 pp.

Veen and Ix, Space Police officers, are called to the city museum on the planet Chel to investigate a robbery. They find that a valuable painting was stolen by use of a time machine. Then Ix becomes obsessed with the idea that his daughter, who was killed in a space car collision, can be brought back to life by this same time machine.

Kelley, Leo P. **Death Sentence.** Illus. Steven Hofheimer. Fearon-Pitman Pubishers, 1979. 58 pp.

The scientists on the planet of New Earth are mysteriously disappearing, only to return a few days later without their scientific knowledge. Officer Ted Prentiss of the Space Police is sent to New Earth to solve this mystery before the planet is destroyed.

Kelley, Leo P. **Sunworld.** Fearon-Pitman Publishers, 1979. 57 pp.

Marsha Brody, a new Space Police officer, is assigned to the worst space station possible. She has heard rumors about Space Station Number Nine and its Commander Kyle. She is soon called to Sunworld to help the humans ward off an alien attack. Many are killed, and one woman is taken captive, but Commander Kyle does nothing. Marsha is disgusted with the whole situation. How was she to know that the aliens were really trying to save the people of Sunworld from a horrible fate? Easy reading.

Kestavan, G. R. **The Pale Invaders.** Atheneum Publishers, 1976. 178 pp.

Old Carz tells stories of the old days when people rolled along in iron boxes on wheels. Children laugh at his unbelievable tales of the past until strangers arrive. These people begin to give threatening evidence that supports what the old man said about life on Earth before the devastating period called the Upheaval.

Key, Alexander. **Jagger: The Dog from Elsewhere.** Westminster Press, 1976. 126 pp.

The earth's surface trembles, cracks, and crumbles, carrying Jagger with it. This great white dog regains consciousness in a place he's never been. But he makes contact almost immediately with Nan by thought transmission and learns he's in Alabama. Nan does what she can to help the wounded Jagger, who is now threatened by hunters. Before long, it's Jagger who needs to help Nan in a world of hatred, suspicion, greed, and violence.

Key, Alexander. **The Sword of Aradel.** Westminster Press, 1977. 144 pp.

Brian, a peasant boy in the Middle Ages, has been cared for and taught by Brother Benedict. Happy in his simple life, Brian is surprised and somewhat disturbed when he is called on to leave the abbey and go on a search for the true sword of Aradel. Merra, a girl with magical powers, says she'll try to help Brian in his quest. Merra's guess is that Cerid hid the sword somewhere in the future. Now Merra and Brian must travel through time to find the sword and then return safely back to their own time. When the two of them, accompanied by the nightingale Tangred, land in downtown Manhattan and try to buy food with gold coins, they are arrested.

Kurland, Michael. **The Princes of Earth.** Thomas Nelson, 1978. 190 pp.

When Adam Warrington, a teenage practical joker from a strict planet, travels to Mars to attend the university, he finds himself involved in a series of adventures. Adam uses all his humor, wit, and courage in his travels around the universe. He even earns the gratitude of Michael, one of the princes of Earth, who is an heir to the throne.

Lee, Robert C. **Once upon Another Time.** Thomas Nelson, 1977. 153 pp.

Middle-aged Bob Crawford, a husband and father, is driving his Mustang when he is hit by a truck. Bob wakes up to discover that he has been transported back in time to World War II, when he was fifteen years old. Bob can't tell if he is dead or just dreaming, and he wonders if he can make it back to the future. Meanwhile, he has his life to live over again, only his knowledge of future events keeps getting him into trouble. When he mentions the atomic bomb, he becomes wanted by both the American government and the Nazis.

Lee, Robert C. **Summer of the Green Star.** Westminster Press, 1981. 127 pp.

A green and gold fireball swept across the summer sky. Most people thought it was just a meteor. David did not think much of it until he met Adrienne and her family. They seemed unusual to him from the start. Slowly, it begins to dawn on David that Adrienne's family and that green-gold "meteor" are somehow related. But he won't let himself believe his suspicions until he can get positive proof that they are extraterrestrial beings.

Lee, Robert C. **Timequake.** Westminster Press, 1982. 160 pp.

When an earthquake hits their camping site, young cousins Randy Walker and Morgan McCormick are separated from their family. They soon find themselves in a strange land in the year 2027. It is a time that mixes the primitive and the high tech as tribes fight with lasers. Randy and Morgan decide to try and live with one group as they search for a way back to 1982.

Lem, Stanislaw (translator Louis Iribarne). **Tales of Pirx the Pilot.** Bard Books. 1981. 206 pp.

Why does Pilot Pirx get all the most dangerous missions? His bosses will tell you it is because Pirx has the crazy ability to bumble through any situation and survive. Pirx's adventures include a trip with a pair of love-crazy horseflies, a voyage to a moon station built by madmen, and a meeting with a rusty old robot whose programming has become confused. Mature reading.

Lucas, George. **Star Wars: From the Adventures of Luke Skywalker.** Del Rey Books, 1977. 220 pp.

Twenty-year-old Luke Skywalker finds himself drawn into the battle between good and evil forces in a galactic civil war. Two personable robots join Luke, Han Solo, and a large and furry Wookiee in an exciting chase across space in search of a beautiful, kidnapped rebel princess. Terrifying space battles and laser duels await these men and women who oppose Darth Vader.

MacCloud, Malcolm. **Gift of Mirrorvax.** Argo Books, 1981. 192 pp.

Michael had lost his self-confidence. On his planet, Vax, he wanted to be bought by the richest of the great business conglomerates. Instead, he is trained as a lawyer and becomes recyclage. Then the computers of three conglomerates begin bidding on him, offering two thousand chronas, an unbelievable amount of money. But Michael soon finds out what he has to do—he is to become an astronaut on a mission to a hidden planet.

MacCloud, Malcolm. **The Tera Beyond.** Argo Books, 1981. 190 pp.

Jawn was only a high schol student, yet he was hunted by CRAC, the government secret service force on his planet, Tera. How had he ever gotten into this mess? Could it really have begun with something as innocent as a biology project? Jawn discovered some exciting information about the two basic kinds of bacteria on Tera. But when he tried to continue his studies, his teacher, his friends, and even the government tried to force him to stop. Jawn begins to wonder just what horrible secret he has stumbled on to.

Mark, Jan. **The Ennead.** Thomas Y. Crowell Co., 1978. 306 pp.

When Isaac nears his fifteenth birthday, he knows that he must find a job. On his planet of Euterpe, unemployment for those Isaac's age is not allowed. His job as his older brother's steward seems perfect, but this work actually brings him closer to danger than if he hadn't found work. Isaac witnesses a romance, and love is a crime on Euterpe. By keeping the secret, Isaac could risk being sent to another planet.

McCaffrey, Anne. **Dinosaur Planet.** Del Rey Books, 1978. 202 pp.

A group of space technicians is sent to the planet Ireta to make a list of the plants and animals and to search for new energy sources. But the crew finds the animal life to be dinosaurlike creatures. And to make things worse, the rescue ship has disappeared. The action becomes more tense as members of the crew begin to change curiously in the darkness of this future world.

Meluch, R. M. **Wind Dancers.** Signet Books, 1981. 166 pp.

It is a strange new universe. The Morts are weird corpses that begin to overrun the planet of Aeolis. Humans there have had control for a long time, but now the Morts threaten to end their rule. So the Serviceship *Halcyon XLV* is sent to Aeolis to solve the mystery of the Morts. But finding the secret behind the Morts could mean the destruction of all the humans on the planet.

Murphy, Shirley Rousseau. **The Ring of Fire.** Atheneum Publishers, 1977. 232 pp.

The Planet Ere is torn by a violent and savage war. But the Children of Ynell are members of a secret race possessing psychic powers and the ability to see the future. Through the use of these forbidden powers, the children help fight the enemy. As they refine their powers through lessons given by the Seer teacher, the children are hunted by the enemy and are eventually forced to gather together and combine their powers.

Niven, Larry. **The Ringworld Engineers.** Holt, Rinehart & Winston, 1980. 357 pp.

Louis Wu escaped from the Ringworld twenty years ago. Now he finds himself kidnapped by a puppeteer who forces Louis to fly a ship, *The Hot Needle of Inquiry,* to the Ringworld, an artificial planet, huge and flat like a ring, rotating around a sun. But because of a mechanical problem, the Ringworld is beginning to tilt and all life on it will eventually be destroyed by the sun. So Louis must try to find the planet's control center. His quest takes him through many battles and adventures with such creatures as the Grass Giants, the City Builders, and the Night Hunters.

Norton, Andre. **Knave of Dreams.** Viking Press, 1975. 252 pp.

Ramsay Kimble is fascinated by his recent dreams; they are so real, unlike any he has known before. Then one day he wakes up in the world of his dreams, a world that exists parallel to his world on Earth. In this other world he is a prince, but he is also hunted by those who would take his right to rule away. Is there a chance to get back to his former life, or should he stay and deal with the adventure and danger of being a prince?

Norton, Andre. **Voorloper.** Illus. Alicia Austin. Ace Books, 1981. 267 pp.

Voor is a new planet declared free and open to settlers by Survey Testers. But the Shadow stalks on Voor, striking without warning at isolated settlements and killing nearly everything. How can anyone stop something that drives those who see it mad?

Parenteau, Shirley. **The Talking Coffins of Cryo-City.** Elsevier/Nelson Books, 1979. 126 pp.

This world is one with perfectly controlled weather. Sunshine and rain are so well regulated that there are even musical instruments that can be played by the wind and the raindrops. But something goes wrong. The spring rains do not arrive, and crops die in the blazing sun. Is young Kallie the only one who questions what is happening? Apparently, since she is sentenced to life frozen in a capsule in Cryo-City, where the ill await cures and criminals await terror.

Pinkwater, Daniel M. **Alan Mendelsohn, the Boy from Mars.** E. P. Dutton, 1979. 248 pp.

> Changing to a new school can be hard, but for Leonard Neeble life is unbearable at Masterson Junior High. Then he meets Alan Mendelsohn, who is just as strange as he looks and who claims to be from Mars. The two friends explore mind control and soon travel to different planes of existence. Then Leonard and Alan are challenged with a race against time to save the people of a different thought-plane from starvation.

Richelson, Geraldine, adapter. **The Star Wars Storybook.** Random House, 1978. 56 pp.

> It is a time of battles between good and evil in outer space. Luke Skywalker, aided by Ben (Obi-wan) Kenobi, fights Darth Vader, the evil Imperial Dark Lord. Starship pilot Han Solo and a two-hundred-year-old Wookiee also attempt to help save Princess Leia from the evil Imperial forces. This text contains color photographs from the popular film. Easy reading.

Schlee, Ann. **The Vandal.** Crown Publishers, 1981. 188 pp.

> What makes Paul set fires? His parents don't know, his psychiatrist doesn't know, and Paul can only say that he feels he has to destroy the darkness with the light from the fire. As Paul seeks to understand his behavior, he comes to question his place in the orderly society of the future in which he lives. (Guardian Award for Children's Fiction)

Shelley, Mary Wollstonecraft. **Frankenstein.** Watermill Press, 1980. 333 pp.

> Dr. Frankenstein is trying to find the secret to the creation of life. Using assorted body parts stolen from fresh graves, the doctor assembles his monster. But this monster is a victim, not a criminal. He is a sympathetic character who, like a child, tries to understand the strange world around him. Originally published in 1818.

Slater, Jim. **The Boy Who Saved Earth.** Illus. Ron Logan. Doubleday & Co., 1981.

> Marcou, a fourteen-year-old boy from a friendly alien planet, has telepathic powers and superintelligence. He has survived a spaceship crash on Earth and seems destined to save the planet from alien invasion. These aliens, the Malagan, are able to possess the

minds of humans and make those humans do their evil bidding. Will Marcou be able to contact his own planet in time to help the Earth? Or will he be captured and have his own mind possessed?

Sleator, William. **The Green Futures of Tycho.** E. P. Dutton, 1981. 133 pp.

Eleven-year-old Tycho finds a strange, egg-shaped object that has the power to transport him back and forth in time. Learning how to use it is fun, but it is also a bit frightening when he discovers futures for himself that he hates. Can the egg change things, or has he been changing them himself somehow? If so, can he undo what he has done?

Sleator, William. **House of Stairs.** E. P. Dutton, 1975. 166 pp.

Peter, Lola, Blossom, Abigail, and Oliver are five teenagers of the twenty-first century who have just been released from state mental institutions. But they are not released into the free world. Instead, they are blindfolded and led into a strange building filled with hundreds of winding staircases with deadly drop-offs. The only food or water they can have must be taken from a machine with flashing lights; and the machine forces them to perform a weird dance before they can have anything. But Peter and Lola make a brave attempt to resist the machine.

Slote, Alfred. **My Robot Buddy.** Illus. Joel Schick. J. B. Lippincott Co., 1975. 92 pp.

What did Jack Jameson really want for his tenth birthday? A robot—one programmed to play ball, to fish, to talk with—a made-to-order friend. On his birthday, Jack's parents take him to Atkins Robots, Inc., where his special robot, Danny, is created to his specifications. It is the happiest day of Jack's life—until the mysterious blue solar car begins coming around. Easy reading.

Stevenson, Robert Louis. **The Strange Case of Dr. Jekyll and Mr. Hyde.** Watermill Press, 1980. 102 pp.

Edward Hyde is a vile and obnoxious person. Henry Jekyll is a reputable doctor, pleasant and well liked. The recent relationship between Jekyll and Hyde has the doctor's friends puzzled. But little do they know that the good doctor has created the weird Mr. Hyde. Originally published in 1886.

Stickgold, Bob, and Mark Noble. **Gloryhits.** Del Rey Books, 1978. 280 pp.

DNA is the substance that helps pass on hereditary traits from parents to children. Charlie and Ann are going to have a child. But a friend of theirs, a doctor, warns them about possible birth defects in the child that could be caused by some contaminated LSD they have taken. Related to Ann and Charlie's problem is the story of some biological warfare experiments conducted by Major Stanley Johnson. The CIA and the Russians are both investigating the use of viruses to kill the enemy in battles. But what connection is there between Charlie and Ann's baby and germ warfare?

Stone, Josephine Rector. **Green Is for Galaxy.** Argo Books, 1980. 170 pp.

This is the story of a great escape into space. Illona has the job of taking care of the goslings, children with strange powers who are allowed to live because they can construct androids. They live on a lost space colony called Willy's World, where people are kept perpetually entertained by the ruler. But when Illona discovers what her goslings will be used for, she knows she must escape with them to another planet. But first she must battle X-Blue-One, who will kill her if he has to, rather than let her escape.

Stone, Josephine Rector. **The Mudhead.** Argo Books, 1980. 140 pp.

Korby had been on many missions with his parents to strange and distant planets. But he especially wanted to go with them on their latest assignment to a primitive world. Once he gets there, however, Korby quickly becomes bored. He is restricted to one section of the base on which they live. And there is no one his own age to play with. So Korby begins to watch the local animals and natives when they come by the base. One day Korby rushes out to rescue a foxlike creature caught in a net, only to discover it is a trap for him. What could his native captors have planned?

Stone, Josephine Rector. **Praise All the Moons of Morning.** Argo Books, 1979. 172 pp.

In a harsh future world, Desta has known nothing but slavery. But a strange bag of crystals reveals a message from her ancestors who had crashed in a spaceship centuries ago. So Desta gathers her courage and sets out on a dangerous journey, battling the demons and the desert to follow the hope of a better life in a free land.

Stone, Josephine Rector. **Those Who Fall from the Sun.** Atheneum Publishers, 1978. 153 pp.

The Techmen take over Earth and control the population through mind-control devices. Those who refuse to be controlled are shipped off to distant planets. Alanna, a young outcast separated from the rest of her family, travels on one ship with an old man she has befriended. Once they arrive at the strange new planet, Alanna must struggle against odd creatures and dangerous Techmen. The actions and decisions that Alanna makes now will determine the future freedom of all the people who have arrived with her.

Townsend, John Rowe. **Noah's Castle.** J. B. Lippincott Co., 1975. 255 pp.

Norman Mortimer and his family face a life of hardship in late twentieth-century England. Prices jump tremendously every month, and paper money is fast becoming useless. Norman decides what he must do to save his family from starvation: he begins to collect huge amounts of food and supplies to save for harder days. When the harder days come, Norman's family is content; except that angry, hungry, begging throngs gather outside his door.

Tuning, William. **Fuzzy Bones.** Ace Books, 1981. 375 pp.

Where did Fuzzies come from? Who were their ancestors? Humans need to answer questions like these before they can fully accept the species *Fuzzy sapiens* as equals on Earth. But looking for the information begins to threaten both humanity and the Fuzzies.

Verne, Jules. **A Journey to the Center of the Earth.** Watermill Press, 1980. 385 pp.

Three daring explorers enter the funnel of an extinct volcano in Iceland and wind their way down into the blackness of the earth's core. Although they may never see daylight again, they continue into this eerie world of prehistoric plants and animals, a subterranean ocean, and sea monsters. But once they arrive thousands of miles below the earth's surface, how will these fearless explorers ever be able to return? Originally published in 1864.

Walsh, Jill Paton. **A Chance Child.** Farrar, Straus & Giroux, 1978. 185 pp.

Creep has spent all of his young life locked in a tiny room beneath the stairs with only his half brother caring enough to bring him scraps of food. Then a wrecking ball working on the building next door accidentally knocks a hole in the wall, freeing him, so Creep runs, but to where? The old barge he finds on the canal not only takes him away from his room, but takes him away in time. The time he finds himself in is cruel, however, for it is England's Industrial Age with its sweatshops, long hours, and abuse of children as a source of cheap labor.

Wells, H. G. **The Invisible Man.** Watermill Press, 1980. 235 pp.

Griffin is a brilliant young researcher and chemist who feels trapped and unappreciated teaching in a small English college. His brilliance leads him to investigations into the properties of light, and eventually he finds the secret of invisibility. Unfortunately, Griffin doesn't realize that the drugs he is taking to achieve invisibility are also driving him mad. Now he is a hunted homicidal maniac; a man caught in a trap of his own genius. Originally published in 1897.

Wells, H. G. **The War of the Worlds.** Watermill Press, 1980. 258 pp.

War machines from Mars descend upon Earth intent on taking over our planet. The humans are defenseless against the Martians' hovering machines, which shoot light rays that destroy anything in their paths. Although the humans fight bravely, no weapon seems to damage the Martian ships. How can the humans possibly hope to win this war with the alien invaders? Originally published in 1898.

West, Carl, and Katherine MacLean. **Dark Wing.** Argo Books, 1979. 242 pp.

Travis seems to fall into trouble without trying very hard. First, he finds himself on spaceport land without a permit to be there. Then, in escaping from a police helicopter looking for trespassers, he finds a wrecked ambulance with two paramedic cases still inside. This creates a problem because practicing medicine has been outlawed in Travis's futuristic society for over seventy years! But Travis decides to ignore the law and becomes involved in black-market medicine.

Wilder, Cherry. **The Nearest Fire.** Argo Books, 1980. 226 pp.

Three earthmen are separated from a fourth on the planet Torin. With the help of two refugees from a penal colony, the earthmen escape capture by the Great Elder. Finally, the men are able to gain the Elder's cooperation for their mission.

Williamson, Jack. **The Humanoids.** Avon Books, 1980. 259 pp.

A generation of robots come to Earth from a distant planet for the purpose of saving humankind from itself. The goal of these humanoids is to bring everlasting peace. The trouble is that these robots are slowly robbing people of their freedom to struggle and to feel. Dr. Forester, a famous scientist, is recruited by a group of people to stop the humanoids.

Winterfeld, Henry (translator Kyrill Schabert). **Star Girl.** Illus. Fritz Wegner. Camelot Books, 1976. 191 pp.

The beautiful little girl huddled beneath the tree in the middle of the forest looks about seven or eight years old. Walter and his friends have ventured far into the forest to pick mushrooms when they see her. Mo tells them she has fallen out of her father's spaceship and the tree broke her fall. And she is not seven or eight—she is eighty-seven! The people on her star, Asra, stay young for hundreds of years. In some ways Mo is very much like humans, but there are ways in which she is different—and those differences nearly destroy her before her father's spaceship returns to pick her up.

Yep, Laurence. **Sweetwater.** Illus. Julia Noonan. Camelot Books, 1975. 201 pp.

You can't see Tyree's planet of Harmony from Earth, but teenage Tyree is a fifth-generation Earth person. He's now become a Silkie on a star colony, and he's the one who feels he must keep the memories of Earth alive in his people. He's also determined to keep alive the memories of Old Sion, the city the commune dwellers are about to abandon. Through music, Tyree and his blind sister discover a past that leads back to the present and to the preservation of the thoughts of the Old Sion and Earth that Tyree wants to protect.

Fantasy and Folklore

Aiken, Joan. **The Stolen Lake.** Delacorte Press, 1981. 291 pp.

Twelve-year-old Dido is aboard the *Thrush* when it is summoned to the aid of the Queen of New Cumbria. The queen is upset because a neighboring king has stolen her lake. She is really Queen Guinevere, and she's been waiting over a thousand years for King Arthur to return to her across the lake. It's up to Dido and the crew of the *Thrush* to get the lake back—or else. But Dido is worried. Why are there no other children around?

Aleichem, Sholom (selected and translated by Aliza Shevrin). **Holiday Tales of Sholom Aleichem.** Illus. Thomas di Grazia. Charles Scribner's Sons, 1979. 145 pp.

These stories, translated from the Yiddish, are of youthful adventures, small-town people, and humorous events that become a part of everyone's life. Illustrations help recreate the highlights of Jewish holidays.

Aleichem, Sholom (editor and translator Curt Leviant). **Old Country Tales.** Paragon Books, 1979. 313 pp.

Advice and stories from Eastern Europe fill this book, including Tevye the Dairyman reading the Psalms, a portion of a romantic story from "The Song of Songs," Jewish children's adventures, old folktales of people in trouble and sorrow, stories of soldiers and the railroads, and news of holiday feasts and village events. The language, culture, and feelings of the Yiddish community captured in these selections are rich in moments of warmth and laughter.

Aleichem, Sholom (editor and translator Curt Leviant). **Some Laughter, Some Tears: Tales from the Old World and the New.** Paragon Books, 1979. 248 pp.

How does a child view the world—a particular child who is an only son of wealthy Jewish parents? The burden of life is nearly too heavy for the boy in "Elijah the Prophet" as he thinks of how he cannot get dirty, or take risks, or go out without a hat. And as the Passover holiday approaches, the pressures force him to make an impossible choice. There are many other Jewish stories here, some brought from Russia, and some about immigrants in the New World. For example, there are stories of how new people here were plotted against, and of how the dream of a land where gold can be scooped up from the pavements fades as these same people are forced to scratch for a living on crowded, noisy city streets.

Alexander, Lloyd. **The First Two Lives of Lukas-Kasha.** Yearling Books, 1982. 213 pp.

Lukas makes a deal with Battisto the Magnificent and finds himself washed ashore in a new land of palaces and hidden treasure. To his astonishment, he is hailed King of Abadan. But his life in the palace is endangered by rivals who threaten to overthrow him. Running for his life, Lukas teams up with the court astrologer, a hot-tempered slave girl, and a poet. Not even in his wildest dreams could Lukas have imagined the strange adventure that is just beginning.

Alexander, Lloyd. **The Kestrel.** E. P. Dutton, 1982. 244 pp.

Augustine, King of Westmark, sends Theo out to tour the land. While Theo sets forth, a war breaks out, and he and Mickle, the future queen, find their lives drastically changed. With the war come betrayals and conspiracies, but also some hope. (ALA Best Book for Young Adults)

Alexander, Lloyd. **Westmark.** E. P. Dutton, 1981. 184 pp.

Theo works as an apprentice to a printer. He does well until he violates the strict laws controlling printing. A dramatic confrontation with the police follows, and Theo becomes a fugitive. While on the run, he encounters dwarfs and fortune seekers. Then his real adventure begins when he enters the kingdom of Westmark.

Alexander, Lloyd. **The Wizard in the Tree.** Illus. Laszlo Kubinyi. E. P. Dutton, 1975. 138 pp.

Mallory is a young girl who believes in wizards, wishes, and witches. When she finds a real wizard who has been trapped inside a hollow tree for centuries, it seems too good to be true. But trouble comes when the innocent little man is accused of murder, and Mallory must depend on her quick thinking and magic powers to save herself and her friend.

Anderson, Margaret J. **In the Circle of Time.** Scholastic Book Services, 1979. 218 pp.

Robert and Jennifer accidentally discovered the secret of the ancient circle of stones. Now they are trapped in the future. Will they ever go home again? Or will they live forever with the inhabitants of a distant time—Kartan, Lara Avara, Panchros, Alloperla, and the Barbaric One?

Babbitt, Natalie. **Knee-Knock Rise.** Illus. by author. Camelot Books, 1974. 118 pp.

Knee-Knock Rise in the Mammoth Mountains is greatly feared because it is the home of the Megrimum. Young Egan, who goes to stay with his aunt and uncle in the village of Instep, decides to climb the Rise and face the demon. But after Egan goes through all this terror and effort, no one believes his discovery. (Newbery Honor Book)

Babbitt, Natalie. **The Search for Delicious.** Camelot Books, 1976. 167 pp.

The King asks twelve-year-old Gaylen to poll the kingdom to find out what the people think is the most delicious food. In his travels, Gaylen encounters more problems than he thought possible: the 900-year-old woldweller who refuses to help him; a peculiar minstrel who offers him a magical key; a cave of dwarfs who lead him to Ardis, the mermaid child of the lake; and even a civil war.

Banks, Lynne Reid. **The Indian in the Cupboard.** Illus. Brock Cole. Doubleday & Co., 1981. 181 pp.

Omri isn't too thrilled with the little plastic Indian he got for his birthday. He's more interested in his other presents: his new skateboard, the mysterious cupboard his brother gave him, and the very old key that, remarkably, fits the cupboard's lock. In fact, he almost forgets about the toy Indian until he decides it's just the right thing to keep in his cupboard. He locks the Indian in the cupboard overnight, and by morning something unbelievable has happened—the Indian has come to life! His name is Little Bear, and he becomes Omri's friend. But the longer Omri knows Little Bear, the more convinced he is that he must do something drastic to keep his Indian friend safe from harm. Easy reading.

Barrie, J. M. **Peter Pan.** Illus. Trina Schart Hyman. Charles Scribner's Sons, 1980. 184 pp.

Who doesn't remember Peter Pan, the boy who did not want to grow up? Following Peter Pan in his playful fun are Tinker Bell and the Darling children. The adventure begins the night that Peter flies into the Darling home looking for his shadow. He decides to teach the children how to fly and takes them back to Neverland with him, where even more excitement is in store for them all involving pirates and treasures. Originally published in 1904.

Baylor, Byrd. **A God on Every Mountain Top: Stories of Southwest Sacred Mountains.** Illus. Carol Brown. Charles Scribner's Sons, 1981. 64 pp.

This book contains stories of the Southwest Indians' sacred mountains. Certain mountains are considered holy places by the Indians, and each mountain has its story. These legends are presented in the form of poetry, and each legend is accompanied by an illustration.

Beamer, Charles. **Magician's Bane: Book One of the Legends of Eorthe.** Thomas Nelson, 1980. 203 pp.

What can three average American children do to save a group of children held captive in the Land of the King? But Jodi, Martin, and Eric are asked by a magician named Waymond to help, and they decide to accept the dangers and risks. On their way to the Land, the three children and Waymond must battle Murks, Wraths, Slashes, and Stenches—all evil creatures led by Grandfather Obit. Lending a hand to overcome Obit and his monsters, however, are a cougar, the King, and the Zooks, an army of children.

Beckman, Thea. **Crusade in Jeans.** Charles Scribner's Sons, 1975. 275 pp.

By some fluke, Rudolf Hefting of Holland finds that a time machine has thrust him into the Rhineland of the early 1200s at the precise moment the Children's Crusade is marching through. As a teenager of the twentieth century, Rudolf uses his special knowledge and skills to help lead the children across Europe. They defy disease, hunger, war, and all kinds of horrors. Through their trials, this huge band of young people develop loyal friendships, a special kind of courage, and a devotion to God. (1974 Gold Medal in the Netherlands)

Beresford, Elisabeth. **Curious Magic.** Elsevier/Nelson Books, 1980. 144 pp.

Andy takes a vacation off the coast of England and is surprised at what awaits him: a Roman fort, pirates, a merboy, a white witch (Mrs. Tressida), and the witch's niece. Andy finds that the spell that now binds the white witch can be broken, but only by a wounded knight. Andy must make himself fit this description, and, to do so, he must deal with magic and time travel.

Bethancourt, T. Ernesto. **Tune in Yesterday.** Holiday House, 1978. 156 pp.

Richie Gilroy and Matty Owens are good friends and jazz musicians. However, life is not going smoothly for them. To escape the boredom of a summer's evening, the boys start out on an adventure that takes them through the town's cemetery. There they happen upon a Gate to the Past guarded by the strange Abner Pew. With Abner's help, they pass through the Gate and find themselves in New York City in the year 1942. World War II is raging across the Atlantic, and great jazz is blaring all over New York. But this world of jazz is soon mixed with espionage for Richie and Matty when they overhear German spies plotting against the United States.

Bond, Nancy. **A String in the Harp.** McElderry Books, 1978. 365 pp.

The mythology and countryside of Wales works its magic on the Morgan children, who move there from the United States with their father shortly after the death of their mother. At first, each member of the family handles grief in a way that separates them. Then Peter finds an ancient harp-tuning key that takes them back to the time of Taliesin, a sixth-century bard who lived in that part of Wales. Will the harp have the power to bring the Morgans back together?

Bradley, Michael. **The Norwood Tor.** Dodd, Mead & Co., 1980. 172 pp.

Jeremy Spiller defies his parents and runs off to search for his missing brother, Paul. Lured by a special magic coming from a strange, disguised creature, Jeremy continues on his search in the company of a bizarre assortment of circus people traveling on a speeding train toward the north. As they race across the countryside, though, Jeremy begins to discover strange secrets among the circus troupe. In spite of these suspicions and fears, though, Jeremy believes he will find Paul at the end of his journey. But when at last Jeremy and Paul meet, Jeremy confronts a chilling surprise.

Byars, Betsy. **The Winged Colt of Casa Mia.** Illus. Richard Cuffari. Camelot Books, 1975. 128 pp.

Serious and bookish, from a series of boarding schools, Charles comes to Texas to visit his Uncle Coot, a former movie stunt man. They have trouble understanding one another until a strange colt is born. This colt has wings! With this strange horse, uncle and nephew go on numerous adventures that bring them closer together.

Caldecott, Moyra. **The Tall Stones: The Sacred Stones Trilogy #1.** Popular Library, 1979. 255 pp.

Kyra, Karne, and Fern, though very young, must join together to fight the evil that has come to their village in the form of a priest not fully approved by the Church. Kyra's powers of sight and mind control are essential to their winning against the priest, yet she is the youngest of the trio and the most afraid. The Lords of the Sun, the source of power in their religion, must be contacted for help; but only Kyra has the ability to do that by letting her mind leave her body and travel to the world in which the Lords dwell.

Carlson, Bernice Wells. **Picture That.** Illus. Dolores Marie Rowland. Abingdon Press, 1977. 143 pp.

Twelve charming folktales from all over the world are featured in this book. Accompanying each tale are a short game or verse and two or more art projects related to the story. It is a mixture of activity, craft, and story designed to put your imagination to work.

Carroll, Lewis. *Alice's Adventures in Wonderland* and *Through the Looking-Glass.* Illus. John Tenniel. Signet Books, 1973. 238 pp.

Follow Alice on her adventures after she falls down a rabbit hole and steps through a looking glass. Join her as she meets some incredible characters: the Mad Hatter, the Duchess, the Mock Turtle, the Queen of Hearts, the Cheshire-Cat, and Tweedledum and Tweedledee. Nothing is ever what it appears to be in the crazy world Alice finds herself in. Both novels were originally published in the mid-1800s.

Chandler, Robert, translator. **Russian Folk Tales.** Illus. Ivan I. Bilibin. Shambhala Publications, 1980. 77 pp.

Vasilisa is a beautiful young girl with wicked stepsisters and an evil stepmother. Together they send Vasilisa to see the horrible Baba-Yaga, who would eat those people who couldn't do her bidding. But Vasilisa is helped by her magic doll to do all that the ugly woman asks her to do. This is just one of seven Russian folktales in this collection.

Chant, Joy. **Red Moon and Black Mountain: The End of the House of Kendreth.** E. P. Dutton, 1976. 277 pp.

The three Powell children are swept from their drab English home into the strange and exciting world of Kendrinh. Penny is captured by the dreadful Hurnei and must escape or die. Oliver must battle the powerful Fendarl to save a small Indian village. Nick wanders around the unfriendly Khentor Lands in search of his brother and sister. Soon, all three children become part of a larger adventure in a land of strangers.

Cole, Joanna, editor. **Best-Loved Folktales of the World.** Illus. Jill Karla Schwarz. Doubleday & Co., 1982. 792 pp.

This collection includes over 200 folk and fairy tales from around the world, selected for their popularity. The old favorites and new tales are arranged geographically, with an index of the subjects of the tales and a title index provided.

Collodi, Carlo (translator and adapter Marianna Mayer). **The Adventures of Pinocchio.** Illus. Gerald McDermott. Four Winds Press, 1981. 122 pp.

Pinocchio, a wooden puppet, wants to become a real boy. But he gets himself into much trouble in his adventures around the town. Helping him get out of tough situations and onto the path to boyhood are the Blue Fairy, Cricket, and his maker, Gepetto. Originally published in 1883.

Cook, Ann, and Herb Mack. **Robot Visits School.** Illus. Irene Trivas. Yearling Books, 1982. 32 pp.

In this story—one of six Robot tales—a robot goes to a grade school and offers to help solve mathematical problems. The children soon discover the robot needs repairs, and they take him to the school nurse and the custodian. But will he be fixed in time to help the children finish their lunchroom survey of favorite foods? Other books in this series are *Robot and the Flea Market, Robot Saves the Day, Robot Goes Collecting, Robot in Danger,* and *Robot Comes to Stay.* Easy reading.

Cooper, Susan. **The Grey King.** Illus. Michael Heslop. McElderry Books, 1980. 208 pp.

In this fourth book in The Dark Is Rising series, Will Stanton is visiting in North Wales, recovering from a severe illness. Will realizes he comes from the Old Ones, immortals dedicated to saving the world from evil. When he hears about a certain harp of gold that people say will be found by a boy followed by a white dog who can see the wind, Will knows he must find the harp and use it to awaken six sleepers in the ancient hills. (Newbery Award)

Curley, Daniel. **Hilarion.** Illus. Judith Gwyn Brown. Houghton Mifflin Co., 1979. 88 pp.

The tailor, the carpenter, the butcher, and the shoemaker all came to America from Linsk to find their fortunes. But instead they found hard times. They were often cold, hungry, and jobless. One night, they are joined in their darkest hour of need by a giant of a man. His name was Hilarion, and he brought with him a most interesting trunk filled with an endless supply of food and warmth and hope for their future. Could Hilarion possibly change their lives permanently and make their dreams come true?

Dawood, N. J. **Tales from the Arabian Nights.** Illus. Ed Young. Doubleday & Co., 1978. 320 pp.

Stories from Persia, India, and Arabia fill this book, including such familiar tales as "Ali Baba and the Forty Thieves" and "Sinbad the Sailor." Other stories focus on mythical beasts, genies, and magicians. Ordinary animals and people are plunged into extraordinary situations in still other tales.

de Paola, Tomie. **The Legend of Old Befana: An Italian Christmas Story.** Illus. by author. Harcourt Brace Jovanovich, 1980. 28 pp.

This is a retelling of an old Italian Christmas story. Where we have Santa Claus, Italian children wait for Befana, an old woman who will bring them candy and gifts—or sticks. Her legend is told here in poetic language and with colorful illustrations.

Dickens, Charles. **A Christmas Carol.** Watermill Press, 1980. 124 pp.

This classic Christmas story begins with an introduction to Ebenezer Scrooge, who has no time for Christmas, or friendship, or anything except making money. He cares for no one except himself. Things begin to change for Mr. Scrooge when he is visited by the Ghosts of Christmas Past, Present, and to Come, who show him his life the way it was, the way it is, and the way it will be. The experiences change Scrooge in surprising ways. Originally published in 1843.

Diop, Birago (translator and editor Rosa Guy). **Mother Crocodile (Maman Caiman).** Illus. John Steptoe. Delacorte Press, 1981. 26 pp.

Because she once snapped at him, Golo-the-Monkey tells the animals that Mother Crocodile is crazy. Now no one will listen to her. When she hears that trouble is approaching, she tries to warn everyone, but even her children refuse to leave with her. Then they hear gunfire and wonder if Mother Crocodile was telling the truth after all. This is a retelling of an Ouolof folktale from Senegal, West Africa. Easy reading.

Dorson, Richard M., editor. **Folktales Told around the World.** University of Chicago Press, 1975. 622 pp.

Over a hundred folktales from forty-six countries are printed here. Many of the stories come directly from the mouths of storytellers. Expert collectors recorded these tales and contributed them to this collection of authentic folk stories. Some background notes are given on the story narrators. Some mature situations.

Dumas, Alexandre (translator Douglas Munro). **When Pierrot Was Young.** Illus. Peter Farmer. Oxford University Press, 1975. 88 pp.

Pierrot, a lovable, clownlike boy who never ages, falls hopelessly in love with Princess Fleu-d'Amandier in fairy-tale Bohemia, but he finds himself in danger because of an evil nobleman. Pierrot must rely on magic and his own resourcefulness to escape.

Eichenberg, Fritz. **Endangered Species and Other Fables with a Twist.** Illus. by author. Stemmer House Publishers, 1979. 128 pp.

Fritz Eichenberg has taken short fables and "twisted" them to speak to our modern world and the weaknesses of people. His own black-and-white woodblocks illustrate each of the twenty-six fables. Hypocrisy, war, corruption, and pride are among the human weaknesses explored in the fables. The animals in these fables take on qualities of humans as a donkey becomes the leader of the other animals, the wolf and the shepherd strike up a money-making scheme, and an owl watches for the neutron bomb.

Fisher, Lucretia. **Two Monsters.** Illus. Thomas Jardine. Stemmer House Publishers, 1976. 25 pp.

This simple fable consisting of only a few lines per page is for anyone who has yearned for a true friend or had to be separated from that friend. Two lonely monsters in a dense forest find themselves separated by a wide chasm. They learn to enjoy one another across the chasm as well as try to find a bridge to reach each other. Easy reading.

Fleischman, Paul. **The Half-a-Moon Inn.** Scholastic Book Services, 1980. 78 pp.

On Aaron's twelfth birthday his mother doesn't return home to their cottage by the sea. Aaron goes out searching for her in a snowstorm and gets lost. A mute, the boy can only write messages—but the people who can help him cannot read. When he thinks he has found shelter at an inn, he meets witchlike Miss Grackle, who traps him so he will be her slave.

Franko, Ivan (translator Bohdan Melnyk). **Fox Mykyta.** Illus. William Kurelek. Tundra Books, 1978. 148 pp.

It is spring, and King Lion Tsar Lev, ruler of all the beasts, says it is the time for all his subjects to bring their complaints to his attention. But Fox Mykyta just wants to sleep. Beast after beast tells the king of crimes committed by Fox—crimes of all kinds, from theft to chicken killing. The king now has to send just the right kind of representative to persuade the sly Fox Mykyta to come and answer these complaints. Fox cleverly fools one royal representative after another, though, and remains safely in his fortress of Foxburg. Then the King Lion tries harsher measures against Fox. How long will Fox's wits keep him and his family secure at Foxburg?

Fregosi, Claudia, adapted by. **Snow Maiden.** Illus. by author. Prentice-Hall, 1979. 27 pp.

In this Russian retelling of the Greek myth of Persephone, the lovely Snow Maiden, daughter of Wind and Frost, envies the children of Earth and wishes to leave her heavenly home to join them. Her parents feel sorry for her and allow her to go, but they warn her never to experience the warmth of love or the warmth of the sun. Her experience on earth is both tragic and beautiful.

Gardner, Nancy, retold by. **Favorite Tales from Grimm.** Illus. Mercer Mayer. Four Winds Press, 1982. 224 pp.

Rapunzel, with her long golden braids hanging out of the window, pines for the King's son. Snow White and Rose Red befriend a clumsy bear, who is really a prince in golden clothing. And the crooked little man, Rumpelstiltskin, teaches the frantic miller's daughter how to spin gold. Meet Cinderella, Hansel and Gretel, Little Briar Rose, the Bremen Town musicians, and more timeless characters in this new collection of old favorites illustrated by award-winning artist Mercer Mayer.

Garner, Alan. **Elidor.** William Collins Publishers, 1979. 148 pp.

Roland, Nick, Helen, and David Watson explore an abandoned Manchester neighborhood. They go inside a large, ruined church and lose each other in the darkness. Strange noises echo around the church, while faint music grows into a wild dance and footsteps sound in a passage somewhere. Then a voice speaks and bids the children through a crack in time. The children enter the strange world of Elidor where Malebron the King gives them a sword, a stone, a spear, and a cauldron—magic treaures that link them to both worlds. He begs them to find the unicorn Findhorn, who must sing his song to release Elidor from its darkness and evil.

Garner, Alan. **The Owl Service.** William Collins Publishers, 1979. 157 pp.

Alison and her stepbrother Roger are vacationing in the country with their parents. Their friend there is the strange and sensitive Welsh boy, Gwyn. Almost at once, a series of weird, seemingly meaningless events begins to happen. After Gwyn searches the attic for mice one day, he finds a set of very old dishes. Alison cleans one of the plates, and the three children see the shape of a painted owl appear. Or is it a flower? In either case, the painted image casts a spell on them. Alison, Roger, and Gwyn are now caught in a power they can't control. (Guardian Award; Carnegie Medal)

Grahame, Kenneth. **The Wind in the Willows.** Watermill Press, 1980. 245 pp.

The world of animals comes to life in the adventures of the Mole, the Rat, the Toad, and the Badger. These four friends represent four different types of human personalities and they philosophize, talk, and act like people. They also get in trouble, just like humans. For example, when the Toad steals a motor car to travel about the world, it takes the combined efforts of his friends to save him from himself. Originally published in 1908.

Gray, J. E. B., retold by. **Indian Tales and Legends.** Illus. Joan Kiddell-Monroe. Oxford University Press, 1979. 230 pp.

This collection of legends involves splendid kings, tigers of great cunning, ten-headed demons, sailors who fish diamonds and gems from the sea, villains and saints, and even cats and tortoises. All the legends and fables here are from the Indian story cycles *Nala and Damayanti* and *Ramayana*.

Green, Lila, retold by. **Tales from Africa.** Illus. Jerry Pinkney. Silver Burdett Co., 1979. 96 pp.

Here are ten tales from Ghana, Ethiopia, Sierra Leone, Zanzibar, the Congo, and West Africa. They include tales of spiders, ungrateful men, wise judges, rabbits, and a prince who wanted the moon. Easy reading.

Green, Lila, retold by. **Tales from Hispanic Lands.** Illus. Donald Silverstein. Silver Burdett Co., 1979. 96 pp.

The nine folktales in this book have been collected from Spain, Puerto Rico, Mexico, Nicaragua, and Uruguay. There are the stories of the rabbit who outsmarted the tiger, the little ant who chased away the billy goat, and the fox who fooled the coyote. Easy reading.

Brothers Grimm. **Household Tales.** Illus. Mervyn Peake. Schocken Books, 1979. 240 pp.

Most of the Brothers Grimm's famous fairy tales are in this collection: "Snow White," "Cinderella," and "Rumpelstiltskin." But also included are less familiar stories like "The Old Sultan," "Pack of Ragamuffins," and "The Twelve Huntsmen and the Turnip."

Grinnell, George Bird, retold by (editor John Bierhorst). **The Whistling Skeleton: American Indian Tales of the Supernatural.** Illus. Robert Andrew Parker. Four Winds Press, 1982. 108 pp.

This collection of nine eerie stories is based on tales from the Cheyenne, Blackfoot, and Pawnee Indians. The tales were written in the same straightforward way storytellers probably told them around a campfire in the nineteenth century. Included are stories about a pile of bones that turn into a whistling skeleton, a talking dog, a deer who cares for a young boy, and medicine animals who restore a boy to life. Easy reading.

Haldeman, Linda. **The Lastborn of Elvinwood.** Avon Books, 1980. 224 pp.

Ian James is a forty-year-old actor in a local theater in England. On a rainy night he follows Mrs. Hubbard and the vicar as they walk into a dark forest. To his astonishment, the vicar and the woman pick up chestnuts, hold them to their lips, and disappear under the ground. Ian James follows their lead and finds himself in a fairy world ruled by Oberon. But these fairies face extinction because they are all too old to have children. Oberon gets Ian James to promise to find a young human bride for the fairy prince.

Hancock, Niel. **Circle of Light-1: Greyfax Grimwald.** Popular Library, 1977. 352 pp.

Bear awakens late one September morning to prepare for the thousand-year trip down the mountainlike side of the sky. He wonders sleepily what the World Before Time is like now. First

Otter, then Dwarf join Bear, and the trio leaves the country of Lorini and dares to cross Calix, the great water that guards strange lands. Soon they enter the evil Palace of Darkness and the town where the dreaded Humans live. This is just the beginning of a great adventure that brings them loyal and courageous friends and fearsome enemies.

Hausman, Gerald. **Sitting on the Blue-Eyed Bear: Navajo Myths and Legends.** Illus. Sidney Hausman. Lawrence Hill & Co., 1975. 130 pp.

Poems, legends, and myths tell the history and tradition of the Navajo Indians. They explain why the evil coyote destroyed the goodness of the young Earth, why rainbows stretch across the sky, and why a boy's voice changes. The medicine men are also described—their chants, their dances, and their natural cure-alls. Another story tells of the four worlds the Navajos believe men are born into before they reach Earth.

Haviland, Virginia, editor. **North American Legends.** Illus. Ann Strugnell. William Collins Publishers, 1979. 209 pp.

Here is a collection of the legends of Eskimos, American Indians, Afro-Americans, and European immigrants. Included are such famous tall tales as those about Pecos Bill, Paul Bunyan, and Davy Crockett. Also presented are legends of Sedna, the Eskimo's sea goddess, an Indian Cinderella who triumphs over her evil sisters, and a number of other lesser-known but fascinating folktales.

Heath, W. L. **The Earthquake Man.** Beaufort Books, 1980. 95 pp.

What are the O'Gradys to do with the troll who has moved in with them? He is making their lives miserable. There are hints of a giant bird, of animals fleeing the area, and of a monstrous catastrophe about to happen. And then a strange little man appears who offers to get rid of the troll—but what are his motives?

Highwater, Jamake. **Anpao: An American Indian Odyssey.** Illus. Fritz Scholder. J. B. Lippincott Co., 1977. 255 pp.

Anpao is a brave young Indian man who undertakes a journey across the face of the ancient world and through space and time in the name of the one he loves, Ko-ko-mik-e-is. Anpao proceeds through a series of legendary adventures that reflects the tales of Indian storytellers throughout the years. (Newbery Honor Book)

Hoban, Russell. **The Mouse and His Child.** Illus. Lillian Hoban. Camelot Books, 1975. 182 pp.

The little toy mouse doesn't want to be sold from the warm and friendly toy store. But he and his father are purchased and are wound so they dance until they break. Then they are thrown away. But the two mice are rescued from the trash by an old tramp who sets them on a journey home. Easy reading.

Ingram, Tom. **The Night Rider.** Bradbury Press, 1975. 176 pp.

When Laura feels a tug on her fishing line, she never suspects that magic is at work. Instead of a fish, she hooks a mysterious bracelet so powerful that it can break the barrier of time. Whenever she puts it on, she is transported into a strange world: a world of black horses, silver daggers, misty riverbanks, and evil forces. But Laura has the key to saving a life in this grim land—if only she can find it.

Ipcar, Dahlov. **A Dark Horn Blowing.** Viking Press, 1978. 222 pp.

One night Nora is taken from her husband and newborn son by the sound of a horn calling to her. She is needed to care for another newborn boy, a prince of a country that Nora finds too strange to be of this earth. It is a magical place where time moves only half as fast, where memory becomes hazy, and where just knowing a person's true name gives one complete control of that individual. But even without a memory, Nora longs for something. After many years her memory of her past life returns, and it is the prince who aids her escape on a magical horse.

Irving, Washington. *The Legend of Sleepy Hollow* and *Rip Van Winkle.* Watermill Press, 1980. 83 pp.

In the first tale you will meet a superstitious schoolteacher, Ichabod Crane, and his rival, Brom Bones. One dark night, as he rides home after hearing ghost stories, Ichabod is certain he meets the Headless Horseman of Sleepy Hollow. The story of Rip Van Winkle is about a good-natured, lazy man who falls asleep and wakes up twenty years later. Now he must adjust to all the changes that took place while he was sleeping. Both stories were originally published in serial form between 1818 and 1820.

Jagendorf, M. A. **Stories and Lore of the Zodiac.** Illus. Anne Bevans. Vanguard Press, 1977. 159 pp.

The word *zodiac* comes from a Greek word that means "a circle of animals." The zodiac actually is a circle or belt in the sky consisting of twelve constellations spaced along the paths of the sun, moon, and planets. People who studied the stars in the past thought they saw shapes in the clusters of stars, and so they named the clusters after those shapes. Special stories and folklore soon grew up around these names. This book takes each sign and explains the story behind its meaning, and the influence it is supposed to have on people's lives.

Jagendorf, Moritz A. **Tales of Mystery.** Illus. Oscar Liebman. Silver Burdett Co., 1979. 96 pp.

These folktales involving the mysterious were collected from around the world. Included are such tales of suspense as "The Coffinmaker's Ghost" from Ireland, "The Courageous Cossack" from Russia, and "The Revenge of the Rocks" from France. Easy reading.

Jansson, Tove (translator Elizabeth Portch). **Comet in Moominland.** Illus. by author. Camelot Books, 1976. 192 pp.

Moomintroll and Sniff set off for the mountains to ask the Professor about comets. To their surprise, they learn that a very dangerous comet is heading straight for Moominvalley. Easy reading. (Hans Christian Andersen Award)

Jansson, Tove (translator Elizabeth Portch). **Finn Family Moomintroll.** Illus. by author. Camelot Books, 1975. 170 pp.

Deep in the forests of Finland live the Moomintrolls who only really become active in the warm months. On one particular spring day, a tall black hat appears (without an owner)—and with it some very strange, unpredictable, and frightening creations. Anything that is placed in the hat, on purpose or accidentally, emerges from it later in a totally new form! How and where can the Moomintrolls get rid of this annoying and frightening hat? Easy reading. (Hans Christian Andersen Award)

Jansson, Tove (translator Kingsley Hart). **Moominpappa at Sea.** Illus. by author. Camelot Books, 1977. 192 pp.

Pappa's island is a strange and eerie place. The silent fisherman, the sea horses, and the Groke make the place weird, but the happy members of the Moomin family are determined to stay in their new home. Easy reading. (Hans Christian Andersen Award)

Jansson, Tove (translator Kingsley Hart). **Moominvalley in November.** Illus. by author. Camelot Books, 1976. 175 pp.

After a long, treacherous journey, Snufkin, Fillyjonk, Mymble, Toft, Humulen, and Grandpa-Grumble reach their destination:

the little house in Moominvalley. All are disappointed when they find that Moominpappa and Moominmama are not there, but the enchanting valley and the rain-dripping forest spellbind them. Together, the six creatures enter into a season filled with surprises and excitement. Easy reading. (Hans Christian Andersen Award)

Jarrett, David. **Witherwing.** Warner Books, 1979. 238 pp.

Witherwing, the youngest of the six princes of Tum-Barlum, is a feared warrior who seeks mysterious power. He also possesses a swanlike wing in place of a left arm. In order to save his enchanted realm from the Ultimate Evil, the prince must battle sorcery, wizards, and half-human creatures.

Johnston, Norma. **The Days of the Dragon's Seed.** Atheneum Publishers, 1982. 191 pp.

This story retells the old Greek myths of Oedipus, who unknowingly kills his father and marries his mother, even after he goes to unbelievable ends to prevent this prophecy from being fulfilled. This happens because Oedipus rids the city of Thebes of thieves and kills the Sphinx that sat at the gate, letting no one enter or exit. The people of Thebes were the dragon's seed—they were born from the teeth of a sacred dragon. Oedipus and his people must answer some difficult questions about humans and gods.

Jones, Diana Wynne. **Drowned Ammet.** Atheneum Publishers, 1978. 255 pp.

Mitt was born on the day of the Holand Sea Festival. It was a day when dummies of folk figures Poor Old Ammet and Libby Bear, his wife, were drowned in the sea. But Mitt's life is hardly a festival. It is a constant struggle. And Mitt grows up with a grudge against the rulers of his land. When his protest against the strict and uncaring government fails, Mitt is forced to run away to Holy Island. In this mysterious place, Mitt begins to learn the true identity and power of those two folk figures that are celebrated by his people at the festival.

Jones, Gwyn, retold by. **Scandinavian Legends and Folk-Tales.** Illus. Joan Kiddell-Monroe. Oxford University Press, 1979. 222 pp.

These folktales, sagas, and legends have been collected from Denmark, Iceland, Norway, and Sweden and are divided into four groups: Princes and Trolls, Tales from the Ingle-Nook, From the Land of Fire and Ice, and Kings and Heroes. All the tales are short, and they include such characters as woodcutters, poets, kings, dogs, bears, geese, and wild swans.

Karl, Jean E. **Beloved Benjamin Is Waiting.** E. P. Dutton, 1978. 150 pp.

The empty caretaker's house at the local cemetery seems spooky, but it is the only place Lucinda can find to hide after a gang of kids terrorizes her. Her mother and brother are gone, so Lucinda begins to confide her feelings to Benjamin, a statue of a small boy who died in 1889. Lucinda's conversations with an iron statue are strange, but even stranger is the fact that the statue seems to respond to Lucinda.

Keidel, Eudene, compiled by. **African Fables That Teach about God.** Illus. Kathy Bartel. Herald Press, 1978. 93 pp.

These tales from Africa use animals to teach spiritual values. The animals in the fables are amazingly clever in resolving the conflicts in their lives. By their solutions, they also teach humans something about life. The fables are rich in African culture, but contain universal thoughts.

Keidel, Eudene, compiled by. **African Fables That Teach about God, Book II.** Illus. Paul D. Zehr. Herald Press, 1981. 111 pp.

The folk stories of Africa are like tales everywhere else: they are timeless because they help people of a common race or nation define who they are and what their values have come to be. More than that, folktales delight the listener or reader. Animals in these African fables get entangled in all kinds of zany problems, like stealing bananas and peanuts, or arguing over everything, or making promises they will never keep. But there are people stories too. One of these tells about how flying ants help a young boy unable to talk suddenly force words off his tongue.

Kennedy, Richard. **Crazy in Love.** Illus. Marcia Sewall. Unicorn Books, 1980. 57 pp.

Diana wishes she could have a husband, and an enchanted woman grants the wish. The new husband, Dan, thinks his wife is crazy, and Diana wonders about his sanity. Both newlyweds now worry about each other and wonder what will happen to their marriage.

Kennedy, Richard. **Inside My Feet: The Story of a Giant.** Illus. Ronald Himler. Harper & Row Publishers, 1979. 71 pp.

Billy is the only one left in his small family, and it seems he will be the next victim of the horrible giant that kidnapped his parents. In every case of a disappearance, the magical boots of the ogre have stomped to the victim's cottage and pulled the prey inside the boots with a weird force. Now Billy must outsmart the clever giant and resist the power of his magical boots. Man-eating rats, puzzling riddles, and a fiery lantern are all part of his daring plan.

Kiesel, Stanley. **The War between the Pitiful Teachers and the Splendid Kids.** Flare Books, 1982. 207 pp.

After attempts to feed the teachers shark-infested rice pudding and to steal all the school's grammar charts fail to defeat the teachers, a group of school children decide to wage open war on their instructors. Each side has fearsome fighters: the teachers have Mr. Forclosure, while the kids have Big Alice. But can the students undermine Mr. Forclosure's dreaded plan to turn them into "Perfect Young People"?

Konwicki, Tadeusz (translators George and Audrey Korwin-Rodziszewski). **The Anthropos-Specter-Beast.** S. G. Phillips, 1977. 201 pp.

Peter is very bored with the world around him, and with trying to handle the problems in his family. His curious adventures begin when a speaking dog, Sebastian, transports him to a remote countryside. Then, Peter takes part in a children's expedition to the moon. There they encounter the unknown and the unknowable. Mature reading.

Lang, Andrew (editor Kathleen Lines). **The Rainbow Fairy Book: A Selection of Outstanding Fairy Tales from the Color Fairy Books.** Illus. Margery Gill. Schocken Books, 1977. 252 pp.

These thirty-seven tales were drawn from the famous color books of Andrew Lang that were originally published between 1889 and 1910. These fairy tales include the familiar and the unfamiliar: the Golden Goose, the Magic Kettle, the Maiden with the Wooden Helmet, the Caliph Stork, the Cats' Elopement, Tritill, Litill and the Birds, and others.

Langton, Jane. **The Fledgling.** Harper & Row, Publishers, 1980. 182 pp.

Georgie wanted to learn to fly more than anything else in life. She practiced in the house and in the yard at every opportunity. Then one night a migrating Canadian goose comes to her window. Georgie climbs onto the back of the "Goose Prince," and the two are soon soaring above Walden Pond. (Newbery Honor Book)

Le Guin, Ursula K. **Malafrena.** G. P. Putnam's Sons, 1979. 369 pp.

Malafrena, Itale's birthplace, is the only peaceful valley in all of a certain European country. Elsewhere the King rules mercilessly and with an iron hand. Itale decides to leave his tranquil home and rebel against the powerful dictator. A bloody battle for freedom involves Itale in a secret newspaper, a dangerous undercover mission, and a near-fatal sickness.

Lilius, Irmelin Sandman (translator Joan Tate). **The Goldmaker's House.** Illus. Ionicus. Merloyd Lawrence Books, 1977. 86 pp.

Herr Turiam, the new owner of the spooky Old Gripander House, is the most feared man in the village of Tulavall. Young Bonadea first encounters the strange old man when she rings the bell at his house to ask permission to get her little bark boat from a stream flowing through his property. From that moment on, Bonadea's life changes dramatically. Herr Turiam, who the villagers say is a sorcerer, offers the young girl the job of maid in his house. Bonadea takes the job, but in it she learns strange things and witnesses bizarre events at the Old Gripander House.

Lilius, Irmelin Sandman (translator Joan Tate). **Horses of the Night.** Illus. Ionicus. Merloyd Lawrence Books, 1979. 137 pp.

In his shack overlooking a Finnish village, Mr. Klingkors schemes to become the next Mayor. Silja and Krullasse, two village girls, try desperately to stop him by using Mr. Klingkors' own dynamite against him. When he hires twenty Russian horsemen for protection, the two girls lose hope. Then watchful spirits from long ago begin moving about to help them.

Lisker, Tom. **Tall Tales: American Myths.** Illus. Jeffrey Gatrall. Contemporary Perspectives, 1977. 48 pp.

Americans are famous for telling tall tales of fishermen, frontier people, cowboys, and loggers. This book explains what tall tales are and how they got started. Following this are retellings of some of the most famous tales of all: Pecos Bill, Paul Bunyan, Johnny Appleseed, and Davy Crockett. Easy reading.

Littledale, Freya, retold by. **Snow White and the Seven Dwarfs.** Illus. Susan Jeffers. Four Winds Press, 1982. 32 pp.

This is a retelling of the story of Snow White, a beautiful girl who is hated by her mean stepmother. After being scared away from home, Snow White meets seven little men who take her into their cottage and protect her. But the evil stepmother decides she has to rid herself of Snow White permanently, so she goes searching for the girl in the forest.

Lively, Penelope. **The Revenge of Samuel Stokes.** Illus. Ionicus. E. P. Dutton, 1981. 122 pp.

Tim Thornton and his family move into a new housing development where everything looks normal. But soon mysterious things begin to happen. The washing machine starts to smell like roast deer meat, tobacco smoke comes from the television set, and a greenhouse becomes a natural temple. The family wonders if a ghost from the eighteenth century is involved.

Mace, Elisabeth. **The Rushton Inheritance.** Thomas Nelson, 1978. 173 pp.

Tom Rushton wishes he could go to London because nothing ever happens in his little village. But there's no hope of leaving, so he keeps doing what he's best at—penmanship and copying. One day, after working especially long and hard for his Grandmother, he notices a figure standing near the dark curtains. It is a stranger, a stranger who seems somehow vaguely familiar. The stranger tells Tom his name is Steve Rushton. But after the boys talk, Steve vanishes into the curtains again, so Tom thinks it's all a dream. But Steve comes and goes often, and Tom learns that Steve is from a future century and has come to search for hidden treasure.

MacDonald, George. **The Stories of George MacDonald.** Chariot Books, 1979. 190 pp.

These Scottish tales include one about Princess Rosamond, who was spoiled, bad tempered, and cruel. One day, when a Wise Woman comes to the palace, the princess disappears. In another story, Princess Irene is in danger from mountain goblins, and her rescue depends on young Curdie and a mysterious old woman.

Manheim, Ralph, editor and translator. **Rare Treasures from Grimm.** Illus. Erik Blegvad. Doubleday & Co., 1981. 99 pp.

Fifteen lesser-known fairy tales from the Brothers Grimm are presented here. In "Thousandfurs," a beautiful princess is covered by a cloak of a thousand skins so she looks like an animal herself. In another story a seemingly pleasant forest becomes a place of terror when hunters begin vanishing among the trees.

Manton, Jo, and Robert Gittings. **The Flying Horses: Tales from China.** Illus. Derek Collard. Holt, Rinehart & Winston, 1977. 172 pp.

The twenty-seven stories collected here are all taken from 4,000 years of Chinese history and literature, and all are accompanied by ancient Chinese poems and verse sayings. The stories include tales about the noble flying horses of the Emperor Wu, building the Great Wall, practical cats, and a cheerful funeral.

Martin, Graham Dunstan. **Catchfire.** Houghton Mifflin Co., 1982. 183 pp.

The Realm of Feydom seems doomed. War, starvation, and disease threaten the entire land. And all this because of a spell put on the country by the wizard Hoodwill. Now young Ewan and witch-girl Catchfire must set out to break the spell. But first they must defeat the monster who guards the spell in the ruins of Midriver Castle.

Martin, Graham Dunstan. **Giftwish.** Houghton Mifflin Co., 1981. 202 pp.

When the wizard Hoodwill asks Ewan to save the land from an evil spell, the young boy is more than willing. No one has ever asked him to do anything important. But Ewan slowly realizes he has been tricked by the wizard. He will not be a hero, but a sacrificial victim. Ewan must now fight the wizard and a sly sorceress to save his life and his homeland. With witch-girl Catchfire and a friendly wizard called Caperstaff, Ewan gets ready to do battle with the forces of evil.

McCaffrey, Anne. **Dragondrums.** Argo Books, 1979. 240 pp.

Piemur is sent to Masterharper Robinton to do political work. He becomes an apprentice to the great master of drums, and soon he learns the basics of reading and sending drum messages. But his education is not limited to this. Piemur is expected to perform many dangerous and unusual missions, which include stealing the eggs of fire-lizards and taking valuable gems from miners. In doing all this he must also escape from the pursuit of dragon-riders.

McCaffrey, Anne. **Dragonsinger.** Atheneum Publishers, 1978. 264 pp.

Menolly is a young girl who comes to live at Harper Hall. While there, Menolly wants to study music under the Masterharper and to plan her future around it. She also would like to reserve time to help her friends. Sequel to *Dragonsong*.

McCaffrey, Anne. **Dragonsong.** Atheneum Publishers, 1978. 202 pp.

The people of Pern developed huge dragons to fight the spores that fell like rain and that could destroy all living matter. Everyone was especially careful during Threadfall, when the spores came. Menolly has other problems. She loves music and wants to be a Harper, but her father forbids it. Menolly makes some important discoveries, such as nine fire-lizards and the fact that she can sing—as well as a new direction for her life.

McCarty, Toni. **The Skull in the Snow and Other Folktales.** Illus. Katherine Coville. Delacorte Press, 1981. 87 pp.

In this collection of folktales from all over the world, the main characters all have something in common: they are all women of courage. You won't meet any princesses who wait to be rescued by a prince here. These women know what they want and they use their own strength and bravery to get it. Easy reading.

McDermott, Gerald. **The Knight of the Lion.** Illus. by author. Four Winds Press, 1979. 50 pp.

Sir Yvain, one of King Arthur's Knights of the Round Table, longs for adventure and glory. But in the course of his travels, Yvain learns there are other important goals to work for in life.

McKillip, Patricia A. **Harpist in the Wind.** Argo Books, 1979. 256 pp.

Morgon has to settle the conflict and unrest that exist throughout the land when wizards and mysterious shape-changers clash. At the same time, he must cope with his own inner conflict as he tries to discover himself and his destiny. Morgon soon finds himself responsible for the dawning of a new age and finds for himself a future more demanding than any he had ever imagined. Volume three in a trilogy.

McKillip, Patricia A. **Heir of Sea and Fire.** Atheneum Publishers, 1977. 199 pp.

Morgon has disappeared. But Raederle will not believe that her fiancé is dead, so she sets out on her own to find him. Her travels make her aware that she too has power, the power to shape fire and to create powerful illusions. She begins to realize that she is a descendant of the shape-changers, the very people who are trying to destroy Morgon. Now, before she finds Morgon, she must be sure that she will not be used to help destroy the one she loves. Volume two in a trilogy.

McKillip, Patricia A. **The Riddle-Master of Hed.** Atheneum Publishers, 1978. 222 pp.

Though he lives in a place where even the princes are farmers and where no one is a hero, Morgon finds that he cannot avoid a destiny that will take him beyond being a simple farmer. The riddle Morgon sets out to solve, and one he stakes his future on, is this:

on his forehead Morgon has three stars; a harp that bears the same three stars can be played by no one but Morgon; and a sword with the stars can be used only by him. So what does this all add up to? Something inside Morgon will not let him rest till he searches for the meaning behind the three stars, the harp, and the sword. Volume one in a trilogy.

McKinley, Robin. **Beauty: A Retelling of the Story of Beauty and the Beast.** Harper & Row, Publishers, 1978. 247 pp.

This is a modern version of the classic tale of Beauty and the Beast. This time, the story is told from the viewpoint of Honour, the youngest of three daughters, whose nickname was "Beauty." Through her experiences with the Beast, she learns a great deal about what makes up true beauty and what ugliness is really all about.

Miles, Bernard. **Robin Hood: His Life and Legend.** Illus. Victor G. Ambrus. Rand McNally & Co., 1979. 125 pp.

Robin Hood is loved and admired for his battles against tyranny and for the poor. Aiding him in his fight are Little John, Maid Marian, Friar Tuck, and Will Scarlet. But his most dangerous enemies, the Sheriff of Nottingham and Prince John, try to have him killed and his band of Merry Men put in prison.

Miller, Steven B. **The Midnight Son.** Four Winds Press, 1981. 128 pp.

Illustrated with over four hundred detailed drawings, this story concerns the odyssey of Phaedran, known as the child of light. He is drawn to the planet Fauna to seek a happiness that now exists only in his dim memory. While on his quest, the boy must contend with a giant monster and a terrifying Firedrake. Through his adventures, Phaedran learns some valuable lessons about life and about his own character.

Mobley, Jane. **The Star Husband.** Illus. Anna Vojtech. Doubleday & Co., 1979. 32 pp.

Once a young Plains Indian girl wished for something more than the other girls had the imagination and daring to want—she wanted the brightest star from the heavens as her husband. One night she falls asleep on a little hill with this dream in her heart, and when she awakens her wish has been granted. Her star husband is kind, gentle, wise, and loving. Soon she bears a son and their son becomes the moon. But something inside the Indian girl makes her spirit restless, so she tells her star husband she must leave him and their son. What she is searching for is unclear, but she knows she must look for it.

Moffitt, Frederick J., retold by. **Tales from Ancient Greece.** Illus. Bill Shields. Silver Burdett Co., 1979. 90 pp.

All the tales in this book deal with the Greek warrior Odysseus. He helped the Greek soldiers win the Trojan War by designing a huge wooden horse and then began a long ten-year trip home in which he encountered the Cyclops, the Skurries, and the Sirens. The first part of his voyage is recorded much as a personal diary, and a navigation chart is included. A glossary gives further information about the gods and mortals. Based on the *Odyssey* of Homer. Easy reading.

Moskin, Marietta D. **Dream Lake.** Atheneum Publishers, 1981. 138 pp.

Hilary has repeatedly had a strange dream. She does not do much in the dream but look out of a window at a lake and mountain. But because of this recurring dream, Hilary has always been a little afraid of going into the country. When her mother takes a job overseas one summer, however, Hilary must go to live with her great-aunt in New Hampshire. Hilary likes her aunt, but her older cousin seems to take pleasure in persecuting Hilary. Even more troubling for Hilary, though, is that her dream has drawn her into a fantasy world of the eighteenth century in which she finds herself a lowly indentured servant. Can this fantasy be showing her a life she once led?

Murphy, Shirley Rousseau. **The Castle of Hape.** Argo Books, 1980. 172 pp.

A monster named Hape is strong enough to blind the minds of the Carriolinians so that the enemy hordes can sweep over their borders. But the leader of the Carriolinians, Ramad of the Wolves, has been called upon to take care of another disaster. The land of Ere is threatened. On his new mission, he meets Telien, whom he falls in love with. But Telien has her own mission to fulfill.

Murphy, Shirley Rousseau. **Caves of Fire and Ice.** Flare Books, 1982. 174 pp.

Skeelie of Carriol lives on the planet Ere, where time travel is possible but unpredictable. When her friend Ramad of the Wolves journeys into time to find his lost love Telien, Skeelie knows she must follow. But how and where will she find Ramad? And who will control the destiny of Ere?

Myers, Walter Dean. **The Legend of Tarik.** Viking Press, 1981. 185 pp.

When the forces of evil and of good go to war, many die. For the medieval villages of Northern Africa, the name of El Muerte brings terror. Those he touches lose their freedom, and then their lives. In his latest slaughter, young Tarik barely survives. Once healed, he desires revenge against El Muerte. But first he must master the arts of self-defense and self-discipline. To help him, Tarik acquires a magic sword, a magnificent horse, the powerful Crystal of Truth, and two strong and faithful friends. But Tarik learns the results of battle are not only triumph, but also despair.

Naylor, Phyllis Reynolds. **Footprints at the Window.** Atheneum Publishers, 1981. 167 pp.

Dan Roberts has lived with some big questions in his life. Will he be stricken with the hereditary disease his father now has? Who are the mysterious gypsies from the present and past who have haunted him in York, England, and at his grandmother's house in Pennsylvania? Unable to live with the tension anymore, Dan decides to find the gypsies again. When he does, he meets a young girl he likes among them named Orlenda. But soon the pair is transported back to medieval England to the time of the plague—the Black Death— and Dan discovers he must save himself and Orlenda from the fatal disease.

Norton, Andre. **Gryphon in Glory.** Argo Books, 1981. 242 pp.

Josian's husband has been wandering the dark and dangerous Waste on a secret mission. Worried, Josian leaves the safety of her Dale to find him. Reunited in the Waste, Josian and her husband have trouble talking to each other. Kerovan seems cold and aloof. He says he must follow his destiny even though it means encountering the evil powers of the Dark. But Josian decides to stay with Kerovan and help him when she can with the power from a small crystal globe on her neck chain.

Norton, Andre. **Red Hart Magic.** Illus. Donna Diamond. Thomas Y. Crowell Co., 1976. 179 pp.

When Chris Fitton meets his new stepsister, Nan Mallory, the two young people do not get along. But a series of time-ways adventures takes them into the past to the time of King James I of England, and these experiences eventually help them with their present-day problems.

Norton, Mary. **The Borrowers Avenged.** Illus. Beth and Joe Krush. Harcourt Brace Jovanovich, 1982. 298 pp.

Imagine that your greatest fear is being spotted by humans ten times taller than you are —then you can realize what it is like to be one of the characters in this book. As in the four previous books about the Borrowers, the miniature Clock family—Pod, Homily, and their daughter, Arriety—are forced to find a new home. Join them in their adventures as they escape from an attic and set out in a knife-box boat with the wicked Platters hot on their trail.

Nye, Robert. **Beowulf: A New Telling.** Laurel-Leaf Library, 1982. 94 pp.

The story of the brave Beowulf and the monster Grendel has intrigued readers for centuries. This new version is said to be an interpretation, not a translation. When Hrothgar, king of the Danes, calls for someone to fight the monster Grendel, only one man dares—Beowulf. And then the battle begins.

O'Brien, Robert C. **Mrs. Frisby and the Rats of NIMH.** Illus. Zena Bernstein. Scholastic Book Services, 1971. 268 pp.

The doctors at NIMH have created a race of superintelligent rats. These rats can read the labels on medicine bottles, the signs on walls, and the instructions on how to open their cages. When they make their escape from NIMH, the rats decide to carry out a plan against humans. Mrs. Frisby is only a mouse, but she has some rat-sized troubles with humans. She decides to ask the rats of NIMH for help. (Newbery Award)

Onassis, Jacqueline, editor. **The Firebird and Other Russian Fairy Tales.** Illus. Boris Zvorykin. Studio Books, 1978. 78 pp.

In "The Firebird," Tsar Vyslav sends his three sons on a mission to catch the elusive Firebird who, every night, plucks the golden apples from the Tsar's favorite tree. "Maria Morevna" concerns a young boy whose mother and father, on their deathbed, command he give his sister to the first person who comes to ask for her hand in marriage. The two remaining stories are about a beautiful maiden created out of snow by a lonely couple who long for a child, and about a young girl whose mother gives her a magic doll that not only talks but also protects the youngster.

Park, Ruth. **Playing Beatie Bow.** Atheneum Publishers, 1982. 196 pp.

Abigail Kirk is confused, hurt, and angry. First her father ran away with another woman. Now that he wants to come back, Abigail cannot believe her mother will let him. To distract herself, Abigail goes off to watch some children play a game called Beatie Bow. She notices a strange child there watching the game. However, when Abigail tries to speak to her, the girl runs away. Abigail decides to follow her, but she soons finds she has run back into another century with the girl. (ALA Best Book for Young Adults)

Pascal, Francine. **Hangin' Out with Cici.** Viking Press, 1977. 152 pp.

Fourteen-year-old Victoria is always in trouble. She cannot believe that her mother was young once or that her mother can understand her problems. Then, after a train ride home, Victoria finds herself thrown into the past. She is alone in this strange world until she meets another girl named Cici who looks very familiar.

Patai, Raphael, editor. **Gates to the Old City: A Book of Jewish Legends.** Avon Books, 1980. 807 pp.

This is a large collection of stories exploring 3,000 years of legends underlying the Jewish culture. It contains selections from the seven main sources of Jewish literature: the *Bible,* the *Apocrypha,* the *Talmud,* the *Midrash,* the *Kabbala,* folklore, and Hasidism. Included in the stories are myths, folktales, parables, animal fables, word games, maxims, and hyperboles. Notes from the editor help clarify the meaning of the stories by explaining certain aspects of Jewish life.

Patten, Brian. **Mr. Moon's Last Case.** Illus. Mary Moore. Charles Scribner's Sons, 1975. 158 pp.

Former police officer Reginald Moon searches for a figure that he saw jump from a bridge onto a moving freight train. While some people say it was a child or small man, he believes it was a leprechaun. But what will he do once he finds the tiny magic man?

Perrault, Charles (translator John Bierhorst). **The Glass Slipper: Charles Perrault's Tales of Times Past.** Illus. Mitchell Miller. Four Winds Press, 1981. 113 pp.

New translations of classic French stories are provided here: "The Sleeping Beauty," "Little Red Ridinghood," "Bluebeard," "Puss in Boots," "Cinderella," "Diamonds and Toads," "Rickety Topknot," and "Hop O' My Thumb." Notes have been added to the stories to fully explain certain cultural points.

Phelps, Ethel Johnson, editor. **Tatterhood and Other Tales.** Illus. Pamela Baldwin Ford. Feminist Press, 1978. 164 pp.

A woman offers a magic spell to a queen who wants to have a child. The queen is overjoyed when twin daughters are born to her. One girl is quiet and lovely, but her twin is always racing around on a goat and wears torn, mud-spattered clothes. She is also loud and careless. When a wicked troll puts a spell on the beautiful princess and takes her away, her sister's strength, courage and inner goodness face a surprising test. There are twenty-six other folktales from such countries as South Africa, China, Ireland, and Pakistan.

Picard, Barbara Leonie. **Stories of King Arthur and His Knights.** Illus. Roy Morgan. Oxford University Press, 1979. 292 pp.

This book takes the famous stories of King Arthur and his kingdom of Camelot and retells them. From the time Arthur pulls the sword from the stone and becomes the new king, adventures begin for the king and his knights. They include the quest of Gawaine against the Green Knight, the story of Lancelot of the Lake, Arthur's marriage to Guinevere, and the quest for the Holy Grail.

Pinkwater, D. Manus. **The Hoboken Chicken Emergency.** Illus. by author. Scholastic Book Services, 1977. 92 pp.

Quick! Call the fire department! Call the police! Arthur's pet, Henrietta, is lost. Frightened and hungry, poor Henrietta wanders around the streets of Hoboken, New Jersey, looking for potatoes or whatever else she can find. Why is there all this fuss over a missing pet? Well, Henrietta just happens to be a 266-pound chicken who is fifteen feet high!

Pinkwater, D. Manus. **Lizard Music.** Laurel-Leaf Library, 1980. 173 pp.

When Victor's parents go on vacation for two weeks, Victor gets to stay up late and watch all the television he wants. He also begins to fantasize that there are lizards everywhere he looks. Things get stranger and funnier when the boy meets the nutty Chicken Man, an odd person with a chicken named Claudia under his hat. And if this isn't wacky enough, Victor discovers that the Pod People have invaded the earth and have taken over a late-night talk show.

Riordan, James, retold by. **Tales from Central Russia: Russian Tales, Volume One.** Illus. Krystyna Turska. Kestrel Books, 1976. 286 pp.

Once storytellers were responsible for telling these tales from village to palace, passing them along by word of mouth. Now they are gathered into a collection that shows the influence of the Russian land and people. The animals have human characteristics and the people struggle against landlords and rich merchants. Witches, ogres, wood sprites, and other creatures frequent these stories.

Riordan, James, retold by. **Tales from Tartary: Russian Tales, Volume Two.** Illus. Anthony Colbert. Kestrel Books, 1978. 171 pp.

These thirty-nine folktales all came from the Tartar region of the Soviet Union, which includes Southern Siberia and the Crimea. Some of the tales are savage and others humorous. They involve a nightingale who comes back to life, a bride who has green toads fall from her mouth, a bear who loses his tail, a cockerel who wants to be the shah, a tailor who outwits a wolf, and a boy with golden knucklebones.

Rosen, Winifred. **Three Romances: Love Stories from Camelot Retold.** Illus. Paul O. Zelinsky. Alfred A. Knopf, 1981. 120 pp.

"What do women want more than anything in the world?" is the question on which King Arthur's life depends and Sir Gawain's future hangs in "The Marriage of Sir Gawain and Dame Ragnell." Then in "Enid and Geraint," perfect love is darkened by suspicion and jealousy when again and again Geraint doubts Enid's faithfulness. In the final story, "Merlin and Niniane," the wizard of Arthur's domain meets his destiny and becomes a prisoner of love. Love's pleasures and pitfalls are revealed in these three tales, which give a lively sampling of life in Camelot.

Rounds, Glen. **Ol' Paul, the Mighty Logger.** Illus. by author. Holiday House, 1976. 93 pp.

In this retelling of the Paul Bunyan tales, the author claims to have known and interviewed Ol' Paul himself. The legendary figure outwits huge mosquitoes, straightens out a wild river, and tames a giant bullsnake. With his faithful blue ox, Babe, he travels across America and even helps form the Rocky Mountains. The two companions are a terrific logging team, but they get some help from Shot Gunderson, Sourdough Sam, and Hot Biscuit Slim. Paul Bunyan is a man who has big adventures—adventures that mix humor and tension.

Rush, Alison. **The Last of Danu's Children.** Houghton Mifflin Co., 1982. 240 pp.

When Kate's sister is bewitched by a boy she thought was her friend and is delivered into the power of Cernunnos, the Horned God,

Kate and Matt set out to rescue her. They enter another world and time, pitting themselves against the servants of the terrible Horned God. Danu's Children, creatures of light, join the battle on their side, but more and more of the fearsome Old Ones awaken, until it seems to Matt that only his own death will be enough.

Sargent, Sarah. **Weird Henry Berg.** Crown Publishers, 1980. 113 pp.

Henry Berg's peaceful life changes suddenly when his grandfather's antique egg hatches into a lizard. The lizard Vincent proves to be the perfect companion until his glowing eyes and wing-like shoulders start attracting too much attention. Then Henry must protect his pet against a university psychologist, an old lady named Millie, and a determined green creature that flies at night. And when Vincent's true identity is revealed, Henry is forced to make the most difficult decision of his life. (Juvenile Book Merit Award, Friends of American Writers; ALA Best Book for Young Adults)

Scott, Bill. **Boori.** Illus. A. M. Hicks. Oxford University Press, 1978. 149 pp.

Boore, an Australian aborigine, undertakes a quest where he encounters savage warriors, the Rainbow Snake, and spirits that oppose his people. Throughout his ordeals, Boori displays the courage and confidence that mark him as a leader of his people.

Selden, George. **Tucker's Countryside.** Illus. Garth Williams. Camelot Books, 1972. 167 pp.

John Robin flies to the Times Square subway station to tell Harry Cat and Tucker Mouse that their good friend Chester Cricket needs their help. A quick trip to Connecticut on the night train reveals to the old friends that the Old Meadow is in danger. Human houses are taking over the animals' land. Bulldozers are destroying their homes. Can John, Harry, Tucker, and Chester stop human progress?

Senn, Steve. **A Circle in the Sea.** Argo Books, 1981. 256 pp.

Robin Shaw's father brings her a rare gift one day—a strange ring he found on an undersea exploration. It is only after she gets the ring that Robin begins to dream she is a dolphin. Robin soon finds it is more than a dream. Her mind actually begins to inhabit the body of a dolphin named Breee. As Breee, Robin learns how dolphins live, communicate, and struggle to survive as humans pollute the waters. Drawn more and more into an undersea world, Robin-Breee decides to help the dolphins and whales fight for their lives.

Senn, Steve. **The Double Disappearance of Walter Fozbek.** Illus. by author. Hastings House Publishers, 1980. 120 pp.

How would you like to wake up one morning to be the only human in a world full of dinosaurs? This is just what happened to Walter Fozbek. His mother, his father, his cousin—everyone was a tyrannosaur, pterodactyl, or some other huge creature. If he cannot return to the period he was in before he fell asleep, Walter just knows he will become the latest exhibit at the local museum!

Skorseth, Theresa. **The Birds of Storm Hill.** Abingdon Press, 1982. 143 pp.

When Dexter and his father released a trapped hummingbird from the roof of their cottage, they never dreamed anything would come of it. But the hummingbird turns out to be Nectar, leader of the elders, a mysterious flock of birds able to assume human form. It is their task to protect England from the spirit of a long-dead evil king. A traitor in their midst has threatened to release the evil king's spirit, and the elders need the help of the spirit of a good king who killed the evil one many thousands of years ago. Will Dexter and his family be able to help the elders find the good king in time to save their country?

Stearns, Pamela. **The Fool and the Dancing Bear.** Illus. Ann Strugnell. Atlantic Monthly Press, 1979. 167 pp.

A spiteful queen has put a curse upon the people of a certain land. The curse drains their intelligence and their spirit. Only April Flower, a clairvoyant, knows how to remove the queen's curse. Court jester Timon, a lovesick king, and a dancing bear join forces to find this clairvoyant and save the kingdom. Their journey is filled with adventures, escapes, disguises, and disillusionment.

Steinbeck, John (editor Chase Horton). **The Acts of King Arthur and His Noble Knights.** Del Rey Books, 1977. 451 pp.

Combining today's language with the exciting adventures of the original King Arthur stories, Steinbeck retells the legendary stories of Merlin's wizardry, Arthur's nobility, Guinevere's beauty and wisdom, and Lancelot's strength and goodness. But human weaknesses and the power of evil combine to destroy Arthur and all he builds. Mature reading.

Sutcliff, Rosemary. **The Chronicles of Robin Hood.** Illus. C. Walter Hodges. Oxford University Press, 1977. 280 pp.

These fourteen brief but adventurous tales of Robert of Locksley originally appeared in "The Lytell Geste of Robyn Hoode," printed in 1495. The familiar stories of the legendary English outlaw who aided the poor and his merry band of followers include such characters as Maid Marian, Little John, and Friar Tuck. Easy reading.

Sutcliff, Rosemary. **The Sword and the Circle: King Arthur and the Knights of the Round Table.** E. P. Dutton, 1981. 260 pp.

The legend of King Arthur and his knights is retold here with stories of their adventures, jousts, loves, and magic. Young Arthur pulls the mysterious sword from the rock to become the true King of England, and he changes Britain forever. He forms the famous Round Table of knights that Lancelot, the world's greatest knight, joins at Camelot, the center of Arthur's kingdom. But various battles, quests, and personal troubles cause problems for all the knights, and King Arthur himself.

Synge, Ursula. **Land of Heroes: A Retelling of the Kalevala.** McElderry Books, 1978. 222 pp.

The Kalevala, which means "Land of Heroes," is Finland's national epic, a collection of tales as old and beautiful as the lakes and the forests of the country they come from. The heroes—Vainamoinen the Singer, Ilmarinen the Smith, and the boastful Leminkainen, who alone dares to cross the River of Death—are magicians whose power is the power of song. They are rivals for the hand of the lovely Maiden of Pohja. But the maiden's mother is Mistress Louhi, sorceress of the bitter North, and she sets almost impossible tasks for each of her daughter's suitors.

Tolkien, J.R.R. (editor Christopher Tolkien). **The Silmarillion.** Ballantine Books, 1977. 458 pp.

This collection of stories—filled with magic, heroes, fairy tales, and romances—identifies the characters who form the mythology and the legends for *The Hobbit* and *The Lord of the Rings.* This volume helps us to understand the fantasy world of Middle-earth created by J.R.R. Tolkien, but it should not be used as an introduction to Tolkien's writings. Mature reading.

Traven, B. **The Creation of the Sun and the Moon.** Illus. Alberto Beltrán. Lawrence Hill & Co. and Creative Arts Book Co., 1977. 65 pp.

When the jealous gods of evil extinguish the sun's light, darkness and destruction begin on Earth. A courageous young man performs impossible deeds to create a new sun. Years later, it is his clever son who prepares for the even more difficult task of creating the moon.

Turnbull, Ann. **The Wolf King.** Scholastic Book Services, 1976. 170 pp.

Long ago, Coll's ancestors had sworn brotherhood with the wolves and called themselves the Wolf Clan. Then one man broke faith with the wolves, and the peace was shattered. Coll, the shepherd boy, is charged with a dangerous mission: he must free his brother from a deadly curse by killing the Wolf King.

Wallace, Barbara Brooks. **Miss Switch to the Rescue.** Illus. Kathleen Garry McCord. Abingdon Press, 1981. 158 pp.

In this fantasy adventure, Miss Switch, a fifth-grade teacher, joins Rupert Brown to find out what has happened to Amelia Daley. Thanks to Rupert's opening of a corked bottle, Amelia has been captured by Mordo the warlock, and she just might be turned into a toad! Easy reading.

Webster, Joanne. **The Love Genie.** Elsevier/Nelson Books, 1978. 125 pp.

When fourteen-year-old Jennie finds a valuable fossil on the beach, she never expects that it is the home of a real genie. Much to her delight, the genie promises to grant her every wish. At first, it is enough to ask for a chocolate bar every day, but then Jennie becomes a little more serious about her wishes. She asks the genie to do her homework and to get Simon Matthews to like her. Then some of the genie's magic backfires, and life becomes more interesting than ever.

Wetherbee, Holden. **The Wonder Ring: A Fantasy in Silhouette.** Illus. by author. Doubleday & Co., 1978. 100 pp.

This unusual book contains no words at all, but it does have 136 silhouettes, black-on-white profile pictures. From the silhouettes a story emerges. This tale begins when a mistreated boy shows kindness to a beggar, so the beggar returns his kindness by giving him a magic ring. All of the illustrations were cut by hand from paper.

Williams, Jay. **The Magic Grandfather.** Illus. Gail Owens. Four Winds Press, 1979. 149 pp.

Eleven-year-old Sam Limner's two obsessions are television and food, that is, until he discovers that his grandfather has an unusual talent. Grandfather Limner has a secret he shares with few others— his gift for performing magic. From the moment his grandfather reveals this gift, Sam's whole life becomes incredibly exciting, challenging, and filled with danger and responsibility.

Wolkstein, Diane, compiled by. **The Magic Orange Tree and Other Haitian Folktales.** Illus. Elsa Henriquez. Schocken Books, 1980.

"Cric?" the Haitian storyteller calls out, "Crac!" the audience answers if ready to hear a story. All these stories are usually told at certain large gatherings in Haiti. The tales include stories of hunger and survival, humor, imagination, silliness, wisdom, and creativity in art, songs, and dances. Some of the story titles alone give a sense of the fantasy flavor in them: "The Monkey Who Asked for Misery," "The Case of the Uncooked Eggs," and "The Singing Bone."

Wood, Colin. **A Confusion of Time.** Thomas Nelson, 1975. 168 pp.

The appearance of Wally, a midget, and his dog, Mullinger, ends Raymond's loneliness during a long illness. By simply moving the screen in the kitchen, the three are able to step into the Victorian home that existed on that spot in England in the 1860s. The trio makes daily trips into the past where the inhabitants of the house take Raymond on a chase after the kidnappers of the house's owner. These people also involve him with many of the people and events of England during the time of the American Civil War.

Wrightson, Patricia. **Journey behind the Wind.** McElderry Books, 1981. 156 pp.

He was already a two-time hero to his people, but once again Wirrun, a young Australian aborigine, is called for help by Ko-in, the ancient spirit-hero. An alien thing with red glowing eyes, no body, and a terrifying face has been wandering the land in the service of a fearsome master. With Murra, a water spirit whom he married, Wirrun rides the wind to his people. But on the way Murra is taken by her sisters, leaving Wirrun sad and unable to think about his duty. Finally, Wirrun decides he can only escape his sadness with work, so he once again takes on the dangerous task of finding the red-eyed alien.

Yolen, Jane. **Dragon's Blood.** Delacorte Press, 1982. 243 pp.

When Jakkin Stewart's father died on his planet Austar IV while training a savage dragon, his mother sold Jakkin and herself into "bond" for support. Now Jakkin lives and works in the dragon barns of his master. While watching the new hatchlings, he decides to "hatch" a plot of his own—to steal a dragon and train it to fight in the famous dragon pits. Then Jakkin would win both money and his manhood as a master. But first he meets a strange girl named

Akki who is related to the planet's ruling class. Will she help Jakkin? (ALA Best Book for Young Adults)

Yolen, Jane. **Dream Weaver.** Illus. Michael Hague. William Collins Publishers, 1979.

For a penny, an old blind Dream Weaver creates dreams for seven sets of people. The seven tales that result from this are much like myths or folklore, and they include stories of a character who can change from animal to human, a boy's deep love for his mother, a princess whose stone heart is changed, an artist who creates his own pottery child, and a man of stone who makes a son out of rock.

The Supernatural

Alcock, Vivien. **The Haunting of Cassie Palmer.** Delacorte Press, 1980. 149 pp.

Does Cassie Palmer have supernatural powers? She doesn't think so until she raises a ghost named Deverill. Deverill says he only wants to serve Cassie, but she soon begins to fear that he is driving her toward sorcery and damnation. Will Cassie be able to discover the right spell in time to rid herself of Deverill?

Arthur, Ruth M. **Miss Ghost.** Atheneum Publishers, 1979. 119 pp.

Was there ever really a Miss Ghost? Elphie was not totally sure after she left the remote area of Scotland where she had been sent as a foster child. But for a long time, Miss Ghost had been the only person Elphie could talk to. No one else in that wild and superstitious place understood her, nor did she understand them. Elphie tried to fit in, and she even took care of the baby of the family with whom she stayed. But it all seemed to be for nothing. Everything she did got her into trouble. Then Miss Ghost came into her life to help her find a way out of loneliness and desperation.

Bawden, Nina. **Devil by the Sea.** J. B. Lippincott Co., 1976. 227 pp.

Hilary and her brother Peregrine are enjoying a day at the beach in a resort town in England when Hilary notices a strange man dressed in shabby clothes. He speaks to the children, and young Peregrine fears that the man is the devil. Then Hilary notices that the old man has taken a young girl by the hand, and he is leading her across the marshes. Later, the young girl is found dead. Hilary is frightened, yet fascinated, by what she has seen and heard. Now she wants to find out if the man actually is the devil.

Christopher, Matt. **The Return of the Headless Horseman.** Illus. James McLaughlin. Westminster Press, 1982. 95 pp.

Steve and Jim set out on what should be an ordinary, relaxing fishing trip. But once they are on their way, strange things begin to happen. The worst is the appearance of a headless horseman—everyone says he is the ghost of a nineteenth-century horse thief. The boys are scared, but they also begin to wonder if this is a real ghost.

Corbett, Scott. **Captain Butcher's Body.** Illus. Geff Gerlach. Atlantic Monthly Press, 1976. 169 pp.

The ghost of Captain Butcher—meanest, vilest of pirates—seems a curious and fascinating legend, fun to joke about but not very real. But when George Crowell and his cousin Leo find an old book that describes Captain Butcher's villainous exploits in great detail, their interest is sparked. According to the book, Captain Butcher's ghost is due for a return to Broadmoor Cove, so George and Leo set out to witness what they never expected would really happen.

Corbett, Scott. **The Discontented Ghost.** E. P. Dutton, 1978. 180 pp.

Sir Simon de Canterville, a respectable ghost, lives in an English manor house called Canterville Chase. There he enjoys his privacy until an American family decides to move in. Sir Simon is furious and tries all sorts of ways to drive them out. He runs into trouble, however, when he has to match wits with the family's young twins.

Cunningham, Julia. **Tuppenny.** Unicorn Books, 1978. 87 pp.

Tuppenny, a mysterious girl with an unknown past, comes to the evil town of Standing. When she works at the house of a well-known businessman, she uncovers a wicked plot that concerns a runaway girl and a selfish mother. In another house, she exposes a terrible secret and restores happiness. Everywhere she goes, lives are changed in some bizarre way. Then Tuppenny goes to a house where a murder has taken place, and she finds herself in grave danger.

Curry, Jane Louise. **Poor Tom's Ghost.** McElderry Books, 1979. 178 pp.

When Roger's family moves into the old deserted house built in England in 1603, they spend many hours repairing cracked wallpaper, fallen plaster, and leaky ceilings. But worst of all, Roger's father seems to be possessed with a strange fear of something lurking in the house. To save his father, Roger must go backwards in time to solve a mystery involving a ghost.

Dolan, Sheila. **The Wishing Bottle.** Illus. Leslie Morrill. Houghton Mifflin Co., 1979. 81 pp.

Nora wants a pony more than anything in the world. And though she works and saves, she finally realizes it will take years to accumulate enough money for a pony. So Nora begins to wish, using her magic wishing bottle. And the magic works, as one morning a pony appears from nowhere. What happens next helps Nora to understand the magic of wanting something very much, and the reality of what must be done to make a wish come true. Easy reading.

Duncan, Lois. **Summer of Fear.** Little, Brown & Co., 1976. 217 pp.

When Julia's gifted aunt and uncle are killed in a tragic car accident, she feels cheated and pained. But now their only child Rachel, whom Julia hasn't seen for years, is coming to live with Julia's family in New Mexico. Rachel turns out to be a mystery. Beautiful and bright, she is also spoiled, demanding, and unpleasant to live with—except when she is around boys and men. Rachel sets out to steal Julia's boyfriend immediately. And it's not long before she's working to get the affection of every male in sight. Meanwhile, though, Julia wonders what Rachel does during those hours she spends alone in their room. Julia begins to suspect Rachel of witchcraft and to fear for the people in her family.

Dunlop, Eileen. **Elizabeth.** Illus. Peter Farmer. Holt, Rinehart & Winston, 1975. 185 pp.

Thirteen-year-old Elizabeth Martin spends the summer with Aunt Kate in a Scottish mansion. She is bored and lonely, until she discovers a magic looking glass that sweeps her into the eighteenth century and changes her into another girl who lived in the mansion. Elizabeth becomes trapped in the past, and she must find her way out of a mystery before she dies a death that really isn't meant for her.

Feil, Hila. **The Ghost Garden.** Illus. Thomas Quirk. Atheneum Publishers, 1976. 236 pp.

Jessica, a quiet girl who loves magic, spends the summer at her aunt's old mansion on Cape Cod. There she meets Christina, and together the two girls read books about ghosts, discover a secret room, and plant a witch's garden. But their plans to contact some ghosts are stopped suddenly when Christina becomes terribly ill. Then Jessica sees the true connection between ghosts, death, and Christina's sickness.

Fisher, Leonard Everett. **Noonan: A Novel about Baseball, ESP, and Time Warps.** Illus. by author. Doubleday & Co., 1978. 125 pp.

In the year 1896, fifteen-year-old Johnny Noonan is a pitcher for the Brooklyn Dutchmen Professional Ball Club. Johnny's promising career is cut short, however, when he is hit on the head by a foul ball. When he wakes up it is 100 years later—1996. Johnny is now playing baseball in a teenage league, and he finds out that the game of baseball has changed since the great oil crisis in 1983. There are no umpires, so the decisions about outs, balls, and strikes are all made by computers. Johnny finds he has changed too: he has ESP powers and can make a baseball stop in midair, or make it go wherever he wants.

Gould, Joan. **Otherborn.** Coward, McCann & Geoghegan, 1980. 160 pp.

Mark and his sister Leggy are stranded on an island they think is deserted. Then they meet Tanary Ariki and Ameeta, two children who look about their own age. But when they learn that the two strangers have actually lived a long life, they also learn the wonderful and mysterious secrets of the island. Mark and Leggy watch as infants are born in bodies of old men and women and as ninety-year-old babies die peacefully. The two children must now struggle to be accepted by the natives of this unusual island.

Griffiths, Helen. **The Mysterious Appearance of Agnes.** Illus. Victor Ambrus. Holiday House, 1975. 160 pp.

Agnes seems to appear in the village from thin air. She cannot tell who she is or where she comes from, for Agnes cannot, or will not, speak. She is a strange child who doesn't play with the other children, nor does she return the love of the kind people who take her in. Agnes is so different that the villagers begin to grow afraid of her. So when they see her dancing in the forbidden forest with a cat, the villagers are sure she is a witch.

Grohskopf, Bernice. **Blood and Roses.** Atheneum Publishers, 1979. 256 pp.

Rob is confused when his teacher and his mother announce their engagement, so he seeks the quiet of the library to sort things out. But the sudden appearance of a ghost in the library transforms the peacefulness into thrilling adventure. Later, while visiting England with his mother, Rob discovers that the ghost belongs to William Caxton, a printer, and he sets out to perform an unusual task for Mr. Caxton that will completely change both of them.

Hall, Marjory. **The April Ghost.** Westminster Press, 1975. 184 pp.

Amanda thought she would never tell her father and her stepmother the secret of what she'd witnessed at the abandoned Denton house while on an errand there. Nor did she ever intend to reveal the secret of her imaginary blond companion Isobelle, who listened to all her problems and joys. Even in 1785 and in Salem, Massachusetts, no sensible person would believe that Amanda had actually seen a disembodied hand move a sugar bowl, or that she witnessed the little tea table moving by itself. But one evening, Amanda's stories slip out, and they signal the beginning of a chain of mysteries.

Hallahan, William H. **Keeper of the Children.** Avon Books, 1979. 188 pp.

When a Tibetan monk has his young followers beg for him, their parents try to interfere, but with sad results. When all of the other parents have met with violent and bizarre deaths, Ed Benson realizes that to fight back he must learn the monk's methods: ESP, psychokinesis, and spirit travel. Any combat between the two men will have to take place when they are outside their own bodies, floating in the spirit world.

Hanlon, Emily. **Circle Home.** Bradbury Press, 1981. 237 pp.

A nine-year-old girl falls from the second story of a building and is pronounced dead, but she later revives. Four years later this same girl, Isabelle Lessing, believes she is Mai from another place and another time. Only Ogon, a snake, seems to know about Mai, and Mai believes Ogon has come to take her home. Is it possible that Isabelle has a second life? And why does a shopping mall seem to be the doorway to the past?

Jackson, Shirley. **The Haunting of Hill House.** Popular Library, 1977. 174 pp.

Hill House is supposed to be haunted. This eighty-year-old house even looks evil, but four people are determined to stay in the house and discover the source of the superstitions about it. This group is led by Dr. Montague, who wants to record any important psychic phenomena. He is joined by Luke, who is an heir to Hill House, and two young women, Eleanor and Theodora. After a number of frightening experiences, Eleanor begins to feel her life is somehow related to that of a young girl who hanged herself from the upper turret of Hill House years ago.

King, Stephen. **The Dead Zone.** Signet Books, 1980. 402 pp.

Johnny is a small boy who by accident is plunged into The Dead Zone. Johnny Smith is a small-town teacher who wins a four-and-a-half-year trip into The Dead Zone. John Smith awakens from a coma, and now he has the strange power to see the future and the fate awaiting humankind in The Dead Zone. How do all these John Smiths relate to each other through their Dead Zone experiences? Mature language and situations.

King, Stephen. **Fire-Starter.** Signet Books, 1981. 404 pp.

A young girl is born with the most destructive power a human being has ever commanded. Her parents want her protected, but the government wants to use her as a weapon. Mature language and situations.

Kotzwinkle, William. **Dream of Dark Harbor.** Illus. Joe Servello. Doubleday & Co., 1979. 44 pp.

Jack finds shelter in a deserted fisherman's shack on a lonely jetty, only to wake to a crashing storm. His survival depends on what he doesn't believe in—ghosts, watery ghosts of sailors from the sea. This eerie fantasy creates an uneasy mood that never lets up.

Levitin, Sonia. **Beyond Another Door.** Atheneum Publishers, 1977. 174 pp.

The plate that Daria won at the carnival looks like an ordinary plate—but it isn't. Soon a strange face begins to appear on the plate, and an unfamiliar voice tells her hidden secrets about her past. How can she explain this to anyone when no one else can see or hear it? Daria searches for a way to escape the terror that now haunts her dreams because of the plate's power over her.

Lively, Penelope. **The Ghost of Thomas Kempe.** Illus. Antony Maitland. E. P. Dutton, 1973. 186 pp.

James Harrison is continually blamed for broken dishes, slammed doors, icy drafts, and other disturbances in the old home his family has recently moved into. Frustrated, he tries to find the source of the trouble. This search leads James to discover the ghost of Thomas Kempe. With the help of two friends and a dog, James tries to send the restless spirit back to its grave.

MacKellar, William. **Kenny and the Highland Ghost.** Illus. W. T. Mars. Dodd, Mead & Co., 1980. 185 pp.

Fourteen-year-old Kenny is unhappy when his father is transferred to the Scottish Highlands. Then Kenny meets Duggie Cameron, and the two boys explore Stratton Castle and find the ghost of Mr. MacDhu, the former Earl of Strathullen. Duggie and Kenny watch the cowardly but mischievous ghost play many pranks before this former Earl of Strathullen is finally put to rest.

MacLeod, Charlotte. **The Withdrawing Room.** Avon Books, 1981. 188 pp.

A woman rents out rooms in her house on Beacon Hill in Boston. But she doesn't know that Death is going to visit and start "evicting" her boarders one by one.

Oppenheim, Shulamith. **The Selchie's Seed.** Illus. Diane Goode. Camelot Books, 1977. 82 pp.

When a rare white whale surfaces near the Sinclore family's private island, Mr. Sinclore thinks it will be gone by the next morning. But it isn't. This is only the beginning of a series of strange events, events somehow connected with the ocean. Marian, the daughter, senses a powerful, magical calling from the water and from the whale. Then a dark secret of the past is revealed, and Marian learns that she has inherited a curse that may tear her from her family and bind her to the sea.

Otfinoski, Steven. **Village of Vampires.** Illus. Chris Kenyon. Fearon-Pitman Publishers, 1979. 59 pp.

Dr. John Laurence is asked to visit Mexico to help provide health and medical care. With his daughter, Sandy, and his young assistant, Paul Ross, Dr. Laurence hopes to stop an epidemic that has killed almost everyone in a certain village. Dr. Laurence is assisted by José, a villager who claims that the people are being turned into vampires. When José becomes a vampire, Dr. Laurence realizes he must act quickly before his former assistant claims his next victim—Sandy. Easy reading.

Owen, Dilys. **Leo Possessed.** Illus. Stephen Gammell. Harcourt Brace Jovanovich, 1979. 150 pp.

There is something strange about the old Georgian town house in England that Leonora and her family move into. That voice crying in the attic must belong to someone. Then two ghosts that Leonora thinks she is only imagining begin to speak to her. Soon one of the spirits, driven by bitter jealousy, begins to invade her mind and body.

Peck, Richard. **The Ghost Belonged to Me.** Viking Press, 1975. 183 pp.

At first, Alexander has no intention of listening to the warnings about the ghost of a drowned girl who lives in his barn. Then he actually meets the ghost, who predicts a horrible accident. Alexander tries to prevent the accident, but the whole town is thrown into an uproar when they hear his ghost story.

Peck, Richard. **Ghosts I Have Been.** Viking Press, 1977. 214 pp.

Above all else, Blossom Culp wishes to possess her mother's gift of second sight. But she is also concentrating on other things, like the gang of boys that is plotting vandalism and the odd girl that appears on Halloween night. Strangely, these events lead her to a startling realization, and soon Blossom is on the road to international fame.

Pierce, Meredith Ann. **The Darkangel.** Atlantic Monthly Press, 1982. 223 pp.

A servant girl named Aeriel finds she must choose between destroying her vampire master for his evil deeds, or saving him for the sake of his beauty and the spark of goodness she sees in him. She hopes, though, to free his thirteen young brides, whose souls are imprisoned in lead vials hanging about his neck. And she wants to release them before the vampire takes a fourteenth bride. Mature situations. (ALA Best Book for Young Adults)

Pope, Elizabeth Marie. **The Perilous Gard.** Illus. Richard Cuffari. Houghton Mifflin Co., 1974. 280 pp.

"Perilous gard" was the phrase used for a castle people feared because of old magic. Kate Sutton is not afraid when she is sent away from the English court and imprisoned in Elvenwood in 1558. But she is not prepared for what she finds at the castle. She has to use her cleverness and wits to deal with a whole new kind of world of the supernatural.

Randall, Florence Engel. **A Watcher in the Woods.** Atheneum Publishers, 1976. 229 pp.

Jan is positive that she didn't just imagine the figure in the woods near her family's new home. Her mother says that it is probably only a trespasser passing through, but Jan is not so sure. She has the feeling that something is watching—something frightening and mysterious. Jan's fears are confirmed when her sister starts to get messages from the strange being. Then Jan unravels the mystery when she discovers a secret that has been hidden in the woods for fifty years.

Read, Mary Lyle. **The Sack Man and the Grave.** Abingdon Press, 1981. 160 pp.

Nine-year-old Victory Carroll visits her great-aunt's estate, Carroll Oaks, and immediately becomes involved in a mystery when she learns about a lost treasure hidden on the property. With the help of an old man and an antique doll possessed by a restless spirit, Victory searches for the hidden fortune.

Roberts, Nancy. **Appalachian Ghosts.** Photographs by Bruch Roberts. Doubleday & Co., 1978. 77 pp.

Gray, misty fog couldn't stop Larry Huff from speeding down Highway 55 out of Campbellsville, Kentucky, on his new Honda. Even though the fog was so thick in some places he could barely see, Larry didn't mind. The quiet and the mist let him be alone with his own thoughts for awhile. Then he spotted a thin, ghostly looking little girl alongside the road and gave her a ride home. Her hands around his waist were cold—you see, Laura had been dead seven years now. Other ghosts besides Laura fill the stories on the pages of this book, stories guaranteed to keep you guessing.

Shecter, Ben. **The River Witches.** Harper & Row, Publishers, 1979. 180 pp.

When Andrew pays a visit to ailing Aunt Elizabeth, the trip turns out to be less boring than he expected. Andrew learns that his aunt is a real witch and that he has the chance to become a warlock! But first he must embark on a journey, a journey that mixes the powers of witchcraft and the threat of death.

Shelley, Mary; **Frankenstein.** Bram Stoker; **Dracula.** Robert Louis Stevenson; **Dr. Jekyll and Mr. Hyde.** Signet Books, 1978. 680 pp.

Three famous horror classics of the nineteenth century are collected here. In *Frankenstein,* a doctor attempts to create life in a laboratory. In *Dracula,* a vampire pursues eternal life by drinking human blood each night. While in *Dr. Jekyll and Mr. Hyde,* a man experiments with drugs and finds there are two sides to his personality—one kind and one murderous.

Sleator, William. **Into the Dream.** Illus. Ruth Sanderson. E. P. Dutton, 1979. 137 pp.

Paul and Francine know that something strange and powerful is at work when they discover that they share the same repeating dream. Bravely, they follow the signs in their dream to an old hotel that they had visited as children. There they dig up secrets of the past that have been buried deep in their minds, especially memories of a UFO and a psychic transfer. Then Paul and Francine discover that their lives rest in the hands of secret agents who will do anything to seize their mental powers.

Swearingen, Martha. **If Anything.** Elsevier/Nelson Books, 1980. 223 pp.

One night Martin Evans loses control of his sports car and runs into a brick wall. He is killed instantly. But a strange woman named Ashgrove Frazier finds him. She is a ghost who tries to convince Martin he is now a ghost too. But he does not believe her and decides to tell the police his story. Both Martin and the police are in for a surprise.

Tannen, Mary. **The Lost Legend of Finn.** Illus. Michael Hostovich. Alfred A. Knopf, 1982. 144 pp.

Fiona and Bran McCool have one mission in mind: to solve the mystery of their unknown father. The only way they can do this is to travel back in time 2,000 years so that Finn can help them. They use their uncle's magic book to work a spell, but the magic goes wild and the two find themselves in the amazing and strange Ireland of 839 A.D. So enchanted are they by the land that they nearly forget their mission. Then one magic night Old Biddy Gwynn, a powerful Druid, chants a haunting spell that transforms the two childred into ravens. As ravens, they see the world through new eyes, and gradually come to understand certain truths about themselves. Sequel to *The Wizard Children of Finn.*

Tannen, Mary. **The Wizard Children of Finn.** Illus. John Burgoyne. Alfred A. Knopf, 1981. 214 pp.

A mysterious whistle from the woods behind their uncle's house lures eleven-year-old Fiona McCool and her brother Bran into the spell of Finn, an enchanted boy. The spell carries the three on a 2,000-year journey back in time to Ireland, Finn's homeland. Here they must escape the clever Sons of Morna, cross swift rivers, battle wild beasts, and find the Wisdom of Salmon. After all this, Finn must set himself up as a leader in this strange land. But is there any magic that can take the sister and brother back home again?

Thorne, Ian. **Dracula.** Crestwood House, 1977. 40 pp.

A count in Transylvania lives hundreds of years by drinking human blood each night. Now he must seek fresh victims in a new area. This is one of a series of short books relating the stories of such famous monsters as Dracula, King Kong, Godzilla, the Wolf Man, Frankenstein, the Mad Scientists, the Creature from the Black Lagoon, and the Mummy. Pictures from films made about each monster are included with the stories. Easy reading.

Waldorf, Mary. **Thousand Camps.** Houghton Mifflin Co., 1982. 197 pp.

Chloe is spending the summer with her uncle and his family on their farm on the California coast. In the daytime everything is normal, but some nights, when the fog swirls in from the sea and the Pigeon Point lighthouse is mysteriously dark, Chloe and her friend Joaquin find that they can slip through the windwall into another world. There they meet the long-ago inhabitants of a small Indian village who teach Joaquin and Chloe that they have a dangerous and important task to carry out—one that will keep a promise made many years ago.

Willard, Barbara. **Spell Me a Witch.** Harcourt Brace Jovanovich, 1979. 142 pp.

When Belladonna Agrimony, the principal of the Academy for Young Witches, goes to a convention, her nine young pupils cast wild spells and get into trouble. Now that Belladonna has come back, she has to cancel all three spells and find her prize student, Angelica, who has vanished into thin air.

Windham, Kathryn Tucker. **Jeffrey Introduces 13 More Southern Ghosts.** Strode Publishers, 1978. 128 pp.

Jeffrey, the ghost-in-residence at the Windham house in Selma, Alabama, introduces the reader to some of his spirit friends who live in other Southern states. Each ghost has a weird adventure story to tell.

York, Carol Beach. **Beware of This Shop.** Thomas Nelson, 1977. 127 pp.

Hester and Isabel discover the gift shop by chance and each purchases a small trinket at the quaint place. Soon, however, they begin to suffer nightmares and illness, so the two girls destroy their purchases. After Isabel goes away, Hester decides to discover for herself exactly what evil is at work in the shop, so she goes to work for Mr. Mordrian, the shop's strange owner.

Humor and Satire

Aragones, Sergio. **Sergio Aragones's** *MAD* **Marginals from Various Places around the Magazine.** Illus. by author. Warner Books, 1980. 192 pp.

This is a collection of visual jokes presented in brief horizontal or vertical panels. This picture humor makes amusing and ironic statements about human beings—from how they act at funeral processions to their experiences on the high seas.

Berg, Dave (editor Albert B. Feldstein). *MAD*'s **Dave Berg Looks at Things.** Illus. by author. Warner Books, 1981. 192 pp.

Cartoonist Dave Berg looks satirically at the trials of ownership, the frustrations of communicating with other people, and the silliness that faces all of us as part of our daily life.

Bierce, Ambrose. **The Devil's Dictionary.** Illus. Ferebe Streett. Stemmer House Publishers, 1978.

The famous Ambrose Bierce takes over a thousand words and gives them new definitions—witty and biting in satire. The definitions include poems, long essays of 400 words, stories, and epigrams. Nearly all the definitions show his use of puns, and all show his skill with the language. For example, a *circus* is defined as "a place where horses, ponies and elephants are permitted to see men, women and children acting the fool," and *armor* is "the kind of clothing worn by a man whose tailor is a blacksmith."

Bishop, Ann. **Hello Mr. Chips: Computer Jokes and Riddles.** Illus. Jerry Warshaw. Lodestar Books, 1982. 50 pp.

Computers seem to be with us for good, and here is a collection of jokes and riddles about computers at work, at play, and in the classroom. Here are some samples: What do you get when you cross a computer with an elephant? A five-ton know-it-all. Why did the computer cross the road? It had the chicken's number.

Bleepers! In Love and **Bleepers! In Space.** Warner Books, 1980. 24 pp.

Ever want to be a comic-book writer? Well, here's your chance. Readers of these volumes ask friends or family members to supply nouns, verbs, and other parts of speech without letting them see the full sentence. The dialogues you create for the comic-book characters will be hilariously crazy every time.

Booth, George. **Pussycats Need Love, Too.** Illus. by author. Avon Books, 1981. 140 pp.

These cartoons capture dogs, cats, and other unusual characters, acting in all sorts of ways—weird, stubborn, wise, and wild. Most of these cartoons first appeared in *The New Yorker* magazine.

Brandreth, Gyles. **Total Nonsense Z to A.** Illus. Lucy Robinson. Sterling Publishing Co., 1981. 96 pp.

The author reveals the secrets of defrosting your dog, raising a pet piranha, and becoming a nervous wreck. There are spoofs of spooky stories (like the spine-tingling tales of the haunted hairpiece and the ghost of the giant Choc-o-Mint Galactic ice cream), a botanical guide to flowers (such as the Manypeeplia Upsidownia), and poems about crazy things (such as strawberries growing in the sea). These outrageous ideas and delightful ditties will keep you seeing the whimsical side of the world.

Collins, David R. **The One Bad Thing about Birthdays.** Illus. David Wiesner. Harcourt Brace Jovanovich, 1981. 28 pp.

David's best present on his birthday would be to have as many wishes as he wants. He tells us what those wishes would be in an amusing and illuminating way. Easy reading.

Corbett, Scott. **Jokes to Read in the Dark.** Illus. Annie Gusman. Unicorn Books, 1980. 69 pp.

What are good manners called in Warsaw? Polish polish, of course. What's a blunderbus? A school bus on the wrong road. If you like puns, limericks, elephant jokes, and one-liners, then this collection of jokes is for you.

Cresswell, Helen. **Absolute Zero: Being the Second Part of The Bagthorpe Saga.** Camelot Books, 1979. 174 pp.

The Bagthorpes are a family living in England. The fun begins for them when Uncle Parker wins a Caribbean cruise for sending in the best slogan for a breakfast cereal. Now all of the Bagthorpes begin to enter contests. Mr. Bagthorpe, jealous of Uncle Parker, tears the labels off of all the canned goods in the larder, and as a result, each meal comes as a fresh, and not always pleasant, surprise. A cheating grandmother, a sister who writes on walls, and a family dog who becomes the biggest contest winner of them all complete this zany family group. (ALA Notable Book)

Cresswell, Helen. **Bagthorpes v. the World: Being the Fourth Part of The Bagthorpe Saga.** Camelot Books, 1980. 193 pp.

The eccentric Bagthorpe family decide to become farmers in England. But nobody quite knows how to go about it. After some humorous mix-ups, the family dog, Absolute Zero, finds his way into this farming project.

Cresswell, Helen. **Ordinary Jack: Being the First Part of The Bagthorpe Saga.** Camelot Books, 1979. 195 pp.

Meet the zany Bagthorpe family and their dog, Absolute Zero. There is one quiet member of this crazy bunch, though, and they call him "Ordinary Jack." But Jack is tired of being a normal boy in an extraordinary family, so he decides to work on a specialty, something to make him stand out. What he comes up with is the idea of becoming the family prophet. And he really does amaze everyone by predicting their future.

Crume, Vic. **The Billion Dollar Hobo.** Scholastic Book Services, 1978. 121 pp.

Vernon's job record is not good—thirty-nine jobs in thirty-four cities. When his short-order cooking sets a diner on fire, his rich Uncle Trayne comes to the rescue. Uncle Trayne, now a billionaire, started out riding the rails, so Vernon decides to follow his example. Vernon is determined that this will be his big chance to pull his life together and make something of himself. Based on the screenplay.

Danziger, Paula. **There's a Bat in Bunk Five.** Delacorte Press, 1980. 150 pp.

For Marcy Lewis, the junior counseling job at the summer camp has many advantages—like the cute lifeguard and the crazy camp activities. But it also harbors disaster in the form of a wild bat, a runaway, and twelve pranksters. Marcy faces the challenge of a lifetime: just living through this summer at camp.

DeBartolo, Dick (editor Nick Meglin). **A *MAD* Guide to Fraud and Deception (And Other Accepted Business Practices).** Illus. Harry North. Warner Books, 1981. 192 pp.

Have you ever bought something that was not what all the ads promised? Have you ever gone to a movie that got good reviews, only to find it was boring? In this book, the people at *MAD Magazine* expose this kind of consumer rip-off in a collection of hilarious illustrated examples.

Doty, Roy. **King Midas Has a Gilt Complex.** Doubleday & Co., 1979.

What kind of rocks all look alike? What kinds of coins snore? What kind of animal can never be trusted? The answers to these wacky riddles are all based on jokes and puns. Cartoons accompany each riddle.

Doty, Roy. **Pinocchio Was Nosey: Grandson of Puns, Gags, Quips and Riddles.** Doubleday & Co., 1977.

What was Camelot famous for? Its knight life. What does your father sing in the bathtub? Pop music. How long does a candle burn? About one wick. If you liked these jokes, you'll enjoy this collection of puns, gags, and riddles. All jokes are illustrated with drawings.

Eckstein, Joan, and Joyce Gleit. **The Best Joke Book for Kids.** Illus. Joyce Behr. Camelot Books, 1977. 32 pp.

This is a collection of favorite elephant jokes and pickle jokes. These jokes often come from an oral tradition, and have been passed down from generation to generation, usually by children.

Evans, Derek, and Dave Fulwiler. **Who's Nobody in America?** Illus. Bob Byrd. Owl Books, 1981. 112 pp.

Everyone has the experience of feeling like a nobody at times. However, this book collects examples of all the humorous "nobody" statistics throughout the United States. In Virginia, Thomas Freeman complains that "In my homeroom's student election of 1977, no one voted for me. Not even the two kids I paid to nominate me." The book is complete with a horoscope for nobodies and survey statistics for nobodies.

Feldstein, Albert B., editor. **Clods' Letters to *MAD*.** Illus. Al Jaffee. Warner Books, 1981. 192 pp.

What kind of weirdo writes to *MAD Magazine?* Well, this book gives you some idea of the wide variety of people who take the time to praise, criticize, yell at, or congratulate the magazine and its writers and illustrators. These letters are often as funny as the subjects they talk about.

Feldstein, Albert B., editor. **The Eggs-Rated** *MAD*. Warner Books, 1981. 192 pp.

The writers and artists of *MAD Magazine* turn their attention to such topics as model building, graduation, and dieting—and they find something funny to say about all.

Feldstein, Albert B., editor. *MAD* **about the Buoy.** Warner Books, 1980.

In this collection from *MAD Magazine,* "Fiddler on the Roof" becomes "Antenna on the Roof"; Mother Goose becomes ecology minded; parents regret their permissiveness; and the power and light company welcomes you to a behind-the-scenes view of its operations.

Feldstein, Albert B., editor. **The Uncensored** *MAD*. Warner Books, 1980. 192 pp.

Televison and movies are two of the main targets of *MAD's* satires in this collection. *MAD* versions of "M*A*S*H" and *American Graffiti* are hilariously accurate.

Fidell, Jeanette. **TAB Joke Book.** Scholastic Book Services, 1979. 122 pp.

This is a collection of jokes on a number of subjects: school, food, words, people, animals, kids, and work. Most are plays on words, and some are accompanied by illustrations. A typical joke: Ad in the classified section—"Lovely kitten desires position as companion to little girl. Will also do light mousekeeping."

Forrest, David. **One of Our Dinosaurs Is Missing.** Avon Books, 1975. 188 pp.

What happens when a microdot containing valuable government secrets is placed on the skeleton of a brontosaurus? What happens here is that the dinosaur is stolen by some British nannies who then become involved in a Chinese spy plot called "The Great Leap Downward." Originally published as *The Great Dinosaur Robbery.*

Gaines, William M. (editor Albert B. Feldstein). **Burning** *MAD*. Warner Books, 1975. 192 pp.

Alfred E. ("What—Me Worry?") Neuman introduces this collection of articles from *MAD Magazine* that includes humorous looks at Father's Day cards and summer camps.

Gaines, William M. (editor Albert B. Feldstein). **Dr. Jekyll and Mr. MAD.** Warner Books, 1981. 192 pp.

What is so funny about driving, Mother's Day cards, and hate? This volume of *MAD* articles will tell you in words and pictures.

Gaines, William M. (editor Albert B. Feldstein). **The Ides of *MAD*.** Warner Books, 1980. 192 pp.

Nothing is sacred when it comes to *MAD*'s humor. Stamp collecting, palm reading, Shakespeare, stereo sets, parking meters, and many more subjects are made light of in this book.

Gaines, William M. (editor Albert B. Feldstein). **The Indigestible *MAD*.** Warner Books, 1981. 192 pp.

Here is another collection of work containing *MAD*'s unique brand of satiric and absurd humor. Explored in this book are parents' predictions for their children, the spy business, and college life.

Gaines, William M. (editor Albert B. Feldstein). **The *MAD* Frontier.** Warner Books, 1980. 192 pp.

MAD Magazine attacks traffic signals and previews new movies. There is also a collection known as "The *MAD* Treasury of Unknown Poetry"—and you will realize why these poems have stayed undiscovered for so long when you read them.

Gaines, William M. (editor Albert B. Feldstein). ***MAD* in Orbit.** Warner Books, 1981. 192 pp.

Who is in the Idiot's Hall of Fame? What can you do with a credit card besides charge things? This book, compiled by the creators of *MAD Magazine,* will tell (and show) you.

Gaines, William M. (editor Albert B. Feldstein). **The Pocket *MAD*.** Warner Books, 1980.

As usual, the people at *MAD Magazine* are making fun of everything in sight. This time they take on Paul Newman, the Avis-Hertz advertising campaigns, Dr. Seuss, Mother Goose, dating practices, and "Star Trek." There are also many sight gags in these pages and pages of cartoons.

Gaines, William M. (editor Albert B. Feldstein). **The Voodoo *MAD*.** Warner Books, 1981. 192 pp.

Special insurance policies for teenagers and comic-strip heroes are only two of the subjects explored with crazy humor in this book.

Illustrations are used in one section to show you how you look to other people—including your teachers.

Garfield, Leon. **The Night of the Comet: A Comedy of Courtship Featuring Bostock and Harris.** Delacorte Press, 1979. 149 pp.

Cassidy is turned docile when he falls in love with a girl named Mary Flatley. But she runs away from him in search of a husband without a wandering eye. So Cassidy and his friend O'Rourke set out to find and capture Mary. Their travels set off a chain of hilarious events including cases of mistaken identities and courtship rituals that leave the characters totally confused over who is in love with whom.

Havis, Allan. **Albert the Astronomer.** Harper & Row, Publishers, 1979. 120 pp.

Sixth-grader Albert Bloom is not popular with his classmates. Even his parents don't understand him. Albert likes to study the stars but spends so much time with his telescope that he is flunking out of school. He makes matters worse by accusing a neighbor of being an alien and of believing that UFOs visit his neighborhood. To top it all off, Albert also believes that he is from outer space and only adopted by his parents. Now, with the help of his new friend, Lenora, Albert the Astronomer is about to astonish the world.

Heide, Florence Parry. **Banana Twist.** Holiday House, 1978. 111 pp.

Jonah D. Krock has a pest of a neighbor named Goober Grube. But Jonah is not much better. When he and Goober first meet, Jonah makes up all kinds of false stories about himself. He tells himself he only stays around Goober because Goober serves him banana splits. But who will have the last laugh?

Hicks, Clifford A. **Peter Potts.** Camelot Books, 1979. 105 pp.

Peter Potts just seems to have a knack for getting into trouble. Take the time he took a hornet's nest to school for science class. It wasn't his fault when it rolled under the radiator and heated up the hornets. Or what about the time he decided to use fishing line, a chicken, and a barbell to remove a tooth, and he ended up removing his friend Joey's tooth instead? Peter begins to wonder if his accidental troubles will ever end.

Jacobs, Frank, and Paul Peter Porges (editor Albert B. Feldstein). *MAD* **around the World.** Warner Books, 1979. 190 pp.

Going around the world with *MAD Magazine* is a wild and crazy trip. Helpful hints for travel come in *MAD*'s handy phrase book for exotic cities like Philadelphia, Las Vegas, Los Angeles, New York, and Washington, D.C. Other chapters reveal how to be a smart tourist instead of a dumb one, where bigots take their tours, and what irritates people most on their trips.

Keller, Charles, editor. **The Best of Rube Goldberg.** Prentice-Hall, 1979. 130 pp.

For over fifty years, Rube Goldberg, an award-winning cartoonist, drew cartoons that presented machines and contraptions of marvelous complexity built to perform such simple tasks as sharpening a pencil or killing a fly. His absurd, yet ingenious, inventions stand as critical commentaries of our mechanical age. This collection of cartoons includes inventions designed to bait a hook, lose weight, open bottles, and whip cream. Each cartoon includes an explanation of the inner workings of the invention.

Keller, Charles, editor. **Growing Up Laughing: Humorists Look at American Youth.** Prentice-Hall, 1981. 189 pp.

This is a collection of humorous stories, cartoons, and poems by some of America's top humorists. Mark Twain, Shel Silverstein, Robert Benchley, Frank Gilbreth, Emma Rounds, Ruth McKenney, and Bill Cosby are all represented in this book, which includes selections titled "Guinea Pigs," "The Chivalry of Adolescence," and "Savage Homecoming."

Kiernan, Joseph. **Lots of Funny Riddles.** Illus. by author. Warner Books, 1981. 125 pp.

Looking for a silly riddle with a funny answer? This book will provide you with hundreds of them. Here is a sample to give you an idea of what is included: "What holiday do vampires like most? Fangsgiving."

Koch, Tom (editor Nick Meglin). **The *MAD* Worry Book.** Illus. Robert Clarke. Warner Books, 1980. 191 pp.

The people at *MAD Magazine* believe that everyone worries, but only about the things they know. However, there are many things for people to worry about that they just aren't aware of. *MAD* has decided to explore these other worries. So dig in and find a worry you have never thought of before.

Lorenz, Lee. **Pinchpenny John.** Illus. by author. Prentice-Hall, 1981. 30 pp.

In this novel suggested by incidents in Chaucer's "The Miller's Tale," an astrology student tricks a penny-pinching old carpenter into believing that a terrible flood is about to occur. Why do all this? Well, it seems the student wants to steal the carpenter's gold. But chaos and excitement result when the plan is set in motion. Easy reading.

Lorenz, Lee. **Scornful Simkin.** Illus. by author. Prentice-Hall, 1980. 30 pp.

In this retelling of Chaucer's "The Reeve's Tale," a certain miller is known and feared as a bully who always steals some of the grain he grinds for his customers. But he will soon be taught a hilarious lesson when two clever university students outwit the miller. Easy reading.

Mankoff, Robert. **Elementary: The Cartoonist Did It.** Avon Books, 1980. 60 pp.

This collection of 111 cartoons, largely from *The New Yorker* magazine, contains sharp attacks on social issues and human weaknesses.

Martin, Don (editor Nick Meglin). *MAD*'s **Don Martin Grinds Ahead.** Illus. by author. Warner Books, 1981. 192 pp.

Is there a doctor in the house? You will need one (or at least an aspirin) after you see what *MAD Magazine* does to the subjects of first aid and modern life, among others.

McCarthy, Eugene J., and James J. Kilpatrick. **A Political Bestiary.** Illus. Jeff MacNelly. Avon Books, 1979.

Common political terms have been matched here to cartoonlike beasts, birds, and fish with humorous results. For example, "inflation" has been matched with a galloping horse, and "the bloated bureaucracy" is illustrated by an overweight fish. Some other terms wittily illustrated are "the loophole," "the staggering deficit," and "the paradox."

Meglin, Nick. **The Sound of** *MAD*. Illus. George Woodbridge. Warner Books, 1980. 192 pp.

What do silent movies, gambling, food, justice, radio, and television have in common? They are all targets for *MAD*'s crazy brand of humor in the selection of pieces from the magazine.

Orwell, George. **Animal Farm.** Signet Books, 1974. 128 pp.

The animals of Manor Farm are sick and tired of their mistreatment at the hands of Farmer Jones, so they revolt. They drive Jones and his workers off the farm and proceed to run the farm themselves. Lying below this plot is a satirical attack on totalitarian governments. The freedom of the animals after their revolt soon becomes nothing more than slavery under new masters, the pigs. As author Orwell puts it, "All animals are equal, but some animals are more equal than others." Originally published in 1946.

Peck, Robert Newton. **Basketcase.** Doubleday & Co., 1979. 94 pp.

Everyone at Graffiti Prep is counting on the wits of Higbee Hartburn, the class joker, to save the school. Unless Graffiti wins the big basketball game, the school goes broke. But what can anyone do with a basketball player who can only dribble to the sound of a schnitzelboop? Or a senior citizen's band in the cheerleading section? Then there are the cheerleaders who wear bloomers. But, believe it or not, they all become part of Higbee's crazy plan to save his school.

Pinkwater, Daniel. **Attila the Pun: A Magic Moscow Story.** Illus. by author. Four Winds Press, 1981. 69 pp.

Norman wouldn't miss working at the Magic Moscow for anything, even though his father tells him he should just hang out with the other kids. There's so much going on at Magic Moscow, and besides, Norman makes piles of money, even if he is underage. But one day when Norman is on duty alone, the scariest guy he has ever seen walks in and orders the house supersnack, a Nuclear Meltdown. Soon, however, Norman and his friends discover they have a ghost on their hands they can't get rid of.

Pinkwater, Daniel. **The Worms of Kukumlima.** E. P. Dutton, 1981. 152 pp.

Ronald Donald Almondotter is in for a surprise when Sir Charles Pelicanstein, a famous explorer, visits his grandfather's factory with a new adventure in mind. Sir Charles wants to search for the intelligent earthworms that are supposed to live in the heart of Africa. So Ronald, his grandfather, and Sir Charles embark on a journey to Africa. Once there, they are aided by strange elephants and peculiar mice, even though a wise man tells them to go home. But the trio finally find an intelligent earthworm, and Ronald learns how amazing they really are.

Powers, John R. **The Unoriginal Sinner and the Ice-Cream God.** Popular Library, 1977. 320 pp.

Tim Conroy has made his way through college, and now he is facing the work world. Everyone keeps advising him to "settle down," but Tim refuses. He knows that what everyone really means by this is to quit doing things your way and do them their way. Tim is assisted in his struggle to remain free by a wonderful, unconventional garage mechanic who doubles as an advisor to the young man.

Robertson, Mary Elise. **Jemimalee.** Illus. Judith Gwyn Brown. Camelot Books, 1979. 122 pp.

Mr. Curtis, a poet, and his family have taken a house out in the country where Mr. Curtis plans to write a book. But he can't seem to get started writing, so it is up to the family cat, Jemimalee, and the dog, McTavish, to help. The two animals talk things over, and Jemimalee begins to slip into Mr. Curtis' study at night to type out poetry. Mr. Curtis begins to believe he has been typing in his sleep. This scheme works so well that Jemimalee and McTavish plan other ways to help the family.

Rosenbloom, Joseph. **Biggest Riddle Book in the World.** Illus. Joyce Behr. Sterling Publishing Co., 1977. 272 pp.

A librarian has collected these riddles from among the favorites of children and young people he has talked to. Here are some samples to whet your appetite: "What can you turn without moving? Milk. It can turn sour." "When do mathematicians die? When their numbers are up." "What is a twip? A twip is what a wabbit takes when he wides a twain." Care for more?

Rosenbloom, Joseph. **Daffy Dictionary: Funabridged Definitions from Aardvark to Zuider Zee.** Illus. Joyce Behr. Sterling Publishing Co., 1977. 256 pp.

"Abalone" is an expression of disbelief (agh, baloney!) and a "forger" is someone who is always ready to write a wrong. A "psychopath" is a crazy road, and "egg white" is Snow White's brother. Over 2,000 of these goofy definitions are provided here. The definitions are usually in the form of puns, jokes, quips, wise sayings, wacky word play, and one-liners.

Rosenbloom, Joseph. **Dr. Knock-Knock's Official Knock-Knock Dictionary.** Illus. Joyce Behr. Sterling Publishing Co., 1977. 128 pp.

"Knock, knock. Who's there? Izzy. Izzy who? Izzy come, Izzy go." If you thought that joke was corny but fun, you'll enjoy the other 500 knock-knock jokes in this collection. In addition to the classic examples of this variety of joke, the book includes knock-knock jokes using dozens of names. Your name is probably included in one of them.

Rosenbloom, Joseph. **The Gigantic Joke Book.** Illus. Joyce Behr. Sterling Publishing Co., 1978. 251 pp.

This large book of jokes presents humor for all kinds of occasions, all kinds of people, and all kinds of moods. There are old and new jokes, crazy and intellectual jokes, and jokes about everything from athletes to space travel to King Arthur. By the way, did you hear the one about the girl who missed the party? When her mother asked why, the girl replied: "The invitation said from three to six—and I'm seven."

Rosenbloom, Joesph. **Monster Madness: Riddles, Jokes, Fun.** Illus. Joyce Behr. Sterling Publishing Co., 1980. 122 pp.

Humans make mistakes, but ghosts make boo-boos. Once a monster nibbled on an electric bulb because he wanted only a light snack. Jokes like these threaten to turn those monsters and ghouls who scare us into objects of fun. This book, packed with riddles and jokes, may do just that.

Schulte, Elaine L. **Zack and the Magic Factory.** Thomas Nelson, 1976. 126 pp.

Zachary Dabble goes to visit his aunt's magic factory and plunges headlong into adventure. Two thieves break into the financially troubled factory and try to steal the latest invention. Soon after this threat, Zachary, his aunt, and a friendly girl embark on a wild chase filled with magic pranks, tricks, and traps.

Schulz, Charles M. **Always Stick Up for the Underbird.** Illus. by author. Holt, Rinehart & Winston, 1977. 185 pp.

Charlie Brown wonders why he is always so unlucky. He also feels everyone just feels sorry for him—that no one really likes him. Then Lucy tells Charlie Brown he's "a decent sort." He feels great, until Lucy adds that being a decent sort is about all he can hope for. There are many more encounters between Charlie, Lucy, Linus, Schroeder, and Snoopy in this collection of "Peanuts" cartoons. (Peanuts Parade #14)

Schulz, Charles M. **And a Woodstock in a Birch Tree.** Illus. by author. Holt, Rinehart & Winston, 1979. 186 pp.

Snoopy, Charlie Brown's crazy beagle, and Snoopy's little bird friend, Woodstock, go on a series of adventures. Snoopy must spend much of his time being a Beagle Scout and leading his troop of birds (including Woodstock) on forest hikes, cookouts, campouts, and the pursuit of merit badges. (Peanuts Parade #23)

Schulz, Charles M. **Don't Hassle Me with Your Sighs, Chuck.** Illus. by author. Holt, Rinehart & Winston, 1976. 188 pp.

That "Peanuts" bunch is back together again in a new collection of cartoons. Snoopy, Charlie Brown, Linus, Lucy, and the rest of the gang show up on the tennis court and the baseball field to play some wild games. And poor Charlie Brown still suffers the humiliation of failure whether he's managing the ball team or trying to outsmart Snoopy, his nutty, tennis-playing dog. (Peanuts Parade #12)

Schulz, Charles M. **Fly, You Stupid Kite, Fly!** Illus. by author. Holt, Rinehart & Winston, 1976. 185 pp.

Charlie Brown wants to practice kicking his football, but the only holder available is Lucy, and he doesn't trust her. She convinces him that she is a changed person, that she would never pull the ball away. Charlie Brown runs for the kick—and Lucy snatches the ball away at the last minute, causing Charlie Brown to fall with an enormous thud. But Lucy tells him she admires his faith in human nature! There are numerous episodes like this in the book involving Charlie Brown and his stubborn kite, his wacky dog, and his crazy friends. (Peanuts Parade #6)

Schulz, Charles M. **How Long, Great Pumpkin, How Long?** Illus. by author. Holt, Rinehart & Winston, 1977. 202 pp.

Linus is spending much of his time and energy waiting for the Great Pumpkin to arrive on Halloween night and give him the goodies he is missing by skipping trick-or-treating and waiting in the pumpkin patch. Also included in this collection of "Peanuts" comic strips is the story of baseball slugger Snoopy, who is trying to break the home-run record. (Peanuts Parade #16)

Schulz, Charles M. **"I Never Promised You an Apple Orchard": The Collected Writings of Snoopy.** Holt, Rinehart & Winston, 1976.

Charlie Brown's dog, Snoopy, has decided to write. But all he seems to get for his efforts are rejection slips. Snoopy also must suffer the criticism of his friends and the bungling efforts of his secretary, Woodstock. Through it all he continues to churn out more stories.

Schulz, Charles M. **It's A Long Way to Tipperary.** Illus. by author. Holt, Rinehart & Winston, 1976. 208 pp.

In this collection of cartoons from the "Peanuts" comic strip, Snoopy has aerial dogfights on his doghouse with the infamous Red Baron. Also, the other "Peanuts" characters—Charlie Brown, Lucy,

Schroeder, and Linus—go through humorous experiences at baseball games, at school, and on vacations. (Peanuts Parade #2)

Schulz, Charles M. **It's Hard Work Being Bitter.** Illus. by author. Holt, Rinehart & Winston, 1977. 185 pp.

Peppermint Patty prepares a speech to give her teacher, criticizing her for not having made Patty any smarter by midmorning than she was before she came to school. Find out about the other crazy efforts of the whole "Peanuts" gang to cope with life in and out of school in this collection of cartoons. (Peanuts Parade #15)

Schulz, Charles M. **A Kiss on the Nose Turns Anger Aside.** Illus. by author. Holt, Rinehart & Winston, 1976.

What happens to Charlie Brown, Lucy, Linus, Schroeder, Snoopy, and the rest of the "Peanuts" characters between Halloween and Christmas? Well, for one thing, Charlie Brown fails to whip together a winning baseball team again, while Schroeder's love for Beethoven threatens to drive a lovesick Lucy crazy. (Peanuts Parade #8)

Schulz, Charles M. **Peanuts Jubilee.** Illus. by author. Holt, Rinehart & Winston, 1975. 222 pp.

Charles Schulz has personally selected his favorite "Peanuts" episodes to fill this twenty-fifth anniversary edition of the "Peanuts" comic strip. In addition to providing the color cartoons contained here, Schulz writes for the first time about his life and his art. He traces the origins of the wacky dog Snoopy and the other principal "Peanuts" characters. Early drawings and cartoons, personal snapshots, and other memorabilia trace the growth of the Schulz style and philosophy that have helped to make Charlie Brown and his pals some of the most famous fictional characters in the world.

Schulz, Charles M. **Race for Your Life, Charlie Brown.** Illus. by author. Holt, Rinehart & Winston, 1978. 220 pp.

Based on the movie of the same title, this book takes the "Peanuts" gang to Camp Remote, high in the Rockies. Wild and action-packed games and contests have opposing camp teams using any means to emerge as winners. Everything builds toward the river raft race, with Peppermint Patty captaining the girls' boat and Charlie Brown commanding the boys' craft. Snoopy and Woodstock pilot their own unique boat. All boats are equipped with radar, both loran and sonar, but the race is hampered by obstacles like thunderstorms, blizzards, rapids, waterfalls, a log jam, and an encounter with a bear. Can they all finish? And who will finally win?

Schulz, Charles M. **Sandlot Peanuts.** Illus. by author. Holt, Rinehart & Winston, 1977. 186 pp.

The "Peanuts" gang plays a brand of baseball—that All-American game—like that of no other team in America. This odd assortment of players, no matter what bad luck comes their way, is always out there trying. Everything imaginable, and unimaginable, happens to them at some point in this collection of Charlie Brown baseball stories, including being forced to take a loss because of a betting scandal.

Schulz, Charles M. **Snoopy's Tennis Book.** Illus. by author. Holt, Rinehart & Winston, 1979.

Snoopy's at it again; this time at the Wimbledon tennis tournament. This nutty dog's wit and wisdom are directed this time toward all aspects of the sport of tennis. Included is "Snoopy's Tournament Tips"—a collection of forgettable tennis advice for those who play in competitions.

Schulz, Charles M. **Speak Softly, and Carry a Beagle.** Illus. by author. Holt, Rinehart & Winston, 1975. 185 pp.

Theodore Roosevelt advised: "Speak softly, and carry a beagle!" or at least that's how Sally remembers it, so she decides to do just that. Her decision leads to a series of predicaments suggesting that carrying a can of mace or a Saint Bernard might be more effective than toting around a beagle, especially when that beagle is Snoopy. The other members of the "Peanuts" gang are also up to their latest tricks in this collection of comic strips. (Peanuts Parade #11)

Schulz, Charles M. **Stop Snowing on My Secretary.** Illus. by author. Holt, Rinehart & Winston, 1977. 202 pp.

Would you like to learn how to play the exciting game of "Ha Ha, Herman"? Well, let Charlie Brown and the rest of the "Peanuts" gang teach you—and you can learn from their hilarious mistakes. Other zany activities involving the group fill the comic strips in this collection. (Peanuts Parade #20)

Schulz, Charles M. **Thank Goodness for People.** Illus. by author. Holt, Rinehart & Winston, 1976. 185 pp.

Having trouble getting along with people? Lucy has some advice. She says her profound philosophy "has been refined in the fires of hardship and struggle" and it is, in simple terms we can all understand, to "live and let live." Can this really be the crabby and selfish

Lucy talking? Find out if Lucy can live up to her philosophy in this collection of "Peanuts" comic strips. Also discover the "Peanuts" gang's many other tips for getting along in this complicated world. (Peanuts Parade #9)

Schulz, Charles M. **There Goes the Shutout.** Illus. by author. Holt, Rinehart & Winston, 1977. 210 pp.

What did the "Peanuts" gang—Charlie Brown, Lucy, Schroeder, Snoopy, and Linus—look like in the 1950s? This collection of early comic strips shows you. The characters look somewhat different, but they were acting as nutty then as they do now. (Peanuts Parade #13)

Schulz, Charles M. **There's a Vulture Outside.** Illus. by author. Holt, Rinehart & Winston, 1976. 202 pp.

Snoopy as a bloodthirsty vulture? In an attempt to change his image, Charlie Brown's lovable dog decides to perch on a tree and try to terrify all who pass. On another tree nearby, his master is having his usual problems with his kite. (Peanuts Parade #3)

Schulz, Charles M. **What Makes Musicians So Sarcastic?** Illus. by author. Holt, Rinehart & Winston, 1976. 185 pp.

What?! Violet shouting insults at Lucy? Charlie Brown and Linus look on, amazed at Lucy's ability to take it. The boys think that Violet has to be the greatest insult yeller of all time. But when she moves in to meet Lucy eyeball-to-eyeball, Lucy belts out a counterattack. Lucy is the winner and still champion! This is just one of the cartoon episodes capturing the "Peanuts" kids in comic situations. (Peanuts Parade #10)

Schulz, Charles M. **What's Wrong with Being Crabby?** Illus. by author. Holt, Rinehart & Winston, 1976.

Lucy's famous bad temper is featured in this "Peanuts" collection. Charlie Brown is, of course, the chief victim of Lucy's anger. But what can he do against the "Queen of the Crabs"? In other episodes, Lucy uses her sharp wit—and sharp tongue—as a soapbox psychiatrist. Only Snoopy is able to remain untouched by Lucy's sarcasm as he dances his way past her insults. (Peanuts Parade #4)

Schulz, Charles M. **Who's the Funny-Looking Kid with the Big Nose?** Illus. by author. Holt, Rinehart & Winston, 1976. 220 pp.

Snoopy, Charlie Brown, school, and baseball mix in this collection of "Peanuts" cartoons to create hilarious episodes of daily life.

Charlie Brown begins to wonder if his team will ever win a ball game with such players as his crazy dog and the ever-complaining Lucy. (Peanuts Parade #1)

Siegel, Larry (editor Nick Meglin). **MAD Clobbers the Classics.** Illus. Angelo Torres. Warner Books, 1981. 192 pp.

The writers at *MAD Magazine* mangle the classics of literature. Would you believe *Mopey Duke, Julius Seesaw,* and *The Scalloped Letter*?

Smith, Robert Kimmel. **Jelly Belly.** Illus. Bob Jones. Delacorte Press, 1981. 155 pp.

Nathaniel Robbins is in the fifth grade and is so overweight that everyone calls him "Jelly Belly." His parents want him to lose weight, so they send him to Camp Lean-to. But with the help of his grandmother and some of the other boys at camp, our hero turns an expected famine into a feast. Easy reading.

Stine, Jovial Bob. **How To Be Funny: An Extremely Silly Guidebook.** Illus. Carol Nicklaus. E. P. Dutton, 1978. 72 pp.

This book answers such questions as "How many elephants can get into a bad mood?" and "What did the kangaroo say to the stuffed pelican?" And with chapters discussing how to be funny at school, at dinner, and with your soup, this book is a funny work itself. The author is the editor of *Bananas* magazine and does not intend for the reader to take his book as a serious instruction manual. What it is meant to be is a crazy example of what humor is all about.

Stine, Jovial Bob, and Jane Stine. **Bored with Being Bored! How to Beat the Boredom Blahs.** Illus. Jerry Zimmerman. Four Winds Press, 1982. 70 pp.

This book is full of fun, jokes, and Boredom Breakers for those dull moments in everyone's life. Find out how to beat the boredom blahs on long, monotonous car trips, at school assemblies, and in doctors' waiting rooms. Learn some interesting answers to the boring questions your relatives always ask you at family get-togethers. Find out which ten gifts grown-ups think are interesting, but kids don't. After reading this book, boredom will never be quite so boring again!

Stine, Jovial Bob, and Jane Stine. **The Sick of Being Sick Book.** Illus. Carol Nicklaus. E. P. Dutton, 1980. 68 pp.

Believe it or not, there is a bright side to being sick. And this book, illustrated with humorous drawings, is a bedside encyclopedia of coping with illness. In one section, you will learn how to squeeze the most sympathy from friends and relatives. Another part reveals all the secrets of getting out of school with even the mildest of illnesses. There is also a guide to bedside visitors. An interesting section explains how to survive daytime television. This little book can help you make the best of being sick.

Thaler, Mike. **Never Tickle a Turtle: Cartoons, Riddles, and Funny Stories.** Camelot Books, 1979. 96 pp.

This is a collection of absurd jokes, riddles, funny stories, and cartoons about animals. Do you have a favorite beast? There is probably something humorous said about it in this book.

Thaler, Mike. **The Yellow Brick Toad: Funny Frog Cartoons, Riddles, and Silly Stories.** Illus. by author. Doubleday & Co., 1978. 94 pp.

What is so funny about frogs and toads? They are green, slimy, and give you warts. Well, this collection of jokes, riddles, cartoons, and humorous stories tries to show the lighter side of these creatures.

Thomas, Karen. **The Good Thing . . . The Bad Thing.** Illus. Yaroslava. Prentice-Hall, 1979. 28 pp.

This book has some good news . . . and some bad news. For instance, eating lots of cookies is a good thing, but it becomes a bad thing when you are too full to eat your delicious supper. The book is filled with situations like these that have both a good side and a bad side.

Trudeau, G. B. **The People's Doonesbury: Notes from Underfoot, 1978–1980.** Illus. by author. Holt, Rinehart & Winston, 1981. 214 pp.

This is a collection of the popular cartoons from the "Doonesbury" series of 1978–1980. Watch the "Doonesbury" characters expose the shady side of politics, the news, and life in the United States—and provide a laugh or two along the way.

Trudeau, G. B. **You're Never Too Old for Nuts and Berries.** Holt, Rinehart & Winston, 1976.

The "Doonesbury" folks are at it again. Duke becomes a "sheik" when oil is discovered in Samoa; Zonker's father moves in with him just before a big exam; and Joanie falls in love.

Twain, Mark. **A Connecticut Yankee in King Arthur's Court.** Signet Books, 1980. 493 pp.

Hank Morgan, hit on the head by a crowbar in nineteenth-century Connecticut, awakens to find himself in the England of King Arthur and the Knights of the Round Table. Can a modern American use his advanced scientific knowledge to change history for the better, or will the violent, evil side of humankind win out? Hank's attempts to adjust to his new world are filled with humor.

Wallace, Barbara Brooks. **The Contest Kid Strikes Again.** Illus. Gloria Kamen. Abingdon Press, 1980. 160 pp.

Young Harvey Small, the contest kid, has won again! He gives his prize chickens to Hawkins, Mrs. Mosley's English butler, to keep, but someone who is trying to get rid of Hawkins uses the chickens for foul purposes.

Wilde, Larry. **The Official Smart Kids/Dumb Parents Joke Book.** Pinnacle Books, 1978. 200 pp.

This collection of jokes manages to poke fun at both kids and their parents. So find out from these books what is so funny about you, your friends, your mother, and your father.

Poetry

Adoff, Arnold. **I Am the Running Girl.** Illus. Ronald Himler. Harper & Row, Publishers, 1979. 34 pp.

Rhonda shares the feelings of joy, pride, and excitement she feels while running. These poems allow us to experience what Rhonda does when she gets out and jogs in the out-of-doors.

Aiken, Joan. **The Skin Spinners: Poems.** Illus. Ken Rinciari. Viking Press, 1976. 83 pp.

This is a group of poems on a variety of topics: simple things, mysterious things, legends, people, and ballads. Each of the poems is aimed at young people.

Atwood, Ann. **Haiku-Vision: In Poetry and Photography.** Charles Scribner's Sons, 1977. 30 pp.

Haiku, which is a popular Japanese unrhymed verse form, and haiga, which are haiku-like drawings, are presented in this book. Accompanying them are color photographs that might have inspired the haiku and haiga. The collection shows that for most writers, haiku is more than an art—it is a spiritual experience.

Belting, Natalia. **Our Fathers Had Powerful Songs.** Illus. Laszlo Kubinyi. E. P. Dutton, 1974. 26 pp.

"The gods sang,/And man had life./They gave him songs,/And he had power." This is what a Southwest Navaho song says about the importance of song in the lives of this country's Indians. Indians have songs for everything—for the hunt, for going to battle, for planting, for joy, for sorrow, for the beginning of a new life, for lifting the dead to another life. The poetry and drawings capture the sense of strength and magic in the Indians' songs.

Cole, William. **A Boy Named Mary Jane and Other Silly Verse.** Illus. George MacClain. Camelot Books, 1979. 63 pp.

Crazy poems, funny rhymes, and also nonsense verse are found in this book. The selections are short and easy to read.

Glenn, Mel. **Class Dismissed! High School Poems.** Photographs by Michael J. Bernstein. Clarion Books, 1982. 96 pp.

These poems convey the emotional feelings of high school students. Topics covered include parents, school, friends, grandfathers, sports, love, and other subjects of importance to most high school students. Mature language and subject matter. (ALA Best Book for Young Adults)

Hill, Helen, Agnes Perkins, and Alethea Helbig, editors. **Straight On till Morning: Poems of the Imaginary World.** Illus. Ted Lewin. Thomas Y. Crowell Co., 1977. 150 pp.

This collection of nearly 100 contemporary American and English poems is intended for younger readers and contains subjects like fantasy and magic. Some section titles give an idea of other topics for the poetry: "Mysteries" and "Funny and Fabulous Friends." And the poems in "What's There in the Dark?" might surprise you. Poets who have contributed to the collection include: Nikki Giovanni, Eve Merriam, Randall Jarrell, and May Swenson.

Holdridge, Larry. **Symphony in B Minor,** *Pathétique:* **The Passion of Peter Ilitch Tchaikovsky.** Illus. Ferebe Streett. Stemmer House Publishers, 1978. 57 pp.

The last musical composition of Tchaikovsky's remains something of a puzzle. The author attempts to create a poem that 'suits the moods of the music. To do this, the poet returns to the past where the king of Ice attacks the Warmlands. The story that emerges in this poem captures the joy, sadness, and despair of the music that inspired it.

Hopkins, Lee Bennett, editor. **I Am the Cat.** Illus. Linda Rochester Richards. Harcourt Brace Jovanovich, 1981. 40 pp.

Do you love cats? Then this collection of poetry is made for you. These cat poems describe how cats play, how they sleep, how they act mysteriously, and how they do other "cat things." Poets represented here include William Carlos Williams, May Swenson, T. S. Eliot, and Myra Cohn Livingston.

Hopkins, Lee Bennett, editor. **My Mane Catches the Wind: Poems about Horses.** Illus. Sam Savitt. Harcourt Brace Jovanovich, 1979. 42 pp.

Twenty-two poems about horses and the wide open spaces fill this book. The illustrated works capture the excitement, beauty, and nobility of horses in a variety of situations.

Hopkins, Lee Bennett, editor. **Moments.** Illus. Michael Hague. Harcourt Brace Jovanovich, 1980. 59 pp.

In celebration of the changing seasons, Lee Bennett Hopkins has selected a group of fifty poems about squirrels, crab apples, wild geese, snowflakes, skiing, Valentine's Day, and the Fourth of July. Read funny, sad, beautiful, and mysterious poems by such authors as Robert Frost, David McCord, Langston Hughes, Nikki Giovanni, Shel Silverstein, and Emily Dickinson.

Hughes, Ted. **Moon-Whales and Other Moon Poems.** Illus. Leonard Baskin. Viking Press, 1976. 83 pp.

Among the familiar yet strange creatures and things that this poet imagines inhabit the moon are moon cabbages. Moon cabbages are not vegetables to eat but are "little old women . . . bundles of great loose lips, yappity-yap-yapping." There are also moon-whales, moon-lilies, moon-mirrors, moon-horrors, moon-diseases, moon-freaks, and moon-clocks. The moon has a special kind of wind, a unique sort of music, and weapons of all kinds that simply appear. And all these moon items are subjects for poetry in this book.

Hughes, Ted. **Season Songs.** Illus. Leonard Baskin. Viking Press, 1976. 77 pp.

This is a collection of twenty-four poems dedicated to spring, summer, autumn, and winter. Such poems as "A March Calf," "Sheep," "Leaves," and "Snow and Snow" represent each of the seasons. The unrhymed poetry is enhanced by black-and-white and color illustrations. (ALA Notable Book)

Janeczko, Paul B., editor. **Dont Forget to Fly: A Cycle of Modern Poets.** Bradbury Press, 1981. 141 pp.

Here is a collection of short and modern poems on such subjects as cats, cemeteries, marriage, Sundays, dentists, suicide, love, insomnia, radar, and swimming. Each poem reveals the hopes and fears that surround the subject, and you just might find yourself in many of the poems.

Janeczko, Paul B., editor. **Postcard Poems: A Collection of Poetry for Sharing.** Bradbury Press, 1979. 106 pp.

Each of the 104 poems in this collection is brief enough for you to put on a postcard, but they are enjoyable enough to be read again and again. Included in the collection are the works of such notable poets as Karl Shapiro, Archibald MacLeish, William Carlos Williams, Theodore Roethke, and Carl Sandburg.

Koch, Kenneth, and Kate Farrell, editors. **Sleeping on the Wing: An Anthology of Modern Poetry with Essays on Reading and Writing.** Random House, 1981. 313 pp.

Poems by twenty-three poets are included in this collection, as are essays explaining the poetry. For example, accompanying Walt Whitman's poetry is an essay that discusses the poems and that might encourage readers to write poems of their own. Most of the featured poetry is modern, including works by Emily Dickinson, Gerard Manley Hopkins, William Butler Yeats, Wallace Stevens, and D. H. Lawrence.

Larrick, Nancy, editor. **Bring Me All of Your Dreams.** Photographs by Larry Mulvehill. M. Evans & Co., 1980. 104 pp.

This collection of poems about daydreams and night dreams includes everything from humor to fantasy to tragedy. The selections contain the poetry of such famous writers as William Stafford, Langston Hughes, Carl Sandburg, and e.e. cummings, as well as writings of an American Indian, a girl in a Nazi concentration camp, and a young Brooklyn boy.

Larrick, Nancy, editor. **Tambourines! Tambourines to Glory! Prayers and Poems.** Illus. Geri Greinke. Westminster Press, 1982. 112 pp.

The spiritual poems and prayers collected here are by well-known religious leaders and writers, writers of fiction, and even children. They contain the words many people like to speak when they are happy, sorry, sad, or in need of counsel.

Lewis, Richard, editor. **The Luminous Landscape: Chinese Art and Poetry.** Calligraphy by Loretta Pan. Doubleday & Co., 1981.

In this book, poets and painters of ancient China write about and paint the spirit they see in nature. Within the two major themes of water and mountains, the poems are carefully matched to the artwork.

Livingston, Myra Cohn, editor. **Callooh! Callay! Holiday Poems for Young Readers.** Illus. Janet Stevens. McElderry Books, 1978. 131 pp.

Want a poem for every holiday? Here they are—verses for New Year's Day, Valentine's Day, Lincoln's Birthday, Washington's

Birthday, your birthday, Easter, May Day, Mother's Day, Father's Day, the Fourth of July, Columbus Day, Halloween, Thanksgiving, and Christmas. Each holiday is honored with several poems ranging from the traditional to the modern. You will learn that there are traditional English carols that are Christmas poems, and that the American song "Yankee Doodle" is really a poem for Washington's Birthday. Modern poems include works by Eve Merriam, Shel Silverstein, and John Updike.

Livingston, Myra Cohn. **4-Way Stop and Other Poems.** Illus. James J. Spanfeller. McElderry Books, 1976. 40 pp.

The short poems in this book reflect many different moods: absurd, humorous, lighthearted, thoughtful, sad. They also include such subjects as dead pets, chewing bubble gum, spoiled sisters, watching television commercials, and singing rats. Easy reading.

Livingston, Myra Cohn. **No Way of Knowing: Dallas Poems.** McElderry Books, 1981. 45 pp.

This collection of poetry reflects the author's remembrances of life in Dallas, Texas, between 1952 and 1964. The verses mirror the life of the black men and women Myra Cohn Livingston came to know as friends. There are poems about fishing at Turtle Creek, family quarrels, people's reactions to the assassination of John Kennedy, and young people falling in love.

Livingston, Myra Cohn, editor. **O Frabjous Day! Poetry for Holidays and Special Occasions.** McElderry Books, 1979. 204 pp.

"O Frabjous day" is a phrase from the poem "Jabberwocky" and is a nonsense way of shouting hurrah in celebration. Over a hundred poems of celebration have been collected in this book, celebrations of popular holidays such as Christmas, Halloween, and Easter, and celebrations of other occasions such as birthdays and the discovery of America. Some of the well-known poets included in the collection are Carl Sandburg, Alfred Lord Tennyson, Walt Whitman, Robert Frost, T. S. Eliot, and Robert Herrick.

Lopez, Barry Holstun. **River Notes: The Dance of Herons.** Bard Books, 1980. 81 pp.

This is a series of poetic stories about men, women, and nature. While the work deals with all aspects of people and their environment, the central symbol of the book—one that ties the individual stories together—is the river.

Merriam, Eve. **Rainbow Writing.** Atheneum Publishers, 1976. 51 pp.

This is a collection of poems about the human experience, especially ordinary moments and simple thoughts. "Twogether" and "Egotripping" are two poem titles that give you an idea about what aspects of people's lives are explored by the works in this volume.

Merriam, Eve. **A Word or Two with You: New Rhymes for Young Readers.** Atheneum Publishers, 1981. 31 pp.

These poems are about parents, friendship, new neighbors, the supermarket, and noise. One poem, "Tube Time," pokes fun at our consumer world by revealing shampoo bottles that cry and a cup of coffee that snores. "Secret Hand" creates a strange mood with images of stripes from tiger trees and drops of orange rain. The poems in this book are both humorous and serious. Easy reading.

Peck, Richard, editor. **Pictures That Storm inside My Head: Poems for the Inner You.** Avon Books, 1976. 189 pp.

Have you ever wanted to share a very private moment but have been afraid to say the words? This collection of over seventy poems is a way of saving special memories of things that have happened. Poets including John Ciardi, James Dickey, and Sylvia Plath express their loneliness, anger, fear, love, and joy—the feelings that are shared by all of us.

A Poison Tree and Other Poems. Illus. Mercer Mayer. Charles Scribner's Sons, 1977. 46 pp.

Twenty well-known poems by such poets as Theodore Roethke, Langston Hughes, William Blake, and Eve Merriam have been chosen for this collection because they all concern emotional experiences: fear, hate, love, delight, guilt. Each poem is illustrated to match the mood the poetry reveals.

Silverstein, Shel. **A Light in the Attic.** Harper & Row Publishers, 1981. 168 pp.

Silverstein's poetry and drawings together provide a humorous view of all kinds of subjects: sword swallowers, anteaters, nailbiters, push buttons, kangaroos, balloons, Blackbeard, lost cats, clams, homework machines, a union for children's rights, and wild strawberries. Silverstein also offers advice in his poems, such as "How to Make a Swing with No Rope or Board or Nails" and "How Not to Have to Dry the Dishes."

Smith, William Jay, editor. **A Green Place: Modern Poems.** Illus. Jacques Hnizdovsky. Merloyd Lawrence Books, 1982. 223 pp.

The title of this book comes from the idea that poetry is "a place that is eternally green." In this collection of twentieth-century poetry from America, Africa, Australia, France, Germany, and Hungary, the wide-ranging subjects include tumbleweeds, floors and ceilings, digging for China, sleeping giants, toasters, mischievous dogs, a goose in a bottle, and clocks and immortality.

Viorst, Judith. **If I Were in Charge of the World and Other Worries: Poems for Children and Their Parents.** Illus. Lynne Cherry. Atheneum Publishers, 1982. 55 pp.

These short poems reveal people's secret thoughts, worries, and wishes. Some of the subjects included in the forty-one poems are cats, spring fever, fairy tales, and good-byes. Easy reading.

Willard, Nancy. **Household Tales of Moon and Water.** Harcourt Brace Jovanovich, 1982. 96 pp.

The everyday life of members of a small household—mother, father, son, and cats—is the focus of this book. Poems feature these characters as they ask questions about their lives and as they observe eggs, plants, fruit, and even soap bubbles. Mature reading.

Willard, Nancy. **A Visit to William Blake's Inn: Poems for Innocent and Experienced Travelers.** Illus. Alice Provensen and Martin Provensen. Harcourt Brace Jovanovich, 1981. 45 pp.

Inspired by the work of eighteenth-century poet William Blake, the author has written a book of magical poems about life at an imaginary inn run by none other than William Blake himself. Blake is helped at the inn by two dragons that brew and bake, two angels that wash and shake the featherbeds, and a rabbit who shows visitors to their rooms. Easy reading.

Wood, Nancy. **War Cry on a Prayer Feather: Prose and Poetry of the Ute Indians.** Doubleday & Co., 1979. 108 pp.

The prose and poetry of the Ute Indians has been collected and made into tone poems about these once formidable hunters and warriors. The Ute Indians lost their dominance early in the nineteenth century, and today the tribe is scattered. The poems observe the old ways of strength and talk about loss of the old life-style and the need for deeper beliefs.

Yevtushenko, Yevgeny (translator Daniel Weissbort). **Ivan the Terrible and Ivan the Fool.** Illus. Hank Virgona. Richard Marek Publishers, 1979. 95 pp.

This is a long historical poem about two Ivans in Russia. One Ivan is Ivan the Terrible, the powerful ruler. The other Ivan is a foolish folk character. Between them, these Ivans reveal much about Russian history, society, and culture. Mature reading.

Plays

Bradley, Virginia. **Holidays on Stage: A Festival of Special-Occasion Plays.** Dodd, Mead & Co., 1981. 255 pp.

These original plays focus on ten American holidays. Imagine Abe Lincoln's beard posing a threat to the junior high basketball team, or Grover the Groundhog refusing to get out of bed on February 2. Consider the Pilgrims celebrating Thanksgiving in the middle of an Arizona sandstorm. These plays demonstrate there can be both serious and humorous ways to celebrate your favorite days.

Cheatham, Val R. **Skits and Spoofs for Young Actors.** Plays, 1977. 194 pp.

Robin Hood has problems with a liberated Ms. Maid Marian; Little Red Riding Hood thinks she has trouble with the wolf until she meets a mobster on the way to Grandma's house; the Pied Piper plays rock music on his kazoo to rid the city of rats. These humorous plots are among the seventeen royalty-free plays presented in this book. All are short and easy to stage. Other plays concern some not-so-fearsome monsters, the tortoise and the hare, a weird Wizard of Oz, and Jack and the beanstalk and his chicken.

Clark, Brian. **Whose Life Is It Anyway?** Bard Books, 1980. 146 pp.

The light humor of this drama covers a serious subject. When a young sculptor, Ken Harrison, is involved in an auto accident that paralyzes him from the neck down, his life's goals and dreams seem as shattered as his body. While the doctors are dedicated to saving his life, Ken wishes only to die. In spite of protests, he engages a lawyer to plead his case—to be allowed to die with dignity. Mature situations.

Davis, Ossie. **Langston.** Delacorte Press, 1982. 146 pp.

Young Langston Hughes wants to be a poet. But his mother, and almost everyone else he meets, finds this an undesirable goal for the boy. So after high school, Langston leaves his mother in the Midwest and goes to live with his father in Mexico. Instead of the encouragement he hopes to find there, however, Langston discovers a father determined to send his son to Columbia University to become an engineer. Once in New York, Langston soon finds inspiration among the artists of Harlem and leaves school to begin his life as a poet.

Kamerman, Sylvia E., editor. **On Stage for Christmas: A Collection of Royalty-Free, One-Act Christmas Plays for Young People.** Plays, 1978. 488 pp.

This collection has over thirty plays dealing with the theme of Christmas. Each script is written with young actors in mind. Included are easily staged dramatizations of famous classics like *A Christmas Carol* and *The Nutcracker.* There are also a spoof of the story of Scrooge, a drama about the first Christmas, and an old-fashioned melodrama involving an evil villain and a pretty herione in distress.

Kamerman, Sylvia E., editor. **Space and Science Fiction Plays for Young People.** Plays, 1981. 220 pp.

Spaceships, astronauts, outer-space travel, and robots are featured in these sixteen one-act, royalty-free plays for young people. In these plays, a teenager's homemade radio telescope picks up signals from another planet, the emotional strain of an outer-space voyage causes trouble among the spaceship crew, and a comic battle takes place between country folk and a computerized "tin man." Included are details for sets, costumes, lighting, sound effects, and properties.

Mahlmann, Lewis, and David Cadwalader Jones. **Folk Tale Plays for Puppets.** Plays, 1980. 142 pp.

This is a special collection of royalty-free plays in which the roles are acted out by hand puppets, rod puppets, and marionettes. Some of the plays included are: "The Gingerbread Boy," "Anansi and the Box of Stones," "Uncle Remus Tales," and "The Rabbit Who Wanted Red Wings."

Mahlmann, Lewis, and David Cadwalader Jones. **Puppet Plays from Favorite Stories: 18 Royalty-Free Plays for Hand Puppets, Rod Puppets, or Marionettes.** Plays, 1977. 204 pp.

Here are eighteen plays for hand puppets, rod puppets, and marionettes. The plays, based on familiar fairy tales or fables, are easy to perform, even for the beginning puppeteer.

Merten, George, **Plays for Puppet Performance.** Plays, 1979. 90 pp.

Get out your own Pinocchio and try one of these ten puppet plays. An introduction explains how puppets are used and how puppet plays differ from other types of plays. Before each play a helpful list is provided that includes the following information: number of acts, types of puppets needed, cast of characters, properties, settings, and production notes. *The King's Dinner, Spider's Eye View, Wiggie in the Jungle, The Magic Book,* and six other plays are included in the collection.

Murray, John, editor. **Fifteen Plays for Today's Teen-Agers: A Collection of One-Act, Royalty-Free Comedies and Mysteries.** Plays, 1979. 352 pp.

This collection of one-act plays includes comedies, mysteries, and adventures. Events threaten passengers in *The Bermuda Triangle Mystery*; an old woman waits for a telephone call from a tomb in *Haunting of Hathaway House;* two jokester vampires save their home and solve a mystery in *The Vagabond Vampires.*

Simon, Neil. **The Collected Plays of Neil Simon, Volume II.** Avon Books, 1980. 737 pp.

So many of Neil Simon's works become hit movies that sometimes people forget he writes plays. This collection includes eight of his humorous works like *The Sunshine Boys, California Suite,* and *Chapter Two.* Mature situations.

Thane, Adele. **Gilbert and Sullivan Operettas Adapted for Half-Hour Performance.** Plays, 1976. 330 pp.

Eight Gilbert and Sullivan musical plays have been modified so that each takes thirty minutes to perform. Before each operetta is the text of the play, and following the text are production notes describing characters, costumes, lights, and scenery. Then the book provides the music, with melodies and chord symbols. Among the operettas presented are: *H.M.S. Pinafore, The Mikado, The Gondoliers, Patience, Trial by Jury,* and *The Pirates of Penzance.*

Thompson, Ernest. **On Golden Pond.** Signet Books, 1981. 191 pp.

Norman and Ethel are in love—and have been for the forty-eight years of their marriage. Norman, a retired professor, has had a cool relationship with his daughter, but now a reunion in the country is planned. However, the daughter and her boyfriend decide to leave the boyfriend's son with the old couple for the summer. The young boy and old man slowly become friends. And it is this relationship that helps father and daughter finally learn to accept one another.

Winther, Barbara. **Plays from Folktales of Africa and Asia: One-Act, Royalty-Free Dramatizations for Young People from Stories and Legends of Africa and Asia.** Plays, 1976. 274 pp.

These one-act plays are adapted from the legends and folklore of two distant continents. Characters in the dramas include warriors, chieftains, villagers, cobras, hares, dragons, flying horses, gods, and goddesses. Many of the plays are adapted from such epics as *The Ramayana, The Arabian Nights,* and the tales of Anansi, the African spider.

Short Story Collections

Abels, Harriette S. **Strangers on NMA-6.** Crestwood House, 1979. 9 booklets.

The adventures of men and women as they reach out into the unknown regions of space are the topics of this series of nine stories. A big blob fleeing from its colony is the problem in one story. In another, the extreme cold of Venus threatens to cripple life support systems on the planet. Still other stories concern space medical emergencies, thieves from an asteroid, and a space station forced out of orbit. Other titles in this Galaxy I series: *A Forgotten World, The Green Invasion, Medical Emergency, Meteor from the Moon, Mystery on Mars, Planet of Ice, The Silent Invaders,* and *Unwanted Visitors.*

Aiken, Joan. **The Faithless Lollybird.** Illus. Eros Keith. Doubleday & Co., 1978. 255 pp.

Meet a sailor who flees from a spiteful woman to return to the litle mermaid waiting for him at sea. Watch what happens when an irate witch changes a family cat into a timber wolf. Read the tales of the seven magpies with short memories, of a falcon whose gift brings unexpected consequences, of the lonely mail carrier who wants a letter for himself, and, of course, of the faithless Lollybird. Who is this Lollybird? One of the twelve stories (and a poem) in this collection will tell you.

Aldiss, Brian, editor. **Evil Earths.** Avon Books, 1979. 318 pp.

Here are fourteen stories about one of the strangest planets— Earth. Such authors as J. S. Campbell, Howard Fast, Philip K. Dick, Fritz Leiber, Arthur C. Clarke, and William Tenn fill their tales of the future with insights, humor, prophecies, and hope. Mature situations.

Aldiss, Brian, editor. **Perilous Planets.** Avon Books, 1980. 350 pp.

Strange viruses feast on the metal skins of space ships. Squidlike aliens plot against all earthlings who come their way. Giant women of Mizar X make life difficult for their male callers. These and other strange tales make up this collection of seventeen short science fiction stories. Represented are works by Frederick Pohl, Robert Silverberg, Damon Knight, and Robert Sheckley.

Alexander, Lloyd. **The Town Cats and Other Tales.** Illus. Laszlo Kubinyi. E. P. Dutton, 1977. 126 pp.

Here is a collection of eight tales about cats who outwit, outmaneuver, and often outclass the humans they come in contact with. From Pescato, the town cat who deals so shrewdly with a petty tyrant, to little Witling, the unlikely apprentice, these stories are full of feline humor and human truths.

Asimov, Isaac, Martin Greenberg, and Charles Waugh, editors. **Science Fiction A to Z: A Dictionary of the Great S. F. Themes.** Houghton Mifflin Co., 1982. 651 pp.

These fifty collected stories all contribute to such great science fiction themes as alien worlds, bionic persons, ESP, invisibility, mutants, mad scientists, robots, star travel, UFOs, Yeti, and others. Stories are by famous authors, including Ray Bradbury, Brian Aldiss, Anne McCaffrey, Andre Norton, H. G. Wells, and Arthur C. Clarke. Mature reading and situations.

Bang, Molly, editor. **The Buried Moon and Other Stories.** Illus. by editor. Charles Scribner's Sons, 1977. 63 pp.

This book contains five folktales gathered from all over the world— Japan, England, India, China. "Wolf in Disguise" is the Japanese version of the Grimm fairy tale "The Wolf and Seven Kids." Other stories feature a priest who has gone completely mad; two princesses, one who can be saved only by marriage, the other only by chopping off her own head; and a clever young woman who outwits the huge and powerful Lord of the Dead. The final story in the book is about a beautiful Moon who is buried in an awful swamp with Quicks, Bogles, and Crawling Horrors, all creatures out to do harm in the darkness of night. The common theme in the tales is their emphasis on the feelings buried deep within us.

Bernard, Christine, retold by. **A Host of Ghosts.** J. B. Lippincott Co., 1977. 256 pp.

This is a collection of twenty-five stories about ghosts and the supernatual. The book includes such chilling tales as "The French Teacher's Double," "The Case of the Bell Witch," and "The Man in the Iron Cage." Some of the stories here claim to be nonfiction, and all are easy reading.

Bradbury, Ray. **The October Country.** Illus. Joe Mugnani. Del Rey Books, 1978. 276 pp.

In nineteen stories, Ray Bradbury deals with ordinary people caught up in fantastic and unreal situations. In "Uncle Einar," for example, the mundane problem of drying the laundry is solved when Uncle Einar trails the string of clothes behind him as he soars into the air on his silken green wings. Another story, "The Lake," fuses past, present, and future as it explores the drowning death of a little girl.

Bradbury, Ray. **The Stories of Ray Bradbury.** Alfred A. Knopf, 1980. 884 pp.

In this selection of stories you will join a space exploration team on Mars, and evil men and women on Earth. Other stories that explore the unknown include: "There Will Come Soft Rains," "The Rocket Man," "The Veldt," "The Wonderful Ice Cream Suit," "All Summer in a Day," and "Mars Is Heaven."

Budbill, David. **Snowshoe Trek to Otter River.** Illus. Lorence F. Bjork-lund. Dial Press, 1976. 83 pp.

Three short stories relate the adventures of twelve-year-old Daniel and his friend Seth while they are camping and canoeing in the North Woods. They find wild creatures in this exciting, but dangerous, place. But they also learn how to survive by living off the land, building their campsite, and identifying animal tracks.

Carr, Terry, editor. **Beyond Reality: 8 Stories of Science Fiction.** Elsevier/ Nelson Books, 1979. 214 pp.

Are there really cracks in time into which a man may crawl? What would it be like to live backwards in time? Can you imagine the possibilities of a man living several minutes ahead of everyone else? Would you be interested in a pill that expands the good times and contracts the bad times? These and other tales about time are found in this collection of eight science fiction stories.

Carr, Terry, editor. **The Infinite Arena: Seven Science Fiction Stories about Sports.** Thomas Nelson, 1977. 191 pp.

In this collection, seven science fiction writers have speculated about how people will live and play in centuries to come. There are stories about a baseball Interbeing League, a fighter who exchanges his body for that of a jockey, and a game of space polo that is master-minded by a group of educated bugs. Sports fans will enjoy the fantastic athletics and fascinating situations in the sports arena created in the tales. Mature situations.

Carr, Terry, editor. **To Follow a Star: Nine Science Fiction Stories about Christmas.** Thomas Nelson, 1977. 151 pp.

Earthlings in "The Santa Claus Planet" find themselves involved in a gift-giving war. "The New Father Christmas" concerns a time when Santa does not leave toys but carries off old people. These and other tales revolving around Christmas are included in this collection of nine science fiction stories.

Carr, Terry, editor. **Planets of Wonder: A Treasury of Space Opera.** Thomas Nelson, 1976. 188 pp.

A human with wings? A lost god? A society of outcasts? These strange beings are all found in this collection of spine-chilling science fiction stories. Ride on a death ship with a team of desperate men, dream of the dreadful future along with a mentally unsound boy, and explore the mysteries of space with a friend from Venus. Each story will sweep you into fantasy and adventure.

Carr, Terry, editor. **Universe 8.** Popular Library, 1978. 224 pp.

Would you like to go on a primitive hunt in a futuristic world that pits age against youth? Or how about loaning someone the use of your mind while you make use of another's body? Or perhaps you'd enjoy a journey to a future senior citizens' home that is anything but peaceful and calm. These and five other unusual tales of the future are presented in this collection.

Carr, Terry, editor. **The Year's Finest Fantasy: Volume 2.** Berkley Publishing Corp., 1979. 265 pp.

Nine stories are included here by such masters of science fiction as Ray Bradbury, Harlan Ellison, and Stephen King. There are stories about young love gone wrong, about a gunslinger chasing a man as he himself is being chased, about a woman who hides a secret of the past, and about a woman and her family forced to live through the history of a certain house. Mature language and situations.

Chute, Marchette. **Stories from Shakespeare.** William Collins Publishers, 1979. 351 pp.

Do you have trouble reading Shakespeare's plays? But do you ever wonder about the kinds of stories Shakespeare told? Here you will find the thirty-six comedies, tragedies, and histories of Shakespeare's First Folio retold in language that you can understand and enjoy. Perhaps when you discover how exciting and funny Shakespeare's plots are, you will take a chance with the original plays.

Cohen, Daniel, editor. **The Headless Roommate and Other Tales of Terror.** Illus. Peggy Brier. M. Evans & Co., 1980. 128 pp.

Need to stay awake at night? Here is a collection of stories to keep you up until sunrise. Nineteen stories of horror and the supernatural are collected here. Many are modern adaptations of classis American tales of terror.

Cormier, Robert. **Eight Plus One: Stories.** Pantheon Books, 1980. 179 pp.

These nine stories center on family situations. In "The Moustache," a teenage boy visits his grandmother in a rest home, and she mistakes him for her husband, who died many years ago. In "Another of Mike's Girls," a father watches as his teenage son breaks off a romance.

de Camp, Catherine Crook. **Creatures of the Cosmos.** Illus. Jay Krush. Westminster Press, 1977. 152 pp.

This collection of science fiction stories concerns weird and unusual creatures from around the universe. A million-dollar pup who looks like a poodle is really an electronic cynoid made for a little girl in a future city. An American black bear can talk and think like a human, but it is frustrated by hands that don't work properly. A green Kweet from Venus has more sense than his young owner. Other stories involve talking dogs, giant ants, tiny dragons, and terrifying sea monsters.

del Rey, Judy-Lynn, editor. **Stellar #4: Science Fiction Stories.** Del Rey Books, 1978. 230 pp.

This is a collection of short stories involving science fiction, suspense, and spectacle. In one story, a Martian assassin has his crime planned perfectly until he learns that his target is a man who will not die. In another story, the earth's sun is going to explode, and an amazing woman's desperate plan is all that can stop the catastrophe. And, would you believe bomb-throwing bunny rabbits as the villains in "Animal Lover"?

del Rey, Lester. **The Best of Lester del Rey.** Del Rey Books, 1978. 366 pp.

This collection of sixteen short stories covers such diverse topics as a visit with a Neanderthal man and the story of man's first landing on the moon. In "Helen O'Loy," del Rey finds that the way for a man to get the ideal mate is to build her. Robots labor to recreate the extinct human species in "Instinct." And in "Hereafter, Inc.," a model of heaven becomes hellish.

Doyle, Arthur Conan. **Adventures of Sherlock Holmes.** Watermill Press, 1980. 237 pp.

Six of Arthur Conan Doyle's most popular Sherlock Holmes detective stories are included in this collection. Holmes's baffling cases always begin with something that seems trivial, but they quickly become complicated and dangerous. For example, a harmless family ritual becomes the basis for a mysterious crime; a strange organization whose membership is all red-headed men deals in bizarre operations; and a lost Christmas goose is related to a jewelry robbery. Doyle's Sherlock Holmes stories were originally published between 1887 and 1927.

Ecke, Wolfgang (translators Stella Humphries and Vernon Humphries). **The Case of the Face at the Window.** Illus. Rolf Rettich. Prentice-Hall, 1979. 128 pp.

Here are some solve-it-yourself mysteries about forged banknotes, book thieves, and jazz trumpets that are perfect practice for any future detective. For example, one story tells about an unknown face that appears at a certain window every night. The clues will point to the guilty one, but only your clever thinking can solve the mystery.

Ecke, Wolfgang (translators Stella Humphries and Vernon Humphries). **The Invisible Witness.** Illus. Rolf Rettich. Prentice-Hall, 1981. 143 pp.

Are you a super sleuth? Here are eighteen chances to find out. This book is chock-full of solve-it-yourself detective stories that will boggle your mind and tease your wit. There's the man who tries to escape by train from the scene of a crime, but what mistake does he make? And there's the mysterious case of the hotel spook. Can you find the clue as the story goes along? All the cases are marked to show their degree of difficulty. See how good you are, super sleuth!

Elwood, Roger, and Howard Goldsmith, editors. **Spine-Chillers.** Doubleday & Co., 1978. 396 pp.

Twenty-three tales of terror are included in this volume. These stories include one about a man saved just in time from snow and a wolf, a coach filled with dead people that rides the moors, a wolf that behaves like a man, and pictures of cats able to kill rats. The authors include Bram Stoker (of *Dracula* fame), Sir Walter Scott, Lafcadio Hearn, and Fitz-James O'Brien. Mature situations.

Engdahl, Sylvia, editor. **Anywhere, Anywhen: Stories of Tomorrow.** Atheneum Publishers, 1976. 301 pp.

Although this collection of five short stories is classified as science fiction, the stories are concerned with today's values, truths, and feelings. One story centers on a boy who is "different" and how a society in the future deals with him. Another story concerns a girl whose parents seem to refuse to let her grow up.

Famous Tales of Terror. Watermill Press, 1980. 135 pp.

Five classic tales of terror are included in this collection: "The Body Snatchers" by Robert Louis Stevenson, "The Mark of the Beast" by Rudyard Kipling, "The Werewolf" by Frederick Marryat, "The Judge's House" by Bram Stoker, and "The Damned Thing" by Ambrose Bierce. These horror stories involve a gentle man who is transformed into a beast, a place filled with rats and containing a hangman's noose, a mysterious evil that reaches out to claim victims, and a werewolf who commits grisly deeds in the night.

Ferman, Edward L., editor. **The Best from** *Fantasy and Science Fiction,* **24th Series.** Charles Scribner's Sons, 1982.

The twenty stories and articles that make up this collection include Isaac Asimov's discussion of robotics (a term he invented), a look at the subtle cruelty of an alien mind, the story of how war is replaced by a game, and a discussion of household appliances that actually travel. Mature language and situations.

Ferman, Edward L., and Barry N. Malzberg, editors. **Graven Images: Three Original Novellas of Science Fiction.** Thomas Nelson, 1977. 151 pp.

A time traveler steps into Beethoven's body and composes a Tenth Symphony in "Choral," one of three novellas contained in this book. Another story examines the life of an actor in a futuristic society where art is strictly regulated. The third novella concerns the misadventures of a painter who is hired by the air force to paint a thunderstorm. Unfortunately, he is accidentally ejected from the F-106 fighter plane and lands years later.

Fox, Paula. **The Little Swineherd and Other Tales.** Illus. Leonard Lubin. E. P. Dutton, 1978. 114 pp.

A country goose becomes a master storyteller when she begins to tell fascinating tales to her friend the duck. As she speaks, wild creatures and far-off places seem to come alive. The goose describes raccoons who play the flute, a cricket who loves to play pranks, and a rooster whose best friend is a mirror. But the lively stories are suddenly stopped when a mysterious question confuses the goose.

Garfield, Leon. **The Apprentices.** Viking Press, 1978. 315 pp.

During the 1800s, boys learned their trades not in schools, but as apprentices under the instruction of master tradesmen. These are twelve stories about the lives of some of these young men. There are tales of a future lamplighter, a carver of mirror frames, a basket-maker, and a bird cage maker.

Gilroy, Tom. **In Bikole: Eight Modern Stories of Life in a West African Village.** Illus. Monica Vachula. Alfred A. Knopf, 1978. 83 pp.

The author of this book was a twenty-one-year-old Peace Corps worker in the West African village of Bikole. During his two years there he came to love the people, the Serrers, whose village story-tellers passed on these tales to him. Most of the stories are sad, as they concern life in a poor African village. But the stories also reveal how people learn to accept sadness and not let it rule them.

Greenberg, Martin Harry, Joseph Olander, and Robert Silverberg, editors. **Dawn of Time: Prehistory through Science Fiction.** Elsevier/Nelson Books, 1979. 224 pp.

This unusual collection of science fiction stories takes the reader into the past rather than into the future. In "A Gun for Dinosaur," big-game hunting is the topic—*very* big game. The hero of "The Day is Done" is the last Neanderthal man. Creating a dinosaur from DNA molecules taken from a tyrannosaurus fossil is the plot of "Paleontology: An Experimental Science."

Greenberg, Martin Harry, Joseph D. Olander, and Patrick Warrick, editors. **Run to Starlight: Sports through Science Fiction.** Delacorte Press, 1976. 383 pp.

In these stories, the Last Super Bowl is played out before empty stands in Hoboken, New Jersey; the Martians can't hit a curve ball to the satisfaction of a Dodgers fan; in combat football, scoring is based on the number of casualties. If you are a sports fan and a science fiction fan, you can read in this book about what sports in the future might be like.

Hamalian, Leo, editor. **Rogues: Stories of Swindlers, Thieves, and Confidence Men.** Thomas Y. Crowell Co., 1979. 245 pp.

This is a collection of twelve lively tales about thieves, con men, and tricksters. Does a clever salesman sell real magic potions? Is a next-door neighbor truly who he says he is? Have the police finally trapped the master burglar? Dodging honesty and the law, rogues like these fill the pages of this book with adventure. Among the authors are O. Henry, P. G. Wodehouse, Jesse Stuart, and John Erskine.

Herbert, Frank, editor. **Nebula Winners Fifteen.** Harper & Row, Publishers, 1981. 223 pp.

This collection of short stories and short novels by the winners of the 1980 Nebula Awards includes Edward Bryant's "giANTS," Barry Longyear's "Enemy Mine," George R. R. Martin's "Sandkings," and others. Frank Herbert provides the introductions to the best in science fiction and fantasy being written today.

Hitchcock, Alfred, editor. **Spellbinders in Suspense.** Random House, 1982. 213 pp.

Film director Alfred Hitchcock gave us films about attack birds and murderous hotel managers. Now he wants us to meet a big-game hunter who suddenly finds that he is being hunted, a dog that inherits a fortune and becomes a target for murder, and a crime buff who foolishly tries to prove that Jack the Ripper is still alive. In this collection, mystery and suspense stories are provided by such writers as: Dorothy Sayers, Roald Dahl, Daphne du Maurier, and Richard Connell.

Hitchcock, Alfred, editor. **Witch's Brew.** Illus. Stephen Marchesi. Random House, 1977.

Alfred Hitchcock has once again collected a group of creepy stories. This time he presents eleven short works about magic, witchcraft, and the supernatural by such writers as Joan Aiken, Robert Bloch, and Lord Dunsany.

Hoke, Helen, editor. **A Chilling Collection: Tales of Wit and Intrigue.** J. M. Dent & Sons, 1980. 140 pp.

A boy who wants to be invisible and manages it. A soldier who refuses to be daunted by the terrors of a ghostly third degree. An ape who keeps house. The ghost of a knight who didn't kill his dragon. A davenport that causes men to vanish. These and many others form the cast of characters in this collection of fantasy tales gathered from both sides of the Atlantic.

Hoke, Helen, editor. **Eerie, Weird, and Wicked: An Anthology.** Thomas Nelson, 1977. 158 pp.

A Tibetan box that houses a murderer? A murky pond overgrown with heart tissue? Anything is possible in this collection of bizarre horror stories. Other tales involve a man who finds a mysterious creature at the bottom of his well and a woman who picks up the telephone and meets a ghostly madman on the other end. The authors of these twelve strange stories include Howard Fast, Mrs. H. D. Everett, Penelope Wallace, and Algernon Blackwood.

Hoke, Helen, editor. **Ghastly, Ghoulish, Gripping Tales.** Franklin Watts, 1983. 160 pp.

This collection contains nine stories by authors as varied as Algernon Blackwood and Idris Seabright. The stories include a haunted trailer, jealousy on the ski lift, strange Egyptian beetles seen by only one man, a devastating army of ants on the move, and the horror at Chilton Castle. Some stories contain violence; all are ghastly, ghoulish, or gripping.

Hoke, Helen, editor. **Mysterious, Menancing, and Macabre: An Anthology.** Elsevier/Nelson Books, 1981. 148 pp.

This collection of nine mystery and horror stories includes "The Tombling Day" by Ray Bradbury, "The Demon Lover" by Elizabeth Bowen, "The Shuttered Room" by H. P. Lovecraft, and "The Way up to Heaven" by Roald Dahl.

Hoke, Helen, editor. **Terrors, Torments, and Traumas.** Elsevier/Nelson Books, 1978. 160 pp.

This awe-inspiring collection of tales of terror introduces some truly horrifying characters. There is Widow Bowen and her "Green Fingers" and the Thing they grow. And the young student Marion and his nighttime visitor who was only "Keeping His Promise." And the crew of slavers who embarked on "The Voyage of the *Deborah Pratt*" and came back—different. This collection of horror stories by such notable authors as Ray Bradbury, Evelyn Waugh, and Franz Kafka is guaranteed to make you panic.

Howard, Jean G. **Too Close Apart: Two Island Stories.** Illus. by author. Tidal Press, 1977. 86 pp.

The two stories in this book, "Private Journey" and "The Visitor," are about old age. Both Charlie and Old Pete have been shaped by many years of Maine life into lonely, isolated men with merely a flicker of the will to live. Charlie and Old Pete fret out their last days with little to comfort them except an ancient dachshund (in Charlie's case) and, for Pete, the memory of an early love affair when he was thirteen. Mature situations.

Hunter, Kristin. **Guests in the Promised Land.** Avon Books, 1976. 124 pp.

Meet a number of interesting young people in this collection of short stories. Junior has just made a hero's return after eighteen months in prison, and he is determined that his younger brother won't follow in his path. Judy, standing impatiently for a dress fitting, does not care about the Debutantes' Ball at all, until she overhears some talk beneath her window. What she hears changes her life dramatically. Tall Carlie finally gets up the nerve to "let it all hang loose" in dancing, and then she decides to retreat to a place in a dark corner. Maurice and Amy feel they are two black kids who don't have black names, likes or dislikes, or physical abilities. Each story in this book shows how it is to be young and an outsider, how it is to be black in a white society.

Ireson, Barbara, editor. **The April Witch and Other Strange Tales.** Illus. Richard Cuffari. Charles Scribner's Sons, 1978. 238 pp.

Fourteen unusual stories are brought together in this collection of works by such authors as H. G. Wells, Ray Bradbury, and Walter de la Mare. They include tales of a child's doll house that cannot be opened even though the dolls can get out, how six people in a subway plunge down among subterranean rocks, and what happens when a statue disappears.

Irwin, Walter, and G. B. Love, editors. **The Best of *Trek* #4: From the Magazine for *Star Trek* Fans.** Signet Books, 1981. 215 pp.

If you enjoyed the adventures of the crew of the Starship *Enterprise* on television or in films, you will find hours of excitement in this collection of short stories. There are new tales about Uhura's romances and careers, the friendship of Kirk and Spock, and the heroism of McCoy.

Jackson, Shirley. **The Lottery.** Popular Library, 1975. 219 pp.

Watch the ordinary turn into the eerie in these supernatural tales. Here you will find a love story with no lover, a housekeeper who becomes a jailer, a vacation that exhausts people, and a village tradition that kills. The stories explore the dark side of the human mind: its fears, its cruelties, its evils, and its weaknesses.

Jansson, Tove (translator Thomas Warburton). **Tales from Moominvalley.** Illus. by author. Camelot Books, 1977. 175 pp.

Imagine a world in which dragons and sea serpents are the most ordinary creatures. That is just the case in Moominvalley, where heulens, mymbles, hattifatteners, whompers, and creeps are seen every day. This book contains nine crazy adventure stories about all these Moominvalley inhabitants. In one story, a heulen falls into an attic filled with hibernating Moomins. Another story concerns Moomins who meet an Invisible Child. (Hans Christian Andersen Medal)

Kahn, Joan, editor. **Some Things Strange and Sinister.** Flare Books, 1982. 223 pp.

These fourteen stories, all "worth shivering over," were written by such famous authors as Agatha Christie, Guy de Maupassant, Andre Maurois, and H. G. Wells. Included in these sinister tales are the ghost of a small boy who starved to death, a cocoon for a human being, and a guest for Dracula. Mature subject matter.

Kahn, Joan, editor. **Some Things Weird and Wicked: Twelve Stories to Chill Your Bones.** Pantheon Books, 1976. 243 pp.

There are both classic horror tales and more recent, less known ones in this collection of chilling short stories. Included are such tales as Jack London's "To Build a Fire," Robert Louis Stevenson's "The Body Snatcher," Frank Stockton's "The Transferred Ghost," and nine others.

Kipling, Rudyard. **Just So Stories.** Watermill Press, 1980. 151 pp.

Take a look at a time when animals were different than they are today. Elephants had big, fat noses instead of long trunks. Leopards did not have spots. Camels did not have humps. These humorous stories go on to tell how these and other animals got their trunks, spots, humps, and skins. Originally published in 1902.

Knight, Damon, Martin H. Greenberg, and Joseph D. Olander, editors. **First Voyages.** Avon Books, 1981. 373 pp.

Ever wonder what the first published stories of famous science fiction writers were like? This collection gives you twenty first efforts by such writers as Arthur C. Clarke, Robert Heinlein, Ursula K. Le Guin, and Brian Aldiss. The stories cover such topics as time travel, alien invaders, monsters, and technological advances. Each story begins with a short account of how the tale came to be written.

Knight, David C. **The Haunted Souvenir Warehouse.** Doubleday & Co., 1978. 85 pp.

These eleven tales are concerned with unusual kinds of hauntings: of golf courses, museums, battlegrounds, gardens, vaults, beaches, and warehouses. The stories feature ghostly figures, rubber daggers, people in tricornered hats, and someone who claims to be Marie Antoinette.

Konigsburg, E. L. **Throwing Shadows.** Atheneum Publishers, 1981. 151 pp.

In these five short stories, teenagers discover who they are. Ned finds himself while on a beach near his home, Antonio on the back of a bus on the Pan American Highway, Avery through his brother, and Phillip among the people in an old folks' home, while William knows what he is about but must help his mother rediscover her own identity.

Lane, Carolyn. **Echoes in an Empty Room and Other Tales of the Supernatural.** Holt, Rinehart & Winston, 1980. 158 pp.

Not all ghosts are spooky. Some—like the prankish O'Haggarty twins and "The Musical Bear of the Catskills"—are downright funny. But most of the stories in this collection are designed to bring shivers, not giggles. Ranging from the fog-shrouded moors of England to the shores of the Mississippi River, and even to a desolate patch of sky over the Pacific Ocean, these stories have one thing in common. All are tales of strange, unearthly happenings that no one has ever been able to explain.

Lem, Stanislaw (translator Michael Kandel). **Mortal Engines.** Bard Books, 1982. 239 pp.

Machines that think for themselves are the subjects of these fourteen short stories. These are no ordinary machines. There are crazy robot kings, sleeping robot princesses, robot monsters, dragon-fighting computers, and even a beautiful robot-assassin who falls in love with the man she is ready to kill.

Lester, Julius. **This Strange New Feeling.** Dial Press, 1982. 149 pp.

Can you imagine being a slave in the United States in the 1800s? Or the elation you would feel if a successful escape were made? This is a collection of three love stories. They are also stories about freedom. What makes these stories even more exciting is that they are based on true events in the lives of three black couples. (ALA Best Book for Young Adults)

Levin, Martin, editor. **Love Stories.** Popular Library, 1975. 505 pp.

This collection of stories explores love in all its forms and all its emotions, from sad to happy to funny. Here it is possible to read of Tarzan's first love—an ape, of course—and of love in the twenty-first century as H. G. Wells thought it would be. There is a love story in this book for everyone, no matter what we think or hope love is.

MacDonald, George. **The Complete Fairy Tales of George MacDonald.** Illus. Arthur Hughes. Schocken Books, 1979. 288 pp.

The author, a nineteenth-century Scottish minister, wrote most of these stories to read to his eleven children. The stories include subjects like amusing courts, comic kings and queens, fairy godmothers, curses, and golden keys. Among the stories collected here are: "The Light Princess," "The Giant's Heart," "The Shadows," "The Carasoyn," "Little Daylight," "Cross Purposes," "The Golden Key," and "The Day Boy and the Night Girl."

Manley, Seon, and Gogo Lewis, editors. **Masters of Shades and Shadows: An Anthology of Great Ghost Stories.** Doubleday & Co., 1978. 214 pp.

Ghosts galore. Ghosts in the form of red-eyed and yellow-eyed dogs, white cats, and lonely children. Ghosts who reveal themselves in smells or in other people. Here are chilling tales by sixteen well-known and respected ghost-storytellers. From Charles Dickens's "To Be Taken with a Grain of Salt" to Shirley Jackson's "The Rock," these stories are the best of their eras.

Mazer, Norma Fox. **Dear Bill, Remember Me? and Other Stories.** Delacorte Press, 1977. 195 pp.

The painful, joyful, and silly moments of life are reflected in this collection of short stories. A ninth-grade girl's private journal, a secret meeting in the park, a family's struggle to keep together, and a hectic first date are all part of these tales of boys and girls growing up.

Mazer, Norma Fox. **Summer Girls, Love Boys and Other Short Stories.** Delacorte Press, 1982. 243 pp.

Mary enjoys a brief romantic rebellion, Marlene runs away to teach her mother a lesson, and a high school assignment leads one girl to discover a surprising incident in her mother's past. Set in one neighborhood, these are short stories about what we love and why we do—whether it is a handsome boy, a best friend, or a mother who makes you toe the line.

Miles, Bernard. **Favorite Tales From Shakespeare.** Illus. Victor G. Ambrus. Rand McNally & Co., 1976. 125 pp.

Here are some exciting stories taken from Shakespeare's famous plays and told in modern language. There are witches, a killing, and a vengeful ghost in *Macbeth*. Lovers, fairies, and tradesmen rehearsing a play are all running around an enchanted forest in *A Midsummer Night's Dream*. In *Romeo and Juliet*, two teenagers who fall in love must deal with the fact that their families hate each other. *Twelfth Night; or, What You Will* is a story of a shipwreck and pair of identical twins. While in *Hamlet* a young man meets his father's ghost and is told that he must avenge his father's murder by killing the new king.

Mohr, Nicholasa. **In Nueva York.** Dial Press, 1977. 192 pp.

These eight short stories are about people who live in the Puerto Rican community on New York's Lower East Side. There are Lali, unhappily married to a man old enough to be her father; Yolanda, trying to get along without the help of drugs; and Rudi, determined not to be robbed no matter what the outcome. Part of the interest of this book is how all of the stories are interconnected.

Neugroschel, Joachim, editor and translator. **The Shtetl.** Richard Marek Publishers, 1979. 572 pp.

Jewish short stories, tales, and excerpts from novels are included in this collection exploring Jewish life from the Middle Ages to the twentieth century. The works range from religious writings and Hassidic yarns to modern fantasy and satire. Most of the stories are set in a "shtetl,"the Yiddish word for small town.

Norton, Andre. **Lore of the Witch World.** DAW Books, 1980. 223 pp.

Ever wonder how witches cast a spell? Or what they brew in those pots? This collection of stories will tell you this and much more. Included here are such tales as "Spider Silk," "Falcon Blood," "Legacy from Sorn Fen," "Sword of Unbelief," and "Changeling."

Otfinoski, Steven. **The Zombie Maker: Stories of Amazing Adventures.** Illus. David Noyes. Bluejeans Books, 1978. 95 pp.

Here are stories about unsolved mysteries from around the world. Each story in this collection has an element of truth in it. One story deals with a series of murders, while other tales are about supernatural events and activities that cannot be explained by logic or science.

Paterson, Katherine, editor. **Angels and Other Strangers: Family Christmas Stories.** Thomas Y. Crowell Co., 1979. 118 pp.

This collection of nine short stories captures the real meaning of Christmas—the loving, the sharing, the doing for others. The title story, "Angels and Other Strangers," is about Julia and her two young children, who have an angel come to their rescue when they run out of gas on a lonely road during a Christmas Eve snowstorm. The trio, in turn, finds that they can be of help to their angel. Other stories concern a minister who comes to the aid of a young boy who has broken a window, a father who decides to look for his runaway son, and a lonely man who decides to take in foster children for the holidays.

Pearce, Philippa. **The Shadow Cage and Other Tales of the Supernatural.** Illus. Ted Lewin. Thomas Y. Crowell Co., 1977. 152 pp.

A green glass bottle locks the eyes of a young boy into an empty stare, while a cookie bin is a source of terror for a small child. A strange illness, an empty attic (or is it really?), and a cage of shadows drive others wild with fear. These stories of horror are only a sample of the strange situtions described in this collection of haunting tales.

Poe, Edgar Allan. **Famous Tales of Mystery and Horror.** Watermill Press, 1980. 132 pp.

Enraged by the harsh look of an old man's eye, a madman silently stalks his victim and one night suffocates him in his bed. After cleverly hiding the body, he is confident that no one will ever find out. But suddenly the slow, steady beat of the dead man's heart begins to be heard. This story, "The Tell-tale Heart," is typical of the terrifying tales written by Poe in the mid-1800s.

Poe, Edgar Allan. **Great Tales of Terror.** Watermill Press, 1980. 132 pp.

A madman tortures his cat and murders his wife in the terrifying tale "The Black Cat." In "The Cask of Amontillado" the desire to taste a rare wine lures Montressor's victim into cold, eerie caverns where death is waiting. A prisoner is tortured in a strange cell with moving walls and a seemingly bottomless hole in its center in "The Pit and the Pendulum." "The Fall of the House of Usher" and "Ligeia" are also included in this collection of classic Edgar Allan Poe tales of terror.

Pohl, Frederik, Martin Harry Greenberg, and Joseph Olander, editors. **The Great Science Fiction Series: Stories from the Best of the Series from 1944 to 1980 by Twenty All-Time Favorite Writers.** Harper & Row Publishers, 1980. 419 pp.

This book contains selections from twenty-two science fiction series stories from such authors as Poul Anderson, Issac Asimov, Arthur C. Clarke, Anne McCaffrey, and Larry Niven. In addition to the stories from such authors as Poul Anderson, Issac Asimov, Arthur C. Clarke, Anne McCaffrey, and Larry Niven. In addition to the example, discusses a story from her Dragon series.

Roach, Marilynne K. **Encounters with the Invisible World: Being Ten Tales of Ghosts, Witches, and the Devil Himself in New England.** Illus. by author. Thomas Y. Crowell Co., 1977. 125 pp.

These spooky stories with a touch of humor are fun to read. Betty Brooker, a local witch who swears to get revenge on the nasty skipper, decides to surprise him with the ride of his life. The Witch of Wellfleet has a strange encounter with demons, and with her magic loom she weaves a frightening spell. A strange ghost haunts the shed belonging to a farmer's family until a mysterious peddler, a bag of bones, and a silver padlock put the spirit to rest. These stories, and many more, are enough to keep any lover of supernatural tales entertained for hours.

Ruby, Lois. **Two Truths in My Pocket.** Viking Press, 1982. 137 pp.

When a black girl and a Jewish boy date, what difficulties do they face? What regrets does Rachel feel after her great-grandmother dies? Is there something really special that Tracy can do for her brother's bar mitzvah? These short stories are about Jewish young people who at one moment have great self-confidence, but at the next moment feel frightening self-doubts.

Sayers, Dorothy L. (editor James Sandoe). **Lord Peter: A Collection of All the Lord Peter Wimsey Stories.** Avon Books, 1972. 487 pp.

This is the complete collection of the Lord Peter Wimsey detective tales. In English upper-class circles of the 1920s and 1930s, Lord Peter investigates and solves complicated and bizarre mysteries, often at the risk of his own life.

Schiff, Stuart David, editor. **Mad Scientists: An Anthology of Fantasy and Horror.** Doubleday & Co., 1980. 300 pp.

In this collection of terrifying tales, you'll find many different kinds of awful characters, including one who must pay a dreadful price for forbidden knowledge and another whose mastery of hypnotism results in a most horrible event. From Karl Wagner's "The Fourth Seal" to Dennis Etchison's "The Dead Line," this book of suspenseful stories will be sure to send shivers down your spine.

Silverberg, Robert, editor. **Earth Is the Strangest Planet.** Thomas Nelson, 1977. 189 pp.

These ten stories of science fiction are about future events on Earth. The collection includes H. G. Well's tale of an empire of ants, a suburban couple who use "time gas" in their home, a man who finds strange intelligent life beneath the sea, and a bicycle that repairs itself. Mature situations.

Silverberg, Robert, editor. **The Edge of Space: Three Original Novellas of Science Fiction by Glenn Chang, Phyllis Gotlieb, and Mark J. McGarry.** Elsevier/Nelson Books, 1979. 224 pp.

Each of the novellas in this collection deals with mystery. In "Acts of Love" (Mark S. McGarry), a space traveler searches for the source of devastating power that blew a hole in the earth's crust at a place that used to be called Omaha. A search for a clone murderer is the main concern in "In the Blood" (Glenn Chang). The novella "The King's Dogs" (Phyllis Gotlieb) is about intelligent cat creatures and a series of strange, unexplainable deaths.

Silverberg, Robert, editor. **Explorers of Space: Eight Stories of Science Fiction.** Thomas Nelson, 1975. 253 pp.

This collection of eight short stories by such authors as Arthur C. Clarke, Poul Anderson, and Isaac Asimov deals with various expeditions to worlds that are strange, treacherous, and strangely compelling. Matchstick humanoids, intelligent life too small to be seen, and lovable mutant bears are only some of the creatures introduced in these short stories.

Silverberg, Robert, editor. **The Infinite Web: Eight Stories of Science Fiction.** Dial Press, 1977. 239 pp.

All acts, no matter how trivial, have their consequences, and all things are tied together by one web of cause and effect. This theory is behind the ecological themes of these eight short stories. The stories not only deal with the common problem of pollution, but they offer a dramatic study of the sometimes tragic results that occur when man alters the delicate balance of nature.

Silverberg, Robert, editor. **Lost Worlds, Unknown Horizons: Nine Stories of Science Fiction.** Thomas Nelson, 1978. 172 pp.

These nine stories center around bizarre situations: a sighted man finds he is the handicapped one in a world of blind people; tickets to the past are for sale at one level of Grand Central Station; a strange spot on Carter Ridge takes people through to the fourth dimension; and a balloon tree is not quite what it is thought to be. All these tales are eerie escapes into fantasy.

Silverberg, Robert. **The Shores of Tomorrow: Eight Stories of Science Fiction.** Thomas Nelson, 1976. 191 pp.

These eight short stories, all by Robert Silverberg, concern the not-too-distant future. In one, a space liner seems doomed as it plummets toward Earth with 150 passengers aboard. "Quick Freeze" concerns an inexperienced captain who lands his rescue vessel on an ice-covered planet and soon finds that he too needs to be rescued. In another story, the United States and China fight over the best method to colonize Mars.

Silverberg, Robert, editor. **Strange Gifts: Eight Stories of Science Fiction.** Thomas Nelson, 1975. 206 pp.

The characters in all of these stories possess extraordinary talents or gifts. These unusual characters include the only man on Earth who is immortal, a hospital patient whose senses are strangely reversed, and a man who discovers that he knows everything about everyone on Earth.

Silverberg, Robert. **Sunrise on Mercury and Other Science Fiction Stories.** Thomas Nelson, 1975. 175 pp.

What do you do if you crave fresh milk on the moon? Why, build a cow, of course. Can you wish yourself and others to the point of death? On a trip to Mercury you might. These are only two plots from this collection of eight short stories by Hugo Award-winner Robert Silverberg. Other stories involve an intergalactic zookeeper, an old woman and her thirty-one sons (all of them the same age), and a robot salesman on an Earth space colony.

Silverberg, Robert, editor. **Trips in Time: Nine Stories of Science Fiction.** Thomas Nelson, 1977. 174 pp.

Stories involving time travel make up this collection. Each author takes a different approach to this common science fiction theme.

One story considers the problem of altering the present by changing the past. In a lighter story, Al Miller is trying to call his finance company when he somehow dials himself into the future. A woman chasing love through the ripples of time is the theme of yet another unusual tale.

Silverberg, Robert, Charles G. Waugh, and Martin Harry Greenberg, editors. **The Science Fictional Dinosaur.** Flare Books, 1982. 224 pp.

These nine science fiction stories reveal what might happen if humans came face to face with dinosaurs. Set in the past and in the future, the tales include one about a pterodactyl that saves a sea-mining camp from disaster; one concerning the adventures of a city man who takes a time-travel vacation to hunt a brontosaurus; and one that traces the discovery of a human skeleton millions of years before humans existed.

Singer, Isaac Bashevis. **The Power of Light: Eight Stories for Hanukkah.** Illus. Irene Lieblich. Farrar, Straus & Giroux, 1980. 87 pp.

Here are eight tales—one for each night of the Hanukkah celebration. These stories, written by a Nobel Prize winner, deal with the friendship shared by two blind children, with two refugees who escape from a Polish ghetto and go to Israel, and with a baby deer.

Sobol, Donald J. **Encyclopedia Brown Carries On.** Illus. Ib Ohlsson. Four Winds Press, 1980. 72 pp.

Give ten-year-old Encyclopedia Brown a case to solve—discovering the hiding place of bank robbers, finding a missing key, or tracking down a greedy Bugs Meany—and Encyclopedia does it. And, of course, he helps his policeman father solve his cases too. For Encyclopedia it's simple—all a matter of gathering the facts, adding some brain power, and then using his imagination to make the connections between the facts and the problem. In one of the ten stories in this collection, the Parent-Teacher Association holds a summer carnival. There are lots of good contests and many great prizes, but Bugs Meany appears to be cheating in some of the events. So Encyclopedia must find a way to catch Bugs in the act.

Sobol, Donald J. **Encyclopedia Brown and the Case of the Midnight Visitor.** Illus. Lillian Brandi. Thomas Nelson, 1977. 96 pp.

Ten-year-old Encyclopedia Brown, "America's Sherlock Holmes in sneakers," is a detective. He charges twenty-five cents to solve crimes and mysteries. In this volume of short stories, he solves ten cases, and the reader is challenged to help the junior detective solve each case. Easy reading.

Sobol, Donald J. **Encyclopedia Brown No. 12: The Case of the Dead Eagles and Other Mysteries.** Illus. Leonard Shortall. Scholastic Book Services, 1975. 96 pp.

Encyclopedia Brown is Idaville's greatest weapon against crime. This young man is filled with facts he uses to solve mysteries. This collection of stories featuring Encyclopedia Brown reveals clues to the readers at the same time Brown finds them and asks that readers try to solve the mysteries before Brown does. Easy reading.

Sobol, Donald J. **Encyclopedia Brown Sets the Pace.** Illus. Ib Ohlsson. Four Winds Press, 1982. 89 pp.

This is a collection of ten short mystery stories featuring young detective Encyclopedia Brown and his partner, Sally Kimball. Can you solve these mysteries along with Encyclopedia and Sally? All the clues you need are contained in each story, and the solutions to the mysteries appear at the back of the book.

Strange Stories of the Supernatural. Watermill Press, 1980. 135 pp.

A strange little trinket from mysterious India, a monkey's paw, has an unusual power. It can grant its owner three wishes. But a person must be very careful, because the paw grants *exactly* what is wished for. "The Monkey's Paw" by W. W. Jacobs is one of the supernatural stories in this collection, which also includes "The Ghost Ship" by Richard B. Middleton, "The Mortal Immortal" by Mary Shelley, "The Dream Woman" by Wilkie Collins, and "The Upper Berth" by F. Marion Crawford.

Synge, Ursula. **The Giant at the Ford and Other Legends of the Saints.** Illus. Shirley Felts. McElderry Books, 1980. 183 pp.

Why was St. Christopher known as "the giant at the ford"? What do a lion and a donkey have to do with St. Jerome? What saint is associated with a flying walking stick? All of these questions are answered in various humorous and dramatic stories about the saints. Did you know, for example, St. William Firmatus first became well known when he tamed a wild boar and saved a village?

Thomas, Piri. **Stories from El Barrio.** Alfred A. Knopf, 1978. 141 pp.

Meet the people from El Barrio—the Puerto Rican neighborhood in New York City. It is a place where people face their problems with energy, ingenuity, and love. In this collection of short stories you'll meet teenage gang members, three unlucky boy scouts on their first camping trip, and two young boxers whose friendship is more important to them than winning a match. In their stories, you'll discover the spirit of El Barrio.

Van Tassel, D., editor. **Computers, Computers, Computers in Fiction and in Verse.** Thomas Nelson, 1977. 192 pp.

Do you have computer mania? Then you might want to look at the stories and poems in this science fiction collection. The stories feature computers that can scheme, play jokes, quote Shakespeare, and play chess with spaceships as game pieces. Included in the book are essays discussing dilemmas with computers and predicting their future. Poets also use their imaginations to give the computers personality in their poems. Mature situations.

Wagenknecht, Edward, editor. **The Stories and Fables of Ambrose Bierce.** Illus. Ferebe Streett. Stemmer House Publishers, 1977. 343 pp.

Ambrose Bierce's sardonic wit, bizarre imagination, and chilling descriptions of death in all its forms have made him one of the most important influences on contemporary American fiction. In this collection are such stories as "Oil of Dog," in which a boy watches as his parents, a baby killer and a dog boiler, combine their professions in a masterful commercial venture until, alas, their greed causes them to consume each other. Included also are such chilling masterpieces as "An Occurrence at Owl Creek Bridge" and "The Monk and the Hangman's Daughter."

Waugh, Carol-Lynn Rössel, Martin Harry Greenberg, and Isaac Asimov, editors. **The Twelve Crimes of Christmas.** Avon Books, 1981. 254 pp.

Twelve well-known writers of mystery have contributed short stories to this collection featuring Christmas crimes. Rex Stout offers another Nero Wolfe adventure, Dorothy Sayers leaves a riddle under the Christmas tree, Edward Hoch presents the problem of a Christmas steeple, and Isaac Asimov has a young hero use his head to uncover a bombing plot set for the thirteenth day of Christmas.

Wuorio, Eva-Lis. **Escape If You Can: 13 Tales of the Preternatural.** Viking Press, 1977. 116 pp.

Thirteen tales of the supernatural world are set in such places as Finland, Lebanon, and Canada. The stories attempt to answer such questions as: What would you do if you realized you were a dog trapped in the body of a person? Would you save all your pocket money to visit a group of petrified people? Or, what would you do if you had no friends at all?

Yarbro, Chelsea Quinn. **Cautionary Tales.** Warner Books, 1978. 255 pp.

This collection of science fiction short stories deals with both inner and outer space. In "Swan Song," a huge black swan is able to hold back evil forces on the other side of death. In "Disturb Not My Slumbering Fair," Diedre must find her dinner in the flesh of a human corpse. Martin, the local madman, becomes the high priest of a small village in "Everything That Begins with an M."

Animals

Allen, Martha Dickson. **Meet the Monkeys.** Illus. by author. Prentice-Hall, 1979. 91 pp.

In this book, thirty-two species of monkeys are illustrated and described. The monkeys discussed include such types as the Uakari monkey of South America, the ghostlike Indri of Madagascar, and the Proboscis of Borneo, whose nose is four inches long. The behavior of these animals is also described. For example, the Woolly monkey hangs its head and sobs like a human, and the Silverback gorilla shows it is becoming angry by pulling a leaf from a plant and putting it between its lips. Easy reading.

Amon, Aline. **Roadrunners and Other Cuckoos.** Illus. by author. Atheneum Publishers, 1978. 87 pp.

The more than 100 species of the cuckoo family have developed varied and unusual ways of life in different habitats around the world. In the southwestern American desert, the roadrunner feeds on snakes, while another variety of cuckoo has adapted to its environment by eating available vegetation. Some cuckoos live in faithful pairs, while others have a number of mates.

Beckmann, Ed. **Love, Praise and Reward.** Coward, McCann & Geoghegan, 1979. 218 pp.

The director of one of the oldest and largest training schools for dogs outlines his procedures for the new off-leash training program. The emphasis here is on teaching the dog to be obedient, to do tricks, and to be happy and healthy. The training methods are based on positive reinforcement and avoid the traditional use of punishment. The text is supplemented with photographs.

Brady, Irene, editor. **Wild Babies: A Canyon Sketchbook.** Illus. by editor. Houghton Mifflin Co., 1979. 50 pp.

Humans rarely get to see a wild animal being born. Nature seems to forbid humans even to touch a wild baby, for the mother will often abandon her little ones in fear if they are handled by humans. But this book allows us to take a close look at infants of the wild and to learn much new and interesting information about them. For example, baby bobcats are called kittens, and each newborn is different in color, pattern, and personality from its sisters and brothers. Newborn bats are just two inches long when they are born into the cupped body of the mother as she clings to the roof of their cave. And did you know that a mother squirrel may decide to move her babies from a nest to get away from fleas?

Brown, Philip. **Uncle Whiskers.** Illus. Eric Tansley. Warner Books, 1979. 150 pp.

Uncle Whiskers was more than just a cat—he was handsome, intelligent, enterprising, and courageous. This remarkable animal not only survived an accident that probably would have killed any other cat, but he adjusted to the loss of his two front legs. Indeed, Whiskers was a very extraordinary and special cat.

Callahan, Philip S. **Birds and How They Function.** Illus. by author. Holiday House, 1979. 144 pp.

A research biologist provides scientific and personal information about all types of birds. The book begins with a chapter on how birds have evolved since prehistoric times. This discussion is followed by information about feathers, flight, eating habits, the nervous system and senses, and patterns of courtship, reproduction, communication, migration, and survival. In his last chapter Dr. Callahan urges that action be taken to save certain birds from extinction. Illustrations, photographs, and charts provide additional information about birds.

Carr, William H. A. **The New Basic Book of the Cat.** Charles Scribner's Sons, 1978. 250 pp.

This book contains all a reader would want to know about cats: how to get one, how to take care of one, first aid, sex and mating, and the history of the cat family in science and in myth. An appendix lists all major organizations and publications concerned with cats.

Chinery, Michael (editor Abigail Frost). **Rand McNally's Picture Atlas of Animals.** Rand McNally & Co., 1980. 44 pp.

This book places animals in their geographic regions around the world and also in their specific environments—forests, polar ice caps, mountains, grasslands, deserts, and oceans. Drawings illustrate how each animal and its habitat look. Easy reading.

Clemens, Virginia Phelps. **A Horse in Your Backyard?** Illus. Thomas Forci; photographs by author. Westminster Press, 1977. 154 pp.

Selecting, boarding, feeding, grooming, and generally taking good care of a horse are all covered in this guide for the new horse owner. But along with all of these responsibilities, this book points out the rewards of owning your own horse. Riding for exercise and competition and showing your horse are two of the rewards discussed in detail here.

Coerr, Eleanor, and William E. Evans. **Gigi: A Baby Whale Borrowed for Science and Returned to the Sea.** G. P. Putnam's Sons, 1980. 128 pp.

Was it worth the risks to capture a baby gray whale in order to learn more about these severely endangered mammals? As you read about her capture and follow her progress at Sea World, it will become obvious that Gigi has her own personality, reactions, preferences, and special friends. What happened when Gigi was released is also reported. Photographs.

Cohen, Daniel. **What Really Happened to the Dinosaurs?** Illus. Haru Wells. E. P. Dutton, 1977. 70 pp.

Dinosaurs roamed the earth for over 100 million years and then suddenly disappeared nearly 70 million years ago. Was the extinction of dinosaurs due to temperature changes, food changes, an epidemic, radiation? Some scientists believe that dinosaurs, through evolution, are our present-day birds. These theories are explained and examined with illustrations. Easy reading.

Curtis, Patricia. **Greff: The Story of a Guide Dog.** Photographs by Mary Bloom. Lodestar Books, 1982. 53 pp.

This story traces the life of a Labrador retriever from birth through training at the Guide Dog Foundation. The dog selected grows up with foster families before meeting his blind owner, Peter. Both dog and master go through a long training period, which is described in detail here. Many black-and-white photos accompany the text. Easy reading.

Davidson, Margaret. **Wild Animal Families.** Illus. Fran Stiles. Hastings House Publishers, 1980. 48 pp.

Mammals share some similarities, but this illustrated book mainly explores their differences. Explained here are the differences in birth of a variety of baby mammals and their feeding, living quarters, protection, training, and entry into the adult world.

Edelson, Edward. **Great Animals of the Movies.** Doubleday & Co., 1980. 134 pp.

Have you ever wondered how animals are trained to act in movies and television? This book discusses such famous animal actors as Rin Tin Tin, Lassie, Mr. Ed, Morris the cat, and also some artificial movie animals like the shark from the movie *Jaws* and Miss Piggy. Easy reading.

Facklam, Margery. **Wild Animals, Gentle Women.** Illus. Paul Facklam. Harcourt Brace Jovanovich, 1978. 127 pp.

Gentle women and wild animals don't seem to go together, but these eleven chapters prove otherwise. Belle Benchley is director of the San Diego Zoo; Ruth Harkness brings the giant panda to the United States from China; the late Jane Goodall lived with the chimpanzees; Eugenie Clark works with live sharks; Kay McKeever risks the wild owls' talons and beaks to learn more about them. The last chapter will help you decide if animal watching is for you.

Farley, Walter. **Walter Farley's How to Stay out of Trouble with Your Horse: Some Basic Safety Rules to Help You Enjoy Riding.** Photographs by Tim Farley. Doubleday & Co., 1981. 65 pp.

So you have a horse of your own and you know how to train it. But do you know how to avoid serious accidents and injuries? Most of them are caused by careless mistakes. By following the safety rules laid down here, you should be able to avoid trouble. Easy reading.

Ford, Barbara. **Black Bear: The Spirit of the Wilderness.** Houghton Mifflin Co., 1981. 182 pp.

The black bear may be North America's smallest bear, but it has roamed our woodlands for thousands of years. It has been both a hunted animal and one that is said to have a magical spirit. This book discusses all aspects of the black bear and includes many black-and-white photographs.

Freedman, Russell. **Farm Babies.** Holiday House, 1981. 38 pp.

In the spring, farms turn into nurseries as animals give birth to their young. With the aid of photographs, the author describes eleven farm animals during their first days of life. You will learn some interesting facts about baby barn owls, horses, cats, pigs, and goats. Easy reading.

Freedman, Russell. **How Animals Defend Their Young.** E. P. Dutton, 1978. 79 pp.

An animal's first duty is to protect and defend its young. Contrary to what most people think, animals do not fight to defend their young except as a last resort. Their first defense is to shelter their young in well-hidden places. Many animals have bodily means of sending signals to others of their species that danger is near. If an enemy threatens attack, many animals are likely to try to run away first. Or they may use some device such as camouflage, bluff, or deception to hide or to outsmart their adversary. Illustrated with photographs.

Freedman, Russell. **They Lived with the Dinosaurs.** Holiday House, 1980. 40 pp.

About 65 million years ago, dinosaurs became extinct. But some of the ancient creatures that lived with them did not disappear. Sharks, cockroaches, dragonflies, crocodiles, and many other animals have survived with little change. This book traces these survivor species through their long histories.

Freedman, Russell. **Tooth and Claw: A Look at Animal Weapons.** Holiday House, 1980. 40 pp.

Unlike humans, most animals have built-in weapons for hunting and self-defense. Although most people are aware of the common weapons of teeth and claws, you will be surprised to learn of some of the secret weapons that animals possess. For example, the bombardier beetle uses three chemicals to put a bad taste in the mouth of any toad that tries to eat it. Other animals that have special weapon systems include the porcupine fish, which can expand its body to twice its normal size to reveal sharp protruding spines, the archerfish, which uses a blast of water to stun its victims, and bulldog ants, which have jaws lined with sharp teeth. Easy reading.

Freeman, Dan. **The Great Apes.** G. P. Putnam's Sons, 1979. 190 pp.

Why are we so attracted to the great apes—the gorillas, chimpanzees, and orangutans? We have been studying them for years and now know a great deal about them, even that the chimpanzees can "talk" in sign language and gorillas can respond to people. This large-sized book, filled with photographs and drawings, treats the history of the great apes, their habitats and habits, their relationship to people, and the need to protect them.

Graham, Ada, and Frank Graham. **Alligators.** Illus. D. D. Tyler. Delacorte Press, 1979. 130 pp.

The alligator, described as "America's last dragon," has remained unchanged since prehistoric times. This book discusses how alligators adapt to the environment and also reveals how the pressures of civilization have made the alligator a "political" animal. Because it faced extinction, the alligator has been protected. But now there is an overabundance of them—some of them even showing up in swimming pools. Is it time to modify the protection laws?

Hartman, Jane E. **How Animals Care for Their Young.** Holiday House, 1980. 84 pp.

There are differences and similarities in the ways insects, reptiles, amphibians, birds, and mammals produce and care for their young. Even within each species there are numerous kinds of behavior. Some animals keep their young near them for an extended time; others force their young out at an early age. Elephants form matriarchal societies where the females of the clan herd together with their children under the oldest and most powerful of females. A male seahorse has an incubation pouch where the female sprays about 200 eggs. The father then gives birth to and cares for the young. Other animals, like robins, share parental responsibilities. What are the same for all animals are the conflicts that arise when the young are finally separated from their parents.

Hartman, Jane E. **Looking at Lizards.** Holiday House, 1978. 122 pp.

Lizards are very adaptable reptiles. There are over 3,000 species, ranging from those that fly to those that swim; from tiny geckos to the Komodo dragon, who weighs about 300 pounds. All kinds of lizards are described in this book, including color-changing chameleons and poisonous iguanas. Also included is a section on how to keep lizards as pets. Types of food, cages, water requirements, and environmental needs are explained. Illustrated with photographs and drawings.

Holmes, Burnham. **The First Seeing Eye Dogs.** Illus. Judith Clark. Contemporary Perspectives, 1978. 48 pp.

Morris was too excited to sleep. His father had just read him an article about German shepherd dogs that could be trained to guide their blind owners. Only nineteen years old and totally blind, Morris set out alone by ship and train and traveled from Nashville, Tennessee, to Switzerland in order to get a dog of his own. This is the

true story of how Morris and his dog, Buddy, pioneered changes
that helped blind people to travel in the United States.

Hopf, Alice L. **Pigs Wild and Tame.** Holiday House, 1979. 127 pp.

Although most people think of pigs as plump pink creatures with
curly tails, pigs come in a variety of sizes, shapes, and temperaments.
The warthog, for example, is a monstrosity with curved tusks
protruding from its cheeks. The pigmy porker, on the other hand,
stands only twelve inches high when fully grown. A number of other
unusual members of the pig family from around the world are
described and pictured.

Howe, John. **Choosing the Right Dog: A Buyer's Guide to All the AKC
Breeds Plus . . .** Rev. ed. Harper & Row, Publishers, 1980. 175 pp.

Each of the breeds registered with the American Kennel Club has a
page of its own with a description of the dog's characteristics and a
picture. The description tells if the dog is obedient or stubborn,
noisy or quiet, easy to housebreak or not, and if the breed is quick
or slow to learn—that is, whatever you need to know to choose the
right dog for you.

Hunt, Patricia. **Tigers.** Skylight Books, 1981. 64 pp.

The tiger is the largest and the strongest member of the cat family.
This book describes where tigers live, how they communicate, and
what efforts are underway to save the tiger. Photographs. Easy
reading.

Jenkins, Marie M. **Deer, Moose, Elk, and Their Family.** Illus. Matthew
Kalmenoff. Holiday House, 1979. 128 pp.

How do deer, moose, and elk lose and grow antlers? What are these
animals' mating habits? Do moose, deer, and elk share similar
patterns of living? This book will answer these questions, and many
more. The ecology of the deer family is also discussed, and such
problems as overpopulation are analyzed.

Keane, John. **Sherlock Bones.** Avon Books, 1980. 240 pp.

John Keane is known as Sherlock Bones because he takes his
sheepdog, Paco, on cases to find missing pets. This pair successfully
tracks down more than 100 runaway and lost pets a year. Bones
includes his ten-step method for finding missing or stolen pets for
those who would rather do their own sleuthing.

Kellner, Esther. **Wild Animal Shelter.** Illus. Heidi Palmer. Scholastic Book Services, 1976. 117 pp.

Three baby raccoons, a groundhog (Sugar), two possums (Little Joe and Susie), a fox squirrel (Ditty), and a cottontail rabbit (Nibby) have all been sheltered at one time or another in the author's home. The true stories in this book about these orphaned animal babies are both humorous and sad. The stories also give plenty of helpful information about how to care for small wild animals in trouble. Originally published as *Animals Come to My House.*

Kevles, Bettyann. **Thinking Gorillas: Testing and Teaching the Greatest Ape.** E. P. Dutton, 1980. 167 pp.

Only since 1925 have Western scientists had an opportunity to study gorillas in captivity. Since that time numerous inquiries into the intelligence of apes have been made, and some amazing facts have surfaced. Some gorillas have been able to learn such skills as eating with utensils and even communicating through sign language systems. This book tells the stories of a dozen gorillas and other apes that have been tested over the years. Photographs.

Kevles, Bettyann. **Watching the Wild Apes: The Primate Studies of Goodall, Fossey, and Galdikas.** E. P. Dutton, 1976. 164 pp.

Not until 1960 did science know much that was accurate about wild apes like chimpanzees, gorillas, and orangutans. At that time three young women began observing these animals in the wild. They discovered patterns of ape behavior that resulted in new ways of thinking about primates—and about humans. This book describes the field research of these women, who practically lived within sight of groups of these sometimes dangerous animals.

Lawrence, R. D. **The North Runner.** Holt, Rinehart & Winston, 1979. 287 pp.

Yukon, a 120-pound half-wolf, half-Alaskan malamute, was the abused pet of an Ojibway Indian when the author decided to buy the dog and try to win the savage beast's trust and friendship. Only after a great deal of patience and frustration does the author succeed. Dog and man begin to work as a team, hauling wood over frozen woodlands, surviving blizzards and a tornado, and exploring thousands of wilderness miles. This true story is filled with adventure, and yet it also is a touching story of affection and respect between a man and a beast.

Lawrence, R. D. **Secret Go the Wolves.** Holt, Rinehart & Winston, 1980. 277 pp.

R. D. Lawrence paid twenty-five dollars and a canoe paddle for the two wolf pups in the bottom of a Cree Indian's canoe. Thus began an amazing adventure for Lawrence, his wife, Joan, and their malamute dog, Tundra, in raising and caring for animals that Lawrence vowed would someday return to the wilderness. Keeping the wolves a secret from neighbors and establishing their position as "alpha male" (or leader) of the pack were just some of the problems Lawrence faced. Much of what Lawrence observed about wolf behavior has never before been documented.

Lawrence, R. D. **The Zoo That Never Was.** Holt, Rinehart & Winston, 1981. 308 pp.

R. D. Lawrence and his wife, Joan, never intended to turn their farm into a zoo—it just happened. They started with two baby raccoons that they found abandoned and starving by the side of the road. Later they added Penny, a skunk, Manx, a lynx who was wounded in a trap, Slip and Slide, a pair of otters, and many other wild animals. But the Lawrences' favorite member of the zoo was Snuffles, a bear cub who actually shared the Lawrences' home with them.

Laycock, George. **Does Your Pet Have a Sixth Sense?** Photographs by author. Doubleday & Co., 1980. 89 pp.

Do you believe that animals can predict earthquakes? Or that they will walk thousands of miles to return to their families? Or that some pets can predict the exact time that their owners will return home? This book describes these events and many more about our pets' unusual abilities.

Leen, Nina. **The Bat.** Holt, Rinehart & Winston, 1976. 77 pp.

Popular legends have done the bat an injustice. These unique mammals with wings are much more intriguing and complex than they are given credit for. Such interesting features of bat life as eating and sleeping habits and care of the young are featured in this text.

Leen, Nina. **Monkeys.** Holt, Rinehart & Winston, 1978. 80 pp.

The lives of monkeys and apes are described in this text. Topics covered include how primates live, how they feed and groom themselves, and how they communicate. Another important section discusses which monkeys and apes scientists consider endangered species and why.

Leen, Nina. **Rare and Unusual Animals.** Holt, Rinehart & Winston, 1981. 80 pp.

Beautiful photographs of exotic animals fill the text of this nature book emphasizing the unique animals of the world. Many of the animals included are so rare that most zoos have never had them for the public to see. But in this book we can see the kinkajou, also known as the honey bear of South America; the pygmy silky anteater, a furry creature with large, curved claws; the okapi, a horse-like creature whose hindquarters are striped like a zebra; and the giant Komodo dragon of Indonesia, a lizard that can measure up to twelve feet long.

Leen, Nina. **Snakes.** Holt, Rinehart & Winston, 1978. 80 pp.

By using many action photographs, this book shows you snakes of all kinds and reveals how they move, feed, reproduce, protect themselves, and hunt. Just about every snake you have ever heard of is included—and a number you probably never knew existed. Care to meet a fer-de-lance? This book will let you know if you would.

MacClintock, Dorcas. **Horses As I See Them.** Illus. Ugo Mochi. Charles Scribner's Sons, 1980. 88 pp.

Using silhouettes instead of the usual photographs, the author traces the biological development of the horse. Also covered here are the numerous breeds of horses, the particular use of each, and the part horses have played in the history of humankind.

MacClintock, Dorcas. **A Natural History of Raccoons.** Illus. J. Sharkey Thomas. Charles Scribner's Sons, 1981. 132 pp.

Self-reliant, curious, intelligent, adaptable, indomitable, and above all, opportunistic, raccoons seem to be a lot like us. Here is an illustrated study of the fascinating creature's habitat and behavior. The author discusses the raccoon's legendary curiosity, its feeding and breeding habits, and talks about how to care for orphaned raccoon cubs.

MacClintock, Dorcas. **A Natural History of Zebras.** Illus. Ugo Mochi. Charles Scribner's Sons, 1976. 124 pp.

Zebras, like people, come in assorted sizes. They assume particular life-styles and family and social patterns, according to their needs.

And did you know they observe strict codes of behavior? Their history, their habitats, and their unique characteristics are revealed here in words and illustrations.

Macgregor-Morris, Pamela, editor. **The Book of the Horse.** G. P. Putnam's Sons, 1979. 208 pp.

Everything you'd ever want to know about the horse? Just about. This large-sized book contains twelve chapters of information from types and breeds to buying a horse—even breaking, schooling, and riding a horse. Each page has several illustrations, 350 in all and 150 in color. All aspects of the horse are covered, mostly by British experts, and even great horses of history are featured—from the movies to winners of famous races. A glossary at the conclusion.

Mars, Charlotte. **A Guide to Raising Your Dog Successfully.** Illus. Nancy Lou Gahan. Richards Rosen Press, 1978. 150 pp.

In this comprehensive guide you can find the answers to nearly every question you may have about dogs. How to choose your dog, and then how to teach, groom, feed, breed, and show it are all covered in this text. The legal responsibilities of owning a dog and possible opportunities for jobs involving dogs are also discussed here.

Mason, Theodore K. **The South Pole Ponies.** Dodd, Mead & Co., 1979. 211 pp.

When dogsleds proved awkward, the explorers on the 1901-1904 expedition to Antarctica relied on the power of Manchurian ponies. Considered dumb and stubborn by many, these ponies endured the long miles and the quickly changing weather conditions of the Antarctic. This is the story, complete with pictures, of two separate British expeditions of the early 1900s, one led by Robert F. Scott and one led by Sir Ernest H. Shackleton.

McCloy, James. **Dogs at Work.** Illus. Sheila Beatty. Crown Publishers, 1979. 74 pp.

Here are the stories of eleven breeds of dog that have worked for people in the past and that continue to work for people in different but equally important ways today. A brief introductory note explains how dogs evolved from wolves and how people bred dogs for their special abilities. Some of the dogs discussed include the Great Pyrenees, Newfoundland, bloodhound, golden retriever, Doberman pinscher, and German shepherd.

McDearmon, Kay. **Rocky Mountain Bighorns.** Photographs by Valerie Geist. Dodd, Mead & Co., 1980. 47 pp.

Take a glimpse into the world of the largest and most abundant bighorn sheep, the Rocky Mountain variety. Information is given about their size, feeding and mating habits, and patterns of fighting and playing, as well as facts about their double blanket coats, which help them to withstand temperatures below zero. The bighorns' remarkable jumping ability is documented here by John Muir, a famous nineteenth-century American naturalist who witnessed a band of them plunging off a 150-foot cliff, one after another, and all landing safely on the rocks below.

McGovern, Ann. **Little Whale.** Illus. John Hamberger. Four Winds Press, 1979. 32 pp.

The little whale here is a baby humpback who weighs one ton when she is born. With color drawings showing this whale and the ocean in which she lives, the author discussses how whales eat, swim, breathe, escape danger, and leap out of the water. Easy reading.

McGowen, Tom. **Album of Reptiles.** Illus. Rod Ruth. Rand McNally & Co., 1978. 61 pp.

What makes a reptile a reptile? How different is the desert-dwelling chuckwalla from the color-changing chameleon? Did you know that huge dragon lizards live today in Indonesia? Should you be afraid of cobras? Do giant constricting snakes like to eat humans? The book tells you all about reptiles—from the glass snake and the crocodile to the primitive tuatara.

McGowen, Tom. **Album of Sharks.** Illus. Rod Ruth. Rand McNally & Co., 1981. 59 pp.

Discover how a shark provided key evidence in a murder mystery and how another teamed up with a swordfish to kill whales. This book contains information about many different kinds of sharks, from prehistoric "leftovers" to ones that glow in the dark. It includes characteristics and habits of such fierce killers as the hammerhead and of such unusual species as the sluggish wobbegong, as well as many anecdotes about these much-maligned creatures.

McGowen, Tom. **Album Of Whales.** Illus. Rod Ruth. Rand McNally & Co., 1980.

Whales come in a variety of sizes and personalities. The gigantic blue whale may be over 100 feet long; the tiny white beluga grows to only about fifteen feet. The bottle-nosed dolphin is happy and smiling, but the killer whale is not so friendly. This book tells about more than forty different kinds of whales and discusses the past, present, and the threatened future of this remarkable mammal.

Meyers, Susan. **Pearson: A Harbor Seal Pup.** Photographs by Ilka Hartmann. E. P. Dutton, 1980. 58 pp.

This book is about Pearson, an orphaned seal pup found on a beach near San Francisco. Dedicted volunteers worked to rehabilitate him at the California Marine Mammal Center. When he was found, Pearson was high-spirited but not very strong or healthy. Returning him to good health was a big challenge to the people at the marine center. Many black-and-white photographs record the attention and help given to Pearson. Easy reading.

Milts, Michael H., and Carl Larsen. **Only a Gringo Would Die for an Anteater: The Adventures of a Veterinarian.** McGraw-Hill Book Co., 1979. 225 pp.

What do the pets of Roy Scheider, Barbra Streisand, and Joel Grey have in common with the wolves at the Flushing Zoo? They all have the same doctor—Dr. Michael Milts. The author describes his many adventures with creatures great and small, from treating an emotionally disturbed camel to setting a cricket's broken leg. Go with the good doctor to the Everglades, Brazil, and the jungles of the Amazon.

Morey, Walt. **Operation Blue Bear: A True Story.** Photographs by Ron Garrison and F. Don Schmidt. E. P. Dutton, 1975.

A rare blue bear in Alaska became famous for raiding garbage cans, so it wasn't long before the trophy hunters were interested in his expensive hide. Word reached staff members at the San Diego Zoo, who dispatched a team there to try to save this rare species. This suspense-filled true story traces the adventure of the zoo team and the unusual blue bear.

Moyes, Patricia. **How to Talk to Your Cat.** Illus. Nancy Lou Gahan. Holt, Rinehart & Winston, 1978. 118 pp.

Beginning with the cat's place in history, and then moving through tips for choosing a cat, communicating with it, listening to it, surviving minor crises, and traveling with it, the author humorously explains how to develop a more rewarding relationship with your feline.

North, Sterling. **Rascal.** Illus. John Schoenherr. Avon Books, 1976. 189 pp.

> This is a true account of an eleven-year-old boy, his raccoon named Rascal, and their problems with his family and friends in the period during and after World War I. (Lewis Carroll Shelf Award; Dorothy Canfield Fisher Children's Book Award)

Ordish, George. **The Year of the Ant.** Illus. Clarke Hutton. Charles Scribner's Sons, 1978. 139 pp.

> The life in an ant nest is studied over a one-year period. The shape of the nest, how the ants find directions, the ants' relationships with other insects, and the care of the queen ant and the young pupae ants are thoroughly explained in this illustrated text.

Patent, Dorothy Hinshaw. **Arabian Horses.** Holiday House, 1982. 75 pp.

> The elegant Arabian horse is noted for its speed, beauty, and endurance. In fact, an Arabian horse was used recently in the popular movie *The Black Stallion.* This type of horse has always been a favorite family horse, and its crossbreeding has contributed strong traits to other breeds. It is able to travel long distances and can perform well in competition. These and other important traits and characteristics of Arabian horses are discussed in this book.

Patent, Dorothy Hinshaw. **Bears of the World.** Holiday House, 1980. 125 pp.

> Although bears are familiar animals to us in many ways, it has only been in the last twenty years that they have been given careful scientific study. We now know something of their life spans, habitats, diets, reproduction and mating, and about how their body structure allows them to go through winter without drinking, eating, eliminating water, or losing strength.

Patent, Dorothy Hinshaw. **Butterflies and Moths: How They Function.** Holiday House, 1979. 145 pp.

> Not all butterflies are beautiful and harmless, while not all moths are ugly and destructive. In most cases it's easy to tell a butterfly from a moth by the way they hold their wings and by the differences in their bodies. But sometimes it's nearly impossible to tell one from the other. They share many of the qualities that all members of the insect family do, like having to shed their outer layers as they grow. But they also have cetain strange and unusual aspects of their lives, such as their manners of courtship and mating, their transformations from caterpillars to winged insects, their ways of survival, and the kinds of enemies and friends they have.

Patent, Dorothy Hinshaw. **Fish and How They Reproduce.** Illus. Matthew Kalmenoff. Holiday House, 1976. 128 pp.

The prehistoric origins of fish, their physical development, and the numerous types of fish reproduction are explained in this book. Illustrations show how different fish look and reveal how they protect their young.

Patent, Dorothy Hinshaw. **Frogs, Toads, Salamanders, and How They Reproduce.** Illus. Matthew Kalmenoff. Holiday House, 1975. 135 pp.

A zoologist explores the varied reproductive methods of frogs, toads, salamanders, and caecilians. The influence of these reproductive methods on embryo development, the evolution of amphibians' bodies, and their environmental adaption are also discussed.

Patent, Dorothy Hinshaw. **Horses and Their Wild Relatives.** Holiday House, 1981. 125 pp.

Although most of us have seen live horses, few people have had the opportunity to see a wild horse or one of its relatives. This book examines the horse family, including asses and zebras. Horses are traced back to their earliest form, and then the author discusses how present-day breeds have evolved and adapted to their environments. Photographs.

Patent, Dorothy Hinshaw. **Horses of America.** Holiday House, 1981. 79 pp.

This book discusses the many breeds of horses in America, including the Thoroughbred, Morgan, Quarter Horse, and Clydesdale. Among the topics covered are how the horses evolved, how they are used in competition, and how horses have been historically important in America. Easy reading.

Patent, Dorothy Hinshaw. **The Lives of Spiders.** Holiday House, 1980. 128 pp.

Fear of spiders is common, although the majority of them are harmless to people. These adaptable little animals can be found almost anywhere. Many facts about different species, their daily lives, their habits, and their enemies are discussed in this book.

Patent, Dorothy Hinshaw. **Raccoons, Coatimundis, and Their Family.** Holiday House, 1979. 127 pp.

The raccoon and all its family members—coatis, kinkajous, ringtails, olingos, cacomistles, pandas, and lesser pandas—are discussed here in great detail. The habits and ancestry of these intelligent animals are described, as well as how their young develop. The possibility of keeping a raccoon as a pet is another topic covered in the book.

Patent, Dorothy Hinshaw. **Reptiles and How They Reproduce.** Illus. Matthew Kalmenoff. Holiday House, 1977. 127 pp.

Are reptiles really "cold-blooded"? Find out in this book exploring the evolution of snakes, lizards, crocodiles, and other reptiles. One of the most interesting sections in the book is on the difference between snakes that lay eggs and snakes that bear live young. The scientific explanations are put in easy-to-understand terms.

Patent, Dorothy Hinshaw. **The World of Worms.** Holiday House, 1978. 124 pp.

Most of us are familiar with the earthworms discussed here, but what do you know about flatworms, flukes, leeches, and parasite worms like tapeworms? This book will tell you how worms live, how they reproduce, and how some worms are used as food. Illustrations.

Patent, Dorothy Hinshaw, and Paul C. Schroeder. **Beetles and How They Live.** Holiday House, 1978. 159 pp.

Many of the insects in our gardens and homes are actually beetles, including fireflies and ladybugs. The authors describe what beetles are, how they adapt to their living areas, how you can collect your own beetles, and how to send for rarer beetles. Illustrations.

Penzler, Otto. **Hunting the Killer Shark.** Troll Associates, 1976. 32 pp.

Sharks have an instinctive urge to kill and eat. Since sharks have existed for over 320 million years, their ability to kill has been refined until it is superior. Scientists study sharks to understand their behavior and to protect humans. And just this kind of scientific study of sharks is covered in this text. Photographs.

Pond, Grace, and Angela Sayer. **The Intelligent Cat.** Perigee Books, 1980. 149 pp.

The writers of this book have devised a series of easy, entertaining tests for finding out a cat's IQ. Also included is a wealth of information about the behavior of cats—how they learn, how they mark their territory, and how they hunt, kill, and eat. There are also some special insights provided into the psychology and language of cats.

Poynter, Margaret. **Too Few Happy Endings: The Dilemma of the Humane Societies.** Atheneum Publishers, 1981. 127 pp.

Since the founding of the New York humane society in 1866, the tasks of humane society members across the country have ranged from lassoing a turkey to finding the right stray dog to become the canine star of *Annie*. This book also describes the daily lives of humane society workers and presents some of their most interesting rescues and stories.

Prince, J. H. **Languages of the Animal World.** Thomas Nelson, 1975. 144 pp.

Animals communicate through sound, vision, odor, movement, and body posture. Mammals, birds, fish, and insects are all carefully examined in this study to reveal their ways of communication. Many unusual and interesting discoveries are included, such as the fact that orangutans belch before fighting, and that hyenas' so-called laughter is really a signal to the pack that food has been found. Illustrations.

Pringle, Laurence. **The Controversial Coyote: Predation, Politics, and Ecology.** Harcourt Brace Jovanovich, 1977. 87 pp.

The coyote is a very adaptable animal that has survived massive control efforts among sheep ranchers in the West. This interesting study of the coyote, of the development of predator control techniques, and of the ecological problems related to coyotes and their control shows how ranchers can be helped without causing the extinction of a very clever animal. Photographs.

Pringle, Laurence. **Dinosaurs and People: Fossils, Facts and Fantasies.** Harcourt Brace Jovanovich, 1978.

This book traces the history of people tracking down the fascinating dinosaur through fossil study. Some stories are triumphs, but others are disasters, such as a Triceratops skull being destroyed by a tornado and a ship carrying two skeletons of duck-billed dinosaurs being torpedoed by a German submarine in 1916. The many illustrations range from actual photographs of fossil sites to pinball-machine art displaying dinosaurs.

Robertson, Alden. **The Wild Horse Gatherers.** Sierra Club Books, 1978. 95 pp.

Wild horses still exist in many parts of the western United States. To help protect them and the land they might overgraze, a yearly roundup is held. Many of these wild horses are caught so that they may be given to qualified people through the Bureau of Land Management's Adopt-a-Horse program. Here is the story, both in words and in pictures, of how this roundup is carried out.

Ryden, Hope. **America's Last Wild Horses.** E. P. Dutton, 1978. 319 pp.

The author of this book sensed a story when a friend called to tell her that 200 wild horses were to be rounded up and sold for dog food. Little did she know that her investigation would eventually lead to a court battle to save the few hundred wild horses left in the United States.

Schick, Alice, and Sara Ann Friedman. **Zoo Year.** Photographs by Joel Schick. J. B. Lippincott Co., 1978. 192 pp.

What kind of stories do zoo workers tell? Some of their stories are collected here, and even though the Metropolitan Zoo is fictional, it is a combination of several real zoos. Many of the events mentioned in this book did take place at real zoos. The stories include one about an eye operation on a young tiger with cataracts, the birth of a baby giraffe, the death of a well-loved elephant, and the wounding of an alligator.

Schlein, Miriam. **Lucky Porcupine!** Illus. Martha Weston. Four Winds Press, 1980. 48 pp.

You will learn about porcupines in this book—what they look like, where they live, and how they protect themselves. Porcupines have many natural enemies, such as owls, eagles, bears, and even dogs. They must be prepared for danger, so the sharp set of quills Nature has provided is very helpful. The text also provides tips and guidelines about looking for traces of porcupine homes and habitats. Easy reading.

Scott, Jack Denton. **The Book of the Goat.** Photographs by Ozzie Sweet. G. P. Putnam's Sons, 1979. 64 pp.

This book suggests that the goat, not the dog, may be man's oldest friend. This domesticated animal is presented as intelligent, clean, affectionate, and valuable. Through photographs and text, the writers trace the history of the goat from its form in 10,000 B.C. to members of a present-day herd on a dairy farm.

Scott, Jack Denton. **Discovering the American Stork.** Photographs by Ozzie Sweet. Harcourt Brace Jovanovich, 1976. 64 pp.

Mycteria americana, or the American stork, is a fascinating bird that lives equally well in a salt-water or fresh-water habitat. This book covers not only the various places where these birds may be found, but also their habits. The photographs provide a close view of one of our most interesting birds.

Scott, Jack Denton. **Discovering the Mysterious Egret.** Illus. Pamela Sweet; photographs by Ozzie Sweet. Harcourt Brace Jovanovich, 1978. 53 pp.

Egrets are beautiful white birds that ride on the backs or walk beside the huge feet of cattle, rhinoceroses, hippopotamuses, and elephants. Little is known about this bird. Although a native of Africa, the egret mysteriously appeared in South America in 1930, and not long after in New England, New Jersey, and Florida. To date, no one has been able to explain how this slender creature managed to cross the Atlantic. The author describes the bird's historical background and its mating, nesting, and feeding habits. Photographs portray the egret against a backdrop of mystery and beauty.

Scott, Jack Denton. **The Submarine Bird.** Photographs by Ozzie Sweet. G. P. Putnam's Sons, 1980. 64 pp.

The cormorant, or submarine bird, may be a descendant of the reptile family. The appearance of the newly hatched birds and their ability to catch fish underwater seem to support this theory. The birds' activities are explained in detail, from how they are born to their mating habits.

Scott, Jack Denton. **The Survivors: Enduring Animals of North America.** Illus. Daphne Gillen. Harcourt Brace Jovanovich, 1975. 110 pp.

Who has best adapted to our continent? This book takes a look at twelve different wild animals who have displayed especially outstanding survival abilities. Why, for instance, has the coyote not only survived but actually increased in number in spite of poison and hunting campaigns, while its cousin, the wolf, has all but disappeared? What is it that allows some animals to adapt to the changes made by humans even as others become extinct?

Selsam, Millicent E. **Night Animals.** Four Winds Press, 1979. 40 pp.

The book describes the nocturnal lives of owls, luna moths, foxes, fireflies, weasels, beavers, bats, flying squirrels, and other animals who are especially active in the evening. Photographs. Easy reading.

Shuttlesworth, Dorothy E. **Gerbils and Other Small Pets.** E. P. Dutton, 1976. 130 pp.

Do you want to know how to raise gerbils and other small pets like hamsters, squirrels, mice, white rats, guinea pigs, and rabbits? This book describes ways to provide a safe home for these animals, how to feed them, and how to keep them healthy. The author also relates a number of personal experiences with these small pets. Photographs show the pets and some of their homes. Easy reading.

Shuttlesworth, Dorothy E. **Playful Animals.** Doubleday & Co., 1981. 114 pp.

This book answers the question "Do animals play?" Various animals and their favorite kinds of recreation are described. Such frisky animals as otters, dolphins, large cats, pandas, and rabbits are described as they play by themselves, with other animals, or with people. Photographs.

Simon, Seymour. **Deadly Ants.** Illus. William R. Downey. Four Winds Press, 1979. 52 pp.

This illustrated book on ants explains the several varieties of dangerous ants. Fire ants sting 10,000 people per year in the United States alone. Their stings can give severe pain and, if a large number of ants attack, can even cause death. Army ants, which live mainly in the tropics, swarm in packs numbering up to 20 million. Any animal that gets in their path will be reduced to a skeleton in a matter of minutes. Easy reading.

Smith, Howard E., Jr. **Animal Marvels.** Illus. Margot Apple. Doubleday & Co., 1981. 48 pp.

Unusual animal behavior and activities are examined in this book. You will read about birds that paint, wasps that make paper, and ants that store food in pots. Also described here are monkeys that howl and whales that sing. Easy reading.

Steneman, Shep. **Garfield: The Complete Cat Book.** Random House, 1981. 90 pp.

With the help of the cartoon character, Garfield, created by Jim Davis, this book provides both serious and humorous information about cats. There are sections about the various breeds of cats and about cats in history. You will find information on how to train your cat and where to locate a cat in the first place. Cat shows are also described, and there is information on what to feed a cat and how to keep your cat healthy. Finally, there are funny stories, essays, and poems about felines, their moods, and their activities.

Taylor, Herb. **The Lobster: Its Life Cycle.** Sterling Publishing Co., 1975. 80 pp.

The lobster's life, from a tiny, slippery egg to a hard-shelled, clawed creature, is detailed in this study. Topics discussed include how lobsters mate, how they shed their shells to grow, and how they regenerate damaged parts of their bodies. Also, the dangers of over-fishing lobsters and efforts to counteract this overfishing are con-sidered at length. Whether you fish for lobster, would like to raise them, or simply order them in your favorite restaurant, this book is of interest.

Teleki, Geza, and Karen Steffy (with Lori Baldwin). **Goblin, a Wild Chimpanzee.** Photographs by Geza Teleki and Lori Baldwin. E. P. Dutton, 1977. 55 pp.

More and more scientists are discovering the value of observing how wild animals behave in their natural setting. For example, the chimpanzee has been observed for a number of years, so it is now possible to give an accurate picture of their daily activities. This is the story, in words and photographs, of one day in the life of six-year-old Goblin, a chimpanzee.

Teleki, Geza, Karen Steffy, and Lori Baldwin. **Leaky the Elder: A Chimpanzee and His Community.** Photographs by Geza Teleki and Lori Baldwin. E. P. Dutton, 1980. 80 pp.

Leaky, a graying, elderly male chimpanzee, is a respected leader among the chimpanzees of his group in Tanzania, East Africa. In this study, we see him going through his daily tasks of searching for food, playing with the young, preventing trouble, and setting an example for the others in his community as though he possessed human wisdom.

Todd, Frank S. **The Sea World Book of Penguins.** Photographs by author. Sea World Press/Harcourt Brace Jovanovich, 1981. 96 pp.

Many people think that penguins are really human because of their tuxedo appearance and their upright manner of walking. This book corrects this image and describes the unique habitats and habits of the many varieties of penguins.

Unkelbach, Kurt. **How to Teach an Old Dog New Tricks: Retraining the Secondhand Dog.** Illus. Sam Savitt. Dodd, Mead & Co., 1979. 144 pp.

According to the author, "It's all a matter of common sense, cun-ning, and timing to teach a secondhand dog a new trick." Patience, love, and persistence are also important factors. This book provides a step-by-step process for the basic training of dogs, new or old. It also includes a list of cautions that are helpful.

Van Wormer, Joe. **Squirrels.** Photographs by author. E. P. Dutton, 1978. 56 pp.

How does a flying squirrel fly? This book provides the answer to that question and to other questions you might have about members of the squirrel family: ground squirrels, chipmunks, tree squirrels, flying squirrels, woodchucks, marmots, and prairie dogs. Topics discussed include physical features, habits, similarities and differences among varieties of squirrels, where they live, and how and what they eat. Easy reading.

Van Wormer, Joe. **Elephants.** Photographs by author. E. P. Dutton, 1976. 58 pp.

They use their trunks to sniff out and pick up food. They travel in herds and live in families within the herd. They are so large that they have no need to fight. They can use their tusks, lose them, and grow new ones. They can walk faster than an Olympic track star can run, yet they can scarcely run and cannot jump at all. They have an acute sense of hearing and of smell, yet they can scarcely see. They are, of course, elephants. Wild elephants spend most of their lives eating, they love taking mud baths, and their worst enemies are tiny mosquitoes and flies.

Wayne, Kyra Petrovskaya. **Max, the Dog that Refused to Die.** Illus. Becky Bristow. Bantam Books, 1983. 86 pp.

Max was dying. It all started out as a vacation—romping through the Sequoia National Forest with his Doberman mate Hildy, his owners George and Kyra, and their young friends Francisco and Carlos. But Max ran ahead of the group, up a darkened path in pursuit of a squirrel, and fell from a cliff. He suffered two broken legs and a shattered hip. Max finds he must not only survive the fall, but also survive being hit by a car, shot at by a dog hater, and attacked by ferocious coyotes. This is a true tale of great animal courage and determination. (Dog Writers Association of America Award)

Weber, William J. **Wild Orphan Babies: Mammals and Birds.** Photographs by author. Holt, Rinehart & Winston, 1978. 160 pp.

Have you ever come upon an injured or orphaned young animal and wondered what you could do to help? Thousands of animals are hurt or abandoned each year. The author, a veterinarian, has spent years caring for animals and giving advice about animal care. In this book he discusses what an orphan is, how to start feeding orphaned animals, how to care for injured animals, and, most important, how to release them when they are to return to nature.

Weber, William J. **Wild Orphan Friends.** Photographs by author. Holt, Rinehart & Winston, 1980. 160 pp.

A veterinarian tells the stories of some of the wild animals he has cared for because of some injury or accident. Each animal is unique, often humorous, and sometimes sad. His animal friends include deer, raccoons, owls, gulls, and rabbits.

Wood, Gerald L. **Animal Facts and Feats.** Sterling Publishing Co., 1978. 256 pp.

Which animals are the fastest, slowest, smallest, oldest, rarest, most ferocious, or most exotic? Facts collected from 197 experts cover mammals, birds, reptiles, fish, and even extinct animals. The most potentially dangerous insect in the whole world? The common housefly. The longest wait between meals? A snake has gone for almost two years between meals. The most artistic? An earthworm earned $100 for its "paintings." Photographs.

Zistel, Era. **Good Companions.** Signet Books, 1981. 117 pp.

Moving from New York City to the Catskill Mountains is quite a change for Era Zistel, so she decides to fill her life with new friends—goats, mice, birds, raccoons, chipmunks, and other wild animals in need of shelter and food. Throughout the years, Era establishes a close relationship with many of these animals, experiencing adventures and hardships with them.

Zistel, Era. **Thistle and Co.** Photographs by author. Little, Brown & Co., 1981. 101 pp.

This book describes the author's friendship with three unusual creatures. There is the raccoon named Thistle who is raised by a mother cat until she leaves to become a member of a wild raccoon family. Next a skunk misnamed Jake surprises the household when "he" becomes a mother. Then there is Poppy the skunk who eventually rules over the many curious family cats.

Biography

Americans

Ancona, George. **Growing Older.** E. P. Dutton, 1978. 48 pp.

Here are remembrances of a group of vital elderly Americans. They come from every part of the United States and from many walks of life. Lulu Mae Craig is 100 years old, yet she still has vivid memories of life in a sod house on the Kansas prairie. Joe Cole remembers the day he rode a deer as a boy on his grandmother's farm in Texas. Millia Davenport remembers hilarious experiences of her school days in Paris. Maybe they had to keep Millia out of the way, for other memories are of the times when she was always running away from home, and they had to tie her to a long line like a puppy.

Bauer, Douglas. **Prairie City, Iowa: Three Seasons at Home.** G. P. Putnam's Sons, 1979. 330 pp.

The author creates a curious and rare opportunity for himself. After he grows up, goes to college, and works in Des Moines and Chicago, he is drawn back to the small-town home of his childhood. He doesn't return simply out of curiosity, though. Instead, he deliberately goes back to live in his hometown for three seasons, hoping to see it now from two points of view—that of the grown-up boy and that of a stranger. The insights he gains from this experience enrich his life, bringing a new appreciation for place, time, and people. Mature situation.

Berg, Jean Horton. **I Cry When the Sun Goes Down: The Story of Herman Wrice.** Westminster Press, 1975. 158 pp.

Herman Wrice is the founder of "The Young Great Society," an organization in Philadelphia that helps the community with housing, job training, day care, drug counseling, and political action. Wrice was brought up in a ghetto where he was a gang member who carried a steel pipe for a weapon. He became the leader of his gang, the Flames, but was also a leader in athletics. Pride made him study, become senior class president, and attend Temple University.

Berman, Edgar. **Hubert: The Triumph and Tragedy of the Humphrey I Knew.** G. P. Putnam's Sons, 1979. 300 pp.

The man many called the "Happy Warrior," Hubert Humphrey, was a senator, vice president under Lyndon Johnson, and, throughout his life, an example of American statesmanship. Although he lost three bids for the presidency, Humphrey never lost his good humor or his gallantry. This biography details the strengths and weaknesses of Humphrey during the last twenty years of his life. The author, a close friend of the senator's, writes honestly of Humphrey's political career with President Johnson and Robert Kennedy, and concludes with an account of Humphrey's losing battle with cancer.

Blackwell, Elizabeth. **Pioneer Work in Opening the Medical Profession to Women.** Schocken Books, 1977. 264 pp.

Elizabeth Blackwell, who lived from 1821 to 1910, is noted for being the first woman to earn a degree from a medical college and so "opened the medical profession to women." Her autobiographical sketches tell of her determination to become a doctor, the difficulties she found as the first woman in medical school, and the comfort and support of her family.

Brough, James. **Consuelo: Portrait of an American Heiress.** Coward, McCann & Geoghegan, 1979. 266 pp.

Consuelo Vanderbilt, who became the heiress to the largest personal fortune America had ever known, had every luxury imaginable except a life of her own. Since her mother was strict and had great social ambitions for her daughter, Vanderbilt couldn't even find freedom in marriage. In order to become an aristocrat, she had to marry into an appropriate family—the Churchills. But even after she became the Duchess of Marlborough, Vanderbilt never found the love and fulfillment she so desperately needed.

Brown, Marion Marsh. **Homeward the Arrow's Flight.** Abingdon Press, 1980. 175 pp.

Susan La Flesche was the first American Indian woman to become a doctor. She was born in the early 1800s on an Indian reservation in Nebraska, the daughter of the last chief of the Omahas. He explained to young Susan that her last name, La Flesche, meant *the arrow.* Her goal in life was to serve her people. She left the reservation to attend boarding school, then Hampton Institute, and, finally, medical school.

Callahan, Dorothy. **Jimmy: The Story of the Young Jimmy Carter.** Doubleday & Co., 1979. 183 pp.

This examination of Jimmy Carter's early life helps explain his climb to the presidency. His hard work at school and on his father's farm, his determination to excel, and his desire to meet the expectations of his parents are described here.

Canada, Lena. **To Elvis, with Love.** Everest House Publishers, 1978. 178 pp.

Karen, a child severely handicapped by cerebral palsy, had been abandoned by her parents. As a result, she was shy and withdrawn and was afraid to trust or love anyone but Elvis Presley. One day she wrote a letter to the famous singer, and he wrote back to her. This is the bittersweet story of the correspondence that developed between Elvis and Karen, and how it brought her happiness in the last few months of her life.

Cavanah, Frances. **The Truth about the Man behind the Book That Sparked the War Between the States.** Westminster Press, 1976. 187 pp.

Harriet Beecher Stowe needed a model for her hero in *Uncle Tom's Cabin,* and she found that real-life hero in Josiah Henson. Henson was a slave boy who taught himself correct English, who suffered cruelty from the slavers, and who grew up to become a courageous and determined man. After escaping from his master, Henson risked his life helping other slaves escape to the North on the Underground Railroad. Josiah Henson was an abolitionist who, through words and deeds, fought against slavery in America.

Chidsey, Donald Barr. **And Tyler Too.** Thomas Nelson, 1978. 158 pp.

"Tippecanoe and Tyler too" was the campaign slogan of William Henry Harrison and his running mate, John Tyler, in the middle 1800s. Tyler was thrust into prominence when Harrison died after only a month in office, and Tyler became president of the United States. This is the story of this "accidental" president and his attempt to be his own man. During his time in the White House, we had no wars, no slaves were freed, and no great social changes were made. But this was a time for officials to learn how to make our government function more smoothly, and a time when America was becoming more secure in its identity as a nation.

Chidsey, Donald Barr. **Andrew Jackson, Hero.** Thomas Nelson, 1976. 203 pp.

Andrew Jackson, son of Irish immigrants, earned each of his nicknames: Old Hickory, Sharp Knife, Hero, and King. Young Andrew never knew his father, went to fight against the British in the American Revolution at thirteen, and lost his mother and two brothers in the same war. A man who set and broke traditions, he was fearless in battle, and he treated the presidency as a battleground. Mature reading.

Chidsey, Donald Barr. **Mr. Hamilton and Mr. Jefferson.** Thomas Nelson, 1975. 207 pp.

What could politicians do about a whiskey rebellion in western Pennsylvania, or a popular French ambassador who tried to stir up trouble on the frontier, or a mosquito-infested swamp along the Potomac? This isn't the plot for an historical soap opera, but some of the interesting events two of America's founding fathers had to contend with in the late 1700s. These, and other dilemmas faced by Alexander Hamilton and Thomas Jefferson, are described in this dual biography.

Coolidge, Olivia. **The Statesmanship of Abraham Lincoln.** Charles Scribner's Sons, 1976. 229 pp.

This biography of Lincoln begins with his inauguration as president and concludes five years later with his assassination. By concentrating on such a short period in Lincoln's life, the author provides an in-depth and not always flattering view of the president. Discussions of his role as commander in chief during the Civil War and his abilities as a skilled politician take up major sections of the book.

Cunliffe, Marcus. **George Washington: Man and Monument.** Mentor Books, 1982. 196 pp.

What was the "father of our country" really like? A man who could inspire both devotion and hatred, Washington is now remembered by most Americans only as the face on the one-dollar bill. This biography shows the complicated man behind that face—a man who was often ambitious, lonely, angry, and uncertain, but always concerned with the fate of the young country he helped create.

Deur, Lynne. **Indian Chiefs.** Fearon-Pitman Publishers, 1978. 103 pp.

Before the eighteenth century, noble Indian chiefs and their tribes lived a peaceful life in North America. Then the white settlers pushed west, driving the native Americans out of their territory, shooting Indian families for government money, and crowding them onto reservations. This book tells of Indian chiefs like Sitting Bull, Crazy Horse, Geronimo, and Black Hawk, who fought for their people—sometimes in peace talks, other times in bloody wars.

Douty, Esther M. **Hasty Pudding and Barbary Pirates: A Life of Joel Barlow.** Westminster Press, 1975. 144 pp.

Although not exactly a household name from American history, Joel Barlow was a poet, statesman, philosopher, and patriot in the exciting times during and after the American Revolution. Because of his liberal writings, he was made an honorary citizen of France. While in France, he helped Robert Fulton develop the steamboat. Later, Barlow became a voluntary hostage to the Barbary pirates in order to rescue American sailors held as slaves. Barlow was a far-sighted American who served his country in its time of greatest need.

Farley, Karin Clafford. **Canal Boy.** Illus. Dennis Bellile. David C. Cook Publishing Co., 1978. 158 pp.

Jim worked along 4,000 miles of man-made channels, locks, and aqueducts that stretched from New York to Illinois. In August of 1848 Jim had only $2 and a dangerous job. He would eventually work out of this situation to become an educator, preacher, general, congressman, and the twentieth president of the United States, James Garfield.

Felt, W. Mark. **The FBI Pyramid: From the Inside.** G. P. Putnam's Sons, 1979. 351 pp.

Author Mark Felt was the first top FBI executive to accept responsibility for the agency's burglaries of suspected terrorist hideouts. This autobiography not only reveals Felt's rigorous training and early assignments as a rookie agent, but recounts the dramatic episodes of thirty years of experience as an FBI agent. Felt includes striking descriptions of the late J. Edgar Hoover, the rise of McCarthyism, and the Watergate era. Photographs.

Fleischer, Jane. **Pontiac: Chief of the Ottawas.** Illus. Robert Baxter. Troll Associates, 1979. 48 pp.

Pontiac, a famous Ottawa Indian chief, led his people to fight with the French against the English just before the Revolutionary War. The English had taken Indian land and paid little for the furs the Indians traded, so Pontiac went to war against the English to try to capture Fort Detroit for his people. Easy reading.

Fleischer, Jane. **Sitting Bull: Warrior of the Sioux.** Illus. Bert Dodson. Troll Associates, 1979. 48 pp.

Chief Sitting Bull's people lived in the Dakota country of the Great Plains. Sitting Bull led his warriors against the whites when gold was found in the Black Hills and the whites began to break treaty rules with the Sioux. This book covers how Sitting Bull became the leader of the Sioux nation and discusses some of his military victories, such as the defeat of General Custer at the Little Big Horn. To complete the picture of the Sioux chief, the author tells of Sitting Bull's desires for peace and freedom for his people, and of his struggles to keep his people alive in the face of starvation and war.

Fleischer, Jane. **Tecumseh: Shawnee War Chief.** Illus. Hal Frenck. Troll Associates, 1979. 48 pp.

Tecumseh was a Shawnee chief who became a general in the British army during the War of 1812. At that time, Tecumseh was trying to save Indian land from American soldiers. But beyond fighting for the British, Tecumseh hoped to protect Indian land and the Indian way of life by uniting all Indians into one mighty nation. Easy reading.

Fox, Mary Virginia. **Lady for the Defense: A Biography of Belva Lockwood.** Harcourt Brace Jovanovich, 1975. 156 pp.

A woman as president of the United States? Still a remote possibility in the 1980s, yet Belva Lockwood was such a candidate in the 1884 campaign. Widowed and a mother at a young age, Lockwood dared to fight for her own rights as a person and to devote her life to civil rights and world peace. She struggled to support her children and to put herself through law school, enduring failures, disappointments, and tragedies. But she also won big victories. She served as a delegate to the first world peace conference and drafted the first legislation to propose a World Court. Here is the story of a woman whose achievements were important, and one who is not as well known as she should be.

Fritz, Jean. **Stonewall.** Illus. Stephen Gammell. G. P. Putnam's Sons, 1979. 152 pp.

Thomas "Stonewall" Jackson was one of the most colorful men in American history. He gained his popularity and fame during the Civil War through his success on the battlefield and because of his numerous eccentricities. He was once called "The Iron Duke" because of his particular way of saluting. He was also known as "Square Box" because of his enormous feet. But his most famous nickname, "Stonewall," was earned at the Battle of Manassas because he stood and faced the enemy like a *stone wall.*

Gordy, Berry, Sr. **Movin' Up: Pop Gordy Tells His Story.** Harper & Row, Publishers, 1979. 144 pp.

This is the true story of an extraordinary black American, the son of a former slave, and the father of the founder of Motown Records. Pop Gordy's story begins during the late 1800s on his father's farm in Georgia helping his family scrape out a living. But Gordy knew how to enjoy everything he did, and when he moved to Detroit in 1922, he took with him his positive attitude and his great capacity for hard work. The story tells of his climb to prominence, a rise that ended with a posthumous "Tribute to a Black American" award in 1979, the year following his death at age 90.

Greenfield, Eloise, and Lessie Jones Little (with Pattie Ridley Jones). **Childtimes: A Three-Generation Memoir.** Illus. Jerry Pinkney. Thomas Y. Crowell Co., 1979. 178 pp.

Three black women—grandmother, mother, and daughter—remember the times when they were children and tell about those times to young people today. These memories include sharp images of burning crosses, baptisms in the river, school and play times, family ghost stories, and the many jobs and houses the family shared. The granddaughter, Eloise Greenfield, is a contemporary author of books for young people.

Hacker, Jeffrey H. **Franklin D. Roosevelt.** Franklin Watts, 1983. 113 pp.

This president was elected to office four different times between 1932 and 1945 and led America through difficult periods of history. This biography of Roosevelt focuses on his politics and personality and shows how they both merged to create his particular leadership skills. Like many other famous people, Roosevelt was the center of both criticism and admiration. Evidence is given of his determination—in overcoming the personal tragedy of polio and in solving national and world problems.

Hanser, Richard. **The Glorious Hour of Lt. Monroe.** Atheneum Publishers, 1976. 170 pp.

James Monroe was at the College of William and Mary in Virginia when the Second Continental Congress called for an army. He enlisted and was with General Washington during the winter of 1776, when the small American army was encamped across the Delaware River from British-controlled Trenton, New Jersey.

Lieutenant Monroe was one of the officers who joined Washington in the secret Christmas crossing of the Delaware to catch the British by surprise. He was also one of the few Americans badly hurt in that battle, but he survived and later became the fifth president of the nation he helped to save.

Harris, Jacqueline L. **Martin Luther King, Jr.** Franklin Watts, 1983. 123 pp.

Martin Luther King, Jr., is best known for his belief, like that of Gandhi, in using nonviolence to solve problems. His life is traced from a young boy in the 1930s whose family was involved in the civil rights movement to his death by assassination in 1968. An enemy of bigotry and a champion of peace, King received the Nobel Peace Prize in 1964. One of his most famous phrases was "I have a dream," and that dream was freedom for all people.

Haskins, James. **Barbara Jordan.** Dial Press, 1977. 215 pp.

Here is the story of the black U.S. representative from Texas who became a national figure during the televising of the Nixon impeachment hearings. Jordan may have captured public attention then, but she had earlier made history when she was elected to the Texas Senate. In 1972 she became one of the first two blacks to be elected to Congress from the South since 1901. This is the account of her triumphs, failures, personal history, and the predictions that have been made about her political future.

Haskins, James. **Fighting Shirley Chisholm.** Dial Press, 1975. 204 pp.

Shirley Chisholm was the first black woman to be elected to the U.S. House of Representatives (1969) and the first black woman to run for the presidential nomination (1972). Here is the story of why and how she attempted these achievements, beginning with her childhood in Brooklyn and Barbados in the 1920s and 1930s. It was not easy for her to accomplish what she did, for both her sex and her race were against her. But she was given the nickname of "Fighting" Shirley Chisholm for a very good reason.

Hocken, Sheila. **Emma and I.** Thomas Congdon Books, 1978. 211 pp.

Sheila Hocken describes how she grew up in a world of darkness, teased by other children, and trying to imagine a world she had never seen, and never expected to see. She did not want to be different, but at last she accepted her need for help. When she is given Emma, a Seeing Eye dog, Sheila feels she receives far more than a pet or a pair of eyes to see for her. And Emma's arrival in

Sheila's life is just the first of three unusual events that take Sheila on a "search for sight."

Hoople, Cheryl G., editor. **As I Saw It: Women Who Lived the American Adventure.** Dial Press, 1978. 187 pp.

This book explores American history to find all kinds of women who used their energy and imagination to build America. Some are famous, such as Abigail Adams and Dolley Madison, but most names are not so familiar even though the women made important observations about their lives through letters, speeches, diaries, and journals. For example, Dame Shirley Clappe writes in her letters about being a part of the 1849 Gold Rush—washing dirt with her own hands and suffering wet feet, torn dresses, ruined gloves, frozen fingers, and other physical hardships.

Hyatt, Richard. **The Carters of Plains.** Strode Publishers, 1977. 320 pp.

This is the story of the Georgia farm boy who surprised millions by winning the Democratic Party's presidential nomination in 1976 and by winning the election itself. Jimmy Carter's story provides inspiration to others who want to become president. Although the Carters didn't have the political connections and national recognition that many presidential candidates have, they were honest, hard-working Americans who had a dream and who worked to make that dream come true. Photographs.

Jassem, Kate. **Chief Joseph: Leader of Destiny.** Illus. Robert Baxter. Troll Associates, 1979. 48 pp.

Chief Joseph of the Nez Percé Indians wanted his people to live in peace and freedom. But fighting broke out between the U.S. Army and the Nez Percé in 1877 as he was leading his people to reservation land. Forced into war, Chief Joseph and 300 warriors had to fight against 2,000 soldiers. Easy reading.

Jassem, Kate. **Pocahontas: Girl of Jamestown.** Illus. Allan Eitzen. Troll Associates, 1979. 48 pp.

Pocahontas, a young American Indian princess, was the daughter of Chief Powhatan. As the early settlers arrived from England in the early 1600s, Powhatan began to fear them and wanted them off his land. Pocahontas stepped in and saved the life of white man Captain John Smith as he was about to be killed by the Indians. She also helped other settlers by giving them food and showing them how to plant crops. These actions angered her father, but this did not stop Pocahontas from helping her new friends. **Easy reading.**

Jassem, Kate. **Sacajawea: Wilderness Guide.** Illus. Jan Palmer. Troll Associates, 1979. 48 pp.

Sacajawea's Indian village was attacked when she was a young girl in the late 1700s. She was captured by an enemy tribe and later was sold to a Canadian trapper. Sacajawea was to earn a place in American history when she helped guide the Lewis and Clark expedition of 1803 to 1806, which was looking for routes west over the Rocky Mountains. In doing so, Sacajawea became the first woman to cross the Rockies.

Jassem, Kate. **Squanto: The Pilgrim Adventure.** Illus. Robert Baxter. Troll Associates, 1979. 48 pp.

Squanto, an American Indian, was fourteen when he saw English ships approach his village in the early 1600s. Although he had never seen a white man before, Squanto was friendly and even helped the new people. Later he was captured by a cruel Englishman in 1615 and was taken to Spain to be sold as a slave. But Squanto fought to find a way to return home. Easy reading.

Katz, William Loren. **Black People Who Made the Old West.** Thomas Y. Crowell Co., 1977. 181 pp.

Black explorers, traders, settlers, prospectors, cowboys, lawmen, soldiers, and other shapers of the frontier are discussed in this combination biography-history book. Also analyzed are these men and women's specific contributions to the growth of our country over the last two hundred years. Photographs. An adaptation of the author's *The Black West: A Documentary and Pictorial History.*

Keller, Helen. **The Story of My Life.** Watermill Press, 1980. 152 pp.

Helen Keller was left deaf, mute, and blind from a childhood sickness, but she learned to read, write, and speak with the help of her teacher, Anne Sullivan. Keller eventually graduated with honors from Radcliffe College in 1904. She spent most of her adult life helping other blind and deaf people. This is her own account of her life—its difficulties and its joys.

Lasky, Victor. **Jimmy Carter: The Man and the Myth.** Richard Marek Publishers, 1979. 419 pp.

The author traces the rise of President Carter from his small-town roots in Georgia to his troubles as a world leader. This controversial book presents a fairly negative view of Carter, and it is highly critical of his campaigning, personal life, and tenure as president.

Lawson, Don. **FDR's New Deal.** Thomas Y. Crowell Co., 1979. 152 pp.

October 1929 was the beginning of the Great Depression, which was brought on by the end of World War I. President Franklin Delano Roosevelt's New Deal policies proved to be the only possible solution. With these New Deal measures, President Roosevelt instituted, for the first time, direct government control over the economy by creating jobs and forcing banks to remain open and provide loans. Photographs.

Lengyel, Cornel Adam. **Presidents of the United States.** Golden Press, 1977.

This book presents a short biography of each U.S. president from George Washington to Jimmy Carter. Details are given about each president's life, and there is a discussion of how each presidential term affected our country. Photographs accompany the biographies.

Levy, Elizabeth. **Lawyers for the People: A New Breed of Defenders and Their Work.** Alfred A. Knopf, 1974. 120 pp.

Short biographies of nine public-interest lawyers demonstrate how the legal profession works to wipe out injustices in American society. Linda Huber works to help juveniles; Bernie Clyne works for and with the poor; Charlie Halpern promotes public-interest law; Tom Kline is trying to make public-interest law self-supporting; Fay Stender concentrates on prison reform; Carol Broege defends radicals; Carol Libow helps women attain their rights; Eleanor Holmes Norton works for equal rights; and Beverly Moore labors for the consumers' best interests.

Levy, Elizabeth, and Mara Miller. **Doctors for the People: Profiles of Six Who Serve.** Alfred A. Knopf, 1977. 108 pp.

These are not just ordinary doctors; each of them reaches into special areas of the profession. A determined black woman, Dorothy Brown, overcomes obstacles and achieves her goals by becoming both a surgeon and a politician. Young medic Sheldon Rosen dedicates his hours and himself to working with the migrant farm workers of the West. A pioneer in the field of genetics, Victor McKusick undertakes to win the trust of the Amish, a group in desperate need of specialized care. Aware of the special needs of women, Marcia Storch devotes herself to developing and promoting medical treatment sensitive to women's needs. And Vince Esposito decides to return to the old ways by becoming a family doctor.

Levy, Elizabeth, and Mara Miller. **Politicians for the People: Six Who Stand for Change.** Alfred A. Knopf, 1979. 113 pp.

You can agree or disagree with these six politicians, but you will probably admire and respect them for believing they can work for change and for doing something about their beliefs. Third-party candidate Moises Morales refuses to be stifled by his opponents' scare tactics, and Nancy Stevenson shows how she ran a tough campaign against three men. Beating a strong political machine became Arthur Eve's objective, while Bill Bradley makes connections between basketball and politics. In the 1960s Tom Hayden was a student radical—and he has not left politics yet. And how can a Chicano activist serve a conservative district? Polly Baca-Barragan tries to answer this question in formulating her political policies.

Lisker, Tom. **Nellie Bly: First Woman of the News.** Illus. Jeffrey Lindberg. Contemporary Perspectives, 1978. 48 pp.

In 1885, seventeen-year-old Elizabeth Cochrane began work as the first female reporter for the *Pittsburgh Dispatch,* and she was given the name Nellie Bly. Her reporting became based on living with the people she wrote about—in factories, slums, and even an insane asylum. She died poverty-stricken in 1922, but she is still remembered for her controversial human-interest stories about social conditions.

Lynch, Dudley. **The President from Texas: Lyndon Baines Johnson.** Thomas Y. Crowell Co., 1975. 169 pp.

On November 22, 1963, John Kennedy was assassinated and Lyndon Baines Johnson became president of the United States. This is the story of Johnson's early beginnings as a politician, his rise to power, and the eventual public disfavor that led him to decide against running for reelection in 1968. Photographs.

Madison, Arnold. **Carry Nation.** Thomas Nelson, 1977. 154 pp.

Was Carry Nation only a hatchet-wielding destroyer of saloons in 1900? What made her turn so strongly against liquor? This book shows us Nation's harsh life as a possible explanation for her actions. Her childhood in the mid-1800s was extremely unstable. Her mother had sudden fits of madness and temper, and Nation was made to feel it was her own sins that caused her mother's outbursts. Nation eventually became very religious, and she would turn to prayer during the many trials in her life, which included an alcoholic husband.

Mails, Thomas E. (with Dallas Chief Eagle). **Fools Crow.** Illus. by author. Discus Books, 1980. 278 pp.

Fools Crow, Ceremonial Chief and medicine man of the Teton Sioux, recalls his boyhood at the turn of the century. He discusses the problems of farming and of how he avoided schools run by whites, and he describes the ancient Indian art of medicine and healing. Fools Crow also shares many other secrets of his culture, tribal traditions, and Teton Sioux philosophies.

Matthew, Scott. **The First Woman of Medicine: The Story of Elizabeth Blackwell.** Illus. Wayne Atkinson. Contemporary Perspectives, 1978. 48 pp.

Elizabeth Blackwell, the first American woman admitted to medical school, became the first woman doctor in 1849—only to discover that no U.S. hospital would hire her. After practicing medicine in Europe, Blackwell opened the first hospital for poor women and continued fighting for women's rights throughout her life.

McCullough, Joan. **First of All: Significant "Firsts" by American Women.** Holt, Rinehart & Winston, 1980. 171 pp.

Over 160 entries chronicle the fascinating and often little-known background of special American women. Included in this book are such unusual stories as that of the first American-born saint, who was a nun and the mother of five children. Or, did you know that the printer of the Declaration of Independence was a woman? And it was Martha Washington, not George, whose picture was first printed on the one-dollar bill.

Morrison, Dorothy Nafus. **Chief Sarah: Sarah Winnemucca's Fight for Indian Rights.** Atheneum Publishers, 1980. 170 pp.

A woman Indian chief? Yes, Chief Sarah was a Paiute Indian woman who was a scout, lecturer, author, educator, and political lobbyist during the nineteenth century. She has been compared to Joan of Arc because of her efforts to gain and protect the rights of her people. She had only three weeks of formal education, yet she started the first Indian school taught and run by the Indians themselves. Photographs.

Morrison, Dorothy Nafus. **Ladies Were Not Expected: Abigail Scott Duniway and Women's Rights.** Atheneum Publishers, 1977. 139 pp.

Abigail Scott Duniway (1834–1915) worked for women's rights, especially for the right to vote in Oregon. Duniway knew the hardships women faced in the territories, and she saw how unfairly they were being treated. Women were not considered as people, but as property. Duniway lived to see the positive results of her work, for she was the first woman to cast a vote in the state of Oregon.

Nies, Judith. **Seven Women: Portraits from the American Radical Tradition.** Viking Press, 1977. 206 pp.

The author of this book has captured the spirit of seven women living during the late 1800s and early 1900s who were considered radicals and were not accepted by society. However, these women laid the groundwork for many of the freedoms that women enjoy today. For example, Elizabeth Cady Stanton was the first woman to wear pants in public and to speak out for women's right to vote and to divorce. Harriet Tubman organized guerrilla operations in the South, led raids against plantations, and was responsible for freeing 300 slaves through the Underground Railroad. The other five women portrayed—Mother Jones, Dorothy Day, Sarah Grimke, Charlotte Perkins Gilman, and Ann Louise Strong—made equally important contributions to social and political change.

Nixon, Richard. **RN: The Memoirs of Richard Nixon.** 2 vols. Warner Books, 1979. 1,392 pp.

Former President Nixon outlines his life from his boyhood in California, through his courtship and marriage, to his political campaigns. Nixon gives his personal views of his tough campaign against John Kennedy and his later triumphs over Hubert Humphrey and George McGovern. The second volume of the autobiography describes Nixon's years in the White House (1969–1974), especially the tumultuous years of the Watergate Scandal. Photographs.

Oppenheim, Joanne. **Black Hawk: Frontier Warrior.** Illus. Hal Frenck. Troll Associates, 1979. 48 pp.

Chief Black Hawk was a Sauk Indian who fought against the Americans in the War of 1812 to protect his people's land from American takeover. Because of his determination, Chief Black Hawk's tribe was one of the last to be pushed west of the Mississippi River. Easy reading.

Oppenheim, Joanne. **Osceola: Seminole Warrior.** Illus. Bill Ternay. Troll Associates, 1979. 48 pp.

During the time of the War of 1812, Little Owl, a Creek Indian, watched his village go up in flames. He was only a young boy when his family and tribe were forced to leave their native Georgia and to live in Florida with the Seminole Indians. Little Owl, renamed Osceola, grew up to become a strong chief and a leader of the Seminoles. He attempted to keep Florida for his people, and this struggle soon grew into a war between the Indians and the Bluecoats, the nickname of the American army troops. Easy reading.

Oppenheim, Joanne. **Sequoyah: Cherokee Hero.** Illus. Bert Dodson. Troll Associates, 1979. 47 pp.

As a young boy in the late 1700s, Sequoyah, unlike his friends, did not dream of becoming a great warrior. He was more interested in the "talking leaves" of the whites—the newspapers and letters used for communication. As a result of this interest, Sequoyah attempted to develop the first American Indian language with an alphabet, so that thoughts could be written down to keep records, record stories, and help in tribal communication.

Patterson, Lillie. **Sure Hands, Strong Heart: The Life of Daniel Hale Williams.** Illus. David Scott Brown. Abingdon Press, 1981. 156 pp.

During hard times in the 1860s, young Dan Williams' family was forced to separate. Williams was busy adjusting to a new home, work, school, and membership in a string band, but he always remembered his father's belief that blacks must become more involved with developing their minds. Williams achieved the honor of being one of the youngest blacks to become a physician and was the first U.S. physician to perform open heart surgery.

Putterman, Ron. **To Find My Son.** Avon Books, 1981. 189 pp.

This is the true story of a single-parent adoption—how Ron volunteered at the County Home for Neglected Children; how he met seven-year-old Alan, a physically perfect but emotionally scarred child who desperately needed love; how Ron became the person who gave that love; how he faced the questioning looks of family and friends, the open hostility and suspicion of county welfare authorities, and lack of understanding of his girlfriend. Everyone questioned how a young, single man could possibly be a parent to a troubled child—everyone, that is except Ron and Alan.

Rice, Edward. **Margaret Mead: A Portrait.** Harper & Row, Publishers, 1979. 204 pp.

More than any other person, Margaret Mead (1901–1978) is given credit for turning anthropology from a stuffy science into a popular subject. Her first study of Samoan teenage girls in the 1920s became a best-selling book, as did almost every study she published. This is the story of a remarkable woman who managed to be both a career woman and a mother, but who was not always able to succeed as a wife. Throughout her life, she expressed the hope that it would one day be possible for all women to succeed at all three endeavors and realize their full potential.

Richardson, Ben, and William A. Fahey. **Great Black Americans.** Thomas Y. Crowell Co., 1976. 344 pp.

The lives of thirty-one black leaders are detailed here. Included are stories about men and women's contributions in the fields of music, art, theater, literature, education, public affairs, science, and sports. Among the famous figures covered are Louis Armstrong, Paul Robeson, Langston Hughes, Malcolm X, George Washington Carver, Muhammad Ali, and Marian Anderson. Originally published as *Great American Negroes*.

Ross, Pat, editor. **Young and Female: Turning Points in the Lives of Eight American Women.** Random House, 1972. 104 pp.

This book contains selections from autobiographies of eight American women including Shirley MacLaine, Shirley Chisholm, Dorothy Day, Emily Hahn, Margaret Sanger, Althea Gibson, Edna Ferber, and Margaret Bourke-White. These women are from different walks of life, but they have some of the same insights into life. All of them are determined to live their lives freely and under their own terms rather than at the dictates of society.

Sobol, Rose. **Woman Chief.** Dial Press, 1976. 108 pp.

Woman Chief was born a Gros Ventre Indian of the prairie, but she was captured when still a child by the Crow Indians. The Crow warrior who adopted her into his family recognized her abilities and trained her as a warrior. She became a chief of the Crow nation and was given the title of Woman Chief for her brave deeds as a hunter and warrior. But life was not easy for this unusual eighteenth-century woman whose strong sense of individuality forced her to make many sacrifices.

Sullivan, Tom, and Derek Gill. **If You Could See What I Hear.** Signet Books, 1976. 183 pp

Tom Sullivan was deprived of sight as a baby, but the blind child still wanted to do everything that other boys did. Although his classmates shunned him, he became a brilliant college student, a natural athlete who excelled in sports, and a musician who won fame and fortune. Then he discovered love. Now this husband and father tells his own story—his hopes and fears, the frustrations and the triumphs, the heartbreaking and the inspiring—in a book that will open your eyes to what courage and life are all about.

Surge, Frank. **Western Outlaws.** Fearon-Pitman Publishers, 1978. 54 pp.

Biographical sketches of widely known outlaws like Jesse James reveal the brief but tumultuous lives of these men and women. Cruel, selfish, and intelligent, they seemed to enjoy life outside the law and society. Ironically, many of them died at the hands of their most trusted friends. Photographs.

Van Rensselaer, Philip. **Million-Dollar Baby: An Intimate Portrait of Barbara Hutton.** G. P. Putnam's Sons, 1979. 285 pp.

Barbara Hutton (1912-1979) was one of America's most famous heiresses. She inherited twenty-five million dollars at the age of ten from her grandfather, Frank Winfield Woolworth. Barbara Hutton went through tens of millions of dollars and seven husbands; she endured the loss of her only son, a legion of selfish friends, and a lifetime of deception. This biography tells the entire story.

Walker, Barbara J. **The Picture Life of Jimmy Carter.** Photographs by Charles M. Rafshoon. Camelot Books, 1978. 47 pp.

When Jimmy Carter first tried for the presidential nomination, nobody knew who he was—or so it seemed. But Carter began to work hard to let people know what he stood for and worked his way from being an unknown Georgia peanut farmer to the presidency. The many photographs in the book follow the rise of this American leader. While in office, the thirty-ninth president was able to achieve many of the dreams he had for making life better for many people. Easy reading.

Warner, Lucille Schulberg, editor. **From Slave to Abolitionist: The Life of William Wells Brown.** Dial Press, 1976. 135 pp.

This biography of William Wells Brown dwells primarily on his days as a slave: the cruelties he endured, the mistreatment he witnessed of his fellow slaves, and his many attempts at escape. His exile in England and his lecture tours are given some attention here also. Only in England, Brown felt, was he really treated as a person.

White, Anne Terry. **Eugene Debs: American Socialist.** Lawrence Hill & Co., 1974. 137 pp.

Eugene Debs was a candidate for the American presidency five times. As a young man in the late 1800s, Debs became interested in helping his fellow workers fight against the large corporations. He became a socialist and he worked for unions and political equality. He was often imprisoned for the strikes he helped carry out against businesses such as the railroads. Photographs.

White, Florence Meiman. **First Woman in Congress: Jeannette Rankin.** Julian Messner, 1980. 95 pp.

She was "one woman against 388 men," as a chapter title puts it. But Jeannette Rankin was determined to use her position as the first woman elected to Congress to further the rights of women and all oppressed people. For the next five decades, Rankin worked in and out of government office as a spokesperson for social reform and was still making speeches in 1972 at age 92. Photographs. Easy reading.

Whitney, Sharon. **Eleanor Roosevelt.** Franklin Watts, 1982. 113 pp.

Eleanor Roosevelt (1884–1962) was one of America's most admired and controversial first ladies. Follow Eleanor as she grows from a painfully shy girl into a powerful woman dedicated to helping the young, the weak, and the poor. The author shows how the goals and values that the Roosevelts shared made them a successful political team, in spite of the personal disappointments Eleanor felt in her marriage.

Wilkins, Roy (with Tom Mathews). **Standing Fast: The Autobiography of Roy Wilkins.** The Viking Press, 1982. 360 pp.

The late Roy Wilkins was a prominent figure in the civil rights movement in the United States. Born in 1901, Wilkins grew up with an aunt and uncle and attended the University of Minnesota, where he began his career in newspaper work as the editor of the school paper. Wilkins became the executive secretary of the NAACP in 1955 and worked long to make advances in justice for all people. He died in September 1981, soon after this autobiography was written. Photographs.

Wilson, Beth P. **Giants for Justice: Bethune, Randolph, and King.** Harcourt Brace Jovanovich, 1978. 97 pp.

Mary McLeod Bethune (1875–1955) had a passion—first a passion for learning and then a passion to make sure black children got a solid education. She worked, she studied, she begged for money, she even gave up her marriage and her home to build a school in the South for black girls. Her fight for educational rights eventually took her to argue her case at the White House. A. Philip Randolph, born in 1889, published a newspaper for blacks' rights, organized the Brotherhood of Blacks, and got blacks into labor unions. Considered by some as the most dangerous of blacks, he never was violent and never lost his personal dignity and quiet manner. Martin Luther King, Jr. (1929–1968), like Randolph, followed the nonviolent protest teachings of Mahatma Gandhi. Early in his life he knew what he must do, and he convinced his talented wife, Coretta, of the value of that mission. King's part in nonviolent marches and other protests ended in his assassination, but also in new rights and freedoms for blacks in the United States. Photographs.

World Figures

Atkin, Mary Gage. **Paul Cuffe and the African Promised Land.** Thomas Nelson, 1977. 160 pp.

Paul Cuffe (1759–1817), whose father had been a slave, set out to earn economic and social independence for himself and his people. His efforts to build a haven for blacks in Sierra Leone are tied to the changing politics of the British, the French, and the Americans during the eighteenth century.

Ayars, James. **We Hold These Truths: From Magna Carta to the Bill of Rights.** Viking Press, 1977. 165 pp.

This book consists of biographies of three men who helped create documents that supported the rights and freedoms of people. The story begins in England in the 1200s with the signing of the Magna Carta, a document stating that even kings must obey the common laws of the country. It was created to protect the people from rulers and leaders who wanted too much power. A number of men influenced, or were influenced by, the Magna Carta: John Langton, archbishop of Canterbury in the thirteenth century; John Lilburne, English supporter of freedom of religion and speech during the reign of Oliver Cromwell in England; and George Mason, the American revolutionary who helped write the U.S. Constitution.

Brooks, Janice Young. **Kings and Queens: The Plantagenets of England.** Thomas Nelson, 1975. 160 pp.

When Mathilda of Flanders refused to marry William the Conqueror, he simply beat her up. Richard III may or may not have murdered his nephews in the Tower of London. Richard the Lionhearted's bride followed him to the Crusades. This book takes a look at some of the kings and queens of England as though they were characters in a royal soap opera. Their stories are colorful and surprising.

Carroll, Raymond. **Anwar Sadat.** Franklin Watts, 1982. 114 pp.

As a boy growing up in the Nile Delta in the 1920s, Anwar Sadat slept on top of the oven in his family's mud-brick home to keep warm. As the president of Egypt, he waged wars and negotiated a difficult peace, winning the admiration of millions and the hatred of many others in the Arab world. Follow one of the most courageous men in history as he becomes a soldier, a prisoner, a revolutionary, a president, and—eventually—the victim of an assassin's bullet in 1981.

Collins, Jim. **The Strange Story of Uri Geller.** Contemporary Perspectives, 1977. 48 pp.

Israeli-born Uri Geller is certainly an unusual man. He bends metal by looking at it, he stops clocks by thinking about them, and he even reads people's minds. He has been doing these things since his youth in the 1950s, and although many people believe he is simply a magician, most people who have witnessed his powers believe in them. Easy reading.

Davidson, Margaret. **The Golda Meir Story.** Rev. ed. Charles Scribner's Sons, 1981. 221 pp.

Golda Meir was an important figure in the struggle to make a Jewish homeland in Palestine—right up to her death in 1978 from leukemia. She always believed in fighting for justice for her people, and she even joined in a fast as a child in Russia to protest the killing of Jews. Meir's girlhood years were spent in Milwaukee, then in 1921 she and her husband immigrated to Palestine. Meir served in every Israeli cabinet from the first election in 1949 and spent five years as prime minister.

de Jonge, Alex. **Fire and Water: A Life of Peter the Great.** Coward, McCann & Geoghegan, 1980. 279 pp.

In 1689 Peter became czar at age seventeen. Peter's greatest desire was to bring Western culture to Russia. He extended Russia's borders; he brought rapid advances in industry, agriculture, medicine, and education; and he built his own city of Petersburg. But Peter was also a victim of his own strong emotions: he never wanted to be alone, he tortured his own son, and he believed others were always in conspiracies against him. Mature situations.

deLeeuw, Adèle. **Carlos P. Romulo—The Barefoot Boy of Diplomacy.** Westminster Press, 1976. 175 pp.

Carlos P. Romulo, foreign minister of the Philippines, is a man of small stature but strong character. Born the son of a guerrilla fighter in 1899, Romulo grew up to become a champion of freedom and self-determination for all people. He became a brilliant newspaper reporter and was the first non-American to win the Pulitzer Prize for reporting. Romulo has become a well-respected diplomat and statesman who acts as a catalyst for change and progress.

Dolan, Edward F., Jr. **Adolf Hitler: A Portrait in Tyranny.** Dodd, Mead & Co., 1981. 228 pp.

Adolf Hitler (1889–1945) was a dictator and a man whose hatred and prejudice brought about World War II and the deaths of millions of people. This book traces how Hitler developed his ideas and how he rose to power in Germany. Photographs.

Ebert, Richard. **Lawrence of Arabia.** Illus. Roy Schofield. Raintree Publishers, 1979. 31 pp.

Thomas Edward Lawrence of England loved history as a small boy in the 1890s. He soon became fascinated with learning about early civilizations, particularly those of Arabia. This interest eventually led him to Arabian lands, where he learned to live and speak as the people there did. In 1916, he went to battle to help the Arabians win their freedom from Turkish oppression. The mission was difficult and dangerous, for the Arabs didn't have enough men and had few weapons. But Lawrence's knowledge and courage, along with his determination, helped the Arabs to victory. Easy reading.

Friedländer, Saul (translator Helen R. Lane). **When Memory Comes.** Discus Books, 1980. 186 pp.

A young Jewish orphan finds himself in Nazi-occupied France in 1940 and decides to prepare to become a Catholic priest. Years later, he travels to Jerusalem to uncover his religious roots. When he gets there, Saul Friedländer wonders how it could have all happened to him. He has changed his identity four times, his religion twice, and his name five times. He wonders who he really is.

Kelen, Betty. **Muhammad: The Messenger of God.** Thomas Nelson, 1975. 259 pp.

The sixth-century Arab world in which Muhammad grew up was a violent one. But, supported by an inner peace, the unschooled orphan boy answered what he felt was God's call to establish a new religion. As he went about his mission, he encountered many trials. People taunted and fought him much of the time. His persistence finally overcame all obstacles, however, and his duty to God was successfully fulfilled.

Keller, Mollie. **Golda Meir.** Franklin Watts, 1983. 110 pp.

Golda Meir, former prime minister of Israel, didn't even go to Israel until later in life. She was born in Russia in 1898 and moved to the United States with her family in 1906. As she grew up, she became interested in Zionism and wanted to immigrate to Palestine to build a homeland there for Jewish people. This book contains personal glimpses of Meir's life, such as her aversion to chickens, her family life with two children, and her determination to work for the country instead of being tucked away in quiet family life. She died at the age of 80, and then it was revealed she had been suffering from cancer for fifteen years. Photographs.

Kherdian, David. **The Road from Home: The Story of an Armenian Girl.** Greenwillow Books, 1979. 238 pp.

Here is the story of the author's mother, who grew up in the Armenian section of Turkey. But in 1915, the Turkish government decided to rid the country of all Armenians. So Veron was deported with her family and suffered many hardships in being displaced. At age sixteen, Veron left for a new life in America as a mail-order bride.

Klüger, Ruth, and Peggy Mann. **The Secret Ship.** Doubleday & Co., 1978. 136 pp.

It is the 1930s, a time of Nazi rule, and a shipload of Jews wait in Romania for the chance to sail for Palestine. But there are dangers ahead. Hitler would like to capture and imprison the group. Ruth Klüger once again tries to help a group of Jews escape Europe. This is the story of an organization, its members, and a woman dedicated to saving lives. Adapted from *The Last Escape: The Launching of the Largest Secret Rescue Movement of All Time.*

Knight, David C. **The Spy Who Never Was and Other True Spy Stories.** Doubleday & Co., 1978. 136 pp.

Ten suspenseful tales of men and women who spied for their countries during wartime are included in this book. Examples are Velvalee Dickinson, who used her exclusive doll shop in New York as a cover for her spying for the Japanese during World War II; Alexander Scotland, who successfully posed as a German officer for twenty years through two wars for Britain; Major William Martin, whose dead body was used by the Allies to plant important forged documents about the invasion of Europe. Other true spies include Nathan Hale; Lydia Darragh, a Quaker woman who spied for

General Washington; Emma Edmonds in disguise for Lincoln; Mata Hari, the famous dancer who was a German spy; Major Peter Ortiz, who spied against the Nazis; Colonel Rudolf Abel, the ingenious Russian spy; and Francis Gary Powers, the amateur spy for the United States.

Knightley, Phillip. **Lawrence of Arabia.** Thomas Nelson, 1977. 96 pp.

Thomas Edward Lawrence became fascinated with the Middle East as a boy growing up in Wales in the 1890s. Later, as a young man, he traveled through Syria and Palestine, learned Arabic, wore the flowing robes of the natives, and worked on archaeological digs. During World War I, Lawrence became involved in the fighting between camel-riding desert fighters and the Ottoman Turks. This short biography traces the life and times of one of modern history's most extraordinary personalities. Photographs.

Lofts, Norah. **Anne Boleyn.** Coward, McCann & Geoghegan, 1979. 192 pp.

When Anne Boleyn was only twenty, King Henry VIII of England demanded that she leave her loved ones and come to the court to become his second queen. Only three years later, in 1536, Anne was accused of adultery and beheaded. By using letters, diaries, and accounts of this sixteenth-century period, the author has reconstructed the story and spirit of Anne Boleyn, the second wife of Henry VIII and the mother of Elizabeth I.

McFarlane, Milton C. **Cudjoe of Jamaica: Pioneer for Black Freedom in the New World.** Enslow Publishers, 1977. 144 pp.

Prior to 1739, the British colony of Jamaica was a slave state. A small group of runaway slaves led by Cudjoe, a brilliant military planner and tribal leader, fought against the British and successfully avoided capture. Cudjoe's use of the art of camouflage and his knowledge of the hills and valleys of the island made his small rebellious army a constant problem for his enemies. Through his extensive use of guerrilla tactics, Cudjoe and his troops eventually forced the British to sign a treaty guaranteeing freedom from slavery on Jamaica.

Poole, Frederick King. **Mao Zedong.** Franklin Watts, 1982. 114 pp.

After 5,000 Chinese Communists were massacred by the authorities, the young Mao Zedong (until recently spelled *Mao Tse-tung* in English) led several hundred peasants into the mountains. There, like the heroes of the adventure stories he had read as a child, he became the leader of an ever-increasing band of outlaws. His revolution changed China forever. Find out how Mao Zedong transformed an economically backward country ruled by feuding warlords into a cohesive, modern nation that is a major power in the world today. The author discusses Mao's character and the motivations behind some of the most controversial policies of China's Communist Revolution.

Roll, Winifred. **Mary I: The History of an Unhappy Tudor Queen.** Prentice-Hall, 1980. 268 pp.

Mary I may be best known for trying to bring Protestant England back to the Roman Catholic Church during her brief reign as Queen of England from 1553 to 1558. She was the only daughter of Katharine of Aragon and Henry VIII, and she grew up in times of uncertainty and insecurity. She was known for her strong principles, religious faith, intelligence, and grace. However, she did earn the title of "Bloody Mary" as a sign of some of the harsh tactics she allowed in order to discourage Protestantism in her country. Photographs.

Rubenstein, Joshua. **Adolf Hitler.** Franklin Watts, 1982. 113 pp.

When Adolf Hitler was a young man in the first years of this century, he dreamed of being an artist. But by the time he was middle-aged, his idealism had turned into a bitter philosophy of hatred, racism, and genocide. The author shows how the boy grew into one of the most feared and despised men in history.

Sullivan, George. **Sadat: The Man Who Changed Mid-East History.** Walker & Co., 1981. 124 pp.

Anwar el-Sadat, president of Egypt, was assassinated in October 1981, after this biography was published. It is the story of the private man as well as the world statesman. Sadat was devoted to his family and his few close friends. But he was also concerned with changing the history of the Middle East with sometimes controversial plans. Photographs show Sadat throughout his life, and maps illustrate the course of Egypt's various wars with Israel.

Toland, John. **Adolf Hitler.** Ballantine Books, 1977. 1,371 pp.

This book is a highly detailed and revealing picture of the world's most infamous leader, Adolf Hitler (1889–1945). Hitler's early years, his family life, and his rise to power are all covered here. A great deal of discussion in the book concerns the workings of the Nazi party, Hitler's relationships with some of the top party officials he appointed, and his plans to become supreme ruler of the world. Photographs. Mature reading.

Topalian, Elyse. **V. I. Lenin.** Franklin Watts, 1983.

Russia's Lenin was an important world leader: he led the famous 1917 Bolshevik Revolution, formulated the official Communist doctrine, and became the first head of the Soviet state. His life is traced from his youth and development to his death on January 21, 1924. One million people made a pilgrimage to pay respects to his body when it lay in state, and the city of Petrograd was renamed Leningrad. For Russians, Lenin was a father figure whose politics and personal characteristics made him revered.

Webber, Andrew Lloyd, and Tim Rice. **Evita: The Legend of Eva Peron (1919-1952).** Avon Books, 1979.

A country girl born out of wedlock, Eva Peron became the second wife of dictator Juan Peron in 1945. She eventually grew to become the most powerful woman in the history of Latin America. Her exciting life inspired the Broadway musical *Evita,* upon which this book is based. Included in the book are photographs of Eva Peron, the story of her rise to power, and lyrics from the musical.

Westwood, Jennifer. **Stories of Charlemagne.** S. G. Phillips, 1976. 152 pp.

Charlemagne, king of the Franks and the Holy Roman Empire, was a powerful historical figure—to some, the greatest man of his time. He believed in civilization, scholarship, and Christianity. Many legends grew up around his name, and some were written down in the twelfth and thirteenth centuries. Four of the lesser-known tales are included in this book, along with two famous ones: "The Song of Roland" and "The Four Sons of Aymon."

Wilson, Pearl Cleveland. **The Living Socrates: The Man Who Dared to Question, as Plato Knew Him.** Illus. Joseph Sheppard. Stemmer House Publishers, 1975. 120 pp.

The Greek philosopher Socrates, who died in 399 B.C., is a well-known name to most people. Strangely enough, he never wrote down a word. His life and teachings have been recorded for us by Plato, who knew him as "the man who dared to question." A list of the people who were around Socrates is given, and many of the dialogues in the book are conversations between Socrates and these companions. Here are Socrates's opinions on love, knowledge, women, the writer's craft, death, courage, and war—topics that concern us even today.

Adventurers

Barron, John. **MiG Pilot: The Final Escape of Lt. Belenko.** Avon Books, 1981. 222 pp.

Lt. Viktor Belenko was a model Soviet soldier. He was a trusted and admired MiG-25 pilot. Time and money were being spent to train and educate him. Then one day, Lt. Belenko took one of the MiG-25 planes and headed for America and freedom. But to get there, he had to get around radar and Soviet fighter planes sent to shoot him down.

Beatty, Jerome, Jr. **From New Bedford to Siberia: A Yankee Whaleman in the Frozen North.** Illus. Eros Keith. Doubleday & Co., 1977. 144 pp.

When fifteen-year-old Daniel Hall left New Bedford on a whaling trip in 1856, he couldn't begin to imagine the adventures that lay ahead. He actually left his ship to find himself alone on the coast of Siberia, with winter coming. This story has been reconstructed from old newspaper accounts, documents, and Hall's own writings.

Frazier, Carla. **To the South Pole.** Illus. Dennis Manton. Raintree Publishers, 1979. 31 pp.

This is the true story of Norwegian explorer Roald Amundsen, who in 1911 was the first person to reach the South Pole. Many illustrations show how Amundsen and his team of explorers traveled by dog sleds and skis to accomplish this long and dangerous journey just thirty-five days before explorer Robert F. Scott arrived at the South Pole. Easy reading.

Gardner, Sandra. **Six Who Dared.** JeM Books, 1981. 62 pp.

This book features six people who could all be described as risk takers: Diana Nyad, Chuck Strange, Kitty O'Neil, Gunther Gebel-Williams, George Willig, and Maxie Anderson. Their accomplishments come in the areas of animal training, stunt work, circus performing, swimming, and flying. Photographs. Easy reading.

Gerson, Noel B. **Sad Swashbuckler: The Life of William Walker.** Thomas Nelson, 1976. 160 pp.

William Walker is a man almost forgotten by historians, yet during his lifetime he was a sensation. He was both respected and hated for his soldier-of-fortune activities. He set himself up as the president of the Central American country of Nicaragua, commanded many battles, and died before a firing squad in Honduras just before the beginning of the American Civil War. He was a strange man who led an unusual and exciting life during a lawless time in our history.

Goodnough, David. **Christopher Columbus.** Illus. Burt Dodson. Troll Associates, 1979. 32 pp.

Christopher Columbus had the dream of proving the earth was round by sailing west from Europe as far as he could. But to do so, he needed money, men, and ships. Queen Isabella of Spain was the only person who would listen to these requests—but her advisers wanted to talk her out of supporting Columbus. She did help, however, and soon Columbus was on a dangerous voyage to unknown regions. Easy reading.

Grierson, John. **I Remember Lindbergh.** Harcourt Brace Jovanovich, 1977. 192 pp.

This story of Charles Lindbergh's life is the story of aviation history. His early barnstorming years, his search for new flight routes, his work with plane and engine developments, and even his efforts at wildlife preservation are all covered in this book, written by a friend and fellow pilot. Lindbergh's most famous accomplishment, the solo flight across the Atlantic in 1927, is described in exciting detail.

Harley, Ruth. **Ferdinand Magellan.** Illus. Hal Frenck. Troll Associates, 1979. 48 pp.

The excitement, dangers, and troubles of Ferdinand Magellan's sea voyage around the world in the years 1519 to 1521 are discussed in this book. Magellan and his crew were the first to accomplish this feat, and their adventures, in a sense, completed what Columbus had begun with his trip across the Atlantic. Easy reading.

Harley, Ruth. **Henry Hudson.** Illus. William Ternay. Troll Associates, 1979. 48 pp.

Henry Hudson was an explorer of the early 1600s who was searching for the Northwest Passage to the Orient. While unsuccessful in reaching the Orient, Hudson entered Chesapeake Bay, Delaware Bay, and New York Bay and was the first white man to sail up the Hudson River. Later he discovered Hudson Bay and set up a trading and land development company. Easy reading.

Hodgman, Ann, and Rudy Djabbaroff. **Skystars: The History of Women in Aviation.** Atheneum Publishers, 1981. 186 pp.

Women fliers have played a role in the history of aviation from the early days to the present. Included in this book are famous and lesser-known women aviators, ranging from those who flew in balloons in the eighteenth century to those who were selected for the Space Shuttle program. Such pilots as Amelia Earhart, Ruth Nichols, Harriet Quimby, Jacqueline Cochran, and Jacqueline Auriol are featured. Photographs.

James, Naomi. **Alone around the World.** Coward, McCann & Geoghegan, 1979. 185 pp.

It is Naomi James' love for the ocean that lures her to the challenge of becoming the first woman to sail alone around the world. The 1977–1978 journey involved a range of experiences, problems, and joys. The radio went dead, leaks developed, errors in navigation occurred, weariness and loneliness at times consumed James. Yet the positive experiences far outnumbered the negative ones. James completed her round-the-world trip as the first solo woman sailor— and set a speed record for the journey.

Jones, Tristan. **The Incredible Voyage: A Personal Odyssey.** Avon Books, 1980. 390 pp.

Tristan Jones wanted to set a record that would not be broken until people found "water amongst the stars." So in the 1950s he set off on a six-year journey in which he would sail a small boat from the Dead Sea (the lowest body of water in the world) to Lake Titicaca (the highest body of water). Along the way, Tristan is thrown into jail, attacked by Arabs, nearly killed by a rat, saved by a crocodile, and starved down to ninety pounds. Mature language and situations.

Jones, Tristan. **Saga of a Wayward Sailor.** Avon Books, 1980. 256 pp.

After his record-breaking around-the-world voyage in the small boat *Cresswell* in the 1950s, Tristan Jones sets off seeking a new adventure. It will be a seven-year voyage that takes Jones from icy Arctic waters to the warm Mediterranean and the steamy Caribbean. Jones begins his trip by joining a drunken Dutch guard in hijacking a shipment of Edam cheese. Other highlights of his voyage include rescuing flood victims in France and following Columbus's path across the Atlantic. Mature language and situations.

Lisker, Tom. **First to the Top of the World: Admiral Peary at the North Pole.** Illus. Gloria Priam. Contemporary Perspectives, 1978. 48 pp.

Robert Peary's journey to the North Pole in 1908 to 1909 is traced in this book, along with his numerous exploratory trips to Greenland and the Arctic region in the late 1800s and early 1900s. His strong desire to be the first at the North Pole influenced most of Peary's adult life, and he made many sacrifices to reach his goal. Easy reading.

Milton, Joyce. **A Friend of China.** Hastings House Publishers, 1980. 120 pp.

How does a girl born in a two-room log farmhouse in Missouri in 1890 grow up to be one of a select group of outsiders to interview Mao Zedong, to travel with units of his guerrilla armies, and to write eyewitness reports of their hardships and dangers? Agnes Smedley was a foreign correspondent in China for ten years during the mid-1900s. She became a national heroine in China for being a person who fought for what she believed in, who saw the world in terms of good and evil, and who sacrificed her own comfort and safety to devote her life to fighting what she saw as injustice and inequality.

Morrison, Dorothy Nafus. **The Eagle and the Fort: The Story of John McLoughlin.** Atheneum Publishers, 1979. 178 pp.

John McLoughlin, the chief agent and administrator of the powerful Hudson's Bay Company from 1824 to 1846, did much to settle the Northwest. He had studied to be a doctor, but when he got into some trouble, he was forced to take a job that would take him away from Quebec. McLoughlin founded Fort Vancouver (now Vancouver, Washington), and it became his headquarters after 1825. He established good relations with the Indians in the region, paving the way for the farmers and settlers that followed. But all of this was done at considerable cost to his personal life and well-being.

Murray, Robert K., and Roger W. Brucker. **Trapped!** G. P. Putnam's Sons, 1979. 335 pp.

In 1925, an amateur cave explorer was caught in a cave-in. This, in itself, was nothing unusual, but the events that followed turned the rescue attempts into a circus of horror. Radio stations carried hourly bulletins and reports. Newspapers for weeks carried conflicting reports and even made up stories to make things more exciting. Here is the true story of how media coverage came to hamper and not help; in fact, it may have contributed to the death of Floyd Collins as the rescue workers came to do things to please the press rather than to follow proven techniques. In the years since, legend has severely distorted the true story. This is an attempt to reconstruct the truth.

Reynolds, Quentin. **The Wright Brothers: Pioneers of American Aviation.** Random House, 1978. 147 pp.

Wilbur and Orville Wright would never take no for an answer because their mother taught them to analyze problems and seek new solutions. They built a sled that went faster and a kite that flew higher. They also invented a newspaper-folding machine to save hours of boring work and put together their own bicycles and printing press. But their wildest dream was that humans could fly, and in 1903 they were the first to fly in a power-driven airplane. Easy reading.

Rosenblum, Richard. **Wings: The Early Years of Aviation.** Illus. by author. Four Winds Press, 1980. 63 pp.

This is an introduction to the many people who had a hand in making the dream of flying come true. Included are Leonardo da Vinci's attempt at making wings, the flights of the Wright brothers, Charles Lindbergh's transatlantic flight, the heroes of World War I (remember the Red Baron?), the "gypsy pilots" who landed in cow pastures, and barnstormers and stunt pilots. The book also discusses pilots' uniforms, insignias, air races and circuses, and air passenger service.

Roth, Arthur. **Great Spy Stories.** Scholastic Book Services, 1981. 122 pp.

These short biographies reveal the lives of Victor Sorge, Buster Crabb, Mata Hari, Gary Powers, Rudolph Abel, Oleg Penkovsky, Cicero, and Belle Boyd—all famous spies during wars and times of danger. Bravery, cunning, luck, and sometimes sheer accident figure into the accounts. Ingenious Belle Boyd, only 19, set up her own intelligence network right in a Confederate prison. She communicated with other prisoners by wrapping tiny notes around marbles and rolling them down the hallways behind the prison guards' backs. Easy reading.

Sakharov, Vladimir, and Umberto Tosi. **High Treason.** G. P. Putnam's Sons, 1980. 318 pp.

The life of Russian counterspy Vladimir Sakharov is detailed here. Sakharov worked as a spy for Stalin, but secretly handed information about the Soviet Union to the United States. In 1977, he escaped the USSR and came to America permanently. He is sought by the KGB—the Russian espionage bureau—to this day.

Scientists

Bernstein, Jeremy. **Experiencing Science.** Basic Books, 1978. 275 pp.

What is the experience of exploring science really like? What are the men and women who conduct these studies and experiments like? This series of biographical profiles reveals the difficulties, the hard work, and the excitement of discovery behind scientific endeavors. Scientists Arthur C. Clarke, Rosalind Franklin, and Johannes Kepler are among those profiled here.

Dank, Milton. **Albert Einstein.** Franklin Watts, 1983. 128 pp.

Nearly everyone knows the name of Albert Einstein, but few people know much about his life. Yet he changed the way people think about the world. In his early childhood there was no sign he would become a genius. He was slow to speak and to develop, and it is said that his parents feared he might be retarded. His genius showed itself in his development of the theory of relativity, published in 1905 when Einstein was twenty-six years old. His life, ideas, fears, and triumphs are all described in this book. Appendixes contain an explanation of the theory of relativity. Photographs.

Haber, Louis. **Women Pioneers of Science.** Harcourt Brace Jovanovich, 1979. 171 pp.

The twelve women in this collective biography represent the fields of industrial medicine, public health, nuclear physics, educational psychology, biochemistry, crystallography, and marine biology. The book points out how important women have always been in science—all the way back to Aspasia, a doctor in the Roman Empire who specialized in medicine for women. But some women had to pose as men and some had to hide their talents in order to do the work they wanted.

Manchester, Harland. **New Trail Blazers of Technology.** Charles Scribner's Sons, 1976. 214 pp.

Everyone seems to know all about great inventors like Thomas Edison and Alexander Graham Bell, but how many people are aware of brilliant scientists who create space-age devices? The author has chosen ten of the most important recent inventions and describes the creative genius of the men and women responsible for their development. Such modern devices as the Xerox copier, the transistor, the Polaroid camera, and the laser are examined in this book. Photographs.

McCoy, J. J. **The Cancer Lady: Maud Slye and Her Heredity Studies.**
Thomas Nelson, 1977. 184 pp.

For thirty years in the first half of the twentieth century, Maud Slye
studied cancer and cared for over 148,000 mice. She had little
money, no assistant, and many odds against her. But she was one of
the first to publish research results indicating that cancer suscepti-
bility was an inherited trait caused by a recessive gene. Her daily
work, her diagnostic tools, and her interactions with other scientists
are detailed in the book.

Morgan, Elizabeth. **The Making of a Woman Surgeon.** G. P. Putnam's
Sons, 1980. 368 pp.

Elizabeth Morgan chose what had often been thought of as a man's
field of work—medicine. Then she took another step and chose
surgery, normally considered the most masculine field of medicine.
She describes her life and her decision—as well as the path that
took her to her practice today. She tells about the humorous and
difficult situations she encountered and her many obstacles involving
both women and men in the field. For the most part, Morgan
appreciates the challenge she finds in medicine and in her particular
field, plastic surgery.

Patterson, Lillie. **Benjamin Banneker: Genius of Early America.** Illus.
David Scott Brown. Abingdon Press, 1978. 142 pp.

Benjamin Banneker, a black man with little formal education, was a
brilliant astronomer, biologist, surveyor, author, and musician
during America's Revolutionary War period. The amazing story
of Banneker's adventures begins with his being taught to read by
his grandmother, an Englishwoman who had come to the colonies
as an indentured servant. The story follows Banneker's achievements in publishing a popular almanac, constructing a clock made
entirely of wood, and saving the original surveyor's design of
Washington, D.C.

Ranahan, Demerris C. **Contributions of Women: Medicine.** Dillon Press,
1981. 118 pp.

Do you know who found the key that led to successful blue-baby
heart operations? Or who created the scoring system used to evaluate
the health of newborn babies? Or who headed an important study
of the safety of birth control pills? All are among the many women
doctors who have made outstanding contributions to the field of
medicine. You can read about five of them in this book: Helen
Taussig, Virginia Apgar, Savitri Ramcharan, Adele Hofmann, and
Olga Jonasson.

Athletes

Adler, Larry. **Man with a Mission: Pele.** Photographs by Bruce Curtis and Joe DiMaggio. Raintree Editions, 1976. 47 pp.

Probably the best known name in soccer is that of Pelé, born Edson Arantes do Nascimento. Pelé began playing soccer in 1945 at age five and became a professional soccer player at fifteen. By sixteen he was a nationally recognized star in his native Brazil and he led his team to world championships in 1958, 1962, and 1970. Pelé retired from Brazilian soccer but came to the United States to play soccer for the New York Cosmos. Easy reading.

Albrecht, Val. **Larger than Life: Joe Namath.** Photographs by Ron Koch and Bruce Curtis. Raintree Editions, 1976. 44 pp.

How does a small-town football player gain instant fame and a spot with the New York Jets? What makes him so great? Why do some people praise him while others scoff at him? There is a price to pay for this kind of achievement, and Joe Namath was willing to pay it. Pain, hard work, long hours, and the grind of being on the road constantly during the playing season have all been a part of Joe Namath's career. Easy reading.

Allen, Maury. **Ron Guidry: Louisiana Lightning.** Photographs by Louis Requena. Harvey House, Publishers, 1979. 71 pp.

Here is a look at the life of a professional baseball pitcher. When Ron Guidry played in the minor leagues, he almost quit baseball. But Guidry's luck changed and his skills improved—and in the 1970s he became a star player for the New York Yankees. Easy reading.

Barrett, Thomas, and Robert Morrissey, Jr. **Marathon Runners.** Julian Messner, 1981. 152 pp.

It takes a special kind of athlete to run more than twenty-six miles in a little over two hours. The runner must endure punishment and pain, as well as enjoy exhiliration. Yet each year, more and more men and women are competing in marathons around the world. Frank Shorter, Bill Rodgers, Walter Stack, and Jay Longacre are four of the best marathoners ever to wear out a pair of shoes. This book tells about the backgrounds of the men and provides the stories behind their great races. Photographs.

Bell, Marty. **The Legend of Dr. J.** Signet Books, 1981. 208 pp.

Julius Erving—or Dr. J.—has been called the most valuable basketball player in the history of the game. But even as a kid in junior high, he seemed headed for big things. Years later, in 1974 and 1976, Dr. J. led the New York Nets to two ABA championships. He then moved on to play exciting basketball for the Philadelphia 76ers. This is his story, told by a sportswriter who has known Dr. J. since high school.

Berger, Phil. **Where Are They Now? Yesterday's Sports Heroes Today.** Popular Library, 1978. 191 pp.

Roger Maris, the only man to hit sixty-one home runs in one season, is now a beer distributor. He and forty-nine other sports heroes tell their own stories, from their early days as rookies to what they are doing today. Other athletes included in this book are Bob Cousy, Elroy "Crazylegs" Hirsch, Jim Ryun, Dan Gurney, and Gale Sayers. Photographs.

Berkow, Ira. **The DuSable Panthers: The Greatest, Blackest, Saddest Team from the Meanest Street in Chicago.** Atheneum Publishers, 1978. 188 pp.

In 1954, the DuSable Panthers were the first all-black basketball team to play at a state high school championship in Illinois. The players were quick and played basketball with the rhythm and style of the famous Harlem Globetrotters. Besides their playing ability, the book discusses the players' characters, their backgrounds, and what happened to them later.

Brown, Fern G. **Racing against the Odds: Robyn C. Smith.** Photographs by Bruce Curtis. Raintree Editions, 1976. 47 pp.

Jockey Robyn Smith didn't enter her first stakes race to lose. But with that victory she won the honor of being the first woman rider ever to win a stakes race. What brought Smith to this point? At a height of 5 feet, 7 inches, she certainly doesn't fit most people's idea of a jockey, and she must work hard to maintain a weight of 105 pounds. Earlier in her life, Smith enrolled in Columbia Studio's acting workshop. The race track is a long way from a Hollywood life of glamour, but Smith is dedicated to her choice.

Brown, Paul (with Jack Clary). **PB: The Paul Brown Story.** Signet Books, 1981. 355 pp.

Paul Brown is a legendary football coach. He turned the Cleveland Browns into the game's all-time super-steamroller during his years as coach, 1946 to 1962, then he made football's greatest coaching comeback with the Cincinnati Bengals, whom he coached between

1968 and 1980. This book is about him and the men he led—Otto Graham, Jim Brown, Lou Groza, and others. It is also about the game he loves—football's explosion into Super Bowl splendor, the profit and the loss, and what it took and still takes to win. Paul Brown's story is the inside story of a great American sport.

Burchard, S. H. **Sports Star: Elvin Hayes.** Harcourt Brace Jovanovich, 1980. 63 pp.

In the 1960s, Elvin Hayes became a great basketball player because of his determination to play hard and intelligently. This book explains how Hayes overcame prejudice, hardships, and challenges to improve himself on and off the basketball court. Photographs.

Burchard, S. H. **Sports Star: George Brett.** Harcourt Brace Jovanovich, 1982. 63 pp.

The Kansas City Royals' third baseman is no average professional ballplayer. He began play in the major leagues in 1973, and a mere seven years later he was named the American League's Most Valuable Player. In between, he had batted over .300 every year but one. George Brett has also been in every American League All-Star starting lineup since 1976. Even after all of these honors, Brett remains excited and enthusiastic about every game he plays. Photographs. Easy reading.

Burchard, S. H. **Sports Star: Tracy Austin.** Harcourt Brace Jovanovich, 1982. 64 pp.

Born into a famous tennis-playing family, Tracy Austin soon became the most famous of them all. She began hitting balls on a court at age two. By age eight, she was winning junior tournaments. At fourteen, she was the youngest person ever to compete at the world's greatest tennis contest, Wimbledon. Two years later, in 1979, she won the United States Open for the first time. This book tells the exciting stories behind these highlights of a remarkable sports figure. Photographs. Easy reading.

Clary, Jack. **The Captains.** Atheneum Publishers, 1978. 178 pp.

Nine great athletes representing baseball, basketball, football, and hockey explain why they are leaders of sports teams. These men describe the great number of responsibilities and duties they must face to be successful at their jobs. And the work doesn't stop once games are over—these captains must look out for their team's welfare on and off the field. Featured are Sal Bando, Bobby Clarke,

Yvan Cournoyer, John Havlicek, Bob Johnson, George Kunz, Bob Lanier, Pete Rose, and Roger Staubach.

Dolan, Edward F., Jr., and Richard B. Lyttle. **Archie Griffin.** Doubleday & Co., 1977. 95 pp.

Archie Griffin was the first collegiate football player to receive the Heisman Trophy twice. In the 1970s Archie played college football at Ohio State University and later played professional football for the Cincinnati Bengals. The stories in this book describe both his moments of success as a football player and his moments of failure. There are also glimpses into Archie's family life and into the personal qualities that have contributed to his football career.

Dolan, Edward F., Jr., and Richard B. Lyttle. **Bobby Clarke.** Doubleday & Co., 1977. 94 pp.

Bobby Clarke has been a key player for the Philadelphia Flyers hockey team since 1969. Although best known for his all-around ability on the ice, Bobby has become one of the greatest centers in the history of the NHL and twice was voted the Most Valuable Player in the NHL. This story of Bobby Clarke begins in Manitoba, Canada, and it follows his development as a hockey player and as a person. Photographs.

Dolan, Edward F., Jr., and Richard B. Lyttle. **Dorothy Hamill: Olympic Skating Champion.** Doubleday & Co., 1979. 95 pp.

Young Dorothy Hamill felt tremendous pressure when she stepped out on the ice for the finals of the 1976 Olympics. Her parents had invested thousands of dollars in skating lessons, while her fans entrusted her with the pride of the United States. And Hamill had pushed herself to a point close to perfection with thousands of hours of practice. But it all seemed worthwhile when she won the gold medal for figure skating and then became a professional skater with the Ice Capades. Her story is one of discipline and sacrifice to achieve her goal—to become one of the greatest figure skaters in the world.

Dolan, Edward F., Jr., and Richard B. Lyttle. **Janet Guthrie: First Woman Driver at Indianapolis.** Doubleday & Co., 1978. 76 pp.

When you think of auto racing, images of roaring engines, gasoline fumes, and daring men come to mind. In the 1970s Janet Guthrie decided to break that last stereotype and prove auto racing doesn't have to be just a man's world. But Guthrie is not your average person, however. She earned a pilot's license, tried out to be an astronaut, and holds a degree in physics. She decided to become a race car driver, and she worked her way through minor races to eventually enter the Indy 500.

Dolan, Edward F., Jr., and Richard B. Lyttle. **Jimmy Young: Heavyweight Challenger.** Doubleday & Co., 1979. 83 pp.

Jimmy Young is a boxer, but he's no ordinary boxer: in 1976 he went fifteen rounds with Muhammad Ali. Young learned to box in the first place to survive against the street gangs in Philadelphia. This story traces Young's boyhood, his decision to turn professional, his training, and his bouts as a heavyweight challenger.

Dolan, Edward F., Jr., and Richard B. Lyttle. **Kyle Rote, Jr.: American-Born Soccer Star.** Doubleday & Co., 1979. 83 pp.

This book presents the life of Kyle Rote, Jr., son of the great football star. The younger Kyle Rote was the first American to win the Most Valuable Player Award in professional soccer during the 1970s. On the way to this award, however, Rote had many personal and professional struggles, though his marriage and his love of soccer kept him optimistic. Photographs.

Dolan, Edward F., Jr., and Richard B. Lyttle. **Scott May: Basketball Champion.** Doubleday & Co., 1978. 85 pp.

Scott May's basketball career from high school to playing for the Indiana Hoosiers is covered in this biography. A highlight of the book is its coverage of May's participation on the 1976 U.S. Olympic basketball team.

Drucker, Malka (with George Foster). **The George Foster Story.** Holiday House, 1979. 111 pp.

George Foster, one of only a few National League baseball players to hit fifty home runs in a single season, did not achieve his great success in professional baseball without some rough periods. Drafted by the San Francisco Giants, Foster was soon traded to the Cincinnati Reds where he slumped and was shipped to the minors. There followed a long period of self-doubt for Foster. Only after receiving guidance from his family and his pastor did he gain the self-confidence to persevere and succeed. George Foster, now in the prime of his career, is considered by many to be the finest all-around outfielder in baseball.

Drucker, Malka (with Tom Seaver). **Tom Seaver: Portrait of a Pitcher.**
Holiday House, 1978. 160 pp.

After thirteen seasons in the major leagues, Tom Seaver held three
Cy Young Awards and was the only pitcher to achieve 200 or more
strikeouts in nine consecutive seasons. As of 1978, he was tenth on
the all-time list of pitchers with the most strikeouts. This is the story
of a boy who, with great determination and concentration, grew
into one of the finest pitchers in the history of baseball.

Evans, Gwen. **Eastern Superstar: Olga Korbut.** Photographs by Heinz
Kluetmeier and Bruce Curtis. Raintree Editions, 1976. 47 pp.

Winning a gold medal in the 1972 Olympics and the applause of
millions has its price—a price paid in Olga Korbut's case by twelve
years of aching muscles, frequent bruises, strict dieting, and hard
practice. In addition, Olga Korbut knew she must perform stunts
no one had seen before to win against the world's best gymnasts.
There was another cost, too—that of being an ambassador of good
will for her country. This meant overcoming her weariness and the
daily pressures of travel. But fame and Olympic gold medals waited
for Olga Korbut along with the hardships.

Geline, Robert, and Priscilla Turner. **Forward: Rick Barry.** Photographs
by Heinz Kluetmeier, Bruce Curtis, and Martin Takigawa. Raintree
Editions, 1976. 47 pp.

Golden State Warrior Rick Barry has the right combination of
ingredients to make him a basketball star—the athletic skills (NBA
leading scorer in 1967), the drive to win, and a secure picture of himself as a person. But it takes more than one person to make a winning
team. And that's what this book is all about. In showing Barry's skills
in playing and living basketball, the book reveals a more general
picture of how people strive together to achieve common goals.

Gemme, Leila Boyle. **King on the Court: Billie Jean King.** Photographs
by Bruce Curtis. Raintree Editions, 1976. 47 pp.

From being a chubby, lonely teenager, Billie Jean Moffitt King
made it to the top in tennis, winning the Wimbledon tournament
six times between 1966 and 1975. But she did all this only by
making the decision to devote herself totally to her goal. Winning,
for King, is a way of life, for she believes that though victory may
be fleeting, "losing is forever." King has set herself even higher goals
to win, however, in fighting for women athletes to have an equal

place with men. How she achieves all these goals is the focus for this biography of a great athlete.

Gorman, Tom (as told to Jerome Holtzman). **Three and Two!** Charles Scribner's Sons, 1979. 216 pp.

Tom Gorman recently retired as a major league baseball umpire. In this book he talks about growing up in a rough New York neighborhood and about his career in baseball. His story involves such baseball heroes as Joe DiMaggio, Don Larsen, Sandy Koufax, and Hank Aaron. Gorman also includes interesting factual material about the techniques umpires use to call plays.

Greenfield, Jeff. **Tiny Giant: Nate Archibald.** Photographs by Heinz Kluetmeier and Bruce Curtis. Raintree Editions, 1976. 47 pp.

There are those who are born to be sports stars, and there are those who have to fight for that spotlight. No one would ever think that a short, skinny, young kid from a poor family and a dangerous neighborhood could make it in the competitive world of sports. But Nate Archibald did just that in a sport made for the tallest people in the world—basketball. And he became the NBA leading scorer in 1973. How he achieved sports success is revealed in this biography.

Hahn, James, and Lynn Hahn (editor Dr. Howard Schroeder). **Ali! The Sports Career of Muhammad Ali.** Crestwood House, 1981. 47 pp.

As a tough and determined young man, Muhammad Ali dreamed of becoming famous at something. He soon found boxing could be the way to attain his goals. This is the story of his rise to the top. Ali won an Olympic gold medal in 1960, then won the world heavyweight championship in 1964, 1974, and 1978. Easy reading.

Hahn, James, and Lynn Hahn (editor Dr. Howard Schroeder). **Brown! The Sports Career of James Brown.** Crestwood House, 1981. 47 pp.

Many people know Jim Brown now as an actor. But before becoming an actor, he was a football player—and he was one of the greatest. This book traces Brown's career in football, highlighting his college career at Syracuse University and his nine seasons playing for the Cleveland Browns between 1957 and 1965. Easy reading.

Hahn, James, and Lynn Hahn (editor Dr. Howard Schroeder). **Chris! The Sports Career of Chris Evert Lloyd.** Crestwood House, 1981. 47 pp.

Who was second only to Babe Didrikson Zaharias in a 1977 sports writers' poll to identify the greatest twentieth-century female athlete? It was Chris Evert Lloyd, the tennis star who won her first Wimbledon title in 1974 and her first U.S. Open in 1975. This is the story behind the headlines of one of the biggest names in tennis. Easy reading.

Hahn, James, and Lynn Hahn (editor Dr. Howard Schroeder). **Sayers! The Sports Career of Gale Sayers.** Crestwood House, 1981. 47 pp.

Here is the story of Gale Sayers, the great halfback who played football for the Chicago Bears between 1965 and 1971. At one time in his career Sayers held nine NFL records, an achievement that helped him earn a place in the Pro Football Hall of Fame. Easy reading.

Herda, D. J. **Free Spirit: Evonne Goolagong.** Photographs by Bruce Curtis, Melchior DiGiacomo, and Jo Anne Kalish. Raintree Editions, 1976. 47 pp.

Here's the story of an Australian woman who seemed to come out of nowhere to become one of the top-rated tennis players in the world. Evonne Goolagong won the title at Wimbledon in 1971 and was a finalist in the U.S. Open in 1973 to 1976. Her methods for winning at tennis differ from those of some other athletes. She relaxes before a match instead of worrying in a hotel room and getting tense; she tells herself she has a *chance* to win, rather than announcing to the world that she *will* win. Her theory about tennis and about life is to *care* about something, not *worry* about it.

Hollander, Phyllis. **100 Greatest Women in Sports.** Grosset & Dunlap, 1976. 142 pp.

Women from around the world participating in twenty different sports are represented in this collection of short biographies. Such stars as Dorothy Hamill, Olga Korbut, Billie Jean King, Suzy Chaffee, and Wilma Rudolph are included, along with dozens of other athletes. Photographs.

Hollander, Phyllis, and Zander Hollander, editors. **Winners under 21.** Random House, 1982. 136 pp.

This book profiles the lives of many sports personalities who became famous while under the age of twenty-one: Moses Malone, Muhammad Ali, Robin Yount, Tracy Austin, Johnny Weissmuller, Wayne Gretzky, Bob Mathias, Steve Cauthen, Al Kaline, and Eric and Beth Heiden. These sports stars share their struggles and their triumphs as they tell their own stories. Photographs.

Hunter, Jim (as told to Marshall Shelley). **A Man against the Mountain.** David C. Cook Publishing Co., 1978. 191 pp.

This is the story of Jim Hunter, the Canadian National Alpine Champion and downhill racer. Hunter describes his early youth, especially the training program designed by his father. As a Christian, Hunter believed that God wanted him to win. But after several races, Hunter was still not a top winner. Then an accident caused him to miss part of a season, and it seemed for a moment as if he might be mistaken in his beliefs. Eventually, however, Hunter's faith and determination pull him back into competition and on to victory.

Ilowite, Sheldon A. **On the Wing: Rod Gilbert.** Photographs by Bruce Curtis and Joe DiMaggio. Raintree Editions, 1976. 47 pp.

Most people would agree that Rod Gilbert is one of hockey's top forwards of the last twenty years, even though his team hasn't had many wins. But what drives this man to play in spite of dangers, injuries, pain, and cruel remarks from critics? What happened in his career to make him a standout among top players? What are the ingredients that combine to form this superstar? This biography answers these questions about an athlete who believes that if you have a love for your profession, you can endure almost any painful test.

Kupper, Mike. **Driven to Win: A. J. Foyt.** Photographs by Heinz Kluet-meier, Lewis Franck, Richard Weening, Vernon J. Biever, and Joe DiMaggio. Raintree Editions, 1975. 47 pp.

He's tough, he's from Texas, and he's known as the best and the most versatile of automobile racers. A. J. Foyt, some say, was "born to squeeze into the cockpit of a race car and try to make it go fast." He was taken to races when he was a baby, and he had his own scaled-down midget car that could do fifty miles an hour when he was only five years old. And that's how it all started. Foyt has fought every step of the way to the top in this dangerous and exciting sport.

Lee, S. C. **Young Bear: The Legend of Bear Bryant's Boyhood.** Strode Publishers, 1978. 135 pp.

How does an Arkansas farm boy who doesn't know the difference between a watermelon and a football grow up to become a legendary college football coach? Maybe from watching his mother stand up for her rights in their town. Maybe from the quiet guidance and strength of his invalid father. Maybe from the fight he had with the bear that gave him his nickname. This book concentrates on the childhood of the late Bear Bryant and shows how these events helped build the determination and enthusiasm he later put into his longtime coaching career at the University of Alabama. Bryant turned down offers to coach professional teams and remained at Alabama until shortly before his death in 1982.

Litsky, Frank. **Winners in Gymnastics.** Camelot Books, 1979. 48 pp.

Seven famous international gymnasts are discussed in this book: Nadia Comaneci, Olga Korbut, Nelli Kim, Cathy Rigby Mason, Nikolai Andrianov, Mitsuo Tsukahara, and Bart Conner. Their backgrounds and the qualities that make them great are explained. Photographs. Easy reading.

Milverstedt, F. M. **In This Corner: Muhammad Ali.** Photographs by Sonia Katchian and Heinz Kluetmeier. Raintree Editions, 1976. 47 pp.

Muhammad Ali, the only heavyweight to win the championship three times (1964, 1974, and 1978), was the most colorful and perhaps the most skilled boxer the world has ever known. Growing up as Cassius Clay, a loudmouthed young fighter from Louisville, he kept his great talents hidden. This book traces Ali's rise to the top, both as a boxer and as a world figure. Photographs. Easy reading.

Milverstedt, F. M. **The Quiet Legend: Henry Aaron.** Photographs by Heinz Kluetmeier. Raintree Editions, 1975. 47 pp.

Henry Aaron took a challenge and won. He displaced the great Babe Ruth as the baseball hitter with the greatest number of career home runs—755. Being a black player in a predominately white man's game made the challenge and the victory even greater. He not only became a record setter, but he went beyond that to become a legend in baseball. This is the story of how a young man developed the dedication and the discipline to attain great things during his baseball career of 1954 to 1976.

Ogan, Margaret, and George Ogan. **Smashing: Jimmy Connors.** Photographs by Melchior DiGiacomo and Bruce Curtis. Raintree Editions, 1976. 45 pp.

Tennis demands physical, mental, and emotional control from its top players. This is the story of one champion—Jimmy Connors. Connors won the title at Wimbledon in 1974 and 1982 and the U.S. Open in 1974, 1976, and 1978. He remains a top competitor today.

Olney, Ross R. **Modern Drag Racing Superstars.** Dodd, Mead & Co., 1981. 111 pp.

Have you wondered what it's like to speed against other race cars in an attempt to be the first driver to reach the end of the racetrack? Six of the biggest superstars of drag racing talk about their sport: Tom "Mongoose" McEwen, Don "Snake" Prudhomme, Shirley Muldowney (the only woman world champion), Gary Beck, Bob Glidden, and Don "Big Daddy" Garlits. A discussion of the career of each superstar is included, along with photographs of them and their performances.

Phillips, Carolyn E. **Michelle.** Signet Books, 1982. 147 pp.

The doctors gave eight-year-old Michelle Price only a 4 percent chance to survive—even after her cancerous leg was amputated. But Michelle had the courage and faith to refuse to give up. Today Michelle is an accomplished horseback rider and has won gold medals in the National Handicapped Skiing Championships. This is the true story of a girl who became a victor, in sports and in life.

Rubin, Robert. **Lou Gehrig: Courageous Star.** G. P. Putnam's Sons, 1979. 160 pp.

Lou Gehrig was a baseball star for the New York Yankees during the 1920s and 1930s. Playing with such other greats as Babe Ruth and Joe DiMaggio, Lou Gehrig set a record for playing in the most consecutive games: 2,130. For his great stamina and courage, Lou Gehrig was called the "Iron Horse." Then Gehrig was struck with a mysterious disease that cut his career short. This is the exciting and dramatic story of one of America's true baseball heroes. Easy reading.

Rudolph, Wilma. **Wilma.** Signet Books, 1977. 172 pp.

Wilma Rudolph is the twentieth of twenty-two children. At six, her leg was in a brace due to a series of childhood illnesses. At sixteen, she ran in the Olympics and won a bronze medal. At eighteen, she became a mother, and her athletic career seemed to be over. At twenty, she ran in the 1960 Olympics and made sports history by winning three gold medals. Rudolph tells her own story of how a black woman athlete can win both in sports and in life.

Schoor, Gene. **Babe Didrikson: The World's Greatest Woman Athlete.** Doubleday & Co., 1978. 185 pp.

Mildred "Babe" Didrikson Zaharias (1913–1956) has been given the title of "world's greatest woman athlete," and with good reason.

Not only did she excel in basketball, where she started, but also in track and field events (winning two gold medals and one silver in the 1932 Olympics) and later in golf (winning the Women's U.S. Open in 1954, just one year after a cancer operation). Her list of accomplishments is truly amazing, as was her courageous fight against cancer.

Schoor, Gene. **Bart Starr: A Biography.** Doubleday & Co., 1977. 211 pp.

Bart Starr became famous as a quarterback for the Green Bay Packers in the years 1956 to 1971. Starr was small as a young boy and didn't look like a potential star football player. But he was determined. After playing football for the University of Alabama's Crimson Tide, Starr was drafted last by Green Bay. No one expected him to stay with the club, so Starr had to gain new confidence in himself as a player. Part of this story details just how he gained the confidence and skills required to be a top football player. Bart Starr also explains his formula for success in life and football.

Schoor, Gene. **Joe DiMaggio: A Biography.** Doubleday & Co., 1980. 207 pp.

This biography of Joe DiMaggio, one of America's most famous baseball stars, begins by discussing his youth in San Francisco and his first years playing minor league baseball. He quickly became a great player and helped his major league team, the New York Yankees, win many league pennants. He was a hard hitter and in 1941 set a record for hitting in fifty-six consecutive games. This, in part, accounts for DiMaggio's nicknames: "Joltin' Joe" and "the Yankee Clipper."

Smith, Beatrice S. **The Babe: Mildred Didrikson Zaharias.** Raintree Editions, 1976. 48 pp.

The Associated Press named her "greatest female athlete of the first half of the twentieth century." That is a long way to come after being so small as a child that everyone called her "Babe." But by the sixth grade, Mildred Didrikson had everyone excited over the way she could hit a baseball, or play well in any sport anyone named— basketball, tennis, golf, running, jumping, swimming, bowling. Later she won three medals in the 1932 Olympics and won the Women's U.S. Open golf championship in 1954, just two years before her death. It may be the fact that her mother had been a superb ice skater in Norway and that her father believed so much in physical fitness that he built a family gymnasium that accounts for the direction Babe's life took. Whatever the reason, the story of this amazing athlete is the story of hard work and victory.

Sorensen, Robert. **Shadow of the Past: True Life Sports Stories.** Bluejeans
Books, 1978. 95 pp.

Thoughts of a troubled past both challenge and worry seven famous
athletes. Olympic runner Wilma Rudolph had to overcome a de-
formed left foot; while football star Rocky Bleier was hit by shrapnel
that paralyzed him. For young gymnast Nadia Comaneci, it is the
shadows of former gymnast stars that must be overcome. Hank
Aaron, too, found he lived with the memory of the great Babe Ruth
and his batting record. And past fears and pains haunt Olympic
diving star Micki King. But all these athletes decide to put up a
fight and free themselves from the past. Photographs.

Staubach, Roger (with Frank Luksa). **Time Enough to Win.** Warner
Books, 1981. 315 pp.

In a 1980 Gallup Poll, Dallas Cowboy player Roger Staubach was
the favorite sports personality among boys and girls ages 13 to 18.
As a professional quarterback in the NFL, Staubach ranked at the
top of the list of all-time passers. In this book, he tells about his
background, his training, the people he has known and played
against, and many of his best moments in football. He also explains
his decision to retire from football and his plans for the future.
Photographs.

Sullivan, George. **On the Run: Franco Harris.** Photographs by Kevin
Fitzgerald, Heinz Kluetmeier, and George Sullivan. Raintree Editions, 1976. 47 pp.

Franco Harris's mother didn't take being a parent lightly. She had
tough rules and she saw that they were obeyed. And the big games
in the Harris neighborhood were games that involved running.
Maybe these were two of the things that turned young Franco's life
toward his career as a great running back for the Pittsburgh Steelers
during the 1970s. Few in the sports world have enjoyed greater
admiration and support from the fans than Harris. This book tells
why he has earned that support, and how it has affected his career
and his life.

Sullivan, George. **Superstars of Women's Track.** Dodd, Mead & Co.,
1981. 130 pp.

The achievements of women in track and field events have been
outstanding in the last decade. This book profiles six of the most
noted women runners in the world: miler Mary Decker, sprinter
Evelyn Ashford, Norwegian cross-country and marathon runner
Grete Waitz, Olympic gold medalist Madeline Manning, hurdler
Candy Young, and 5,000-meter star Julie Shea. Photographs.

Talbert, Peter. **Tracy Austin: Tennis Wonder.** Photographs by Bruce Curtis. G. P. Putnam's Sons, 1979. 47 pp.

Tracy Austin was a cover girl at age four. The caption beneath her photo said that she had been playing tennis for two years. Surrounded by a family of parents, sisters, and brothers who all excelled in tennis, young Tracy saw tennis as a way of life. Her mother says they never told Tracy to play; instead, it was Tracy who begged to play. At age fifteen she was beating the top women players, and in 1981, at age nineteen, she won the U.S. Open tennis title.

Tatum, Jack (with Bill Kushner). **They Call Me Assassin.** Avon Books, 1980. 193 pp.

Jack Tatum, the free safety for the Oakland Raiders until the early 1980s, discusses the dark and violent side of football. But he defends his brutal tackling style as all part of doing his job. Tatum believes a good hit is when the victim wakes up on the sidelines with the sound of a train whistle blowing in his head.

Thacher, Alida. **In the Center: Kareem Abdul-Jabbar.** Photographs by Bruce Curtis and Ron Koch. Raintree Editions, 1976. 47 pp.

How would you like to be center for your basketball team and go up against someone who was 7 feet, 2 inches tall? To live inside that frame all day, every day, can prove even more of a challenge than to face it on a court. This book traces the career of Kareem Abdul-Jabbar and discusses some of the obstacles and advantages of being the tallest man in basketball. Abdul-Jabbar played for the Milwaukee Bucks and the Los Angeles Lakers, and was named the Most Valuable Player six times between 1971 and 1980.

Thacher, Alida M. **Raising a Racket: Rosie Casals.** Photographs by Bruce Curtis and Melchior DiGiacomo. Raintree Editions, 1976. 47 pp.

One of the brightest and most outspoken women tennis players of the 1970s was Rosie Casals. She was a real crowd pleaser, not only with her flashy tennis skills but also with her outgoing personality. This book tells of her early upbringing by an aunt and uncle and traces her career through problems and successes. Color photographs accompany the text. Easy reading.

Twyman, Gib. **Born to Hit: The George Brett Story.** Random House, 1982. 131 pp.

As a young baseball player, George Brett has everything going for him: great athletic ability, an easygoing temper, and the drive to succeed. But in his first season with the Kansas City Royals he is batting only .205. Can coach Charley Lau turn Brett around and help him make it in the majors? Follow Brett as he struggles to improve his batting average and eventually becomes Most Valuable Player of 1980.

Artists

Boston, L. M. **Perverse and Foolish: A Memoir of Childhood and Youth.** McElderry Books, 1979. 140 pp.

Lucy Boston, a distinguished writer and poet, looks back from her eighty-fifth year to remember her childhood in the early 1900s in a strict English household. She sees all her experiences, including a period as a nurse during World War I, contributing to her writing by providing the raw material and emotional background.

Brown, E. K. (completed by Leon Edel). **Willa Cather: A Critical Biography.** Avon Books, 1980. 276 pp.

Willa Cather's novels, originally published between 1913 and 1935, are still read widely and are studied in high schools and universities around the world. This biography reveals her fascination with Nebraska and the Southwest and discusses her attitudes toward religion, the world, and her work as managing editor of a magazine. Perhaps what is most clearly revealed about Cather, though, is her strong belief in the importance of the past—a belief that is reflected in novels like *My Antonia, O Pioneers,* and *Death Comes for the Archbishop.*

Carpenter, Humphrey. **Tolkien: A Biography.** Ballantine Books, 1977. 327 pp.

The strange world of hobbits and Middle-earth are explained through this complete biography of J.R.R. Tolkien (1892–1973). The reader is guided through Tolkien's early years of education and into the mind of the creative genius who gave birth to *The Hobbit, The Lord of the Rings,* and *The Silmarillion.* Photographs.

Christie, Agatha. **Agatha Christie: An Autobiography.** Ballantine Books, 1977. 656 pp.

Agatha Christie, one of the most famous mystery writers, reveals here another side of her charm and wit through anecdotes and reminiscences. Although she had no ideas about becoming a writer in her childhood in England in the early 1900s, she wrote over sixty novels and one hundred short stories before she died in 1976. Photographs.

Chute, Marchette. **An Introduction to Shakespeare.** E. P. Dutton, 1951. 123 pp.

What did William Shakespeare do in his spare time? How did he get started writing plays? These questions, and many more, are answered in detail in this book. Insights into Shakespeare's daily life in the sixteenth century, specific comments on characters in his plays, and descriptions of the busy theater life of Elizabethan England are also provided.

Clarke, Arthur C. **The View from Serendip.** Del Rey Books, 1978. 247 pp.

Arthur C. Clarke's autobiographical reminiscences are full of his characteristic wit and wisdom. But besides himself, Clarke writes about such other science fiction greats as Ray Bradbury and Isaac Asimov. Comments on trends in science fiction and science fact are also an important part of the memoirs of the man who wrote *2001*.

Davenport, Marcia. **Mozart.** Avon Books, 1979. 380 pp.

When Wolfgang Amadeus Mozart was born during the bitterest of winter days in 1756, his parents were afraid he wouldn't survive. But he did, much to the gratitude of centuries of music lovers. Mozart's boyhood home was warm, happy, and filled with music. When his orchestra-director father began teaching three-year-old Mozart's sister Marianne to play, the little boy would imitate the chords he had heard when the lesson was done. By age four, Wolfgang himself began receiving instructions. From that day forward, Mozart felt his career was settled. He went on to compose countless symphonies, concertos, chamber works, and operas like *The Magic Flute*, *Don Giovanni*, *The Marriage of Figaro*, and *Così fan tutti*.

Davenport, Marcia. **Too Strong for Fantasy.** Discus Books, 1979. 470 pp.

Contemporary writer Marcia Davenport includes many well-known figures in her autobiography, saying that the book might be uninteresting if she remained the central character. Of herself, Davenport begins by saying that she was born in June, a Gemini, and that this may explain the multiple personalities she feels she has. Born in New York, she loves the countryside of both Vermont and Italy. But her restlessness won't allow her to live anywhere longer than six months, and she always finds herself returning to New York to work. Mature language and situations.

Duncan, Lois. **Chapters: My Growth as a Writer.** Little, Brown & Co., 1982. 263 pp.

Lois Duncan, author of many contemporary novels, stories, and articles, answers questions about how a writer begins and comes up with ideas. She begins with her life from age thirteen and traces her successes and failures as a writer from that point. Duncan stresses that a writer needs many and varied personal experiences to influence and develop his or her work, and she talks about her own experiences, both good and bad, as proof of this. Included in *Your Reading* are four of her novels: *Daughters of Eve, Killing Mr. Griffin, Summer of Fear,* and *They Never Came Home.* (ALA Best Book for Young Adults)

Forrester, Helen. **Minerva's Stepchild.** Beaufort Books, 1981. 300 pp.

Helen was lucky—she was the oldest child of a wealthy English family and was pampered by parents and servants alike. But then came the Great Depression, and her family was plunged into poverty overnight. The worst part was that her sick and frantic parents expected Helen to be the housekeeper for the rest of the family, to grow up uneducated and unskilled, to be the old-maid sister who sacrificed for everyone else. Here, in her autobiography, writer Helen Forrester tells how she rebelled against this way of thinking and won a life of her own.

Gaeddert, LouAnn. **A New England Love Story: Nathaniel Hawthorne and Sophia Peabody.** Dial Press, 1980. 150 pp.

Nathaniel Hawthorne, a recluse, and Sophia Peabody, a semi-invalid, fell in love and transformed each other's life. With her encouragement and faith, he attempted to make something of his writing, and with his love and care, she slowly battled her way out of illness. The author bases her story of this nineteenth-century couple on their letters and journals.

Gerson, Noel B. **Harriet Beecher Stowe.** Popular Library, 1976. 255 pp.

Prior to the Civil War, it was unthinkable for a woman to speak out about slavery and other social ills, but that did not stop Harriet Beecher Stowe from writing *Uncle Tom's Cabin* and other books. Through her tireless crusades for human rights and dignity, Stowe earned the respect and admiration of the world's great leaders.

Goodman, Saul. **Baryshnikov: A Most Spectacular Dancer.** Harvey House, Publishers, 1979. 71 pp.

He left his home not knowing whether he would ever be allowed to return. By 1974, when he was only twenty-six years old, he was recognized as one of the greatest dancers of all time. He appeared in a motion picture for the first time and was nominated for an Academy Award. He dances before millions of people each year on television and in live performances. He is known wherever he goes. He is Mikhail Baryshnikov, one of the most incredible dancers in our time. This is the story of his personal and professional life.

Graffman, Gary. **I Really Should Be Practicing.** Avon Books, 1982. 344 pp.

What is it like to be a concert pianist? Gary Graffman recalls his boyhood in New York, his teachers, his friends, and his pianos. He remembers the musical giants Toscanini and Rachmaninoff, and looks back on friendships with Van Cliburn, Vladimir Horowitz, and Eugene Ormandy. This is a memoir of the extraordinary, unexpected, and hilarious events in his thirty years of concert tours.

Hancock, Carla. **Seven Founders of American Literature.** Illus. Ted Trinkaus. John F. Blair, Publisher, 1976. 207 pp.

Seven nineteenth-century writers, all with different characters and experiences, created literature that was distinctly American: Washington Irving, James Fenimore Cooper, Edgar Allan Poe, Herman Melville, Walt Whitman, William Cullen Bryant, and Samuel Clemens, who wrote under the name of Mark Twain. This book provides a biographical sketch of each writer.

Harris, Janet. **The Woman Who Created Frankenstein: A Portrait of Mary Shelley.** Harper & Row, Publishers, 1979. 210 pp.

Mary Wollstonecraft Shelley is best known as the creator of *Frankenstein*. She wrote the novel of terror as part of a contest with her husband, the famous Romantic poet Percy Bysshe Shelley, and with two other male writers—to see who could write the best horror story. In her original novel, Shelley named the doctor Victor Frankenstein; his creation, the Monster, was supposed to be a beautiful, perfect person. This book traces Mary Shelley's life—from her birth in 1797 as the daughter of the English author and feminist Mary Wollstonecraft, to her death in 1851. Mature situations.

Haskins, Jim. **James Van DerZee: The Picture-Takin' Man.** Photographs by James Van DerZee. Dodd, Mead & Co., 1979. 256 pp.

Through the pictures taken by black photographer Van DerZee, discovered in 1967 by the art community, Americans have learned about another Harlem, one that was not a slum, but a place of comfort, beauty, and pride. Van DerZee opened his first studio in Harlem in 1909, and during the next sixty years he recorded thousands of images of daily life in Harlem.

Henry, Marguerite. **The Illustrated Marguerite Henry.** Illus. Wesley Dennis, Robert Lougheed, Lynd Ward, and Rich Rudish. Rand McNally & Co., 1980. 128 pp.

A popular writer of many stories about horses and other animals, Marguerite Henry takes time to pay tribute to the four artists who have illustrated her books, including one who originally came to her attention as the young author of a glowing fan letter. She reveals answers to questions most people ask about how a writer and an illustrator work together to make a book. She also includes many of the illustrations discussed in this book.

Hlibok, Bruče. **Silent Dancer.** Photographs by Liz Glasgow. Julian Messner, 1981. 64 pp.

This book describes the experiences of a ten-year-old deaf girl studying ballet at the Joffrey Ballet School. Nancy tells the story from her point of view—from the alarm clock in the morning that awakens her early with a flashing light, through the difficult practice sessions, to the change of clothes in a dressing room at the end of a day. Easy reading.

Holme, Bryan. **The Kate Greenaway Book.** Viking Press, 1976. 140 pp.

Part biography and part anthology, this book recounts the life story of Kate Greenaway—a writer, illustrator, and editor of children's verses and stories during the second half of the nineteenth century. Also included in the book are many samples of the pictures, songs, rhymes, and sketches that have made Greenaway famous in her field.

Hürlimann, Bettina (translator Anthea Bell). **Seven Houses: My Life with Books.** Thomas Y. Crowell Co., 1977. 262 pp.

Bettina Hürlimann, an internationally acclaimed editor and author of books for children, recalls her fascinating life in phases that correspond to different houses. She begins with artists and intellectuals at her parents' home in Germany in the early part of this century and concludes with the grandchildren in her current home. Hürlimann details her love of children's books and her appreciation of those children's authors and illustrators she has come to know around the world.

Katz, Jane B., editor. **This Song Remembers: Self-Portraits of Native Americans in the Arts.** Houghton Mifflin Co., 1980. 202 pp.

How are artists—performing artists, visual artists, literary artists—alike? And how are modern native American artists like those of other nationalities? How are they different? This book contains interviews with an influential group of American artists to discover some answers to these questions. Each artist has inherited a strong cultural tradition, but adds to it a style of his or her own. They come from all sections of the country: the Navajo sculptor and painter R. C. Gorman from the Southwest, Tlingit dancer Cecilia White from the Northwest, pipe-carver Amos Owen from the Plains, and many more.

Kilby, Clyde S. **Tolkien and *The Silmarillion*.** Harold Shaw Publishers, 1977. 90 pp.

In words and pictures, this book provides biographical images of the life and work of J.R.R. Tolkien, the author of such works of fantasy as *The Hobbit*, *The Lord of the Rings*, and *The Silmarillion*. This work also talks of Tolkien's relationship with friends and fellow writers like C. S. Lewis and Charles Williams.

Lambert, Gavin. **The Dangerous Edge.** Grossman Publishers, 1976. 271 pp.

How their personal lives influenced nine mystery writers and filmmakers is the subject of this group biography. The writers/filmmakers included are: Wilkie Collins, Sir Arthur Conan Doyle, G. K. Chesterton, John Buchan, Graham Greene, Eric Ambler, George Simenon, Raymond Chandler, and the "Master of Suspense," Alfred Hitchcock.

Lisca, Peter. **John Steinbeck: Nature and Myth.** Thomas Y. Crowell Co., 1978. 245 pp.

John Steinbeck received the Nobel Prize for literature in 1962 and is recognized all over the world as an important novelist. This book discusses all of Steinbeck's major novels and short stories and points out how Steinbeck used nature, legend, and myth as important parts of his fiction. Among the works covered are: *The Grapes of Wrath, Of Mice and Men, The Red Pony, The Pearl,* and *East of Eden.* Photographs.

O'Connor, Flannery (editor Sally Fitzgerald). **The Habit of Being.** Vintage Books, 1980. 596 pp.

This collection of letters by a well-known and celebrated short story writer, Flannery O'Connor, reveals much about the author, whose stories were written in the 1950s and 1960s. Her observations of the small farm she was confined to for the last ten years of her life due to illness, her feelings about her own writings, her comments about her strong Catholic faith, and the humor for which she was noted are all found in her letters.

Pohl, Frederik. **The Way the Future Was: A Memoir.** Del Rey Books, 1979. 293 pp.

Frederik Pohl, the award-winning author, recalls his experiences in the world of science fiction. Fans of this kind of writing will be interested in what Pohl has to reveal about the details of the publishing business, and about his often amusing fellow science fiction writers. The author traces his involvement with science fiction—from the early years of writing "space opera" for pulp magazines to his most recent successes. Photographs.

Rudström, Lennart. **A Family.** Illus. Carl Larsson. G. P. Putnam's Sons, 1980. 32 pp.

Swedish artist Carl Larsson (1853–1919) lived, taught, and painted in several countries. Here was a man who always knew what his career would be. Yet he decided he needed to find a way to combine painting and making a living with raising his children. He finally found that way—by using his family as the subject of his works.

Schulz, Charles M. (with R. Smith Kiliper). **Charlie Brown, Snoopy and Me: And All the Other Peanuts Characters.** Doubleday & Co., 1980. 126 pp.

Charles Schulz talks about his cartoons and gives advice to young people who want to do this kind of creative work. His ideas on inspiration, work habits, and jobs are interesting and often humorous. The creator of Charlie Brown, Snoopy, and the other members of the "Peanuts" gang also talks about his characters, his inspirations, and his own development as a cartoon artist. Illustrations from his comic strips are used to explain Schulz's discussions about his creative growth.

Scott, John Anthony. **Woman against Slavery: The Story of Harriet Beecher Stowe.** Thomas Y. Crowell Co., 1978. 169 pp.

When *Uncle Tom's Cabin* was published in 1852, it was as if a torch had been put to a smoldering national issue. For the first time, millions of Americans were made conscious of the human suffering of slaves. But who was the woman behind the book? Harriet Beecher Stowe's rigidly Christian girlhood instilled in her a lifelong commitment to social justice. As a wife and mother trying to cope with overwhelming domestic responsibilities, she began to write. Her compulsion to speak out could not be suppressed in deference to husband, children, and the demands that poverty made on her time. This book shows how a nineteenth-century woman struggled to discover herself through her own powers.

Sive, Helen R. **Music's Connecticut Yankee: An Introduction to the Life and Music of Charles Ives.** Atheneum Publishers, 1977. 141 pp.

The music of American composer Charles Ives (1874–1954) is considered to be some of the first truly American music because Ives did not imitate the music of European composers. Instead, he experimented with traditional American tunes like hymns, folk songs, and military marches. You never know when you will hear a bit of "The Stars and Stripes Forever," "My Old Kentucky Home," or even "The Star-Spangled Banner" in one of Ives's compositions.

Tudor, Bethany. **Drawn from New England: Tasha Tudor.** William Collins Publishers, 1979. 96 pp.

An artist and writer with over sixty books to her credit, Tasha Tudor is best known for her illustrations of rural New England scenes. Her daughter Bethany shares vivid scenes from Tasha's life—her childhood, her artistically creative teen years, her raising of four children, and her love of the simple country-dweller way of life in a house without running water or central heating. Included are family photographs and some of Tasha's drawings.

Yates, Elizabeth. **My Diary—My World.** Westminster Press, 1981. 187 pp.

What is a well-known writer like in her childhood years? What does it feel like to be a teenager during World War I? Why would wealthy parents make their daughter wait on tables? This is the story of a woman who wanted to be a writer more than anything else. But Elizabeth Yates's diary entries also create a general picture of life in America between 1917 and 1925.

Yeo, Wilma, and Helen K. Cook. **Maverick with a Paintbrush: Thomas Hart Benton.** Doubleday & Co., 1977. 125 pp.

When he was a young boy growing up in Missouri in the late 1800s, Thomas Hart Benton enjoyed making charcoal paintings on his mother's wallpaper. Of course he got into trouble, but he kept on drawing. Over the years, Benton has become one of America's most popular, yet most controversial, painters. He is best known for paintings of people in realistic American scenes such as factories, bars, churches, and city streets. He is also noted for his murals and other large wall paintings. This book reveals Benton's thoughts about art and what happened to him as a result of his art. A color photograph section reproduces some of Benton's most famous paintings.

Entertainers

Berman, Connie. **Diana Ross: Supreme Lady.** Popular Library, 1978. 174 pp.

Diana Ross grew up in a Detroit ghetto, determined to make something of herself. Here is the story of how determination, hard work, and talent made Ross a star first as a member of the Supremes, then as an actress in such films as *Lady Sings the Blues* and *The Wiz*. This is also the story of her disappointments and loneliness. Behind her all the time, though, were her family and friends.

Bonderoff, Jason. **Alan Alda: An Unauthorized Biography.** Signet Books, 1982. 246 pp.

Who is the man behind *M*A*S*H*'s Hawkeye Pierce? This is Alan Alda's story, from childhood to the present. It tells of Alda's crippling illness as a child, of his relationship with his movie star father, of his early failures as an actor, and of his eventual successes in film and on television.

Burns, George. **The Third Time Around.** G. P. Putnam's Sons, 1980. 220 pp.

He broke into show business at age twelve as a singer, dancer, yodeling juggler, and roller skater accompanied by a seal. Some seventy years later he is still an active entertainer, playing such film roles as a master bank robber, a washed-up vaudevillian, and even God. This comic genius is, of course, George Burns. This autobiography includes intimate memories, zany anecdotes, and public triumphs, all told with the typical George Burns wit. Photographs.

Cross, Helen Reeder. **The Real Tom Thumb.** Illus. Stephen Gammell. Four Winds Press, 1980. 92 pp.

Charles Sherwood Stratton was a very clever boy and a joy to his family. But he didn't grow. In the 1840s, when he was almost five years old—and still less than 25 inches tall—he was discovered by the fabulous P. T. Barnum, founder of Barnum and Bailey's Circus. Before long, Charles Sherwood Stratton was known to the world as Tom Thumb. Everyone, including President Lincoln and Queen Victoria, wanted to meet him. His life was an extraordinary one, at times lonely and at times as enchanted as a dream come true. You may not believe that it all really happened—but it did!

Edmonds, I. G. **The Magic Brothers: Carl and Alexander Herrmann.** Elsevier/Nelson Books, 1979. 159 pp.

A man in a black cape lined with red satin swirls silently from the cab, whisks upstairs and into the bedroom of the sleeping eleven-year-old boy, and carries him off. The kidnapper is Carl Herrmann, a young German magician of the mid 1800s. The boy he kidnaps is his brother Alexander. Alexander worships his famous brother, so he works as Carl's assistant, taking great risks, enduring discomfort and pain, and working ceaselessly. To the brothers, though, it is not work they are doing, but fun! Carl is determined to be the best in his profession, and he's constantly working up new tricks and trying variations on old ones. But Alexander, much as he loves his brother, intends that one day *he* will be the best.

Ewers, Carolyn H. **Sidney Poitier: The Long Journey.** Signet Books, 1981. 140 pp.

For actor and director Sidney Poitier, it was a long struggle from his boyhood in the Bahamas to stardom in Hollywood. When he began acting, there were few good parts for black actors. But he kept trying to break into theater and film. Finally, he was offered important parts in the play *A Raisin in the Sun* and in films like *The Defiant Ones* and *Edge of the City.* Then, in 1963, Poitier won the Academy Award for his role in *Lilies of the Field*—the first black to do so since 1939.

Gutman, Bill. **Duke: The Musical Life of Duke Ellington.** Random House, 1977. 184 pp.

Duke Ellington may not have been the father of jazz, but he certainly was one of the most important musicians who contributed to the growth of this music's popularity among all types of people. This book looks at Ellington's youth in the early 1900s, describes his early successes in small all-black clubs, and shows his evolution into one of America's greatest jazz band leaders and jazz composers. Ellington's long career ended with his death in 1974. Photographs.

Haskins, James. **I'm Gonna Make You Love Me: The Story of Diana Ross.** Laurel-Leaf Library, 1982. 182 pp.

Diana Ross is such a glamorous superstar that it's hard to believe she used to be just "a skinny kid from the Detroit projects." She was poor and shy and black, and she felt like a nobody. In fact, the only things she had going for her were her beautiful singing voice and her determination to be somebody. How she got to be that somebody when just about everything else seemed to be against her is an inspirational story.

Herz, Peggy. **TV 79.** Scholastic Book Services, 1978. 108 pp.

Peggy Herz interviews and writes about some of television's biggest stars: Erik Estrada of "CHiPs," Melissa Gilbert of "Little House on the Prairie," Haywood Nelson of "What's Happening," Ron Glass of "Barney Miller," Joyce DeWitt of "Three's Company," and characters from such programs as "Mork and Mindy" and "The Hardy Boys." These talks with the stars reveal their personal interests and the inside story of their lives as television personalities.

Lennon, Cynthia. **A Twist of Lennon.** Avon Books, 1980. 190 pp.

Four Liverpool dropouts got together and formed a musical group that proceeded to rock the world during the 1960s. These strange-looking young men made their American debut on the Ed Sullivan show as the Beatles. John Lennon's ex-wife, Cynthia, has written their story from her position as their constant companion at the beginning of their rise to fame. Little-known anecdotes about each of the Beatles give the reader insights into the ordinary people behind the superstar images.

Lynn, Loretta (with George Vecsey). **Loretta Lynn: Coal Miner's Daughter.** Warner Books, 1980. 244 pp.

Country-western singer Loretta Lynn tells how she reached wealth and stardom after being a "nobody from nowhere." She explains what it means to grow up in a coal miner's family in a small mountain town. Loretta married at the age of fourteen and immediately had to assume the responsibilities of being a wife and mother when she herself was scarely more than a child. She tells how, as an uneducated and painfully shy girl, she began her career in country singing, and talks about the pain she suffered as the price for fame. But she says she'd do it all over again. Mature situations.

Maiorano, Robert. **Worlds Apart: The Autobiography of a Dancer from Brooklyn.** Coward, McCann & Geoghegan, 1980. 173 pp.

Robert Maiorano was a tough street kid growing up in gang-ridden Brooklyn in the 1950s. His early goal was to become a Brooklyn Dodger, but he grew up to become another type of athlete—a ballet dancer. This is the story of the hard work and family problems during Maiorano's first sixteen years as a dancer. Currently a soloist with the New York City Ballet, the author describes his endless training, his successes, and his failures.

Marvin, Edgar. **When the Movies Began: First Film Stars.** Illus. Meredith Nemirov. Contemporary Perspectives, 1978. 48 pp.

Television actor Shaun Cassidy learns that a film star's life is always busy, as Lola Pearsons explains the early career of Norma Talmadge, one of the biggest stars of silent movies. Lola tells how the actors struggled for opportunities and stardom in the early part of this century.

Miller, Jim, editor. **The *Rolling Stone* Illustrated History of Rock 'n' Roll.** Rev. ed. Random House, 1980. 474 pp.

This book contains biographical information about the individual stars and the groups of rock 'n' roll, beginning in the early 1950s and going through to disco and New Wave. Some of the people and groups discussed are Elvis Presley, Buddy Holly, James Brown, The Doors, Bob Dylan, Janis Joplin. This book also contains information on the blues revival, rock festivals, and the heavy metal movement in rock. A list of albums and singles follows each mini-biography of the singers and groups. Photographs.

Nesbitt, Cathleen. **A Little Love and Good Company.** Stemmer House Publishers, 1977. 252 pp.

As an Irish sea captain's daughter in the late 1800s and later as a British stage and film actress, Cathleen Nesbitt has led a life of romance and adventure. Yet she has retained a set of simple values to live by. Love and family life remain at the center of this actress's world. In her own words, she tells of her intense romance with the poet Rupert Brooke and shares some of the poetry and the letters he wrote her. But her story is not only of her personal life, but also of a life in the theater. Nesbitt talks about meeting and working with other famous theater people like Richard Burton, Rex Harrison, Audrey Hepburn, and Noel Coward. Photographs. Mature situations.

Pollock, Bruce. **The Face of Rock 'n' Roll: Images of a Generation.** Holt, Rinehart & Winston, 1978. 178 pp.

Rock 'n' roll of the last two decades is recorded here through pictures and words. The authors of this book use color pictures of actual album covers to illustrate the different people and movements in rock 'n' roll. An index lists the stars featured in this group biography.

Pollock, Bruce. **When Rock was Young: A Nostalgic Review of the Top 40 Era.** Holt, Rinehart & Winston, 1981. 214 pp.

The first rock 'n' roll singers and songs are featured in this book. This history of top-40 popular music focuses on the songs that became hits between 1955 and 1963. Singers interviewed for the book include Phil Everly of the Everly Brothers, Dave Guard of the Kingston Trio, Little Anthony of Little Anthony and the Imperials, Neil Sedaka, and Brenda Lee.

Rather, Dan (with Mickey Herskowitz). **The Camera Never Blinks: Adventures of a TV Journalist.** Ballantine Books, 1979. 362 pp.

In this autobiography, Dan Rather relates many of his experiences as a television journalist. He covers many political events, including Watergate and President Nixon's resignation. He also explores the issue of civil rights, and comments on Martin Luther King's death. As part of his job, Rather traveled to the jungles of Vietnam and covered the war. Finally, this television anchor man discusses his famous colleagues: Walter Cronkite, Barbara Walters, Eric Sevareid, Mike Wallace, and David Brinkley. Mature reading.

Ronan, Margaret. **Superstars.** Scholastic Book Services, 1978. 140 pp.

What does young Academy Award-winner Tatum O'Neal think of making films with her father, Ryan? How did Sally Field break away from her Flying Nun image? What does John Travolta want from his career? This series of short profiles of famous film, television, and recording stars gives you a quick behind-the-scenes look at the real people behind the famous faces.

Schaffner, Nicholas. **The Boys from Liverpool: John, Paul, George, Ringo.** Methuen, 1980. 184 pp.

Here is the story of the Beatles—from their beginnings in small clubs in the late 1950s, to their worldwide success in the 1960s, to their individual lives and careers just before the death of John Lennon in 1980. This book examines the impact they had on the form of popular music and upon the attitudes of young people around the world.

Stein, Cathi. **Elton John.** Popular Library, 1975. 159 pp.

From a pudgy little boy from Middlesex, England, Elton John worked his way to music stardom on the strength of his talents as a pianist, singer, and songwriter. This book traces his often bumpy rise from obscurity to the center of the rock world. Among the topics discussed are his family and friends, his rock 'n' roll image, and the cost of his success.

Terkel, Studs (with Milly Hawk Daniel). **Giants of Jazz.** Rev. ed. Thomas Y. Crowell Co., 1975. 210 pp.

Jazz is America's most original music form. It developed from combining European songs, dances, and marches with the complex and exciting rhythms brought by slaves from Africa. The public and private lives of such jazz greats as Count Basie, Billie Holliday, Duke Ellington, and Benny Goodman are presented here in tracing the development of this music in America. Through dialogue and anecdotes, the author recreates the simple beginnings, triumphs, and failures of thirteen legendary musicians. Rare photographs accompany the biographies.

Terry, Walter. **Frontiers of Dance: The Life of Martha Graham.** Thomas Y. Crowell Co., 1975. 176 pp.

From the first time that she saw Ruth St. Denis dance on stage in the early 1900s, Martha Graham knew that all she wanted to do in life was dance. And she did just that for half a century. Graham became one of America's pioneers of modern dance. She was respected around the world not only as a performer, but as a teacher and choreographer as well. Photographs.

Warren, David. **The Great Escaper.** Illus. Annabel Large. Raintree Publishers Group, 1979. 31 pp.

Who was the greatest magician and escape artist who ever lived? Most people would say Harry Houdini, who lived from 1874 to 1926. This book describes many of Houdini's dramatic escapes from locked cells, coffins, and water traps.

Williams, Hank, Jr. (with Michael Bane). **Living Proof: An Autobiography.** G. P. Putnam's Sons, 1979. 222 pp.

Here, in his own words, is the story of Hank Williams, Jr., and what it meant to be the son of a famous and highly regarded country-western singer. Even as a young boy he was pushed by family and friends to follow in his father's footsteps and his life has shown the strain. In an attempt to escape the pressures, Hank Jr. began to turn to alcohol and drugs. This path almost cost him his life, but he finally stopped to examine his life and to change it. Mature language and situations.

York, William. **Who's Who in Rock Music.** Charles Scribner's Sons, 1982. 413 pp.

Arranged alphabetically, the entries in this book include essential facts about more than 12,000 performers and groups—from popular bands to people who have recorded only one album. Entries for the individual performers include information on instruments played, band memberships, and solo albums. The more popular performers and groups are discussed in longer essays.

Fine Arts

Theater and Music

Allport, Alan J. **Model Theaters and How to Make Them.** Charles Scribner's Sons, 1978. 96 pp.

The magic and movement of a live play can be recreated through the construction and operation of a model theater. This book explains in detail how to build the stage, backstage, orchestra, and scenery. Illustrated instructions for creating actors and planning their on-stage movements allow the reader to begin his or her own production of a play. Included are instructions for producing Shakespeare's *Romeo and Juliet, The Merchant of Venice,* and *A Midsummer Night's Dream* on a model stage.

Bebey, Francis (translator Josephine Bennett). **African Music: A People's Art.** Lawrence Hill & Co., 1978. 184 pp.

An eight-stringed harp of Nigeria, the musical shouting of many Pygmy voices, and xylophones made with calabashes from Senegal are but three of the many unique musical features of Africa. This fully illustrated book explains the natural links between the vocal and speech patterns of people of African nations and the music that they create.

Berger, Melvin. **The Story of Folk Music.** S. G. Phillips, 1976. 118 pp.

Folk music is special because it is created for and by average people. Folk music changes, flows with the times. And folk music always has a purpose, whether it be to express joy or sorrow, to record history, or to criticize social injustice. Folk music is usually sung, but certain instruments may accompany the voice or voices. This book traces the history of folk music, discusses its qualities, and tells us how we can join in the composing and singing of it.

Bierhorst, John. **A Cry from the Earth: Music of the North American Indians.** Four Winds Press, 1979. 112 pp.

American Indian music can be enjoyed as an art form or as a way to interpret Indian life. This study of Indian music and dance includes discussions of the instruments used to play the music, as well as descriptions of the music itself and the uses of the music. If other American traditions are dying, this book reveals that Indian music is still very much alive. The many photographs include reproductions of musical scores and the figures of dance steps.

Blocher, Arlo. **Jazz.** Troll Associates, 1976. 32 pp.

The history and development of jazz is just one of the musical forms covered in this series of books concerned with popular music. Each book takes a different type of music and examines its beginnings, its changes over time, and its current status. The artists and performers who have been closely associated with each type of music are also discussed. This Troll Jam Session series includes books on country music, folk music, and rock 'n' roll. Easy reading.

Greenberg, Jan Weingarten. **Theater Business: From Auditions through Opening Night.** Holt, Rinehart & Winston, 1981. 210 pp.

For most people in the audience viewing a theatrical production, the months of preparation by the actors and technicians are taken for granted. This book presents a detailed backstage view of a theater production, from the earliest stages of the production on through to opening night. Explained here are how actors get their jobs, how plays are financed, how scripts are obtained, and how the show is publicized.

Headington, Christopher. **The Performing World of the Musician.** Silver Burdett Co., 1981. 114 pp.

This book focuses on the musician's life. Information is provided about pursuing a career in vocal or instrumental music, in composing or performing. The book also explores the history of the performance of music and profiles the careers of composer Andrew Lloyd Webber and rock musician Jerry Harrison.

Judy, Susan, and Stephen Judy. **Putting on a Play: A Guide to Writing and Producing Neighborhood Drama.** Charles Scribner's Sons, 1982. 147 pp.

Everybody likes plays—producing them, acting in them, writing them, and watching them. The authors draw on their experience in the theater to suggest ways to develop your imagination, and transform your ideas into different kinds of plays. They also provide advice on how to present your finished product to an audience. A glossary of stage terms is included at the end of the book.

Lewis, Robert. **Advice to the Players.** Harper & Row, Publishers, 1980. 174 pp.

Anyone who dreams of one day acting on Broadway or in Hollywood must first become fully trained in the art of acting. This book guides you through the control of the body and the emotions, and provides exercises and suggestions to develop acting and stage presence. Such areas as concentration, the use of the senses, self-criticism, improvisation, and the role of the imagination in acting are covered in depth.

Luttrell, Guy L. **The Instruments of Music.** Thomas Nelson, 1977. 127 pp.

This book begins with a discussion of the greatest musical instrument—the human voice. From there it moves to cover all the major instruments, giving a history of each and explaining how each instrument works by diagrams and pictures. The final topic addressed is how musical sound is created electronically.

McGann, Mary. **Enjoy the Arts: Theater.** Illus. Adele Myers. Richards Rosen Press, 1977. 146 pp.

If you are serious about drama, this book will help you get the most from your theater studies and theatergoing. In addition to tracing the history of the theater from ancient Greece to Broadway, this book discusses the structure of plays, famous playwrites, the art of stage direction, theatrical trends and fads, and theater around the United States.

Olfson, Lewy. **You Can Put On a Show.** Illus. Shizu Matsuda and Santa De Haven. Sterling Publishing Co., 1976. 144 pp.

Here is everything you need to know to stage your own show for money, or just for fun. All of the different jobs that need to be done are described, and tips about acting are also provided. There are ideas for shows using many people, and for shows needing only one. There are even some scripts to help you begin.

Schaaf, Peter. **The Violin Close Up.** Photographs by author. Four Winds Press, 1980. 26 pp.

The author of this book has photographed a violin from a variety of angles to give the reader a close and instructive view of the instrument and its parts.

Stolzenberg, Mark. **Exploring Mime.** Photographs by Jim Moore. Sterling Publishing Co., 1979. 128 pp.

Mime, a theatrical art of communication without words, is one of the most complex and imaginative of the performing arts. Unlike in most dramatic arts, the voice is of no value to the performer here. Only his or her control of the body is important to make an audience imagine a scene that is not really there. Over two hundred photographs help to illustrate the basics of this art form. Some mime routines that you can try are explained and described in detail.

Swift, Clive. **The Performing World of the Actor.** Silver Burdett Co., 1981. 113 pp.

Would you like to be an actor or actress? Find out what it's really like to work in theater, movies, television, and radio. This book provides an illustrated history of the dramatic arts, career information, and revealing portraits of Glenda Jackson, Jack Mitchell, and Sara Coward.

Uslan, Michael, and Bruce Solomon. **Dick Clark's The First 25 Years of Rock 'n' Roll.** Dell Publishing Co., 1981. 465 pp.

What was rock 'n' roll like in 1955? In 1967? Who had the biggest hits in 1979? Get a look at rock 'n' roll's biggest stars, as seen on Dick Clark's television program, "American Bandstand," and see how the sounds have changed over the last twenty-five years.

Willson, Robina Beckles. **The Voice of Music.** Illus. Jeroo Roy. McElderry Books, 1977. 224 pp.

This book covers the wide range of music from pop to classical. Whatever the category, music in both its written and performed stages is treated. Music popular in different centuries is also analyzed.

Dance

Berger, Melvin. **The World of Dance.** S. G. Phillips, 1978. 190 pp.

Here is the history of dance in both words and pictures—the dances of Greeks, Romans, Hebrews, Orientals, and Americans. Included are many stories about famous ballets and about the important personalities of modern dance, people such as Isadora Duncan and Martha Graham.

Bullard, Brian, and David Charlsen. **I Can Dance.** G. P. Putnam's Sons, 1979. 128 pp.

Words and pictures portray the basic ballet postions, exercises, and movements. If you follow the instructions in this book, you will be able to dance and feel better about your general body movements. Three short dances that use the movements taught in the book are described at the end so you can test your own skills, and maybe even put on your own performance.

Davis, Jesse. **Classics of the Royal Ballet.** Coward, McCann & Geoghegan, 1980. 80 pp.

Text and black-and-white photographs share the space in this book, which contains the plots of six ballets: *The Nutcracker, Swan Lake, La Fille Mal Gardée, Giselle, Romeo and Juliet,* and *Sleeping Beauty.* Photographs of performances by the Royal Ballet accompany each ballet plot.

Fischer-Munstermann, Uta (translator Dale S. Cunningham, editor Liz Williamson). **Jazz Dance and Jazz Gymnastics, Including Disco Dancing.** Illus. Guntram Herold. Photographs by Rupert Leser. Sterling Publishing Co., 1979. 120 pp.

Here is a how-to book that teaches the various steps and movements involved in jazz and disco dancing. Included are the basic exercises that will enable you to master the various movements and the more advanced techniques involved in improvisation and choreography.

Jessel, Camilla. **Life at the Royal Ballet School.** Photographs by author. Methuen, 1979. 144 pp.

To become a member of England's Royal Ballet School it is not necessary to have had any ballet lessons, but it is necessary to meet the strict requirements of height, agility, coordination, flexibility, and attitude. Once accepted at the age of ten, each member must practice daily, as well as attend regular classes and continue to show promise as a dancer. Here is the complete story of the Royal Ballet School from auditions to finished performance.

Kline, Nancy Meders. **Enjoying the Arts: Dance.** Illus. Laura Eynon. Richards Rosen Press, 1975. 159 pp.

The many forms of dance are explored in this book from traditional ballet to modern dance. Ten dances—five ballets and five modern dances—are compared and discussed. Details of the choreography of these dances are provided. Mature reading.

Lowe, Jacqueline, and Charles Selber. **The Language of Show Dancing.** Photographs by Martha Swope. Charles Scribner's Sons, 1980. 38 pp.

Can you do "six o'clocks," "hitchkicks," "cakewalks," and "barrel turns"? These dance steps are used in the musical theater and also in ice skating, cheerleading, roller skating, and disco dancing. This book contains photographs of show dancing's best-loved steps.

Lustgarten, Karen. **The Complete Guide to Touch Dancing.** Photographs by Bernie Lustgarten. Warner Books, 1979. 127 pp.

Step-by-step instructions make it easy to learn twelve partner dances. Everything from the fox-trot to the cha-cha is explained here. Even if you will never be a Fred Astaire or a Ginger Rogers, this book will improve your ability to maneuver around any dance floor.

Shreeves, Rosamund. **Movement and Educational Dance for Children.** Plays, 1980. 235 pp.

This discussion of terms and basic dance movements gives detailed instructions to those who want to work with beginning dance students. Types of dance patterns, special dancing activities for different occasions, and methods for teaching dance are covered in this book.

Walker, Katherine Sorley, and Joan Butler. **Ballet for Boys and Girls.** Photographs by Costas and others. Prentice-Hall, 1979. 96 pp.

If you have ever seen a ballet on television or on the stage, you may not have understood very much about this complicated dance form. If so, then this book will help. It explains the basic positions of the legs and arms, the jumps, and many of the dance steps. It also distinguishes between the dancing required of the men and women performers. Some of the more popular ballet stories are described, along with a history of their performances.

Painting and Other Art Forms

Batterberry, Ariane Ruskin, and Michael Batterberry. **The Pantheon Story of American Art for Young People.** Pantheon Books, 1976. 159 pp.

This book explores the history of art in the United States, including the contributions of the Indians and the early settlers. Sections of the book cover art movements and important individual artists in the eighteenth, nineteenth, and twentieth centuries. The text is illustrated with many art reproductions.

Bennett, Peter. **The Illustrated Child.** Illus. Dreadnaught. G. P. Putnam's Sons, 1979. 128 pp.

Children have been the subjects of illustrations throughout the years. These illustrations often reveal much about the illustrators and the times in which they lived. For example, in the Middle Ages, children were seen as small-scale adults. So, in many ways, this is a story of the perceptions of illustrators and of how ideas about children changed throughout the years. Over 200 illustrations—from books, magazines, posters, advertisements, chapbooks, and comic strips—are included in the volume.

Holme, Bryan. **Enchanted World: Pictures to Grow Up With.** Oxford University Press, 1979. 95 pp.

The artists represented in this book range from a fourteen-year-old girl to Leonard Da Vinci, from medieval tapestry makers to artists working today in New York. The works of art also come from many different countries, such as Japan and Peru. But in them all, people, animals, or battles seem to come to life and to reveal the personality of the artist. The text contains ninety-six illustrations, forty-four in color.

Horwitz, Elinor Lander. **Contemporary American Folk Artists.** Photographs by Joshua Horwitz. J. B. Lippincott Co., 1975. 142 pp.

Art takes many forms. This book talks about one form that is enjoying a renewed popularity—folk art. Folk art is untrained, is unconcerned with the conventional rules, and is seldom realistic, yet it has beauty, strength, and emotional impact. Folk art is still alive in America, and in this book you can read about those who paint it, carve it, and create it out of anything and everything they find around them—from a rusted clock, to old tires, to tin cans.

Price, Christine. **Arts of Clay.** Charles Scribner's Sons, 1977. 64 pp.

Pottery is an ancient art form that is still practiced and prized today. Here is the story of pottery making as it is done around the world to create works of art and practical items for the home.

Price, Christine. **The Mystery of Masks.** Charles Scribner's Sons, 1978. 64 pp.

Magical, powerful, and mysterious—masks can change their wearers into spirits, animals, or even gods. These stories and drawings about masks from around the world help us discover their importance in the lives of people.

Vaizey, Marina. **100 Masterpieces of Art.** G. P. Putnam's Sons, 1979. 119 pp.

The author has chosen 100 paintings that she feels are representative of the greatest Western painters from the thirteenth century to the present day. Each painting and its artist are discussed, as are the art movements that many of these pictures helped create or popularize.

Mass Media

Fenten, D. X., and Barbara Fenten. **Behind the Television Scene.** Crestwood House, 1980. 47 pp.

This is one of a series of books that lives up to its title. It really does take you behind the scenes to show you everything that must be done in order to produce a television show. Many people are involved besides the performers, who are usually the only people the audience sees. This book describes them all. Other subjects in the Behind the Scenes series are radio, sports, newspapers, and the circus. Easy reading.

Fireman, Judy, editor. **TV Book: The Ultimate Television Book.** Workman Publishing Co., 1977. 402 pp.

Although television is barely fifty years old, virtually thousands of shows have been developed, produced, broadcast, and canceled. This book looks at many of these programs and their stars through articles by 150 different authors who have experience behind the scenes and in front of the camera. Over 1,200 photographs.

Jahn, Mike. **How to Make a Hit Record.** Bradbury Press, 1976. 118 pp.

The process of making a hit record is described from start to finish by using the story of a fictional singer, Steve Harrison. Steve begins as a local entertainer who, with hard work and good guidance, becomes famous with a hit single. From this point, Steve's story is filled with valuable advice from such actual performers as Carly Simon and James Taylor, as well as from the people involved in the production and promotion of a big record. Even though Steve isn't real, the details provided about the recording industry are.

Larson, Rodger, Lynne Hofer, and Jaime Barrios (editor Joan Platt). **Young Animators and Their Discoveries: A Report from Young Filmmakers Foundation.** Photographs by Alfonso Barrios. Charles Scribner's Sons, 1976. 159 pp.

Young filmmakers describe how they make animated movies—from the early stages of writing a script, to the creating of artwork, to the recording of a soundtrack. An animated film attempts to create movement by photographing a subject or object, moving it, and then filming it again and again, or by photographing a series of drawings. Also included are interviews with twelve young filmmakers.

LeBaron, John, and Philip Miller. **Portable Video: A Production Guide for Young People.** Illus. Mary Aufmuth. Prentice-Hall, 1982. 157 pp.

If you've ever wanted to produce your own television program, this is the book for you. You'll find out how video works, how to collect and connect the pieces of a portable video system, how to handle and position the camera to get the kind of shots you want, how to plan video productions, and more.

Marx, Samuel. **Mayer and Thalberg: The Make-Believe Saints.** Warner Books, 1980. 336 pp.

Here is the story behind M-G-M, the greatest Hollywood film studio during the 1920s and 1930s. Through the activities of studio chiefs Louis B. Mayer and Irving Thalberg, M-G-M developed great stars and created memorable films—Clark Gable, Greta Garbo, Jean Harlow, Joan Crawford, *Grand Hotel, Mutiny on the Bounty, Camille, The Good Earth.* The stories and anecdotes collected in this book show both the hard work and the glamour that go into making movies.

Medved, Harry, and Michael Medved. **The Golden Turkey Awards: Nominees and Winners—The Worst Achievements in Hollywood History.** Perigee Books, 1980. 223 pp.

The Golden Turkey awards are given for the worst performances or the worst movies. Categories include such crazy honors as: "The Worst Rodent Movie of All Time," "The Most Ridiculous Monster in Screen History," "The Most Brainless Brain Movie of All Time," and "The Worst Vegetable Movie of All Time." In each category, the nominees are examined and a winner (or is that loser?) is named.

Miklowitz, Gloria D. **Movie Stunts and the People Who Do Them.** Harcourt Brace Jovanovich, 1980. 64 pp.

Motorcycle crashes, people leaping from burning buildings, cowboys diving from runaway horses. All common sights on television and in movies. The daring men, women, and children who make these adventures look so realistic are the subjects of this informative book. The preparations for the stunts, as well as the amazing stunts themselves, are explained and illustrated with photographs.

O'Connor, Jane, and Katy Hall. **Magic in the Movies: The Story of Special Effects.** Doubleday & Co., 1980. 145 pp.

Have you ever sat in a movie and wondered just how a particular scene was filmed? Special effects and how they were accomplished are described in detail in this book. Learn about the shark in *Jaws,* the space invaders in *Close Encounters of the Third Kind,* the burning of Atlanta in *Gone with the Wind,* the invisible man in *The Invisible Man,* and lots, lots more.

Schudson, Michael. **Discovering the News: A Social History of American Newspapers.** Basic Books, 1978. 228 pp.

Has newspaper reporting remained the same in America over the years? This book reveals that journalism in this country has changed, yet is the same in some ways. In some periods, the gathering and reporting of news was viewed as a type of entertainment. In other eras, the purpose of newspaper reporting was seen as strictly informative. But no matter what the approach, American journalists always seem to be guided by the ideal of objectivity.

Seuling, Barbara. **You Can't Show Kids in Underwear: And Other Little-Known Facts about Television.** Illus. by author. Doubleday & Co., 1982. 93 pp.

Did you know about 40,000 television commercials are made each year? Or that over 73 million people watched the Beatles when they first appeared on American television? Or that Mary Tyler Moore's legs were the only part of her the audience saw on her first television series? These and hundreds of other strange and interesting bits of television trivia are collected in this book. By the way, that "wild and crazy" Steve Martin is a former philosophy student.

Weiss, Ann E. **The School on Madison Avenue: Advertising and What It Teaches.** E. P. Dutton, 1980. 128 pp.

If Madison Avenue, the center of the ad business, is a school, then we are all its students because we learn from advertising every day. But is it helpful or harmful? Or both? This book contains a brief history of advertising, and then focuses on twentieth-century methods of selling things. This book calls for more intelligent and effective regulations of advertising. Photographs.

Weiss, Ann E. **Tune In, Tune Out: Broadcasting Regulation in the United States.** Houghton Mifflin Co., 1981. 122 pp.

What kind of regulation do we have today for broadcasting? This book first traces the history of regulation. For example, did you know one minute can cost $500,000 today compared to $50 for ten minutes years ago? The book then goes on to discuss different regulatory groups, presenting arguments for and against regulation. Also included here are insights into how new technology is affecting broadcasting and its regulation. Photographs.

Religion

Boone, Pat. **Pray to Win: God Wants You to Succeed.** G. P. Putnam's Sons, 1980. 237 pp.

Singer-actor Pat Boone explains his belief in prayer. Boone tells personal stories of people who have used prayers and have been successful in business, health, and competitions. Two special communication codes that people have used with God, Boone explains, are meditation and speaking in tongues. Prayer probes, action prayers, prerequisites for power prayer, and supernatural answers are also explained and analyzed here.

David-Neel, Alexandra (translators H. N. M. Hardy and Bernard Miall). **Buddhism: Its Doctrines and Its Methods.** Discus Books, 1979. 299 pp.

Disguised as a beggar traveling through Tibet in the 1920s, author David-Neel was the first Westerner to penetrate the sacred city of Lhasa. She wrote this book to help Westerners understand the deepest mysteries of Buddhism, a highly personal religious philosophy based on the beliefs that suffering is inherent in life but that one can be liberated by mental and moral self-purification. After a brief summary of the life of the Buddha (who lived in India in the fifth century B.C.), the author discusses the theory of Interdependent Origins, the concept of Karma, and the way to attain Buddhahood or perfect enlightenment.

Dickinson, Peter. **City of Gold and Other Stories from the Old Testament.** Illus. Michael Foreman. Pantheon Books, 1980. 188 pp.

Here are fresh retellings of thirty-three Old Testament tales as they might have been told by people who were part of the events, or by those who had just heard about them. The story of the parting of the Red Sea, for example, is told by a fisherman who was there at the time. Noah's tale of the Great Flood is passed on from one professional entertainer of 550 B.C. to his rival. And a song conveys the story of the plague of Egypt.

485

Efron, Marshall, and Alfa-Betty Olsen. **Bible Stories You Can't Forget: No Matter How Hard You Try.** Illus. Ron Barrett. E. P. Dutton, 1976. 79 pp.

Bible stories have been around for a long, long time, and they've been told in many different ways in many different languages. The authors selected eight of the most memorable, exciting, and popular of these stories for retelling in a modern fashion. Included are the story of the Great Flood and Noah's Ark; the story of the Tower of Babel; the story of Joseph and the Coat of Many Colors; and the romance of Samson and Delilah. A map helps the reader to understand where these stories are said to have taken place.

Evslin, Bernard. **Signs and Wonders: Tales from the Old Testament.** Illus. Charles Mikolaycak. Four Winds Press, 1981. 337 pp.

This book takes stories from the Old Testament (including some from the Apocrypha) and uses dialogue and additional description to retell the stories. The characters in these stories include Adam, Eve, Moses, Deborah, Samson, David, Solomon, Esther, Judith, and Daniel.

Farah, Caesar E. **Islam: Beliefs and Observances.** Barron's Educational Series, 1970. 306 pp.

This book provides an introduction to Islam as a religion and a political force. The beliefs, ceremonies, and writings of Islam are described here. The book contains footnotes, a glossary, and recommended readings to help further your understanding of this important movement in world history.

Goldreich, Gloria, editor. **A Treasury of Jewish Literature: From Biblical Times to Today.** Holt, Rinehart & Winston, 1982. 243 pp.

From Biblical times to the modern day, Jewish literature has been written and collected. The literature collected here includes selections from Canadian and American Jewish literature, literature of the Holocaust, literature of Zionism, Yiddish literature, and selections from the Talmud, the Apocrypha, and the Prophets. Brief introductions provide the reader with historical background and cultural insights into the selections.

Greenfeld, Howard. **Bar Mitzvah.** Illus. Elaine Grove. Holt, Rinehart & Winston, 1981. 32 pp.

The origins and significance of the Jewish ceremony of bar mitzvah are explored in this book. This celebration marks the day when a

Jewish boy assumes an adult role in the Jewish community. A similar ceremony for Jewish girls, called the bas mitzvah, is also explained.

Greenfeld, Howard. **Passover.** Illus. Elaine Grove. Holt, Rinehart & Winston, 1978. 32 pp.

Passover is the most widely celebrated of all Jewish holidays, and it has been celebrated for more than 3,000 years. The first part of this book retells the history behind the holiday that came into being when the enslaved Israelites left Egypt. The second part of the work describes how the holiday is observed and explains the meaning of the different traditions associated with it.

Greenfeld, Howard. **Rosh Hashanah and Yom Kippur.** Illus. Elaine Grove. Holt, Rinehart & Winston, 1979. 31 pp.

Unlike most of the Jewish holidays, Rosh Hashanah and Yom Kippur have no story connected to them. Yet, they are two of the most important holidays because they are related to very spiritual concepts. Why they are so meaningful to the Jewish faith is explained here, as well as how these two holidays are observed.

Holden, William Curry. **Teresita.** Illus. José Cisneros. Stemmer House Publishers, 1978. 219 pp.

When Santa Teresa died at the age of thirty-three, the funeral report said the cause of death was consumption. But those who loved and revered her said that her spirit had worn itself out by her ceaseless service to her people. The illegitimate daughter of Don Tomas Urrea and a young Indian girl, Teresita was not someone people would expect to become a worker of miracles. Yet, even as a young girl in Mexico, Teresa displayed the unusual power to foresee events. As a teenager, Teresa fell into an extended trance-like state for several months. When she awoke, she remembered nothing of the visitations form the Virgin Mary she had spoken of, nor of the miraculous healings she herself performed. But at this point she did feel determined to dedicate her gifts to helping people.

Holland, Isabelle. **Abbie's God Book.** Illus. James McLaughlin. Westminster Press, 1982. 80 pp.

Twelve-year-old Abigail Tyrrell's father asked her to write down all the questions that she wanted to ask him about God. So Abigail began writing down her converstions and thoughts about God. The result is not a novel, or a story with a plot, but a series of a young girl's personal ideas about a very important subject, God.

Meyer, Carolyn. **Amish People: Plain Living in a Complex World.**
Photographs by author, Michael Ramsey, and Gerald Dodds.
McElderry Books, 1978. 138 pp.

Different religious beliefs have separated groups of people from one
another throughout history. The Amish people, with their strict
beliefs about dress, behavior, marriage, and even ownership of
machinery, form a distinct religious group. These people do as
much as they can to separate themselves from the worldliness of the
other people of America, whom they refer to as "the English."
Because of their withdrawal, not much is really known about the
Amish and their customs. This book discusses what is known of
these very unusual people, and it puts to rest some of the untruths
that have been believed by outsiders for years.

Moore, Joan André. **Astronomy in the Bible.** Illus. by author. Abingdon
Books, 1981. 160 pp.

This book combines a study of science with a study of the Bible.
The chapters cover information about the stars, moon, sun, planets,
and constellations in the time of Amos, Job, and Jesus. The book
even discusses that special star, the Christmas star.

Moskin, Marietta D. **In Search of God: The Story of Religion.** Atheneum
Publishers, 1979. 142 pp.

This book is about the search for God made by many different
religions. It explains how and why different religions come about
and what they provide for their followers. Holy objects, religious
laws, and other common elements are discussed. This book points
out that an understanding of religion is the beginning of knowledge
of human society. Photographs.

Rifkin, Jeremy (with Ted Howard). **The Emerging Order: God in The
Age of Scarcity.** G. P. Putnam's Sons, 1979. 272 pp.

The American Dream may have been falsely interpreted to justify a
greedy point of view that allows us to ravage the land. This book
suggests that if America continues on its present course, the possible
result is self-destruction. The authors propose that we drasticlly
reorder our values and take seriously our tasks as protectors of all
God's creations. Religion, they charge, must play the major role in
changing the disorder that reigns today.

Wangerin, Walter, Jr. **The Bible: Its Story for Children.** Rand McNally
& Co., 1981. 416 pp.

This is an illustrated version of the Old and New Testaments with a modernized and simplified text. In this book you will find most of the famous stories from the Bible.

Weiss, Ann E. **God and Government: The Separation of Church and State.** Houghton Mifflin Co., 1982. 132 pp.

What happens when religious beliefs come into conflict with the individual liberties of others? No one answer fits all cases, but readers of this book are urged to think clearly about these issues. The book traces the history of American attitudes toward religion from colonial days to the present, and it looks at how the Constitution provides for separation of church and state. The question of how the constitutional regulations on this issue are applied today is also covered here.

Personal Improvement and Health

Abrams, Joy, Ruth Richards, and Pam Gray. **Look Good, Feel Good: Through Yoga, Grooming, Nutrition.** Illus. Betty Schilling. Holt, Rinehart & Winston, 1978. 128 pp.

By developing a caring attitude for your body, a peaceful state of mind, and a few sensible health routines, you will be well on the road to looking and feeling good. This three-part handbook will help you get started on such a health program.

Arehart-Treichel, Joan. **Poisons and Toxins.** Holiday House, 1976. 160 pp.

Poisons are all around us in our homes and in the environment. This book discusses all kinds of poisons and toxins and their use in gardens, murders, suicides, warfare, households, and other places. This volume also provides a glossary and a list of related readings for those who want to pursue the subject of poisons further.

Azerrad, Jacob. **Anyone Can Have a Happy Child: The Simple Secret of Positive Parenting.** Warner Books, 1981. 222 pp.

No more tantrums, no more guilt! This author provides a simple, sensible alternative to traditional child-rearing methods. He exposes the myths of parenting and teaches parents what really makes a child happy. He gives step-by-step instructions to improve a child's behavior and covers such topics as fighting with brothers and sisters, lying, nightmares, eating problems, defiance, and more. The secret to successful parenting is a lot easier than you think!

Bayrd, Edwin. **The Thin Game: Dieting Scams and Dietary Sense.** Avon Books, 1979. 199 pp.

The facts about being overweight and the advice about taking off those excess pounds, and keeping them off, are presented in this book. Fad diets are examined and shown to be unreliable in the long run, even though they may be initially successful. If you are one of the 70 percent of Americans who are either on a diet or thinking about going on one, there are some good tips to follow.

Berk, Juliene. **The Down Comforter: How to Beat Depression and Pull Yourself out of the Blues.** Avon Books, 1981. 256 pp.

Have you ever felt lonely, listless, angry, lazy, or bored? We all have. But if these feelings drag on, they can lead to depression. This book offers advice and tips on dealing with depression and some of its side effects like eating, smoking, drinking, and worrying too much. There is also advice on how you might help friends out of their depressed moods.

Bershad, Carol, and Deborah Bernick. **Bodyworks: The Kids' Guide to Food and Physical Fitness.** Illus. Heidi Johanna Selig. Random House, 1979. 220 pp.

What you eat, when and where you eat, and how you eat all affect your life. This book lets you have fun while you learn all about different health life-styles, how your body works, physical fitness, where food comes from, eating habits, and nutrition. For example, this book discusses such things as what puts the pop in popcorn and where the gas in beans comes from. Originally published as *From the Inside Out.*

Betancourt, Jeanne. **Smile: How to Cope with Braces.** Illus. Mimi Harrison. Alfred A. Knopf, 1982. 84 pp.

Braces seem to be a standard part of many teenagers' lives. This book presents the typical problems and solutions related to wearing braces. There are many humorous illustrations and interesting facts and suggestions given here.

Bowe, Frank. **Comeback: Six Remarkable People Who Triumphed over Disability.** Harper & Row, Publishers, 1981. 172 pp.

The six people profiled in this book are disabled. They have a variety of handicaps: near-total paralysis, mental retardation, deafness and blindness, childhood polio, severe loss of vision, and major hearing loss. But all are outstanding people who have achieved in spite of their disabilities. These men and women include a poet, a theoretical physicist, a sex counselor, a social activist, a busboy, and a neurochemist. The author, who himself is deaf, intends to show that disabled people can do far more than we realize.

Burns, Marilyn. **Math for Smarty Pants.** Illus. Martha Weston. Little, Brown & Co., 1982.

Ever been terrified by numbers? The author of this book believes that math makes sense, or can make sense, if you put your mind, not your emotions, to it. Done in cartoon and comic-book style, this volume includes games, logical puzzles, memory quizzes, riddles, probabilities, twists, and many other intriguing problems to help anyone become at ease with numbers.

Carlson, Dale. **Boys Have Feelings Too: Growing Up Male for Boys.** Illus. Carol Nicklaus. Atheneum Publishers, 1980. 165 pp.

The male image, especially the "macho" image, is examined here by looking at the past, present, and future views of the male. The author discusses how sexual equality can free boys from the traditional tough and cool image and give them freedom to be more aware of their emotional side, and to express it more openly.

Carlson, Dale. **Where's Your Head? Psychology for Teenagers.** Illus. Carol Nicklaus. Atheneum Publishers, 1977. 215 pp.

In easy-to-understand language, this book presents famous psychologists' opinions and views—people like Freud, Jung, and Adler. It will help a teenager understand the mind, how it grows and develops, and where our problems come from. There are sections on behavior theories, culture, abnormal psychology, and the uses of psychology.

Carr, Rachel. **Wheel, Camel, Fish, and Plow: Yoga for You.** Photographs by Edward Kimball. Prentice-Hall, 1981. 95 pp.

Does your body need some shaping? Through thirteen fundamental yoga exercises, you can stretch and tone your body, improve your posture, and even develop your ability to concentrate better. The best part is that the program suggested in this book needs only half an hour a day.

Carton, Lonnie. **Raise Your Kids Right: Candid Advice to Parents on How to Say No.** G. P. Putnam's Sons, 1980. 250 pp.

Believe it or not, many parents have trouble saying no to their children, even though many times that is really the answer the child wants to hear. Here is advice for parents on how to say no, and also some ground rules for both parents and their children to follow to become better individuals and to improve their relationships.

Cohen, Daniel. **How to Buy a Car.** Photographs by Maureen McNicholas. Franklin Watts, 1982. 87 pp.

Should you buy a new or used car? Where should you buy it? How can you pay for it? What about car insurance, registration fees, and other details? Here are the answers to all your questions about buying and maintaining a car.

Crichton, Michael. **Five Patients: The Hospital Explained.** Avon Books, 1981. 209 pp.

Here are five fascinating and true cases of patients at a major city hospital. You will meet Ralph Orlando, Sylvia Thompson, Edith Murphy, Peter Luchesi, and John O'Connor and follow their experiences in emergncy rooms, surgery, and examinations. Their combined stories provide a clear and revealing picture of how hospitals in America work for, and sometimes against, their patients.

Daitzman, Reid J. **Mental Jogging: 365 Games to Enjoy, to Stimulate the Imagination, to Increase Ability to Solve Problems and Puzzles.** Richard Marek Publishers, 1980. 230 pp.

Mental jogging is like physical jogging. Mental warm-up exercises can be done to get the mind moving at a faster and more spontaneous pace. Maybe one of the best things about this group of daily mental exercises is that there are no right or wrong answers to the problems—the jogger uses his or her imagination to produce novel and unique solutions to ordinary problems. Another favorable point is that the exercises can be done alone or with other people. The author promises that regular performance of these exercises can result in a more agile and flexible mind.

de Vries, Madeline, and Eric Weber (with Lucretia Robertson). **Body and Beauty Secrets of the Superbeauties.** Illus. Catherine Clayton Purnell. G. P. Putnam's Sons, 1979. 223 pp.

Eleven women who have achieved stardom and who are generally considered to be beautiful share with you their ideas on makeup, diet, exercise, hair care, and fashion. Through interviews with each, you also learn a little about what it is like to be Suzanne Somers, Cheryl Ladd, Mary Tyler Moore, or Ann-Margret.

Donahue, Parnell. **Sports Doc: Medical Advice, Diet, Fitness Tips, and Other Essential Hints for Young Athletes.** Illus. Mimi Harrison. Alfred A. Knopf, 1979. 177 pp.

Whether you are an athlete in an organized sport or just a person concerned with your body, this book will be a valuable guide. The author explains the medical facts behind nutrition, rest, pains and sprains, skin problems, internal injuries, and fractures. He also gives clear advice about dealing with sports injuries and how to prevent them from occuring.

Dorr, Lynn Clark. **How to Enjoy Life between 12 and 20: Your Inner Beauty, Your Outer Image.** Corwin Books, 1976. 370 pp.

Why be miserable as a teenager or young adult? Since the number one requirement for being a well-adjusted person is to like and respect yourself, the author of this book talks about developing both inner and outer pride. This includes paying attention to personal awareness, communication skills, manners, poise, physical fitness, complexion, cosmetics, hair, wardrobe, and career goals. Also included is a calorie-counting list of foods, as well as suggested exercises for keeping in shape.

Eagan, Andrea Boroff. **Why Am I So Miserable If These Are the Best Years of My Life? A Survival Guide for the Young Woman.** J. B. Lippincott Co., 1976. 251 pp.

Has someone ever told you to "just be yourself"? Unless you really know who you are and what you want, this is pretty frustrating advice. Here is a guide to help teenage girls learn the basics that are needed when making decisions and to avoid a few pitfalls along the way. Sections are included on relationships with friends and parents, sex, menstruation, birth control, pregnancy, venereal disease, and legal rights.

Farkas, Emil, and Margaret Leeds. **Fight Back: A Woman's Guide to Self-Defense.** Holt, Rinehart & Winston, 1978. 159 pp.

The chapters of this self-defense text describe the various techniques covered in the lessons: "The Fighting Stance," "Use of Arms, Elbows and Hands," and "Use of Legs, Knees and Feet." Another section explains how to apply self-defense techniques when being attacked. The lessons are presented with photographs to illustrate the various maneuvers. A method of scheduling and planning a series of these lessons is also included.

Gallant, Roy A. **Memory: How It Works and How to Improve It.** Four Winds Press, 1980. 108 pp.

Whether you want to be able to memorize a page in the telephone book as a stunt, or simply memorize names and dates for a history test, this book can be a valuable tool. Through the use of such memory-assisting techniques as word rhyming, pictorial images, and key words, you can learn to improve your memory skills. In addition, information about memory itself will lead to a better understanding of the function of that area of brain activity.

Graedon, Joe (with Teresa Graedon). **The People's Pharmacy-2.** Avon Books, 1980. 468 pp.

This text provides information concerning such topics as over-the-counter medications, drug interactions, vitamins, drugs and children, drugs and older people, and arthritis and medication. This information is up-to-date medical and clinical data concerning the most common drugs people take. Warnings about drug abuse are also presented, and tips on the safe use of drugs are provided.

Harrington, S. W. **How to Get Your Parents to Give You Everything You've Ever Wanted.** Atheneum Publishers, 1982. 165 pp.

Want to learn how to handle family blowups, demanding fathers, troublesome brothers and sisters, and overprotective mothers? Then this is the book for you. There are tips on using diplomacy, humor, and battle tactics to keep from always getting the worst of family situations. Beyond their use in dealing with parents and siblings, the ideas in this book can help you better work with everyone.

Hauser, Gayelord. **The Gayelord Hauser Cook Book: Good Food, Good Health, Good Looks.** Perigee Books, 1980. 294 pp.

The twenty-four chapters in this cook book cover standard dishes such as fish, poultry, and vegetables and less commonly prepared juices, health foods, and yogurt dishes. The preparations for each dish are detailed yet clear. An interesting feature of this book is that brown sugar replaces white sugar in the dishes and natural flour and grains are recommended instead of bleached flour. All recipes stress cooking with your five senses and your common sense.

Hayden, Torey L. **Somebody Else's Kids.** Avon Books, 1982. 333 pp.

A seven-year-old boy who can only repeat what other people say . . . an abused little girl who can't learn to read . . . a ten-year-old boy who had seen his stepmother murder his father . . . a twelve-year-old girl who becomes pregnant—these are the "problem children" in Torey Hayden's class. Together they give each other the love they could find nowhere else. Mature situations. (A Literary Guild Selection)

Klein, Aaron E., and Cynthia L. Klein. **Mind Trips: The Story of Consciousness-Raising Movements.** Doubleday & Co., 1979.

Consciousness is being aware of your own existence and of what is around you. This book gives information about consciousness-raising movements in general and focuses on transcendental meditation (TM). There is also a brief discussion of several other popular movements: kung fu, yoga, Hare Krishna, martial arts, est, Zen, and Arica.

Kounovsky, Nicholas. **Instant Fitness: How to Stay Fit and Healthy in Six Minutes a Day.** Illus. Mickey Surasky. Paragon Books, 1979. 77 pp.

The human body is like a machine. When it sits still too much, or moves to excess at other times, it has to be taken in for repairs. The author has devised a method for physical fitness that each person can adapt to his or her own needs. The program of exercises is based on developing six areas: endurance, suppleness, equilibrium, strength, speed, and skill or coordination. The clearly and simply drawn illustrations show readers exactly how to do each exercise and let them decide which ones are most appropriate for their individual strengths and weaknesses.

Krementz, Jill. **How It Feels When a Parent Dies.** Alfred A. Knopf, 1981. 111 pp.

If you've lost one of your parents through death, you probably felt guilty, angry, and confused when it happened. You're not alone in these feelings; they are completely normal. Here are the stories of sixteen children who have also lost their father or mother. These boys and girls speak honestly about their feelings and experiences and tell how they learned to go on, remembering some things and forgetting others.

Leckart, Bruce (with L. G. Weinberger). **Up from Boredom, Down from Fear.** Richard Marek Publishers, 1980. 272 pp.

Why are we bored? Are there kinds of boredom? This author uses different theories of psychology to explain these questions and identifies the personality types coping with bordom as "juicers, eggheads, players, and goalies." Then he explains how to overcome boredom and make life meaningful. Some of the chapter titles are "Dr. Jekyll, Meet Mr. Hyde," "Getting to Know the Sane Me," "Stuck in the Mud," "Talking to Yourself," and "Taking the Plunge." Some mature reading and subject matter.

Levenkron, Steven. **Treating and Overcoming Anorexia Nervosa.** Charles Scribner's Sons, 1982. 205 pp.

The author is a psychotherapist who has treated anorexics, people who become obsessed with dieting. Today anorexia nervosa is striking one out of every 250 adolescent girls in the United States. It is serious enough to cause death in some cases. The book describes an approach called nurturant-authoritative therapy, which is working to help cure the disease. Then six patient cases are discussed. The book concludes with a direct letter to any anorexic.

Lyttle, Richard B. **The Complete Beginner's Guide to Physical Fitness.** Doubleday & Co., 1978. 151 pp.

Anyone who cares about good health can benefit from the suggestions given in this book on knowing your body, on learning how best to feed the body, and on exercising the body. The exercises here stress pliometrics, miometrics, and aerobics along with yoga, isometrics, and weights.

MacCracken, Mary. **Lovey: A Very Special Child.** Signet Books, 1977. 245 pp.

Hannah was a "hopeless" child. Everyone agreed on that—the schools, the doctors, and even the mother who loved her but could not reach her. Everyone, except one remarkable teacher who understood what it was like to be eight years old and hurt and angry and confused. One child. One teacher. Just enough to make a miracle.

Marcus, Rebecca. **Being Blind.** Hastings House Publishers, 1981. 119 pp.

What is it like to be blind? There is no one answer to this question. Blindness is a slightly different experience for each person. This book attempts to separate truth from myths and misunderstandings by discussing such questions as: What causes blindness? Can the blind feel colors? Do they have a "sixth sense"? Would the blind rather do everything without help?

Morrison, Carl V., and Dorothy Nafus Morrison. **Can I Help How I Feel?** Illus. James McCrea and Ruth McCrea. Atheneum Publishers, 1976. 124 pp.

Everyone must face the stress and strain of growing up. This book carefully analyzes common problems faced by young people and attempts to suggest methods of dealing with them. If there are not always complete solutions for all the frightening feelings teenagers have, this book suggests that there is at least the comfort of knowing that a person is not alone in having these problems.

Myers, Irma, and Arthur Myers. **Why You Feel Down—And What You Can Do about It.** Charles Scribner's Sons, 1982. 115 pp.

Ever feel depressed? It sometimes seems to come with being an adolescent. This book begins with a discussion about understanding depression and where it comes from. Then there are suggestions on doing something about it. Some of the topics treated are changes in physical, intellectual, and emotional life, changing relationships in the family, the influence of friends, and the demands made on the adolescent, and receiving mixed messages from people.

Naylor, Phyllis Reynolds. **Getting Along with Your Teachers.** Illus. Rick Cooley. Abingdon Press, 1981. 94 pp.

That person standing in front of the classroom each day is a stranger the first day of school. This book tells you how to discover the human being behind the stranger without becoming a "teacher's pet." A teacher has far more to give you than facts, but it is up to you to find out what. Teachers can be personal counselors, friends, career advisors, morale boosters, and much more, if you know how to go about developing a good relationship with them.

Nieburg, Herbert A., and Arlene Fischer. **Pet Loss: A Thoughtful Guide for Adults and Children.** Harper & Row, Publishers, 1982. 147 pp.

Is grieving for a lost pet silly or unreasonable? No, according to this book. It is important to express the feelings that a pet's loss brings, and come to terms with that grief. This book discusses the various ways a person can lose a pet, and how one can learn to accept a new pet. Making arrangements with the veterinarian after the death of a pet is also discussed here.

Passwater, Richard. **The Easy No-Flab Diet.** Richard Marek Publishers, 1979. 270 pp.

This author does not count calories. He counts "FLAB units," which help you burn fat while preserving the lean tissue you need. Guidelines are provided for preparing to diet and for exercise, taking the FLAB units into account. Recipes for no-flab diets are included.

Paul, Aileen. **The Kids' Diet Cookbook.** Illus. John DeLulio. Doubleday & Co., 1980. 180 pp.

This book was written for young people who are overweight and who want to lose pounds. There are weight and activity charts, menus, recipes, sound advice, and an overall plan to follow to take weight off sensibly.

Peavy, Linda, and Ursula Smith. **Food, Nutrition, and You.** Charles Scribner's Sons, 1982. 191 pp.

Do you know how much bike riding it takes to burn off the calories from a hamburger and a milkshake? How McDonald's became the international fastfood giant it is today? What foods are best for fueling a winning effort in sports? This book explores proteins, carbohydrates, fats, vitamins, and minerals and discusses such topics as food additives and weight problems.

Penney, Peggy L. **Surgery, From Stone Scalpel to Laser Beam.** Thomas Nelson, 1977. 134 pp.

Surgery began in prehistoric times when sharpened stones served as scalpels, and was based on magic and superstition. As surgery developed from prehistoric times—through the era of Greek physician Hipprocrates, to the barber-surgeons, to organ transplants—it became the story of men and women who made valuable discoveries and changes in medical procedures.

Rayner, Claire. **Everything Your Doctor Would Tell You If He Had the Time.** G. P. Putnam's Sons, 1980. 224 pp.

Why does hair turn gray? What are those brown patches on skin? Why do I get travel sickness? Why do I blush? Your doctor may not have time to answer all the questions that you think of. This book provides answers to all these questions, and the more than 300 illustrations provide additional information. Because of her newspaper column, this author is known as Britain's medical "Dear Abby."

Reuben, David. **Everything You Always Wanted to Know about Nutrition.** Avon Books, 1979. 263 pp.

In a candid question-and-answer format, Dr. Reuben explores and analyzes the food industry today. This is a book for those who wish to stay well. What foods are hurting us and how we should control our diets are discussed in this nutrition guide.

Richards, Arlene Kramer, and Irene Willis. **Boy Friends, Girl Friends, Just Friends.** Atheneum Publishers, 1979. 155 pp.

Being a friend and having friends are not easy. This book looks at some of the reasons why this is so, and it gives some advice on how to make it less difficult to keep up a relationship, whether your friend is of the same sex or of the opposite sex.

Richards, Arlene Kramer, and Irene Willis. **Leaving Home.** Atheneum Publishers, 1980. 163 pp.

Everyone has to leave home eventually to become a completely developed, independent person. But getting ready to take this step takes lots of time and planning. This book is filled with advice and suggestions about "leaving the nest." It discusses the painful parts of the process, as well as the exciting ones. Case histories are presented of young people who are in the process of separating from their parents or who have already done so.

Rosenfeld, Isadore. **The Complete Medical Exam.** Avon Books, 1979. 375 pp.

For many people, going to see a doctor is a frightening and expensive experience. This handbook, which was written by a doctor, is not intended to replace your doctor, but to help you make use of your doctor's skills more efficiently. The book explains how to tell your doctor what's wrong with you, how to evaluate his or her competence, and how to understand the various tests and medicines prescribed by the doctor.

Schowalter, John E., and Walter R. Anyan, Jr. **The Family Handbook of Adolescence.** Alfred A. Knopf, 1979. 303 pp.

This book, written by two physicians, describes that period of growth that takes people out of childhood and into adulthood. The book clearly explains what happens to the body and to the personality as well. Special issues concerning things like friends, school, hobbies, jobs, sports, and religion undergo vast questioning and changes during this crucial period, all of which can be troublesome to teenagers. This book discusses these changes, and goes into detail about such related subjects as medical care, special physical problems, and those problems associated with sex. Also covered are ways to cope with psychological problems such as depression and drinking.

Seide, Diane. **Looking Good! The Everything Guide to Beauty, Health and Modeling.** Thomas Nelson, 1977. 160 pp.

If you sleep right, eat right, and make the most of your good points, you may be able to be a professional model someday. But this guide is also for girls who just want tips to look their best. It can be a helpful guide to becoming a professional model, though, if that is your goal. Photographs.

Shurkin, Joel N. **The Invisible Fire: The Story of Mankind's Victory over the Ancient Scourge of Smallpox.** G. P. Putnam's Sons, 1979. 448 pp.

Smallpox is a disease we do not take seriously today because a vaccine has been discovered to protect us against it. But the disease has had a frightening history. It killed entire populations, disfigured people for life, and even affected battles and the fates of nations. Only through the medical teamwork among scientists of all nations was the virus that causes smallpox finally destroyed. The last person to contract a case of smallpox was quarantined and cured in Africa in 1977.

Silverstein, Alvin, and Virginia Silverstein. **Cancer.** Rev. ed. Illus. Andrew Antal. John Day Co., 1977. 102 pp.

What do we know about cancer today? This book examines all the recent information we have at hand about the various forms of cancer, their symptoms, possible causes, and treatment. The discussion includes new discoveries, especially about Red Dye Number Two and the successful use of CMF. The book also provides suggestions to readers about how they can protect themselves against cancer.

Silverstein, Alvin, and Virginia B. Silverstein. **Allergies.** J. B. Lippincott Co., 1977. 128 pp.

If roses make you sneeze, if strawberries make you break out in a rash, or if aspirin gives you a headache instead of making one go away, you are probably suffering from an allergy. One out of five people shares your problem—a problem that can mean only a little discomfort, or that can be so severe as to cause death. This book helps explain allergies: what they are, how they are diagnosed, how they are treated, and the research that is being done in the hope of someday eliminating allergies altogether.

Silverstein, Alvin, and Virginia B. Silverstein. **Epilepsy.** J. B. Lippincott Co., 1975. 64 pp.

Epilepsy is a much misunderstood disease that has caused unnecessary suffering for those who have it. This book contains information on the disease, its causes, its symptoms, and its treatment. It also includes chapters on living with epilepsy and on encouraging friends, family, and employers to treat epileptics like anyone else so that they have a chance to lead normal lives.

Silverstein, Alvin, and Virginia B. Silverstein. **So You're Getting Braces: A Guide to Orthodontics.** Photographs by authors. J. B. Lippincott Co., 1978. 112 pp.

Orthodontics is the branch of dentistry that deals with straightening teeth. Orthodontic treatment in the form of wearing braces may be uncomfortable, but it can eliminate physical and psychological problems. The history, the mechanics, and the importance of orthodontics are explained in this book.

Solomon, Neil. **Dr. Solomon's High Health Diet and Exercise Plan: How to Make Cholesterol Work for You.** G. P. Putnam's Sons, 1980. 206 pp.

Dr. Solomon talks about some astonishing new discoveries about diet, exercise, and human health. Cholesterol is a dirty word in America today, but Dr. Solomon explains how there are good kinds as well as bad kinds of cholesterol, and he explains ways to make this element work for healthier bodies. This book offers a total health program that includes facts about nutrition and diet, as well as offering a complete exercise program. Recipes for healthy foods are also included.

Somekh, Emile. **The Complete Guide to Children's Allergies: Care and Treatment for Your Allergic Child.** Corwin Books, 1979. 206 pp.

This book supplies answers to the many questions that anyone with allergies might have. Terms are first explained, and then information is given on skin testing; allergies affecting the skin, nose, and lungs; desensitization; drugs; vaccines; allergy journals; breathing exercises; camps for allergic children; and types of pollen. A glossary of terms and special notes are included.

Stiller, Richard. **Pain: Why it Hurts, Where it Hurts, When it Hurts.** Thomas Nelson, 1975. 162 pp.

In this book, doctors and surgeons discuss how their patients cope with pain in different situations. Unusual facts about pain, nerves, psychological connections, and methods of treatment shed a new light on this subject. Tips on how to cope with pain are also included.

Stiller, Richard. **Your Body is Trying to Tell You Something: How to Understand Its Signals and Respond to Its Needs.** Harcourt Brace Jovanovich, 1979. 128 pp.

We need to pay attention to our bodies because they give us important messages. Those messages are in the form of headaches, skin problems, sleeplessness, and anxiety. The author concentrates on the symptoms young people suffer. He explains the causes and suggests what to do about these symptoms. Guidelines for medical and psychological counseling are provided as well as a glossary of technical terms.

Warner, Lucille, and Ann Reit. **Your A to Z Super Problem Solver.** Illus. by authors. Scholastic Book Services, 1978. 104 pp.

Teenage problems from acne to zest are talked about frankly and constructively. Are you embarrassed about your height, unable to talk to your parents, worried about school? This book includes some interesting answers to these problems.

Weinhold, Barry, and Gail Andresen. **Threads: Unraveling the Mysteries of Adult Life.** Richard Marek Publishers, 1979. 123 pp.

Most people at some time in their lives feel caught in patterns that restrict and seem continually self-defeating. This book shows how to unravel those confining threads, and how to change those destructive patterns to allow a person the freedom to achieve. This book's sections cover such topics as the permission theory, the ways to solve life's mysteries, techniques for achieving growth and change, and ways to apply these techniques to the various roles in life one plays.

Weinstein, Grace W. **Money of Your Own.** E. P. Dutton, 1977. 99 pp.

Why does your allowance disappear so fast? Is there anything you can do about it without asking for a raise? Sure—learn to manage the money you have. This book helps you learn how to use your good sense to stretch your dollars further. The author describes the best methods of shopping, saving, using credit, and managing your allowance and earnings.

Wentzler, Rich. **The Vitamin Book.** Dolphin Books, 1979. 224 pp.

Can vitamin C cure the common cold? Is megavitamin therapy useful? Which are the best vitamins for you to take? The answers to these and hundreds of other questions about vitamins are covered in this handbook of vitamins, minerals, and essential nutrients. From vitamin A to zinc, this book explains, describes, and suggests which vitamins will help you in what ways. Charts and graphs accompany the text.

Westin, Jeane Eddy. **Finding Your Roots: How Every American Can Trace His Ancestors at Home and Abroad.** Ballantine Books, 1978. 291 pp.

Have you ever wondered if you were related to some famous person? Do you know who your great-great-great-grandparents were? The only way to answer these and other questions about your ancestry is to research your own family's roots. The author outlines a step-by-step procedure to follow your personal history back in time. The effective use of libraries, government records, family health records, and genealogical societies is explained in detail.

Winston, Stephanie. **Getting Organized: The Easy Way to Put Your Life in Order.** Warner Books, 1979. 256 pp.

Who does not feel the need to become organized? This book discusses organizing principles in terms of time and paperwork, money, the home, rooms, and even children. But the volume begins with a short quiz to find out how organized you are. Not too surprisingly, the author is founder and director of a consulting firm called The Organizing Principle.

Wolf, Barbara. **Living with Pain.** Seabury Press/a Continuum Book, 1977. 144 pp.

Why do some people suffer more pain than others? Why do certain medicines relieve pain for some people and not for others? Does concentrating on pain tend to intensify the discomfort? These and other questions are discussed in this excellent guide to the physical and emotional aspects of adapting to persistent pain.

Wolf, Beverly. **Connie's New Eyes.** Photographs by Bernard Wolf. J. B. Lippincott Co., 1976. 96 pp.

Alison Gooding, a New Jersey farm girl, decides to raise puppies for the Seeing Eye program. Her first dog is a golden retriever named Blythe. It isn't easy to say good-bye to Blythe at the end of a wonderful year together. But Alison knows Blythe is needed and that when she gives Blythe up, she will receive a new puppy to train. At the Seeing Eye Center, Connie David—blind since birth and now about to begin her first job as a primary school teacher—has been receiving her training as a guide dog's owner. She is nervous, excited, and happy. Blythe will help Connie be independent in her new career and in her new life.

Worth, Jennifer. **Emergency Room.** Elsevier/Nelson Books, 1980. 126 pp.

Imagine yourself sitting at the desk in a hospital emergncy room night after night for ten years. One night a man comes in with a knife plunged so deeply into his abdomen that only the handle shows. Children come in, sometimes with a small stone or bean stuck up their noses, sometimes as the victims of abusive parents. Then there are the babies born in the back seat of cars. But besides the drama of the patients, this book also reveals the drama of the nurses, doctors, and orderlies who must quickly deal with each of these cases.

Zeleznak, Shirley. **Jogging.** Crestwood House, 1980. 31 pp.

Everyone wants to be healthier and happier, and jogging can be one way to reach these goals. Before beginning to jog, though, a person needs to learn something about this popular exercise. Jogging can be done alone or with others, fast or slow, in competion or not, and at nearly any time or place. The author discusses techniques of jogging, correct clothing, exercises, and mental attitudes. She emphasizes the importance of making running a habit—a way of life.

History and Government

Archer, Jules. **Watergate: America in Crisis.** Thomas Y. Crowell Co., 1975. 306 pp.

On August 9, 1974, Richard M. Nixon secured for himself a place in history by resigning as president of the United States. The author explores the people and facts behind this event to create a fascinating account of presidential politics during the Watergate period. Although this book is clearly factual, it reads like a suspenseful detective story. The book begins the complicated story with the discovery of the break-in at the headquarters of the Democratic Party in the Watergate, and it continues to unfold with the details that led to Nixon's eventual resignation. Photographs.

Archer, Jules. **Washington vs. Main Street: The Struggle between Federal and Local Power.** Thomas Y. Crowell Co., 1975. 201 pp.

Here is an examination of different aspects of the battle for power between federal and local governments. Topics covered include schools, welfare, civil liberties, war, taxes, minorities, homes, farmers, labor, consumers, and pollution. Alternatives used to cope with these problems in certain Scandinavian countries are also explained.

Bentley, Judith. **American Immigration Today: Pressures, Problems, Policies.** Julian Messner, 1981. 190 pp.

As they have for centuries, people today migrate in search of better jobs, better living conditions, and the freedom to choose their own way of life. In the past, immigration helped to relieve population pressures in other countries. Today, few countries encourage immigration. The book describes the human experience of immigrating to a new land and reviews the current laws enacted to control these moves. Photographs.

Bornstein, Jerry. **Unions in Transition.** Julian Messner, 1981. 179 pp.

Trade unions struggled to be born in order to make life decent for thousands of overworked and underpaid people. As their functions and structure grew, unions became more complex, powerful, and sometimes corrupt. Today much controversy surrounds the idea of labor unions. Are they still dedicated to making life better for the average worker? What does the future hold for unions? This book addresses all these topics.

Brown, Dee (adapted by Linda Proctor). **Lonesome Whistle: The Story of the First Transcontinental Railroad.** Holt, Rinehart & Winston, 1980. 144 pp.

In 1869 the last spike needed to complete the first transcontinental railroad linking the East and West coasts was pounded into place. The story that leads up to this last spike is filled with adventure, frustration, corruption, and success. This book describes how the railroad began, how it was built with the labor of immigrants, how it was plagued by outlaws, and how it helped destroy the lands of Indian tribes. Photographs.

Chen, Jack. **The Chinese of America.** Harper & Row, Publishers, 1980. 274 pp.

This book gives an historically accurate account of the Chinese contribution to the development of America: their pioneering of the West Coast fishing industry, their value as farm laborers, and the important part they played in building the transcontinental railroad system. Sections on the economic, social, and political problems faced by Chinese-Americans since the 1860s include discussions on youth gangs, Chinatowns, senior citizens, and garment sweatshops.

Daugherty, James. **The Landing of the Pilgrims.** Random House, 1978. 151 pp.

Based on journals of the Pilgrims, this book relates the history of the Plymouth settlers. These adventuresome people first fled England in 1608 and traveled to Holland in search of religious freedom. In 1620 they crossed the ocean and landed at Plymouth, Massachusetts. Once they arrived, the Pilgrims had to endure hunger, disease, and fighting with the Indians.

Davis, Burke. **Black Heroes of the American Revolution.** Harcourt Brace Jovanovich, 1976. 80 pp.

This is an account of the adventures of black Americans who participated in the struggle for independence from England. Included are tales of black soldiers, sailors, spies, scouts, guides, and wagoners. Easy reading.

Davis, Burke. **Our Incredible Civil War.** Ballantine Books, 1978. 172 pp.

As it says on the cover, this is an "almanac of incidents, accidents, oddities, and rarities" about the American Civil War. Information presented includes lists of firsts: the first use of railroad artillery, repeating rifles, flame throwers, land-mine fields. There are also descriptions of soldiers, military leaders, and battles. Folklore about the war is provided, as are personal stories that might not appear in regular history texts.

Davis, Daniel S. **Behind Barbed Wire: The Imprisonment of Japanese Americans during World War II.** E. P. Dutton, 1982. 129 pp.

December 7, 1941, was an historic date—it was the day Pearl Harbor was bombed by the Japanese. But soon there was another historic date: June 1942, when 120,000 Japanese-Americans were put behind barbed wire in "relocation" camps. These Japanese-Americans had to abandon their homes and possessions and live in primitive conditions until the end of World War II. But they were determined to survive, and this is the story of that struggle. Photographs. (ALA Best Book for Young Adults)

Delear, Frank J. **Airplanes and Helicopters of the U.S. Navy.** Dodd, Mead & Co., 1982. 143 pp.

This is the story of U.S. Naval aviation—its beginnings, growth, achievements, and the current array of aircraft making up one of our nation's first lines of defense. Various planes from the past as well as modern Navy planes are described and displayed by use of photographs and drawings.

Doty, Roy (with Leonard Maar). **How Much Does America Cost?** Illus. by author. Doubleday & Co., 1979. 63 pp.

You may be surprised at how much money it takes to run the United States. How this is done, including what your taxes pay for, is described in this guide to our country's economy.

Dunn, Harold. **Our Hysterical Heritage: The American Presidential Election Process, out of the Mouths of Babes.** Illus. Victor Curran. Stemmer House Publishers, 1980. 81 pp.

"George Washington said no president should be sentenced to more than two terms in the Big House. . . . Every four years America is struck by presidential campaigns. . . . The people who are expected to help the president sometimes are locked up in his cabinet." The author has selected his young students' funniest and most penetrating comments on American presidential elections, candidates, and the voting public.

Fincher, Ernest B. **The Presidency: An American Invention.** Abelard-Schuman Books, 1977. 210 pp.

Almost every aspect of the presidency of the United States is covered by this book. It discusses such topics as great campaigns, veto power, "the presidential disease," controlling the power of the president, and written and unwritten rules about who may be president. Also included are forecasts of presidents to come, a ranking of past presidents, and a chart showing important information about the first thirty-nine American presidents. Photographs.

Fisher, Leonard Everett. **The Hospitals.** Illus. by author. Holiday House, 1980. 62 pp.

In the first half of the nineteenth century, many people avoided hospitals because they were considered dirty and disease-ridden. Later, these conditions changed dramatically. This book discusses the hospital reforms brought about by scientific discoveries, human caring, and government legislation. (Nineteenth Century America series)

Fisher, Leonard Everett. **The Unions.** Illus. by author. Holiday House, 1982. 62 pp.

The story of the labor movement in America in the nineteenth century is one filled with strikes and riots. But labor did not give up the struggle for a fair standard of living for workers. By the end of the century, the American Federation of Labor had been founded, and the country was celebrating its first Labor Day. This book traces the history and influence of the union movement in America during the nineteenth century.

Freedman, Russell. **Immigrant Kids.** E. P. Dutton, 1980. 67 pp.

Kids who came to America from Europe a century ago had to act like miniature adults. They had to work hard and long at all kinds of jobs, from peddling newspapers to laboring in sweatshops. How the children came to America and what their lives were like living in crowded immigrant neighborhoods are described here in words and photographs. What kept most of them going through poverty and hardships was the belief that in America their lives one day could and would be better.

Gerson, Noel B. **The Trial of Andrew Johnson.** Thomas Nelson, 1977. 159 pp.

When Abraham Lincoln was assassinated in 1865, Vice President Andrew Johnson became president. Many people felt the government would now punish the South because of the Civil War, but Johnson upheld the laws guaranteed by the U.S. Constitution. Yet there were those in government who opposed Johnson, including the secretary of war, Edwin Stanton. Johnson fired Stanton and was then charged with committing crimes against the nation. Because of this charge, he was impeached by Congress. This book details this momentous event in our history.

Gidley, M. **With One Sky above Us: Life on an Indian Reservation at the Turn of the Century.** Photographs by Edward H. Latham. G. P. Putnam's Sons, 1979. 159 pp.

Through recently discovered photographs and letters of an Indian agency physician, the author has been able to draw an accurate picture of life on an Indian reservation at the end of the 1890s. The book focuses on the Nez Percé Indians of the Pacific Northwest at a time when Indians across the country were struggling to retain their culture against the enormous pressures placed on them by the U.S. government to do things like cut their braids, live in houses, and become Christians—in short, to be like whites.

Goode, Stephen. **The New Federalism: States' Rights in American History.** Franklin Watts, 1983. 146 pp.

Should power be distributed among states? Or should it be invested in a strong, centralized national government? This relationship between the states' powers and the power of the national goverment is the keystone for our constitutional system. This book begins with the 1787 Constitutional Convention and ends with our federalism of the 1980s—the "New Federalism" of President Reagan. Views of both critics and proponents are included.

Hagan, William T. **American Indians.** Rev. ed. University of Chicago Press, 1979. 193 pp.

The history of American Indians is traced from their early abuse at the hands of the Pilgrims and Puritans to their present search for the political power to control their own lives. Foreign manipulation, broken treaties, and neglect by the U.S. government have finally given way to national concern for Indian welfare.

Hamalian, Leo, editor. **In Search of Eden.** Mentor Books, 1981. 372 pp.

How do foreigners see America? This book presents our country from a number of fresh and interesting viewpoints, covering the period from the early explorers to the present. You can discover how a German governess described America during the Revolution. Or how a French official viewed the California Gold Rush. Or what an Englishwoman had to say about slavery in the South. Or what a modern English writer sees as the end of the American Dream of success.

Haskins, Jim. **The Long Struggle: The Story of American Labor.** Westminster Press, 1976. 160 pp.

The development of American labor unions from their beginnings in the 1700s to their powerful influence today is traced here. Unions have become especially concerned over a complex labor situation that stems from growing automation, the elimination of jobs, boring and tedious work on assembly lines, and the new influx of women into the labor market. This book looks at the strengths and weaknesses of unions and examines the struggle of the American worker to gain understanding and respect in society.

Highwater, Jamake. **Many Smokes, Many Moons: A Chronology of American Indian History through Indian Art.** J. B. Lippincott Co., 1978. 125 pp.

The author, who is of Blackfoot/Cherokee heritage, traces American Indian history through Indian art from 35,000 B.C. to 1973. This book shows how Indians see the whole world in terms of their cultural heritage. Included are many black-and-white photographs of Indian art.

Hilton, Suzanne. **Getting There: Frontier Travel without Power.** Westminster Press, 1980. 192 pp.

Westward ho! But how did our ancestors make the long and hazardous trip West? This book discusses all the means the pioneers used to travel: canalboats, covered wagons, sailing ships, stagecoaches, horses, and even feet. There are also sections describing what people took along on these journeys. Many actual letters and entries from diaries and journals are included to give you a firsthand taste of what is was like to travel the frontier in the days before gas, steam, or mechanical transportation.

Hilton, Suzanne. **We the People: The Way We Were, 1783–1793.** Westminster Press, 1981. 205 pp.

America is independent of the British! Now what happens in the next ten years? What was it like to be a young person in those days when there was no capital city, no army, no legal rights, and books had to be brought from England? This book covers amusements, marriage, fashions, housekeeping, schools, government, fires, funerals, and everyday life in the eighteenth century.

Horwitz, Elinor Lander. **The Bird, the Banner, and Uncle Sam: Images of America in Folk and Popular Art.** J. B. Lippincott Co., 1976. 167 pp.

The bald eagle, the Stars and Stripes, and Uncle Sam are among the many symbols that stand for America. Our nation has a large family of patriotic images, and this book traces and describes them all. The author tells how the eagle was chosen as our national bird (the runner-up was the turkey!), how a dusky female Indian evolved into Miss Liberty, and how a federal meat inspector became Uncle Sam. Illustrated by more than 160 photographs.

Horwitz, Elinor Lander. **On the Land: American Agriculture from Past to Present.** McElderry Books, 1980. 132 pp.

This book traces the history of farming in the United States, including a discussion of the problems facing farmers and all Americans today. Is modern agricultural technology beneficial? Has the strong role of government in shaping farming policies been too much? Alternatives for farming in the future are presented, and recommendations are made for further reading on the subject. Photographs.

Katz, William Loren, and Jacqueline Hunt Katz, editors. **Making Our Way: America at the Turn of the Century in the Words of the Poor and Powerless.** Dial Press, 1978. 170 pp.

What was life like in the early days of the twentieth century for a farmer's wife, a black sharecropper, a coal miner, a cowboy, a sweatshop worker, and a tramp? In this book, these people speak in their own words about their daily struggles to survive. The tales they have to tell about themselves and their country reveal their dreams, hopes, anger, sense of humor, and bitterness. Taken together, the stories show a picture of America different from that in most history books.

Lasky, Kathryn. **Tall Ships.** Photographs by Christopher G. Knight. Charles Scribner's Sons, 1978. 64 pp.

Excitement and danger alternated with boredom aboard the tall-masted ships, which sailed the world before the invention of the steam engine. This book explores life aboard the tall ships, the design of the ships, their construction, and the men who built and sailed them. Portions of the diaries, journals, and letters of past and present-day sailors are included, as are photographs taken aboard the *Regina Maris,* a modern tall ship.

Lawson, Don. **The United States in the Civil War.** Illus. Robert F. McCullough. Abelard-Schuman Books, 1977. 186 pp.

The issue of slavery grew more and more controversial in the 1800s until the South finally abandoned the Union to form its own government. The war that followed was dominated by the North, mainly because the North was able to mass-produce war machinery. Besides providing details on the slavery issue and the industrial question, this history of the Civil War covers the battles, the generals, and the statesmen involved in what many historians call the most traumatic war in the our country's history.

Lawson, Don. **The United States in the Mexican War.** Illus. Robert F. McCullough. Abelard-Schuman Books, 1976. 145 pp.

The Mexican-American War of 1846 to 1848, or "Mr. Polk's War," was not a popular one. President Polk wanted to expand America's borders to include Texas, California, and New Mexico. However, many citizens and politicians felt this wasn't a good enough reason to engage in a costly and bloody war. But through the aid of such men as Davy Crockett and Jim Bowie, the United States succeeded in winning the new land. Covered here is the fall of the Alamo in 1836, an event leading to the Mexican-American War.

Lawson, Don. **The United States in the Spanish-American War.** Illus. Robert F. McCullough. Abelard-Schuman Books, 1976. 140 pp.

Most of the major events leading up to the Spanish-American War are described in detail in this book. This war, begun in 1898, resulted in the United States finally becoming a major world power and led to U.S. involvement in the Philippine Insurrection and the Boxer Rebellion. Spain, on the other hand, lost most of its world influence by its defeat in the war. This account illuminates our nation's involvement in a war during a largely ignored period in our history.

Levison, Andrew. **The Full Employment Alternative.** Coward, McCann & Geoghegan, 1980. 252 pp.

Unemployment has become one of America's most chronic and severe economic problems. This book traces the history of unemployment from the breadlines of the Great Depression to present-day problems of unemployment among American youth. It also explores the economic systems of various European governments and suggests that a solution to our crisis would be to devise a uniquely American combination of business, labor, and government with a goal of full employment.

Loeb, Robert H., Jr. **Meet the *Real* Pilgrims: Everyday Life on Plimoth Plantation in 1627.** Doubleday & Co., 1979. 101 pp.

Thanks to the people who have preserved Plimoth Plantation, it is possible for us to visit that early colony and see what life was like in 1627. This book takes us on a tour of this living museum where the people who live there now speak to us in Elizabethan English and work, play, eat, celebrate holidays, and even marry as the original Pilgrims did.

May, Charles Paul. **The Uprooted.** Westminster Press, 1976. 160 pp.

Not all Americans came to this country of their own free will. Here is a look at people who have been brought to America or who have been forced to move and live in certain areas of the country. Included are early European settlers, African slaves, Asian settlers, Japanese nisei, and Vietnamese refugees. There are discussions of why certain minorities were relocated or interned, and what these events meant (and still mean) to American history.

McKay, Ernest A. **Carrier Strike Force: Pacific Air Combat in World War II.** Julian Messner, 1981. 191 pp.

It took only a year after the 1941 sneak attack on Pearl Harbor for the Japanese to gain control of the Pacific Ocean in World War II. To meet this threat, the United States Navy developed an aircraft carrier task force that could hit and run. These carriers were as tall as seventy-story buildings and could carry a hundred planes each. This book is the story of these mighty ships and their successful missions.

Meltzer, Milton. **Violins and Shovels: The WPA Arts Projects.** Delacorte Press, 1977. 160 pp.

During the Great Depression, the Works Progress Administration provided jobs for millions of people. The WPA also provided an opportunity for artists, musicians, actors, and writers to work together and create an American art form. The problems of the WPA arts program and the difficulties the artists suffered are discussed in this book, as are some of the great contributions of this program.

Munves, James. **Thomas Jefferson and the Declaration of Independence.** Charles Scribner's Sons, 1978. 135 pp.

This book shows the actual writing and editing of the document that turned out to be the Declaration of Independence. The author has recreated, through letters, notes, and manuscripts, the seventeen days in which the document was written and revised. The book also highlights the life of Thomas Jefferson, the major draftsman of the document, and how his life influenced his writing of the Declaration of Independence.

Murphy, Keith. **Battle of the Alamo.** Illus. Trevor Parkin. Raintree Publishers, 1979. 31 pp.

Setting themselves up in an old fort in Texas in 1836, a small group of men made the decision to stand up against a large Mexican army and to fight for the independence of Texas. The group of sharp-shooters inside the walls of that fort were led by Davy Crockett. Several of the men, including Crockett, took turns playing songs to keep up the spirits of the small band of Texans. For nearly two weeks they held their ground, but the battle ended as a bloody massacre. What happened during those tense days is described in this book.

Nabokov, Peter, editor. **Native American Testimony: An Anthology of Indian and White Relations—First Encounter to Dispossession.** Thomas Y. Crowell Co., 1978. 242 pp.

Using historical documents, this book attempts to reveal some of America's history through the eyes of the American Indian. In anecdotes and interviews, the attitude of Indians toward white explorers, missionaries, traders, soldiers, settlers, and government diplomats is revealed. Photographs.

Namias, June. **First Generation: In the Words of Twentieth-Century American Immigrants.** Beacon Press, 1978. 234 pp.

Why do people choose to immigrate to America? To find out, the author interviewed thirty-one first-generation immigrants who entered the United States between 1900 and the 1970s and some of their children. These interesting first-person oral histories are stories of hope, suffering, disappointment, and happiness.

Neal, Harry Edward. **The Secret Service in Action.** Elsevier/Nelson Books, 1980. 144 pp.

What kinds of cases does the Secret Service get involved in? Agents have had shoot-outs with people who threatened to kill public figures. They have saved a president's daughter from a wild elephant. They have trained dogs for the Canine Unit to hunt criminals. And they have even become trapped in an illegal mine shaft. The author, a former assistant chief of the Secret Service, recalls these and other exciting moments in the organization's 125-year history in this book.

Neuborne, Burt, and Arthur Eisenberg. **The Rights of Candidates and Voters.** Rev. ed. Avon Books, 1980. 188 pp.

This extensive handbook of the American Civil Liberties Union describes the rights of voters in the United States and the rights of those who wish to run for office. Other related topics covered include access to the ballot, the right to fair representation, and the financing and conducting of political campaigns.

Paylin, Jolie. **Cutover Country: Jolie's Story.** Iowa State University Press, 1976. 168 pp.

Every day is an adventure for eleven-year-old Jolie Paylin when her father moves his family from a conservative Illinois farm community to a stretch of isolated and half-cleared land in northern Wisconsin in the 1920s. Life is harsh, and the work hard, and so Jolie fears her mother will want to leave this land of exciting challenges. This true personal history of a family offers insights into the pioneer spirit that has never quite left the American people.

Perrin, Linda. **Coming to America: Immigrants from the Far East.** Delacorte Press, 1980. 182 pp.

Has America always welcomed poor and oppressed people from around the world? This book focuses on Asian immigrants from China, Japan, the Philippines, and Vietnam who often suffered harassment and discrimination when they came to the United States. The author examines the changing history of Asians in America from 1849, when news of the Gold Rush in California reached China, to the resettlement of the Vietnamese "boat people" in 1979. Much of the information has been taken from diaries, letters, books, and interviews.

Phelan, Mary Kay. **The Story of the Boston Massacre.** Illus. Allan Eitzen. Thomas Y. Crowell Co., 1976. 136 pp.

Boston, 1770. Residents feel insulted and angry over British authority—from the problem of unjust taxation to the pressures of tight military surveillance. Name-calling, threats, and scuffles between the factions grow. Distrust builds and tension grows so great that the slightest frown might have the power to touch off a full-scale battle. Then one bitter March Monday, there is another exchange of angry insults. A dare shouted to fire is mistaken as an order to begin shooting. The British soldiers' muskets open on the throng of angry citizens, many of whom are wounded or killed. Later, during the trial, Paul Revere, Sam and John Adams, and many others are involved in what is to become a crucial moment in our history.

Phelan, Mary Kay. **Waterway West: The Story of the Erie Canal.** Illus. David Frampton. Thomas Y. Crowell Co., 1977. 125 pp.

When the construction of a mile-long canal across the upper region of New York is proposed to the U.S. government in 1813, the plan is scorned. Almost everyone is convinced that it is ridiculous. Only one man, De Witt Clinton, has enough courage to fight for the plan. Through war, debate, and severe hardship, he leads a team of men shovelful by shovelful to link Lake Erie with the Hudson River.

Remini, Robert V. **The Revolutionary Age of Andrew Jackson.** Avon Books, 1977. 188 pp.

America was not at war during the fifty years between the War of 1812 and the Civil War, yet it was a time of revolution. People weren't rioting or killing one another, but enormous changes in the American character were taking place. Such men as Andrew Jackson, Henry Clay, John C. Calhoun, and Daniel Webster tried to handle the difficult questions of the period: What was the nation to do about the Indians? How do you rationalize slavery in a free nation? Could America be made truly democratic? Was it possible to solve the power struggles between the president and the Congress? The way that these and other questions were answered has helped to determine the modern American way of life.

Sabato, Larry J. **The Rise of Political Consultants: New Ways of Winning Elections.** Basic Books, 1981. 379 pp.

Contrary to popular belief, the "best man" still wins elections. In modern politics, however, the "best man" isn't the candidate, but the candidate's political consultant. Professional consultants are hired by candidates to help them handle the media, take polls, create campaign strategy, and send direct mailings to voters. This book contains interviews with some of the most successful political consultants, who discuss the new political campaign technology that makes or breaks America's politicians.

Santoli, Al. **Everything We Had: An Oral History of the Vietnam War by Thirty-Three American Soldiers Who Fought It.** Random House, 1981. 265 pp.

Here is a collection of transcribed tape-recorded accounts of thirty-three American men and women who served in the Vietnam War. Their stories begin in 1962, at the beginning of U.S. involvement in Vietnam, and they end in April 1975. These are personal accounts of battles and living conditions by soldiers, sailors, and nurses. When viewed together, the stories accurately reveal what happened to many Americans in Vietnam. Mature language and situations.

Seymour, Forrest W. **Sitanka: The Full Story of Wounded Knee.** Christopher Publishing House, 1981. 194 pp.

This is an account of the major events before, during, and after the battle at Wounded Knee in 1890—not altogether as the United States Army told it, and not altogether as the Indian survivors remembered it. The facts in this book come from numerous sources, including personal interviews with Wounded Knee participants. Finally, here is the full story of Wounded Knee.

Sullivan, George. **The Supercarriers.** Dodd, Mead & Co., 1980. 160 pp.

The giant aircraft carriers that populate our navy have changed the strategies of modern defense and warfare. Beginning with a tiny biplane taking off from a wooden ramp of a battleship in 1910, the history of carrier aviation is one of constant growth in number and size. The author traces the influences of carriers in World War II, Korea, Vietnam, and in the future. Also discussed are the details of life on a supercarrier and the current controversy over their cost and effectiveness. Photographs.

Supree, Burton (with Ann Ross). **Bear's Heart: Scenes from the Life of a Cheyenne Artist of One Hundred Years Ago with Pictures by Himself.** J. B. Lippincott Co., 1977. 64 pp.

Bear's Heart, a Cheyenne Indian imprisoned at Fort Marion, Florida, in 1876, used pictures to record scenes from the life of the Plains Indians before and after the arrival of the settlers and soldiers. The accompanying text explains the Indians' activities on the Great Plains and their imprisonment in Florida.

Surge, Frank. **Western Lawmen.** Fearon-Pitman Publishers, 1978. 62 pp.

When guns were the loudest law in the West, brave and just people worked to create order out of chaos. Some were more lawless than outlaws, and each was a colorful and unique figure. Many met violent deaths, even though the one thing they shared was the promise to use a gun only as the last resort. Photographs.

Tamarin, Alfred, and Shirley Glubok. **Voyaging to Cathay: Americans in the China Trade.** Viking Press, 1976. 184 pp.

As a brand-new nation, the United States had to have commerce in order to survive. To some, China seemed the answer. Many young men risked their lives sailing around Cape Horn to get to the port of Canton, where they traded goods for exotic treasures to take home. Many made their fortunes, and many lost their lives. But they all had exciting adventures in a land largely unknown to them—a land of silks, spices, porcelain, and other rare arts. This book traces the earliest contacts between the United States and China from the years following the American Revolution until the arrival of the steamship.

terHorst, J. F., and Ralph Albertazzie. **The Flying White House: The Story of Air Force One.** Coward, McCann & Geoghegan, 1979. 350 pp.

This is the story of Air Force One, the president's private plane, and it includes descriptions of the specific airplanes that have carried U.S. presidents from Franklin Roosevelt to Jimmy Carter. Also collected here are descriptions of memorable flights of the presidents, including Nixon's departure from the White House following his resignation.

Tunis, Edsin. **Indians.** Rev. ed. Illus. by author. Thomas Y. Crowell Co., 1979. 153 pp.

In lively style and with numerous detailed illustrations, the daily lives of the major tribes of North American Indians before the Europeans arrived are described in this book. The reader will discover information about their homes, clothes, dances, music, war ceremonies, and methods of worship.

Van Every, Dale. **Disinherited.** Discus Books, 1980. 302 pp.

The Cherokees, Chickasaws, Choctaws, and Seminoles were among the tribes of American Indians who lost their lands. This book explains the problems these Indians encountered when they came into contact with white settlers and were forced by the U.S. government to give up their lands.

Weingarten, Arthur. **The Sky Is Falling.** Popular Library, 1977. 282 pp.

On July 28, 1945, an Air Force B-25 bomber with three men aboard flew into the Empire State Building in New York City. As a result, fourteen people were killed and twenty-six were injured. This is the story of why it happened, how it happened, and why it should never happen again. The book also provides information about those people who lost their lives, those who survived, and those whose heroic efforts kept down the number of fatalities.

The Western Writers of America. **Water Trails West.** Discus Books, 1979. 347 pp.

During America's first 100 years, travel around the country was so difficult that it was easier to travel from New York to England than to travel from New York to the Appalachians. But our country's waterways soon played a key role in the exploration and settlement of the frontier. This book is a collection of documented, historically accurate stories about some of America's great waterways. Included are details of cross-country canoe trips, travels via the Erie Canal, voyages across the Great Lakes, steamboating on Texas rivers, and dangerous journeys on the rough and wild rivers of the far West. Photographs.

World

Baldwin, Margaret. **The Boys Who Saved the Children.** JeM Books, 1981. 62 pp.

Can you imagine soldiers bursting into your house and taking away your father or mother or sister right in front of your eyes? That was happening to everyone in young Ben Edelbaum's neighborhood in Lodz, Poland, in 1940. A group of boys decide to try to resist. And these children find they are able to defy the Nazis—at least for a little while.

Barbary, James. **Puritan and Cavalier: The English Civil War.** Thomas Nelson, 1977. 192 pp.

This history of the English Civil War gives vivid details of the plots, the personalities, and the battles that took place throughout England during the 1640s. It was the time when King Charles and his pro-Catholic army tried to prevent the Puritan army, representing the Parliament, from ruling England.

Barber, Noel. **The Fall of Shanghai.** Coward, McCann & Geoghegan, 1979. 248 pp.

Prior to its takeover by the Communist forces in 1949, Shanghai was a city of incredible contrast: wealth and abject poverty, splendor and squalor, gluttony and starvation. It was a city open to business, both legal and criminal; a city in which people made a fortune or died penniless. Prostitution and drugs were openly allowed. The revolution was to change all that. Here is the story of the Communist takeover and the effect it had on the people who lived in this unique international city.

Bendiner, Elmer. **The Fall of Fortresses: A Personal Account of the Most Daring—and Deadly—American Air Battles of World War II.** G. P. Putnam's Sons, 1980. 258 pp.

The author recalls his personal experiences during World War II as the navigator of a B-17, known as a flying fortress because of its huge size and devastating power. One of his missions was to bomb the ball bearing factories at Schweinfurt, Germany. By searching both German and U.S. archives and interviewing military survivors, the author explains the complexities of the mission and the horror of making the bombing runs through flak and ground fire. Photographs.

Bethell, Nicholas. **The Palestine Triangle: The Struggle for the Holy Land, 1935–48.** G. P. Putnam's Sons, 1979. 384 pp.

This book looks at the historical period of 1935–1948 in which three groups of people—the Arabs, the Jews, and the English—vied for the control of Palestine. The author explains the history of the capital city of Jerusalem and describes some of the reasons for recent problems there and around the Palestine region. Mature reading.

Blau, Melinda. **First over the Oceans.** Illus. Jon Gampert. Contemporary Perspectives, 1978. 48 pp.

The 1947 journey of the *Kon-Tiki* across the Pacific, the first voyage around the world by Magellan, and the first steamship race across the Atlantic by the *Sirius* and the *Great Western* in 1838 are all described here. Interesting anecdotes and facts are presented about each journey.

Botjer, George F. **A Short History of Nationalist China, 1919–1949.** G. P. Putnam's Sons, 1979. 312 pp.

China has gone through many periods of great change, often due to rebellion and warfare. In 1919, the Japanese took control over part of China; soon thereafter the Chinese Communist Party was founded. Within a few years the Communists were fighting against the Chinese Nationalists, led by Chiang Kai-shek. More than twenty years of civil war followed, and in 1949 the Communists drove Chiang Kai-shek and the Nationalists off the mainland to set up their government on the island of Taiwan. This history book looks at all the plots and intrigues that occurred in China between 1919 and 1949, and discusses their effects on the country's politics—and its people.

Carroll, Raymond. **The Palestine Question.** Franklin Watts, 1983. 88 pp.

People have been fighting each other over the small strip of land known as Palestine for centuries—almost as long as the land has been inhabited. The conflict between the Jews and the Arabs is explained and traced through the years. Other aspects discussed are the British control (1920–1948), the UN partition plan, the war of 1948–1949, the Palestine Liberation Organization, and the Israeli military action against the PLO in Lebanon in 1982.

Casewit, Curtis W. **The Saga of the Mountain Soldiers: The Story of the 10th Mountain Division.** Julian Messner, 1981. 151 pp.

The Tenth Mountain Division of the U.S. Army contributed more to the downfall of the Germans in Italy than any other division in World War II. They were known as the "Magnificent Tenth" and were trained in Colorado and Texas, where they had to cope with blizzards, subzero weather, and eighty-pound packs on their backs. Many of these heroic soldiers had been famous skiers, skilled hunting guides, or experienced foresters before joining the army, and they used this experience to their advantage in fighting mountain warfare. Here you'll learn all the details of their dangerous but true adventures.

Cohen, Daniel. **The Body Snatchers.** J. B. Lippincott Co., 1975. 159 pp.

These are historical "horror stories" of grave robbers through the centuries. The book presents information concerning burial customs and attitudes towards death throughout history, then discusses religious, economic, scientific, and political motives for body snatching and grave robbing. Early grave robbers often were medical students looking for bodies to dissect. Other grave robbers were looking for money, either by selling bodies or by stealing valuables buried with the dead.

Collins, Larry, and Dominique Lapierre. **Freedom at Midnight.** Avon Books, 1976. 596 pp.

When Great Britain freed India from the British Empire in 1947, civil wars, riots, and countless murders followed. The people and the events that brought about this tumultuous turning point in Asian history are all explained in detail here. The story of Britain's three-and-one-half-century rule of the Indian subcontinent is also analyzed.

Dillon, Eilis. **Rome under the Emperors.** Thomas Nelson, 1975. 186 pp.

A view of life in Rome in 110 A.D. is recreated in this book. At the center of this combination history book and novel are the stories of four boys. We first meet fifteen-year-old Lucius, whose father is a Roman senator. The daily routine of his wealthy family's life is described, including the type of clothes they wear and Lucius's studies with his tutor. Gallus is also fifteen, and his father is a businessman. The father of fifteen-year-old Tullin is a farmer, so the book allows us to follow the work of producing food for the Empire. Finally, we meet Quintus, whose father is a stallholder in the marketplace. Between these four stories, a vast, yet personal, picture of life in ancient Rome is presented.

Dornberg, John. **The Soviet Union Today.** Dial Press, 1976. 275 pp.

The Soviet Union is filled with contrasts. For example, there is some degree of profiteering in a supposedly nonmaterialistic society. And a huge gap exists between the rich and poor in a country that denies class difference. The Soviets try to modernize, but they suffer from pollution, delinquency, alcoholism, and a rising divorce rate, as we do in the United States. There is more freedom now than under the rule of the czars, but some educated people continue to try to gain more freedom from the government.

Forman, James D. **That Mad Game: War and the Chances for Peace.** Charles Scribner's Sons, 1980. 225 pp.

This book gives an overview of both war and peace throughout history. It then examines the causes of wars and of the various attempts that have been made to abolish war permanently. Also discussed is the nature of humans and what makes them so aggressive. On the other hand, there is a discussion of how peace, love, and reason are developed in human personalities.

Goldston, Robert. **Next Year in Jerusalem: A Short History of Zionism.**
Atlantic Monthly Press, 1978. 242 pp.

For two thousand years the Jewish people have searched for a
homeland where they could live in freedom and peace. Jews have
been enslaved, dispersed, forced to live in ghettos, and massacred
because of their faith. Throughout all this, Jewish people maintained
their burning desire for a Jewish state. This book traces the history
of Zionism from its beginnings to the establishment of Israel.

Goldston, Robert. **Sinister Touches: The Secret War against Hitler.** Dial
Press, 1982. 214 pp.

Included in this book are the stories of how Nazi codes were
cracked, how espionage was carried out in New York and other
cities, and how tricks outwitted such Nazi spies as the famous
"Cicero." The strategies used to mislead Hitler about Allied plans,
the race for atomic power, and individual wartime acts of courage
are also discussed in this account of the underground battle against
Nazi power in the 1940s. (ALA Best Book for Young Adults)

Graff, Stewart. **The Story of World War II.** E. P. Dutton, 1978. 83 pp.

This book provides a brief history of World War II from 1939 to
1945. The author discusses the beginnings, the big battles, and the
conclusion of the war. There are sections on Germany under Adolf
Hitler and on Japan's attack on American ships at Pearl Harbor.
Photographs. Easy reading.

Hall, Grover C., Jr. **1000 Destroyed: The Life and Times of the 4th
Fighter Group.** Aero Publishers, 1978. 384 pp.

Even before the United States entered World War II, there were
American pilots fighting the Germans and the Japanese. These
American fliers were volunteers who made up the Eagle Squadron
and who flew in the Royal Air Force of Great Britain. When the
United States declared war, the Eagle Squadron became the 4th
Fighter Group of the United States Army Air Force. This book
contains many stories about how this fighter group became the
German Air Force's most hated and feared enemy. Photographs.

Hauser, Thomas. **The Execution of Charles Horman: An American
Sacrifice.** Discus Books, 1980.

The research done for this book presents evidence that there was a
plot to have journalist Charles Horman executed in 1973 and that
his death was actually without reason. Horman supposedly had
overheard too much about American involvement in the military

overthrow of the Chilean government and the assassination of President Salvadore Allende of Chile. The book insinuates that the Nixon administration and the CIA were instrumental in getting the successful military coup organized, and implies that the fear that Horman would make public what he heard led to a conspiracy between our government and the Chilean military to have Horman kidnapped and killed. The movie *Missing* is based on this book.

Hilton, Suzanne. **Here Today and Gone Tomorrow: The Story of World's Fairs and Expositions.** Westminster Press, 1978. 191 pp.

World's fairs and expositions have been a part of our history since 1851, when London was the host for the Crystal Palace Exposition. The telegraph was a big exhibit at that fair, as were many other appliances and inventions people soon came to use every day. This book traces the many world's fairs since the 1851 fair, including the fairs at St. Louis, Seattle, Osaka, Montreal, and Paris.

Hoyt, Edwin P. **The Men of the Gambler Bay.** Avon Books, 1981. 278 pp.

It is World War II and the fighting in the Pacific is becoming more and more fierce. The leaders of the United States Navy plan a dangerous but necessary mission to be called the Battle of Leyte Gulf. One ship—the *Gambler Bay*—is to experience much combat. This book traces the story of this ship, from construction to destruction at sea under Japanese fire. This is also the story of the brave men on the ship and their heroic deeds.

Japanese Broadcasting Corporation (NHK), editor. **Unforgettable Fire.** Pantheon Books, 1977. 110 pp.

Those who survive a tragedy tell of its horror best. Thirty years after the most terrible bombing known to man took place in 1945 at Hiroshima, Japan, some survivors relive its tortures. Through words and vivid drawings made at the time of the catastrophe, these people share their experience with the rest of the world as a warning, for they realize that today's weapons might wreak even greater destruction upon the earth.

Joyce, James Avery. **The War Machine: The Case against the Arms Race.** Avon Books, 1982. 251 pp.

The human race has stockpiled weapons with a destructive power equal to three tons of TNT for every person on this planet—all controlled by one button in Washington and one button in the Kremlin. How did it come to this? Joyce discusses the military establishment, our political leaders, and the multinational arms manufacturers in this urgent plea for participation in the worldwide campaign against the arms race.

Kurzman, Dan. **Miracle of November: Madrid's Epic Stand, 1936.** G. P. Putnam's Sons, 1980. 352 pp.

Madrid, the capital and heart of Spain, was a besieged city in the fall of 1936. General Franco's rebel Fascist army believed that the taking of the city would be a routine matter. They did not expect to encounter the unified and enraged citizens of Madrid, who refused to bow under pressure. This is the story of how the city's men, women, and children dug trenches, built barricades, and generally prepared to stop the Fascist troops at all costs.

Lawson, Ted W. (editor Bob Considine). **Thirty Seconds over Tokyo.** Random House, 1971. 201 pp.

Bomb Tokyo? That was the top-secret mission of Army Captain Ted Lawson and his crew. Thousands of people had been killed in Japan's sneak attack on Pearl Harbor in 1941, so the United States had to strike back fast. But our Pacific fleet had been wiped out. The solution was a daring raid on Japan's largest city by a squadron of U.S. fighter pilots. This is Captain Lawson's own story, and he tells just how he flew his bomber over Tokyo. This edition of the book has been prepared especially for young readers. Photographs.

Lidz, Richard. **Many Kinds of Courage: An Oral History of World War II.** G. P. Putnam's Sons, 1980. 266 pp.

The author used taped interviews to record the stories of people who displayed courage in World War II. Included are tales of Hitler's rise to power in Germany in the 1930s, the story of the English evacuation from Dunkirk, France, and the bombing of Pearl Harbor. Other stories concern firsthand accounts of life in concentration camps and the Normandy invasion. These individual stories are all connected by the author's running narrative on the broader background of events discussed in the stories.

Marrin, Albert. **The Airman's War: World War II in the Sky.** Atheneum Publishers, 1982. 203 pp.

This story tells exactly how World War II was fought in the skies by the U.S. Air Force. Included are discussions of strategic plans, bomber crews, fighter pilots, and all the different kinds of planes. The book also includes the stories of British and American nonstop bombing raids over Germany, and the slow island-by-island battles in the Pacific. Photographs.

McIntosh, Dave. **Terror in the Starboard Seat.** Beaufort Books, 1980. 184 pp.

This is the true story of the 418th Squadron of the Canadian Air Force and their battles in World War II. The author describes his exploits as a navigator aboard a two-man fighter plane, a Mosquito, that was used to raid at night. Mature language and situations.

Murphy, E. Jefferson. **Understanding Africa.** Rev. ed. Illus. Louise E. Jefferson. Thomas Y. Crowell Co., 1978. 211 pp.

For years Africa has been misunderstood. Most people are confused by false ideas of who and what the Africans are. Since 1960, however, ideas about Africa have been changing, largely because of the growing independence movements among the various African peoples. This book tries to clarify the story of Africa by describing its geography, history, population, natural resources, and cultures, with special emphasis on the countries to the south of the Sahara.

Noble, Iris. **Interpol: International Crime Fighter.** Harcourt Brace Jovanovich, 1975. 116 pp.

The purpose of Interpol, the International Police, remains a mystery to many people. Instead of being a super detective agency, it is really a network of communication centers in 117 nations that assists local police in tracking down criminals who flee across national boundaries. The American center, in Washington, D.C., is one of five major communication centers in the world. Some of Interpol's cases, such as a raid on a Michigan pizza parlor, are also presented in this book.

Poynter, Margaret. **Gold Rush! The Yukon Stampede of 1898.** Atheneum Publishers, 1979. 91 pp.

In 1898 the stampede for gold was on in the Yukon Territory. This is the exciting story of gold hunters in Canada and Alaska. This society of sourdoughs and gold miners is thoroughly described with attention to how these people with a common goal helped each other in times of need. The first gold strikes are discussed, and descriptions of the different types of mining are given.

Reiss, Johanna. **The Journey Back.** Thomas Y. Crowell Co., 1976. 212 pp.

From personal experience, the author tells what it was like after World War II when everyone who had been in hiding, or who had lived through the horrors of the Nazi concentration camps, came home. After so many years even members of the same family were strangers. The author had been so young when she had gone into hiding that she felt her real family were the people who had hidden her. Her mother was now dead; her oldest sister had converted to Christianity; her father was courting a new wife; and even her sister Sini, who had been in hiding with her, was different, going out every night to dance with the Canadian soldiers. Hiding had been hard, but readjusting to a family of strangers was somehow harder.

Rice, Edward. **Babylon, Next to Nineveh: Where the World Began.** Four Winds Press, 1979. 186 pp.

This interesting and informative tour of the land between the Tigris and Euphrates rivers provides a historical picture of a civilization that is twelve thousand years old. The cities, people, and leaders of Mesopotamia are discussed in terms of their contributions to the growth and development of this historic area.

Roberson, John R. **China from Manchu to Mao (1699–1976).** Atheneum Publishers, 1980. 208 pp.

This history of China begins in 1699 during the reign of Emperor Kang Xi at a time when the influence of foreigners in China began to grow. During the three centuries since then, Western nations have constantly tried to influence Chinese affairs. In this period, Chinese history includes such well-known names as the Dowager Empress Ci Xi, Sun Yat-sen, Chiang Kai-shek, and Mao Zedong, a library assistant who changed China. Photographs.

Ross, Josephine. **The Tudors: England's Golden Age.** G. P. Putnam's Sons, 1979. 184 pp.

The Tudors were a family of three kings and two queens whose reigns marked a particularly exciting time in England. The Tudor dynasty was begun by Henry VII, who became king of England in 1485, and it ended with Elizabeth I's death in 1603. In between reigned Henry VIII, Edward VI, and Mary I. During their reigns England changed from a medieval kingdom to a great European power, largely because of the sharp minds, spirits, and decisions of the five Tudors. Photographs.

Roth, Russell. **Muddy Glory: America's "Indian Wars" in the Philippines, 1899–1935.** Christopher Publishing House, 1981. 273 pp.

America's wars in the Philippines from 1899 through 1935 converted this country's Indian-fighting veterans into trained soldiers who would defend our country's ideals in two world wars. But they also taught lessons that have been too soon forgotten—lessons in the skills and agonies of modern guerrilla warfare. The author shows how American soldiers saw the wars, the Filipinos, and each other and discusses the strengths and weaknesses of the prominent commanders, politicians, and journalists.

Ryan, Cornelius. **The Longest Day.** Popular Library, 1975. 350 pp.

June 6, 1944, was indeed "the longest day" for hundreds of thousands of Allied troops. It was a day when thousands would die, tons of bombs would explode, and millions of bullets would be fired. It was the day on which the Allies launched their first counterattack on the German forces occupying Western Europe by landing on the beaches of Normandy. This book describes this one day in history in extreme detail, revealing to the reader a multitude of facts, little-known anecdotes, and unusual views of the battle that led to the end of World War II. The text is complete with pictures, illustrations, maps, and even a listing of D-Day veterans.

Simpson, William P. **Island "X"—Okinawa.** Christopher Publishing House, 1981. 271 pp.

Operation Rice Paddy was the code name for a huge assault on a mysterious Pacific island near the military's final goal—Japan. On Island "X," air raid alerts, kamikaze attacks, swarms of biting insects, tropical rains, typhoons, primitive huts, mudholes, and dangerous, unprotected native wells made things difficult for the men as they tried to do their jobs. The author was stationed in the Pacific during the last half of World War II and provides a firsthand picture of the men and machines that helped to win the war.

Spencer, William. **The Islamic States in Conflict.** Franklin Watts, 1983. 88 pp.

The Islamic people, like many other people, have had their quarrels for years. There are many sources for these quarrels and conflicts: different ideas about Islam and about politics, differences of race and culture, and rivalries of all kinds. This book focuses on the Arab states of Iraq, Lebanon, Syria, Jordan, Saudi Arabia, Egypt, and non-Arab Iran. Their unity and divisions throughout history are presented.

Stevenson, William. **A Man Called Intrepid: The Secret War.** Ballantine Books, 1976. 541 pp.

This is the story of a combined American and British intelligence operation just before and during World War II. This book explains in great detail the ways spies worked for both the Allies and the Nazis. Specific incidents discussed include the destruction of the

German battleship *Bismarck* and the assassination of Reinhard Heydrich. How agents broke enemy codes and the use of counter-espionage measures are also described here.

Taylor, Theodore. **Battle in the Arctic Seas: The Story of Convoy PQ 17.** Illus. Robert Andrew Parker. Thomas Y. Crowell Co., 1976. 151 pp.

In the summer of 1942, a convoy of cargo ships carrying guns and war equipment to the Soviet Union left from a port in Iceland. This true story tells about the adventures of an American sailor, Ensign Carroway, and the cargo ship *Troubador*. His ship had few guns, but it found itself in danger from German planes and submarines. When Convoy PQ 17 breaks formation, the *Troubador* must fight its own way through the hazardous Arctic seas to the Soviet Union.

Theis, Dan. **The Crescent and the Cross.** Thomas Nelson, 1978. 180 pp.

Pope Urban II begins almost two hundred years of war when he calls for the Crusades to free the Holy Land from Muslim control. The political and religious bickering, the thirst for power by certain leaders, and the problems of the Crusaders themselves are discussed as possible reasons for the terrible bloodshed and folly of this massive adventure. Lasting for the entire twelfth and thirteenth centuries, the Crusades produced many romantic heroes and warriors who tried to win back the Holy Land, including Bohemond I, Alexius, Raymond IV of Toulouse, and Godfrey of Bouillon.

Toliver, Raymond F. (with Hanns J. Scharff). **The Interrogator: The Story of Hanns Scharff, Luftwaffe's Master Interrogator.** Aero Publishers, 1978. 384 pp.

This is the story of Hanns-Joachim Scharff, who was the master interrogator of the Allied pilots captured by the Germans during World War II. He broke down prisoners who were trained to remain silent with a method so efficient that after the war he was invited by the U.S. Air Force to lecture senior officers of the Pentagon on POW interrogation techniques. Photographs.

Worth, Richard. **Israel and the Arab States.** Franklin Watts, 1983. 96 pp.

Exactly what is going on between Israel and the Arab states? This book answers that question by focusing on Arab-Israeli relations, rather than Israeli-Palestinian relations. The author traces the history through all the acts of terrorism as well as through four wars (the War of Independence in 1948, the Sinai War of 1956, the Six-Day War of 1967, and the October War of 1973). The historic meeting of Anwar Sadat and Menachem Begin with Jimmy Carter at Camp David is highlighted.

Ziemian, Joseph (translator Janina David). **The Cigarette Sellers of Three Crosses Square.** Avon Books, 1977. 140 pp.

Few Jews are alive in the harsh world of Nazi-occupied Poland in 1943. But out of the Warsaw ghetto, where dead bodies lie unburied in the street, a group of children escapes. Surviving by wits and courage, sleeping in cellars and attics, this small band of friends makes a living by working right under the noses of their enemies, selling cigarettes to Nazi officials.

Hobbies and Crafts

Albin, Len. **Secrets of the Video Game Super Stars.** Illus. Ernest Haim. Avon Books, 1982. 186 pp.

This book shows you how to master the twenty-six most popular video games. Learn to spot enemy attack patterns, outmaneuver advancing phalanxes, improve your score, and sharpen your eye-hand coordination. Find out how the games are designed and how they work. Get all the secrets from the stars themselves.

Alkema, Chester Jay. **Masks.** Photographs by author. Sterling Publishing Co., 1978. 48 pp.

Humans have found methods to disguise or hide their faces since the beginnings of history. For many reasons—religious, dramatic, or just plain fun—colorful masks and headdresses have found their way into virtually every culture. This is an illustrated book of making masks from a variety of materials. You can create simple paper bag masks or complicated paper collage masks by following simple construction techniques. Color photographs of the masks accompany the text.

Alkema, Chester Jay. **Puppet-Making.** Sterling Publishing Co., 1976. 48 pp.

What do cartoons, sticks, paper bags, newspaper, sawdust, socks, clay, food, spoons, and tongue depressors have in common? They can all be used to make a variety of puppets. With step-by-step instructions and many illustrations, this book guides you through the process of creating puppets for theater performances or just for your own amusement. Easy reading.

Allison, Linda. **The Sierra Club Summer Book.** Illus. by author. Sierra Club Books, 1977. 160 pp.

Summer is that time of year when kids can stay up late, sleep long into the morning, and still have hours and hours of daylight to enjoy. But summer can bring boredom with all those extra hours to fill. This book will not only provide dozens of entertaining ideas to occupy the time, but it will also teach you some things you may want to know once summer rolls around. For example, how would you like a dozen methods for keeping cool on a hot day? Or maybe you'd like to be able to tell the temperature by using a gum wrapper? Or perhaps you'd enjoy becoming an inner-city naturalist? These and dozens of other intriguing ideas can be found in this book.

Ames, Lee J. **Draw 50 Airplanes, Aircraft and Spacecraft.** Illus. by author. Doubleday & Co., 1977. 50 pp.

Easy-to-follow directions for drawing fifty airplanes, other aircraft, and spacecraft take you from simple geometric forms to a completed, detailed drawing. And while you do all this, you will be able to gain some valuable insights into the proportions and perspectives used generally in drawing and sketching.

Ames, Lee J. **Draw 50 Boats, Ships, Trucks and Trains.** Illus. by author. Doubleday & Co., 1976. 50 pp.

Ever want to draw your favorite truck, boat, or train? Well, now you can learn how to with a few simple step-by-step instructions. So, go ahead, take your pencil in hand, and start drawing that Mack truck, the *Titanic,* or that little red caboose.

Ames, Lee J. **Draw 50 Dinosaurs and Other Prehistoric Animals.** Illus. by author. Doubleday & Co., 1977. 50 pp.

Draw your way back into the Stone Age. This guide helps you recreate the time when dinosaurs ruled the earth. You will learn how to sketch a tyrannosaurus rex, a pterodactyl, or a brontosaurus.

Ames, Lee J. **Draw 50 Dogs.** Illus. by author. Doubleday & Co., 1981. 50 pp.

Have you ever tried to draw a picture of a dog, only to be disappointed with the results? This book can show you how to draw a fleet-footed greyhound, a shaggy Old English sheepdog, a heroic St. Bernard, and many others. All you need to do is follow the author's step-by-step instructions—and you'll be proud of your picture!

Ames, Lee J. **Draw 50 Famous Cartoons.** Illus. by author. Doubleday & Co., 1979. 50 pp.

Now you, too, can be the creator of Popeye, Archie, and other cartoon characters. Just follow the easy directions provided in the manual, and you are on your way to creating new adventures for your favorite comic characters.

Ames, Lee J. **Draw 50 Famous Faces.** Illus. by author. Doubleday & Co., 1978. 50 pp.

There are many famous people, from all walks of life, for you to draw in this step-by-step guide. Do you think people are too hard to draw? Well, in nine easy steps you'll find out you can draw people very skillfully—and well-known people at that.

Ames, Lee J. **Draw 50 Famous Stars.** Illus. by author. Doubleday & Co., 1982. 50 pp.

Would you like to draw famous actors and actresses so perfectly that anyone could recognize them instantly? Now you can! Lee J. Ames shows you a foolproof method for sketching the stars. By following his step-by-step instructions, you can make professional-looking drawings of Woody Allen, Carol Burnett, Robert Redford, and many more.

Backhouse, Andrew. **Illustrated Card Games.** Illus. Clarissa. Thomas Nelson, 1976. 126 pp.

Here is a book for the beginning card player or the expert. The history of cards is covered, from their original use in telling fortunes to their being banned as instruments of the devil. And if you would like to join the card-playing ranks, this book will teach you seventeen different games. These games range from those that are easy to those that are more difficult, and from those requiring one player to those that can be played by as many as nine.

Bahadur, Dinesh. **Come Fight a Kite.** Harvey House, Publishers, 1978. 56 pp.

Everyone has heard of flying a kite, but have you heard of fighting a kite? After an introduction describing the four basic kite designs, this book discusses how to use these designs to make fighter kites. Other sections cover launching and kite-fighting techniques. There are also tips on how to fight one-on-one and in teams.

Baron, Nancy. **Getting Started in Calligraphy.** Sterling Publishing Co., 1979. 95 pp.

You don't have to be a great artist to letter with beauty, grace, and style. Beginning with a list of the materials you will need, this guide goes on to instruct you in sitting positions, the proper angles for the pen, and loosening-up exercises. There are five different styles of decorative lettering to choose from.

Barr, Stephen. **Puzzlequiz: Wit Twisters, Brain Teasers, Riddles, Puzzles, and Tough Questions.** Illus. Colos. Thomas Y. Crowell Co., 1978.

Test your skill and memory in history, literature, math, science, and puzzles of all sorts. Can you describe the first U.S. flag, for instance? Or what animal climbs itself? Do you really think you know what Cinderella's slipper was made of? You may be surprised by the answers to these and over five hundred other problems.

Barry, Sheila Anne. **Super-Colossal Book of Puzzles, Tricks and Games.** Illus. Doug Anderson. Sterling Publishing Co., 1978. 640 pp.

With this huge collection of games and puzzles, you'll never have to be bored again on a rainy Saturday. Thousands of entries are designed for children aged six and older. Included are optical illusions, card tricks, word games, personality tests, number games, and dozens of other things to do. The answers to all of the problems are provided at the end of the book.

Berloquin, Pierre. **100 Geometric Games.** Illus. Denis Dugas. Charles Scribner's Sons, 1976. 144 pp.

This is a collection of mind benders. The puzzles have been carefully selected so as not to be too difficult for even nonmathematicians, but at the same time they are not so easy that they could be solved immediately.

Berman, Norman, and Andrew Pinto. **Art from Clutter.** Richards Rosen Press, 1977. 95 pp.

Beauty is indeed in the eye of the beholder when it comes to creating works of art from odds and ends found lying around a house. Pasta wall hangings, tin-can organizers, nail sculptures, and plaster castings are all described and illustrated with photographs. You will find here that simple techniques and unusual materials make for some interesting creations even a novice can construct.

Bowman, Bruce. **Toothpick Sculpture and Ice-Cream Stick Art.** Illus. by author. Sterling Publishing Co., 1977. 64 pp.

With some toothpicks or ice-cream sticks and a bottle of white glue you can create all sorts of interesting works of art—from a weeping willow tree or giraffe to a jewelry box or a basket. The author has included step-by-step instructions and detailed illustrations for making a number of interesting objects.

Broadwater, Elaine. **Clay Craft at Home.** Photographs by author and Lisa Petranoff. Chilton Book Co., 1978. 140 pp.

A lump of clay seems irresistible to anyone of any age. That appeal can be satisfied by making clay modeling a hobby. The basic kinds of clay, supplies, modeling techniques, decorating methods, bead-making, kilns, firing, and ways to use molds are all clearly explained and illustrated. A similar craft, glass stretching, is also described in this book. Lists of supply sources, suggested readings, and terms used in clay and glass crafts close this guide.

Bruun-Rasmussen, Ole, and Grete Petersen. **Make-up, Costumes and Masks for the Stage.** Photographs by Jens Bull. Sterling Publishing Co., 1978. 96 pp.

Here are lots of ideas for transforming yourself and your friends into many interesting characters and animals with the aid of makeup, costumes, or masks. Written instructions are provided along with diagrams, pictures, and patterns for you to follow. Though primarily aimed at theatrical productions, these costuming tips would also come in handy at Halloween or for parties.

Campbell, Gail. **Salt-Water Tropical Fish in Your Home.** Sterling Publishing Co., 1976. 138 pp.

While this handbook is prepared for beginning hobbyists, it has information for experienced aquarists, too. The author, a marine biologist, describes the latest equipment available, demonstrates how to select fish that are healthy and compatible with one another, and discusses how to establish a favorable environment for them. This book also explains how to treat different diseases, how to care for over 100 species of fish, and how to breed the fish. Photographs.

Chatterton, Pauline. **Coordinated Crafts for the Home.** Richard Marek Publishers, 1980. 208 pp.

The crafts explained here can help you redecorate your room or provide distinctive gifts for friends. Basic designs can be knitted, crocheted, embroidered, latchhooked, or patched and then used for pillows, pictures, seats, or afghans. This book comes complete with directions, photographs, and drawings displaying designs of Scandinavian, American, and African origin. Instructions and techniques are carefully and clearly explained so that even beginners can turn out craft creations to be proud of.

Cosman, Madeleine Pelner. **Medieval Holidays and Festivals: A Calendar of Celebrations.** Charles Scribner's Sons, 1981. 135 pp.

Twelve medieval holidays and festivals are discussed in this book. For February there is the still-celebrated Valentine's Day. But have you ever heard of Lammas Day (August) or St. Swithin's Day (July)? Descriptions of each holiday include discussion of foods, decorations, costumes, music, and dances. The last chapters provide instructions for making banners and costumes and even offer recipes so any of these traditional celebrations can be recreated today.

Currell, David. **Learning with Puppets.** Plays, 1980. 207 pp.

Step-by-step instructions are provided for making all types of puppets. There are also excellent directions for making simple puppet theaters and scenery, and suggestions on staging shows with minimum preparation and rehearsal.

Davis, Edward E. **Into the Dark: A Beginner's Guide to Developing and Printing Black and White Negatives.** Atheneum Publishers, 1979. 210 pp.

Developing your own black-and-white negatives and making your own prints can be cheaper, faster, and better than a professional developing lab. This book takes the reader step by step through a duscussion of necessary equipment, how to set up a darkroom, and how to develop negatives and make contact prints. Photographs.

Del Re, Gerard, and Patricia Del Re. **The Christmas Almanack.** Illus. Doug Jamieson. Doubleday & Co., 1979. 402 pp.

While there are twelve days of Christmas, there are only eleven sections to this Christmas book. But everything is covered here from how Christmas is described in the gospels, to Christmas celebrations around the world. Traditional Christmas recipes, decorations, stories, television specials, and music are all discussed in this collection. There are even sections on Christmas superstitions and how to say "Merry Christmas" in many foreign languages.

Dexler, Paul R. **Yesterday's Cars.** Photographs by author. Lerner Publications Co., 1979. 48 pp.

Three classifications of older cars are featured in this book: antique cars, classic cars, and special-interest cars. Tips are given for collecting and restoring old cars. Information about old-car competitions across the country is included as well. Easy reading.

D'Ignazio, Fred. **The Creative Kid's Guide to Home Computers: Super Games and Projects to Do with Your Home Computer.** Illus. Stan Gilliam. Doubleday & Co., 1981. 130 pp.

Home computers are growing in popularity as they become more affordable. With this guide and a home computer, anyone can draw computer pictures, invent games, compose music and poetry, and even build a robot. Written in nontechnical language, the book is easy to understand and is illustrated with drawings and photographs.

DiNoto, Andrea. **Anytime, Anywhere, Anybody Games.** Illus. Marina Givotovsky. Golden Press, 1977. 48 pp.

All types of games are described here. Some games are simple and may be played alone. Others require a little bit of equipment and several players. Some of the games are "brain teasers," including such memory games as "Twenty Questions" and "I Packed My Bag." Other games highlight the use of muscles, speed, and agility. There are also games that require wit and knowledge to play.

Donner, Michael. **Bike, Skate, and Skateboard Games.** Illus. Lynn Matus. Golden Press, 1977. 48 pp.

Whether you pedal, pump, or glide to get your wheels moving, this book has games for you. These games give young people a chance to improve their skills and further enjoy their bikes, roller skates, and skateboards. Along with the entertainment pointers, some safety tips are given for bicycle riding and skateboarding. Easy reading.

Eckstein, Joan, and Joyce Gleit. **Fun with Making Things: An Activity Book for Kids.** Illus. Stan Tusan. Camelot Books, 1979. 135 pp.

There are over fifty things for kids to make and do in this collection. There are practical objects that can be made out of tin cans, wood, paper clips, aluminum foil, papier-mâché, and much more. With this book, there will always be something to do or to make, whether you are inside, outside, by yourself, or with a friend.

Edelhart, Mike. **What Your Handwriting Says about You.** Prentice-Hall, 1979. 119 pp.

Handwriting is a key to personality, and this study of handwriting analysis explains the peculiarities of writing and what they reveal about the writer. Interesting historical stories, party activities, and the many applications of handwriting analysis are included.

Etkin, Ruth. **Playing and Composing on the Recorder.** Sterling Publishing Co., 1976. 72 pp.

The recorder is one of the easiest instruments to play, and you can even start composing the moment you pick it up. This easy-to-follow book shows you exactly how to finger and blow each note and how to write music. It even tells you how to care for your recorder and how to make a case for the instrument, how to construct a music stand, and how to compile a notebook for your music.

Fixx, James F. **Solve It! A Perplexing Profusion of Puzzles.** Doubleday & Co., 1978. 95 pp.

Which is heavier, lead or gold? The answer may surprise you. Can you name three English words that have no rhymes? How can four fives equal fifty-six? These and other brain teasers are included in this book of puzzles. Also provided are the author's ten general rules for problem solving.

Foley, Ellen, and Peggy Anne Streep, editors. **The Golden Book of Hand and Needle Arts.** Golden Press, 1977. 160 pp.

Instructions on how to make many hand and needle projects are included here, along with step-by-step diagrams for the beginner. None of the projects is simple, so some experience or adult help is necessary. Crocheting, appliqué, quilting, embroidery, macramé, lace making, and inkle weaving are all covered, as well as some lesser-known techniques such as reverse appliqué and hardanger embroidery.

Foshee, John H. **You, Too, Can Canoe: The Complete Book of River Canoeing.** Strode Publishers, 1977. 435 pp.

This instruction book in canoeing is organized into the following four sections: the basics, including selection of a canoe and needed equipment; techniques, with information on paddle strokes, rivers, and how to handle a canoe on the river; safety, repair, and logistics, including rescue and repair techniques, and information on where you might go to canoe; and the final section of information on being a trip leader, and including a glossary of canoeing terms. Photographs and illustrations.

Fujimura, Kobon (editor Martin Gardner; translator Furie Adachi). **The Tokyo Puzzles.** Charles Scribner's Sons, 1978. 184 pp.

The author has collected ninety-eight puzzles that are designed to tease, confuse, and frustrate, but all in good fun. Some of the puzzles will test your math ability, others require detective work, while a few ask for logic and common sense. Answers are provided at the back of the book.

Garden, Nancy. **The Kids' Code and Cipher Book.** Holt, Rinehart & Winston, 1981. 163 pp.

Ever wanted to be a spy? Send and receive hidden messages? Crack secret codes? Well, this book may not make you James Bond or Mata Hari, but it does present a variety of codes and ciphers, along with messages to encode and decode for practice.

Gardner, Pat, and Kay Gleason. **Dough Creations: Food to Folk Art.** Chilton Book Co., 1977. 149 pp.

Bread has been the basis of people's diet since they turned from hunting to farming. In addition, it has been made into a form of artistic expression and a highly valued craft. Here is a history of the art of breadmaking, as well as instructions for creating your own works of art in both edible and inedible forms.

Ghinger, Judith. **Hooray Days: New Year's to Christmas—Things to Make and Do.** Illus. Marina Givotovsky. Golden Press, 1977. 48 pp.

Every holiday has its own kind of magic—a special game or song, decorations, or some kind of celebration. This book is full of that kind of fun to take you out of the ordinary all through the year. There are brand-new things to make and do, plus some old-fashioned favorites with a new twist.

Goodenough, Simon. **Military Miniatures: The Art of Making Model Soldiers.** Chilton Book Co., 1978. 127 pp.

Model soldiers are really not toys. Because of their astonishing attention to accurate historical detail, it takes the finest craftspeople to produce these greatly prized collector's items. This book will introduce the reader to the craft and hobby of creating and collecting military miniatures. The text includes instruction on painting techniques, on molding and casting, and on the construction of realistic settings for the miniatures. Diagrams and photographs.

Grainger, Sylvia. **How to Make Your Own Moccasins.** J. B. Lippincott Co., 1977. 125 pp.

This how-to book includes detailed directions for making ten different moccasins that are based on actual Indian styles, but that use modern materials and techniques. An explanation of the materials that need to be used is provided, as well as step-by-step instructions for making patterns and cutting out, sewing, and decorating the moccasins. Diagrams and photographs.

Hillman, Howard (with Shannon O'Cork and Dana Shilling). **The Cook's Book.** Illus. Anistatia Gallegos. Avon Books, 1981. 559 pp.

Here is a handy, alphabetically arranged encyclopedia that tells you about the origins, availability, storage, preparation, and uses for over 1,000 food items and cooking ingredients. You may not be a gourmet cook after reading this book, but it will help you become a better and smarter consumer.

Hilton, Suzanne. **Who Do You Think You Are? Digging for Your Family Roots.** Westminster Press, 1977. 189 pp.

History in a textbook may not be interesting to you, but the lives of your ancestors might be. Have you ever wondered where your great-great-great-grandparents came from? Here is a book to help you find out. It tells you how to start filling in that family tree, and where to go or write to fill in any gaps. You might find a president or even a chicken thief among your forebears, but you will never know unless you start looking.

Hobson, Burton. **Getting Started in Stamp Collection.** Sterling Publishing Co., 1977. 144 pp.

For anyone who's curious about the world, then and now, and for anyone who is a collector at heart, stamp collecting is one hobby that combines these two interests. Stamps tell stories of the past, and of fascinating people, places, and events of the present. They also reveal information about religions, inventions, plants, animals, holidays, and just about any subject you could name. Not only that, the hobby of collecting stamps can gain you new friends, and may become profitable also. This book is for anyone who wants to use stamps for more than mailing letters.

Hodgson, Mary Anne, and Josephine Ruth Paine. **Fast and Easy Needlepoint.** Photographs by Michael Pitts and Richard Fowlkes. Doubleday & Co., 1978. 96 pp.

This simple craft book tells everything a beginner needs to know about covering a canvas with bright designs. The authors explain what needlepoint is and describe exactly what things are needed to get started on this creative and fun craft. After learning seven basic designs, beginners can create their own designs by combining colors and charting original design ideas. These bright creations can find both decorative and practical uses as cases for eyeglasses, pictures, guitar straps, or book covers.

Holtje, Adrienne, and Bert Holtje. **Cardcraft: Twenty-two Techniques for Making Your Own Greeting Cards and Notepaper.** Chilton Book Co., 1978. 180 pp.

Here is the book for people interested in making their own greeting cards, party invitations, or fancy notepaper. Several techniques of design are described, and some all-purpose designs are provided, along with lessons on lettering techniques. You can choose the techniques and design that best suit your abilities and tastes.

Holz, Loretta. **Make It And Sell It: A Young People's Guide to Marketing Crafts.** Photographs by author. Charles Scribner's Sons, 1978. 142 pp.

This informative book provides clear examples of how you can sell the craft items you make. Specific information includes ways to start your own business and how to go into a partnership and share profits. There are examples of methods of breaking in at flea markets and bazaars, and how you can best set up a booth to show your products. Explanations are also provided about how to sell on consignment and how you and your business relate to the laws: child labor statutes, income tax, Social Security, sales tax, and copyrights.

Hoople, Cheryl G. **The Heritage Sampler: A Book of Colonial Arts and Crafts.** Illus. Richard Cuffari. Dial Press, 1975. 129 pp.

We want and need to preserve our past. Provided in this book are recipes for foods like johnnycakes, apple fritters, and homemade butter; methods for making a patchwork pillow, cornhusk dolls, and hot pads; ways to weave and to make braided or hooked rugs; and techniques for making candles, silhouettes, and popcorn and paper decorations. Or how about trying some old-fashioned maple sugar candy? A special Christmas section gives ideas that allow your whole family to spend the holiday season the same way your great-grandparents did.

Horner, Deborah R. **Masks of the World to Cut Out and Wear.** Charles Scribner's Sons, 1977. 9 pp.

An Alaskan ceremonial dance mask appears to be a laughing Oriental monster. The Ganesh mask of India is an elephant-headed god, complete with trunk. The fangs on the mask of the bright red Rangda, Queen of the Witches, could frighten away the bravest soul in Bali. These and other colorful masks are printed in this book on heavy cardboard—ready to be cut out, put together, and worn.

Horowitz, I. A., and Fred Reinfeld. **First Book of Chess.** Sterling Publishing Co., 1976. 128 pp.

Have you always thought chess was too complicated to learn? This easy-to-follow book clearly explains how to play chess. Diagrams illustrate various table moves, while the text explains strategies for playing and winning this international game.

Hoyt, Edwin P. **Coins, Collectors, and Counterfeiters.** Thomas Nelson, 1977. 142 pp.

This book traces the production, collection, and counterfeiting of coins from 700 B.C. to the present. It tells of the problems of early kings in having coins made, the cleverness of the first counterfeiters, and the difficult production methods used for ancient coins. Tips for collectors are also included: information on the most valuable coins, advice on starting a collection, and a discussion of how coins increase in value.

Huang, Paul C. **The Illustrated Step-by-Step Beginner's Cookbook.** Illus. Joseph Daniel Fiedler with Michael McQuaide. Four Winds Press, 1980. 96 pp.

Ever read a recipe and not really understand what you are supposed to do? This book solves that problem by providing illustrations for every recipe given. Recipes include Japanese, Chinese, French, Italian, and South American dishes—from simple ones like hard-cooked eggs to such difficult dishes as beef lo mein.

Hutton, Darryl. **Ventriloquism.** Sterling Publishing Co., 1977. 128 pp.

How do you "throw" your voice? How can you speak clearly without moving your lips? Are parts of the body other than the vocal organs used in ventriloquism? You will find the answers in this book, along with all the information you need to know about handling dummies and hand puppets, creating an act, and using lighting and sound effects. There is even a section on how to combine ventriloquism and magic tricks.

Jacobs, Patricia. **The Best Bread Book.** Corwin Books, 1978. 95 pp.

Since the author has lived in England and the United States, these bread recipes come from both countries. A glossary explains all the special terms used. The book includes all kinds of breads as well as advice about storing bread, measurements, ingredients, shapes and sizes of tins, and even failures (and how to prevent them). Ever heard of Soya Semolina Bread? Flower Pot Wholewheat Loaves? Herb Soda Loaf?

James, Elizabeth, and Carol Barkin. **A Place of Your Own.** Photographs by Lou Jacobs, Jr. Skinny Books, 1981. 92 pp.

Who hasn't thought of having their own personal spot that reflects their taste and interests? This book suggests ways to decorate an apartment or a room with easy-to-make furniture and inexpensive accessories. Having a place of your own takes work, but it can be fun and stimulate your imagination and creativity.

Judd, Wallace. **Games Calculators Play.** Warner Books, 1979. 128 pp.

In addition to helping with math homework, a calculator can become a favorite new toy. With the help of this book, you can spell out rhymes, solve riddles, play calendar games, and even trick your friends with your calculator. The book also explains how calculators work and what to look for when purchasing a new calculator.

Judy, Susan, and Stephen Judy. **Gifts of Writing: Creative Projects with Words and Art.** Charles Scribner's Sons, 1980.

Assembled here is a collection of activities designed to encourage creative writing and to present that writing in an attractive form. The authors believe that people sharing their ideas, feelings, and personality through writing is one of the most important gifts someone can give. Projects described here include designing stationery, posters, greeting cards, family trees, Easter eggs with original messages, and books of all kinds.

Katz, Ruth J. **Make It and Wear It.** Illus. Sharon Tondreau. Walker & Co., 1981. 47 pp.

What would anybody like? Fashion at a reasonable price! This book discusses and illustrates how to make vests, backpacks, disco bags, camisole tops, and many other items—all from such familiar materials as pot holders, file folders, handkerchiefs, and placemats. How about a backpack from an old pair of blue jeans?

Kern, Marna Elyea. **The Complete Book of Handcrafted Paper.** Coward, McCann & Geoghegan, 1980. 224 pp.

Junk mail, old handkerchiefs, and last year's Christmas cards now have a practical use—recycle them into handcrafted paper. With a kitchen blender, easily constructed molds, and the instructions in this book, you can create beautiful stationery, notepaper, and placemats. Whether you're interested in a new, unique hobby or a money-making business, this book explains all aspects of handcrafted paper with step-by-step instructions and pictures.

Kubey, Craig. **Scoring Big at Pac-Man: How to Munch the Monsters.** Warner Books, 1982. 46 pp.

Pac-Man has more machines operating than any of the other roughly 400 coin-operated video games in the United States—about 100,000 in this country alone. This booklet has advice and tips about playing and winning a Pac-Man game. Black-and-white illustrations of this video game help explain the text.

Kubey, Craig. **The Winners' Book of Video Games.** Warner Books, 1982. 270 pp.

Are people still superior to machines? This book provides evidence that the human can still win in a test of wits—even over video games. The book provides an eight-point plan of action in playing video games with adaptations for each game and specific insights for such games as Asteroids (hit the small fast rocks before you try for the drifting slow ones). There is also information included here about game history and terminology, along with quick quizzes.

Kuslan, Richard, and Louis Kuslan. **Ham Radio: An Introduction to the World beyond CB.** Prentice-Hall, 1981. 95 pp.

Amateur radio, according to this book, is an exciting and rewarding hobby. The book takes the reader on a tour of an established radio station, pointing out the various pieces of equipment and explaining how an antenna is erected. Suggestions on where to get expert advice to begin your own radio transmitter-receiver is also provided. A glossary explains many of the strange terms used in the hobby, such as "moonbounce" and "Elmers."

Lamb, Geoffrey. **Secret Writing Tricks.** Thomas Nelson, 1975. 87 pp.

Who isn't intrigued by the idea of secret messages? This book is full of codes and message tricks involving symbols and words. There is information about the codes used by the Greek Spartans, by the Bishop of Chester, and even by Sherlock Holmes himself. Sample codes are provided that can be used to puzzle family and friends.

Larson, Randy. **Backpacking for Fun and Glory.** Photographs and illus. by John R. Henshaw. Harvey House, Publishers, 1979. 77 pp.

Why not try backpacking instead of doing the same old things on your next vacation? But before you do, there is some information provided here on how to prepare for your hike and, perhaps, for nights spent outdoors in the wilderness. Other information in the book includes tips on what types of clothing, shelter, and food to take, how to get where you want to go, and how to read maps and a compass. There are also suggestions and commonsense rules about safety on backpacking trips, and on how to leave the land in good shape for others to enjoy.

Lasson, Robert (with Sidney Shupak). **Glue It Yourself: Woodworking without Nails.** Illus. Jeff Murphy. E. P. Dutton, 1978. 91 pp.

This book, completely illustrated with photographs, describes the tools and techniques needed for a variety of woodworking projects that do not require assembly with nails. Projects ranging from a pencil box to a simple attaché case are described in step-by-step detail.

Laycock, George. **The Complete Beginner's Guide to Photography.** Doubleday & Co., 1979. 149 pp.

Photography need not be a mystery to the newcomer if a good beginning handbook, such as this one, is used as a guide. The author introduces the reader to types of cameras, different lens choices, photographic accessories, and types of film. In addition, developing and printing techniques are clearly explained. Although black-and-white photography is emphasized, color photography is also discussed.

Lear, Edward. **Edward Lear's Book of Mazes.** Illus. Gyles Brandreth and David Farris. Sterling Publishing Co., 1980. 109 pp.

Nonsense poems, rhymes, and limericks accompany thirty complicated picture mazes. If you get too frustrated tracing your way through the waves of the high seas or the knots of an old man's beard, you'll find relief in the solutions given at the back of the book.

Lieberman, Jethro K., and Neil S. Rhodes. **The Complete 1980 CB Handbook.** Avon Books, 1980. 493 pp.

Anyone interested in CB radios can find something of value in this illustrated handbook. Included are chapters on types of equipment, how to shop for equipment, CB language, the installation of equipment, and CB etiquette. Specific mention of equipment by brand name and model number is particularly helpful to the reader interested in purchasing CB units.

Lyttle, Richard B. **The Complete Beginner's Guide to Stereo.** Doubleday & Co., 1981. 152 pp.

One of the most expensive purchases that many teenagers make is a stereo system. But trying to get straight answers from fast-talking salespeople is often impossible. This guide will help you sort through the facts and figures, the terminology, and the basic principles of stereo. Is it best to buy a stereo receiver with a built-in tuner or a separate tuner and amplifier? What's the difference between various speaker designs? What should you look for in selecting a component system? These and other frequently asked questions are answered clearly in nontechnical language. Photographs and diagrams.

Maar, Len, and Nancy Maar. **Out-of-Sight Games: New and Exciting Action Games for Kids.** Illus. John Lane. Doubleday & Co., 1981. 63 pp.

Try your skills at Moon Rocks Relay or Space Chain Walk. This collection of new and exciting action games can help relieve the boredom of a long afternoon. Rules, scoring, and an explanation of tactics are provided for these mind and body twisters.

MacDonald, Margaret, editor. **Whistler's Mother's Cook Book.** G. P. Putnam's Sons, 1979. 144 pp.

Here is a collection of eighty-nine of the original recipes of Anna McNeill Whistler, most famous through the portrait painted of her by her son, which is popularly called "Whistler's Mother." Whistler says that these recipes made up her basic cooking file. The recipes include such interesting items as Collard Eels, Floating Island, Pint Cake, and Gambles I, along with the usual apple pie, pudding, and gingerbread. A prologue describes the Whistler household in detail.

Math, Irwin. **Morse, Marconi, and You.** Charles Scribner's Sons, 1979. 80 pp.

Using this clear, illustrated, step-by-step guide, a young experimenter can build telegraph, telephone, and radio sets that really work. Starting with information concerning the basics of electricity, this book takes you through a series of experiments and projects using common hardware-store items and inexpensive commercial devices.

Maurer, Diane Philippoff. **Fiber Arts: Macrame, Crochet, Wrapping, Coiling, Weaving.** Chilton Book Co., 1978. 158 pp.

Only recently has the art world considered creations of fiber as works of art, rather than as crafts. This attitude is discussed at some length and with humor by the author, herself a fiber artist. Here are encouragements, instructions, and ideas on beginning to create fiber art of your own. Instructions are also here on how to card, spin, and even dye your own yarns so that the work can be a total expression of your creativity.

McCaslin, Nellie. **Act Now! Plays and Ways to Make Them.** Illus. Daty Healy. S. G. Phillips, 1975. 120 pp.

If you would like to act or put on plays, but think that you have to buy a stage, costumes, makeup, and a script, then this book is for you. Here are pages filled with theatrical ideas for you and your friends to do alone or in groups. The ideas start with some simple activities and go on to a play complete with all the stage directions. Even an entire play can be done with the barest of essentials.

McLeod, William T., and Ronald Mongredien. **Chess for Young Beginners.** Illus. Jean-Paul Colbus. Golden Press, 1977. 60 pp.

Want to learn to play chess? This book provides clear pictures and understandable instructions to help you begin to learn the complicated game of chess. Chess terms and playing concepts are listed and defined at the back of the book.

McLoone, Margo, and Alice Siegel. **Sports Cards: Collecting, Trading, and Playing.** Holt, Rinehart & Winston, 1979. 78 pp.

Back in 1880, when cigarette manufacturers started putting picture cards in their cigarette packages to stiffen them, who would have thought that one hundred years later these same sports cards would be worth hundreds of dollars? Millions of people around the world have been collecting sports cards for decades. This little book can help collectors understand the cards they have and can even help them increase their collections. Included are games to play with sports cards, information on how to get your cards autographed, and tips on how to keep up a collection.

Meyer, Carolyn. **Lots and Lots of Candy.** Illus. Laura Jean Allen. Harcourt Brace Jovanovich, 1976. 96 pp.

The history of candy is explained in this book, along with the development of different kinds of candy throughout the world. In addition, there are forty-four recipes for those who want to try making their own candy.

Meyer, Carolyn. **Mask Magic.** Illus. Melanie Gaines Arwin. Harcourt Brace Jovanovich, 1978. 88 pp.

As far back as the history of humankind reaches, masks have been used. Masks have been used to horrify, beautify, hide, disguise, or create a new identity. Masks for all seasons and reasons are discussed here. Autumn has been the season for spirit masks, whether pagan or Christian. With the coming of winter came the carnival, or head, masks. But the most joyous and most elaborate masks were created in the spring to celebrate life. Whether you try making a few or all of the masks here, you'll have fun with your hands and with your imagination.

Meyer, Carolyn. **The Needlework Book of Bible Stories.** Illus. Janet McCaffery. Harcourt Brace Jovanovich, 1975. 87 pp.

Nine biblical stories are used as the models for needlework projects. The directions for the needlework are simple, and the materials required are readily available. Even beginners can follow the designs and do the stitching that will create the illustrated biblical tales on fabric.

Millard, Adele. **Plants for Kids to Grow Indoors.** Illus. Gregory Thompson. Photographs by Glenn Lewis and Bud Millard. Sterling Publishing Co., 1977. 124 pp.

You can turn a vegetable into a fern, grow roses in a teacup, or even build a rock garden in your home. Indoor gardening has become a very popular hobby for people to enjoy, no matter where they live. There is great satisfaction in learning about why plants grow as they do. This guide will provide the instructions for many plant projects that can teach you about nature as you grow them indoors.

Murphy, Jim. **Weird and Wacky Inventions.** Crown Publishers, 1978. 148 pp.

A hat that can tip itself, a pair of protective eyeglasses for chickens, and a cow decoy that is a hunting device are some of the strange and unusual inventions described in this book. Also provided are illustrations of inventions that allow you to see if you can guess what the inventions really are. Another section of the book talks about certain inventions and the changes and developments that were made over time in those inventions, including a look at the way the bicycle was invented and how it has changed.

Murray, Jerry. **Getting into Radio-Controlled Sports.** G.P. Putnam's Sons, 1979. 128 pp.

Everything you need to know about the construction, operation, and competition of radio-controlled models is included in this illustrated handbook. Included are explanations of how radio control operates, instructions for choosing equipment, and information regarding radio-controlled models for land, sea, and air.

Needleman, Carla. **The Work of Craft: An Inquiry into the Nature of Crafts and Craftsmanship.** Discus Books, 1981. 142 pp.

The personal perspective is emphasized in this book on crafts— what the individual artist and craftsperson brings to such tasks as weaving, design, and woodcarving. The craft items are a reflection of the artist's inner being. The book also points out what ways crafts can be used to educate people.

Ness, Evaline. **American Colonial Paper House to Cut Out and Color.** Illus. by author. Charles Scribner's Sons, 1975. 23 pp.

Having fun making and creating your own American colonial-style house depends upon having the right tools combined with a sense of imagination. This book provides basic structures and tips on how to build the house and how to furnish it. It is left up to you to add or create the details and special touches to make that house uniquely yours. A list of tools and suggested building techniques keeps your project moving smoothly forward until you have a complete colonial house of your own.

Ness, Evaline. **Four Rooms from the Metropolitan Museum of Art to Cut Out and Color.** Illus. by author. Charles Scribner's Sons, 1977. 28 pp.

A Spanish room of the eighteenth century, a Syrian room, a French salon, and a Venetian bedroom (complete with a secret door) are all historic rooms in the Metropolitan Museum of Art. They are all elegant, and they are all here to color, cut out, and glue together. Directions and a list of supplies make your job easier and fun. Added colored paper, carpet scraps, and your own craft work can make the rooms even more elegant and more your own.

Newcomb, Duane. **The Complete Vegetable Gardener's Sourcebook.** Avon Books, 1980. 340 pp.

All aspects of gardening are explained in this useful book. Information on soil preparation, tools, pest control, greenhouses, and seeds, and the addresses of garden supply warehouses and manufacturers, are provided to help make vegetable gardening an easier, more enjoyable activity. Photographs and illustrations.

Paraquin, Charles H. (translator Paul Kuttner). **Eye Teasers: Optical Illusion Puzzles.** Illus. by author. Sterling Publishing Co., 1978. 96 pp.

"Believe only what you see" is an old saying. But the eye can't always believe what it sees because it may be teased, as proven by the optical illusions presented in this book. After the author explains optical illusions, he illustrates a number of them to show how unreliable the reader's eye is. Discussions of these optical puzzles are found at the back of the book.

Parker, E. M. **Letters and Numbers for Needlepoint.** Charles Scribner's Sons, 1978. 93 pp.

People who are hooked on needlepoint or who have just started learning about it will find that the patterns for letters and numbers in this book have an old-fashioned charm well suited to the art of needlepoint. The patterns are varied, easy to follow, and of different sizes and styles. This book explains the stitches used in these century-old patterns, including the tent stitch and the cross stitch. Also described are the types of fabrics that might be best to highlight the patterns.

Paust, Gil. **Model Railroading: How to Plan, Build, and Maintain Your Trains and Pikes.** Doubleday & Co., 1981. 146 pp.

Model railroaders can find valuable information about their favorite hobby in this book. Types of locomotives, accessories, safety and maintenance procedures, and organizations for model railroad enthusiasts are all clearly explained. Photographs.

Pettit, Florence H. **Christmas All around the House: Traditional Decorations You Can Make.** Illus. Wendy Watson. Photographs by Robert H. Pettit. Thomas Y. Crowell Co., 1976. 226 pp.

This is not the usual kind of Christmas crafts book. Instead, instructions are provided for making traditional Christmas decorations, foods, and ornaments from around the world: a Mexican piñata, an English kissing ball, and Moravian Christmas cookies, to name a few. Most are easy enough to make in a few hours using simple tools and materials.

Pettit, Florence H. **The Stamp-Pad Printing Book.** Illus. by author. Photographs by Robert M. Pettit. Thomas Y. Crowell Co., 1979. 153 pp.

Stamp-pad printing today is just a version of an art form that is thousands of years old. Rather than rubber, the early printer-artists used blocks of wood, clay, bone, or leather. Pigments, or colors, were obtained by using such things as plants, grasses, or berries. This book details some of the materials the modern artist will need to try this form, and it includes some basic practice designs. Step-by-step instructions are given for making valentines, decorative notepaper, signs, posters, greeting cards, and much more. Instructions are also given for printing in two colors, sewing together a folder or booklet to cover memo pads, and printing cloth banners.

Popular Mechanics **Complete Car Repair Manual.** Avon Books, 1978. 328 pp.

Ever wonder what makes engines run and how you could repair them? This simplified manual is put out by the editors of *Popular Mechanics* magazine, and they have used photographs, diagrams, and step-by-step procedures to cover almost any automotive problem. Even if you have little or no mechanical experience, you will be able to read and make sense of the suggestions.

Purdy, Susan. **Christmas Gifts for You to Make.** J. B. Lippincott Co., 1976. 96 pp.

A gift becomes very special when you take time and use your talents in creating that gift. Here is a book with many suggestions and detailed instructions for making a variety of gifts—from glove finger puppets and dough designs to decorative note pads, bib aprons, and tick-tack-toe wall hangings. Pictures and diagrams accompany the step-by-step instructions. Also included are some clever ideas for wrapping your gifts.

Rapp, Joel. **Mother Earth's Hassle-Free Vegetable Cookbook.** Illus. Marvin Rubin. Avon Books, 1981. 211 pp.

Here is a cookbook for anyone interested in a meatless diet. But this book is not strictly vegetarian, as eggs and dairy products are included. None of the recipes requires the skills of a French chef or fancy equipment. There is lots of advice on how to get started on this type of diet, as well as how to select the best vegetables, cheeses, and eggs, and it is all done in a light, entertaining manner.

Raymond, Jennifer. **The Best of Jenny's Kitchen: Cooking Naturally with Vegetables.** Avon Books, 1982. 180 pp.

Jenny's kitchen includes only one kind of cooking—vegetable cooking. She provides nutritional information for vegetables and planning meals around vegetables. Recipes are included for soups, salads, sauces, breads, entrées, and desserts. Substitutions and equivalents are listed, as are additional sources of information on vegetarian cooking.

Ris, Thomas F. **The Neat Stuff Something-to-Do Book.** Illus. Deborah Bratlein, Dale Nordell, Marcia Pomeroy, Kelly Smith, John Smith. Wanderer Books, 1979. 82 pp.

Based on a nationally syndicated Neat Stuff newspaper feature, this book includes jokes, riddles, and games from the column. Also provided are experiments, arts and crafts projects, special recipes, and clever ways to earn money. Directions are included to organize a Neat Stuff club with your friends.

Ritchie, Carson I.A. **Making Scientific Toys.** Thomas Nelson, 1976. 169 pp.

Toys using laws of science to function are usually easy to make and inexpensive. Often the parts are items that can be found around the house. This book explains how to make toys using optical, acoustical, and chemical laws of nature. Principles of flying, balance, weather, climate, and heat are also considered when making these toys.

Rosenberg, Arthur D. **Chess for Children and the Young at Heart.** Illus. Howard Berelson. Photographs by Marianne Groher. Atheneum Publishers, 1977. 150 pp.

Using step-by-step pictures and explanations, this book takes you through the basics of identifying chess pieces, to simple moves, and then on to planning game stretegy by chess charts and good opening moves. Since the book contains a minimum of text and a maximum of pictures, the beginner can absorb the information rapidly and can be playing the game of chess in no time.

Ruthberg, Helen. **The Book of Miniatures: Furniture and Accessories.** Chilton Book Co., 1977. 231 pp.

If you are fascinated with tiny things—furniture, mirrors, clocks, dishes, curtains, shelves, planters, jewelry, clothes—this book describes everything a miniaturist could want explained. Careful and detailed building instructions and patterns for these small items fill the pages of this guide. The book also shows how to care for and store these precious furnishings.

Samtur, Susan J. (with Ted Tuleja). **Cashing In at the Checkout.** Warner Books, 1980. 174 pp.

Saving coupons, using promotions, watching for sales, and reading shoppers' newsletters can help save lots of money at the supermarket.

This book explains how you can organize these various methods of receiving payments from manufacturers each month, while still buying only the products you want and will actually use.

Sandler, Martin W. **The Story of American Photography: An Illustrated History for Young People.** Little, Brown & Co., 1979. 314 pp.

This large-sized book, complete with over 200 black-and-white photographs, covers the history of photography from its invention in 1839 and from the first pictures, called *daguerreotypes,* to the present. Many famous masters such as Alfred Stieglitz are described, and samples of their photographs are included. Lesser-known photographers are also featured, and some of their photographs are reproduced for the first time.

Sarnoff, Jane, and Reynold Ruffins. **A Great Aquarium Book: The Putting-It-Together Guide for Beginners.** Charles Scribner's Sons, 1977. 47 pp.

Selecting an aquarium and the proper fish for it are described in this book. Color pictures of fish will help you decide which types of fish you want, and information on fish species will help you identify which fish can be kept together in the same tank. Also included are discussions of the furnishings for an aquarium, types of fish food, how to keep an aquarium clean, and how to keep your fish healthy. Easy reading.

Schleicher, Robert. **Model Car, Truck and Motorcycle Handbook.** Chilton Book Co., 1978. 161 pp.

This book provides a step-by-step guide to model cars, trucks, and motorcycles. Beginning with the basic tools and work areas you need and covering assembling, painting, detailing, and displaying models, the book is thorough and specific in its instructions. Everything you need to know to produce a realistic model is here.

Schleicher, Robert. **Model Railroading Handbook.** Chilton Book Co., 1975. 227 pp.

Here is an introduction to the various scale sizes of model railroads and the kinds of kits and assembled models available. Model railroading as a hobby is discussed, as are places to find advice about this popular hobby. Most of the book, though, shows you how to use materials to construct pieces of equipment not available in kits. This information includes track planning, scenery making, painting, and decal application.

Schleicher, Robert. **Model Railroading Handbook, Volume II.** Chilton Book Co., 1978. 177 pp.

Illustrations and examples teach you how to build model railroad layouts. You will also learn how to convert model railroad pieces from kits into your own unique models. Besides all this, the book has discussions of hand and remote-control switching and of realistic scenery and backgrounds. Finally, there is information about simplified electronic and sound systems.

Schmitz, Dorothy Childers. **Kite Flying.** Crestwood House, 1978. 32 pp.

Kites can be of many sizes, shapes, colors, and materials. They can be used for many things—from predicting the weather, to taking pictures, to sending signals, to celebrating holidays. How to make kites, how to use them, and the kinds of kites made throughout history are all discussed in the pages of this book. Photographs. Easy reading.

Schumann, Walter (translator Evelyne Stern). **Gemstones of the World.** Sterling Publishing Co., 1977. 256 pp.

This is a guide to over 1,400 of the world's gemstones in both their rough and cut states. The book contains full details on where they are found, how they are mined and cut, how they are often imitated, how they are identified and classified, and what their characteristics and physical properties are. So if you are a lover of jewels, this book will give you a more educated eye when you look at them.

Schwartz, Paula Dunaway. **You Can Cook: How to Make Good Food for your Family and Friends.** Illus. Byron Barton. McElderry Books, 1976. 192 pp.

Here is a cookbook for young beginning cooks who would like to sharpen their skills and eventually cook for the family. The recipes are simple and fall into seven categories, from soups to desserts. All directions are clear and easy to follow. The book also provides a few sample menus so it is possible to cook an entire meal.

Shriberg, Linda K., and Carole Nicholas. **Kids in the Kitchen.** Illus. Robert Cavey. Julian Messner, 1980. 129 pp.

Now even young people can plan and prepare complete menus. With this book as a guide, the menu can be as American as hamburgers, or it might transport the entire family for an evening in the Orient, Italy, Greece, Ireland, or Mexico. How about a complete Hawaiian luau? Directions are also provided for substituting ingredients, reducing portions, and timing dishes.

Solomon, Hannah. **Bake Bread!** Photographs by Edward Stevenson. J. B. Lippincott Co., 1976. 79 pp.

Nothing in the world tastes, smells, or feels like home-baked bread. If any activity is better than eating homemade bread, it's preparing and baking breads. This book explains with illustrations and step-by-step details how to make basic bread. Once this is mastered, the craft of baking bread is limited only by the baker's imagination, for with many different kinds of flour, and additions like nuts, cinnamon, or raisins, you can make all kinds of shapes, sizes, and flavors.

Speca, Bob, Jr. (with Berg Sugar). **The Great Falling Domino Book.** Warner Books, 1979. 118 pp.

World champion Bob Speca set up, then knocked down, 97,450 dominoes to set the current record in the *Guinness Book of World Records.* His book is a complete guide to beginning domino hobbyists as well as advanced players. Through diagrams and pictures, the reader is shown complicated domino setups such as the Mousetrap, Walking the Plank, The High Dive, and The Elevator.

Tennissen, Anthony C. **Colorful Mineral Identifier.** Photographs by Werner Lieber. Sterling Publishing Co., 1975. 224 pp.

This basic introduction to identifying colorful minerals will make studying or collecting them more meaningful. There are more than 120 common minerals pictured in this authoritative guide. Each mineral is discussed according to physical properties, crystal system, and areas where it is commonly found.

Torre, Frank D. **Woodworking for Kids.** Doubleday & Co., 1978. 132 pp.

Bird houses, telephone stands, adjustable book racks, tool organizers, and ecology boxes are just some of the wooden items you can make with the aid of this book. Each project is complete with information about the amount and type of wood and tools needed for the job. There are pictures and diagrams that help describe the projects step by step. At the beginning of the book is information about the basic woodworking tools—hammers, saws, planes, clamps, measuring tools, and important material about wood and how to finish wood.

Uston, Ken. **Mastering Pac-Man.** Illus. by author. Signet Books, 1982. 128 pp.

Learn how to increase your score on the most famous computer game of them all—Pac-Man. This book provides tips on beating the monsters, playing fast and slow games, creating your own game patterns, and playing the new Puc-One game. Numerous illustrations help make the lessons clear.

Van Ryzin, Lani. **Starting Your Own Band: Rock, Disco, Folk, Jazz, Country and Western.** Walker & Co., 1980. 64 pp.

If you sing or play an instrument, you have probably thought about starting your own band. Whether you play country, rock, or folk music, the glamour and excitement of a music career is certainly attractive. This book explains what equipment, skills, and personalities it takes to get your group started. Included is information on promotion careers in the music business, lighting techniques, and sound systems. Photographs.

von Bornstedt, Marianne, and Ulla Prytz (translator Kenneth T. Dutfield). **Folding Table Napkins.** Photographs by Ollie Akerström. Sterling Publishing Co., 1976. 48 pp.

Here are the instructions and diagrams you need to be able to fold cloth and paper napkins in twenty-eight different styles suitable for the most formal of dinners—and the most informal. Napkins, artfully arranged, are an easy, inexpensive way to dress up your table.

Walker, Braz. **Tropical Fish Identifier.** Sterling Publishing Co., 1976. 256 pp.

Any aquarium owner will find this book a valuable guide to tropical fish. The fish are pictured in 120 full-color plates. With the pictures is information about species names, physical descriptions, habits, feeding needs, water temperatures, and health care for each species.

Weiss, Harvey. **Games and Puzzles You Can Make Yourself.** Thomas Y. Crowell Co., 1976. 56 pp.

If you are tired of all your old games, or if some of the game pieces from these games are missing and you don't have the money to buy new ones, then this book is for you. Three dozen different games are described here. Each can be played with everyday objects found around the house. If you want to make the games permanent to keep or to give as gifts, then there is information on how to do this. The games range from the very easy to the complex.

Weiss, Harvey. **How to Run a Railroad: Everything You Need to Know about Model Trains.** Thomas Y. Crowell Co., 1977. 127 pp.

For those of you who are tired of watching your model train just go round and round the same track, this book can help. Here is everything you need to know to build miniature hills and mountains, lakes and streams, trees and shrubs, and farms and towns to surround your tracks. There are instructions for bridges and elevated tracks, so that your train and its rails can expand in all directions. Also included is valuable information on the workings of the train itself and on how to keep it running smoothly.

Weiss, Harvey. **Model Airplanes and How to Build Them.** Thomas Y. Crowell Co., 1975. 90 pp.

Learn how to build several types of airplanes and helicopters out of cardboard or wood. These planes are not meant to fly, but the models illustrated here should still give you the feel and the spirit of flying. Some of the airplanes you can build from the diagrams provided include jet-powered planes, Sopwith Camels, the Red Baron's Triplane, and the Wright Brothers' plane. Easy reading.

Weiss, Harvey. **Model Buildings and How to Make Them.** Illus. by author. Thomas Y. Crowell Co., 1979. 95 pp.

Whether you are a budding architect, or just interested in building a town for your model railroad, you will find careful instructions and many helpful ideas here. Materials used for the structures described here can be cardboard or wood, and either can look remarkably good when enough attention is paid to decorating details. This book can help you as well with certain special school projects in history or geography.

Williams, Barbara. **Cornzapoppin': Popcorn Recipes and Party Ideas for All Occasions.** Photographs by Royce L. Bair. Holt, Rinehart & Winston, 1976. 160 pp.

This is a cookbook for popcorn lovers. It begins by tracing the history of popcorn, and then it gives advice for growing, buying, storing, popping, and even flavoring the corn. All the recipes are arranged by month, with a recipe for each holiday and event. Instructions and illustrations show the artistic popcorn arrangements suggested in some of the recipes.

Williams, Barbara, and Rosemary Williams. **Cookie Craft: No-Bake Designs for Edible Party Favors and Decorations.** Photographs by Barbara Williams. Holt, Rinehart & Winston, 1977. 190 pp.

Using store-bought cookies and frostings, and following the directions in this book, you can create party decorations and favors that are clever, funny, or pretty—and ones that can be eaten, too. The directions provided are detailed, and there are plenty of pictures to help you along. All you need supply besides the cookies and glaze is plenty of patience.

Wiseman, Ann. **Making Musical Things: Improvised Instruments.** Illus. by author. Charles Scribner's Sons, 1979. 63 pp.

Music expresses every mood and feeling. And you don't have to be rich to own instruments, or extremely talented to learn to play them. You can be your own music maker by following the clear directions and illustrations in this book, and by using things you find around the house. Imagine creating your own chimes, drums, horns, and guitars—or any one of fifty basic instruments—and then playing tunes upon them with only a little practice. With the help of this book, you could even start your own neighborhood do-it-yourself band.

Yerkow, Charles. **Fun and Safety on Two Wheels: Bicycles, Mopeds, Scooters, Motorcycles.** Photographs by author. G. P. Putnam's Sons, 1979. 142 pp.

The central idea behind this book is that safe riding can also be fun. Many accidents are caused by simple neglect or lack of knowledge about the basics of bicycles, mopeds, scooters, or motorcycles. This book teaches you to know the parts of your machine and how they should work properly. Also included are rules for safe riding in and out of traffic. Finally, there are sections on long-distance touring and on racing.

Occupations and Careers

Abrams, Kathleen S. **Career Prep: Electronics Servicing.** JeM Books, 1981. 61 pp.

To help you decide whether electronics servicing is a career you might be interested in exploring, this book takes you on a guided tour of this profession. You will meet people who do this work and find out how they feel about it. Also discussed here is where electronics work is done, what kinds of interests and abilities it takes to do the job, and where someone would get the training for such a job. Methods of looking for work in electronics servicing are also covered in this guidebook.

Ancona, George. **And What Do You Do? A Book about People and Their Work.** Photographs by author. E. P. Dutton, 1976. 47 pp.

While most jobs require some special training, many rewarding jobs do not call for a college degree. This book describes twenty-one different people at work on different jobs where a college education is not necessary. It shows what the work involves and explains how you can get the training to do each job. The kinds of jobs covered include: barber, chef, computer operator, illustrator, farmer, welder, zoo keeper, costume designer, and tugboat deckhand.

Association for Academic Health Centers. **A Guide to Education for the Health Professions.** Acropolis Books, 1979. 139 pp.

This comprehensive book describes the job duties and professional training required for careers in a number of medical fields: allied health, dentistry, health services administration, nursing, optometry, osteopathic medicine, pharmacy, podiatric medicine, public health, and veterinary medicine. The book also discusses future trends in these job fields. (Addresses of specific institutions with medical/health education programs are listed.)

Barton, Peter. **Staying Power: Performing Artists Talk about Their Lives.** Photographs by author. Dial Press, 1980. 210 pp.

A ballerina, a bass player, a Shakespearean actor, a country-and-western guitarist, a blues singer. Twelve actors, dancers, and musicians tell us why they chose to be performing artists and why they struggle ahead in their difficult, though rewarding, careers. They talk about their first infatuation with music, theater, or dance and about the hard, painful work required to develop their talents. They discuss misadventures and setbacks, career breakthroughs, emotional and financial highs and lows. Most of all, they share with us the excitement of performing and the satisfaction of surviving against great odds and fierce competition.

Berger, Melvin. **Medical Center Lab.** John Day Co., 1976. 103 pp.

A medical center contains around-the-clock dramas of life and death that demand the skills, knowledge, quick thinking, and compassion of many women and men in interrelated jobs. Two types of labs must operate efficiently in a medical center to save lives. The clinical lab deals directly with the patient—testing, diagnosing, and treating each emergency case. The research lab carries on a series of experiments to find ways of improving methods of treatment of special diseases like cancer, heart diseases, and diseases of the brain. This book describes all the procedures of the labs and tells of the doctors, nurses, and technicians who staff them.

Berger, Melvin. **Police Lab.** John Day Co., 1976. 127 pp.

Correct analysis of a tiny carpet fiber can be what finally catches a murderer. Police work is often combined with the latest scientific methods and equipment in order to solve crimes. This book tells how different crimes are solved through the use of laboratory techniques and the skills of scientific specialists.

Blackwood, Alan. **The Performing World of the Singer.** Silver Burdett Co., 1981. 113 pp.

Have you ever thought you could be a professional singer? This book provides information and suggestions about careers in music, popular and classical. There are also sections on the history of songs and singers, along with chapter-long profiles of opera star Sherrill Milnes, club singer Terri Balash, and rising classical singer Matthew Best.

Blanchard, Nina. **How to Break into Motion Pictures, Television, Commercials and Modeling.** Avon Books, 1980. 254 pp.

This is a complete manual of everything an aspiring star needs to know to get a chance to succeed. Written by a top Hollywood agent, the book takes an in-depth look at interviews, presenting yourself, writing a résumé, seeking out opportunities, choosing an agent, and several other areas important to beginning a career. Included is an index to acting and modeling schools, workshops, and agencies.

Campbell, Patricia J. **Passing the Hat: Street Performers in America.** Photographs by Alice Belkin. Delacorte Press, 1981. 260 pp.

We've all seen those entertainers on the street—the ones who sing, dance, juggle, and perform magic or mime. As this book points out, these *buskers*, as they are known, are part of an ancient tradition. They learn how to hold a crowd's attention with tricks passed from generation to generation. The author tells the reader about the best spots for buskers, such as Boston and New Orleans, and shows the dedication and skill needed for any good street act. There is also a discussion of the problems these buskers often have with the law.

Cassedy, Sylvia. **In Your Own Words: A Beginner's Guide to Writing.** Doubleday & Co., 1979. 214 pp.

For anyone who enjoys writing, this book is for you. The author believes that if you are someone who carefully notices the world around you, you may have developed a special way of looking at people and events that is one of the primary tools of the good writer. The book discusses how to write poetry, myths, legends, tall tales, science fiction, fantasy, ghost tales, letters, essays, and school reports. From all of these forms of writing, you should be able to find one perfectly suited to expressing your imagination.

Catalyst Staff. **Marketing Yourself: The *Catalyst* Women's Guide to Successful Résumés and Interviews.** G. P. Putnam's Sons, 1980. 185 pp.

This book offers advice to women in the areas of choosing, launching, and advancing a career. The first part of the book deals specifically with the preparation of a résumé, and it considers this résumé in light of the particular problems facing a woman in today's job market. The book's second major section explains techniques of presenting yourself effectively at an interview. Included is advice on setting goals, understanding body language, and gaining the competitive edge. This book comes complete with sample applications, résumés, and role-playing situations.

Cavallaro, Ann. **The Physician's Associate: A New Career in Health Care.** Elsevier/Nelson Books, 1978. 160 pp.

A young woman dressed in a white coat, stethoscope around her neck, is taking a patient's blood pressure, reading his case history, and writing a prescription for medicine. Is she a doctor? A nurse? No, she is a physician's associate, a member of a new and rapidly growing medical career. The physician's associate is not a half-educated doctor, but a highly trained member of the medical profession who takes some of the pressure off doctors by taking care of more routine medical problems that would usually require a physician's full attention. So, if you are looking for a career in medicine, this book can be helpful in explaining another job possibility open to you—one you may not have known about.

Claypool, Jane. **How to Get a Good Job.** Photographs by Maureen McNicholas. Franklin Watts, 1982. 89 pp.

Finding just the right job is important. This book will help you match your skills and talents with those demanded by a particular job and will help you find a job that brings satisfaction rather than just money. Part-time, summer, and full-time employment is discussed, and suggestions are given for determining job goals and obtaining the necessary training. Typical interview questions are listed as are checklists of questions to ask yourself. Photographs. Easy reading.

Clemens, Virginia Phelps. **Behind the Filmmaking Scene.** Westminster Press, 1982. 153 pp.

What goes on behind the scenes in the making of the films we see at local theaters and on television? This guide describes the work of the producer, director, screenwriter, actor, set designer, hairstylist, cinematographer, and film editor. Also included in the book is information about the education, experience, and personal traits needed in each behind-the-scenes film job.

Curtis, Patricia. **Animal Doctors: What It's Like to Be a Veterinarian and How to Become One.** Delacorte Press, 1979. 170 pp.

Veterinarians engaged in many different kinds of practices relate through personal stories what it is like to treat and care for animals. Their stories should make it easier for you to decide if this is a career for you, as they reveal the hardships, as well as the pleasures, of the profession. Also included are the names and addresses of the schools that provide training in veterinary medicine. Photographs.

Dean, Anabel. **Fire! How Do They Fight It?** Westminster Press, 1978. 112 pp.

In this book you will meet the earliest firefighters in colonial

America, the men who organized the first unpaid voluteers in 1717. Then meet the people who operate the enormous superpumpers in New York City today. In between, you will find out all about fires and how people have fought them over the centuries.

Deming, Richard. **The Paralegal.** Elsevier/Nelson Books, 1980. 142 pp.

Paralegals have more legal responsibilities than a legal secretary, although they do not have a law degree and cannot offer all the services provided by a lawyer. These specialists provide legal and administrative assistance to lawyers in government, in the public sector, and in private practice. Their functions and responsibilities include such fields of practice as antitrust, civil rights, consumer protection, insurance, real estate, and taxation. The career of the paralegal is examined in detail, with a discussion of salaries, duties, and schools that provide training.

Edmonds, I. G., and William H. Gerhardt. **Broadcasting for Beginners.** Holt, Rinehart & Winston, 1980. 182 pp.

The communications industry is an attractive career choice for many young people today. Although television may seem more glamorous than radio, there are many more jobs available in the radio business. This guidebook will tell you how to get started in radio—how to train your voice, keep station logs, write radio copy, and practice on-the-air techniques. The book also includes information about broadcasting schools, deejaying, sportscasting, and broadcast journalism. Photographs.

Fenten, Barbara, and D. X. Fenten. **The Team behind the Great Parades.** Westminster Press, 1981. 89 pp.

How do they make the huge balloons for the Macy's Thanksgiving Day Parade? Who puts all those flowers on the floats in the Tournament of Roses Parade? Here you will find the answers to these and other questions about America's most famous parades and learn how even you can apply for a chance to be in a great parade. Easy reading.

Fenten, Barbara, and D. X. Fenten. **Tourism and Hospitality—Careers Unlimited.** Westminster Press, 1978. 160 pp.

Thousands of careers exist in the areas of tourism and hospitality. Included are jobs in transportation services, information gathering and distribution, recreation, and food service. This guide describes what qualifications are needed to enter the field, and what hard work and fringe benefits you can expect to encounter with each job.

Fenten, D. X. **Ms. Architect.** Westminster Press, 1977. 128 pp.

Although less than 5 percent of the architects in the United States are women, it is a career that women can and do excel in, and one they are now being encouraged to enter. Here are some answers to questions you might have about becoming an architect, as well as advice about how to get more information. Also included are a list of schools that offer degrees and a chapter on related careers that do not require an architecture degree.

Folse, Nancy McCarthy, and Marilyn Henrion. **Careers in the Fashion Industry: What the Jobs Are and How to Get Them.** Harper & Row, Publishers, 1981. 270 pp.

Models are not the only people involved in the fashion industry. Behind each beautiful face is a troupe of skilled professionals who make the "look" that sells the products. The authors survey the entire industry, including textiles, apparel manufacturing, retailing, publicity, and photography. Explained are how each operation works, what education or training is needed, and what salaries can be expected. An appendix lists colleges and trade schools that offer training in various aspects of the fashion industry.

Foxworth, Jo. **Boss Lady: An Executive Woman Talks about Making It.** Warner Books, 1979. 250 pp.

A woman who wants to succeed in the business world today may have an easier time of it than she would have twenty years ago, but the fact remains that the odds are still against her. This book offers some helpful pointers and good advice for those who might wish to achieve business success. The areas covered include how to handle an interview, the sexist attitude, the drinking lunch, and how to dress to ensure that you are taken seriously.

Friedman, Sara Ann, and David Jacobs. **Police! A Precinct at Work.** Photographs by Alex Webb. Harcourt Brace Jovanovich, 1975. 183 pp.

The police department is on duty twenty-four hours a day in New York City. Police men and women on duty at 1 a.m. deal with a different world from those on the 1 p.m. shift. But all cops must handle such people as winos, robbers, and wife-beaters every day. And police officers must learn to enforce the law, not interpret it— sometimes a difficult task. Besides this, each kind of police duty, combined with the personality of the cop carrying it out, creates various conflicts within and among the levels of any police department. By following fifteen police officers in their jobs through a full day, this book lets readers get an idea what life is like as a cop in a major city.

Germann, Richard, and Peter Arnold. **Bernard Haldane Associates' Job and Career Building.** Harper & Row, Publishers, 1980. 241 pp.

Nobody should have to stay in a job they don't like. Men and women change jobs and careers today more than ever before. Step-by-step methods to make this a relatively simple process are included in this guide, as is information for getting that first job.

Gilbert, Sara. **Ready, Set, Go: How to Find a Career That's Right for You.** Four Winds Press, 1979. 145 pp.

Finding a job that you will enjoy can be the most difficult task of your life. This book introduces you to the various aptitude, achievement, and vocational-interest tests that you can take to find out more about your interests and abilities. The book also discusses which tests you should avoid. Questions answered here are ones like: How do I get the job I want? How do I get started once I've decided what I want to do? How do I apply for a job? How do I create a résumé?

Glasner, Lynne, and Marilyn Thypin. **Ready to Go: Auto Mechanic's Helper.** Photographs by Bernard Vidal. Fearon-Pitman Publishers, 1976. 60 pp.

In this first book in a series about jobs, Joe gets work after school and on weekends as an auto mechanic's helper. The reader learns about cars and other aspects of the job with Joe. A glossary is included in each book that illustrates and defines words associated with each job. A cassette tape is also available with the complete text of each book. Other books in the series discuss working as a waitress, supermarket stock clerk, duplicating room worker, short-order cook, baker's helper, gardener, sewing machine operator, porter/janitor, and day-care center aide. Easy reading.

Gleasner, Diana. **Breakthrough: Women in Writing.** Walker & Co., 1980. 155 pp.

Five noted women writers—Judy Blume, Erma Bombeck, Erica Jong, Jessamyn West, and Phyllis Whitney—discuss their careers in writing. They talk about the personal sacrifices they have needed to make in order to write and how they helped fight the existing prejudice against women writers. These five writers also share their feelings about the rewards of writing.

Hahn, James, and Lynn Hahn. **Aim for a Job with a Telephone Company.** Richards Rosen Press, 1979. 155 pp.

The story of how Alexander Bell invented and established the telephone in 1876 has a fairy-tale quality. Today we take this miracle for granted. This elaborate system now offers not only a source of rapid communication for all of us, but a variety of career opportunities as well. These jobs are anywhere and everywhere in the country, and they're as varied as equipment installers, linepersons, repairpersons, operators, clerks, bookkeepers, stenographers, typists, computer programmers, office machine workers, and teletype operators. There are also jobs as salespeople, truckdrivers, and security workers. One chapter tells what actual employees say about their jobs to help you decide if one may be the right job for you.

Haldane, Bernard, Jean Haldane, and Lowell Martin. **Job Power Now! The Young People's Job Finding Guide.** Acropolis Books, 1978. 176 pp.

Traditional job questionnaires and new "Job Power" forms are described in this guide. New methods and strategies are suggested for settling old problems in applying for jobs, such as the lack of work experience. Under the "Job Power" method, young people are asked to describe their strengths and experiences that relate to the job in question, such as setting goals, working on a schedule, and working toward and achieving goals. These descriptions can be based on such achievements as making the track team or helping with family chores. The "Job Power" guide is intended to start you looking at where you show potential as a future worker.

Harmon, Margaret, editor. **Working with Words: Careers for Writers.** Westminster Press, 1977. 153 pp.

When most of us think of writers, we imagine free-lance novelists and poets, some starving and some wealthy. But the surprising fact is that most writers today are staff writers who work full time and who receive a regular paycheck from their employers. This book is a collection of articles written by working authors who explain their particular fields. Writing for newspapers and magazines, for advertising firms, for radio and television, and for industry are all covered here. Opportunities, necessary skills, and salaries are also discussed.

Harrison, C. William. **Here Is Your Career: The Building Trades.** G. P. Putnam's Sons, 1979. 125 pp.

Men and women in the building trades represent the largest group of skilled workers in America's labor force. The author takes a look at the career opportunities available today in the construction industry and describes the skill requirements and the rewards of each job, from bricklayer to plumber, from safety engineer to general contractor.

Holmes, Burnham. **Early Morning Rounds: A Portrait of a Hospital.** Photographs by Janet Beller. Four Winds Press, 1981. 80 pp.

What really goes on inside a hospital? Find out as you follow several medical students on their assignments to different areas of the hospital. This is their time to leave the classroom behind and get firsthand experience in setting a bone, stitching a wound, and delivering a baby.

Horn, Yvonne Michie. **Dozens of Ways to Make Money.** Harcourt Brace Jovanovich, 1977. 83 pp.

From selling weeds to washing windshields, here are dozens of practical job ideas. The hints on advertising and selling provided here will be helpful to those who want to strike out on their own. Every idea has been successfully tested—all it takes is a small investment and a little imagination to start you on your way to making extra cash.

Horn, Yvonne Michie. **Sing for Your Supper: Earning Your Living as a Singer.** Harcourt Brace Jovanovich, 1979. 137 pp.

Have you thought it might be nice to "sing for your supper"? There are many young people who do just that—in many ways and on many levels. You don't have to be a superstar to have a career doing something you enjoy. Thirteen young singers describe their many styles and methods of singing for a living in this book. Some use music to do therapy work, some teach music, some write songs and lyrics. The author then describes guidelines for creating your own pattern for success in a music career.

Hummel, Dean L., and Carl McDaniels. **How to Help Your Child Plan a Career.** Acropolis Books, 1979. 177 pp.

Although this book is geared toward parents, it can be of great help to students as well. It explores such areas as potential occupational interests, job testing, resources for further information about specific careers, and forecasting the future labor market. One interesting feature of this book is a career game that will help direct your job thoughts.

Jaspersohn, William. **A Day in the Life of a Marine Biologist.** Little, Brown & Co., 1982.

A marine biologist's life includes both adventure and routine work. This book follows a typical day in the life of Arthur Humes, a marine biologist with the Boston University Marine Program at Woods Hole, Massachusetts. The day includes a field trip, the lab session where specimens are identified and studied, and time spent at a typewriter writing a scientific paper. Photographs.

Jenness, Aylette. **The Bakery Factory: Who Puts the Bread on Your Table.** Photographs by author. Thomas Y. Crowell Co., 1978. 69 pp.

Probably one of the items in our lives we all take for granted is bread. Did you ever wonder who makes that stuff we toast for breakfast, use for sandwiches at lunch, enjoy in the form of rolls at dinner, or devour hot with jam as a snack? This book takes readers on a tour of a bakery and lets them in on conversations with workers about their jobs. You will discover that baking on an enormous scale with big vats of dough, huge ovens, and machines of all kinds is far different from what happens in your kitchen.

Katz, Judith A. **The Business of Show Business: A Guide to Career Opportunities behind the Scenes in Theatre and Film.** Barnes & Noble, 1981. 254 pp.

Acting is not the only career in show business. Many other exciting jobs exist in administration, production, and supporting services for the theater and film industries. Here you'll meet the people who hold these jobs, find out what the jobs are really like, and even get some tips on getting started in show business yourself.

Keith, Judith. **"I Haven't a Thing to Wear!"** Illus. Lee Wydra. Avon Books, 1981. 311 pp.

With this book, a girl will never have to say, "I haven't a thing to wear!" The author is a radio and television personality who shows how to dress with very little money and lots of imagination. Her advice ranges from using small scarves for accent to step-by-step instructions for coordinating entire outfits. Tips on diet and exercise are also included.

Keyes, Fenton. **Your Future in a Paramedic Career.** Richards Rosen Press, 1979. 149 pp.

Paramedics are in large demand today. This book looks at the various types of paramedic careers available and the educational background and training required for each. These careers range from such jobs as ambulance assistant to specialized therapist. A personality checklist will help you decide if paramedics might be a career for you. There is also information on schooling and training for paramedicine and available scholarships.

Klein, David, and Marymae E. Klein. **Yourself Ten Years from Now: A Career Planning Book.** Harcourt Brace Jovanovich, 1977. 152 pp.

It is not too early to begin planning for your future now, and this book offers some sound advice for you in starting this career planning. The book asks you first to examine your likes and dislikes, your personal needs and values, and the pressures of your family and friends. It then gives you some valuable information regarding all these concerns to help you make a more informed decision. A final chapter suggests the places you might go to find out more about the kind of career you think might be suitable for you.

Klever, Anita. **Women in Television.** Westminster Press, 1975. 142 pp.

Thirty-seven women, ranging from unknown technicians to superstars, describe how they got into television, what kinds of jobs they do, and what kind of training they had to prepare them for their jobs. This book covers all types of jobs held by women, not just the glamorous, on-camera ones. If you are interested in a career in television or think you might be, this book will give you a realistic picture of the profession.

Lee, Mary Price. **Ms. Veterinarian.** Westminster Press, 1976. 139 pp.

A woman who wants to be a veterinarian faces many obstacles. There are fewer than twenty veterinary schools in the United States, and all have traditionally been male oriented. This book examines the role of women in veterinary medicine, past and present, and discusses how you might best go about pursuing a career in this area if you are female.

Lehrman, Steve. **Your Career in Harness Racing.** Atheneum Publishers, 1976. 148 pp.

This book discusses harness racing—the racing of horses harnessed to two-wheeled carts called sulkies. Information includes the duties of grooms, trainers, and drivers. Information about related careers is also provided. Photographs and illustrations help explain what it's like to be involved with this type of horse racing.

Lobb, Charlotte. **Exploring Vocational School Careers.** Richards Rosen Press, 1979. 154 pp.

What is it like to attend a vocational school? Detailed information is provided on available courses, facilities, job placement opportunities, and the amount of homework you can expect. Some thirty course possibilities are described, and about 1,500 possible careers based on these courses are suggested. Also included is information about obtaining financial assistance to attend a vocational school.

London, Mel. **Getting into Film.** Ballantine Books, 1977. 178 pp.

Do you want to be in pictures? Have you ever wondered about how you could get involved in the glamorous world of the movies? Whether you intend to seek a job in the film industry or are simply a film buff, this book will answer hundreds of questions about the growing, changing world of film production. Included is information about training programs, job hunting, film workshops, and the free-lance market. Also, the basic aspects of cinematography, special effects, makeup, animation, and acting are presented in everyday language. Photographs and illustrations.

Matteson, George. **Draggermen: Fishing on Georges Bank.** Illus. by author. Four Winds Press, 1979. 138 pp.

Come along on a voyage of the *Elsie G,* a modern fishing boat, and learn about the exciting occupation of commercial fishing. The type of fishing described here is called trawling, where huge nets are used to drag the bottom of the sea to haul in fish like cod and haddock. The use of these nets can be dangerous, and each member of the crew has important duties. Ecology is also important to these people, so the book describes the limits imposed on fishing, as well as the methods being used to protect endangered fish.

Miklowitz, Gloria D., and Madeleine Yates. **The Young Tycoons: Ten Success Stories.** Harcourt Brace Jovanovich, 1981. 124 pp.

Do you think you are too young to be a millionaire? You will think differently after you read these stories of men and women in their teens and twenties who made it big in business. One even started making money at age eleven. These people built successful careers in areas as varied as photography, construction, flowers, cleaning, pets, and even discos. While each junior tycoon has a different story, their experiences all show that financial success requires someone who recognizes opportunity, accepts challenges, and exercises ingenuity.

Mitchell, Joyce Slayton. **See Me More Clearly: Career and Life Planning for Teens with Physical Disabilities.** Harcourt Brace Jovanovich, 1980. 284 pp.

This book was written especially for teenagers with physical disabilities. It begins with a discussion of sexuality, because this important topic is often confusing to the disabled. The book then goes on to other topics designed to help disabled teenagers choose a career and a plan for living that will allow them self-sufficiency and fulfillment.

Moore, Charles Guy. **The Career Game: A Step-by-Step Guide up the Ladder of Success.** Illus. Joan O'Connor, Anne Green, and Fred Haynes. Ballantine Books, 1978. 263 pp.

Knowing how our economic system works can be an aid in making intelligent career decisions, because knowledge of the system will help identify which professions will be in demand in the future. In addition to providing general economic information, this book discusses the salaries and job security of particular professions and helps readers in rating jobs.

O'Connor, Karen. **Working with Horses: A Roundup of Careers.** Photographs by Kelle Rankin. Dodd, Mead & Co., 1980. 121 pp.

Horses continue to be popular, so there are a variety of jobs available for people who want to work in the horse industry. Such jobs include farrier, wrangler, riding instructor, and veterinarian. Here are brief descriptions of these jobs and discussions with the people who hold them. This book also includes a list of places to write for more information about careers with horses.

Paige, David. **A Day in the Life of a Forest Ranger.** Photographs by Michael Mauney. Troll Associates, 1980. 32 pp.

Take a closeup look at the duties and concerns of a national park ranger, from morning until night. A ranger's more dangerous tasks are described here, as well as the routine activities. You will learn that a ranger's duties include everything from paperwork to relocating wild animals. Easy reading.

Paige, David. **A Day in the Life of a Rock Musician.** Photographs by Roger Ruhlin. Troll Associates, 1980. 32 pp.

What a rock musician might experience in one full day of work is the subject of this book. This musician does everything from writing a new song, to recording another, to performing before a live audience. The members of a typical group are introduced along with their instruments, as are the other people it takes to make a group a success. Easy reading.

Pelta, Kathy. **There's a Job for You in Food Service: A Career Guide.** Dodd, Mead & Co., 1979. 181 pp.

Here is a career guide for people interested in food service. The book describes all types of jobs connected with feeding people, from busperson to restaurant manager. Sections of the book look at specific food jobs, such as the duties of a waiter or waitress. Also included is information on training for specific positions like chef or caterer. Photographs.

Potter, Neil. **Oil Rig.** Macdonald Educational, 1977. 47 pp.

Oil is a part of our everyday lives, as a source of energy and as a component in such products as plastic and polyester. Oil is found almost everywhere in the world—below the surface of oceans and seas, in jungles and deserts, in steaming swamps, and in freezing Arctic regions. Various jobs related to oil can also be found around the world. There are the geologists who first search for the oil, then there are the members of the drilling team and the divers on the ocean rigs. There must also be those who serve and supply these specialty workers. Finally, the oil must be transported and refined by still other workers. Photographs and diagrams help explain the entire process of drilling for oil.

Rafferty, Robert. **Careers in the Military: Good Training for Civilian Life.** Elsevier/Nelson Books, 1980. 256 pp.

More and more jobs today require technical knowledge and experience that are sometimes difficult to obtain. One option available to young people is a career in the armed forces. In this book you will find information concerning educational opportunities, pay scales, fringe benefits, and comparisons with civilian jobs. This book also examines the military opportunities for women, including their potential for becoming officers.

Reed, Arthur. **Airport.** Macdonald Educational, 1978. 47 pp.

Because so many kinds of activities are going on in an airport every day, many kinds of jobs are available there. Some of these jobs require highly specialized training, while others are less complex and don't require much training or experience. This book explains how an airport operates and, using photos and diagrams, describes some of the jobs going on there. Airport careers include everything from the most visible jobs as part of the flight crew or passenger-handling staff, to positions in air traffic control, plane maintenance, security and customs, and business management.

Rennert, Amy. **Making It in Photography.** Illus. Bruce Curtis. G. P. Putnam's Sons, 1980. 125 pp.

The field of photography is fast becoming one of the most popular careers for young people. This book focuses on several professional photographers in various areas of the field, including photojournalism, fashion photography, and travel photography. This book also explores some of the related photography career areas such as camera repair and teaching photography. Included is a directory of degree and nondegree programs.

Roberts, W. G. **The Quest for Oil.** S. G. Phillips, 1977. 157 pp.

This study traces the beginnings of the oil industry and shows how it is currently operating. Other sections explain the drilling process, the complex refining procedure, and the transportation of crude oil and its by-products, while stressing the need for conservation. The need for good geologists, chemists, and engineers is also stressed in this illustrated survey of the industry.

Schleier, Curt. **The Team behind Your Airline Flight.** Westminster Press, 1981.

Ever wondered what it takes to get a plane in the air and down again safely? This book explains air travel from the trip to a travel agent to the moment the plane lands at its destination. Even the midair meal and the people behind it are discussed here. Black-and-white photographs of airline personnel accompany the description of their duties.

Schmidt, Peggy J. **Making It on Your First Job: When You're Young, Inexperienced and Ambitious.** Avon Books, 1981. 258 pp.

Do you sometimes dream (or worry) about what you will do when you finish school? Do you want to trade your blue jeans for a briefcase? This book covers such topics as courses to take before graduation, zeroing in on the right job for you, and where and how to look for work.

Skurzynski, Gloria. **Safeguarding the Land: Women at Work in Parks, Forests, and Rangelands.** Harcourt Brace Jovanovich, 1981. 162 pp.

Here is a book for women who prefer the outdoors and who would like to choose a career that would keep them there. Three women who have already done just that—a park ranger, a wildlife specialist, and a range conservationist—talk about their jobs and the education they needed to prepare for these jobs once reserved for men.

Smith, Betsy Covington. **Breakthrough: Women in Television.** Walker & Co., 1981. 140 pp.

Do you ever dream of being a TV star? The eight women in this book all have major jobs in television—but not necessarily in front of the camera. They share their experiences as camera operator, anchor, news correspondent, screenwriter, producer, artist, promotion manager, and programmer.

Smith, Elizabeth Simpson. **Breakthrough: Women in Aviation.** Walker & Co., 1981. 155 pp.

This book discusses nine women who have very different jobs in aviation—aeronautical engineer, aerial refueler, astronaut, air traffic controller, FAA inspector, and pilots in commercial, air force, corporation, and cargo flying. Described here are their lives and their difficulties on the job. Photographs.

Sullivan, George. **How Do They Package It?** Westminster Press, 1976. 144 pp.

Since the turn of the century, a revolution in shipping and buying habits has demanded new product packaging. Some 25,000 colorful containers compete for the consumer's dollars. This behind-the-scenes account of the packaging industry also looks at such issues as the ecological results of the 5.3 pounds of trash discarded by each family every day and the psychology of packaging.

Summers, Clyde W., and Robert J. Rabin. **The Rights of Union Members.** Discus Books, 1979. 202 pp.

In a question-and-answer format, this book presents the rights and responsibilities of workers who belong to labor unions. Even though each individual labor contract is different in its specifics, federal law regulates the basic principles behind these contracts, and that is what this book is largely about. In addition, the book tells you how to protect your individual rights as a union member.

Terkel, Studs. **Working.** Avon Books, 1975. 762 pp.

For three years Studs Terkel traveled throughout the United States talking with people, all kinds of people, to find out how they felt about their jobs, their lives, and themselves. Their stories are recorded in their own words. You will hear from farmers, food workers, factory workers, writers, nurses, teachers, lawyers, executives, sports figures, musicians, and many others. There are also interesting stories from police officers, doorkeepers, and janitors. Mature language.

Trainer, David. **A Day in the Life of a TV News Reporter.** Photographs by Stephen Sanacore. Troll Associates, 1980. 32 pp.

Want to be a Barbara Walters or a Dan Rather? What it takes to get the news on the air is described here. The job of the reporter is the primary subject, but the behind-the-scenes jobs of the camera operator, sound engineer, and director are also included. Easy reading.

Ward, Brian. **Hospital.** Macdonald Educational, 1978. 47 pp.

Once a hospital was a place to go to die. Either your illness or accident killed you—or the hospital itself would. Today the opposite is true, as people go to the hospital to receive treatment, to get better, to return home to a normal life. Today's hospitals have become huge complexes that serve many kinds of patient needs. And many kinds of people now work in a hospital besides the doctors and nurses. There are jobs for technicians, receptionists, cleaners, dieticians, and many more. This book explains all these hospital jobs with the help of drawings and photographs.

Williams, Barbara. **Breakthrough: Women in Archaeology.** Walker & Co., 1981. 168 pp.

Interested in studying past cultures by examining old tools, pottery, and other relics? The lives and work of six women archaeologists are discussed in this book. Each chapter covers the career of one of these women, explaining the importance of their work and its difficulty. The women also offer advice to young women considering the field of archaeology. The book contains over forty black-and-white photographs, a glossary, information on archaeological field schools, a list of colleges that have archaeology departments, and a list of museums with major archaeological holdings.

Witty, Margot. **A Day in the Life of an Emergency Room Nurse.** Photographs by Sarah Lewis. Troll Associates, 1980. 32 pp.

Every day can have the tension and drama of an episode of "M*A*S*H" for certain people. This is an account of what might be a typical day for an emergency room nurse. Provided here is an overview of the nurse's duties and concerns when people are brought in with a variety of problems—all requiring immediate treatment. Easy reading.

Wright, Carol. **Hotel.** Macdonald Educational, 1979. 47 pp.

> Hotels and inns can be traced back many centuries. Today they range from luxury hotels to small homey inns with few rooms. But wherever they are, whatever size or style, hotels require a staff of people who work with the public. There can be people who work as housekeepers and desk clerks and those who work in the kitchen, restaurant, or bar. Keeping the whole place running smoothly also demands a well-trained hotel manager. This book describes many kinds of hotels, their services, and the jobs available on their staff.

Wright, John W. **The American Almanac of Jobs and Salaries.** Avon Books, 1982. 775 pp.

> Choosing an occupation is one of the most important decisions you will make. Before making such a choice, you should have all of the facts about the various occupations available to you. This lengthy, up-to-date text lists hundreds of jobs and provides such information as the salary ranges for each. Also included is some commonsense advice about the prospects of gaining employment in your chosen field.

Yeomans, William N. **Jobs '80-'81.** Paragon Books, 1979. 319 pp.

> It is never too early to make career plans. While no one has found a simple formula for finding the ideal job, this book does offer a guide to the requirements for particular occuptions, their salaries, and the benefits of various careers. Information about colleges and other sources of training, how to prepare for interviews, and the ways to use employment agencies, newspaper ads, and career counseling services is also included. Special sections cover career opportunities for women and minorities. Let this book show you how to evaluate your job skills and objectives in order to find the area of work best suited to you.

Young, Pam, and Peggy Jones (editor Sydney Craft Rozen). **Sidetracked Home Executives: From Pigpen to Paradise.** Warner Books, 1981. 157 pp.

> The authors originally were two disorganized and frustrated sisters and wives. One day, they realized the reason they never seemed to do anything right at home was that they did not look at their lives in the proper way. They were really "Home Executives," with a job like anyone else. So the pair analyzed their jobs and set up a schedule that arranged their chores on a daily, weekly, and monthly basis. In this book, the sisters offer their example as a guide for others who want to reorganize their lives.

Zimmermann, Barbara, and David B. Smith. **Careers in Health: The Professionals Give You the Inside Picture about Their Jobs.** Beacon Press, 1978. 239 pp.

Various professionals who make up the health industry give readers the inside information about their occupations. Included is information about the duties and responsibilities of a physician's assistant, nurse-midwife, laboratory technologist, hospital administrator, and other professionals with health-related careers.

Places and People of the World

Alotta, Robert I. **Old Names and New Places.** Illus. Lee deGroot. Westminster Press, 1979. 112 pp.

Here is an explanation of some of the different sources used in naming towns, streets, rivers, and many other places in the United States. Some names are humorous, some are patriotic, while some are merely informative. The last two chapters provide hints on how to trace the origin of place-names in your own community.

Archer, Jules. **Legacy of the Desert: Understanding the Arabs.** Little, Brown & Co., 1976. 214 pp.

The Arabs and the Middle East have become more and more important to us as we have become more and more dependent on their oil, yet the people and the land may not be familiar to us. This book does much to explain the Arab people by discussing their religion, their history, and their culture in easily understood language.

Atmore, Anthony, and Gillian Stacey. **Black Kingdoms, Black Peoples: The West African Heritage.** Photographs by Werner Forman. G. P. Putnam's Sons, 1979. 128 pp.

The authors write of the African kingdoms of West Africa—their people, trade, crafts, art, and religions. The book points out the differences among various groups in Africa, as well as noting their similarities. Photographs.

Barker, Carol. **Arjun and His Village in India.** Illus. by author. Oxford University Press, 1979. 32 pp.

Twelve-year-old Arjun tells us what it is like to live in rural India. He discusses how people work and the ways they obtain and prepare food. The various religious ceremonies and beliefs of India are also covered by Arjun. Easy reading.

Bell, Neill. **The Book of Where; or, How to Be Naturally Geographic.** Illus. Richard Wilson. Little, Brown & Co., 1982. 119 pp.

Geography is a subject that often confuses many people with its charts, maps, and graphs. This book begins with questions about our own houses, streets, cities, or towns. From the familiar, the book then takes the reader to the less familiar world at large. The book provides a trip around the world in 119 pages of cartoons, maps, and interesting explanations.

Bourne, Miriam Anne. **The Children of Mount Vernon: A Guide to George Washington's Home.** Illus. Gloria Kamen. Doubleday & Co., 1981. 56 pp.

Mount Vernon, Washington's home, was a plantation where the president's grandchildren, Nelly and Wash Custis also lived. This book traces a day in their lives as they play hide-and-seek and go about seeking other recreation and adventures. Through their story, the reader learns much about Mount Vernon's buildings and grounds, and the people who worked there in the early days of the American nation. Easy reading.

Bowen, David J. **The Land and People of Chile.** Rev. ed. J. B. Lippincott Co., 1976. 159 pp.

Chile is a country in South America that stretches 2,600 miles from its northern tip to its southern tip at Cape Horn. The customs and life-styles of the people of Chile are presented in this book. Included are discussions of rituals, ceremonies, occupations, clothing, foods, and geography.

Cheney, Cora. **Alaska: Indians, Eskimos, Russians, and the Rest.** Dodd, Mead & Co., 1980. 143 pp.

This history of Alaska looks at the arrival of the first people to Alaska and traces their places of origin. It discusses the role of the Russians and Americans in Alaska during the past century and the building of the oil pipeline during the 1970s. Also included are true stories of explorers and some bits of Alaskan mythology. Photographs.

Clifford, Mary Louise. **The Land and People of the Arabian Peninsula.** J. B. Lippincott Co., 1977. 191 pp.

Years ago we may have associated the people of the Arabian peninsula with genies and magic lamps, but our dependence on Arab oil has changed all that. The eight nations of Arabia are presented in this book in a more realistic light. The geography, religion, language, and political history that set this region apart from all others are described here as well as the cultural shock the Arabian people face as they try to adjust to the modern society so abruptly brought to them because of their recent oil-based wealth and power.

Cornell, James. **Lost Lands and Forgotten People.** Sterling Publishing Co., 1978. 224 pp.

Mysterious rock paintings in the middle of the Sahara, gigantic heads in the jungles of Mexico, castles swallowed up in the sands of Arabia—this book is a fascinating chronicle of lost civilizations. It asks the eternal questions: Where did they come from? Where did they go? Wander through abandoned pyramids in Mexico, Guatemala, and Honduras. Explore deserted cities in China and India. And wonder, as the author does, what will eventually become of our *own* civilization.

Cornell, James. **Where Did They Come From? Mysterious Origins of Ancient People.** Scholastic Book Services, 1978. 108 pp.

Many interesting legends about Stone Age people are explained and evaluated in this book. Creatures who lived thousands or millions of years ago, according to anthropologists, could be our ancestors—relatives of ours who evolved to become what we now call *homo sapiens* or human beings. Such possible ancient relatives of humans as the "Peking Man" and the "Bog People" are described and discussed in this book. Easy reading.

Dornberg, John. **Eastern Europe: A Communist Kaleidoscope.** Dial Press, 1980. 311 pp.

The "Iron Curtain" countries of Poland, Hungary, Czechoslovakia, Bulgaria, and Romania are discussed in this book. These countries are under Soviet influence and may be unfamiliar to Americans. The author, who has traveled extensively in Eastern Europe, describes each country's history, politics, economics, and industry, as well as revealing what day-to-day life is like for the average person in these countries.

Dresang, Eliza T. **The Land and People of Zambia.** J. B. Lippincott Co., 1975. 159 pp.

Here is an introduction to the history and people of Zambia. In the 1880s British explorer David Livingston claimed this portion of South Africa for Great Britain. The British ruled the country until granting independence to Zambia in 1964. Now the country is caught up in a struggle to modernize. Zambia feels the need to develop its natural resources and its industry to keep up with the rest of the world.

Engel, Dolores. **Voyage of the Kon-Tiki.** Illus. Gary Bale. Raintree Publishers, 1979. 31 pp.

The mystery of the origin of the Polynesian settlers has long puzzled even experts. A young Norwegian named Thor Heyerdahl believed that the first people had come from South America to the islands of the South Pacific by raft hundreds of years before. To prove this to the many doubters, Heyerdahl persuaded five other adventurers to join him in making such a voyage in a boat made like the one these early people would have used. The men made the ship themselves and, in the spring of 1947, embarked on an adventure that might easily have cost them their lives, but nothing could stop them—not the scorpions and alligators of the jungle, or the storms and sharks of the seas, or the natives they encountered on the islands. Easy reading.

Erdoes, Richard (editor Marvin L. Reiter). **The Native Americans: Navajos.** Photographs by author. Sterling Publishing Co., 1978. 83 pp.

The Navajo way is to "walk in beauty in a beautiful land." But the Navajos' peace of mind is often shattered in the conflict of being caught between two cultures. In many ways, the Navajos are finding a way to blend the old and the new, to combine their way and the white people's way. The text and photographs in this book explain the harsh beauty of the arid Navajo land, the people at work and at play, and the legends and traditions the older Navajos keep alive and pass on to their children and grandchildren.

Ferguson, Linda. **Canada.** Charles Scribner's Sons, 1979. 242 pp.

Canada, one of our closest allies and nearest neighbors, is a more interesting country than many Americans realize. With a wide variety of topographical and wildlife wonders, Canada's ecological balance has been a major concern that has guided the nation's growth and progress. This book explores Canada's history, environment, culture, and accomplishments and helps to make the nation's value and importance fully understood. Maps and photographs.

Garver, Susan, and Paula McGuire. **Coming to North America from Mexico, Cuba, and Puerto Rico.** Delacorte Press, 1981. 161 pp.

Hispanics make up the fastest-growing minority group in the United States today. Why do they come? What do they find? How do they adapt to life here? In their own words, this book tells of their hopes and fears, their sufferings and successes.

Goldston, Robert. **The Sword of the Prophet: A History of The Arab World from the Time of Mohammed to the Present Day.** Dial Press, 1979. 246 pp.

From the time of the seventh century to the recent Mideast wars, the Arab nations have had a rich and exciting history. The author believes these nations were rediscovered by the Western world only after World War II, so he fills in the gaps for us before and after that period.

Grout, Phil. **A Spell in Plains.** Photographs by author. Stemmer House Publishers, 1978. 150 pp.

In words and pictures, this book provides us with some idea of the land and people of Plains, Georgia, so that we may better understand one famous man who came from there, Jimmy Carter. But Carter and his family get little direct mention. It is his neighbors and their ideas and actions that are described here. Their combined stories, however, go to show how the former president is a product of a certain environment.

Gyles, Anna Benson, and Chloë Sayer. **Of Gods and Men: The Heritage of Ancient Mexico.** Harper & Row, Publishers, 1981. 231 pp.

Mexico is filled with mysterious traditions dating back to before the time of Christ. The civilizations of the Toltec, Maya, and Zapotec had legends and customs that still exist in some form among many of the Indian tribes of Mexico. This book gives an overview of these ancient civilizations of pre-Hispanic Mexico and discusses what remnants exist in the country today. Photographs.

Huynh Quang Nhuong. **The Land I Lost: Adventures of a Boy in Vietnam.** Illus. Vo-Dinh Mai. Harper & Row, Publishers, 1982. 115 pp.

Here are the personal memories of a boyhood filled with adventure and humor in the highlands of Vietnam. These tales include friendly and dangerous snakes, a gentle pet water buffalo named Tank, man-eating crocodiles, and the author's eighty-year-old grandmother, who uses a secret talent in karate and some sharp thinking to handle bandits that break into the house.

Jenness, Aylette, and Lisa W. Kroeber. **A Life of Their Own: An Indian Family in Latin America.** Illus. by authors and Susan Votaw. Thomas Y. Crowell Co., 1975. 133 pp.

The authors of this book spent many days living and talking with the Hernandez family, an Indian family in Guatemala. The daily life of the family is described first—the work they do, the type of food they eat, and the way the family members treat one another. Some of the many photographs and illustrations will aid the reader in making craft objects similar to those made by the Hernandez family. On example is a *barridette,* which is a type of kite.

Kahn, Kathy. Hillbilly Women. Discus Books, 1980. 151 pp.

Nineteen women live in the coal-mining and cotton-milling areas of Appalachia talk about their lives. Their language is frank, and so are their feelings about life. Despite enormous abuse and overwhelming poverty, these women's spirits remain undaunted.

Kraske, Robert. The Twelve Million Dollar Note: Strange but True Tales of Messages Found in Seagoing Bottles. Thomas Nelson, 1977. 96 pp.

What is a bottle worth—a few cents when you return it to the supermarket? Miguel returned a bottle that made him the richest boy in the Azores Islands. Another bottle introduced a lonely American man to an Irish farmer's daughter. One man wrote his will on a blank check and threw it overboard in a bottle when his fishing boat got into trouble. Next time you go beachcombing, you may want to look for more than shells!

Linn, Christopher. The Everglades: Exploring the Unknown. Troll Associates, 1976. 32 pp.

The Florida Everglades today look the same as they did in prehistoric times. Plants and animals there must still survive extensive wet and dry seasons. Many photographs show the beauty and the dangers of the Everglades, as the text discusses the remarkable variety of wildlife that inhabits this swampy region. Easy reading.

Loescher, Gil (with Ann Dull Loescher). China: Pushing toward the Year 2000. Harcourt Brace Jovanovich, 1981. 160 pp.

Ever since recent negotiations with China, there has been a new and keen interest in the People's Republic of China. But in order to understand China's role in current world events, we must have some knowledge of its history and political devlopment. This book discusses past and present leaders' responsibilities for the current condition of the nation and its people. Early encounters with the West, Chinese nationalism, revolutions, invasions, civil war, and Chinese communism are all major topics covered in the book. Photographs.

Loescher, Gil. (with Ann Dull Loescher). **The World's Refugees: A Test of Humanity.** Harcourt Brace Jovanovich, 1982. 145 pp.

What happens to the millions of people who have to leave their homes because of war, lack of water and food, or other disasters? This book describes the events that have caused the refugee crisis, how and where the refugees have traveled, and what life is like in refugee camps. The attitudes and traditions of Americans regarding refugees are also discussed. Photographs.

Lyttle, Richard B. **People of the Dawn.** Illus. Heidy Fogel. Atheneum Publishers, 1980. 181 pp.

How do we find out about early people, people of the dawn of civilization? Through intensive archaeological studies, according to this book. Sites where traces of prehistoric people were discovered are described here along with the methods for dating the objects found. The book also shows how conclusions are drawn from these objects about the kind of life these people lived. A bibliography is provided that suggests further reading on the subject.

Macaulay, David. **Pyramid.** Houghton Mifflin Co., 1975. 80 pp.

This book describes in detail the painful and complicated occupation of building a pyramid. The black-and-white illustrations reveal the process of pyramid building step by step. Knowledge of how these architectural wonders were constructed also helps in the understanding of all aspects of Egyptian culture.

Mangurian, David. **Children of the Incas.** Four Winds Press, 1979. 73 pp.

The Inca empire flourished in Peru and surrounding areas between 1200 and 1500. But when the Spanish conquest began in the 1530s, this once-mighty civilization was nearly destroyed. Now only one small village of 104 people high in the mountains near Lake Titicaca remains. Thirteen-year-old Modesto describes what it's like to live in that village where old life-styles continue to be followed. Many people die there from disease, from hunger, from poverty. And Modesto's story, illustrated with black-and-white photographs, reveals the harshness of the life there. Most of the village children go to school only through the fifth grade. But Modesto's dream is to go to the city, get a full education, and do something to make life better for his people.

Mann, Peggy. **Easter Island: Land of Mysteries.** Holt, Rinehart & Winston, 1976. 224 pp.

Easter Island, a tiny speck in the southeast Pacific, has been the center of much interest. It is the prehistoric people of that island who are of most interest to historians, sociologists, and anthropologists. They had their own unique writing system and created giant stone statues unlike any others in the world. The mystery has been why these 1,000 statues were created. Many other mysteries and legends are discussed here, with theoretical answers provided based upon known historical facts.

Mathews, Janet. **Wurley and Wommera: Aboriginal Life and Craft.** Illus. Walter Stackpool. William Collins Publishers, 1977. 127 pp.

A *wurley* is a hut, and a *wommera* is a spear-grip for a weapon; both terms are used by the aborigines of Australia. The aborigines first came to Australia 40,000 years ago and had to adapt to a harsh land. This book explores their daily life, tools and weapons, and fights and battles. Their life-style has changed little over the centuries, but now the twentieth century is endangering their way of life.

Nance, John. **The Land and People of the Philippines.** J. B. Lippincott Co., 1977. 192 pp.

The story of the Philippines is a tale of traders from Asia, settlers from Malaysia, craftspeople from China, and conquerors from Spain, the United States, and Japan. The history, life, and future promise of this country of seven thousand islands and its people are captured in this study of the Philippines.

Nance, John. **Lobo of the Tasaday: A Stone Age Boy Meets the Modern World.** Photographs by author. Pantheon Books, 1982. 56 pp.

Pictures and words tell the exciting story of a young boy who belongs to a recently discovered tribe in the Philippine jungles. Lobo's tribe still live as people did in the Stone Age, using crude tools and weapons to provide themselves with fire, food, and shelter. When Lobo and his people meet outsiders from the modern world, both groups find they have much to learn from each other.

Nelson, Richard K. **Hunters of the Northern Ice.** University of Chicago Press, 1975. 429 pp.

The Eskimos of northern Alaska have long depended on hunting to supply food, clothing, and other necessities. Hunting techniques and hunting expeditions for the arctic fox, polar bear, white whale, seal, and walrus are explained in this book. The author lived with and studied the Eskimos near Wainwright and Point Barrow, Alaska, where he learned about the dangers of shifting ice, methods for predicting weather conditions, and how to survive in emergency weather conditions. He describes the daily life of the Eskimos and the harsh environment in which they live, and he shows how today's life-styles and emphasis on ecology are changing the traditional Eskimo life.

Orlob, Helen. **The Northeast Passage: Black Water, White Ice.** Thomas Nelson, 1977. 141 pp.

The attempts since 1553 to sail the Arctic Ocean above the Soviet Union, from the Atlantic to the Pacific, are described in this book. Many people lost their lives in these frozen seas, but today, with the help of ice breakers, passage is made in as little as ten days. And such voyages are necessary to maintain life in the mineral-rich lands of Siberia. Here is a story of true adventure and discovery by courageous men and women.

Pace, Mildred Mastin. **Pyramids: Tombs for Eternity.** Illus. Radu Vero and Mirela Zisu. McGraw-Hill Book Co., 1981. 192 pp.

Why were the pyramids of Egypt built? What did they look like in their original state? Do they have special powers? On this journey into the past, you will read about the world's oldest boat and the first stone building.

Packard, Jerrold M. **The Queen and Her Court: A Guide to the British Monarchy Today.** Charles Scribner's Sons, 1981. 221 pp.

This book contains everything you ever wanted to know about the British queen and her court: their lives, personalities, houses, customs, jewel collections, maintenance costs, ancestors, descendants, titles, and other interesting facts. For example, did you know that running Buckingham Palace requires the same staff and cost as running a large hotel? There are 337 full-time and 126 part-time employees there who earn a total of over one million pounds a year.

Poynter, Margaret. **Search and Rescue: The Team and the Missions.** Photographs by Jerry Newcomb. Atheneum Publishers, 1980.

This is a story of volunteers on mountain search and rescue teams in Southern California. These volunteers are trained in search procedures and use equipment as varied as helicopters and dogs. Several rescue stories are included in this book, such as one concerning a three-year-old boy who wandered into the desert, one about two backpackers who were trapped in a snowstorm in the High Sierras, and the tale of a snapped cable on an aerial tramway at Squaw Valley that left half a car dangling high above the valley floor.

Ross, Frank, Jr. **Arabs and the Islamic World.** S. G. Phillips, 1979. 222 pp.

The Arab countries are some of the world's oldest and newest nations. With a history dating back to 2,500 B.C., the Arab empire endured for several centuries, conquering other nations in Europe and Africa. Then, after being conquered itself by powerful invaders, Arabia remained a quiet and secluded area of the world until the twentieth century. With the discovery of oil in the region and the founding of Israel, the Middle East has again taken on worldwide significance. This book traces the history of the region and the development of the Arab culture up to the 1977 Camp David Accords. Maps and photographs.

Spier, Peter. **People.** Illus. by author. Doubleday & Co., 1980. 40 pp.

The four billion people in the world lead quite different lives from one another. This colorfully illustrated book discusses the many tribes, nationalities, and ethnic groups and explores their life-styles and daily activities. (National Conference of Christians and Jews National Mass Media Award; Christopher Medal; American Book Award nomination)

Stephens, John H. **Towers, Bridges and Other Structures.** Sterling Publishing Co., 1976. 288 pp.

What are the greatest construction feats of all time? The Great Wall of China? The Louisiana Superdome? This book discusses the most spectacular feats of civil engineering and the most spectacular construction disasters. The descriptions include information on above-ground structures, below-ground engineering, and hydraulic works. The story behind the building of each structure is included, and there are numerous photographs.

Stewart, Katie (with Pamela and Maurice Michael). **The Joy of Eating.** Stemmer House Publishers, 1977. 288 pp.

People throughout history have eaten not just to stay alive, but for the joy of eating. Even back in Grecian times, meals and utensils were as elaborate as today. This book presents pictures of people eating, representing various cultures around the world. Included are the foods of ancient times, medieval cooking, Islamic and Indian meals, Chinese and Japanese dishes, and North American cooking. Accompanying the text are 111 recipes.

Swanson, Glen. **Oil and Water: A Look at the Middle East.** Illus. Jill Shaffer. Prentice-Hall, 1981. 44 pp.

Oil and water are both important to life—especially in the Middle East. That area contains over half of the world's crude oil reserves, but it suffers from a shortage of water. How the Middle East has attempted to balance the oil and water question yesterday and today is the focus of this book. A glossary of terms related to oil production and a list of petroleum uses conclude the discussion.

Switzer, Ellen. **Our Urban Planet.** Photographs by Michael Switzer and Jeffrey Gilbert Switzer. Atheneum Publishers, 1980. 279 pp.

Why do people live in cities? Will they continue to want to do so? When did cities begin? What kinds of cities survive best? What future do cities have? This book deals with these questions and other urban problems and offers possible solutions. Featured are Venice, Amsterdam, Hong Kong, and New York City. (Children's Science Book Award)

Thorne, Ian (editor Howard Schroeder). **Bermuda Triangle.** Crestwood House, 1979. 47 pp.

To many ship captains, airplane pilots, and average people, the name "Bermuda Triangle" is linked to fear and mysterious activities. This triangle is an area between Florida, Bermuda, and Puerto Rico in which many planes and boats have disappeared over the years. This book traces the history of the area, focusing on the sea and air disasters that have occurred within it. Easy reading.

Thum, Marcella. **Exploring Literary America.** Atheneum Publishers, 1979. 317 pp.

Ever wonder where famous writers lived? This travel and reference guide describes the landmarks that honor many American authors from the eighteenth to the early twentieth centuries. Included are indexes for geographic location, author, title, and subject. Black-and-white photographs and maps.

Traub, James S. **India: The Challenge of Change.** Julian Messner, 1981. 150 pp.

India is a land that fascinates and puzzles outsiders. The country's vastness and diversity seem to invite comparison to the United States. Yet this book reveals how the two countries are opposites in most areas. While the U.S. finds itself trying to slow down to prevent "future shock" and the loss of traditions, India finds it must force its people out of ancient patterns of living. The book provides a clear view of India today by discussing the country's history, geography, religions, social system, government, national art and architecture treasures, and overcrowded city slums.

Tsunetomo, Yamamoto (translator William Scott Wilson). **Hagakure: The Book of the Samurai.** Discus Books, 1981. 180 pp.

Written by a real Japanese samurai warrior who lived three hundred years ago, this book presents a collection of his observations about the samurai way of life. It covers both war activities and peacetime pursuits.

Vlahos, Olivia. **Far Eastern Beginnings.** Illus. George Ford. Viking Press, 1976. 292 pp.

The continent of Asia is rich with history, cultures, and languages. It is a place of soldiers, monks, merchants, travelers, sailors, and craftspeople. This book discusses many aspects of life in the Far East, but always with an emphasis on its people.

Yungmei, Tang. **China, Here We Come! Visiting the People's Republic of China.** G. P. Putnam's Sons, 1981. 64 pp.

A group of thirteen-year-olds raised money for a trip to China. Once there, they visited the cities of Beijing, Nanjing, Hangzhou, and Shanghai. This book follows their journey to landmarks such as the Great Wall of China, a silk factory, the Hangzhou zoo, a tea commune, Children's Palaces (for extracurricular instruction after school), and the Arts and Crafts Research Institute. These students also visited schools and say they were impressed with the discipline and the fact that students go to school six days a week. The teenagers also were allowed to watch students studying theater, ballet, acrobatics, martial arts, and sports. Photographs. Easy reading.

Sciences

Adams, Florence. **Catch a Sunbeam: A Book of Solar Study and Experiments.** Illus. Kiyo Komoda. Harcourt Brace Jovanovich, 1978. 77 pp.

Sixteen solar experiments are described in this book. But first there is an explanation of a variety of facts concerning solar energy. Some of the experiments outlined include using the sun to find directions, constructing a solar furnace, and using the sun to cook your food. These experiments require only simple materials, and they are fully illustrated.

Adler, Irving. **How Life Began.** Rev. ed. Illus. Ruth Adler and Peggy Adler. John Day Co., 1977. 130 pp.

This book opens with a discussion of the concepts of life and death. This section leads to a general examination of what life is, how it began, and what distinguishes life from death. The book's purpose is to ensure that people will aid in the protection of life in the future and help increase the quality of that life.

Aero, Rita. **The Complete Book of Longevity.** Perigee Books, 1980. 200 pp.

Everyone seems to want a longer life, and to know about whatever anyone thinks contributes to longevity. This book contains all the suggestions people have come up with for prolonging life, health, and vigor—from high-potency drugs to simple exercises. Also included are discussions about the oldest people in the world today and where they live. Current medical research on longevity is another topic covered. Even very strange and unorthodox practices to prolong life, such as blood transfusions from young to old in South America, are discussed.

Anderson, Norman D., and Walter R. Brown. **Halley's Comet.** Dodd, Mead & Co., 1981. 78 pp.

Halley's comet is on its way! It will be visible in the mid-1980s—for the first time since 1910. This time astronomers will be able to photograph and study it with equipment that was not available on its last visit. Scientists now know that comets have little effect on Earth, but in ancient times people thought the presence of a comet meant certain death. Find out more about comets so you will be ready for the next visit of Halley's comet. Photographs.

Archer, Jules. **Epidemic! The Story of the Disease Detectives.** Harcourt Brace Jovanovich, 1977. 149 pp.

Disease detectives, scientifically known as epidemiologists, trace the source of infectious diseases from all over the world in order to prevent their spread. The thirty interesting investigations in this book provide examples of the methods epidemiologists use in their scientific detective work. Included are such outbreaks as Lassa fever, bubonic plague, and hepatitis. Photographs.

Arnold, Caroline. **Sex Hormones: Why Males and Females Are Different.** Illus. Jean Zallinger. William Morrow & Co., 1981. 122 pp.

What makes men and women different from each other? Why are we different in some ways but not in others? Sex hormones have a lot to do with the way we look, think, and act. The author discusses how hormones relate to aggression, puberty, sexual maturity, pregnancy, and other characteristics.

Asimov, Isaac. **How Did We Find Out about Oil?** Illus. David Wool. Walker & Co., 1980. 61 pp.

Due to concern over energy use, the subject of oil is a topic of almost everyone's conversation. Isaac Asimov, scientist and science fiction writer, answers some basic questions about this precious natural resource. What is oil? Where does it come from? How did we find out about it? What will we do when it runs out? Photographs.

Asimov, Isaac. **The Sun Shines Bright.** Discus Books, 1983. 242 pp.

Things are not always what they seem to be! For instance, "Out, Damned Spot!" is not necessarily a line from *Macbeth*. Neither is "A Long Day's Journey" part of a play title by Eugene O'Neill. Nor is "Siriusly Speaking" a serious misspelling. Instead, these are some of the titles of fascinating essays (about sunspots, the tidal influence of the moon upon the earth, and the brightest star in the sky) that this book contains.

Aylesworth, Thomas G., and Virginia L. Aylesworth. **The Mount St. Helens Disaster: What We've Learned.** Franklin Watts, 1983. 75 pp.

On May 18, 1980, Mount St. Helens, a long dormant volcano, blew up. It is estimated that the eruption released 500 times more energy than the atomic bomb that destroyed Hiroshima. This detailed description of the event includes background information on volcanoes, new breakthroughs in scientific monitoring, the damage done to humans and wildlife, and weather changes. Predictions are made regarding future behavior of the volcano.

Baird, Eva-Lee, and Rose Wyler. **Going Metric the Fun Way.** Illus. Talivaldis Stubis. Doubleday & Co., 1980. 128 pp.

Many Americans think "going metric" means difficulty and serious work. Here is a collection of riddles, tricks, puzzles, jokes, and other activities that make learning metrics fun. Comic illustrations featuring such characters as Klondike Mike and Morton the Moron will have you going from ounces to grams in no time at all.

Berger, Melvin. **Disease Detectives.** Thomas Y. Crowell Co., 1978. 81 pp.

In 1976 at an American Legion convention in Philadelphia, a strange disease struck the legionnaires, killing about twenty and making others seriously ill. The Center for Disease Control in Atlanta, Georgia, immediately set out to find the cause of the illness and to determine a cure. Bacteriologists, virologists, environmentalists, and toxicologists worked night and day to solve the mystery, and this book describes their efforts.

Berman, Arthur I. **Space Flight.** Illus. by author. Doubleday/Anchor Books, 1979. 206 pp.

If you are fascinated by space flight, this book will interest you. It begins by explaining some of the simple principles that are part of what keeps planets, satellites, and meteors on their paths. There is also information about how spaceships have moved toward Titan, the giant moon of Saturn. In fact, this book explains all about space flight—how it works and what it can do for us on Earth.

Bernstein, Jeremy. **Science Observed: Essays out of My Mind.** Basic Books, 1982. 376 pp.

The author takes the reader on a tour of scientific imagination and addresses such questions as: Can TV really teach science? With a mixture of humor and philosophy, Bernstein also discusses Einstein's work, film director Stanley Kubrick's use of scientific material in *Dr. Strangelove* and *2001: A Space Odyssey,* and scientific cranks.

Blumberg, Rhoda. **The First Travel Guide to the Moon: What to Pack, How to Go, and What to See When You Get There.** Illus. Roy Doty. Four Winds Press, 1980. 83 pp.

Although it may seem unlikely now, in the not-too-distant future you may be able to take a tour of the moon. What will you need? What should you pack? What might you find there when you arrive? This book answers questions like these in a humorous manner, while providing some factual information about the moon at the same time. Cartoons illustrate the text.

Bova, Ben. **Science—Who Needs It?** Westminster Press, 1975. 114 pp.

Some people are saying that science has gotten us into a mess. They say it is time people left science alone. To decide whether science is beneficial or destructive, this book first explores how the earth was in the beginning of time and discusses what a world without science would be like. The book then discusses what science is, how it has revolutionized life on earth, and the kinds of people scientists are. Also covered here are the problems people face today with science and the responsibilities we all share in dealing with those problems. The book concludes by suggesting that a world without science would probably mean the death of most people in the world today.

Branley, Franklyn M. **Color: From Rainbows to Lasers.** Illus. Henry Roth. Thomas Y. Crowell Co., 1978. 87 pp.

The fascinating science of color is the subject of this book. It describes how scientists separate the different colors in a ray of light, bend colored rays, and use different types of light-catching prisms in their experiments. These same scientists also study how the eye absorbs color, and they can recreate the vision of a color-blind person. Also included is information on color photography, colors of pigment and primary colors, the psychology of color, and optical illusions.

Branley, Franklyn M. **Jupiter: King of the Gods, Giant of the Planets.** Illus. Leonard D. Dank. Elsevier/Nelson Books, 1981. 90 pp.

Jupiter, the name of the king of the gods, is also the name given to the planet that is 1300 times larger than Earth. What we know about Jupiter is discussed in this book—as are some possibilities for future explorations. The Pioneer and Voyager probes of the planet in the 1970s are also covered, and the information that was gained on these trips is analyzed.

Branley, Franklyn M. **Space Colony: Frontier of the 21st Century.** Illus. Leonard D. Dank. Elsevier/Nelson Books, 1982. 103 pp.

If space will be our future frontier, what will it be like? This book uses scientific imagination to look at the first colonies in space. They will be huge structures with towns, factories, and farms. Described and discussed are how the colonies will be built, what kind of work will take up people's time, and the best ways of surviving in this new environment.

Calder, Nigel. **Nuclear Nightmares: An Investigation into Possible Wars.** Penguin Books, 1981. 168 pp.

What types of nuclear weapons have been produced? How do they work? Is the risk of world destruction by such weapons becoming greater or lesser? This book explores the important, and often frightening, subject of atomic power. Though progress has been made in nuclear arms negototians among countries, the threat of nuclear war is still very much with us.

Caras, Roger. **Mysteries of Nature: Explained and Unexplained.** Harcourt Brace Jovanovich, 1979. 64 pp.

Certain mysteries of nature still puzzle scientists after hundreds of years: sperm whales who beach themselves, strange screams in North American forests, South African sea serpents, and strange animal drawings of Wodi Mukkateb. But some of these puzzles have possible explanations, and this book presents them for consideration. Photographs.

Chapman, Clark R. **Planets of Rock and Ice: From Mercury to the Moons of Saturn.** Charles Scribner's Sons, 1982. 221 pp.

What we have learned thus far about the planets and what this knowledge reveals about the planet Earth is examined in this book. For example, Io, one of Jupiter's twelve known moons, exhibits volcanic activity thirty times more powerful than any on Earth. And the state of things on Venus and Mars may be forecasts of future stages in the Earth's development. Photographs.

Cherrier, François (translator E. W. Egan). **Fascinating Experiments in Chemistry.** Photographs by author. Sterling Publishing Co., 1978. 96 pp.

Fifty safe chemical experiments are explained in this book. These experiments, which can be done at home or at school, are explained step by step and are accompanied by photographs and illustrations. The materials used for the experiments are either household items, like soap and glassware, or materials that can be purchased at any drug store. Among the experiments included in the book are ten recipes for making invisible ink, how to make small fireworks, how to make a miniature volcano, and how to make crystals and underwater forests.

Cherrier, François (translator E. W. Egan). **Fascinating Experiments in Physics.** Photographs by author. Sterling Publishing Co., 1978. 96 pp.

Using many household materials, you can perform over fifty experiments in physics. You can learn to create a rainbow, construct hot-air mobiles, make magnetic sculptures, build musical instruments, and experiment with light and sound. Each experiment in this book is explained step by step and demonstrated in illustrations and photographs.

Cobb, Vicki. **Magic . . . Naturally! Science Entertainments and Amusements.** Illus. Lance R. Miyamoto. J. B. Lippincott Co., 1976. 159 pp.

Here is an introduction to thirty acts of magic, all of them based on science. These magic acts are simple and use materials you can find around the house. One of the most interesting of these tricks is to break a pencil with a dollar bill. Other feats you can learn about include tricks with invisible ink, ways of changing the color of liquids, and how to perform an act called the Devil's Handkerchief, where a glowing piece of wood is held against a handkerchief for a few seconds without the material getting scorched.

Cobb, Vicki. **More Science Experiments You Can Eat.** Illus. Giulio Maestro. J. B. Lippincott Co., 1979. 126 pp.

Science experiments usually conjure up images of test tubes and unpleasant odors. But this book describes experiments that help you see and understand scientific principles—and then let you enjoy eating the results! For example, you can make cheeses or preserve foods like beef jerky and frozen zucchini while learning how various substances affect smells and tastes and how your taste buds work. Diagrams, charts, and drawings make doing the experiments fun, easy, and delicious.

Cohen, Daniel. **A Close Look at Close Encounters.** Dodd, Mead & Co., 1981. 175 pp.

Ever since the UFO phenomenon began in 1947, literally thousands of people have claimed to have seen or encountered aliens from other worlds. These close encounters range from simple sightings of lights in the sky to claims of actually being taken aboard flying saucers. This book reports on several of the more unusual and less publicized cases, including a California hunter who claims to have spent a night in a tree after being chased by two aliens, and a Kentucky family who say that their house was attackd by gnome-like creatures. Drawings and illustrations.

Cohen, Daniel. **The World of UFOs.** J. B. Lippincott Co., 1978. 160 pp.

Unidentified flying objects—are they visitors from other worlds, or are they simply natural phenomena? This book presents a number of theories and introduces you to famous figures who have been involved with UFOs. Included are summaries of Air Force investigations into UFOs as well as theories involving ancient astronauts who might have visited earth 40,000 years ago.

Collins, Jim. **First to the Moon.** Contemporary Perspectives, 1978. 48 pp.

This study of rockets and space travel looks at the development of the first rockets and traces their use in such space adventures as the launching of *Sputnik,* the first moon landing, and the journey of *Pioneer 10* as it travels continuously out into space.

Coombs, Charles. **Gold and Other Precious Metals.** William Morrow & Co., 1981. 126 pp.

Would you like to know how to prospect for gold? If you are successful in your treasure hunt, do you know what the gold could be used for besides jewelry? Do you know why gold, silver, and platinum are so valuable? Included in this book are stories of how precious metals have been used in the past and tales of how early Americans searched for gold. Photographs.

Cowle, Jerry. **Discover the Trees.** Illus. Mike Anderson. Sterling Publishing Co., 1977. 94 pp.

Believe it or not, trees have personalities and characteristics as different from each other as human beings have. For example, the American sycamore, or button bull tree, sheds its outer bark each year and grows new bark; the bald cypress has knobby "knees"; and lightning likes to strike oak trees best (so don't seek shelter there during a thunderstorm!). Certain trees can live on parts of the earth where others would never survive. And trees serve humans in a thousand different ways, from producing fruit, nuts, and syrup to supplying warmth, coolness, and even entertainment.

Cox, John. **Overkill: Weapons of the Nuclear Age.** Thomas Y. Crowell Co., 1978. 208 pp.

What kind of science went into making nuclear weapons? The author, a British engineer, explains the development of nuclear power, which became possible after the splitting of the atom. Included in the book are such topics as the atomic bomb, atomic missiles, and delivery systems such as ICBMs, MIRVs, LRCMs, and SLBMs. The book argues for complete nuclear disarmament to make the world safe. Photographs.

Dean, Anabel. **Submerge! The Story of Divers and Their Crafts.** Westminster Press, 1976. 111 pp.

This comprehensive study begins with stories of Greek divers who took air-filled goatskins underwater when diving. Then the book turns to descriptions of underwater vehicles, dwellings, and explorers. Did you know that private industries, government agencies, universities, and scientific organizations are all working on experiments in underwater living? This book provides a fresh view of a whole frontier that people have been exploring along with outer space.

D'Ignazio, Fred. **Working Robots.** Elsevier/Nelson Books, 1982. 149 pp.

Can a robot really think? What does the inside of its brain look like? Will robots ever replace all humans at work? This book provides loads of information about what robots are and what their place in the modern world is. There are sections on how you can build your own working robots and teach them to do various jobs.

Dowden, Anne Ophelia. **This Noble Harvest: A Chronicle of Herbs.** Illus. by author. William Collins Publishers, 1979. 80 pp.

Herbs have been used by people throughout the ages for healing, cooking, killing, and providing fragrance. This book tells the history of herbs, the superstitions about them, and their uses in medicine, magic, religion, and the kitchen. Have you ever heard of mandrake, St. John's wort, monkshood, and cowslips? All are unfamiliar herbs that are discussed here. Practical advice is also given about growing, drying, and preserving herbs. Color pictures of herbs are included in the text.

Edmonds, I. G. **The Mysteries of Troy.** Thomas Nelson, 1977. 191 pp.

Was there really a Trojan Horse? Legends, archaeological findings, history, and literature about Troy are discussed in order to examine some of its many mysteries. German archaeologist Heinrich Schliemann's discovery of the nine layers of Troy in the 1870s seemed to provide more questions than answers about the ancient city. And to this day, men and women continue to search for answers.

Engdahl, Sylvia, and Rick Roberson. **The Subnuclear Zoo: New Discoveries in High Energy Physics.** Atheneum Publishers, 1977. 98 pp.

People are forever curious about how things are made. But can we ever hope to understand and use particles so small that they cannot be seen? In a clear and readily understandable manner, this book explains how matter is composed, describes the particles outside atoms, shows ways to observe what is invisible, and explores some of the mysteries yet unsolved in the field of high energy physics. With an understanding of these topics comes the knowledge of why it's important to study these tiny particles and to discover ways they can be used to benefit everyone. Illustrations.

Engdahl, Sylvia, and Rick Roberson. **Tool for Tomorrow: New Knowledge about Genes.** Atheneum Publishers, 1979. 91 pp.

Scientists are discovering many things about genes—things that can work for the good of individuals and society or that have the power to destroy humankind. Because genes concern life itself and ways of altering life forms, scientists and doctors must exercise enormous care and responsibility when experimenting with them. Perhaps this knowledge can solve the problem of hunger by breeding foods in new ways, like crossing plant genes with animal genes. Perhaps a safe genetic way to recycle waste products into fuel can solve the problem of energy shortages. Knowledge of altering genes may also prevent disease and deformities in animals and in human beings. But if scientists find they can clone human beings, would society want to do it? Who or what would be cloned? Who would decide? And on what criteria? This book discusses these and other important questions about genetic studies.

Facklam, Margery, and Howard Facklam. **The Brain: Magnificent Mind Machine.** Harcourt Brace Jovanovich, 1982. 118 pp.

How do we know what we know? How do we learn? How do we remember? These and many other questions about the human brain are discussed here. The history of brain experiments is also traced from electrical energy experiments on frogs in the 1770s to recent work in split brain studies. There are chapters on biofeedback, sleep and dreams, electroshock therapy, brainwashing (including a discussion of cults and the ways they control people), and even hypnosis.

Facklam, Margery, and Howard Facklam. **From Cell to Clone: The Story of Genetic Engineering.** Illus. Paul Facklam. Harcourt Brace Jovanovich, 1979. 128 pp.

The clones are coming! Not in science fiction books, but in laboratories at major universities and private companies. Although once thought to be only a farfetched dream, modern genetic engineering has become a science that can alter the way we live. When the structure of DNA was found, it unlocked the secrets of life and made possible research that may someday cure cancer or slow the aging process to a standstill. Clones of plants and animals have already been successfully created, and who knows what the potential of human clones might be? This book traces the history of genetic science and speculates on its future. Diagrams and photographs.

Foster, Genevieve. **The Year of the Flying Machine: 1903.** Illus. by author. Charles Scribner's Sons, 1977. 96 pp.

The inventions, discoveries, and changes in political, social, and economic ideas of the early 1900s are covered here. The Wright brothers, Teddy Roosevelt, Marconi, Lenin, Ford, the Curies, Einstein, Freud, Peary, and Tzu Hsi are all discussed as major characters who helped shape the new century.

Freedman, Russell. **How Birds Fly.** Illus. Lorence F. Bjorklund. Holiday House, 1977. 62 pp.

With the help of many diagrams, this book explains how birds take off and land, glide, soar, and dive. Bird flight is compared to the flight of planes, allowing readers to understand both animal and mechanical flight at the same time.

Fuller, Curtis G., et al., editors. **Proceedings of the First International UFO Congress.** Warner Books, 1980. 440 pp.

From June 24 through June 26, 1977, the International UFO Congress met in Chicago to review the past and consider the future. This book contains the best of the lectures given there. These talks cover widely differing and often conflicting views. Actual cases of UFO sightings are included, and there are chapters that deal with the questions of "hard evidence," reported encounters with UFO aliens, UFO myths and messages, and UFOs as mind phenomena. A concluding chapter predicts where UFO studies may go in the future.

Gale, Mort. **Moon Power.** Warner Books, 1980. 240 pp.

This book suggests that the moon not only influences the earth's tides, but it also can influence plant, animal, and human behavior. Charts and graphs help illustrate the various positions of the moon and their corresponding effects upon human behavior. Also provided are discussions of common personality characteristics of people who are born during the moon's different phases.

Gallant, Roy A. **The Constellations: How They Came to Be.** Four Winds Press, 1979. 196 pp.

This book takes you through the evening sky season by season. It teaches you how to find the constellations and what to look for in each—a famous nebula, a distant galaxy, or the remains of a star that exploded centuries ago. Here also are nearly fifty myths from ancient Greece and Rome, from the Sumerians, Babylonians, Chinese, Hindus, Mayas, Egyptians, Scandinavians, Arabs, and North American Indians. More than forty-four constellations and eighty-five stars are included in the easy-to-use star charts. Now you can become an astronomical expert and watch the night sky as it revolves like a picture book filled with mystery and adventure.

Gallant, Roy A. **The Planets: Exploring the Solar System.** Four Winds Press, 1982. 176 pp.

This book explores our solar system—one central source of heat and light, nine known planets with about forty-five moons circling them, millions of rock-metal fragments called asteroids and meteoroids, and billions of "dirty snowballs" of ice and dust that we call comets. Here is up-to-date information gathered from both U.S. and Soviet space probes and from radio and optical telescopes. The mysteries that still surround our solar system are also discussed.

Gardner, Robert. **Space: Frontier of the Future.** Illus. Jeffrey Brown. Doubleday & Co., 1980. 158 pp.

At the turn of the century, no one believed that people could leave the face of the earth and actually walk in space. Now humankind's survival may depend on being able to do just that. The West is no longer humankind's frontier—space is. This book describes what has been done in space, and it explains how people might live in space stations in the not-too-distant future.

Gardner, Robert. **This Is the Way It Works: A Collection of Machines.** Illus. Jeffrey Brown. Doubleday & Co., 1980. 119 pp.

For most of us, machines are mysteries. We dial a telephone and expect a familiar voice to reach us. We snap on a light switch, push the button on an automatic washer, pour hot or cold liquids into a vacuum bottle, pull up a zipper, or strike a match—and unthinkingly expect results. Then there are the more sophisticated kinds of machines like artificial lungs, heart valves, and kidney machines—machines that can save and sustain lives. We are awed, grateful, or indifferent about machines every day. This book tries to help us understand them no matter what our emotions.

Glenn, Jerome Clayton, and George S. Robinson. **Space Trek: The Endless Migration.** Warner Books, 1980. 256 pp.

The next twenty years may be the most exciting in human history, largely because the exploration and exploitation of space will become a major part of our lives. This book explains the present status of space programs and space debates. It reveals the dangers of certain programs and discusses what the future might be like with, and without, space migration. The text includes pictures, diagrams, charts, and illustrations.

Golden, Frederic. **Colonies in Space: The Next Giant Step.** Illus. Kiyo Komoda. Harcourt Brace Jovanovich, 1977. 145 pp.

Will space colonies alleviate population explosion and energy problems on Earth? This author thinks so. He shares with the reader the dream of many colleagues to establish extraterrestrial colonies and perhaps eventually to create a human-made planet. This book intermingles the possibilities of the future (such as space-shuttle travel in the year 2030) with a history of our fascination with space (including the launching of *Sputnik 1,* the world's first satellite) and *Skylab*'s record eighty-four-day orbit of Earth. Many photographs (made available by the National Aeronautics and Space Administration) and a glossary of space terms are included.

Goldin, Augusta. **Geothermal Energy: A Hot Prospect.** Harcourt Brace Jovanovich, 1981. 128 pp.

In today's search for new energy sources, we often forget one that lies beneath our feet—the heat energy from natural steam, hot water, magma, and hot rocks beneath the earth's surface. Such power is already being used in Iceland, Japan, Italy, New Zealand, Alaska, and some other parts of the United States. Just how this energy is tapped and the problems in doing so are discussed in this book. Illustrations.

Goldin, Augusta. **Oceans of Energy: Reservoir of Power for the Future.** Harcourt Brace Jovanovich, 1980. 144 pp.

The ocean is filled with energy that can be tapped for electric power and methane gas. Energy from tidal power has already been extracted in France and Russia. Scientists are still studying the production of electricity from ocean waves and ocean currents and the extraction of natural gas from ocean kelp farms. This book highlights the facts about water power, showing that there are no simple solutions to our energy problems, only intelligent choices.

Gottlieb, William P. **Science Facts You Won't Believe.** Franklin Watts, 1983. 128 pp.

Did you know the primary colors are *not* red, yellow, and blue? That astronauts are weightless in outer space, but *not* because they escape gravity? That we do *not* have five senses? Hundreds of similar misconceptions are explored in this book—all concerned with science "facts" that are not facts at all but misinformation. What's more, we don't breathe with our noses, and ostriches do not stick their heads in sand.

Gribbin, John. **Weather Force: Climate and Its Impact on Our World.** G. P. Putnam's Sons, 1979. 190 pp.

Climatology is the study of the forces of weather. This book looks into patterns in climate and analyzes cycles that lead to weather disasters. Also investigated are collections of weather oddities such as electric rain in Spain that hit the ground and gave off a distinct crack and bright sparks. The book concludes with a discussion of the problem of industrial activities affecting the earth's climate and the possibility of another ice age as a result. Photographs.

Grillone, Lisa, and Joseph Gennaro. **Small Worlds Close Up.** Crown Publishers, 1978. 60 pp.

From hypodermic needles to cork, small objects provide interesting viewing when greatly magnified. Through close-up photography, the reader can see exactly where and how venom shoots through a snake's fang, how a small lizard clings to glass panes, why opals sparkle, and why a dolphin's skin is so beautiful. (This book was selected an outstanding 1978 science trade book and was chosen as one of the best books of that year by *School Library Journal.*)

Grossman, Peter Z. **In Came the Darkness: The Story of Blackouts.** Four Winds Press, 1981. 146 pp.

Blackouts come about when electricity is lost in a major area. What happens to major metropolitan areas that suffer blackouts? What happens to the people who are caught in these blackouts? Here are the facts about the causes of power failures and stories that show human weakness and strength in dealing with an environment without electricity.

Harmon, Margaret. **The Engineering Medicine Man—The New Pioneer.** Westminster Press, 1975. 222 pp.

Today's "medicine man" is the bioengineer. These men and women deal with different fields in the hard sciences and the life sciences in carrying out their jobs. They have developed devices such as a simple zippered sheet to move patients more gently and a computer that analyzes blood instantly. Pacemakers can also be credited to the work of bioengineers. A large appendix lists colleges and universities that offer bioengineering training.

Heintze, Carl. **The Biosphere: Earth, Air, Fire, and Water.** Illus. Wayne Harmon. Thomas Nelson, 1977. 128 pp.

Our biosphere is composed of earth, air, fire, and water. The development and interaction of these elements is so complex that without one of them life could not exist on our planet. This book explains the various functions of these forces and shows how human carelessness could cause an imbalance in them that would lead to a major disaster.

Heintze, Carl. **The Bottom of the Sea and Beyond.** Thomas Nelson, 1975. 144 pp.

The ocean floor holds many secrets of the earth's development, like information about the shifting of continents, the location of minerals, and the changing of weather patterns. This description of past and present ocean explorations is interesting because it points out vital scientific questions that may be answered by future discoveries beneath the ocean floor.

Heppenheimer, T. A. **Colonies in Space.** Warner Books, 1980. 321 pp.

After an introduction by science fiction writer Ray Bradbury, who challenges all of us to become citizens of the universe, this book explains the various ways we may travel and live in space and presents scientific information concerning space exploration and colonization. Chapters discuss such ideas as homes in space, recreation in space ports, moon mining, and colonizing the stars.

Herbert, Don. **Mr. Wizard's Supermarket Science.** Illus. Roy McKie. Random House, 1980. 91 pp.

Moldy soup, a bag of beans, a bottle of vinegar, a cereal box, and an egg—Mr. Wizard clearly explains and demonstrates how to perform magic tricks and experiments with supplies from the kitchen. By learning how to update the egg-into-the-bottle trick, for example, even a novice can dazzle family, friends, and teachers.

Hess, Lilo. **Small Habitats.** Charles Scribner's Sons, 1976. 47 pp.

Did you know that you can create your own miniature world—one you can observe, enjoy, and control? All you need is a square or rectangular container such as a fish tank. Then decide whether you want to have a meadow, woodland, tropical jungle, tropical coastline, desert, or marshland environment. Each type would need to be supplied with its own variety of plants and animals that are compatible with each other and the environment. And this book will tell you all you need to know about setting up one of these habitats. Placed in this small world, these plants and animals and their continuing cycles of life and death can be studied in a way that is nearly impossible to duplicate outdoors.

Heuer, Kenneth. **Thunder, Singing Sands, and Other Wonders: Sound in the Atmosphere.** Dodd, Mead & Co., 1981. 124 pp.

Ever wonder how certain natural sounds are produced—sounds like the rumbling of a thunderstorm, the sizzle of snow in a blizzard, the murmuring of winds in forest trees, or the boom of desert sand dunes? This book explains these and many other examples of atmospheric acoustics. In simple-to-understand terms, the phenomenon of meteorological sounds is described. Illustrtions.

Hirsch, S. Carl. **He and She: How Males and Females Behave.** Illus. William Steinel. J. B. Lippincott Co., 1975. 155 pp.

Did you know that female bees do all the work in the hives, and male bees do all the loafing? That the father sea catfish cares for and carries the eggs in his mouth? That in certain societies women hold the power and choose the men they want for husbands? The author describes an astonishing variety of behaviors in earth's creatures, and one fact becomes clear—males and females do not all fit into prearranged, fixed roles. Is the behavior of men and women inherited, or do we learn how to act from our culture? Here is the latest scientific evidence to shed light on this and other questions.

Hoagland, Mahlon B. **The Roots of Life.** Discus Books, 1979. 152 pp.

How does life begin? What are genes made of? How do some cells "decide" to become brain cells, while others "decide" to become skin cells or nerve cells? The author describes the structure and behavior of cells, touching upon the possible causes and cures for cancer, as well as on the realtionship between mental illness and brain chemistry. Mature reading.

Humphrey, Henry, and Deirdre O'Meara-Humphrey. **When Is Now? Experiments with Time and Timekeeping Devices.** Doubleday & Co., 1980. 80 pp.

Before there were modern digital clocks and watches, man used other ingenious devices to tell time. Egyptians devised a sun clock that divided the day into twenty-four hours. Others used water clocks, nocturnals, and astrolabes to tell time and also to determine their location while at sea. This book explains these devices and shows you how they can be made at home. Pictures and illustrations are provided with the text.

Hutton, Richard. **The Cosmic Chase.** Mentor Books, 1981. 225 pp.

Who will be the first to colonize space—the Soviet Union or the United States? This book offers some possible answers to the question, as well as discussing other future events in the space race. But before speaking of the future, the book traces the history of space exploration from the Soviet Union's successful launching of *Sputnik* to America's achievements with *Mercury, Gemini, Skylab,* and the *Apollo* mission that put a person on the moon.

Jargocki, Christopher P. **Science Brain-Twisters, Paradoxes, and Fallacies.** Illus. Richard Liu. Charles Scribner's Sons, 1976. 183 pp.

Which is heavier, humid air or dry air? Is it easier to push or pull a wheelbarrow? Why is shortwave reception better at night? Do you think you know the answers to these and other science-related questions? You might just be surprised. This book of math and science problems will test the knowledge of even the best of students. One hundred and sixty-nine problems are presented here in both words and illustrations.

Jenkins, Marie M. **Embryos and How They Develop.** Holiday House, 1975. 194 pp.

The growth of a single, fertilized cell has some similarities in almost every animal. The development of single-celled animals, more complex animal species, and human beings is compared in order to see the sources of embryo development and the reasons why reproductive cells mature as they do.

Jespersen, James, and Jane Fitz-Randolph. **Mercury's Web: The Story of Telecommunications.** Illus. Judith Fast. Atheneum Publishers, 1981. 226 pp.

Did you know that your bathroom scale, thermometer, and camera, as well as your telephone, radio, and television, are all part of a complicated network of communications sytems? Many scientists believe that these devices and thousands of others that store, gather, and transmit information are just the start of a new Information Revolution that will change the way we relate to our fellow humans. This book traces the history and importance of communications from yodels and smoke signals to satellites and computers.

Jespersen, James, and Jane Fitz-Randolph. **Time and Clocks for the Space Age.** Atheneum Publishers, 1979. 178 pp.

Past, present, future are all broad measurements of time. But what about the specific measurement of time used today? It is the atomic second, defined as so many vibrations of the cesium atom. This book discusses the history of measuring time, ways of precise measuring, and some scientific studies about the concept of time. The table of contents is a clue to the interesting topics contained in this book: "Smart Machines," "How Clocks Conduct the Symphony," "Is a Minute Really a Minute?" "Time Stops," and "Blurred Time." (Children's Science Book Award of the New York Academy of Science)

Kaplan, Marshall H. **Space Shuttle: America's Wings to the Future.** Aero Publishers, 1978. 215 pp.

The National Spaceline is a project to begin space shuttles, or delivery rockets, from Earth into space and back. The shuttles will carry people and equipment to space stations and places like the moon. They will be used in the collection of space data and raw materials from space and possibly in space colonization. This book takes a very technical look at the rockets used and tests being conducted in this area of space exploration. A glossary of space terms is provided to help your understanding of the material. The book also includes biographical information about the men and women who are candidates to be astronauts for the space shuttle.

Kavaler, Lucy. **A Matter of Degree: Heat, Life, and Death.** Harper & Row, Publishers, 1981. 226 pp.

Life as we know it on Earth exists within a very narrow temperature range. This book explores the ways we survive great heat, and the ways animals, plants, and microbes adapt to life at high temperatures. It explains how heat affects conception and the relationship between heat and violence. The book also explores the medical uses of heat, the risks of getting a perfect suntan, and how a person might survive in a jungle.

Kiefer, Irene. **Global Jigsaw Puzzle: The Story of Continental Drift.** Illus. Barbara Levine. Atheneum Publishers, 1978. 79 pp.

Recent research shows that earlier theories about continental drift are correct. Plate tectonics, the study of the floating, rigid plates that compose the earth's surface, indicates that the continents are moving. Additional research on this geological process will aid in locating mineral deposits and possibly will help prevent earthquakes.

Klein, Aaron E. **The Complete Beginner's Guide to Microscopes and Telescopes.** Doubleday & Co., 1980. 225 pp.

Sometimes we need help in seeing some of the most beautiful things in the universe. The diamondlike beauty of a grain of salt exposes itself only under the scrutiny of a microscope. Telescopes are required to reveal the wonders of the heavens. This guide offers the reader information on choosing microscopes and telescopes and provides tips for using these insturments properly to get the best results.

Knight, Bernard. **Discovering the Human Body.** Lippincott & Crowell, Publishers, 1980. 181 pp.

This book is more than diagrams and explanations about how the human body works. It is also a history of the many discoveries made through the ages and a history of the people who made those discoveries such as Langerhans (islets of Langerhans), Hoboken (valves of Hoboken), Purkinje (who discovered muscle fibers that make the heart contract), and Broca (who located the part of the brain where speech arises). Photographs and illustrations.

Knight, David C. **Viruses: Life's Smallest Enemies.** Illus. Christine Kettner. William Morrow & Co., 1981. 127 pp.

Did you know that the simplest form of life known to science is also the major cause of human disease? Or that the three types of viruses cause illness not only in people but in plants and animals as well? This book also reports the latest research findings on the use of drugs to fight harmful viruses—including the serious side effects that some drugs cause and the difficulty in designing a drug that will stay in a cell long enough to be effective.

Kraske, Robert. **Is There Life in Outer Space?** Harcourt Brace Jovanovich, 1976. 85 pp.

Because the universe is so large, and because there are so many UFO sightings, many scientists believe that intelligent life exists in outer space. These scientists are now trying to find out where that life is and what it might be like. The exciting challenges of contacting and communicating with other beings are described and discussed in this book.

Langone, John. **Human Engineering: Marvel or Menace?** Little, Brown & Co., 1978. 149 pp.

If we are able to make bold changes in the human body and mind, *should* we make those changes? These changes might include organ transplants, altering brain functions, increasing intelligence, sharpening memory, cloning, producing test-tube babies, and manufacturing, combining and manipulating genes. For each daring new possibility, this book provides some historical background, as well as a discussion of the hazards involved.

Larsen, Sherman J. **Close Encounters: A Factual Report on UFOs.** Raintree Publishers Group, 1978. 94 pp.

This book provides a factual treatment of the subject of UFOs— Unidentified Flying Objects. It describes what a UFO is, includes a short history of UFOs, and explains how researchers study a UFO report. Black-and-white and color photographs of UFO sightings are used throughout the book. Also included is a glossary of technical terms and a listing of UFO organizations around the world. Easy reading.

Lauber, Patricia. **Journey to the Planets.** Crown Publishers, 1982. 90 pp.

Did you know the surface of Venus was covered with red-hot rocks? Or that Mars may have had water on it at one time? Or that Pluto takes 248 years to orbit the sun? This book describes the history and physical characteristics of all nine planets and their moons. The numerous illustrations clearly show many of the wonders discussed, while revealing the similarities and differences of each planet.

Leakey, Richard E., and Roger Lewin. **People of the Lake: Mankind and Its Beginnings.** Avon Books, 1979. 238 pp.

Here is the story of the scientists who search for the remains of early humans. What they find are only fragments, but with painstaking effort they can piece together what our ancestors must have looked like and how they lived, communicated, and interacted with each other and their surroundings. With this information we can also learn something about ourselves, and why we think and respond the way we do.

Limburg, Peter R. **Farming the Waters.** Beaufort Books, 1980. 223 pp.

Humans have long farmed the land and raised animals on it for food, but they have settled for only what they could catch from the waters. Today all that is changing, and many fish, shellfish, mollusks, and even seaweed are being raised on ocean farms. This underwater farming is called aquaculture—the raising of water-dwelling life for profit. This book discusses both how this is done on a large scale and how an individual can do it in his or her backyard.

Limburg, Peter. **The Story of Your Heart.** Illus. Ellen Going Jacobs. Coward, McCann & Geoghegan, 1979. 95 pp.

We feel our heart beating and hear about our heart, and then we take it for granted. What does it really do? This book gives a clear explanation of the heart and its functions, with line drawings and diagrams to illustrate major points. It also discusses heart defects and problems and provides a history of human heart surgery from 1872 to the present. Did you know that the first heart surgery was done to remove a three-inch sewing needle from the heart of a man who had been injured in a brawl?

Lyttle, Richard B. **Waves across the Past: Adventures in Underwater Archaeology.** Illus. by author. Atheneum Publishers, 1981. 207 pp.

How true are stories about sea monsters, pirate ships, and lost continents and seaports? Answering questions like these is part of the work of underwater archeologists. In its early days, this kind of exploration had to be done in heavy diving suits and with a limited oxygen supply. But during World War II, scuba gear helped free the underwater explorers to go into new areas of the sea and to discover lost cultures and treasures. Besides tracing the history of undersea archaeology, this book includes the adventures of private treasure hunters looking for sunken gold and silver.

Madison, Arnold, and David L. Drotar. **Pocket Calculators: How to Use and Enjoy Them.** Thomas Nelson, 1978. 145 pp.

Almost every household now has a pocket calculator that is used for homework, budgeting, or figuring out taxes. Yet most of us who use a calculator do not really understand it. What do the terms mean? Which model is right for what job? Both practical and game ideas related to calculators are given in this book, along with the history of mechanical aids to arithmetic. It is the story of progress from the abacus to the silicon chip.

Math, Irwin. **Wires and Watts: Understanding and Using Electricity.** Illus. Hal Keith. Charles Scribner's Sons, 1981.

This book begins with some basic information about electricity and magnetism. Then instructions for making working models of objects like miniature lamps to light a dollhouse and electirifed games and puzzles are provided to put the principles of electricity to practical use.

McDonald, Lucile. **Windmills: An Old-New Energy Source.** Illus. Helen Hawkes Battey. Elsevier/Nelson Books, 1981. 120 pp.

Although they date back as far as the fourteenth century, windmills are being thought of as a new energy source in our energy-hungry world. Here is the story of wind power's use and development, from the crude stone towers of medieval Europe to the 200-foot high towers with their giant blades that produce 2,500 kilowatts of electricity for the state of Washington. The future use and development of this cheap energy source are also discussed in this book.

McFall, Christie. **Wonders of Dust.** Dodd, Mead & Co., 1980. 80 pp.

If your only encounter with dust has been connected with housework, then you will be amazed to find that dust comes in many different shapes and sizes, originates from many different sources (even the ocean), is found everywhere in the universe, and is actually increasing in our environment. The whys and hows of all this, how dust affects people and the environment, and much more can be found in this book on a material we usually take for granted, or try to get rid of.

McGowen, Tom. **Album of Astronomy.** Rev. ed. Illus. Rod Ruth. Rand McNally & Co., 1981. 64 pp.

This album of facts and stories provides an introduction to the stars, the sun, the planets, the universe. You will learn about asteroids, comets, black holes, and quasars. Drawings and diagrams are provided to help you enjoy learning about the various stars that form patterns in the sky.

McGowen, Tom. **Album of Rocks and Minerals.** Illus. Rod Ruth. Rand McNally & Co., 1981. 59 pp.

Rocks are more interesting than they might first appear. Not only are their formations intriguing, but their uses range from the creative and the practical to the destructive. Do you know about the burning stone or the moon's metal? Which metal is most precious? Which mineral do we eat? After you read this book, you will know how difficult life would be without the rocks and minerals we take for granted.

McMullen, David, and Susan McMullen. **First into the Air: The First Airplanes.** Illus. Jeffrey Gatrall. Contemporary Perspectives, 1978. 48 pp.

Two first flights are described and explained in this book: the first powered flight in an airplane in 1903 and the first motorless flight of a pilot-powered airplane in 1977. The *Kitty Hawk* and the *Gossamer Condor* are compared, and the book includes photographs of other early planes and gliders.

Milton, Joyce. **Here Come the Robots.** Illus. Peter Stern. Hastings House Publishers, 1981. 118 pp.

This book introduces readers to actual robots just as exciting as any seen in movies. People have learned to use robots for many jobs, and the list of robot records provided here proves how well they do their tasks. Now robots can wash family cars, explore planets, help a fourth-grade class with schoolwork, and substitute for firefighters or police officers. Easy reading.

Moorman, Thomas. **What Is It Really Like Out There? Objective Knowing.** Atheneum Publishers, 1977. 87 pp.

How do we "know" anything? What is "truth"? These questions have been around for a long time and they really have no permanent answers. But there are ways you can try to seek truth and look for objective knowledge. To lead you in this search for truth, this book discusses such related subjects as brainwashing, prejudices, theories of truth, subjectivity, objectivity, personal growth, and the habit of truth.

Morgenstern, Steve. **Metric Puzzles, Tricks and Games.** Illus. Joyce Behr. Sterling Publishing Co., 1978. 128 pp.

An argument for changing to the metric measurement system opens this book. Then it provides the metric measurements while familiarizing the reader with the meanings of units. From here on, the book is filled with puzzles, games, tricks—all presented in hope that practice will cause more people to use the metric system every day.

Navarra, John Gabriel. **Earthquake.** Doubleday & Co., 1980. 95 pp.

The thought of an earthquake can bring fear and terror. This book helps you understand what causes an earthquake and how the huge dislocations in the earth's crust are measured, studied, and predicted. Did you know that there are now measures and techniques that can help prevent most of the destruction from an earthquake? This book also provides practical suggestions for anyone caught in an earthquake. Easy reading.

Oleksy, Walter. **Treasures of the Land: Archaeology Today in America.** Julian Messner, 1981. 223 pp.

Numerous archaeological excavations in the United States have uncovered clues to the life-styles of our ancestors. Here is an introduction to the field of archaeology—what an archaeologist does, what goes on at a dig, and career possibilities in this field for young people. Black-and-white photographs.

Oleksy, Walter. **Visitors from Outer Space? Is There Life on Other Planets?** G. P. Putnam's Sons, 1979. 152 pp.

Some people believe that formations like those at Stonehenge and Easter Island indicate that Earth had visitors from outer space centuries ago. And there are those who believe that we continue to have such visitors. Although evidence of sightings has been recorded throughout history, the sighting of what is now called an unidentified flying object (UFO) first happened in 1947, and it set off a series of reports of sightings of strange objects in the sky, of mysterious disappearances of people, and of unusual kinds of evidence left behind at supposed spacecraft landing areas. Then there are the mysteries surrounding the Bermuda Triangle and the Great Lakes Triangle to be considered in relation to possible beings from outer space. What is known about all these UFO-related experiences is described and analyzed in this book.

Olney, Ross R. **They Said It Couldn't Be Done.** E. P. Dutton, 1979. 134 pp.

Throughout history there have always been people of vision, people who believe in trying to do the impossible. Just twenty years ago there were those who believed it was impossible to land a spaceship on the moon. Yet in 1969 the impossible was achieved. This book is a collection of stories about the moon landing and nine other successes of modern engineering, including the creation of the

Mount Rushmore National Monument, the Holland Tunnel, the Brooklyn Bridge, and the Astrodome. Photographs.

Osis, Karlis, and Erlendur Haraldsson. **At the Hour of Death.** Discus Books, 1979. 244 pp.

Life after death is examined in this study. Witnesses give incredible reports based on their observations of the dying, who seemingly begin to view another existence beyond death.

Ostrander, Sheila, and Lynn Schroeder. **Psychic Experiences: E.S.P. Investigated.** Sterling Publishing Co., 1977. 243 pp.

Whether it's learning about the plant that witnessed a murder and testified against the killer, or reading of those who can bend steel simply by thinking about it, the reader will be amazed to learn what certain people believe invisible waves in the air have the potential to do. This book includes major chapters on mental telepathy, clairvoyance, psychic energy, seeing into the future, interpreting messages from the dead, collecting information about UFOs, and providing information about other lives and lost civilizations. This field may hold enormous potential for the future as it develops and gains scientific credence.

Pallas, Norvin. **Calculator Puzzles, Tricks and Games.** Illus. Joyce Behr. Sterling Publishing Co., 1978. 95 pp.

Calculators can be tools or toys. They can easily and quickly solve problems that might have taken hours or days in the past. So, the new owner of a calculator needs to learn all about the calculator and then decide how to use it most effectively. Once its practical use is mastered, then it can also be the source of tricks, puzzles, and games. It can help with shopping or with taxes, and it can also calculate sports statistics or amaze people with number puzzles.

Patent, Dorothy Hinshaw. **Bacteria: How They Affect Other Living Things.** Holiday House, 1980. 127 pp.

Would you believe that life would be impossible without bacteria? Although many people think of bacteria only as disease-carrying germs, actually most bacteria are helpful organisms. This text discusses the function of bacteria in the life cycles of plants and animals, as well as bacteria as a food source. Illustrations.

Patent, Dorothy Hinshaw. **Evolution Goes On Every Day.** Illus. Matthew Kalmenoff. Holiday House, 1977. 156 pp.

Evolutionary changes are still going on in the animals and plants we see today. This book looks at the evolutionary aspects of genes, DNA, mutations, viruses, bacteria, plant breeding, cloning, and cell fusion. The controversies of sociobiology and genetic engineering are also discussed in some detail. A glossary of scientific terms is included.

Place, Marian T. **Mount St. Helens: A Sleeping Volcano Awakes.** Dodd, Mead & Co., 1981. 158 pp.

How do you cope with an active volcano in your backyard? This is what some people in the state of Washington had to find out when Mount St. Helens erupted in May 1980 with the force of a ten-megaton bomb. Read all about this amazing event—the eyewitness accounts of the eruption, the search-and-rescue operations that went on, and scientists' ongoing search for clues to when Mount St. Helens and related volcanoes will erupt again.

Playfair, Guy L., and Scott Hill. **The Cycles of Heaven.** Avon Books, 1979. 364 pp.

Can the orbits of distant planets predict earthquakes? Does the solar cycle determine the composition of human blood? Is the secret of all life to be found in electromagnetic waves? This book examines these and other questions and provides very detailed, scientific explanations. The various forces of the universe appear to affect us in strange or unknown ways, touching upon birth and suicide rates, weather patterns, radiation, Kirlian auras, cancer, and biorhythms. This book attempts to show the relationships between certain earthly conditions and cosmic events.

Rahn, Joan Elma. **Eyes and Seeing.** Illus. by author. Atheneum Publishers, 1981. 114 pp.

How do we see? Do we see the same as other animals? This book begins with a discussion of the basic principles of seeing and then goes on to describe such different kinds of eyes as those of flatworms and those of humans. Information is included on light and on how simple experiments can be done with light in its relation to sight. A glossary includes all the scientific and medical terms used, and a bibliography directs the reader to other books on the subject.

Rahn, Joan Elma. **Grocery Store Zoology: Bones and Muscles.** Illus. Ginny Linville Winter. Atheneum Publishers, 1977. 130 pp.

This book helps you learn about the bones and muscles of the human body by comparing them to the bones and muscles of the meat brought home from the grocery store. Experiments use chicken, beef, pork, lamb, and rabbit to get an idea of what our skeletal system is like. There are many illustrations to help you identify the animals' anatomy.

Rahn, Joan Elma. **The Metric System.** Illus. Ginny Linville Winter. Atheneum Publishers, 1976. 79 pp.

Most of the world weighs and measures by the metric system, why not you? After beginning with a history of the system, this book explains length, area, volume, weight, temperature, and time in relation to the metric system. A helpful appendix includes definitions, symbols, and conversion tables.

Renmore, C. D. **Silicon Chips and You.** Beaufort Books, 1980. 129 pp.

The watches we wear on our wrists, the calculators we carry in our pockets, the video games we play on television sets, and the computers we use at home—these are only a few of the devices that rely on silicon chips to function. And there seem to be infinite possibilities for the use of these chips on the job, at home, at school, in health care, in communications, and in war. This book reveals the revolution in human life caused by one small slice of pure silicon less than a centimeter square and just half a milimeter thick.

Risedorf, Gwen. **Born Today, Born Yesterday: Reincarnation.** Raintree Childrens Books, 1977. 48 pp.

Are people able to come back from death and to live a new life? This collection of astounding stories about reincarnation examines the case histories of people who believe that they lived in former times and returned to live again. Easy reading.

Rosen, Stephen. **Weathering: How the Atmosphere Conditions Your Body, Your Mind, Your Moods—and Your Health.** M. Evans & Co., 1979. 354 pp.

How are we affected by the weather? This book looks at physique, temperament, social class, age, and sex and relates all these characteristics to the changes in weather. It also illustrates practical ways of living with the weather, such as tips of what foods to eat, drugs to avoid, clothes to wear, and vacation spots to pick, depending on climatic conditions. Illustrations.

Ross, Frank, Jr. **Oracle Bones, Stars, and Wheelbarrows: Ancient Chinese Science and Technology.** Houghton Mifflin Co., 1982. 175 pp.

The ancient Chinese were marvelous inventors. Their soldiers went into battle armed with rocket launchers; they had ironclad warships;

their bridges hung from iron cables; and their physicians used drugs not even discovered in the West for hundreds of years. The many achievements of the Chinese in astronomy, medicine, mathematics, and technology are discussed here.

Rovin, Jeff. **Mars!** Corwin Books, 1978. 244 pp.

Mars has interested people from ancient times to today. This mysterious planet is discussed, described, and illustrated in this book. Facts are provided about the planet, but the many fantasies about Mars are also explored. The book reveals how scientists, science fiction writers, comic-strip artists, and filmmakers have all been intrigued with the one planet whose surface humankind can see.

Sagan, Carl. **The Dragons of Eden: Speculations on the Evolution of Human Intelligence.** Ballantine Books, 1977. 271 pp.

Speculations about the history and function of the human brain are the main concerns of this book. There are discussions about such things as the reasons for sleeping and dreaming, the definition of death, cloning, animal communication, and people's most feared beasts. Illustrations.

Salvadori, Mario. **Building: The Fight against Gravity.** Illus. Saralinda Hooker and Christopher Ragus. McElderry Books, 1979. 150 pp.

Have you ever wondered what makes buildings and bridges stand up? Why don't skyscrapers sway or buildings sink into the ground? This book provides an explanation of the basic principles of architecture, such as the characteristics of building materials like stone or wood. Readers are then shown how to make models out of materials readily available to them. (Childrens Science Book Award)

Scheffer, Victor B. **A Natural History of Marine Mammals.** Illus. Peter Parnall. Charles Scribner's Sons, 1976. 157 pp.

Over a period of 60 million years, warm-blooded mammals left the land on which they lived and adjusted to life in the sea. This book tells how the sea forced these mammals to adapt their shape and bodily functions in order to survive.

Segan, Ann. **One Meter Max.** Prentice-Hall, 1979. 39 pp.

For years the U.S. government has been encouraging its citizens to convert to the metric system of weights and measurements. Max Meter, Minnie Millimeter, Cedric Centimeter, and Katie Kilometer will help you get used to the metric system. Easy reading.

Sherrod, P. Clay (with Thomas L. Koed). **A Complete Manual of Amateur Astronomy: Tools and Techniques for Astronomical Observations.** Spectrum Books, 1981. 319 pp.

What kind of research can an amateur astronomer conduct? Here are more than a dozen research projects that use modest equipment to search for comets, study the rotational rate of Jupiter, or hunt for extragalactic supernovae. The sky's the limit.

Shurkin, Joel N. **Jupiter—The Star That Failed.** Westminster Press, 1979. 110 pp.

Here is the complete story of the planet Jupiter, from its formation billions of years ago, through the earliest discoveries about it, to the thorough investigations done by the *Pioneer* space probes. Through reading this book, you will discover that Jupiter is not only the largest planet in our solar system, but one of the most interesting.

Shurkin, Joel N. **Update—Report on the Planet Earth.** Westminster Press, 1976. 155 pp.

This book explains many geologic theories central to science, beginning with the formation of the universe and our solar system and continuing with discussion of many of the phenomena still occurring on the planet Earth. Topics covered here include continental drift, plate tectonics, earthquakes, volcanoes, and the methods scientists use to measure, observe, and learn more about these forces.

Shuttlesworth, Dorothy E., and Lee Ann Williams. **The Moon: Steppingstone to Outer Space.** Doubleday & Co., 1977. 110 pp.

People have long been fascinated with the beauty and mystery of the moon. This book explains what a moon is and discusses the legends and myths about our moon, as well as the historical theories about it. It also traces the steps people have taken to reach the moon and what new facts and possibilities successful moon missions have produced. But planets other than Earth have moons. Are these moons like ours? What about our satellites? Do they count as moons? And what, if any, value for the average person is there in the discoveries about the arid desolation of Earth's moon? The book explores these questions and more.

Silverstein, Alvin, and Virginia Silverstein. **The Genetics Explosion.** Illus. Constance Ftera and Richard Erik Warren. Four Winds Press, 1980. 142 pp.

Each year science is discovering so much about genes and their behavior that it is hard to keep up with how all this knowledge can change, and is changing, our lives. Maybe you've heard about clones and test-tube babies, but this book also gives basic facts and commonsense information about genetics. Among other topics, the book discusses how doctors and scientists are beginning to have control over what happens in cases concerning victims of genetic diseases. Also presented are some interesting ideas of how to improve the very nature of human life through genetics. There are those who say people have no right to tamper with nature, while others say that with the knowledge comes the responsibility to use it to help those who suffer. This book provides one way to learn the facts about a controversial area of scientific knowledge and draw your own conclusions.

Silverstein, Alvin, and Virginia Silverstein. **The World of Bionics.** Methuen, 1979. 116 pp.

Although a totally bionic person like the "Six Million Dollar Man" is not yet a reality, you will be surprised at how close science is to doing this. The new science of bionics has been around for only about twenty years, yet already complex robots, mechanical hearts, and functional artificial limbs have been developed and are in everyday use. Here is the story of the development of this science with predictions about its applications. Photographs.

Simon, Seymour. **The Long View into Space.** Crown Publishers, 1979. 42 pp.

Here is an illustrated guide to the earth as viewed from outer space, the moon, the stars, the constellations, and other objects in the universe. Large telescopes make it possible to see even the rocks and dust on the moon, the great red spot that whirls over the surface of Jupiter, and the huge clouds of gas that lie among the stars. Easy reading.

Smith, Howard E., Jr. **Balance It!** Photographs by George Ancona. Four Winds Press, 1982. 49 pp.

How does a scale work? Why do tightrope walkers carry a pole in their hands? What is a center of gravity? This book tells you about weight, symmetry, and gravity and gives easy-to-follow instructions for making a letter scale, balancing dolls, a floating sculpture, and a mobile.

Stiller, Richard. **Habits: How We Get Them, Why We Keep Them, How We Kick Them.** Thomas Nelson, 1977. 157 pp.

We behave in certain ways because of habits—learned patterns of acting, thinking, or feeling. The brain activity that is involved and the forming and breaking of habits are all explained in this book.

Streuver, Stuart, and Felicia Antonelli Holton. **Koster: Americans in Search of Their Prehistoric Past.** Signet Books, 1980. 249 pp.

More than 7,000 years before Christ was born, there was a great civilization that lived in what is now the American Midwest. For the past ten years, scientists and volunteer student workers have been exploring one of the sites of this prehistoric culture on a farm in west central Illinois. The group has made some amazing discoveries that are helping them find out what these prehistoric people ate, how they made tools, how they cured diseases, and how they buried their dead.

Sullivan, George. **How Do They Find It?** Westminster Press, 1977. 160 pp.

Today, with modern technology at our fingertips, we are able to locate needed minerals and oil with remarkable accuracy. In another area, newly developed radar and sonar devices allow scientists to detect approaching violent weather such as hurricanes and tornadoes. X-ray equipment is now used to detect concealed weapons, while simple electronic metal detectors let novices become treasure hunters at the beach or in the park. So whether you are interested in exploring ancient sunken wrecks or understanding complex airline tracking systems, this book will provide an introduction to the subject of recent technological advances.

Taylor, John G. **Black Holes.** Avon Books, 1975. 208 pp.

A black hole is a huge star that has collapsed and that begins to exert a tremendous gravitational pull. Nothing can escape it, not even light. According to this book, black holes may be very dangerous to us. More knowledge of black holes is needed. It might even help us understand our beginnings and give us vital information on the creation, and the possible destruction, of the universe.

Taylor, L. B., Jr. **Gifts from Space: How Space Technology Is Improving Life on Earth.** John Day Co., 1977. 130 pp.

Electronic implants, biological isolation garments, flame-retardant materials, lightweight insulation materials, computer chips, and energy-producing devices are some of the by-products of the space program. These discoveries of space research are now put to practical use in our everyday lives. This book discusses how these seemingly complex scientific discoveries have many simple uses, even around your own house. Photographs.

Taylor, L. B., Jr. **Space: Battleground of the Future?** Franklin Watts, 1983. 128 pp.

Will wars of the future be fought in space? We already have satellites put to military use, "spy" weather satellites, antisatellite devices (called "killer satellites"), laser weapons, and command posts in space. Are we turning space into a battleground? Photographs.

Taylor, L. B., Jr. **Space Shuttle.** Thomas Y. Crowell Co., 1979. 119 pp.

This book explains NASA's space shuttle program for the 1980s. It discusses what the program means, why it is necessary, and who will be involved, and describes some of the products coming from the program that can benefit us all.

Thorne, Ian. **UFO's.** Crestwood House, 1978. 47 pp.

Many mysterious sightings caused the Air Force to begin a study of UFOs as early as 1947. Since then, many sightings have been explained, but there still are many questions to be answered. Pictures and stories from those who reportedly saw UFOs or who were involved in the Air Force investigations are included.

Tichy, William. **Poisons: Antidotes and Anecdotes.** Sterling Publishing Co., 1977. 192 pp.

Did you know that in Renaissance Italy poisoning was a popular and routine crime? Poison comes from many sources: minerals, plants, animals, and people. The author traces the story of poison through the ages and lists famous poisoners such as Cesare Borgia, and even Leonardo da Vinci. The book also has a list of practical ways to prevent and counteract a poisoning. Illustrations.

Trefil, James S. **Living in Space.** Illus. Gloria Walters. Charles Scribner's Sons, 1981. 130 pp.

When will it be possible to live in a space colony? What will life be like there? This book provides details on how a space colony might be created. It discusses such areas as construction, energy, food, recreation, and work. For example, in athletics, there would be no hiking, backpacking, climbing, or hunting on these colonies. However, there would be jogging, track and field, team sports, space polo, and even a unique kind of swimming.

Vergara, William C. **Science in Everyday Life.** Harper & Row, Publishers, 1980. 306 pp.

The world around us poses many questions that are not always easy to answer. This book provides concise and clear answers to many of these scientific questions. How does a nuclear breeder reactor work? Do animals ever commit mass suicide? How did agriculture begin? The book answers these and other questions in nontechnical language and with diagrams that help make certain principles of science easier to understand.

Walsh, Martin. **Stranger Than Fiction II.** Scholastic Book Services, 1978. 107 pp.

This collection of short factual stories focuses on strange events and mysteries that scientists have been unable to explain. Topics include foretelling the future, communicating with spirits, and discovering a lost tribe in the Philippines.

Warner, Matt. **Flowers, Trees, and Gardening.** Golden Press, 1975. 48 pp.

This book explains the wonders of plants—from giant trees to flowers, fruits, and vegtables. Directions for growing your own garden indoors or outdoors add to the usefulness of this book.

Weiss, Ann E. **The Nuclear Question.** Harcourt Brace Jovanovich, 1981. 160 pp.

Nuclear energy is a subject of much controversy, and this book helps to explain why. It covers both the advantages and disadvantages we face as a nation interested in developing this energy source. In addition, the historical development of nuclear energy is traced here, as well as its cost in dollars. This information should help you make up your own mind about how you feel about the uses of nuclear power. Photographs.

Weiss, Malcolm E. **Seeing through the Dark: Blind and Sighted—A Vision Shared.** Harcourt Brace Jovanovich, 1976. 84 pp.

Our minds enable us to see better. Both blind and sighted people share certain ways of sensing their surroundings. Through touch, memory, and the vibrations of sound waves, we can all see in the dark. This book's explanation of sensing tries to make us all see more and understand the enormous capacities of our senses. Photographs.

Weiss, Malcolm E. **Why Glass Breaks, Rubber Bends, and Glue Sticks: How Everyday Materials Work.** Illus. Paul Plumer. Harcourt Brace Jovanovich, 1977. 74 pp.

This book looks at some everyday materials and explains why they look and act as they do. For example, why is salt cube shaped? Why is caramel candy like glass? Why do we bounce back and not keep on going through a trampoline? How can diamonds, coal, and pencil lead be made out of the same material and all look so different? There are answers to these and other questions.

Wohlrabe, Raymond A. **Exploring the World of Leaves.** Photographs by author. Diagrams by John F. McTarsney. Thomas Y. Crowell Co., 1976. 140 pp.

A well-known science writer explains what science knows about leaves and their functions, from controlling the earth's water loss, to adding to the energy and food supplies. The beginning botanist will appreciate the clear technical information and the suggested experiments and science projects using leaves.

Wulforst, Harry. **Breakthrough to the Computer Age.** Charles Scribner's Sons, 1982. 185 pp.

What kind of people and events make up the history of the electronic computer? This is a story of inventors, experimenters in laboratories, and large corporations. Many computer pioneers were interviewed for this book, among them George Stibitz, John von Neumann, J. Presper Eckert, and John Mauchly. Events cover the "kitchen table" computer of 1937, to UNIVAC's 1952 breakthrough in computer engineering.

Yates, Madeleine. **Earth Power: The Story of Geothermal Energy.** Illus. Bettye Beach. Abingdon Press, 1980. 64 pp.

Volcanoes, geysers, and hot springs are similar natural pheonomena locked away in the earth since the beginning of time. Both by accident and by instinct, people from ancient times to the present have found ways to channel this kind of natural pressure as a means of energy. Scientists wonder if these geothermal sources could be one answer to our energy needs. Right now, Iceland is using "earth energy" as a power source for things like heating homes, cooking food, and heating hot water. Amazing as its many uses and advantages are, though, geothermal energy has its problems and its dangers. When everything positive and negative is taken into account, will this buried treasure find a permanent place in our lives?

Yates, Madeleine. **Sun Power: The Story of Solar Energy.** Illus. J. S. Laughbaum. Abingdon Press, 1982. 80 pp.

Although many people think of solar energy as a modern idea, it is actually as old as civilization itself. This book explains in very simple terms how solar energy works to heat and light our homes and gives a simple but accurate description of what makes the sun shine. It also explores possible future uses of solar energy.

Languages

Brandreth, Gyles. **The Biggest Tongue Twister Book in the World.** Illus. Alex Chin. Sterling Publishing Co., 1978. 128 pp.

How many pecks of pickled peppers did Peter Piper pick? This collection contains both easy and difficult tongue twisters. For those who are interested in verbal challenges, the tongue twisters are all fun, even if occasionally frustrating.

Fronval, George, and Daniel Dubois (translator E. W. Egan). **Indian Signs and Signals.** Photographs by George C. Hight. Illus. Jean Marcellin and George Catlin. Sterling Publishing Co., 1978. 80 pp.

The Plains Indians have been communicating up to the present day without a common verbal tongue. Their sign language is given here both in print and in the photographs of a Kiowa chief and his family in tribal dress using the sign language. Over 800 signs are explained and illustrated. Also included are other nonverbal means of communicating such as smoke signals, feathers, trail markings, and body paint.

Hazen, Barbara Shook. **Last, First, Middle and Nick: All about Names.** Illus. Sam Weissman. Prentice-Hall, 1979. 130 pp.

Everyone has a name—two, three, four, or even more names. Who has the longest name? the shortest? What does your name mean? Or have you thought about changing your name but don't really know how to do it legally? All of these questions and more are answered in this book about names.

Katan, Norma Jean (with Barbara Mintz). **Hieroglyphs: The Writing of Ancient Egypt.** McElderry Books, 1981. 92 pp.

The ancient Egyptians used a system of writing called hieroglyphs (meaning "sacred writings"). There are over 700 of these signs or letters that can be seen today on many Egyptian objects in museums, especially on tombs and statues. Hieroglyphs remained a mystery for over 2,000 years. Then, in 1799, some of Napoleon's soldiers found a stone at Rosetta that helped scholars decode the hieroglyphs. Many black-and-white pictures and illustrations capture examples of this important form of writing, which some believed had magical power. The book explores the origins of hieroglyphs and presents instructions for drawing them.

Kraske, Robert. **The Story of the Dictionary.** Harcourt Brace Jovanovich, 1975. 67 pp.

We all use the dictionary—in fact, it is the second most popular book in the English language. Here is a book that traces the history of the dictionary and describes how a dictionary is prepared. In addition, the pronunciation, meaning, and source of a number of words in the English language are provided. You might be surprised to discover where certain words came from. Photographs.

Lehman, Charles L. (with Donald Cowles and Gertrude Hildreth). **Handwriting Models for Schools.** Alcuin Press, 1976. 156 pp.

Handwriting, as it is described in this book, is a form of language. The shapes of letters and even the spaces between them have meanings. A brief history of handwriting, along with sample styles, is also given.

Leokum, Arkady, Paul Posnick, and Stanley J. Corwin. **Where Words Were Born.** Corwin Books, 1977. 60 pp.

This heavily illustrated book traces the roots of over 110 words. For example, *piano* and *flu* come from Italian, *braille* and *sandwich* from people's names. *Jalopy* is traced to a small town in Mexico, while *abracadabra* is a coined or made-up word. *Alligator* is so named because it looks like a sea lizard, and a *secretary* is supposed to keep secrets. Easy reading.

Meadow, Charles T. **Sounds and Signals: How We Communicate.** Westminster Press, 1975. 94 pp.

Communication is a vast subject and includes radio, telephone, television, speech, writing, computers, and even more. This book discusses what basic communication is and then explores some ideas for the future of communication. The chapters include the topics of codes, levels of communication, the noise factor, language, pictures, and new worlds of information. Illustrations.

Pizer, Vernon. **Take My Word for It.** Dodd, Mead & Co., 1981. 125 pp.

What do the following words have in common: *shrapnel, guillotine, chauvinism, boycott, poinsettia, silhouette,* and *leotard?* All are words brought into the English language from famous people's names. Jules Leotard was a twenty-one-year-old French acrobat who changed circus history by introducing the flying trapeze and a one-piece, thin garment that clung to him like a second skin—the leotard. The stories of the famous name-givers are organized into chapters on the rank and file, thinkers and tinkers, politicians, pleasure seekers, and the women whose names have entered the English vocabulary.

Rosenbloom, Joseph. **Twist These on Your Tongue.** Illus. Joyce Behr. Thomas Nelson, 1978. 91 pp.

This clever collection of colorful tongue twisters tests the reader's ability to speak clearly and not to stammer while stifling laughter. The phrases included here have varying degrees of length and difficulty, so if you have never tried a tongue twister before, you can begin slowly.

Safire, William. **On Language.** Avon Books, 1981. 331 pp.

This is a collection of comments on the American language. The author writes about the ways Americans use the language, how our language differs from one part of the country to another, and how we use slang terms. Sections on usage, style, word origins, pronunciation, jargon, and dialect are included here. The book also includes letters from readers of the author's language articles that appeared in the *New York Times Magazine*.

Sammons, Martha C. **A Guide through Narnia.** Harold Shaw Publishers, 1979. 164 pp.

Narnia is the well-known but imaginary land of C.S. Lewis's *Chronicles of Narnia*. Even though a fantasy land, the place-names, maps, chronology, and people of Narnia make it seem real. This book discusses the life of the author of the seven Narnia books, summarizes the history of Narnia, and describes what the Pevensie children learn during their adventures there.

Schwartz, Alvin. **Chin Music: Tall Talk and Other Talk.** Illus. John O'Brien. J. B. Lippincott Co., 1979. 127 pp.

According to some American folklore, a dentist is a "tooth carpenter," a doctor is a "pillroller," a school is a "knowledge box," and a steady boyfriend is a "yahoo." Here is a collection of American folk words and sayings, including illustrations of many of the meanings. In addition, the author explains the part of the country where certain words originated. You will be able to find a few interesting ones from your area.

Scott-Giles, C. W. **The Wimsey Family.** Avon Books, 1979. 88 pp.

British writer Dorothy Sayers is perhaps best known for creating the character of Lord Peter Wimsey, an amateur detective who often solved mysteries that baffled the authorities. This book chronicles his family by collecting all the references to the Wimseys in the Lord Peter mysteries and by correspondence with author Sayers. If you're a Lord Peter fan, you may want to know more about the Wimsey family.

Steckler, Arthur. **101 More Words and How They Began.** Illus. James Flora. Doubleday & Co., 1980. 48 pp.

The amusingly intricate historical or trivial origins of 101 words are explained in this study of our language. Some of the most common words come from the strangest places. Read this book and find out about a few of them.

Thomas, Sidney R. **Styles for English Language: Developing Techniques in Prose, Drama and Verse.** Blandford Press, 1979. 167 pp.

Style in writing does more than reflect the individual who is doing the writing; it must also fit the form: magazine article, story, business letter, formal report. Here is a book designed to help you develop style while keeping form in mind. Perhaps the lessons here will help you improve your writing.

Tyler, J.E.A. **The New Tolkien Companion.** Illus. Kevin Reilly. Avon Books, 1980. 650 pp.

This book includes an alphabetical dictionary as a guide for those readers who enjoy the works of J.R.R. Tolkien, which include *The Hobbit, The Lord of the Rings* trilogy, and his last work, *The Silmarillion.* Anyone who takes a journey through Tolkien's Middle-earth needs this guide to its legends, history, languages, and people.

Weiss, Ann E. **What's That You Said? How Words Change.** Illus. Jim Arnosky. Harcourt Brace Jovanovich, 1980. 48 pp.

Did you ever want to know where a certain word came from? This light-hearted look at the origins of English words is a pleasant introduction to the history of our language. Easy reading.

Wolk, Allan. **Everyday Words from Names of People and Places.** Elsevier/Nelson Books, 1980. 315 pp.

Could you guess what words were taken from these men's names: George Ferris, Joel Poinsett, Nicholas Chauvin, and Louis Pasteur? *Ferris wheel, poinsettia plant, chauvinism,* and *pasteurization.* This book traces many of our words to the names of people or places. From politics to clothing to the mineral and vegetable world, the history of hundreds of words has been collected. New words can be learned—such as *toledo,* which is a finely tempered sword named for the city of Toledo, Spain, where sword making has been a fine art since ancient times.

Wolk, Allan. **The Naming of America.** Thomas Nelson, 1977. 192 pp.

Ever wonder about the names of cities, towns, and other places? There are many reasons for choosing place-names: inspiration, whim, a desire to honor famous people, and memories of other places. Many of these stories are humorous; others are strange or astonishing. You will find stories about your own state here and about many of the towns within your state. For example, Pie Town, New Mexico, was named for the fruit pies that were sold there. And Why, Arizona, was so named because everyone wanted to know *why* anyone would live there.

Nature and Ecology

Bergon, Frank. **The Wilderness Reader.** Mentor Books, 1980. 372 pp.

These articles, stories, and journal entries are about life and activities in the wilderness. The material comes from explorers, naturalists, hunters, philosophers, and conservationists. Included are selections from early writers like Henry David Thoreau and Meriwether Lewis. Isabella Lucy Bird talks about a woman's life in the Rockies in the nineteenth century, and John McPhee explores the lost American frontier in twentieth-century Alaska.

Borland, Hal. **The Golden Circle: A Book of Months.** Illus. Anne Ophelia Dowden. Thomas Y. Crowell Co., 1977. 53 pp.

This book contains colorful paintings of nature in miniature that accurately record the various months of the year. These pictures of flowers, trees, and vines are accompanied by twelve essays that help describe and explain the changing of the seasons.

Busch, Phyllis B. **Wildflowers and the Stories behind Their Names.** Illus. Anne Ophelia Dowden. Charles Scribner's Sons, 1977.

Sixty wildflowers are illustrated in this book, and information is provided about the origins of their names and other historical facts associated with them. Many flowers have intriguing names, such as touch-me-not, bedstraw, goatsbeard, and dandelion, and the stories behind the names are just as interesting.

Dinneen, Betty. **The Family Howl.** Illus. by author. Macmillan Publishing Co., 1981.

Ever wondered about the jackal, an animal that is found in Africa and South Asia? Here is the story of Silverback, Russett, and their four pups, who lived in the Nairobi National Park of Kenya. The author followed this jackal family for a year and witnessed the animals giving birth, scavenging, hunting, playing, and struggling for survival. Some interesting facts are presented: jackals sleep by day, forage by night; the father stays with the pups while the mother hunts; and the family joins together to howl under the moon.

Dowden, Anne Ophelia. **State Flowers.** Illus. by author. Thomas Y. Crowell Co., 1978. 85 pp.

In this small book, each state flower is presented on the left page in full color. On the right page is the origin, history, and special uses of the flower. If you wonder about why a certain state chose a particular flower, the exact wording of the legal statutes that made the flower official is included. As an example, Illinois adopted the violet after a vote by its schoolchildren in 1907. They chose the violet rather than the wild rose or goldenrod.

Elbert, Virginia Fowler. **Grow a Plant Pet.** Illus. by author. Doubleday & Co., 1977.

How about considering a plant for your next pet? A plant grows, changes, and needs the same care as any other kind of pet. Eleven chapters contain information on the selection and care of popular indoor plants such as spider plants, cacti, aluminum plants, marigolds, and Chinese bean sprouts. Light, soil, water, food, pests, trimming, and starting new plants are discussed for each kind of plant.

Fodor, R. V. **Angry Waters: Floods and Their Control.** Dodd, Mead & Co., 1980. 64 pp.

Although water is necessary for survival, too much water causes death and destruction. This book discusses the various causes of floods, the many methods of flood control, attempts at flood forecasting, and the use of flood warning systems when all else fails. Photographs.

Gallant, Roy A. **Earth's Changing Climate.** Four Winds Press, 1979. 226 pp.

Climatologists are people who study the climate—temperature, wind, atmospheric conditions, and, particularly, climate changes that will possibly occur in the future. For example, if there were melting of the polar ice caps, the sea level would rise, and a coastal city like New York might be completely submerged. Of major interest in the book is its description of the ways we are trying to control the weather. We may eventually tame hurricanes, but what consequences will we suffer for tampering with nature?

Galston, Arthur W. **Green Wisdom.** Illus. Lauren Brown. Basic Books, 1981. 217 pp.

Green plants must have something going for them to have survived on the earth after billions of years. But most people aren't aware of the marvels of plant life. This book takes the reader on a guided tour of plants in such chapters as "The Language of Leaves," "The Immortal Carrot," and "Rotten Apples and Ripe Bananas."

Giblin, James, and Dale Ferguson. **The Scarecrow Book.** Crown Publishers, 1980. 55 pp.

Scarecrows are as old as the history of farming. They have been made out of straw, wood, animal bone, cloth, and metal. In colonial times, whole families of Pilgrims acted as scarecrows and took turns guarding their fields from morning until night. In their long history, scarecrows have often been so frightening that they could scare people as well as birds. To this day, myth and superstition surround them. This book covers the myths and superstitions surrounding the scarecrow. Photographs. Easy reading.

Goldin, Augusta. **Grass: The Everything, Everywhere Plant.** Thomas Nelson, 1977. 176 pp.

This carefully researched book presents a wealth of uncommon information on the many varieties of this familiar form of plant life. For instance, did you know that sugar cane comes from a tall grass the Chinese described as "a rare and precious plant"? Corn, too, is a grass, as are oats, barley, and wheat. The author also discusses the relationship of grasses to a balanced ecosystem of plants, animals, soil, water, and minerals. Photographs.

Hays, James D. **Our Changing Climate.** Atheneum, 1979. 101 pp.

Is the earth slowly cooling off? Are we headed for another ice age? Why does climate change? Although most people take the weather for granted, our climate is affected by numerous factors. Even today with all our advanced scientific procedures, not all the answers about certain climate questions are evident. This book attempts to discuss these and other questions in easy-to-understand language. Diagrams and photographs.

Heintze, Carl. **Summit Lake.** Photographs by Richard Heintze. Thomas Nelson, 1976. 160 pp.

Summit Lake lies at the top of the Donner Pass in the Sierra Nevadas, where the wilderness has not been spoiled by the careless hand of people. The author spent a year observing the cycle of nature from one spring to the the next. This is a poetic account of these few acres of land and water where visitors can leave civilization behind and experience nature. Photographs.

Helfman, Elizabeth S. **Apples, Apples, Apples.** Thomas Nelson, 1977. 149 pp.

We take apples for granted. They have been around since the era of cave dwellers and they come in many shapes, flavors, and colors. Apples can be transformed into delicious dishes, and are a staple in holiday celebrations, legends, folklore, and mythology. They can represent love or symbolize sin. The interesting story of the apple in fact and fiction is presented in this book. Illustrations.

Hellman, Hal. **Deadly Bugs and Killer Insects.** M. Evans & Co., 1978. 191 pp.

We are surrounded by potential killers. No guns can protect us. We sit and wait for the enemy to attack, helpless to fight back effectively. The enemy? Insects, of course. The common housefly is potentially more dangerous than a black widow spider or a scorpion. Fire ants already infest areas of the South. Killer bees have been found in southern Texas. Hundreds of other species of biters, burrowers, and bloodsuckers surround us. But don't panic yet. According to this book, we should be able to live in peace with the enemies—for a while at least!

Hogner, Dorothy Childs. **Endangered Plants.** Illus. Arabelle Wheatley. Thomas Y. Crowell Co., 1977. 83 pp.

Why would plants be endangered? Because they are overpicked, destroyed by industry, trampled, and ignored. This book provides a history of some endangered plant species, as well as discussing what can be done to protect them. Illustrations help the reader identify these plants.

Holmes, Anita. **Cactus: The All-American Plant.** Illus. Joyce Ann Powzyk. Four Winds Press, 1982. 178 pp.

The cactus is more than a spiny plant growing in a desert. There are many varieties of this plant from the lace cactus to the horse crippler. This book describes the types of cacti, how and where they grow, and their many uses. There is also a guide to home cultivation of cacti, and a list of places where cacti can be observed in nature. The book even has a few recipes for cactus dishes.

Hopf, Alice L. **Nature's Pretenders.** G. P. Putnam's Sons, 1979. 96 pp.

Here is a look at eighteen species of animals that disguise themselves in order to survive. For example, the octopus can change color, shoot out a black fluid as a smoke screen, and even break off an arm without permanent injury. Other masqueraders include insects who look like sticks or twigs, a spider that actually lassos prey with a string of silk, a fish that has a line dangling from the end of its snout to catch its own dinner, and a harmless snake that has grown to resemble a deadly poisonous snake. Photographs.

Hosking, Eric (with Kevin MacDonnell). **A Passion for Birds: Fifty Years of Photographing Wildlife.** Coward, McCann & Geoghegan, 1979. 224 pp.

The author has assembled over 80 color and 200 black-and-white photographs of some of the world's most beautiful and exotic birds. This large book includes action pictures of the snow owl, the Spanish imperial eagle, the Galapagos penguin, the peregrine falcon, and dozens of other colorful and elusive feathered creatures. An accompanying text explains how the author was able to capture each of his photographs.

Hussey, Lois J., and Catherine Pessino. **Collecting for the City Naturalist.** Illus. Barbara Neill. Thomas Y. Crowell Co., 1975. 72 pp.

Not all naturalists make their observations in the widerness. The natural environment of a city can also be studied, as this book points out. You might be interested in a snowflake collection, where snowflakes are collected on glass and then impressions are made of them by use of a chemical solution. Or you could collect spider webs or animal tracks. This book describes urban natural experiments, record-keeping procedures, and methods for storing specimens so that city dwellers can observe and enjoy their environment.

Hutchins, Ross E. **Nature Invented It First.** Dodd, Mead & Co., 1980. 111 pp.

We often think of people as great inventors. But nature was usually there first. This book points out how various plants and animals have developed certain characteristics or behaviors to adapt better to their special ways of life. For example, the woodpecker finch is a tool-using bird; firefly beetles have light-making organs in their tails, and the skunk discovered chemical warfare first, long before humans did.

Jackson, Bart. **White Water: Running the Wild Rivers of North America.** Walker & Co., 1979. 127 pp.

Did you ever dream of riding the rapids of a river in a canoe or on a raft? The information in this guide to seventy-two exciting white-water rivers includes sporting class description, standard run, location, and running season. An additional bonus in the book is the glossary of river terms, as well as tips about how to read a river, safety, competition, and clubs.

Jobb, Jamie. **My Garden Companion: A Complete Guide for the Beginner.** Illus. Martha Weston. Sierra Club Books, 1977. 350 pp.

Being a gardener is like being a magician. You end up with something very different from what you started with. And gardeners, like magicians, need all the help they can get. This book provides information on all the whens, wheres, whats, and hows of planting and even suggests some strange things to grow such as popcorn, peanuts, bamboo, and chewing gum plants.

Kiefer, Irene. **Energy for America.** Atheneum Publishers, 1980. 200 pp.

Does America have enough energy for the future? This book argues that although the United States has resources of fossil fuels, the costs of extracting them are rising as the supplies dwindle. Energy alternatives like wind, water, sun, and the atom are then discussed as possible solutions to the expected power crisis. Photographs.

Kiefer, Irene. **Poisoned Land: The Problem of Hazardous Waste.** Atheneum Publishers, 1981. 90 pp.

Hazardous wastes—chemicals that are poisonous, flammable, or corrosive—are like time bombs waiting to explode. And they could be building up in your backyard! This book covers the history of the chemical industry and traces how its waste has led to such famous chemical disasters as Love Canal and the Valley of the Drums, in which hundreds of people were physically and mentally affected. Also covered are new methods being developed for dealing with the waste and what the government is doing about the problem.

Kohl, Judith, and Herbert Kohl. **The View from the Oak: The Private Worlds of Other Creatures.** Illus. Roger Bayless. Sierra Club Books, 1977. 110 pp.

This book describes how animals behave in their environment—a science called *ethology*. The authors ask the reader to slow down and look around carefully. Activities are presented that will help the reader appreciate the "other world" of the creature being discussed, whether rattlesnake, mole, spider, or golden retriever. (National Book Award)

List, Albert, and Ilka List. **A Walk in the Forest: The Woodlands of North America.** Illus. by authors. Thomas Y. Crowell Co., 1977. 197 pp.

For most people, a casual walk in the woods doesn't seem to reveal much. The authors, who are naturalists, suggest questions that young people might ask about the forest and then take the reader on a guided tour to answer those questions. Photographs and drawings illustrate the tour.

Lopez, Barry Holstun. **Desert Notes: Reflections in the Eye of a Raven.** Bard Books, 1981. 78 pp.

In a series of naturalist stories that read as narrative poems, this book describes the many moods and scenes of the desert. The author recreates his fascination with the desert, its animals, its flora, its weather, and its terrain.

Lopez, Barry Holstun. **Of Wolves and Men.** Charles Scribner's Sons, 1978.

Wolves have been a source of fascination, fear, and romantic legend. This book discusses the wolf of folkore as compared and contrasted to the wolf in nature. People create stories about wolves that reflect what they want or need to see, rather than how wolves really are.

McClung, Robert M. **The Amazing Egg.** E. P. Dutton, 1980. 116 pp.

What do snakes, penguins, hens, and humans have in common? They all use eggs in the reproduction process. Eggs come in all shapes and sizes. While most mammals' eggs are held within the mother's body, many other species of animals hatch from eggs outside the mother's body. Some animals produce thousands of eggs at one time, while others have only a single egg. Sketches and diagrams help explain the egg and its functions in reproduction.

Milne, Lorus J., and Margery Milne. **Dreams of a Perfect Earth.** Illus. Stephanie Fleischer. Atheneum Publishers, 1982. 120 pp.

What can help make life better on Earth? The authors of this book feel it depends on our willingness to support the balance of nature in our forests, rivers, deserts, oceans and shorelands, mountains, and grasslands. And we must be willing to change and even sacrifice some of our habits to do this.

Nagel, Shirley. **Tree Boy.** Sierra Club Books, 1978. 50 pp.

This true story describes how a young man, Andy Lipkis, and his other young friends are helping to save the pine trees in Southern California. Andy was frustrated in his early attempts to get other people and governmental and civic agencies to help him plant trees that could resist smog. But because of his dedication, research, and hard work, he was able to set up a nature foundation that exists today. This book demonstrates how people can have a real effect in helping to save our natural resources if they have enough persistence.

Nixon, Hershell H., and Joan Lowery Nixon. **Glaciers: Nature's Frozen Rivers.** Dodd, Mead, & Co., 1980. 60 pp.

It starts with the drifting of tiny snowflakes. It's so cold that the snow doesn't melt, and the flakes turn into ice crystals, eventually forming a solid field of ice. As the weight of the snow on top of the ice field increases, the mass of ice begins to move. It has become a glacier. This book explains the types of glaciers, how they move, where they are found, and the use of glaciers for water supplies. Photographs.

Patent, Dorothy Hinshaw. **Hunters and the Hunted: Surviving in the Animal World.** Holiday House, 1981. 64 pp.

According to this book, even though there are more than a million different species of animals on earth, there are really only two major categories: those who hunt and those who are hunted. Virtually every animal is part of the food chain of another one. Just as the hunters have developed their skills to become more effective at capturing food, the hunted have developed their skills of escape. Some animals protect themselves by emitting a chemical that tastes bad, while others protect themselves by blending into their environments. This book explains the role of each category of animal in the great pattern of the balance of nature. Photographs.

Penner, Lucille Recht. **The Honey Book.** Illus. Ronnie Ann Herman. Hastings House, Publishers, 1980. 160 pp.

Honey, the world's first sweetener, was believed to be a food of the gods by the Greeks, was used by women as a beauty aid, and was thought to cure baldness. The author chronicles the story of honey from its role in mythology to its modern production and use. Included are fifty recipes using honey—some from the ancient world, some from the Middle Ages, and some from the national cuisines of the peoples of the world today. Illustrations.

Polseno, Jo. **Secrets of a Cypress Swamp: The Natural History of Okefenokee.** Golden Press, 1976. 60 pp.

This book takes you on an illustrated tour through the mysterious

Okefenokee Swamp in Southern Georgia. The description provided of the area includes discussions of the birds, animals, moss, and trees that create the spell of mystery there. Easy reading.

Russell, Helen Ross. **Foraging for Dinner: Collecting and Cooking Wild Foods.** Illus. Doris Shilladay Ross and Robert S. Russell. Thomas Nelson, 1975. 249 pp.

Dinner is as close as your own backyard, or the neighborhood park. This book tells you how to find and identify the more common edible plants. There is a guide that tells you where and when to look for each plant and shows you what the plant looks like. And you don't even have to live in the country to find them all. Many recipes are included for each plant.

Samson, John G. **The Pond.** Illus. Victoria Blanchard. Alfred A. Knopf, 1979. 134 pp.

The book takes you through the cycle of the seasons as you watch the changes that occur in the plants and animals living near a pond. In one section, you will discover the strange things that happen during the winter, while you learn about some of nature's laws. Other sections treat the effects of spring, summer, and autumn on the same area. Illustrations.

Sattler, Helen R. **Nature's Weather Forecasters.** Illus. by author. Thomas Nelson, 1978.

Clues exist all around us to help predict the weather. Wildlife, pets, insects, the wind, the sky, and even our own bodies can predict changes in the weather. For example, locusts sing only when the weather is hot and dry; birds will feed late in the day before a snowstorm; spiders take down their webs before a heavy rain; and air pressure drops cause tissue swelling and pain in our bodies. The last chapter deals with myths of weather prediction and separates those that have some wisdom from those that are purely fantasy.

Schlein, Miriam. **Antarctica: The Great White Continent.** Hastings House, Publishers, 1980. 61 pp.

Antarctica is a frozen continent today, but it was not always so, as the biologists and geologists who have studied it can tell us. It was once warm and green with trees and plants familiar to us all. Because it is so cold and hostile today, it was the last continent to be explored, studied, and settled. Here is the story of Antarctica and of the people who explored it. Photographs. Easy reading.

Shuttlesworth, Dorothy E. **Zoos in the Making.** E. P. Dutton, 1977. 116 pp.

Zoos are very special places, and this book takes the reader behind the scenes of some outstanding zoos in the world including the Arizona-Sonora Desert Museum, the National Zoo in Washington, D.C., and the Bronx Zoo. It is surprising to learn of all the big plans for the zoos of tomorrow. But facts are also provided in this book about the zoos of today. Did you know it takes twenty pounds of bamboo a day to satisfy one hungry panda? Photographs.

Singer, Marilyn. **The Fanatic's Ecstatic Aromatic Guide to Onions, Garlic, Shallots and Leeks.** Illus. Marian Parry. Prentice-Hall, 1981. 262 pp.

What can you do with an onion besides use it in cooking? Ancient Egyptians placed onions in a mummy's tomb. General Grant used onion juice to clean wounds. Some farmers predict the coming weather by examining the skins of onions. This book will tell you all you could possibly want to know about the members of the allium family: their history, folklore, structure, literary appearances, festivals, and, yes, even how to cook them.

Smith, Don. **The Grand Canyon: Journey through Time.** Troll Associates, 1976. 32 pp.

Called one of the Seven Natural Wonders of the World, the Grand Canyon is fascinating for its beauty, size, mystery, danger, and history. This book describes the formation of this natural phenomenon and explains the canyon's caves, the formations, the strata of earth and rock, and the river that formed the canyon. Also discussed is the canyon's history from the time of its discovery to what has happened since that event. Photographs. Easy reading.

Sturges, Patricia Patterson. **The Endless Chain of Nature: Experiment at Hubbard Brook.** Westminster Press, 1976. 146 pp.

Tucked away in the White Mountains of New Hampshire is a place protected from the world of technology. Hubbard Brook Forest, though, is not protected from nature's activities or from people studying those activities. The area is filled with plants, animals, and a group of people in a controlled scientific study. Here in the closed ecosystem, students, researchers, university scientists, and Forest Service workers are observing the mysteries of nature's relationships and cycles. This team of researchers will attempt to use their findings to help formulate a plan for the wise use of the earth's energy.

Torrey, Volta. **Wind-Catchers: American Windmills of Yesterday and Tomorrow.** Stephen Greene Press, 1981. 226 pp.

With the ever-rising cost of energy, people are looking to alternative sources. One of the almost forgotten sources of power is the windmill. Although in the past used only to grind grains or to pump water, today the windmill is being used to generate power for more than one family's electrical needs. This book traces the history of these wind catchers in America. Illustrations.

Watson, Jane Werner. **Living Together in Tomorrow's World.** Abelard-Schuman, 1976. 159 pp.

Beginning with past developments in community living, transportation, and communication, this book goes on to discuss the current situation and the problems in each area and to predict what the future holds. How will we live in the future? Will it be in large, overcrowded cities, or in small cluster communities? How will we move around? Will it be on rapid transit, curbside buses, or bicycles? How will we communicate with the increasing numbers of people in the world? These and many other vital questions concerning our future are examined.

Weber, William J. **Attracting Birds and Other Wildlife to Your Yard.** Photographs by author. Holt, Rinehart & Winston, 1982. 147 pp.

Would you like to talk to the animals like Dr. Doolittle, but can find none around? This book helps you get some animals to come to you, while you help them. It tells you how to choose bird feeders, seeds, plants, and trees that can be used to attract animals and birds to your backyard. You will learn how to lure such birds as hummingbirds, bluebirds, and woodpeckers. There is also information on attracting squirrels, rabbits, raccoons, and other mammals. This book also provides plans and directions for making a bird feeder and a birdhouse. And, when December rolls around, the book will tell you how to make a Christmas tree for your collection of creatures!

Wexler, Jerome. **Secrets of the Venus's Fly Trap.** Dodd, Mead & Co., 1981. 61 pp.

Flies, wasps, bees, grasshoppers—these insects are the food of a plant called the Venus's-flytrap. With large photographs and a clear text, this book carefully explains this plant's life cycle and how it captures and digests its prey. The book also describes how you can train a Venus's-flytrap to accept lean meat from your refrigerator—should you want to keep one as an indoor "pet." Easy reading.

Wilkins, Marne. **The Long Ago Lake: A Child's Book of Nature Lore and Crafts.** Illus. Martha Weston. Sierra Club Books, 1978. 160 pp.

Here is a true story of one person's memories of a childhood in Wisconsin. The events remembered here include tours around secret lakes and other summer adventures. Besides stories of places, this book provides instuctions on how to build things like reflector ovens and make things like tassel dolls. The book just might help you appreciate the world all over again.

Social Issues

Adams, Carol, and Rae Laurikietis. **The Gender Trap: A Closer Look at Sex Roles.** 3 vols. Illus. Andy Johnson. Academy Press, 1977. 116 pp., 117 pp., 117 pp.

Book 1: Education and Work points out that girls and boys have little opportunity to question their roles in life because the education they receive at home, at school, and in everyday life constantly tells them that boys become doctors and businessmen while girls become nurses and secretaries. This book takes a look at how we think about sex roles and what might be done to modify mistaken ideas. *Book 2: Sex and Marriage* talks about the double standard that exists in society for boys and girls. We don't see men in bathing suits selling toothpaste and tractors, but we do see women. There is even a double standard when it comes to marriage or not getting married; a man is a "bachelor," but a woman is an "old maid." The authors discuss ways to improve and change these kinds of attitudes. In *Book 3: Messages and Images,* the topic is the ways in which women, and boys and girls, are pictured in jokes, on television, in stories, and in the movies. Women are "dumb blondes," "old hags," gossips, or sex symbols. Men are not portrayed so often in such stereotypical roles. Although we don't take most of these labels too seriously, the authors feel that such images do subconsciously affect attitudes toward women, and thus these images should be changed.

Anonymous. **Go Ask Alice.** Avon Books, 1972. 189 pp.

This book is based on the diary of a young girl who was hooked on drugs. The diary tells her tragic story—how she began taking drugs and the awful things that happened to her as a result. It is a story that shows the realities of the drug scene and, therefore, contains some harsh language.

Archer, Jules. **Hunger on Planet Earth.** Thomas Y. Crowell Co., 1977. 205 pp.

If you have ever gone hungry for a day, you know that soon your lack of energy will make you simply want to sit. You cannot play, work, or even think clearly. This problem exists daily for millions around the world. There are hungry people in large numbers not only in places like South America, Africa, India, and China, but right here in the United States. This book describes the problems of world hunger, its causes, and some possible solutions.

Archer, Jules. **Who's Running Your Life? A Look at Young People's Rights.** Harcourt Brace Jovanovich, 1979. 168 pp.

Do children and young adults have the same rights as everyone else? What are their rights in the areas of family life, school, and work? A discussion of the rights and obligations of young people is intermixed in this book with various comments by teens, parents, and educators.

Archer, Jules. **You and the Law.** Harcourt Brace Jovanovich, 1978. 178 pp.

Most of us don't pay attention to the law until we are personally involved in some way—serving on a jury, testifying as a witness, being sued, or being the victim of a crime. This book tries to take the mystery out of the law, explaining clearly what to expect from our system, and tries to provide a realistic view of how justice works today in the United States. Many actual court cases are described, and one chapter includes information on the rights of students. A glossary explains repeated legal terms.

Atkinson, Linda. **Your Legal Rights.** Photographs by Maureen McNicholas. Franklin Watts, 1982. 85 pp.

What should you do if your employer is treating you unfairly? Can you be excused from the draft? Do your parents have the right to collect your earnings? What should you do if you are arrested? As a minor, you have some rights that adults don't have. But there are also many things that the law won't allow you to do. This book informs you of your legal rights regarding school, money, driving, alcohol and drugs, sex, marriage, and other issues.

Berger, Melvin. **Censorship.** Franklin Watts, 1982. 84 pp.

Censorship comes from the same word as *census*—to take count or to assess. But censorship controls and restricts what can be written, shown, or said; it assesses and then restricts. The author gives a history of the whole problem of censorship, whether by governments, religious and political leaders, or special-interest groups. Discussed are the issues of language, obscenity, libel, espionage, national security, pornography, and student rights.

Brancato, Gilda, and Elliot E. Polebaum. **The Rights of Police Officers.** Discus Books, 1981. 208 pp.

Does a police officer have to accept mandatory duty in one-person patrol cars or in dangerous places? How much warning must an officer give before using deadly force? Can a police officer safely "blow the whistle" on corruption, criticize the department, or voice political beliefs? Police officers have a serious responsibility to the people they protect, but they also have rights—both as public employees and as private citizens. This American Civil Liberties Union handbook explains what officers can and cannot do.

Browning, Frank, and John Gerassi. **The American Way of Crime.** G. P. Putnam's Sons, 1980. 539 pp.

This book talks about crime in a new way—not about who commits crime and how many times, but about how we as Americans decide what is a crime. For example, in the seventeenth century it was a crime to doubt your religion. In 1859 it was acceptable to own, beat, and even kill slaves, but it was a crime to help them escape. In 1877 it was a crime for workers to strike for better wages, but it was legal for Pinkerton detectives to threaten, assault, and even murder strikers. It would seem then that crime is not a question of simple morality, but depends on something else. This book examines just what that might be.

Burgess, Linda Cannon. **The Art of Adoption.** Acropolis Books, 1977. 154 pp.

As the title indicates, this book is for the adult who is going to adopt or give a child up for adoption. But it is also appropriate for anyone interested in adoption. Numerous case histories from the author's experience add to this thorough account of the adoption process.

Burgess-Kohn, Jane. **Straight Talk about Love and Sex for Teenagers.** Beacon Press, 1979. 219 pp.

In a question-and-answer approach, this book deals with various thoughts and feelings about love and sex. Objective information is provided in order to clarify doubts and correct false concepts about sex.

Carlson, Gordon. **Get Me Out of Here! Real Life Stories of Teenage Heroism.** Illus. David Noyes. Bluejeans Books, 1978. 94 pp.

This collection of seven stories tells how brave teenagers behaved in dangerous situations. Although these young heroes were not all successful at their task, they deserve praise for their willingness to risk their lives in an effort to save others.

Carmichael, Lucianne Bond. **McDonogh 15: Becoming a School.** Discus Books, 1981. 204 pp.

McDonogh 15 was an ill-equipped, poor, and rundown public school in New Orleans in the 1970s. The kids who attended it were the ones nobody cared about. But principal Lucianne Bond Carmichael decided she could help the school. She dreamed of creating a child-centered school that brought art, life, and excitement to the students. This book is the story of Carmichael's quest for a better education for the kids of McDonogh 15.

Cavin, Ruth. **A Matter of Money: What Do You Do with a Dollar?** S. G. Phillips, 1978. 80 pp.

If you have trouble understanding the money concerns of your parents, this book will help. It tells you how money works, from simple barter to credit cards and investments. It also explains inflation, deflation, taxes, and how to use your bank account, and it does all this in easy-to-understand terms.

Clark, Phyllis Elperin, and Robert Lehrman. **Doing Time: A Look at Crime and Prisons.** Hastings House, Publishers, 1980. 158 pp.

Keeping criminals locked up costs money, money that many feel is wasted, since some prisoners are released only to return after committing yet another crime. What is wrong? Is there a better way? This book takes a look at jails and ideas about punishment in the past and the present. It also discusses some new ideas about criminal justice being tried in other countries, as well as in a few places in the United States. Illustrations.

Claypool, Jane. **Unemployment.** Franklin Watts, 1983. 96 pp.

Unemployment is a major problem in the United States. In 1982, the unemployment rate was 10.8 percent—12 million people were out of work. This book defines unemployment and explains how the unemployment figures are computed. Relationships between the unemployment rate and inflation, a recession, a depression, and other factors are also given. Causes and safeguards are offered. Some of the unemployed even tell their stories. Photographs.

Conroy, Pat. **The Water Is Wide.** Avon Books, 1979. 316 pp.

This is a true story about author Pat Conroy, a white man who became a teacher in an all-black school on an island off South

Carolina. The author wanted to do something with his life by helping other people, so he decided to go to a remote place in America
where the students could hardly read and write. Most did not even
know what country they lived in. Conroy had two tasks: to educate
the children as best he could and to help the young blacks of
Yamocrow Island adjust to a changing world. The story focuses
upon Conroy's attempts to communicate with children who had
been given up by the traditional school system. Mature language.

Craig, Eleanor. **One, Two, Three . . .: The Story of Matt, a Feral Child.**
Signet Books, 1979. 229 pp.

Matt is a fictional character whose story is based on a number of
real cases. Everyone said six-year-old Matt was hopeless. He was
brought to the center after being raised in a darkened room by his
frightened mother. Matt appeared to be a wild child who could not
speak and who behaved like an untamed animal. Caseworker
Eleanor Craig decided to ignore the advice of the people around her
and try to help Matt. But where to begin?

Curtis, Patricia. **Animal Rights: Stories of People Who Defend the Rights
of Animals.** Four Winds Press, 1980. 148 pp.

Although the seven characters are imaginary, they are typical of
people working to defend the rights of animals. There is Jennifer
McNair, a veterinarian working to improve factory farms where
cows, sheep, and chickens live out confined and miserable lives. Jeff
Alexander is a law enforcement agent who protects movie animals.
Nora Clausen, an illustrator, works against painful traps used to
hold and kill animals. And Bill Davidson, a medical student, exposes
the maiming of millions of animals in experimental laboratories.

Davison, Jane. **The Fall of a Doll's House: Three Generations of Women
and the Houses They Lived In.** Discus Books, 1982. 240 pp.

What has been the historical and social relationship between women
and houses? How has the role of housewife changed with each
generation? This book explores these questions from the first era of
modern housewives in 1900–1920 to the "Last of the Red-Hot
Housewives" of the present, who are faced with overcomplicated
technology and economic problems.

Deming, Richard. **Women: The New Criminals.** Thomas Nelson, 1977.
179 pp.

Women have always been considered nonviolent, incapable of committing any crime except shoplifting, prostitution, and drug abuse.

Now all that is changing. Although women still commit fewer crimes than men, the increase in crimes by women in recent years is alarming. What is causing this change? This book offers many ideas that center on our society and its changing attitudes toward women.

Dolan, Edward F., Jr. **Matters of Life and Death.** Franklin Watts, 1982. 119 pp.

Do we have the right to decide if a person should not be born? Or to decide that a person should die? These are just two of the difficult questions this book discusses. Where do you stand on these issues, and how can you contribute to their solution? This book presents information that can help you decide. Mature subject.

DuPrau, Jeanne. **Adoption: The Facts, Feelings, and Issues of a Double Heritage.** Julian Messner, 1981. 127 pp.

How does adoption work today? Do adopted children have any special emotional problems that nonadopted children don't face? Do they have a right to look for their birth parents? This book examines these and other common concerns about adoption and finds that there are no easy answers.

Edwards, Gabrielle I. **The Student Biologist Explores Drug Abuse.** Illus. Nancy Lou Gahan. Richards Rosen Press, 1975. 112 pp.

This book describes the difference between medical and abusive drug use by explaining how various drugs change our chemical system. Among the drugs described are hallucinogens, amphetamines (stimulants), barbiturates (sedatives), heroin, cocaine, alcohol, and tobacco. The uses and effects of these types of drugs are explained as they relate to the idea of drug abuse.

Ehrlich, Paul R., and S. Shirley Feldman. **The Race Bomb: Skin Color, Prejudice, and Intelligence.** Ballantine Books, 1978. 254 pp.

These authors confront the belief that certain races are innately less intelligent. Skin color has no bearing on intelligence. The problem is that some people, even some scientists, believe that intelligence may be determined by such biological factors as skin color. This can lead to prejudice and unequal treatment. This book offers information about the concept of how intelligence is determined through testing, and how these race/intelligence problems have become a pressing international issue.

Fincher, Jack. **Lefties: The Origins and Consequences of Being Left-Handed.** Perigee Books, 1980. 221 pp.

Left-handed people throughout history have been a forgotten minority in a world geared—from handshakes to scissors—to the right-handed. They have even been regarded as sinister and evil. Here is a book that examines the facts, legends, and lore about the left-handed, while discussing new findings of scientific research on the subject. Originally published as *Sinister People*.

Fleming, Alice. **Alcohol: The Delightful Poison.** Delacorte Press, 1979. 138 pp.

Legend says that an ancient Persian king discovered alcohol and named it "the delightful poison." Alcohol has been used, and mis-used, by people for at least 7,000 years. This book explores the discovery of alcohol, the customs and ceremonies that surround its use, and the vocabulary pertaining to alcohol and drinking. It traces the history of alcohol in America, from colonial breweries to Pro-hibition, and studies the mysteries of alcoholism and the myths and mistakes about alcohol. Illustrations.

Francis, Dorothy B. **Shoplifting: The Crime Everybody Pays For.** Elsevier/ Nelson Books, 1979. 128 pp.

Shoplifting is on the increase in the United States, costing us all an added 15 percent on everything we buy. This book examines the crime of shoplifting and its punishments. New electronic methods of watching shoppers are covered here, as is the myth that a person can get away with taking a few things. Included is information about consumer attitudes toward shoplifting, community programs, and case histories of shoplifters.

Friedman, Milton, and Rose Friedman. **Free to Choose: A Personal Statement.** Harcourt Brace Jovanovich, 1980. 338 pp.

This book explains the mysteries of economics on a personal level. Topics covered include old-age pensions, why the Federal Reserve doesn't control inflation, why some industries and workers get different kinds of labor and contract arrangements than others, and many other issues related to money. The authors believe our free society is in economic danger, and they analyze that danger and suggest remedies.

Gibson, Karon White, Joy Smith Catterson, and Patricia Skalka. **On Our Own.** Avon Books, 1982. 210 pp.

As young resident nurses in the psychiatric ward of a Chicago hospital, Karon and Joy wanted nothing more than to use their hard-earned training. But the demeaning salary and the abuse by arrogant, insensitive doctors slowly turned their dreams into anger and frustration. So Karon and Joy decided to fight back. The authors mingle their personal and professional lives in this astonishing story of two women who stand up for their rights and ideals against the entire medical establishment—and win.

Goddard, Donald. **Easy Money.** Popular Library, 1978. 384 pp.

George Ramos's ambition is to be wealthy, and the quickest way he knows of is to deal drugs. Until recently the drug market belonged exclusively to the Mob, but blacks and Spanish-Americans are becoming more involved in drug dealing. Here is the story of a black, Frank Matthews, and a Spanish-American, George, who in 1972 attempted to smuggle nearly three tons of heroin into the United States. This is also the story of the people and the police work that stopped them.

Griffin, John Howard. **Black like Me.** Rev. ed. Signet Books, 1976. 188 pp.

What is it really like to be black? The author, a white man, decided to find out in the most direct and dramatic way possible—he medically darkened his skin and went to the South in the late 1950s. The experiences he encountered made him realize that the poverty, hopelessness, fear, and prejudice under which blacks struggled every day of their lives was even more shocking than most people knew.

Hamilton, Virginia, editor. **The Writings of W.E.B. Dubois.** Thomas Y. Crowell Co., 1975. 298 pp.

W.E.B. Dubois—a prominent black political figure, activist, and humanitarian—discusses such issues as suffrage, education, socialism, peace, black self-sufficiency, and his own personal experiences and travels. This collection is made up of excerpts from his essays, articles, speeches, and other writings produced in the seventy years before his death in Ghana, Africa, in 1963.

Haskins, James (with J. N. Stifle). **The Quiet Revolution: The Struggle for the Rights of Disabled Americans.** Thomas Y. Crowell Co., 1979. 144 pp.

The right to an education, to the prevention of disease, to employment, and to easy access to transportation is something most Americans take for granted. Yet thousands of American citizens who are handicapped must fight for these rights every day of their lives. This book tells the story of the handicapped in America. Now, with such laws as the Rehabilitation Act of 1973, the disabled are beginning to lead lives of dignity and independence.

Haskins, James. **Who Are the Handicapped?** Doubleday & Co., 1978. 109 pp.

Often people fear or dislike someone because he or she is different. Sometimes this difference is physical and in the form of a handicap. This book looks at handicapped people and explains some of the types of handicaps such as blindness, deafness, brain or nerve problems, epilepsy, cerebral palsy, and multihandicaps. Also included is a discussion of people's prejudices against the handicapped and of some changing attitudes that are leading to a new awareness of the needs and the contributions of handicapped people.

Hayden, Torey L. **One Child.** Avon Books, 1981. 221 pp.

Six-year-old Sheila never spoke, she never cried, and she seemed filled with hate and anger. Sheila had already been abandoned by her mother and abused by her alcoholic father when she was placed in a class for the hopelessly retarded. Everyone had given the girl up as hopeless—except for teacher Torey Hayden. Sensing something valuable beneath the rage, Torey worked closely with Sheila in an attempt to reclaim the lost child.

Hayden, Trudy, and Jack Novik. **Your Rights to Privacy.** Avon Books, 1980. 185 pp.

What kinds of information are included in school records? Can students see their own records? Do parents have the right to see their child's records? Do you know how to go about finding out? In a question-answer format, this American Civil Liberties Union handbook provides guides for action in three basic areas of personal privacy. A section on the privacy of personal records includes discussions of such documents as school records, social services records, medical and employment records, and Social Security numbers. Part two, covering the topic of intrusion into personal thoughts, looks at polygraphs, psychological-stress evaluators, and psychological testing and questionnaires. The final section, on collection and control of government information, focuses on the filing away of government information about individuals. Sample request and appeal letters are provided at the end of the book.

Hayes, Billy (with William Hoffer). **Midnight Express.** Popular Library, 1977. 320 pp.

Billy Hayes, a young American in Istanbul, Turkey, has the perfect plan to smuggle hashish, a narcotic, out of the country. All goes well until his bus reaches the plane and a search party surrounds it.

He is caught and placed in a Turkish prison. Billy understands little of Turkish laws, and his mistake nearly costs him his life. Mature situations.

Horwitz, Elinor Lander. **Madness, Magic, and Medicine: The Treatment and Mistreatment of the Mentally Ill.** J. B. Lippincott Co., 1977. 191 pp.

There have always been mentally ill people, but different societies have reacted differently to their plight. The author traces the history of the treatment of the mentally ill, from times when they were caged and imprisoned to the latest modern therapy, which enables 400,000 mental patients to be released from hospitals each year to live in communities.

Howard, Marion. **Only Human: Teenage Pregnancy and Parenthood.** Avon Books, 1979. 232 pp.

One out of every ten girls under age eighteen becomes a mother. Through fictionalized case stories, this book describes three very different sets of young couples who discover they are to be parents and what they decide to do about it. They find ways to tell their parents and weigh whether they should have an abortion, or consent to adoption, or commit themselves to marriage. Later, they must choose health care facilities and decide about school and finances. These stories also describe the stages of pregnancy, giving birth, and the first year of being parents.

Hull, Kent, and Paul Hearne. **The Rights of Physically Handicapped People.** Discus Books, 1979. 253 pp.

This comprehensive guide to the rights of physically disabled people is an American Civil Liberties Union handbook. Covered in detail are those rights that allow the physically handicapped the same access to places, buildings, and streets as those who are not handicapped. The handbook also looks at the handicapped person's rights of equal education, equal employment, and the right to live on equal terms in the world.

Hunt, Bernice Kohn. **Marriage.** Holt, Rinehart & Winston, 1976. 144 pp.

Is marriage old fashioned? Is it becoming a thing of the past? According to statistics it is very much alive. It also seems to be a necessary part of life to fulfill the needs of all societies. However, today there are profound changes in the system and many alternatives to conventional marriages. This book begins with the history of marriage and covers such topics as rituals of mating and courtship, weddings in America, and marriage by contract.

Hyde, Margaret O. **Juvenile Justice and Injustice.** Franklin Watts, 1983. 110 pp.

What is a juvenile delinquent? This book reviews case histories of juvenile offenders—girls, boys, violent offenders, and other young lawbreakers. It also looks at our juvenile justice system and describes many programs that have been successful in helping these juveniles return to society.

Hyde, Margaret O. **The Rights of the Victim.** Franklin Watts, 1983.

Although crime affects one out of every five families in the United States, only one out of five people who commit a crime is arrested. And, only one in a thousand goes to jail. This book looks at the rights of the victim of crime and discusses the relationship of criminal to victim, ways to reduce the risk of becoming a victim, and services available to the victim.

Ingalls, Robert P. **Hoods: The Story of the Ku Klux Klan.** G. P. Putnam's Sons, 1979. 127 pp.

For over 100 years the Ku Klux Klan has been a mysterious and controversial brotherhood that has inspired some and terrified others. This secret organization has resorted to both legal and illegal methods to attack those who have threatened its view of the American way of life. This book traces the Klan's history and development in America and separates the truth from the fiction that surrounds the modern Ku Klux Klan.

Jampolsky, Gerald G., editor. **Children as Teachers of Peace.** Celestial Arts, 1982. 96 pp.

"Peace is love that is passed on from generation to generation," writes Clifford, age eight and a half. "Peace is sleeping with your dog," says Michael, age seven. The editors invited children throughout the country to send in their thoughts, advice, drawings, and poems about peace. The result is a sometimes funny and always moving collection of children's reflections on the meaning of peace.

Jordan, June. **Dry Victories.** Avon Books, 1975. 115 pp.

The Reconstruction period after the Civil War and the civil rights movement of the 1960s are often thought of as victories for black people. But this book calls them "dry victories," not really victories at all because black people were not given land and their own economic base, or jobs that would make them truly free. This point of view on American history is told through photographs and a dialogue between two young blacks.

Jungk, Robert (translator Christopher Trump). **The New Tyranny: How Nuclear Power Enslaves Us.** Warner Books, 1979. 261 pp.

In this discussion of nuclear energy, the author very clearly shows his negative feelings about this form of power. While most of the examples are European, there are references to American nuclear accidents, particularly the occurence at Three Mile Island. This book covers all possible areas of nuclear mishap—political, environmental, sociological, genetic.

Kavaler, Lucy. **The Dangers of Noise.** Illus. Richard Cuffari. Thomas Y. Crowell Co., 1978. 83 pp.

This is a book about sound and sound pollution, which we commonly call noise. It also discusses our sense of hearing and what noise does to it. Finally, the book analyzes how we use sound and how we can control the noise that can do us harm. We can close our eyes against light, but it is difficult to close our ears, so we must work to reduce the level of noise around us.

Kavanaugh, Dorritt, editor. **Listen to Us! The *Children's Express* Report.** Workman Publishing Co., 1978. 255 pp.

In this book kids give their opinions about what parents should be like; about friends, enemies, and relatives; about themselves; and about such varied subjects as school, sex, happiness, justice, money, and runaways. Each child tells about his or her own worries and ideas. For example, Martin, age eight, feels adults don't see children as people, but as pets—or maybe they do not *see* children at all. Some adults, he adds, don't care much about children, but they don't even seem to care about each other either.

Kelly, Gary F. **Learning about Sex: The Contemporary Guide for Young Adults.** Rev. ed. Barron's Educational Series, 1977. 188 pp.

This clearly written approach to sex education has an introduction by Dr. Mary Calderone of the Sex Information and Education Council of the United States. The book presents unbiased information for young people about human sexuality and sexual relationships.

Langone, John. **Bombed, Buzzed, Smashed, or . . . Sober.** Avon Books, 1979. 157 pp.

Why do some people want to get "bombed" every weekend? Why do others fear even sipping an alcoholic beverage? Why, how, and when did drinking alcohol get started? What is an alcoholic? How can drinking affect you? This book provides information you can use to begin to answer these key questions and to make some important decisions of your own about drinking.

Langone, John. **Thorny Issues: How Ethics and Morality Affect the Way We Live.** Little, Brown & Co., 1981. 220 pp.

This book discusses a number of key issues that are difficult, troublesome ones with no clear-cut answers. It discusses medical ethics; lawful killing; capital punishment; ethics in business, government, technology, and the press; and human rights. A short history of ethics is also included. Examples are provided to illustrate all the sticky problems presented.

Larson, E. Richard, and Laughlin McDonald. **The Rights of Racial Minorities.** Discus Books, 1980. 253 pp.

This American Civil Liberties Union guide explains and describes the civil rights of individuals. It tells you what action can be taken if your rights are violated. Some specific areas covered include jobs, education, voting, housing, and trials. One appendix lists the federal agencies responsible for upholding the rights of racial minorities, and a second appendix offers information about where a person may seek legal help.

Levi, Maurice. **Economics Deciphered: A Layman's Survival Guide.** Basic Books, Inc., 1981. 306 pp.

In these days of high inflation and high unemployment, it is difficult to cut through all of the charts and graphs to understand what that mysterious term economics really means. How is the value of money determined? What is the reason for rising interest rates? Who benefits from inflation? This book attempts to answer these and many other questions in everyday language. Through the use of concrete examples, the book explains some of the most complicated theories of modern economics in terms everyone can understand.

Levine, Suzanne, and Harriet Lyons, editors. **The Decade of Women: A *Ms.* History of the Seventies in Words and Pictures.** Paragon Books, 1980. 253 pp.

Here is a look at women's achievements in the United States during the last ten years in such areas as sports, politics, and religion. The text and photographs emphasize feminist activism and explore changes in family life and in the roles of men and women. Mature subject matter.

Lipman, Ira A. **How to Protect Yourself from Crime.** Avon Books, 1982. 248 pp.

What is the safest lock you can get for the money? What should you do if you hear an intruder? While you're on vacation, how can you make a burglar think you're at home? What should you do if your car breaks down on a dark street? This book tells you everything you need to know before crime strikes—and what to do when it does.

Liston, Robert A. **The Charity Racket.** Thomas Nelson, 1977. 147 pp.

Thousands of organizations benefit from charity each year. Cures for disease are found, starving people are fed, and museums add to their exhibits. Yet sometimes charity money is collected and never put to such beneficial use; instead, it goes straight into the pockets of greedy profiteers. This book outlines both the good and bad ways charity money can be used.

Liston, Robert A. **Promise or Peril? The Role of Technology in Society.** Thomas Nelson, 1976. 160 pp.

Is technology an evil that has brought on air pollution, crowded cities, and junk yards, or is it the tool that will save humanity and bring about a better life for nearly everyone? This book tries to answer this question as it discusses warfare, hunger, agriculture, unemployment, and think tanks. The book points out some of the chilling realities of technology, as well as its possible roles in the future.

Liston, Robert A. **Terrorism.** Thomas Nelson, 1977. 157 pp.

It seems that each week we see the headlines of newspapers reporting another major act of terrorism somewhere around the world—bombings in movie theaters, skyjackings for ransom, school children held as hostages. These are no longer the plots of fiction, but brutal facts of life. Who are these ruthless people? What do they hope to accomplish? Can they be stopped? This book investigates terrorist activity and attempts to answer the major questions concerning terrorism in the world today.

Livsey, Clara. **The Manson Women: A "Family" Portrait.** Richard Marek Publishers, 1980. 244 pp.

In 1969, Charles Manson's cultish followers invaded a private home in California and murdered its occupants. Manson's cult attracted a certain type of person like Lynette Fromme, who attempted to assassinate President Ford, and Sandra Good, who made violent threats against businessmen. This book is an in-depth study of the individual members of the Manson "family" produced through personal interviews and psychological studies.

Loescher, Gil (with Ann Loescher). **Human Rights: A Global Crisis.** E. P. Dutton, 1978. 130 pp.

This book explains the concept of human rights and examines the rising number of violations of these rights around the world. The efforts of several international rights organizations to combat these violations are described, along with the impact of these organizations on the world public. Photographs.

MacCracken, Mary. **City Kid.** Signet Books, 1982. 247 pp.

Seven-year-old Luke was a withdrawn child with a past history of arson and robbery. No adult could seem to reach him or control him. Teacher Mary MacCracken wondered if she could ever get Luke to respond to her attempts at friendship. His continuing silence and anger began to discourage her until she decided to ask Luke to tell her his side of the story.

Meltzer, Milton. **The Truth about the Ku Klux Klan.** Franklin Watts, 1982. 112 pp.

The Ku Klux Klan has existed in America since 1865, preaching a message of white supremacy. What is the Ku Klux Klan? Where did it come from? Why is it reborn again and again? The author answers these questions and discusses some of the ways in which Americans can fight against the Klan's violent racism.

Meyer, Carolyn. **The Center: From a Troubled Past to a New Life.** McElderry Books, 1980. 193 pp.

This story is based on actual experiences at the Vitam Center in Connecticut, which reaches out to help people of all ages. David Peterson is in real trouble when his parents bring him to the Center. He refuses to stay and refuses to change or progress. But eventually he makes friends, gains status, and learns to love—but not without new problems arising. Mature language and situations.

Moorman, Thomas. **How to Work toward Agreement.** Atheneum Publishers, 1979. 158 pp.

Would you like to learn how to get along with other people? This book presents ideas, techniques, and suggestions on ways to work toward agreement. It considers the issues of prejudice, limited viewpoints, faulty reasoning, and other factors that could contribute to conflict. Various methods for compromise and decisions by concensus are also described.

Murari, Timeri. **Goin' Home.** G. P. Putnam's Sons, 1980. 192 pp.

Alma and Arthur Stanford and their small son, Tavis, are discouraged by life in Boston. A few years ago, Boston was their escape from the South and its prejudice. Now they read that many black people are returning home, that it's different in the South now, that things have changed. So they put their furniture in storage and drive to the farm of Arthur's parents, hoping to get jobs, a nice home, and a good education for Tavis. But as the days wear on, the family's situation goes from bad to worse. Can you really ever go home again? the Stanfords begin to wonder. Mature reading.

Phillips, Joel L., and Ronald W. Wynne. **Cocaine: The Mystique and the Reality.** Discus Books, 1980. 290 pp.

In a society where drugs have become a way of life, it becomes each individual's responsibility to know what drugs do and what the dangers of their abuse are. Cocaine may be especially dangerous because it produces a particularly pleasant feeling and is therefore all the more tempting. This book examines all aspects of this drug. Part one describes the use of cocaine in the past and traces the growth of its popularity through the centuries of Indian migration, during the height of the Inca Empire, and following the Spanish conquest. Part two focuses on cocaine use in Europe and its growing popularity throughout the world in the last years of the nineteenth century. Laws and regulations regarding cocaine use came into being at this time, as did the medicinal use of the drug. The remaining section focuses on cocaine's use and abuse today.

Pomeroy, Wardell B. **Boys and Sex.** Rev. ed. Delacorte Press, 1981. 187 pp.

This book is a guide for both boys and their parents to those complex and confusing years of puberty and young manhood. In simple and direct language, Dr. Pomeroy discusses such topics as dating, masturbation, intercourse, and homosexuality as they relate to sexual and social development.

Rofes, Eric E., editor. **The Kids' Book of Divorce: By, for, and about Kids.** Lewis Publishing Co., 1981. 122 pp.

Twenty kids between the ages of eleven and fourteen wrote this book because they felt divorce had affected each of them in some way. The book took two years to write and contains all kinds of advice, facts, and suggestions to other kids in the midst of divorce problems. It also disscuses how to handle special issues such as homosexual parents. What these kids have all discovered is that divorce has changed them, but has helped most of them mature through the pain.

Sale, Kirkpatrick. **Human Scale.** Coward, McCann & Geoghegan, 1980. 542 pp.

Growthmania, according to this author, is what's happening to us. Everything is growing too large. For example, just since 1971 there are 53,000 new products of one kind or another. The chapters include economics, politics, and society, along with the burden of bigness. The author suggests ways to shape a more livable society built to the human scale. Mature reading.

Segerberg, Osborn, Jr. **Living with Death.** E. P. Dutton, 1976. 122 pp.

Death remains a mystery. This book provides information on the subject in eight chapters dealing with science and death, death revival, what is considered a good death, coping with death, and considering one's own life and death, among other topics. The book uses examples from religion and literature to analyze these major areas relating to the subject of death and dying.

Shanks, Ann Zane. **Busted Lives: Dialogues with Kids in Jail.** Photographs by author. Delcorte Press, 1982. 212 pp.

Did you know that one out of nine teenagers will appear before a juvenile court judge before reaching the age of eighteen? This collection of interviews with thirteen young people who are behind bars tells how they got into trouble, how they feel about themselves and the people in their lives, and what their hopes and fears are for the future. Included is a long list of agencies, organizations, and special programs that can provide help.

Shanks, Ann Zane. **Old Is What You Get: Dialogues on Aging by the Old and the Young.** Photographs by author. Viking Press, 1976. 110 pp.

Both young and old people discuss their feelings about growing old. The author interviewed and photographed people of different ages and with different social and economic backgrounds. Recorded in the book are these people's thoughts about death, fears, grandparents, loneliness, nursing homes, sex, retirement, and work.

Silverstein, Alvin, and Virginia B.Silverstein. **Alcoholism.** J. B. Lippincott Co., 1975. 128 pp.

Alcohol is America's major abused drug—not marijuana, heroin, or cocaine. It is a drug that is usually little understood by the people who use it. What does it do to the body? Why do some people become alcoholics and not others? Why did Prohibition not work? Why don't we do a better job of teaching people how to use alcohol intelligently? The answers to these questions and many more are presented in this book.

Sobol, Harriet Langsam. **Grandpa: A Young Man Grown Old.** Photographs by Patricia Agre. Coward, McCann & Geoghegan, 1980. 63 pp.

Grandparents, seventeen-year-old Karen believes, are special people. Her grandmother is dead now, and Karen knows her grandfather is lonely, but he keeps going on with his life. He lives alone and gets up early each day to go to his office. He spends time with his children and his grandchildren. Her grandfather often speaks to them about himself and his past—how he came to the United States from Poland and how he supported his mother, sisters, and brothers when his father failed to do so. He also talks about the depression, his courtship, and how he sacrificed to go to college but could never have the career he wanted, nor the one he studied for, because he had to care for a family. Actual family photographs accompany the text.

Solomon, Louis. **The Ma and Pa Murders and Other Perfect Crimes.** J. B. Lippincott Co., 1976. 157 pp.

What is a "perfect crime"? It is one that has never been solved, and this book presents six of them—two murders, a hijacking, two robberies, and a kidnapping. Was each of the six a result of flawless planning or just luck? You may recognize some famous names involved in the cases, such as Lizzie Borden, D. B. Cooper, and Serge Rubinstein. Originally published as *Great Unsolved Crimes.*

Stiller, Richard. **The White Minority: Pioneers for Racial Equality.** Harcourt Brace Jovanovich, 1977. 120 pp.

George Washington Cable, John Harlan, and Albion Tourgee were three nineteenth-century whites who warned of national suffering if racial inquality continued in the United States. Their unsuccessful efforts to correct the problem and the results of their failure are traced in this book to the 1970s, where there seem to be the beginnings of a new hope for racial harmony. Photographs.

Stwertka, Eve, and Albert Stwertka. **Genetic Engineering.** Franklin Watts, 1982. 90 pp.

Can we "engineer" people through genes? Our new technology can bring benefits and dangers. The story began in 1962 when three young scientists won the Nobel Prize for discovering DNA, the substance that carries the genetic information of living matter and determines the details of that life. This book discusses the application of this technology, including genetic counseling and test-tube babies, and the controversy surrounding these discoveries.

Toma, David (with Irv Levey). **Toma Tells It Straight—With Love.** Books in Focus, 1981. 207 pp.

David Toma became a famous former police detective as a result of two television series—"Toma" and "Baretta"—and three books that have been based on his experiences as an undercover policeman in New Jersey. Toma talks about his own life, his drug addiction and its cure, and the dangers of drugs. He explains why marijuana is dangerous, how to stop drug and alcohol abuse, how over 80 percent of high school students get pressured into using drugs, and how to spot signs that let you know whether kids are using drugs.

Wright, Lawrence. **City Children, Country Summer: A Story of Ghetto Children among the Amish.** Charles Scribner's Sons, 1979. 203 pp.

The Amish farming community rests in the Kishacoquillas Valley of Pennsylvania. Isolated from the outside world of fashions, television, movies, electric appliances—even the daily news—the people here build their lives around their religion and their work. Families and friends are close-knit, and they make their own recreation. But each summer, for two weeks, a case of culture shock hits the little village when it is visited by a troop of young ghetto children in the Fresh Air program. These city children protest at first. How can they manage without TV? fast foods? crowds? The two groups don't even seem to speak the same language. Is the project worth it? During one particular summer, Tyrone, Darrell, Macy, and the other children in the program slowly realize theirs is a story of an experiment in caring.

Sports

Adler, Irene. **Ballooning: High and Wild.** Troll Associates, 1976. 32 pp.

Ever wonder what it would be like to soar above the rooftops, drifting along in whatever direction the wind decided to take you? This book can introduce you to the adventure of hot-air ballooning. It is just one in a series of books focusing on exciting and sometimes dangerous sports. Other titles in the series include *Diving the Great Barrier Reef, Challenge! The Big Thunderboats,* and *Bobsledding: Down the Chute!*

Allen, Anne. **Sports for the Handicapped.** Walker & Co., 1981. 80 pp.

There are 35 million physically limited people in the United States, and many of them are enjoying challenging sports such as skiing, basketball, swimming, track and field, football, and horseback riding. Besides discussing the lives of many of these individuals, this book provides addresses and information for thirty-seven organizations and programs throughout the country that are devoted to sports for the handicapped. Photographs.

Anderson, Dave, Murray Chass, Robert Creamer, and Harold Rosenthal. **The Yankees: The Four Fabulous Eras of Baseball's Most Famous Team.** Rev. ed. Random House, 1981. 210 pp.

The New York Yankees are the winners of thirty-two pennants and twenty-two World Series. No other baseball team in the world is as well known—or as controversial. In this book, four journalists view the Yankees from the era of Babe Ruth and Lou Gehrig, to the four world championships earned during Joe DiMaggio's reign, through the Mickey Mantle-Casey Stengel years, and up to the present George Steinbrenner era. Photographs and a complete 1981 Yankee roster accompany the text.

Angell, Roger. **The Summer Game.** Popular Library, 1972. 320 pp.

Here is a book about baseball that focuses on the personalities that make up professional baseball—the rookies, the veterans, the coaches, and the fans. Spring training and the hopes that baseball clubs have for each new season are also revealed. Individual games and players are described, as well as the feelings of being a fan. A discussion of ways to improve baseball for the fan's benefit concludes the book.

Arnosky, Jim. **Freshwater Fish and Fishing.** Illus. by author. Four Winds Press, 1982. 63 pp.

Do you enjoy fishing? Among other things, this book shows you how to fish for trout and how to tie a fly. It also shows you how to fish for sunfish and how to make a cork-popping bug. There is additional information on fishing for pike, perch, catfish, and carp. And, once you have caught the fish, you will also learn how to clean your fish. Illustrations.

Ashe, Arthur (with Louie Robinson). **Getting Started in Tennis.** Photographs by Jeanne Moutoussamy. Atheneum Publishers, 1977. 102 pp.

Here is a simple, illustrated guide to the fundamentals of tennis. Professional tennis star Arthur Ashe describes the proper equipment needed, exercises that help tennis players, and strategies in playing tennis. These explanations are aimed at young readers. Chapters include individual lessons on the forehand, backhand, volley, and footwork. There are quizzes at the end of some chapters so you can check to see if you fully understood the tips.

Barrett, Frank, and Lynn Barrett. **How to Watch a Football Game.** Illus. Robert Evans and Phillip McDonel. Owl Books, 1980. 240 pp.

Do you ever wonder what everybody is so excited about at football games? This book will help you understand the game. It is a step-by-step guide that describes and illustrates what happens and who does what during a game. Offensive and defensive positions, and basic running, passing, and kicking plays are explained. Rules and penalties are also covered. Besides this, over 500 football terms are defined.

Bass, Howard. **Ice Skating.** Rand McNally & Co., 1980. 45 pp.

Here is a book that describes skating in pairs, skating alone, dancing on skates, speed skating, ice hockey, and competitive skating. If you are just learning how to skate, it tells you how to choose skates, how to go forward and backward, and how to stop. And if you are an experienced skater, it tells you what to expect from professional or competitive skating. It is full of photographs and informative diagrams that cover every aspect of the ice sports.

Benson, Rolf. **Skydiving.** Lerner Publications Co., 1979. 48 pp.

In skydiving, divers jump out of airplanes and fall in a long free glide before they release their parachutes to land on earth. This book describes skydiving training, the equipment needed for safe diving, and ways to improve skydiving skills. There are many photographs and diagrams that illustrate the text, as well as a glossary of terms used in skydiving.

Berger, Melvin. **The Photo Dictionary of Football.** Methuen, 1980. 55 pp.

Like most sports today, football has a technical language all its own. Terms like *red-dog, lateral, gridiron,* and *scrimmage* are all common in football, but may be meaningless to a newcomer to the sport. This short book defines and illustrates with photographs the jargon used in the game of football.

Bridge, Raymond. **The Complete Canoeist's Guide.** Charles Scribner's Sons, 1978. 301 pp.

This guide illustrates various types of canoes and their uses, from pleasure paddling on a lake to running white-water rapids. Canoeing safety is stressed, and methods of controlling canoes and using them as transportation are explained. Technical terms, when used, are clearly defined, and illustrations are used extensively to support the text. Special sections of the book cover planning canoe trips and building your own canoe.

Bridge, Raymond. **The Complete Guide to Kayaking.** Charles Scribner's Sons, 1978. 312 pp.

The kayak is a water craft, somewhat like a canoe, that may be used for pleasure and competitive sport. Through diagrams, photographs, and descriptions, this guide demonstrates various types of kayaks, the techniques for using them, and the various methods for paddling and controlling kayaks. There is also information on safety procedures in using kayaks, such as the Eskimo roll, which is used to upright the kayak if it should tip over in the water. The author includes a section explaining how to build your own kayak.

Bridge, Raymond. **The Runner's Book.** Charles Scribner's Sons, 1978. 218 pp.

All aspects of the sport of running are covered in this handbook. The first part of the book deals with choosing the right shoes, training techniques, and working yourself into shape to run. Part

Two is directed toward competitive running. This book is worthwhile reading for both the occasional jogger and the serious marathoner. Photographs.

Broun, Heywood Hale. **Tumultuous Merriment.** Richard Marek Publishers, 1979. 278 pp.

Heywood Hale Broun, ex-sportscaster for CBS, has written a humorous and informative look at sports in America. Short anecdotes about such personalities as Vince Lombardi, Joe DiMaggio, Ted Williams, Jackie Robinson, and O. J. Simpson highlight the book. Broun covers virtually all major sports—boxing, tennis, golf, football, hockey, horse racing, basketball, baseball, and auto racing. But no matter what the sport, Broun discusses it with a mixture of criticism and praise.

Bunting, Glenn, and Eve Bunting. **Skateboards: How to Make Them, How to Ride Them.** Harvey House, Publishers, 1977. 39 pp.

Skateboarding need not be taken lightly, even though it is an enjoyable sport. Skateboarding lets you be creative, once you master the skills of using the skateboard and caring for it. This book tells and shows you how to do it all—make your skateboard, care for it, and go from a beginning to an advanced rider, or from a creative to a competitive one.

Campbell, Gail. **Marathon: The World of the Long-Distance Athlete.** Sterling Publishing Co., 1978. 175 pp.

What do some people do for fun that can cause nausea, extreme dehydration, weight loss, cramps, blisters, torn ligaments, and periods of unconsciousness? Running a marathon, of course. In addition to covering the 26-mile-plus running event from its beginning in ancient Greece to the modern Olympics, this book discusses distance swimming and distance bicycle racing. Why do people put themselves through such torture voluntarily? Conversations with many of these dedicated athletes help reveal the answer to that question. Photographs.

Carroll, Theodus. **Firsts under the Wire: The World's Fastest Horses (1900–1950).** Contemporary Perspectives, 1978. 48 pp.

The racing careers of four of the fastest horses in racing history are described in this book: Man O'War, Stymie, Seabiscuit, and Citation. The great horses demonstrate how they are able to win races throughout their careers, while others only have brief periods of top performance. Easy reading.

Chiefari, Janet, and Nancy Wightman. **Better Synchronized Swimming for Girls.** Photographs by Ann Hagen Griffiths. Dodd, Mead & Co., 1981. 62 pp.

There is one sports activity in which girls still predominate—synchronized swimming. It is an exciting, beautiful, and unique sport officially recognized in the 1940s but only recently added to the Olympics. With photographs and written instructions, this book reveals how to perform all the basic body positions, swim in time with music, plan a routine, and perform in competition. Many of the photographs are underwater shots.

Clark, Steve. **Illustrated Basketball Dictionary for Young People.** Illus. Frank Baginski. Harvey House, Publishers, 1977. 125 pp.

Both college and professional basketball terminology is listed and defined in this book. The illustrations show common game strategies as well as various basketball techniques.

Collins, Ed. **Watch the Ball, Bend Your Knees, That'll Be $20 Please!** Caroline House Books, 1977. 216 pp.

The author is a West Coast tennis professional who has put together 100 practical and entertaining tennis lessons to help improve your game. He uses simply worded explanations of the basic and more complicated aspects of the game and provides illustrations of them all. Included in the lessons are such aspects of the game as doubles play, net play, tactics, and the psychological aspects of match play.

Counsilman, James E. **The Complete Book of Swimming.** Atheneum Publishers, 1979. 178 pp.

All levels of swimmers, from beginner to competitive can benefit from this clear, well-illustrated instructional manual. The basic swimming strokes as well as training techniques, practices, and the organization of a competitive swimming meet are covered in detail.

Crawford, Teri. **The First Wild West Rodeo.** Illus. Russell Charpentier. Contemporary Perspectives, 1978. 48 pp.

Ever consider how rodeos get started? This book discusses how the daily work of cowboys gradually became a contest among them and then turned into a formal sporting event, the rodeo. What was probably the first rodeo was held at Prescott, Arizona, in 1886. Today there are many different rodeo events for men and women, and they receive cash prizes for top performances. Easy reading.

DeLeeuw, Dianne (with Steve Lehrman). **Figure Skating.** Atheneum Publishers, 1978. 157 pp.

Ice skating is a way of life for Dianne DeLeeuw. At age four she was circling the rink where her Dutch mother skated for recreation. The Olympics soon became an inevitable goal for DeLeeuw, a goal she was able to attain. Now as a professional show skater, she shares her skills, knowledge, and love of her sport to bring joy to others. In this book, she describes such details as equipment, clothing, and safety tips—all the things beginners need to know. Next, DeLeeuw provides complete instructions for skills like sculling, stroking, crossovers, stops, and turning, and describes how to do rolls, jumps, spins, and the spiral. The skater can also learn details about competitive skating, as well as about ice dancing.

Denyer, Brian Lindsay. **Basic Soccer Strategy: An Introduction for Young Players.** Illus. John Lane. Doubleday & Co., 1976. 134 pp.

As in any sport, no one can play soccer without knowing the basic skills and rules. The author, a British soccer coach in the United States, concentrates on offensive and defensive moves and explains the reasons behind them. He also explains when a player should pass instead of dribble, and how to make the most of a free kick or throw-in. Illustrations accompany each explanation of a basic skill.

Depel, Jim. **The Baseball Handbook for Coaches and Players.** Illus. Jean Simpson. Charles Scribner's Sons, 1976. 96 pp.

This is an easy-to-use guide to playing and coaching baseball. It is approved by Little League Baseball, the National Baseball Congress, and the Pony Baseball League. The book includes tips on batting and fielding, offensive and defensive plays, and various drills used to improve skills. Diagrams show various techniques for individual and team use. There is also information on baseball equipment like the field, pitcher's mound, and batter's cage. One important section outlines playing rules.

Devaney, John. **Secrets of the Super Athletes: Soccer.** Laurel-Leaf Library, 1982. 128 pp.

Did you ever wonder if the soccer pros have some inside information? Now the pros share their secrets and give their soccer strategies. Sting goalkeeper Paul Coffee emphasizes gloves; Vladislav Bogicevic of the Cosmos suggests saving energy since most games are won or lost in the last ten minutes; Kyle Rote, Jr., talks about

ankle weights in running laps. The book also includes a quiz at the
end to test the reader's knowledge of soccer. Photographs.

Dolan, Edward F., Jr. **Basic Football Strategy: An Introduction for
Young Players.** Illus. John Lane. Doubleday & Co., 1976. 131 pp.

Success in playing (or even in watching) football is far more than
knowing the rules of the game. Football is a matter of knowing
what to do, how to do it, and when to do it. It's a game that
requires knowledge, awareness, and intelligence. Football demands
self-confidence, courage, and a body that's in top physical condition.
This book provides an introduction to the game, offensive and
defensive strategies, and ways of mental and physical preparation.
For the spectator, it provides an understanding and appreciation of
the game and its players.

Dolan, Edward F., Jr. **The Complete Beginner's Guide to Gymnastics.**
Photographs by James Stewart. Doubleday & Co., 1980. 194 pp.

At least 5,000 years old and probably originating in Egypt, gymnastics was nearly forgotten following the fall of the Roman Empire.
But recent Olympic stars have brought this daring and challenging
skill back into the spotlight. Many come to gymnastics for fun and
personal pleasure; others hope to excel and to compete. The sport
has changed throughout its history, and it continues to change. This
book examines gymnastics past and present, and discusses how
gymnastics differs for male and female participants and for younger
and older people. The book begins with a description of basic
exercises and proceeds to discuss intermediate and advanced skills.

Edmonds, I. G. **Motorcycle Racing for Beginners.** Holt, Rinehart &
Winston, 1977. 190 pp.

Motorcycle racing has become one of America's fastest growing
sports. With more and more youngsters becoming interested in this
sometimes dangerous sport, it is important to learn the best and
safest way of getting involved. There are a variety of motorcycle
races: road racing, for speed; motocross, for thrills; trials, for preci-
sion; and enduros, for pathfinders. This handbook discusses all
aspects of these different methods of motorcycle racing. Photographs.

Etheredge, Randy, and Warren Etheredge. **The Football Quiz Book.**
Hawthorne/Dutton, 1980. 128 pp.

So you think you know a lot about pro football? Well, try some of
these: Who was the first black to play pro football? What offensive

line was known as "the electric company"? Who has the nickname of "Hacksaw"? In addition to questions like these, this book includes football word searches, play diagrams, and multiple-choice quizzes. And, if you turn out not to be the expert you think you are, the answers are included as well.

Fenten, Don, and Barbara Fenten. **Behind the Sports Scene.** Crestwood House, 1980. 47 pp.

Have you ever wondered how many people it takes—besides the players—to put together a major league baseball game? There are the trainers, who take care of injured players; the scouts, who look for new players; the manager, who has to plan strategy; and the team owner, who has to worry about everything. And that's not all; here you'll also read about all the other important people necessary for the game to go on. Easy reading.

Flanagan, Henry E., Jr., and Robert Gardner. **Basic Lacrosse Strategy: An Introduction for Young Players.** Illus. John Lane. Doubleday & Co., 1979. 132 pp.

Contrary to common belief, lacrosse is not a brutal and completely physical sport played by huge men. It is a sport for the thinking man or woman of any size. The keys to success in lacrosse are intelligence, knowledge of game strategy, and precise stickwork. The author covers the essentials of the game with clear explanations and diagrams.

Fleischer, Jack, editor. **Pro Football at Its Best: The Greatest Games by 15 Top Coaches.** Acropolis Books, 1978. 201 pp.

Fifteen football coaches describe the best professional football games they coached or participated in. For example, John Madden describes how he coached his Oakland Raiders to a 32–14 win over Minnesota in Super Bowl XI. Other coaches who describe their most memorable games include George Allen, Paul Brown, Weeb Eubank, Chuck Fairbanks, George Halas, Tom Landry, Don Shula, Hank Strom.

Fodor, R. V. **Competitive Weightlifting.** Photographs by author. Sterling Publishing Co., 1979. 160 pp.

The comparative strength of men and women has been tested in sports throughout the ages. But no sport so accurately tests strength against strength as weight lifting does. This book explains the various types of weight lifting, how to get started in the sport, and how to establish a training schedule for competition. Five competitive lifts are presented in detail: the snatch, the clean and jerk, the squat, the bench press, and the deadlift.

Free, James Lamb. **Training Your Retriever.** Rev. ed. Coward, McCann & Geoghegan, 1980. 351 pp.

Information is provided to help you select a good retriever and train the dog. Skill tasks and training practices are described and illustrated, and they range from simple to complex skills. An appendix provides additional information concerning retriever clubs and a list of books for further reading on the subject.

Friedman, Arthur (with Joel H. Cohen). **The World of Sports Statistics: How the Fans and Professionals Record, Compile and Use Information.** Atheneum Publishers, 1978. 302 pp.

The statistics provided here reveal how well or how poorly athletes and teams performed during individual games or entire seasons. This book tells how to keep and interpret statistics for a better understanding of sports events. Included are entertaining stories from the author's career as a professional statistician.

Frommer, Harvey. **The Martial Arts: Judo and Karate.** Atheneum Publishers, 1978. 125 pp.

With the help of photographs, this general look at judo and karate explains body positions and falling, throwing, blocking, and kicking techniques. The book describes the development and philosophy of the martial arts and briefly summarizes kung fu, tae kwan do, kendo, and aikido.

Frommer, Harvey. **Sports Lingo: A Dictionary of the Language of Sports.** Atheneum Publishers, 1979. 303 pp.

More than fifty sports are covered here alphabetically, from the *A* of archery to the *W* of wrestling. All the words used as part of each sport are included with the definitions. An introduction discusses how all the different sports languages tend to overlap, with similar concepts being given slightly different terms in each sport.

Frommer, Harvey, and Ron Weinmann. **A Sailing Primer.** Atheneum Publishers, 1978. 99 pp.

Wherever there is water and wind, there is sailing. One of the most popular sports in the world, sailing can be relaxing or fiercely competitve. This volume is a beginning handbook for sailors that covers such areas as buying and maintaining a boat, safety rules, vocabulary of the sea, and points of sailing. Basic sailing strategy is explained in text and pictures.

Gardner, James B. **Illustrated Soccer Dictionary for Young People.** Illus. David Ross. Harvey House, Publishers, 1976. 125 pp.

This book begins with a brief explanation of soccer history. For example, the first soccer rules were made in 1863 when a man named J. C. Thring sat down to put some regulations on paper. The game was first called Association Football and then nicknamed *asoc* before it became *soccer*. In this book, all the rules, positions, people, and strategies are listed alphabetically, with humorous illustrations to accompany each explanation.

Garfinkel, Charles. **Racquetball the Easy Way.** Illus. Elana Mildenberger. Photographs by Mickey Osterreicher. Atheneum Publishers, 1978. 148 pp.

One of the reasons that racquetball is a rapidly growing sport is that it can be fun from the very start—all you need is a racquet, a ball, and a court. This book begins with a discussion of the basics of the game, including its rules, equipment, strokes, and serves. Once the basics are mastered, the player is ready to learn about tactics and doubles play. Photographs and diagrams.

Gregory, Stephen. **Racing to Win: The Salt Flats.** Troll Associates, 1976. 32 pp.

The Bonneville Salt Flats in Utah provide the setting for new land speed records from a strange variety of vehicles. These vehicles and their support crews are examined and pictured in many exciting action photographs. Easy reading.

Herkimer, L. R., and Phyllis Hollander, editors. **The Complete Book of Cheerleading.** Doubleday & Co., 1975. 285 pp.

Being a cheerleader takes more than a loud voice and the ability to leap high. Cheerleading demands strong basic personality and physical skills, a sense of rhythm, stamina, dedication, and a knowledge of certain techniques and style. When done correctly, cheerleading has the power to turn a team and a school around. This book tells and shows how this might be done. There are ideas for cheers and uniforms, for money-making projects, and for skits and stunts, besides discussions of all the basic moves and the variations on those moves. Photographs show complete step-by-step cheerleading techniques.

Hollander, Phyllis, and Zander Hollander, editors. **The Masked Marvels: Baseball's Great Catchers.** Random House, 1982. 129 pp.

Everyone always forgets the catcher, but the catcher's job is one of the most dangerous in all sports. This book traces the careers of some of the best catchers in baseball history: Carlton Fisk, Johnny Bench, Roy Campanella, Thurman Munson, and Yogi Berra, among others. Photographs.

Hollander, Zander, editor. **The Baseball Book.** Random House, 1982. 157 pp.

This book, arranged from A to Z, is really an encyclopedia of baseball's great moments—stars, teams, techniques, language, and stories. Many black-and-white photographs illustrate key personalities and terms of baseball.

Hollander, Zander, and David Schulz. **Sports Teasers: A Book of Games and Puzzles.** Illus. Marsha Cohen. Random House, 1982. 184 pp.

What baseball team had a Murderers' Row? What woman has won the most tennis titles at Wimbledon? What sports did Burt Reynolds and Kirk Douglas play in college? Discover the answers to these and hundreds of other sports questions in this book. Also test your wits on the sports puzzles and word games.

Holmes, Burnham. **The World's First Baseball Game.** Illus. Frank Springs. Contemporary Perspectives, 1978. 48 pp.

Alexander Cartwright, with some help from Robin Carver, wrote the original rules for baseball games. Cartwright also umpired the first game played by these rules in 1846 between two New York teams. The success of these rules assured his fame in the sport of baseball.

Huss, Sally Moore. **How to Play Power Tennis with Ease.** Illus. by author. Harcourt Brace Jovanovich, 1979. 95 pp.

Can a pair of knotted jeans or a sweater help your tennis game? Will a karate chop or a frying pan make you a winner on the court? Well, according to the tennis pro who wrote this book, the answer to these questions is "yes." The book uses simple aids such as everyday clothing and kitchenware to help teach the basic components of the game of tennis.

Isaacs, Neil D., and Dick Motta. **Sports Illustrated Basketball.** Harper & Row, Publishers, 1981. 111 pp.

This book on basketball is one of many in a series on sports from the *Sports Illustrated Library*. Chapters here include fundamentals, rebounding, defense, basic playmaking, and basketball for the spectator. Each chapter contains black-and-white photographs of well-known players.

Jenner, Bruce (with R. Smith Kiliper). **The Olympics and Me.** Doubleday & Co., 1980. 152 pp.

Bruce Jenner, the 1976 Olympic decathlon gold medalist, writes about the Olympic Games, explaining some of the history of the games and describing the various events in which athletes compete. In addition, he gives the reader an insider's view of the tragic killing of Israeli athletes that marred the Munich Olympics. A section is included in which Jenner tells young athletes how to train for a decathlon and about each of the ten track and field events the decathlete must perform. Photographs.

Jerome, John. **The Sweet Spot in Time.** Avon Books, 1982. 348 pp.

In sports, the "sweet spot" is that moment when every sense and every muscle work together to produce a perfect and harmonious movement that can lead to superhuman feats. This book explores the drive for physical perfection in athletics and discusses the work of scientists, doctors, and trainers to understand the "sweet spot" phenomenon.

Kaplan, Janice. **Women and Sports.** Discus Books, 1980. 192 pp.

In this book, a woman sportswriter discusses the current status of women's sports, their drawbacks, and their rewards. For too long women have been told that being athletic is not feminine and that it is harmful to their bodies. By the examples of women athletes, both amateur and professional, this book tries to disprove these ideas. Being involved in a sport is as good for women as it is for men, and just as necessary for their health and general feeling of well-being. Every aspect of women's involvement in sports is examined here, from diet to physiology to psychology.

Keith, Harold. **Sports and Games.** Rev. ed. Thomas Y. Crowell Co., 1976. 313 pp.

From badminton to wrestling, sixteen different sports and games are explained in this book. There is something here for the novice, who can begin by learning the rules, and for the experienced player, who can polish his or her techniques. The book also includes some history, amusing anecdotes, and information about the players who have excelled in each sport.

Kowet, Don. **The Soccer Book.** Illus. Charles McVicker. Random House, 1978. 156 pp.

The history, stars, techniques, and strategies of the game of soccer are presented. The book discusses the equipment you need for the game, outlines the skills you have to work on to improve your dribbling, trapping, receiving, and kicking. Illustrations show you how to play the game.

Laitin, Ken, and Steve Laitin (with Lindy Laitin). **The World's #1 Best-Selling Soccer Book.** Illus. Renee Foulks. Julian Messner, 1981. 127 pp.

Two young players explain soccer fundamentals and game strategies. A vocabulary section defines the terms commonly used in the game of soccer. This is a solid introductory book because it covers all major areas of soccer and is written by young people.

Lang, Jack. **Baseball Basics.** Illus. Bill Gow. Prentice-Hall, 1981. 48 pp.

Baseball has been a favorite American team sport for years. The author has written about baseball for almost two generations, and he shares his knowledge of baseball players' skills, strategies, hustle, and even courage. He also includes tips for economical dress and basic equipment. Photographs. Easy reading.

Lieberman, Nancy (with Myrna and Harvey Frommer). **Basketball My Way.** Photographs by Kimberly Butler. Charles Scribner's Sons, 1982. 193 pp.

The author won an Olympic silver medal in basketball and was the first woman to play in the all-male New York Professional Summer League. Known as "Lady Magic," Lieberman reveals her philosophy of basketball and discusses the skills that brought her to her high ranking. Other information Lieberman provides includes tips on nutrition and conditioning, a glossary of basketball terms, a complete set of rules, and court diagrams.

Linehan, Don. **Soft Touch: A Sport That Lets You Touch Life.** Illus. David Brandon. Acropolis Books, 1976. 109 pp.

Basketball is an activity for all ages and groups—school children, old people, and the handicapped. This book may not make you a basketball star, but it will demonstrate some ways to become a better basketball player, both physically and mentally. The information in the book is based on actual game experiences and includes such tips as how to build your own home basketball court and how to select a basketball clinic or camp.

Liss, Howard. **They Changed the Game: Football's Great Coaches, Players, and Games.** J. B. Lippincott Co., 1975. 160 pp.

A modern football fan would hardly have recognized the game 100 years ago. It had few rules, no organized plays, little equipment, and no officials. The changes that have come about in the game are the result of great coaches like Amos Alonzo Stagg, Knute Rockne, and Vince Lombardi. And great players like Jim Thorpe, Red Grange, and Clark Shaughnessy played the game with such energy and skill that football became popular with most Americans. This book gives the history of the game, including play-by-play calls of some of the greatest football games on record.

Liston, Robert A. **The Great Teams: Why They Win All the Time.** Doubleday & Co., 1979. 243 pp.

All the great sports teams have character and a unifying force that makes them legendary. There is a blending of abilities that makes a team greater than any of its players. The Yankees, Celtics, Colts, and Canadiens are some of the teams examined for the qualities that build a winning tradition.

Loken, Newton C. **Gymnastics.** Rev. ed. Sterling Publishing Co., 1978. 104 pp.

Detailed instructions and black-and-white photographs take you from the very basic to the more advanced routines in men's gymnastics. Also included are the international and general rules of competition, scoring methods, judging standards, detailed descriptions of the apparatus, and information on what is desirable and undesirable in a performance.

Lorimer, Larry, and John Devaney. **The Football Book.** Illus. Charles McVicker. Random House, 1979. 158 pp.

This encyclopedia-style picture book includes a little bit of everything about football. Famous stars, teams, and coaches of both professional and college rank are represented. The rules, strategies, and great moments of the game are also explained and illustrated with black-and-white photographs.

Lorimer, Larry. **The Tennis Book.** Illus. Elizabeth Roger. Random House, 1980. 160 pp.

If your game is tennis, this book will interest you. It is a complete encyclopedia of the game from *ace* to *WTT*. Included are hundreds of black-and-white pictures of past and present players, strategies, and tournaments.

Lyttle, Richard B. **Basic Hockey Strategy: An Introduction for Young Players.** Illus. John Lane. Doubleday & Co., 1976. 131 pp.

Before playing competitive hockey one must master the fundamentals of the game and acquire an adequate knowledge of how to conduct strategy without risking injury, picking up bad habits, or becoming discouraged over the inability to perform. This book teaches the basics in both defensive and offensive strategies, while describing the kinds of physical and mental preparation necessary to play the game. Diagrams illustrate the detailed discussions.

Lyttle, Richard B. **Basic Volleyball Strategy: An Introduction for Young Players.** Illus. John Lane. Doubleday & Co., 1979. 126 pp.

Volleyball is an exciting game for boys and girls, men and women. This book begins by describing the offensive strategies of serving, passing, setting up, and spiking, along with basic and advanced attacks. For defense, the reader learns about blocking, digging, receiving the serve, and playing defensive patterns. Drills, sample game plans, and conditioning to prepare the player physically and mentally are also included.

Marcus, Joe. **Total Soccer!** Photographs by Nury Hernandez. Popular Library, 1976. 127 pp.

Soccer's history, fictional stories about soccer, and tales about soccer championship games are all included here. Soccer rules and strategies are also explained, as well as position responsibilities and training tips. A glossary of soccer terms is included.

Mazer, Bill, and Stan Fischler. **The Amazin' Bill Mazer's Football Trivia Book.** Warner Books, 1981. 158 pp.

This is a football quiz book that presents questions about events and people in the world of football. Answers to the questions are given, and they all provide interesting and sometimes little-known information about the game. A sample question: How did certain players, and teams, get their nicknames?

Meyer, Gladys C. **Softball for Girls and Women.** Charles Scribner's Sons, 1982. 308 pp.

A highly experienced softball player and coach has written this complete guide to throwing, catching, fielding, pitching, defensive strategy, batting, base running, offensive strategy, training, conditioning, injuries, equipment, and organizing play. In the past ten years, softball has become a fast growing sport for girls and women. This book covers all aspects of the sport for all its new converts.

Morgan, Joe (editor Joel H. Cohen). **Baseball My Way.** Photographs by J. Scott Crist. Atheneum Publishers, 1976. 263 pp.

Author Joe Morgan played second base for the 1975 world champion Cincinnati Reds. That year he was selected for the National League's Most Valuable Player Award. In this book, Morgan describes the special abilities and techniques required in three areas of baseball: fielding, hitting, and base running. In each of these areas, the author describes the right and the wrong ways of playing the game. He also provides tips and suggestions for ways young players can improve their overall ability in the sport.

Morris, Greggory. **Basketball Basics.** Illus. Tim Engelland. Photographs by Brent Jones. Prentice-Hall, 1976. 48 pp.

If you are just getting started learning the sport of basketball, then this book will be an excellent source of information. The book is well illustrated and provides suggestions and drills aimed at the beginning player. Such fundamentals as dribbling, shooting lay-ups and jump shots, passing, and faking are covered here. As the title suggests, this book covers only basic skills and is not intended for the more advanced player.

Myers, Gail Andersen. **A World of Sports for Girls.** Westminster Press, 1981. 159 pp.

Are you ready for a lifetime relationship with sports? This book has loads of information that a young sportswoman should know about starting in sports, training, finding coaches, getting sports scholarships for college, and competing. There are many true-life stories of women athletes.

Naden, C. J. **Rough Rider: The Challenge of Moto-Cross.** Troll Associates, 1980. 32 pp.

Motocross is a type of rugged motorcycle racing including steep hills, sharp turns, and mud. Color photographs are provided to help illustrate the types of safety equipment the riders wear and the kinds of motorcycles used in motocross. The book describes races and the dangers of the dirt track. Easy reading.

Nentl, Jerolyn. **Freestyle Skiing.** Crestwood House, 1978. 32 pp.

Freestyle skiing could be called a new sport. But it is important that a person should first be able to ski well before trying freestyle skiing. As part of freestyle techniques, the book explains in clear and simple terms how to do mogul or bump skiing, aerials, and ballet. A freestyle skier can do anything within the limits of imagination, athletic ability, and the rules of safety. However, the freestyle skier also has to be willing to take plenty of spills!

Nentl, Jerolyn. **Skydiving.** Crestwood House, 1978. 32 pp.

The diver leaps, arms and hands stretched into the air, and floats
and flies, doing a somersault or sometimes a loop—maybe even
hooking up with other divers to make stars or boxes. A parachute
opens, and the fall slows so the diver can enjoy the beauty of the
earth. Most people fear the sport of skydiving or parachuting, but
this book explains the wide appeal of the sport, its beginnings, the
equipment needed, and the methods and steps involved in a dive. It
tells the reader how to experience the thrill of the sport and still be
safe.

Olgin, Joseph. **Illustrated Football Dictionary for Young People.** Illus.
Larry Sutton. Harvey House, Publishers, 1975. 125 pp.

Most of the technical terms used in the modern game of football
are defined and illustrated clearly and simply in this book. Included
is a list of some of the greatest players of all time, with a short
biographical sketch provided for each name.

Olney, Ross R. **Illustrated Auto Racing Dictionary for Young People.**
Illus. David Ross. Harvey House, Publishers, 1978. 125 pp.

Stock car, Formula One, and Indy 500 are among the types of
racing represented in this dictionary. Both racing terms and general
automotive vocabulary are included and illustrated.

Olney, Ross R. **Modern Racing Cars.** E. P. Dutton, 1978. 98 pp.

Second only to soccer with fans throughout the world is the sport
of auto racing. This is a sport that has changed much since its early
days. Fourteen different types of race cars and their special capa-
bilities are described in this introductory book. It also tells something about the men and women who are recognized as outstanding
race car drivers. Photographs.

Orlick, Terry. **The Cooperative Sports and Games Book: Challenge
without Competition.** Photographs by Ron and Terry Orlick.
Pantheon Books, 1978. 129 pp.

The idea behind this book is simple: people should play together,
not against each other. To show you how enjoyable and challenging
this can be, the author has created and collected over 100 new
games based on cooperation, not competition. There are games for
people of any age and ability, from preschoolers to senior citizens.
There are games here that can be played in the gym, on the beach,
in the swimming pool, around the playground, in the classroom, in
the backyard, or even in the living room. The instructions are clearly
written, and the games require no fancy or expensive equipment.

Owens, Jesse (editor Dick O'Connor). **Track and Field.** Atheneum Publishers, 1979. 120 pp.

Jesse Owens, the 1936 Olympic track star, explains basic training exercises for young athletes. He also gives tips on how to improve performance in the different track and field events.

Parker, Kathryn. **We Won Today: My Season with the Mets.** Photographs by Chester Higgins, Jr. Doubleday & Co., 1977. 212 pp.

By living with the Mets day by day for a whole season at Shea Stadium during the 1970s, the author is able to reveal firsthand information about the players and those working with them. The men at first resented this young woman's invasion into their private world. But then they began to tolerate her, to trust her, and even to like her. She, meanwhile, grew to love them as a family. This book describes her time with the Mets as she watches each player and how he operates, explores the coaches' and the wives' views, and provides verbal sketches of Bruce Boisclair, Bud Harrelson, Tug McGraw, and Ron Swoboda.

Paulsen, Gary. **Sailing: From Jibs to Jibing.** Illus. Ruth Wright Paulsen. Julian Messner, 1981. 159 pp.

It is surprising how easy it is to sail a small boat. After you learn a few basic rules of sailing, you are ready for the thrill of skimming across the water, powered only by the wind. This book includes all the basic elements of the sport, from learning the parts of a boat to fine tuning it for best performance.

Penzler, Otto. **Hang Gliding: Riding the Wind.** Troll Associates, 1976. 32 pp.

The fundamentals of the exciting sport of hang gliding can actually be learned in a single day. The lessons and safety precautions provided in this book give anyone a chance to glide through the air like a bird. There are also photographs to explain the details of this airborne activity. Easy reading.

Pezzano, Chuck, and Herm Weiskopf. **Sports Illustrated Bowling.** Photographs by Heinz Kluetmeir. Harper & Row, Publishers, 1981. 129 pp.

Bowling is one sport that people of all ages and abilities can enjoy equally. This is a comprehensive, fully illustrated handbook of the fundamentals of the approach, the release, and scorekeeping. The book also covers the more complex geometry of making spares.

Phillips, Betty Lou. **Go! Fight! Win! The National Cheerleaders Association Guide for Cheerleaders.** Photographs by Francis Shepard. Delacorte Press, 1981. 243 pp.

All the tips that anyone would ever need to be a good cheerleader are contained in this guide. Details of what to expect at a tryout session are given, as are ideas for creating cheers. Hints on posture, dress, and attitude are also provided for future spirit-rousers.

Phillips, Louis. **Baseball: Records, Stars, Feats, and Facts.** Illus. Paul Frame. Harcourt Brace Jovanovich, 1979. 174 pp.

Such famous baseball players as Reggie Jackson, Mickey Mantle, Pete Rose, Willie Mays, Stan Musial, Babe Ruth, and Ted Williams are featured in this book. Also included are records for batting, base stealing, and fielding. In addition, there is a section dealing with records for the worst in baseball, such as the most errors by a team or a player. Easy reading.

Phillips, Louis, and Arnie Markoe. **Football: Records, Stars, Feats, and Facts.** Illus. Paul Frame. Harcourt Brace Jovanovich, 1979. 172 pp.

This book focuses on famous football players, including George Blanda, Terry Bradshaw, Jim Brown, Dick Butkus, Earl Campbell, Bob Griese, Vince Lombardi, Joe Namath, Gale Sayers, O. J. Simpson, Bart Starr, and Fran Tarkenton. In a section on records, facts, and feats, there is statistical information about such achievements as the most points scored by one player, the most points scored in one game, and the most passes attempted and caught. Also of interest are the history of early football teams and little-known facts such as the sources of football players' nicknames.

Phillips, Louis, and Karen Markoe. **Women in Sports: Records, Stars, Feats, and Facts.** Illus. Paul Frame. Harcourt Brace Jovanovich, 1979. 174 pp.

After a brief introduction about women in the history of sports, this book provides biographical sketches of some famous women athletes: Nadia Comaneci, Chris Evert Lloyd, Peggy Fleming, Wilma Rudolph, Babe Zaharias, Nancy Lopez, Miki King, Olga Korbut, Althea Gibson, Sonja Henie, and Dorothy Hamill. There are also records and statistics provided for many international and Olympic sports. Easy reading.

Prestidge, Pauline. **Better Gymnastics.** Photographs by Jim Prestidge. Plays, 1979. 91 pp.

In this book, the former coach of the British national gymnastics team discusses how to develop basic and advanced gymnastics skills. Step-by-step directions and pictures help to show the correct postures and positions for each movement.

Roberts, David. **Deborah: A Wilderness Narrative.** Vanguard Press, 1970. 188 pp.

A 1964 mountaineering expedition undertaken by the author and his best friend to the eastern side of Mount Deborah in Alaska is the basis for this story of adventure and friendship. This detailed account of the treacherous climb is really the story of one person's dependence on another. Their difficult journey up a mountain also made the climbers see themselves differently. Photographs.

Rosen, Charles. **Players and Pretenders: The Basketball Team That Couldn't Shoot Straight.** Holt, Rinehart & Winston, 1981. 305 pp.

Everyone has heard of the basketball teams of UCLA, North Carolina, and Kentucky. But what about the one at Bard College? Bard College is a small liberal arts college in upstate New York, and it is not by any means an athletic powerhouse. When the author agreed to coach their team in 1979, he was not prepared for the motley group of individuals with various degrees of skills who made up the team. This book is a diary of the 1979-1980 season, which saw Rosen lead his team to a hilarious, yet educational, record of one win and sixteen losses. It is a bittersweet account of a group of young men learning that winning is not everything.

Rosenbloom, Joseph. **Sports Riddles.** Illus. Sam Q. Weissman. Harcourt Brace Jovanovich, 1982. 64 pp.

Why are baseball pitchers good at making flapjacks? Because they know their batter. This book is full of riddles that involve such favorite sports as baseball, football, and basketball. But you don't have to be a sports lover to be amused by these riddles. So learn a few, and pass them along to your friends.

Ryan, Frank. **Jumping for Joy.** Illus. Elizabeth T. Hall. Charles Scribner's Sons, 1980. 59 pp.

At track and field events around the world, only four jumps are featured: the high jump, the pole vault, the long jump, and the triple jump. The author, a former athlete and coach, provides the history of each jump and points out techniques that develop skills in them. For example, poles for pole vaulting were originally made of bamboo; these then gave way to metal ones. However, since the Olympic Games in Rome in 1960, fiberglass poles have been used.

Savitt, Sam. **One Horse, One Hundred Miles, One Day.** Illus. by author. Dodd, Mead & Co., 1981. 90 pp.

The Tevis Cup Endurance Ride in Squaw Valley, California, is the toughest and most demanding ride in the world. Every year more than 200 contestants try to complete the 100 rough miles within the twenty-four hour limit. Follow along on this ride through the High Sierras and meet the men, women, and horses who compete.

Savitz, Harriet May. **Wheelchair Champions: A History of Wheelchair Sports.** Photographs by Jim McGowan. Thomas Y. Crowell Co., 1978. 117 pp.

Lou Neishlom, Mike Demsy, and Darlene Ziunlan are all exceptional athletes. But it is not any ordinary sport that they excel in. They are champions of wheelchair sports, which include such events as archery, bowling, basketball, and track. This book describes the hard work and the tough conditioning of these courageous wheelchair heroes, and their struggle to achieve their sports dream.

Scagnetti, Jack. **Bicycle Motocross.** E. P. Dutton, 1976. 100 pp.

Here is just about everything you need to know to get involved in the relatively new sport of bicycle motocross racing, which involves racing by bike across rugged, hilly terrains. The author includes information on buying the various parts of the bicycle to assemble yourself, maintaining the bike in racing condition, and getting races started in your area. Also provided in the book are safety tips, racing tricks that can make you a winner, and the rules of the sport. Photographs.

Scagnetti, Jack. **Soccer.** Harvey House, Publishers, 1978. 54 pp.

Soccer may be the world's most popular sport. It is played in 140 countries by more than 250 million registered players. This book discusses the history of soccer from its beginnings in ancient Rome, field and equipment requirements, playing the game, learning basic skills, selecting playing positions, and the importance of team play. Photographs. Easy reading.

Shapiro, Neal, and Steve Lehrman. **The World of Horseback Riding.** Atheneum Publishers, 1976. 99 pp.

This nontechnical book introduces the new rider to pleasure riding, jumping, showing, and maintaining a horse. It also explores the different types of horses and how to select equipment for each. There is also advice on how to ride, with regular practice suggested to gain new skills and sharpen old ones.

Slocombe, Lorna. **Sailing Basics.** Illus. Art Seiden. Photographs by Vick Owens. Prentice-Hall, 1982. 48 pp.

Who hasn't wished at one time or another for a sailboat to skim across the water? This book discusses the history of sailing, then goes on to reveal how to develop an understanding of wind and water. A short course on how to sail is also included, as are mention of water traffic rules and proper sailing clothes. Photographs.

Smith, Don. **Surfing, the Big Wave.** Troll Associates, 1976. 32 pp.

Information about surfing language and methods, along with some action photographs, makes this an excellent introduction to surfing. This is one sport where excitement and danger combine to create a challenging situation for the athlete. Easy reading.

Solomon, Abbot Neil. **Secrets of the Super Athletes: Baseball.** Laurel-Leaf Library, 1982. 128 pp.

What's the secret to Dodger pitcher Fernando Valenzuela's screwball? Why does Yankee Dave Winfield swing a sledgehammer in the on-deck circle? How did a radar gun and a stopwatch make Expos rookie Tim Raines one of the best base stealers in the league? From the first pitch to the last out, learn the secrets and inside tips of baseball—from the stars themselves.

Solomon, Abbot Neil. **Secrets of the Super Athletes: Football.** Laurel-Leaf Library, 1982. 128 pp.

What makes Earl Campbell the most talked-about running back? Why does superstar Walter Payton think twice before taking on Mean Joe Green one-to-one? What is Dave Jennings's secret for making every punt count? Learn these and other secrets and tips from professional football stars.

Stambler, Irwin. **Racing the Sprint Cars.** G. P. Putnam's Sons, 1979. 127 pp.

Although sprint cars don't have the power of dragsters, the flowing lines of Indy 500 cars, or the raw speed of stock cars, sprint car racing provides thrills for millions around the country. The author describes setting up and driving sprint cars, as well as information about some of the world famous racers who started in the sprints. Photographs.

Sullivan, George. **Better Basketball for Boys.** Dodd, Mead & Co., 1980. 64 pp.

Basketball continues to be one of the most popular sports in America today for both boys and girls. This book explains all aspects of the game, beginning with the basics of dribbling, passing, and shooting. Other sections of the book illustrate jump-ball situations, rebounding, footwork, and the free throw. The book concludes with a discussion of game strategy, offensive and defensive skills, and practice drills. Photographs.

Sullivan, George. **Better Field Events for Girls.** Dodd, Mead & Co., 1982. 63 pp.

One of the reasons that records in women's field events are being established so frequently is that training methods have vastly improved. This book illustrates techniques for the long jump, high jump, discus, shot put, triple jump, and javelin. Included are instructions for conditioning and a list of the current records for the various field events.

Sweeney, Karen O'Connor. **Illustrated Tennis Dictionary for Young People.** Illus. David Ross. Harvey House, Publishers, 1979. 125 pp.

All the tennis terms from *ace* to *zoning* are defined simply and clearly by the author. Short biographies of some of the most famous tennis players are included. So, if you are planning to join the ranks of Chris Evert Lloyd and Jimmy Connors, it might help to check the information in this book first.

Swinburne, Laurence, and Irene Swinburne. **America's First Football Game.** Illus. June Gallagher. Contemporary Perspectives, 1978. 48 pp.

This book traces football in America to the first college game in 1869 between Princeton and Rutgers. The book also discusses football's similarity to rugby and soccer, along with describing gradual changes in the game and the big reorganization of rules in 1906 after eighteen young men died as a result of football injuries. Easy reading.

Traetta, John, and Mary Jean Traetta (editor Arvid Knudsen). **Gymnastics Basics.** Illus. Bill Gow. Photographs by Don Carter. Prentice-Hall, 1979. 64 pp.

Exercises and body movements for gymnastics are explained and illustrated in this book. Floor exercises, vaults, the uneven and horizontal bars, balance beam, pommel horse, parallel bars, and still-ring exercises are also described so the beginner can understand the basic elements of gymnastic events.

Tretyak, Vladislav (with V. Snegirev; translator Anatole Konstantin). **The Hockey I Love.** Lawrence Hill & Co., 1977. 189 pp.

The author, a Soviet athlete who is possibly the greatest goalie in hockey, gives his impressions of North American hockey, especially its players and the way they differ from their Soviet counterparts. Tretyak describes the Soviet love of sporting competition in hockey players of different ages and ability levels and suggests that their eagerness for competition is the reason for the many victories of Soviet teams. Photographs.

Turner, Stephen C. **Great Beginnings: Olympics to Super Bowl to World Series to . . . .** Julian Messner, 1981. 64 pp.

Have you ever wondered how the Olympics got started? How about the World Series? The Rose Bowl? Find out more about these and other great "firsts" in sports. Look at the old photographs and see what these contests were really like in the beginning. Easy reading.

Ullyot, Joan L. **Running Free: A Book for Women Runners and Their Friends.** G. P. Putnam's Sons, 1980. 288 pp.

The author, a world-class marathoner, answers all kinds of questions women runners might ask. For example, women can begin running at any age and often record their best times as they get older. She also discusses the newest developments in training and equipment, how running affects your whole life, and the difference between male and female runners.

Van Steenwyk, Elizabeth. **Illustrated Skating Dictionary for Young People.** Illus. David Ross. Harvey House, Publishers, 1979. 123 pp.

The terminology of ice skating, roller skating, and skate boarding is listed and defined in this illustrated dictionary. The author indicates when the various terms are used in more than one field of skating.

Van Steenwyk, Elizabeth. **Stars on Ice.** Dodd, Mead & Co., 1980. 140 pp.

What does it take to be a world champion figure skater? After reading the stories of the men and women in this book, you will begin to understand that it takes someone willing to sacrifice social life, education, and even family for a day-to-day, year-in, year-out schedule of practice and training. Is it worth it? All skaters have their own ideas. Some of the ice stars included here are Scott Cramer, Dorothy Hamill, Charles Tickner, and Linda Fratianne. Photographs.

Walker, Henry. **Illustrated Hockey Dictionary for Young People.** Illus.
Frank Baginski. Harvey House, Publishers, 1976. 125 pp.

In this book, the technical vocabulary of ice hockey is clearly
explained, and it is illustrated with drawings. Also included here are
listings of Stanley Cup winners and Hall of Fame players.

Weber, Bruce. **All-Pro Basketball Stars, 1979.** Scholastic Book Services,
1979. 89 pp.

This book covers recent information about the teams of professional
basketball. Among the material presented is data on the 1978 all-
pro team, the 1978 all-rookie team, and the 1977-78 standings,
1977-78 general statistics, and the team rosters of NBA teams.
Although some changes in team personnel have taken place since
this book was published, there is still valuable material here. Of
particular interest are the photographs and short informational
sections on such stars as Julius Erving, Walter Davis, Bill Walton,
Kareem Abdul-Jabbar, David Thompson, Pete Maravich, and
George Gervin.

Williams, Lee Ann. **Basic Field Hockey Strategy: An Introduction for
Young Players.** Illus. John Lane. Doubleday & Co., 1978. 105 pp.

The clear, complete, and illustrated descriptions in this guide make
the strategies for playing field hockey easy to follow. Now a game
largely for girls and women in this country, field hockey is a game
with ancient beginnings and a worldwide popularity. To play field
hockey well involves an understanding of the terminology and
equipment, a knowledge of each player's position and responsibility,
and an awareness of offensive and defensive techniques. This book
will help you develop the effective playing methods that can bring
both tangible and intangible rewards to the team and to each player.

Yannis, Alex. **Soccer Basics.** Illus. Bill Gow. Prentice-Hall, 1982. 47 pp.

This book provides a brief history of soccer and a clear explanation
of how it is played, its regulations, and methods of scoring the
game. Basic individual skills are also emphasized. Giorgio Chinaglia,
forward of the New York Cosmos, has written the introduction.
Black-and-white photographs capture various moments of soccer
action.

Zeleznak, Shirley. **Backpacking.** Crestwood House, 1980. 31 pp.

Backpacking is an individual or group outdoor sport that can be
done by nearly anyone, at nearly any time of year, in nearly any

place, and for nearly any length of time. Before undertaking back-packing as a project, though, the novice must learn about the various aspects of the sport such as gathering the necessary equipment, choosing proper clothing, selecting kinds of foods to use, planning routes, deciding the most effective way to walk, and memorizing some rules for safety. When you prepare for back-packing properly, it can be an exhilarating experience that is a test of both body and spirit.

Witchcraft, Magic, and the Occult

Avent, Sue. **Spells, Chants, and Potions.** Contemporary Perspectives, 1977. 48 pp.

The forms of magic from spells of ancient Egypt, to African voodoo, to American Indian chants are described in this book. A brief history of magic with specific examples explains why certain people believe in magic. There is also a recipe book of magic spells provided here, including a love spell, a spell to make money, and a good luck spell. Photographs. Easy reading.

Berger, Melvin. **The Supernatural: From ESP to UFOs.** John Day Co., 1977. 117 pp.

The author, who has written over thirty books, has interviewed many people who have experienced or seen unusual events. Chapters in this book deal with ESP, parapsychology, astrology, psychokinesis, spiritualism, faith healing, witchcraft, and UFOs. Also included are lists of books of interest in the area of the supernatural and addresses of groups to which you can write for further information on the subject.

Branley, Franklyn M. **Age of Aquarius: You and Astrology.** Illus. Leonard Kessler. Thomas Y. Crowell Co., 1979. 59 pp.

Are you fated to be a world leader? A world traveler? A scientist, tycoon, or doctor? This book covers the subject of astrology, which teaches that by knowing the date and time of your birth, you can tell many things about your personality and your destiny. The history of astrology and tips on making and reading your own astrological charts are included in the book. Easy reading.

Cashion, Cathy. **Card and Coin Tricks.** Illus. Pat Lee. Golden Press, 1977. 48 pp.

Ever wonder how magicians could guess what card you were holding? Or how they could pull a coin from your ear? This book explains simple card and coin tricks. Easy directions and illustrations also help you learn these tricks yourself. The coin tricks described include such tricks as "The Disappearing Dime" and "The Nine-Cent Surprise."

Cashion, Cathy. **Magic.** Illus. Sally Shimizu. Golden Press, 1977. 48 pp.

Here are instructions for a number of easy magic tricks. These tricks require little practice and few materials. One simple trick discussed is how to make a word disappear. All that is needed for this trick are pencils, paper, and glue. Another interesting trick is called "The Water Charmer," where you turn over a water bottle without spilling a drop.

Cohen, Daniel. **Ceremonial Magic.** Four Winds Press, 1979. 152 pp.

Magic practiced as a part of some kind of ritual is considered ceremonial magic. In this book ceremonial magic is explored as it relates to the ancient Egyptians, demons, crime, black magic, and the Faust legend. Also included is an examination of the question of the purpose of magic.

Cohen, Daniel. **Everything You Need to Know about Monsters and Still Be Able to Get to Sleep.** Illus. Jack Stokes. Doubleday & Co., 1981. 118 pp.

Monsters have terrified and excited people for centuries. Horror films and novels starring vampires and werewolves continue to attract huge audiences ready to be scared. This book contains information about all types of monsters, including mummies, artificial men, sea creatures, and beasts that roam the land. The book covers the topic from historical, fictional, and scientific perspectives.

Cohen, Daniel. **Ghostly Terrors.** Dodd, Mead & Co., 1981. 126 pp.

Thirteen supposedly true tales of ghostly terror have been collected in this book. They include the stories of a strange woman in black on a railway car, a corpse missing from the mortuary, and a haunted submarine. Photographs and drawings. Easy reading.

Cohen, Daniel. **The Great Airship Mystery: A UFO of the 1890s.** Dodd, Mead & Co., 1981. 212 pp.

Could there have been an airship seven years before the Wright brothers' *Kitty Hawk*? Tens of thousands of people in the United States reported seeing a mysterious airship cruising overhead between November 1896 and May 1897. Newspaper explanations ranged from hoaxes to a widespread belief in spaceships from other worlds. Could this be related to the continuing mystery of the UFOs today?

Cohen, Daniel. **Young Ghosts.** E. P. Dutton, 1978. 84 pp.

> Children and young people see ghosts with surprising frequency. Often there *are* ghosts. In Europe, for example, there are the strange legends of the Radiant Boys, ghosts who appear surrounded by a glowing flame or light. And in America, there is the tale of the talkative Bell Witch, who troubled a family in Tennessee in 1817. She slapped faces, pulled hair, and threw things around violently. All the stories in this book are true in the sense that someone somewhere believed them. You can decide for yourself whether to believe them or not.

Dolan, Edward F., Jr. **The Complete Beginner's Guide to Magic.** Doubleday & Co., 1977. 148 pp.

> You don't have to know witchcraft to do magic tricks—all it takes is time to learn and to practice. Those willing to spend the time can do magic tricks that make them the hit of a party. This guide explains and illustrates puzzle and game magic, stunt magic, string and silk magic, coin magic, and mind magic. It also provides some advanced sleight of hand and more complicated equipment tricks.

Dolan, Edward F., Jr. **Let's Make Magic.** Photographs by Jay Irving. Doubleday & Co., 1981. 95 pp.

> Have you ever wondered how magicians perform their tricks? Have you ever wanted to make magic yourself? Here you'll find step-by-step instructions to mystify your family and friends with all kinds of card, coin, and number tricks. You will even be able to convince them that you can see right through a solid object! Easy reading.

Edmonds, I. G. **D. D. Home: The Man Who Talked with Ghosts.** Thomas Nelson, 1978. 182 pp.

> Was Daniel Douglas Home truly in contact with the spirit world? Or was he just a very clever fraud? He was the most famous medium of the nineteenth century, and he never accepted payment for his services. He was never caught trying to fool anyone, and many strange things happened during his séances. Did Home really have occult powers?

Edmonds, I. G. **The Kings of Black Magic.** Holt, Rinehart & Winston, 1981. 192 pp.

> Black magic, according to this author, is science of the occult, and many of the "magicians" were sincere scientists as well as evil men. Among the most famous of these practitioners of black magic were Johann Faust, John Dee (magician to Queen Elizabeth I), Paracelsus

(a great healer), author Edward Bulwer-Lytton, Emperor Julian, and Aleister Crowley, known as the wickedest man in the world. All tried to use magic to find hidden secrets. Photographs.

Edmonds, I. G. **The Magic Makers: Magic and the Men Who Made It.** Thomas Nelson, 1976. 188 pp.

Everyone thinks of the name Houdini first when thinking of people involved in magic. But there were many other people who experimented with magic throughout history: the priests of Egypt; Roger Bacon, the scientist; the Herrmann brothers; Pinetti, who made his own head vanish; and Von Kempelen, who built the extraordinary Chess Player. This book not only discusses these people's acts, but it even explains how some of their tricks were developed.

Edmonds, I. G. **Second Sight: People Who Read the Future.** Thomas Nelson, 1977. 160 pp.

This book discusses people who have an ability to see into the future. Included are the prophets of old, the snake women of Delphi, Nostradamus, Cheiro, Edgar Cayce, Jeanne Dixon, and even contemporary science fiction writers. Can they really foresee what will happen?

Garden, Nancy. **Devils and Demons.** J. B. Lippincott Co., 1976. 160 pp.

Did you know that some Chinese demons live in furniture? People of all ages and from all parts of the world have believed in devils and demons. They've blamed these demons for all kinds of human and natural catastrophes, from crop failure to human illness. This book looks at popular beliefs about demons and gives many accounts of odd events that are related to a devilish source. For example, Cootchie is a disease demon of Australia who must be chased away by whacking the earth with a kangaroo tail, while Pretas is a Siamese hunger demon twelve miles tall but invisible because it is so thin.

Gilbert, George, and Wendy Rydell. **Great Tricks of the Master Magicians.** Golden Press, 1977. 160 pp.

From this book the beginning magician can learn how to make handkerchiefs disappear, how to read a closed book, or how to escape after being tied in ropes. Over 150 magic tricks are explained in detail and with complete illustrations. Emphasis is placed on practicing tricks to present convincing illusions. Although the reader won't learn the secrets of levitation or sawing people in half, this book does reveal the mysteries behind some of the other fascinating feats of magic.

Gross, Henry. **Pure Magic! The Sleight-of-Hand Book of Dazzling Tricks and Captivating Routines.** Charles Scribner's Sons, 1978. 225 pp.

Perform magic tricks that will amaze your family and friends. An experienced magician explains how to create illusions by describing and illustrating methods for practicing and presenting sleight-of-hand tricks with cards, coins, bits of cloth, and other common objects.

Hoffman, Elizabeth P. **This House Is Haunted!** Contemporary Perspectives, 1977. 48 pp.

A woman dreams of a house she has never seen; two years later her family discover the same house for sale, so they buy it. But then strange things begin to occur and the family start to believe the house is haunted. Soon a strange woman who looks like a ghost appears in the night. A psychic comes to visit the house and claims the ghost is real. Then stranger events occur. What is going on exactly? This book makes some interesting guesses about the spirit in this haunted house.

Houdini's Book of Magic. Corwin Books, 1976. 110 pp.

The balanced quarter, growing flowers instantly, vanishing water, obedient matches, putting an egg in a bottle, the mystic banana. All are magic tricks described and illustrated in this book. The first half features tricks performed by the famous magician Harry Houdini. Other magicians' tricks are presented in the second half.

Hunter, Norman. **The Wizard Book of Magic.** Illus. Jill McDonald. Sterling Publishing Co., 1978. 127 pp.

Magic looks easy when someone else does it, but the truth is that magic takes knowledge, skill, and lots of practice. But anyone can perform magic who really wants to do it and is willing to work at it. This book gives general advice about doing magic tricks before showing the reader ways to do tricks with ordinary and extraordinary things. The author promises that those who practice magic regularly will become good enough to trick anyone.

Klein, Aaron E. **Science and the Supernatural: A Scientific Overview of the Occult.** Doubleday & Co., 1979. 184 pp.

This book presents a factually based analysis of the subjects of the occult and the supernatural. The chapters include stories and legends of the possessed, the obsessed, vampires, werewolves, witchcraft, and astrology. Photographs.

Kristos, Kyle. **Voodoo.** J. B. Lippincott Co., 1976. 113 pp.

Voodoo is an intriguing and mysterious practice that is feared and misunderstood. Some people believe that it is simply superstitious silliness, while others believe that voodoo is an evil devil cult associated with black magic. Actually, voodoo is a major religion practiced by eight million people on the island of Haiti alone. It is a religion concerned with all aspects of daily life, as well as with death and the afterlife. The book separates the facts from the fiction about voodoo. Illustrations.

Lamb, Geoffrey. **Table Tricks.** Thomas Nelson, 1975. 86 pp.

Magic is really of two types: professional or formal, and amateur or informal. The tricks in this collection are informal; they can be performed with very little preparation. These tricks will appear to be thought up on the spur of the moment and they can be performed with everyday objects. Mastering these tricks is easy, and they will make it possible for you to turn any occasion into a mystifying experience. Originally published as *Your Book of Table Tricks.*

Laycock, George. **Mysteries, Monsters and Untold Secrets.** Doubleday & Co., 1978. 158 pp.

Does the Lost Dutchman Gold Mine really exist out there in the Superstition Mountains of the southwestern United States? Hundreds of people believe it's there, but so far no one has found it. What, if anything, is buried on tiny Oak Island in Nova Scotia? Since digging began more than two hundred years ago, people have unearthed wooden platforms every ten feet—nothing more. Is there really a Loch Ness monster? A Bigfoot? A Big Bird of Texas? Why do so many ships and planes disappear in the Bermuda Triangle? The author talks about these and many more riddles that puzzle even the experts.

O'Connell, Margaret F. **The Magic Cauldron: Witchcraft for Good and Evil.** S.G. Phillips, 1976. 192 pp.

Witchcraft has long been linked with evil. But there is evidence to suggest that many witches were good and that many of their beneficial contributions to past civilizations have been glossed over or forgotten. The witch was often a healer of the common people, but her brews could also kill. What did witches really do? Do they still exist? Read about the witch as earth mother, the witch in ancient Greece and Rome, burning witches at the stake, witches and the devil in seventeenth-century politics, the witch hunt in Salem, and witches of yesterday, today, and tomorrow.

Polansky, Joseph. **Sun Sign Success: Your Astrological Pathway to Better Living.** Destiny Books, 1977. 221 pp.

If you believe in astrology, you will want to read this book so you can better use your sun-sign knowledge in areas such as finance, business, and communication. The book also tells you how to use astrology to prevent being victimized by consumer frauds. The basic purpose of this work is to help you use the positive aspects of your astrological sign, while turning any negative aspects of the sign into strengths.

Reed, Graham. **Magic for Every Occasion.** Illus. Dennis Patten. Elsevier/ Nelson Books, 1981. 110 pp.

Magic seems to be appropriate for many occasions, from a business meeting to a dinner party. This book contains valuable clues about how and when to perform magic tricks and what tricks to perform. The magic discussed includes gags, tricks with cards, impromptu tricks for friends, tested trickery, and many more. Tips for collecting props are also provided.

Reiff, Stephanie Ann. **Visions of the Future: Magic Numbers and Cards.** Contemporary Perspectives, 1977. 48 pp.

With this book you will learn about the power of cards and numbers. For example, by following step-by-step instructions, you will learn how to find a person's "Personality Number." And did you know that by using the numbers in your name, you can discover interesting information about your present and future? The last section of the book discusses tarot cards, a special deck of cards used to predict good and bad things about people's lives. Various tarot cards are illustrated by photographs and charts. Easy reading.

Roberts, Nancy. **Southern Ghosts.** Photographs by Bruce Roberts. Doubleday & Co., 1979. 70 pp.

Phantom stallions? Ex-president Jimmy Carter's mansion haunted? A bracelet turns into poisonous beetles? Mysterious deaths of six husbands? These thirteen well-known Southern ghost stories are accompanied by black-and-white photographs of the areas of the hauntings or of the ghostly appearances. Did the events really happen? Easy reading.

Sarnoff, Jane, and Reynold Ruffins. **Take Warning: A Book of Superstitions.** Charles Scribner's Sons, 1978. 159 pp.

There have been superstitions as long as there have been people. They probably are among the oldest form of human thought, and they are an important part of folklore. This book, arranged in alphabetical order, reveals that there is not much in life that escapes being touched by superstitions.

Simon, editor. **The Necronomicon.** Avon Books, 1977. 218 pp.

This is a reproduction of an ancient book of chants, charms, and incantations. It is filled with myths and rituals that supposedly can evoke incredible beings, demons, and monsters. Accompanying this text is a complete explanation of terms, comparison charts, notes on pronunciations—and words of warning!

Simon, Seymour. **Strange Mysteries from around the World.** Four Winds Press, 1980. 58 pp.

This book contains ten mysteries that are true: frogs and fish rain down from the skies; an entire ship's crew disappears; a crystal Indian skull seems to have strange qualities and powers; human fire walkers are not burned or injured. Black-and-white photographs accompany each story, and possible explanations for the strange events are offered. Easy reading.

Stadtmauer, Saul A. **Visions of the Future: Magic Boards.** Contemporary Perspectives, 1977. 48 pp.

Magic boards, often called Ouija boards, contain numbers and letters, and some people claim you can contact the spirits of the dead by using such boards. This book discusses some people who reportedly have reached spirits in this manner and presents a short history of how Ouija boards have been used. The book also shows you how you can make your own magic board and provides sample questions for use in an attempt at discovering information about the future by magic board. Easy reading.

Thorne, Ian. **The Loch Ness Monster.** Crestwood House, 1979. 47 pp.

This is one of a series of books on mysterious subjects like the Loch Ness Monster, Bigfoot, and the Bermuda Triangle. The truth that is known about each monster or strange place and the stories that have been told about it are covered in each book. In this book, the history of "Nessie," a prehistoric creature who is supposed to be residing in a lake in Scotland, is covered in detail.

Watson, Jane Werner, and Sol Chaneles. **The Golden Book of the Mysterious.** Illus. Alan Lee. Golden Press, 1976. 144 pp.

This book is designed as an encyclopedia that treats the strange and weird in certain categories: creatures of mystery, mysterious powers of mind and spirit, mysteries science cannot explain, witchcraft and the occult, and mysterious disappearances. The selections are all short, easy to read, and accompanied by colorful illustrations.

White, Carol Hellings. **Holding Hands: The Complete Guide to Palmistry.** Illus. Susan Swan. G. P. Putnam's Sons, 1980. 157 pp.

Here is just about everything you will need to know to read your fortune by the lines in the palm of your hand. Perhaps after you reveal the secrets of your own lifeline, you can ask for a volunteer among your family and friends. Many diagrams and pictures make it easy to master this ancient form of fortune-telling.

White, Laurence B., Jr., and Ray Broekel. **The Surprise Book.** Illus. Will Winslow. Doubleday & Co., 1981. 87 pp.

Would you like to know how to hypnotize a handkerchief, or make a wastebasket produce strange sounds, or be a fortune-teller? If so, this book will show you how to do these and seventy other tricks and practical jokes.

Wilcox, Tamara. **Bats, Cats, and Sacred Cows.** Contemporary Perspectives, 1977. 48 pp.

The topic of this book is seemingly unexplainable animal behavior, especially acts of unusual loyalty to and friendship with humans. This is just one title in a series of books on the occult and the unusual. In each, the author discusses the history of the topic, how it is regarded in today's world, the misconceptions that surround it, and the facts. When appropriate, how-to instructions are given. Other titles in the series include *Palm Reading, The Magic and Meaning of Voodoo, Black Cats and Other Superstitions,* and *Ghosts and Ghouls.* Easy reading.

Williams, Selma R., and Pamela J. Williams. **Riding the Nightmare: Women and Witchcraft.** Atheneum Publishers, 1978. 208 pp.

Most people have heard of the Salem Witch Trials of 1692. This book shows that from the late Middle Ages until the Salem trials, witchcraft was believed in and was used as a reason for persecuting women. Chapters contain legends, myth, folklore, history, and politics that show the relationship of women, witchcraft, and the loss of power. Illustrations. Mature reading and subject matter.

Information Please

Asimov, Isaac. **How Did We Find Out about Comets?** Illus. David Wool. Camelot Books, 1981. 64 pp.

The ancient Greeks called comets "hairy stars." To the superstitious of all centuries, they were a sign of bad times. Modern scientists continue to be fascinated by these spectacular objects. This book provides a history of famous comets and tells about some of the scientists who first spotted them. It also explains what comets are made of and why they act as they do. Easy reading.

Aylward, Jim. **Things No One Ever Tells You.** Warner Books, 1981. 140 pp.

Here is a collection of hundreds of humorous and little-known facts from throughout history and from around the world. Did you know that in ancient Arabia people who took baths regularly didn't have to pay taxes? Or that George Washington died while taking his own pulse? Or that bus drivers in Johannesburg, South Africa, are given a bonus if they hit a hyena? Well, these are all true!

Barber, Richard. **A Companion to World Mythology.** Delacorte Press, 1979. 300 pp.

Arranged in alphabetical order are the names of mythological figures from all parts of the world, from the Irish Cuchulain to the Indian Ganesha. Along with many of the names are summaries of the tales in which the characters appear. Illustrations in black and white and in color line the sides of each page. Here you will find familiar names such as the Greek characters Jupiter and Penelope as well as new names, such as Payatamu (Navaho Indian), Itzli (Aztec), Isis (Egyptian), Gua (West African), and Sennin (Japanese).

Blackburn, Graham. **The Parts of a House.** Illus. by author. Richard Marek Publishers, 1980. 191 pp.

This book is an alphabetically arranged anatomy of a typical house described in words, pictures, and architectural drawings. The color-keyed drawings give a clear picture of how a house is put together, and they also help clarify the vocabulary that builders, designers, and inspectors use.

Brooks, Tim, and Earle Marsh. **The Complete Directory to Prime Time Network TV Shows, 1946-Present.** Ballantine Books, 1979. 848 pp.

How many seasons did "Gilligan's Island" run? Tim Conway appeared in eight different network shows. Can you name them? Name the original cast of "The Mod Squad." If you can't answer these questions and are a television fan, you need this guidebook. Facts and figures about virtually every network television show are listed, summarized, and discussed. Included in this book is a chart showing the networks' prime-time schedules for each year starting with 1946.

Brown, Fern G. **The Great Money Machine: How Your Bank Works.** Julian Messner, 1981. 96 pp.

Have you ever wondered what goes on behind the scenes at a bank? What happens to the money you put in your savings account? Here you'll learn all about banking—from vaults, to checking accounts, to the Federal Reserve System. Easy reading.

Calderone, Mary S., and Eric W. Johnson. **The Family Book about Sexuality.** Rev. ed. Illus. Vivien Cohen. Bantam Books, 1983. 367 pp.

This book answers the questions that most members of any family would have about sex. It includes chapters on how human sexual responses develop and work, human reproductive systems, family planning, marriage, sexual problems, and making sexual decisions.

Carter, David, editor. **The Dell Book of Super Winners.** Laurel-Leaf Library, 1982. 191 pp.

Who won the Grammy Award for Album of the Year in 1981? Who were the most popular soap opera stars? What sports awards were given? Who was Miss America? This annual listing of award winners from sports, film, literature, science, and fashion includes complete statistics and photographs.

Clarke, Joseph F. **Pseudonyms: The Names behind the Names.** Thomas Nelson, 1977. 247 pp.

Pseudonym means "false name," and this book contains a total of 3,499 such false names. Half the collection is made up of pen names of writers, one-third of the collection is stage names, and the rest belong to people in politics, sports, crime, painting, sculpture, and music. People usually take pseudonyms that seem more fitting to their occupation or that sound more glamorous. Others take pseudonyms to protect their real identity or even to avoid confusion with someone else who has a similar name. For example, Ellery Queen, the popular American mystery writer, was actually the pen name of two American lawyers, Manfred Lee and Frederic Dannay. Famous soccer player Pelé was born Edson Arantes do Nascimento, and movie star John Wayne was born Marion Morrison.

Foster, Robert. **The Complete Guide to Middle-Earth: From** *The Hobbit* **to** *The Silmarillion.* Del Rey Books, 1979. 575 pp.

This volume is an alphabetized glossary to the fantasy works of J.R.R. Tolkien. Every character, place, and unusual thing from *The Hobbit* to *The Silmarillion* is listed, discussed, and cross-referenced.

Funk and Wagnalls Standard Dictionary. Signet Books, 1980. 1,112 pp.

This is a very complete paperback dictionary that has 82,000 entries, including abbreviations, slang terms, and geographical names. Most entries include a pronunciation guide and an indication of the word's historical roots, in addition to a full definition.

Gentle, Ernest J., and Lawrence W. Reithmaier. **Aviation and Space Dictionary.** Aero Publishers, 1974. 272 pp.

Over 6,000 definitions and twenty pages of pictures and illustrations are included in this technical reference book. Terminology covering such areas as computer technology, meteorology, navigation, air traffic control, and astronomy is represented here.

Gots, Ronald, and Arthur Kaufman. **The People's Hospital Book.** Avon Books, 1981. 206 pp.

Most people feel conflicting emotions when they or someone they love is faced with a stay in the hospital. On one hand, there is comfort in knowing that experts are there with the best available technology. On the other hand, there is that fear of the unknown— of pain, discomfort, and perhaps even death. The best plan, then, is to learn everything possible about hospitals. This book is a guide to every phase of hospital care—even the food—from the day of admission to the day of release, and beyond that to paying the bill and arranging posthospital care.

Hagerman, Paul Stirling. **The Odd, Mad World of Paul Stirling Hagerman.** Illus. Arthur Friedman. Signet Books, 1981. 194 pp.

Did you know that some people cure a toothache by eating a mouse? That a can of foot powder was once elected to political office? That in Tibet it's polite to stick your tongue out at a guest? Truth *is* stranger than fiction! Hundreds of other unusual facts are presented in this book.

Harrison, David L. **What Do You Know! Mind-Boggling Questions! Astonishing Answers!** Illus. Rod Ruth. Rand McNally & Co., 1981. 255 pp.

This book asks you provocative questions—and it gives you the answers. Included are such questions as: Do all sharks live in the sea? Is Transylvania a real place? Who invented gum? and Can loud music damage our hearing? The answers may amaze you. There are many illustrations included that add to your enjoyment of the information in this book.

Heron House, editors. **The Odds on Virtually Everything.** G. P. Putnam's Sons, 1980. 319 pp.

If you like to bet on sure things, then here is the information you need. All the odds for and against a particular thing happening are listed in this book. Just about every subject is covered: money, work, play, accidents, and marriage, to name a few.

Jaffe, Evan. **Illustrated Ballet Dictionary.** Illus. Phyllis Lerner. Harvey House, Publishers, 1979. 128 pp.

After a brief history of ballet, this book explains the terms most frequently used in ballet. For example, *saute* means "jumped," so any direction for a movement followed by this word means the action must be performed in the air. Well-known composers like Igor Stravinsky, dancers like Edward Villella, and famous ballets like *Sleeping Beauty* are also included in the alphabetical list of ballet terms.

Kendig, Frank, and Richard Hutton. **Life Spans; or, How Long Things Last.** Holt, Rinehart & Winston, 1980. 265 pp.

How long do things last these days? This book takes all kinds of subjects—from jogging shoes to the scales on a fish—to determine how things age. The book also deals with human beings, plants, and weather phenomena, in terms of duration. Did you know that a tornado has a life span of about nine hours? Or that a football for a National Football League game lasts about six minutes of playing time? Or that the hair that extends beyond the surface of your scalp is already dead? You will discover much more fascinating life and death information in this book.

Lee, Kay, and Marshall Lee. **The Illuminated Book of Days.** Illus. Kate Greenaway and Eugene Grasset. G. P. Putnam's Sons, 1979. 213 pp.

Did you know that bees should be informed when a death occurs and be invited to the funeral? That in many parts of Europe May Day is Labor Day? Or that on January 20, St. Agnes's Eve, a girl who goes to sleep without supper will dream of the man she is to marry? Would you like a recipe for rosé wine? Any trivia buff will get hooked on this book—and so will anyone who loves fantasy, who likes to cook or to eat, or who needs to laugh. For every day of the year, the book is filled with a potpourri of facts and fun.

Leokum, Arkady. **The Curious Book.** Corwin Books, 1977. 256 pp.

We are all curious and wonder about certain things—even if we don't ask about them. This book is full of curious facts about people, places, and things of the world. Among other things, it tells you that you can eat hippopotamus, that boys between fifteen and nineteen are the chief victims of drowning, that sumo wrestlers in Japan usually weigh 300 pounds each, and that more people die in the United States in the months of January and February than in any of the other months. Photographs.

Lucaire, Edward. **Celebrity Trivia: A Collection of Little-Known Facts about Well-Known People.** Warner Books, 1980. 528 pp.

This book contains surprising information about movie stars, athletes, politicians, writers, and other public personalities. The material is aphabetized by name, and each entry provides facts that will keep you amazed.

Marsh, Dave, and John Swenson. **The *Rolling Stone* Record Guide.** Random House, 1979. 631 pp.

With the cost of record albums higher than ever, it's important to make wise choices at the store before you bring that hit record home and play it. This guide rates 10,000 currently available rock, soul, country, jazz, blues, and gospel albums. Each is rated from five stars to none. Included is a bibliography of books on rock music, a glossary of rock terms, and a separate list of 300 five-star albums that could make up a basic library of rock.

McCullough, Prudence, and Lowell Miller. **Shop New York by Mail.** Avon Books, 1981. 253 pp.

Interested in buying a custom suit of armor, or having a necktie restyled, or finding an antique fringed umbrella? There is only one place to look for such unusual things—New York City. And you don't have to live there to shop the great stores of the Big Apple. This book is a catalog of hundreds of stores and shops that offer special deals and hard-to-find services to the public by mail order. Also included in this book is some commonsense advice concerning buying through the mail.

McLachlan, Christopher A. B. **Inflation-Wise: How to Do Almost Everything for Less.** Avon Books, 1981. 244 pp.

With inflation eating away a greater and greater part of a person's salary or allowance each month, it is becoming even more important to be a wise consumer. This book is an encyclopedia of money-saving tips and information. What's the best way to negotiate for a used car? How can you save money on entertainment? Where can you get your clothing for less? Hundreds of questions like these are answered clearly and concisely throughout the book.

McWhirter, Norris, and Ross McWhirter. **Guinness Book of Amazing Achievements.** Illus. Kenneth Laager. Sterling Publishing Co., 1978. 95 pp.

This book of amazing records discusses seemingly impossible feats accomplished by human beings. Learn about all these achievements, from something as trivial as who has the longest fingernails in the world, to the hungriest sword swallower, the fastest woman on water skis, and the person who lifted the heaviest weight. Do you know who has the highest known IQ, or the name of the creator of the comic strip published for the longest period? What all these human achievements seem to demonstrate is that people have not yet reached the limits of what they can do.

McWhirter, Norris, and Ross McWhirter. **Guinness Book of Phenomenal Happenings.** Illus. Kenneth Laager. Sterling Publishing Co., 1978. 96 pp.

The authors actually checked every one of these unusual happenings in the twenty years they traveled the world in search of the astounding. The feats range from Mike Musselman devouring twenty-seven doughnuts in 7 minutes 16 seconds to become the doughnut-eating champion, to the greatest performer in Olympic history, pentathlon champion András Balczó of Hungary, who won six world titles and won gold medals in 1960, 1968, and 1972.

McWhirter, Norris, and Ross McWhirter. **Guinness Book of Startling Acts and Facts.** Illus. Kenneth Laager. Sterling Publishing Co., 1978. 95 pp.

Here is a collection of interesting and amazing facts about animals, inventions, events, and unusual people. Easy reading.

McWhirter, Norris, and Ross McWhirter. **Guinness Book of World Records: 1979 Edition.** Sterling Publishing Co., 1978. 704 pp.

The largest ball of string—the greatest number of children born to one mother—the longest toy balloon flight. Here is a new edition of world records. If you like to argue with your friends over the heaviest, the hottest, or the tallest, this book will help you find the correct answer. Incidentally, it is the fastest-selling book ever published.

McWhirter, Norris, and Ross McWhirter. **Guinness Book of Young Recordbreakers.** Illus. Kenneth Laager. Sterling Publishing Co., 1978. 96 pp.

This collection of record-breaking accomplishments indicates the creativity and stamina of young people. Each new record is illustrated, and each one is the achievement of a person who is younger than nineteen. You might find a record here you would like to break!

Merriam, Eve. **AB to ZOGG: A Lexicon for Science-Fiction and Fantasy Readers.** Illus. Al Lorenz. Atheneum Publishers, 1977. 41 pp.

This short book is full of fantasy, science fiction, and whimsy—all the way from *AB* (the abominable Abonaut) to *ZOGG* (the last world). Many more words used in fantasy and science fiction are defined and arranged in alphabetical order.

Miller, Victor. **The Book of Worries: Hundreds of Horrible Things That Can Happen to You.** Warner Books, 1981. 211 pp.

Here are many ideas and possibilities for you to worry about. Information is included in the following categories: financial worries, personal worries, medical worries, natural worries, legal worries, and mechanical worries. So if you need something to get upset over, this book is a feast of ulcer-inducing tidbits.

The New American Webster Handy College Dictionary. Signet Books, 1981. 640 pp.

This dictionary includes abbreviations, geographical names, foreign words and phrases, and forms of address. Of course it also supplies the spelling, syllabication, pronunciation, and meaning of the most common words in the English language as it is spoken in the United States.

Nicholls, Peter, general editor. **The Science Fiction Encyclopedia.** Dolphin Books, 1979. 672 pp.

For science fiction buffs, here is a vast collection of information on authors, editors, magazines, periodicals, motion pictures, television, and characters. Illustrations. Mature situations.

Ogilvie, Bruce, and Douglas Waitley. **Rand McNally Picture Atlas of the World.** Rev. ed. Rand McNally & Co., 1981. 96 pp.

Drawings accompany topographical, political, cultural, and wildlife maps of the seven continents. This atlas is a good beginning guide to the world for those of you developing a taste for faraway places.

Oxford American Dictionary. Avon Books, 1980. 816 pp.

This is a very complete paperback dictionary of the American language. Definitions are accompanied by notes on usage and points of grammar. The large type makes for easy reading.

Partnow, Elaine, editor. **The Quotable Woman: An Encyclopedia of Useful Quotations Indexed by Subject and Author, 1800–1975.** Corwin Books, 1977. 539 pp.

These 8,000 quotations, authored by 1,300 women contributors from all walks of life, are arranged chronologically, beginning with Catherine Beecher (1800–1875) and ending with Octavia Waldo, a contemporary American. A biographical index identifies all the women, and a subject index allows the reader to quickly find quotations on a more limited topic.

Paton, John, editor. **Rand McNally's Children's Encyclopedia.** Rand McNally & Co., 1980. 60 pp.

Find out what you want to know about the past, the present, and even the future in this book. Fascinating facts and illustrations reveal information about such topics as the earth, its moon, and the sun; the world of plants and animals; the regions of the earth; the ancient humans and their lives; and the development of all kinds of transportation. One two-page section, for example, illustrates and describes something of the vast world of the sea—its deep-sea fish, the middle waters where the really big creatures live, and the top level where the fish we eat and fish like the shark dwell.

The Random House Dictionary: Concise Edition. Random House, 1980. 1,070 pp.

Its completeness, conciseness, and clarity are advantages of this recent edition of a basic tool for all students. Adding to its practicality is a manual of style that defines and explains rules in such areas as punctuation, capitalization, and paper preparation. Also included are proofreaders' marks, forms of address, a table of weights and measures, a table of signs and symbols, and a listing of alphabets from around the world.

The Random House School Dictionary. Random House, 1978. 908 pp.

This dictionary is designed for use by middle school and junior high students. All entries are given in one A to Z listing, including all biographical and geographical entries, abbreviations, and contractions. Definitions are written in clear, concise language, and the parts of speech each word can be are given in order of frequency, with the word's more common uses appearing first. A valuable students' guide to the dictionary is provided at the front of the book. There are also activities suggested so that you can learn how to use your dictionary more efficiently.

Riker, Tom, and Richard Roberts. **The Directory of Natural and Health Foods.** Paragon Books, 1979. 320 pp.

This book contains articles on nutrition, diets, natural foods, and other health subjects. Information is also included about retail stores that sell health and natural foods. There are charts, graphs, and discussions relating to the use of such foods as grains, cereals, dried fruit, soy bean products, organic produce, honey, syrup, preserves, dairy products, meat, and meat substitutes. The text includes addresses where you can write or visit to buy products or to get more information concerning natural and health foods.

Rosenbloom, Joseph. **Bananas Don't Grow on Trees: A Guide to Popular Misconceptions.** Illus. Joyce Behr. Sterling Publishing Co., 1978. 155 pp.

We all have mistaken ideas or misconceptions about many things around us. This book explores how certain misconceptions have sprung up around plants, animals, science, history, the United States, food, and just about everything. For example, the toughest gem is not diamond but jade; twelve other metals are heavier than lead; the stingray causes more human deaths in the sea than sharks; Paul Revere did not ride alone; and the greatest mountain range is not the Himalayas but an underwater range called the Mid-Atlantic Ridge.

The Signet/Hammond World Atlas. Rev. ed. Signet Books, 1982. 272 pp.

This atlas contains full-page, full-color maps of every country and continent, detailed maps of all fifty states and the Canadian provinces, and special maps indicating world distribution of population, occupations, languages, religions, climate, and natural vegetation. An extra bonus in the atlas is material on the 1980 U.S. census.

Smith, Elsdon C. (editor Stephen C. Brice). **The Book of Smith.** Illus. Frank Baginski. Paragon Books, 1979. 218 pp.

There are over two million Smiths in the United States and Canada. But even if your name is not Smith, you will enjoy all the information, poems, riddles, and historical stories related to the name Smith. Even Mother Goose included a rhyme about John Smith, and several ailments have been given the name of Smith. The last chapter is a glossary of the names that have Smith in them.

Sobol, Donald J. **Encyclopedia Brown's Second Record Book of Weird and Wonderful Facts.** Illus. Bruce Degen. Delacorte Press, 1981. 144 pp.

Are you interested in weird facts and in discovering things that other people don't know? This book will provide you with little-known information about sports, unusual events, animal oddities, and human achievements. For instance, the book describes chickens who wear contact lenses and girls who wrestle on boys' teams.

Spencer, Donald D. **Computer Dictionary for Everyone.** Charles Scribner's Sons, 1979. 191 pp.

Over 2,500 words, phrases, and acronyms relating to computers are found in this alphabetically arranged dictionary. Computer language has become more and more common, and everyone will soon need to know certain new terms in order to talk about computers. Do you know what a ROM is? A floppy disc? A SNOBOL? A Hollerith card? If not, then this dictionary will help you become an up-to-date member of the computer age.

Sueling, Barbara. **You Can't Count a Billion Dollars and Other Little-Known Facts about Money.** Illus. by author. Doubleday & Co., 1979. 93 pp.

The buffalo on the 1938 buffalo nickel was "Black Diamond" from the Bronx Zoo. The life expectancy of a dollar bill is about eighteen months. In medieval times, doctors sometimes gilded pills to make them more acceptable to rich customers. Here is a book of surprising and zany facts about money.

Tracy, Jack, editor. **The Encyclopedia Sherlockiana; or, A Universal Dictionary of the State of Knowledge of Sherlock Holmes and His Biographer, John H. Watson, M.D.** Avon Books, 1979. 409 pp.

In dictionary form, this book compiles entries on people, places, phrases, and objects related to the famous fictional detective Sherlock Holmes and his adventures. There are more than 3,500 main entries, 8,000 story citations and cross-references, and 200 illustrations to interest any Sherlock Holmes fan.

Urdang, Laurence. **The Basic Book of Synonyms and Antonyms.** Signet Books, 1978. 374 pp.

This book is a reference aid for students and professional writers. It contains alphabetical entries of words and lists words that have similar meanings (synonyms) or opposite meanings (antonyms). The words are also used in sentences, so their exact meaning becomes clear. Even if you aren't a frequent writer, this book will help you expand your vocabulary.

Directory of Publishers

Abelard-Schuman Books. Imprint of Harper & Row, Publishers, Inc. Orders to: Keystone Industrial Park, Scranton, PA 18512

Abingdon Press, Customer Service Dept., 201 Eighth Ave. S., Nashville, TN 37202

Academy Chicago Ltd., 425 N. Michigan Ave., Chicago, IL 60611

Ace Books, c/o Berkley/Jove Publishing Group, 200 Madison Ave., New York, NY 10016

Acropolis Books Ltd., Colortone Bldg., 2400 17th St. N.W., Washington, DC 20009

Aero Publishers, Inc., 329 W. Aviation Rd., Fallbrook, CA 92028

Alcuin Press. Distributed by ISBS, Inc., P.O. Box 555, Forest Grove, OR 97116

Argo Books. Imprint of Atheneum Publishers. Distributed by The Scribner Book Companies, 201 Willowbrook Blvd., Wayne, NJ 07470

Atheneum Publishers. Distributed by The Scribner Book Companies, 201 Willowbrook Blvd., Wayne, NJ 07470

Atlantic Monthly Press. Distributed by Little, Brown & Co., 200 West St., Waltham, MA 02154

Avon Books, 959 Eighth Ave., New York, NY 10019

Ballantine Books, Inc. Division of Random House, Inc. Orders to: 400 Hahn Rd., Westminster, MD 21157

Bantam Books, Inc. Orders to: 414 E. Golf Rd., Des Plaines, IL 60016

Bard Books. Imprint of Avon Books, 959 Eighth Ave., New York, NY 10019

Barnes & Noble Books. Division of Harper & Row, Publishers, Inc. Orders to: Keystone Industrial Park, Scranton, PA 18512

Barron's Educational Series, Inc., 113 Crossways Park Dr., Woodbury, NY 11797

Basic Books, Inc. Orders to: Keystone Industrial Park, Scranton, PA 18512

Beacon Press, Inc. Distributed by Harper & Row, Publishers, Inc. Orders to: Keystone Industrial Park, Scranton, PA 18512

Beaufort Books, Inc. Orders to: Scribner Distribution Center, Vreeland Ave., Totowa, NJ 07512

Berkley Publishing Group, 200 Madison Ave., New York, NY 10016

John F. Blair, Publisher, 1406 Plaza Dr., Winston-Salem, NC 27103

Blandford Press. Distributed by Sterling Publishing Co., Inc., 2 Park Ave., New York, NY 10016

Bluejeans Books. Imprint of Xerox Educational Publications, 245 Long Hill Rd., Middletown, CT 06457

Books in Focus. Distributed by Harper & Row, Publishers. Orders to: Keystone Industrial Park, Scranton, PA 18512

Bradbury Press. Distributed by E. P. Dutton, 2 Park Ave., New York, NY 10016

Camelot Books. Imprint of Avon Books, 959 Eighth Ave., New York, NY 10019

Caroline House Publishers, Inc., 920 W. Industrial Dr., Aurora, IL 60506

Celestial Arts, 231 Adrian Rd., Millbrae, CA 94030

706

Chariot Books. Imprint of David C. Cook Publishing Co., Book Division, 850 N. Grove Ave., Elgin, IL 60120

Chilton Book Co. Orders to: 150 Parish Dr., Wayne, NJ 07470

Christopher Publishing House, 1405 Hanover St., Box 1014, West Hanover, MA 02339

Clarion Books. Imprint of Houghton Mifflin Co. Orders to: Wayside Rd., Burlington, MA 01803

William Collins Publishers, Inc., 2080 W. 117th St., Cleveland, OH 44111; 200 Madison Ave., Suite 1405, New York, NY 10016

Thomas Congdon Books. Imprint of E. P. Dutton, 2 Park Ave., New York, NY 10016

Contemporary Perspectives, Inc. Distributed by Silver Burdett Co., 250 James St., Morristown, NJ 07960

David C. Cook Publishing Co., 850 N. Grove Ave., Elgin, IL 60120

Corwin Books. Distributed by Independent News, 75 Rockefeller Plaza, New York, NY 10019

Coward, McCann & Geoghegan, Inc., The Putnam Publishing Group. Orders to: One Grosset Dr., Kirkwood, NY 13795

Crestwood House, Inc., P.O. Box 3427, Hwy. 66 South, Mankato, MN 56001

Thomas Y. Crowell Co. Imprint of Harper & Row, Publishers, Inc. Orders to: Keystone Industrial Park, Scranton, PA 18512

Crown Publishers, Inc., 1 Park Ave., New York, NY 10016

DAW Books. Distributed by New American Library. Orders to: 120 Woodbine St., Bergenfield, NJ 07621

John Day Co. Imprint of Harper & Row, Publishers, Inc. Orders to: Keystone Industrial Park, Scranton, PA 18512

Del Rey Books. Imprint of Ballantine Books, Inc. Orders to: 400 Hahn Rd., Westminster, MD 21157

Delacorte Press. Imprint of Dell Publishing Co., 1 Dag Hammarskjold Plaza, 245 E. 47th St., New York, NY 10017

Dell Publishing Co., Inc., 1 Dag Hammarskjold Plaza, 245 E. 47th St., New York, NY 10017

J. M. Dent & Sons Ltd., Aldine House, 33 Welbeck St., London W1M 8LX, England

André Deutsch Ltd. Distributed by E. P. Dutton, 2 Park Ave., New York, NY 10016

Dial Press, 1 Dag Hammarskjold Plaza, 245 E. 47th St., New York, NY 10017

Dillon Press, Inc., 500 S. Third St., Minneapolis, MN 55415

Discus Books. Imprint of Avon Books, 959 Eighth Ave., New York, NY 10019

Dodd, Mead & Co., 79 Madison Ave., New York, NY 10016

Dolphin Books. Imprint of Doubleday & Co., Inc., 245 Park Ave., New York, NY 10167

Doubleday/Anchor Books. Imprint of Doubleday & Co., Inc., 245 Park Ave., New York, NY 10167

Doubleday & Co., Inc., 245 Park Ave., New York, NY 10167

E. P. Dutton, Inc., 2 Park Ave., New York, NY 10016

Elsevier/Nelson Books, 2 Park Ave., New York, NY 10016

Enslow Publishers, Inc., Bloy St. and Ramsey Ave., Box 777, Hillside, NJ 07205

M. Evans & Co., Inc. Distributed by E. P. Dutton, 2 Park Ave., New York, NY 10016

Everest House Publishers. Orders to: Box 978, 424 Raritan Center, Edison, NJ 08818

Farrar, Straus & Giroux, Inc., 19 Union Square, W., New York, NY 10003

Fearon-Pitman Publishers, Inc., 6 Davis Dr., Belmont, CA 94002

Feminist Press, SUNY/College at Old Westbury, Box 334, Old Westbury, NY 11568

Flare Books. Imprint of Avon Books, 959 Eighth Ave., New York, NY 10019

Four Winds Press. Imprint of Scholastic Book Services. Orders to: 906 Sylvan Ave., Englewood Cliffs, NJ 07632

Golden Press. Imprint of Western Publishing Co., Inc. Orders to: Dept. M, 1220 Mound Ave., Racine, WI 53404

Greenwillow Books. Division of William Morrow & Co., Inc. Orders to: William Morrow & Co., Inc., Wilmor Warehouse, 6 Henderson Dr., West Caldwell, NJ 07006

Grossman Publishers. Division of Viking Press. Orders to: Viking/Penguin, Inc., 299 Murray Hill Pkwy., East Rutherford, NJ 07073

Harcourt Brace Jovanovich, Inc., 757 Third Ave., New York, NY 10017

Harper & Row, Publishers, Inc. Orders to: Keystone Industrial Park, Scranton, PA 18512

Harvey House, Publishers. Orders to: 128 W. River St., Chippewa Falls, WI 54729

Hastings House Publishers, Inc., 10 E. 40th St., New York, NY 10016

Hawthorn/Dutton. Distributed by E. P. Dutton, Inc., 2 Park Ave., New York, NY 10016

Herald Press, 616 Walnut Ave., Scottdale, PA 15683

Lawrence Hill & Co., Inc., 520 Riverside Ave., Westport, CT 06880

Hiway Books. Imprint of Westminster Press. Orders to: Order Dept., P.O. Box 718 Wm. Penn Annex, Philadelphia, PA 19105

Holiday House, Inc., 18 E. 53rd St., New York, NY 10022

Holt, Rinehart & Winston, Inc., 383 Madison Ave., New York, NY 10017

Houghton Mifflin Co. Orders to: Wayside Road, Burlington, MA 01803

Iowa State University Press, 2121 S. State Ave., Ames, IA 50010

JeM Books. Imprint of Julian Messner; division of Simon & Schuster, Inc. Orders to: Simon & Schuster, Inc., Total Warehouse Services Corp., Farragut Ave., Bristol, PA 19007

Alfred A. Knopf. Orders to: 400 Hahn Rd., Westminster, MD 21157

Laurel-Leaf Library. Imprint of Dell Publishing Co., Inc., 1 Dag Hammarskjold Plaza, 245 E. 47th St., New York, NY 10017

Lerner Publications Co., 241 First Ave., N., Minneapolis, MN 55401

Lewis Publishing Co. Division of Stephen Greene Press, Old Post Rd., Brattleboro, VT 05301

J. B. Lippincott Co. Orders to: 2350 Virginia Ave., Hagerstown, MD 21740

Lippincott & Crowell, Publishers. Imprint of J. B. Lippincott Co. Orders to: 2350 Virginia Ave., Hagerstown, MD 21740

Little, Brown & Co. Orders to: 200 West St., Waltham, MA 02154

Lodestar Books. Imprint of E. P. Dutton, 2 Park Ave., New York, NY 10016

Macdonald Educational. Imprint of Macdonald & Co., Ltd., Holywell House, Worship St., London EC2A 2EN, England

Macmillan Publishing Co., Inc. Orders to: Front and Brown Sts., Riverside, NJ 08370

Richard Marek Publishers, The Putnam Publishing Group. Orders to: 1050 Wall St. W., Lyndhurst, NJ 07071

McElderry Books. Imprint of Atheneum Publishers. Distributed by The Scribner Book Companies, 201 Willowbrook Blvd., Wayne, NJ 07470

McGraw-Hill Book Co. Orders to: Hightstown, NJ 08520; Manchester Rd., Manchester, MO 63011; 8171 Redwood Hwy., Novato, CA 94947

Mentor Books. Imprint of New American Library. Orders to: 120 Woodbine St., Bergenfield, NJ 07621

Merloyd Lawrence Books. Imprint of Seymour Lawrence Inc. Distributed by Addison-Wesley Publishing Co., Inc., Jacob Way, Reading, MA 01867

Methuen Inc. Distributed by Transworld Distribution Services, Inc., 80 Northfield Ave., Raritan Center, Edison, NJ 08817

Thomas Nelson, Inc., P.O. Box 14100, Nelson Place at Elmhill Pike, Nashville, TN 37214

North Country Books, P.O. Box 506, Sylvan Beach, NY 13157

Owl Books. Imprint of Holt, Rinehart & Winston, Inc., 383 Madison Ave., New York, NY 10017

Oxford University Press, Inc. Orders to: 16-00 Pollitt Dr., Fair Lawn, NJ 07410

Pantheon Books. Division of Random House, Inc. Orders to: Random House, Inc., 400 Hahn Rd., Westminster, MD 21157

Paragon Books, The Putnam Publishing Group. Orders to: 1050 Wall St. W., Lyndhurst, NJ 07071

Parnassus Press. Imprint of Houghton Mifflin Co. Orders to: Houghton Mifflin Co., Wayside Rd., Burlington, MA 01803

Penguin Books, Inc. Orders to: Viking/Penguin, Inc., 299 Murray Hill Pkwy., East Rutherford, NJ 07073

Perigee Books. Imprint of The Putnam Publishing Group. Orders to: 1050 Wall St. W., Lyndhurst, NJ 07071

S. G. Phillips, Inc., P.O. Box 83, Chatham, NY 12037

Pinnacle Books, 1430 Broadway, New York, NY 10018

Plays, Inc., 8 Arlington St., Boston, MA 02116

Popular Library, Inc., Unit of CBS Publications, 1515 Broadway, New York, NY 10036

Prentice-Hall, Inc. Orders to: Box 500, Englewood Cliffs, NJ 07632

Puffin Books. Imprint of Penguin Books, Inc. Orders to: Viking/Penguin, Inc., 299 Murray Hill Pkwy., East Rutherford, NJ 07073

G. P. Putnam's Sons, The Putnam Publishing Group. Orders to: 1050 Wall St. W., Lyndhurst, NJ 07071

Raintree Childrens Books. Imprint of Raintree Publishers Group. Orders to: Raintree Group Distribution Center, 424 N. Fourth St., 6th Floor, Milwaukee, WI 53203

Raintree Editions. Imprint of Raintree Publishers Group. Orders to: Raintree Group Distribution Center, 424 N. Fourth St., 6th Floor, Milwaukee, WI 53203

Raintree Publishers Group. Orders to: Raintree Group Distribution Center, 424 N. Fourth St., 6th Floor, Milwaukee, WI 53203

Rand McNally & Co., P.O. Box 7600, Chicago, IL 60680

Random House, Inc. Orders to: 400 Hahn Rd., Westminster, MD 21157

Richards Rosen Press, Inc., 29 E. 21st St., New York, NY 10010

Schocken Books, Inc., 200 Madison Ave., New York, NY 10016

Scholastic Book Services. Division of Scholastic Inc. Orders to: 906 Sylvan Ave., Englewood Cliffs, NJ 07632

Charles Scribner's Sons. Orders to: Shipping and Service Center, Vreeland Ave., Totowa, NJ 07512

Sea World Press, 1250 Sixth Ave., San Diego, CA 92101

Shambhala Publications, Inc. Distributed by Random House, Inc. Orders to: 400 Hahn Rd., Westminster, MD 21157

Harold Shaw Publishers, Box 567, 388 Gundersen Dr., Wheaton, IL 60187

Sierra Club Books. Distributed by Charles Scribner's Sons. Orders to: Shipping and Service Center, Vreeland Ave., Totowa, NJ 07512

Signet Books. Imprint of New American Library. Orders to: 120 Woodbine St., Bergenfield, NJ 07621

Signet Vista Books. Imprint of New American Library. Orders to: 120 Woodbine St., Bergenfield, NJ 07621

Silver Burdett Co., 250 James St., Morristown, NJ 07960

Skinny Books. Imprint of E. P. Dutton, 2 Park Ave., New York, NY 10016

Skylight Books. Imprint of Dodd, Mead & Co., 79 Madison Ave., New York, NY 10016

Spectrum Books. Imprint of Prentice-Hall, Inc. Orders to: Box 500, Englewood Cliffs, NJ 07632

St. Martin's Press, Inc., 175 Fifth Ave., New York, NY 10010

Stemmer House Publishers, Inc., 2627 Caves Rd., Owings Mills, MD 21117

Sterling Publishing Co., Inc., 2 Park Ave., New York, NY 10016

Strode Publishers, 720 Church St., N.W., Huntsville, AL 35801

Tempo Books. Imprint of Grosset & Dunlap, Inc., The Putnam Publishing Group. Orders to: 1050 Wall St. W., Lyndhurst, NJ 07071

Tidal Press, Cranberry Isles, ME 04625

Triumph Books. Imprint of Bantam Books, Inc. Orders to: 414 E. Golf Rd., Des Plaines, IL 60016

Troll Associates, 320 Rte. 17, Mahwah, NJ 07430

Tundra Books, 1434 St. Catherine St. W., Suite #308, Montreal, Quebec, H3G 1R4 Canada

Unicorn Books. Distributed by E. P. Dutton, 2 Park Ave., New York, NY 10016

Vagabond Books. Imprint of Scholastic Inc. Orders to: 906 Sylvan Ave., Englewood Cliffs, NJ 07632

Vanguard Press, Inc., 424 Madison Ave., New York, NY 10017

Viking Press, Inc. Orders to: Viking/Penguin, Inc., 299 Murray Hill Pkwy., East Rutherford, NJ 07073

Vintage Books. Division of Random House, Inc. Orders to: 400 Hahn Rd., Westminster, MD 21157

Walker & Co., 720 Fifth Ave., New York, NY 10019

Wanderer Books. Division of Simon & Schuster, Inc. Orders to: Simon & Schuster, Inc., Total Warehouse Services Corp., Radcliffe St., Bristol, PA 19007

Warner Books, Inc., 666 Fifth Ave., New York, NY 10103

Watermill Press. Imprint of Troll Associates, 320 Rte. 17, Mahwah, NJ 07430

Franklin Watts, Inc., 387 Park Ave. South, New York, NY 10016

Westminster Press. Orders to: Order Dept., P.O. Box 718 Wm. Penn Annex, Philadelphia, PA 19105

Wildfire Books. Imprint of Scholastic Inc. Orders to: 906 Sylvan Ave., Englewood Cliffs, NJ 07632

Windward Books. Imprint of Random House, Inc. Orders to: 400 Hahn Rd., Westminster, MD 21157

Workman Publishing Co., Inc., 1 W. 39th St., New York, NY 10018

Yearling Books. Imprint of Dell Publishing Co., Inc., 1 Dag Hammarskjold Plaza, 245 E. 47th St., New York, NY 10017

Author Index

711

Title Index

71663

DATE DUE

GAYLORD
PRINTED IN U.S.A.